PHYSICAL GEOGRAPHY

FOURTH EDITION

Stacks and cliffs of Old Red Sandstone near Duncansby Head, Caithness.

PHYSICAL GEOGRAPHY

BY

PHILIP LAKE

FOURTH EDITION

UNDER THE EDITORSHIP OF

J. A. STEERS

CAMBRIDGE
AT THE UNIVERSITY PRESS
1971

Published by the Syndics of the Cambridge University Press
Bentley House, 200 Euston Road, London NW1 2DB
American Branch: 32 East 57th Street, New York, N.Y. 10022

ISBN 0 521 055091

First edition 1915
Reprinted 1919 1922 1925 1929
1933 1936 1941 1943
1945 1946 1947
Second edition, revised, enlarged and reset 1949
Third edition 1952
Reprinted 1955
Fourth edition, revised, enlarged and reset 1958
Reprinted 1961 1965 1971

Printed in Great Britain
at the University Printing House, Cambridge
(Brooke Crutchley University Printer)

PREFACE TO THE THIRD AND FOURTH EDITIONS

The only important difference between the second and third editions was the addition in the third edition (1952) of a chapter on river régimes compiled by Mr W. V. Lewis and myself.

In this, the fourth edition, the main part of the book has not been altered in form, but a considerable number of additions and corrections have been made in order to bring the subject-matter reasonably up to date. These changes are more numerous in the sections devoted to the oceans and to land forms. In this work I received much help from Mr Cameron Ovey.

Three entirely new chapters have been added at the end of the volume, of which ch. XVII is by Mr A. T. Grove, and ch. XVIII by Mr A. J. Lee.

The physiographical effects of storms, whether inland or along the coast, are perhaps not sufficiently emphasised in text-books. I have attempted to collect some relevant material of recent storms in this country in order to demonstrate how effectively transport, erosive and depositional processes are speeded up at such times.

The other new chapters represent a link between the physical and biological aspects of geography. The importance of soils to the geographer, and the link that they make between the study of land forms and ecology, is a main theme in Mr Grove's contribution. Mr Lee has shown how important a proper understanding of submarine topography and oceanic circulation is if we are to appreciate the life in the oceans and the economic value of fisheries of all types.

No one would wish to underestimate the importance of a purely physical study of land forms and oceans, but the link between the physical and the human branches of geography is all important especially if the student is to understand, as he should, the necessity of basing human geography, *sensu lato*, on a firm physical foundation. To a large extent that link must be made through what is sometimes called biogeography. Mr Grove is a University Lecturer in Geography in the Cambridge department, and has studied problems relative to the subject-matter of his chapter both in Northern Africa and in these islands. Mr Lee, after reading Geography at Cambridge, entered the Fisheries branch of the Ministry of Agriculture, Fisheries, and Food and is an authority on the interrelation of geographical, physical, and biological aspects of the seas. His research takes him frequently into distant waters.

J. A. STEERS

CAMBRIDGE
January 1958

PREFACE TO SECOND EDITION

Philip Lake's *Physical Geography* first appeared in 1915. It has frequently been reprinted, but until now no major revision has been undertaken. It is no exaggeration to say that this book, known familiarly to generations of geographers, has had a greater influence than any other on the teaching of physical geography, in advanced classes at school and in the early stages at the University. It became a standard work at once and has remained in that class ever since.

When the University Press approached me about making a revision, I accepted on the understanding that I could have the help of Professor G. Manley and Mr W. V. Lewis. All three of us knew that it would be no easy task. It must always be difficult to edit another man's book; here we were faced with the problem of bringing up to date a well-known book, and one, moreover, written with great simplicity and clarity. The fact that three of us were concerned in this revision was bound to imply differences of style which I, as editor, could not have eliminated, even had I wished to do so. The unavoidable differences from Lake's own style will probably strike the reader even more forcibly because of this. But as far as was consistent with the changes we have had to make, wherever we could we have left Lake's own writing untouched. The book, we believe, remains substantially what it was.

Many minor changes have been made, and several entirely new chapters have been written. Professor Manley has been responsible for the section on the atmosphere; Mr Lewis for the revision of that on the lithosphere, apart from ch. III. Ch. III, with the remainder of the book, has been my responsibility. Many of the text-figures are new, and all the original plates have been replaced, since many of the old blocks had worn badly.

Whether we have succeeded is for others to judge. It has certainly been a great pleasure to do this work. All three of us at one time or another were Philip Lake's pupils, and anyone who has had that experience will know that the clarity and lucidity which gives his writing character was even more strikingly apparent in his teaching and lecturing. Few men had his gift of clear exposition, whether to elementary or advanced classes. Moreover, with his keen sense of humour he often succeeded, in the lecture room and on less formal occasions, in driving home a difficult subject in a way that was at once clear and memorable.

Mr Lake died on 12 June 1949 while this edition was in final proof: he had not taken any part in the revision. What had to be done was left entirely in our hands. We have tried to bring it up to date, and yet at the same time to keep as much of the original as possible, and we hope we shall have succeeded in handing on to future geographers something of what those of our own time knew to be the best.

I am grateful to all who have supplied photographs for the new plates. Acknowledgement is made in the list of plates on pp. xvii–xix.

J. A. STEERS

CAMBRIDGE
1949

PREFACE TO FIRST EDITION

There are many books on Physical Geography in the English language, but most of them are intended for the use of junior classes in schools and are accordingly of a very elementary character. It is with the object of providing for the needs of somewhat older students that the present book has been written.

Certain preliminary matters which are often treated under the head of Physical Geography, but which do not properly belong to that subject, are omitted. It is assumed, for instance, that the reader understands the principles of the barometer and the thermometer, and that he has some acquaintance with the motions of the earth and the moon. But no one who has been through a general elementary course in science, such as is now given in most secondary schools, should meet with any difficulty.

A few words as to the arrangement adopted may be of use, especially to teachers who may wish to know how far the book will be serviceable in their own classes. The book falls naturally into three sections dealing respectively with the atmosphere, the ocean and the land. Logically the study of physical geography may begin either with the atmosphere or with the land, and it is mainly a matter of convenience which of these courses should be followed. The two branches of the subject are to so large an extent independent that, if desired, the section on the land may be read before the section on the atmosphere. But the study of the atmosphere should always precede that of the ocean.

In planning a course, however, there is one consideration that should be borne in mind. It is easy to arrange a useful series of laboratory lessons upon the atmosphere or the ocean; but in the case of the land comparatively little laboratory work is possible and the most valuable form of practical work consists of excursions in the field. Consequently, there are advantages in dealing with the atmosphere during the winter months and with the land during the summer. But much depends upon the circumstances under which the course is given.

With regard to the order of the individual chapters, considerable latitude is permissible both in the section on the ocean and in the section on the land. But in the section on the atmosphere the mode of treatment requires that the chapters should be taken in the order in which they appear. According to my own experience the method adopted is the simplest and easiest for the student.

In a book of this kind the question of units is always one of some difficulty. In English-speaking countries climatological data are usually recorded in English measures, and I have accordingly used English measures throughout. But owing to the recent adoption of the C.G.S. system, except as regards temperature, in the Daily Weather Report of the Meteorological Office, I have added a short appendix upon the units employed in that publication.

For the photographic illustrations* I have many friends to thank. Pls. 1–4 are taken from the beautifully illustrated *Cloud Studies* of Mr A. W. Clayden, Principal of the Royal Albert Memorial College at

* The figure numbers refer to the illustrations in the first edition and the author's wording remains unaltered.

Exeter, and for permission to reproduce them I am indebted to the author and his publisher, Mr John Murray. Pl. x, fig. 1, is from a photograph by Mr T. J. Roberts. The photographs of Himalayan glaciers, pl. XII and pl. XIII, fig. 1, were supplied by Mr T. D. La Touche, formerly of the Geological Survey of India. Pl. XIV, showing some of the Antarctic glaciers, I owe to my colleague at Cambridge, Mr C. S. Wright, who was with Captain Scott's last expedition. Pl. XVI, fig. 1, was given to me by Dr A. W. Rogers, Assistant Director of the South African Geological Survey. Pl. XVI, fig. 2, and pl. XVII are from illustrations in *The Duab of Turkestan* by Mr W. R. Rickmers, published by the Cambridge University Press. Both of the figures on pl. XVIII and fig. 2 on pl. XIX are from photographs by the late Dr Tempest Anderson, whose photographic studies of volcanoes are so well known. For permission to reproduce them I am indebted to his executors. Two of these figures and also pl. XIX, fig. 1, have already appeared in the *Text Book of Geology* by Mr Rastall and myself, and both Mr Rastall and our publisher, Mr Arnold, very kindly consented to the use of electros from the blocks prepared for that work. Pl. XX is from models in the Sedgwick Museum.

But most of all I am indebted to Professor S. H. Reynolds of Bristol University, who supplied eleven of the photographs which appear in the plates. To him and to the other friends who have helped me I offer my heartiest thanks.

The maps of isobars and isotherms at the end of the volume are based chiefly upon the maps of Buchan, Mohn and the National Antarctic Expedition of 1901–4.

PHILIP LAKE

CAMBRIDGE
9 November 1914

CONTENTS

PART I. THE ATMOSPHERE

Chapter I

Chapter II

Chapter III

Chapter IV

Chapter V

Chapter VI

Chapter VII

Chapter VIII

Chapter IX

PART II. THE OCEAN

Chapter I

Chapter II

Chapter III

Chapter IV

Chapter V

Chapter VI

PART III. THE LAND

Chapter I

Chapter II

Chapter III

Chapter IV

Chapter V

Chapter VI

Chapter VII

Chapter VIII

Chapter IX

Chapter X

Chapter XI

Chapter XII

Chapter XIII

Chapter XIV

Chapter XV

Chapter XVI

Chapter XVII

Chapter XVIII

LIST OF PLATES

LIST OF FIGURES IN THE TEXT

MAPS

(*At the end of the volume*)

(*a*) Alto-stratus, with alto-cumulus bands at a lower level.

(*b*) Bands of alto-cumulus merging into alto-stratus, and some cumulus below.

(*a*) Small cumulus showing little vertical growth.

(*b*) Valley fog. Note steam from a locomotive in the valley rising above the upper surface of the fog.

(*a*) Cumulus clouds with a growing tendency.

(*b*) Cumulo-nimbus, the top of which has become hybrid cirrus (anvil cloud).

Cumulus clouds with base about 2000 ft. developing on a sunny June morning over north-eastern France. In the background are high cirrus, and cirro-stratus, with other layer clouds below. These layers are part of a frontal system about 100 miles distant. The photograph was taken at 26,000 feet.

(*a*) Hope Islands, Great Barrier Reefs, Queensland. Shingle ridge resting on reef. Young mangroves in foreground. Note dry-land vegetation on shingle.

(*b*) The surface of Arlington Reef, Great Barrier Reefs, Queensland. Photo taken at low water. The upper surface of the reef shows but little living coral.

(*a*) Near Hobbie Geo, East Coast of Caithness. Low cliffs in nearly horizontally bedded Old Red Sandstone. Note the bedding, and two sets of joints along which the sea is cutting.

(*b*) Cliff, almost vertical, in Liassic beds, Marcross, Glamorgan. The thicker beds are limestones, the thinner are shales. The grassy slope is the side of a stream valley. The level top may represent part of the surface of a raised platform.

(*a*) Summit of Rough Tor, Camelford, Cornwall. A perfect example of a Cornish granite tor, showing the characteristic horizontal weathering. The structure is really developed underground, a little below the surface. The loose material between the blocks is washed away as the rock is exposed. It is thus able to remain dry as a rule, and is harder than that immediately below the soil.

(*b*) Castle Point, Dunstanburgh Castle, Northumberland. A sea cliff of columnar Whin Sill overlying sandstone.

(*a*) Rock platform of marine erosion with overlying gravels of the 100-foot, or late glacial, raised beach. In the foreground, the grassy platform of the 25-foot beach. To the right, on the shore, is the modern storm beach of white quartzite shingle. Looking west from near Port a'Chotain, two miles west of Rhuvaal lighthouse, on the north coast of Islay.

(*b*) Ancient sea-caves in quartzite cliff at edge of 25 foot raised beach, near Brein Phort, north of Loch Tarbert, west coast of Jura.

(*a*) Ro Wen, Fairbourne, Merioneth. Note the dunes, and also that the spit is set back from the general line of the coast.

(*b*) Hurst Castle Spit, Hants. Note the recurved shingle ridges and the salt marshes.

(*a*) Liassic cliffs and wave-cut platform near Marcross, Glamorgan. At high water the waves undercut the cliff causing rock falls which supply the shingle beach at the foot of the cliff. As the cliff recedes the wave-cut platform in the foreground is widened.

(*b*) A delta formed when a tributary stream entered the former glacier-dammed lake in Glen Roy, Inverness-shire. When the lake waters drained away the stream cut terraces in the old delta.

(*a*) Crags and scree slopes of Moine-schist, and alluvial flood plain of the River Feshie, $2\frac{1}{2}$ miles S.S.E. of Glen Feshie Lodge, near Kingussie.

(*b*) The Screes, Wast Water, North of Wasdale Hall, Cumberland. These famous screes, which are made up of material derived from the crags of the Borrowdale volcanic rocks, begin at about 1500 feet O.D. and descend to below lake level. The slope of the screes is about 38°.

(*a*) Thornton Force, Ingleton, Yorkshire. The water falls over the massive beds of the *Michelinia* zone of the Carboniferous Limestone. These rest unconformably on highly inclined Ingletonian Grits and Flags. A conglomerate intervenes forming the undercut portion of the face.

(*b*) Giggleswick. Viewpoint just south of Blackriggs Plantation. Giggleswick Scar and view down Ribblesdale. Looking along line of South Craven Fault. Carboniferous Limestone on left and Millstone Grits (grit and shale) forming lower ground on right. Note also fair weather cumulus showing little vertical development.

(*a*) Cheddar Gorge, Somerset. The resistant Carboniferous Limestone beds form fine vertical cliffs nearly 400 feet high in places.

(*b*) Above Malham Cove, Malham, Yorkshire. Clint formation in Great Scar Limestone. Note the direction of the main joints.

The steep northern face of the Eiger, Mönch, and Jungfrau. Cirque glaciers nestle wherever the snow is able to accumulate in any quantity. The great U-valley of Lauterbrunnen lies between the camera-station and the partially wooded Alpine pastures in the left middle distance.

(*a*) Piz Bernina and the Tschierva Glacier, Engadine, Switzerland, showing the gathering ground and typical mountain glaciers. Note the crevasses (ice-fall) where the glacier leaves the collecting basins, and also the medial and lateral moraines.

(*b*) The end of Heillstuggubreein, Jotunheim, showing a medial moraine and two small moraines brought to the surface by the overriding of the ice along a thrust-plane in the steep front of the glacier. Note also the U-section of the main glacier (the valley of which curves upwards to the right), and the hanging tributary glacier, and the snow gullying on the valley side.

(*a*) A mountain range almost submerged by the Antarctic ice-cap. An ice-filled cirque has bitten deeply into the isolated Nunatak on the right.

(*b*) Cape Alexandra, West Grahamland. Snow and ice fall from the steeply sloping ice masses and contribute to the ice-foot below, which is further augmented by direct snowfall.

(*a*) Grooves and striations, some crossing each other, cut into an ice-smoothed rock surface recently uncovered by the Svellnosbreein (Jotunheim) seen in the background.

(*b*) An erratic block of Silurian Grit perched on the Carboniferous Limestone, Norber, near Austwick, Yorks. The surface has been lowered about 2 feet since the ice carried the rock into position.

(*a*) Roches moutonnées cut in the north side of Glen Nevis; view looking downstream showing the glacially smoothed rock surfaces.

(*b*) The same roches moutonnées looking upstream at the plucked faces. A half pot-hole formed by water flowing between the ice and the rock is shown suspended at the top of the rock mass in the centre of the photograph.

(*a*) A general view of the Culbin Sands, Moray Firth. Note the steep face of the dune advancing from right to left.

(*b*) Blakeney Point, Norfolk. In the middle distance, small dunes mainly gathering round clumps of marram grass. In the foreground, older and higher dunes. Note the patchy cover of vegetation.

(*a*) Desert landscape evolution (1). Dissected edge of limestone plateau bordering the Nile. A lower-level erosion surface is eating into the plateau by the enlargement of wadis and gullies.

(*b*) Desert landscape evolution (2). A typical wadi, or erosional trench, carried into horizontally bedded Nubian Sandstones. The high-level plateau is eaten away by enlargement and extension of these wadis. Central Libyan Desert.

(*a*) Desert landscape evolution (3). A more advanced stage of erosion-surface development. The old high-level plateau has been carved into remnants, the smaller ones becoming conical hills. Central Libyan Desert.

(*b*) Desert landscape evolution (4). The penultimate stage. The plateau has been completely cut up, and conical hills in varying stages of removal now dot the encroaching lower-level surface.

(*b*) Nyamlagira, Belgian Congo.
Lava and fissures.

(*a*) Dying mud volcanoes, Iceland.

(*a*) Java: Bromo and Batok cones in the Sand Sea, an expanse of dark-grey volcanic sand, in which the individual grains are much the same size as those of the sea shore, but instead of being formed by the wind and the waves, they consist of lava, blown into dust by explosions. The cones rise like islands from the sand. Note the furrowing, by rain, of the flanks of the cones.

(*b*) The Hot Springs of the Yellowstone National Park. The cone built by Orange Spring; growth is still going on.

(*a*) A near view of the crater which forms the centre of White Island, Bay of Plenty, North Island, New Zealand. It is mainly built of ashes, and its outer slopes are much dissected. Note the enlarged and breached crater.

(*b*) Mts Ngauruhoe and Tongariro. Lake Taupo in the background. North Island, New Zealand. Ngauruhoe is mainly an ash cone on the flank of the broad-topped Tongariro Mountain.

(*a*) Mt Lassen, California. An active volcano which erupted violently in 1914–16. Since then it has emitted steam and mud from fissures.

(*b*) The Great Tarawera Chasm crosses the Tarawera group of rhyolite domes and extends several miles. It was formed in 1886.

PART I

THE ATMOSPHERE

CHAPTER I

INTRODUCTION. COMPOSITION OF THE ATMOSPHERE

Introduction. The planet upon which we live consists of a large core surrounded by two thin coverings or envelopes. The outer envelope is gaseous and is called the atmosphere. The inner envelope is liquid, and is known as the hydrosphere: it is formed by the oceans, but unlike the atmosphere it is incomplete and does not entirely cover the globe. The core itself is solid, at least externally, and is often called the lithosphere.

The specific gravity of the earth as a whole is 5·67, but the specific gravity of the rocks which form the outer part of the lithosphere averages less than 3. The interior therefore must be considerably denser than the exterior. It is, moreover, certain that in the interior the pressure must be very great and there is evidence that the temperature is also very high. The interior must, accordingly, be different from the exterior, and many writers limit the term lithosphere to the outer part of the earth, where the rocks are more or less similar to those which are visible at the surface, and separate the inner portion under the name bathysphere, centrosphere, or barysphere.

Beyond the facts that the materials are dense, that the pressure is great and the temperature probably high, but little is known as to the nature of the bathysphere, and very different views have been held concerning its constitution. Some writers believe it to be solid; others imagine that it is molten; and some have even supposed that it may be gaseous, though owing to the enormous pressure it does not behave like a gas on the surface of the earth. Whatever the condition of the bathysphere may be, tidal observations show that the earth as a whole is as rigid as a solid ball of steel of the same size.

The geographer, however, is concerned with the surface of the earth and not with its interior, and in general he has only to consider the atmosphere, the hydrosphere and the visible portions of the lithosphere, or in other words, the air, the ocean, and the land.

Owing to the effects of perspective, vertical heights usually seem to us considerably greater than equal distances measured along the ground. Partly for this reason and partly because we see so small a part of the earth's surface at a time, few people realise how shallow the ocean and the atmosphere are, compared with the size of the whole earth. If the earth is represented by a globe a foot in diameter, the ocean on a corresponding scale would nowhere be more than $\frac{1}{100}$ of an inch in depth. The atmosphere has no well-defined limit (see p. 7), but assuming it to extend to a height of 200 miles, its thickness on the same scale would be about $\frac{3}{10}$ of an inch.

Composition of the atmosphere. Except for the water-vapour present, the composition of the atmosphere near the surface of the earth is practically uniform throughout the globe. Wherever a sample is taken, the air, after it has been freed from water-vapour, has very nearly the following constitution:

Nitrogen	78·03	per cent	by volume.
Oxygen	20·99	,,	,,
Argon	0·94	,,	,,
Carbon dioxide	0·03	,,	,,
Hydrogen	0·01	,,	,,

It is only in enclosed spaces, or in the immediate neighbourhood of a volcanic vent or of a factory chimney, or in other places where gases of various kinds are poured out, that any important variation in the composition of dry air is found. The uniformity is due partly to the winds and partly to the rapidity with which gases diffuse and mix with one another. It has recently been estimated that the atmospheric content of carbon dioxide has increased by 10 per cent in the past century, on account of domestic and industrial outpourings of the gas from the combustion of coal and oil.

Up to a height of some 20,000 feet the composition remains practically the same. At still greater altitudes it has been supposed on theoretical grounds that there must be differences, and it is known that carbon dioxide is virtually absent. Moreover, there is practically no-water-vapour, or water in any form, above the atmospheric boundary known as the tropopause (defined in the next paragraph) which is found at an average height of about 25,000 feet in polar regions, and rises to 55,000 feet over the equator. At these heights, however, oxygen and nitrogen are still found in almost the same proportion as at the surface.

It is found that when an aircraft or balloon, carrying instruments, rises from the surface, the temperature falls off with little interruption at a rate which, taking the average of many ascents, lies close to 1° F. for 300 feet up to a height varying between 4 and 11 miles (21,000–58,000 feet). With continued ascent, however, the temperature remains steady or shows a slight tendency to rise again. This level, at which the fall of temperature with height ceases to prevail, is called the tropopause; the part of the atmosphere below is called the troposphere, while that above has been called the stratosphere. It will be shown later that all the weather changes we know associated with the formation and disappearance of cloud and precipitation are confined to the troposphere.

Although the composition of dry air at the surface of the earth is almost constant, there are great differences in the amount of water-vapour present. The pressure and the temperature also vary greatly from time to time and from place to place. In the study of the atmosphere from the geographical point of view there are accordingly three main factors to be considered, viz. the pressure, the temperature, and the humidity.

CHAPTER II

ATMOSPHERIC PRESSURE AND ITS INFLUENCE ON WINDS

Barometric pressure. Since the time of Guericke it has been known that the air has weight. Under ordinary circumstances a cubic foot of air weighs about an ounce and a quarter.

As the air has weight it follows that the atmosphere must press upon the surface of the earth, and the pressure at any point will depend upon the amount of air above. It will be less on the top of a mountain than at the foot. But even at sea-level the pressure varies from day to day.

The pressure of the atmosphere is measured by means of the barometer. The greater the pressure the higher the mercury in the barometer stands. The pressure of the atmosphere is in fact the same as the pressure exerted by a layer of mercury as deep as the mercury column in the barometer is high. When, for example, the barometric reading is 30 inches the atmospheric pressure is equal to that of a layer of mercury 30 inches deep. It is usual therefore to express the pressure of the atmosphere in inches or millimetres of mercury. Since the density of mercury is known, it is easy to convert this into pounds per square inch. The average pressure at sea-level is about 29·9 inches, which is equal to about 14·7 pounds per square inch. Since 1910 the millibar has gradually come into use as a convenient unit of atmospheric pressure. It represents a force of 1000 dynes acting on one square centimetre, or very nearly the weight of one gram on the same area. Atmospheric pressure fluctuates on either side of 1000 mb., which is the equivalent under standard conditions of 29·53 inches of mercury. It may rise to about 1070 mb. on occasions in the Siberian winter anticyclones or fall to about 950 mb. in the deepest depressions in temperate regions.

Measurement of heights by means of the barometer. When a barometer is taken to the top of a hill it will always be found that the reading is less at the top than it is at the bottom, because the amount of air above is less and therefore the pressure is less. Consequently the barometer may be used for measuring heights. Near the level of the sea a layer of air 9 feet thick is approximately equal in weight to a layer of mercury $\frac{1}{100}$ inch thick. Therefore for every 9 feet that the barometer is raised the barometric reading will be $\frac{1}{100}$ inch less. Thus we get a rough and ready rule for determining heights. Read the barometer both at the top and the bottom of the hill; take the difference in hundredths of an inch and multiply this by nine. The result will be the height in feet of the top above the bottom.

But the rule assumes that the air is always and everywhere of the same density, which is far from being the case. Air is readily compressed, and when compressed into a smaller space its density is naturally increased. At sea-level the air has the whole pressure of the atmosphere above it; at a height of 10,000 feet the pressure is much lower. Therefore at 10,000 feet the density is much less than at sea-level and 9 feet of air is no longer equivalent to $\frac{1}{100}$ inch of mercury, and the rule becomes altogether inaccurate. Moreover, the density of the air is affected also by the temperature. In order to determine heights with greater accuracy, the mean pressure and mean temperature of the layer of air between the two stations must be known. Table 1,[1] which is small enough to be put into the case of a pocket aneroid, will give results correct to within about 1 per cent.

Table 1

Mean temperature, Fahr.	30°	40°	50°	60°	70°
Mean pressure 27 in.	9·7	9·9	10·1	10·3	10·6
28 in.	9·3	9·5	9·8	10·0	10·2
29 in.	9·0	9·2	9·4	9·6	9·8
30 in.	8·7	8·9	9·1	9·3	9·5

Read both barometer and thermometer at the two stations. The mean of the barometer readings may be taken as the mean pressure of the intermediate air and the mean of the thermometer readings as the mean temperature. Look up in the table the number corresponding with this

[1] From the *Pocket Altitude Tables*, by G. J. Symons.

mean pressure and mean temperature, and use this number instead of 9 in the rule already given. The following is an example:

	Pressure	Temperature
Upper station	28·00 in.	45°
Lower station	30·00 in.	55°
Mean	29·00 in.	50°
Difference	2·00 in.	

Factor for mean pressure 29 inches and mean temperature 50° = 9·4.
200 × 9·4 = 1880 = difference of altitude in feet.

Altimeters for use in aircraft are sensitive aneroid barometers, suitably graduated. In millibar units, 1 mb. change of pressure results from a change of altitude of 30 feet. This rule is sufficiently close for working purposes up to 5000 feet or so. But at levels between 15,000 and 20,000 feet the rate of change of pressure with height is only about half what it is at the surface; 1 mb. for 60 feet can be taken as a working approximation.

The pilot must take into account the fact that his apparent altitude above the ground may be in error owing to variations in the density of the air-column in which he is flying. A short consideration of the facts shown in the above table will quickly lead to the conclusion that if a pilot is flying on a very cold day he should be prepared to find his altitude reading too high.

Height of the atmosphere. If the atmosphere were of the same density throughout, it would be easy to calculate its height; for, since $\frac{1}{100}$ inch of mercury corresponds with about 9 feet of air, 29·9 inches of mercury will correspond with 26,910 feet of air, i.e. rather more than 5 miles. But because the pressure decreases upwards the density also decreases and the same weight of air occupies a larger space. At a height of about 3½ miles the pressure is half what it is at sea-level, that is to say half the atmosphere (measured by weight and not by volume) is below and half above. At 7 miles the pressure is about one-quarter of the pressure at sea-level, at 10½ miles one-eighth and so on. If we imagine the atmosphere divided into horizontal layers about 3½ miles thick the lowest layer contains half the atmosphere (by weight), the second a quarter, the third an eighth, the fourth a sixteenth and so on. If such a law as this, which is approximately true near the earth's surface, holds at all altitudes, there can be no definite limit to the atmosphere, and it must extend upwards in an extremely attenuated form until the attraction of the earth is overpowered by that of some other heavenly body. But long before this point is reached the pressure must be far lower than has ever been attained experimentally, and the behaviour of gases at such low pressures is not accurately known.

There is, however, definite evidence that the atmosphere extends beyond 100 miles. Meteorites or shooting stars are small solid bodies which travel through space at great velocities. In space they are cold and invisible to us, but so great is their speed that when they enter the atmosphere the friction of the air and the compression of the air in front make them white-hot and they become visible, and this is sometimes found to be the case at heights greater than 100 miles. They have even been observed at an altitude of 188 miles.

Barometric variations. Although the average pressure at sea-level is about 29·9″ or 1012 mb. there are considerable variations from day to day, and in England the barometer seldom remains steady for any length of time. It has long been observed that there is some connection between the fluctuations of the barometer and the changes in the weather; but the connection is not so simple as is usually supposed. It is often said that when the barometer stands high the weather will be fine, and when it stands low the weather will be wet; and accordingly many barometers are marked with the words Fine, Change, Rain, etc., but very little reliance can be placed on these indications.

Another common belief, for which there is more justification, is that a rising barometer foretells fine weather and a falling barometer wet. But even this rule has many exceptions.

There is indeed a very close connection between the weather and the barometric pressure. But, to take London as an example, it is not the actual pressure in London that determines the weather there, but the distribution of pressure throughout the surrounding region. If the barometer stands at 29·5 inches the weather may be fine or it may be wet. It will depend to a very large extent upon the pressure in the places round about.

Isobars. The distribution of pressure is determined by taking simultaneous readings of the barometer at a number of different places. After certain corrections these readings are telegraphed to a central office—in England to the Meteorological Office—and are plotted upon a chart. In order to show the distribution of pressure clearly, isobars or lines of equal barometric pressure are drawn through all places where the pressure is the same.

The method of drawing the isobars is illustrated in fig. 1. In this figure the readings of the barometer at the different points shown are given. It is usual to draw isobars for each tenth of an inch, and in this figure isobars for 29·8, 29·9, and 30·0 (as shown) would be drawn. None of the places of observation has these readings; but it is assumed that for short distances the change in the pressure is gradual and fairly regular.

If then it is 29·97 at *A* and 30·3 at *B* the isobar for 30·0 will pass half-way between these points. In this way we obtain the isobars as shown. It should be noticed that all the numbers on the right of the 30·0 isobar are above 30·0, and all the numbers on the left are less than 30·0; and similarly with the other isobars.

But in a single town there may be two barometers, one on the top of a hill and the other at the bottom. The barometer on the hill will always read less than the barometer at the foot, and there is no reason why one reading should be taken as the pressure for that town rather than the

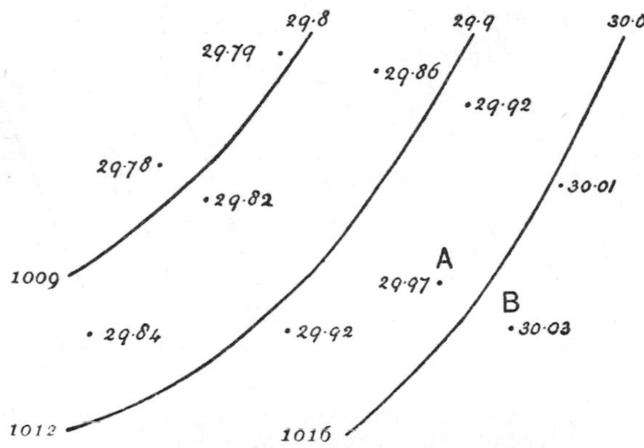

Fig. 1. Method of drawing isobars. Millibar equivalents approximate.

other. It is evident, therefore, that in comparing barometers some allowance must be made for altitude. On the top of Ben Nevis the barometric pressure will always be less than in London and no deductions concerning the weather could be drawn from that fact.

For this reason the pressures plotted on the chart are not the actual readings taken. In every case they are 'reduced to sea-level', that is, an allowance is made for the altitude of the place; and the number plotted is the pressure which there would be at that place at the bottom of a pit reaching to the level of the sea.

Isobars on an ordinary weather-chart are therefore lines drawn through places where the barometric readings, with all necessary corrections, including reduction to sea-level, are the same.

Isobaric charts have been prepared daily in England and other countries for many years, and comparison with the weather for each day has gradually shown that particular forms of isobaric arrangement are usually associated with particular types of weather. Weather-forecasting was for long based on this general principle. Latterly much more attention has been given to the characteristics of the various types of air or air-masses coming within the area covered by the chart.

Relations of wind to isobars. Of all the weather conditions the one which is most evidently and directly dependent upon the distribution of pressure is the wind, and the reason for this is simple. If the pressure in one place is high and in the surrounding area low, then the air will be squeezed outward, as it were, from the higher pressure, and will flow towards the lower. Accordingly we always find that the winds blow from high pressure to low pressure.

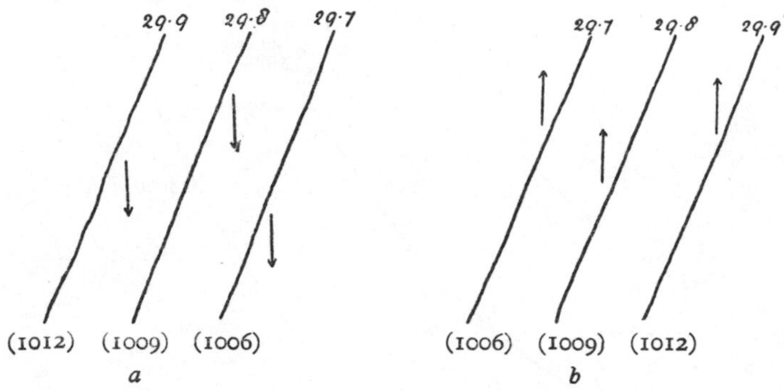

Fig. 2. Relation of surface winds to isobars in the northern hemisphere. Millibar equivalents approximate.

If this were all, the wind would blow straight from the high pressure to the low pressure at right angles to the isobars. But the direction is modified by the rotation of the earth. In the northern hemisphere every wind is deflected to the right of the course which it would take if the earth were still; in the southern hemisphere the deflection is to the left. The cause of the deflection will be explained later: its consequence is that the winds are not at right angles to the isobars but are inclined as in figs. 2*a* and 2*b*. We can accordingly formulate the following rule:

Stand with your back to the wind; if you are in the northern hemisphere there will be high pressure to your right and low pressure to your left; if you are in the southern hemisphere the high pressure will be to your left and the low pressure to your right.

This is known as Buys Ballot's law. It must not be supposed, however, that the actual centre of highest pressure will be exactly to your right or to your left. It is more likely to lie a little backwards also.

When the wind is known, Buys Ballot's law enables us at once to infer the approximate direction of the high pressure. If, for example, the wind in England is from the north, then there is high pressure over the

Atlantic towards the west or north-west; if the wind is from the south, the high pressure is over the continent towards the east or south-east.

When the air is almost still, with only very light and gentle breezes, the direction of these breezes may show no apparent relation to the isobars on the ordinary weather-charts. They are caused by local differences of pressure, too small to appear upon the chart. In the valleys of a mountainous district, or in the streets of a town, the direction of the wind is influenced by the valleys or streets and is not determined entirely by the pressure. But when no such local causes interfere, Buys Ballot's law is almost universally true.

The amount of the deflection is not always the same. Sometimes it is so great that the surface winds are almost parallel to the isobars. As a general rule it may be said that over the sea the average direction is about 10° from the course of the isobars, over land 30°. It will be shown that on a perfectly smooth earth the wind should flow along the isobars, and that the difference in the average deflection given above arises from the decreased hindrance to motion over the sea or, in other words, to an increased drag over the land caused by the friction of air over its irregular surface.

Barometric gradient. Since the winds are due to differences of pressure, the strength of a wind will depend upon the amount of the difference. In order to express this numerically the term barometric gradient, or pressure gradient, has been introduced. The barometric gradient is the rate of fall of the barometric pressure measured in a direction at right angles to the isobars. (The unit of barometric gradient was a fall of $\frac{1}{100}$ inch in 15 nautical miles.) To take an example, a pressure gradient of a tenth of an inch in 30 miles, or 10 mb. in 100 miles, measured in a direction at right angles to the isobars, is well above the average and would be called steep.

On any weather-chart it will usually be found that where the isobars are close together and the gradient is therefore high, the winds are strong, and where the isobars are far apart and the gradient low, the winds are light. In general, the higher the gradient the stronger are the winds.

Deflection of the winds: Hadley's explanation. The first reasonable explanation of the effect of the rotation of the earth upon the direction of the winds is due to Hadley.

At the equator everything that appears at rest upon the earth is really moving eastward with the earth at a rate of about 1000 miles an hour. At 60° from the equator, the eastward velocity is only 500 miles an hour.

Looking down upon the North Pole as in fig. 3 every part of the earth is moving in the direction of the arrow, completing the circle in a day. In three hours, or an eighth of a day, everything at rest at A will move to A' and everything at rest at B will move to B'. If in addition to this movement we give to a particle at A an impulse towards the pole N, that would bring it to B in three hours; it will be carried the distance AB towards the pole, but it has also an eastward motion sufficient to take it to A' in the same time. Consequently, it moves northwards the distance AB and eastwards the distance AA', which is equal to BC. Therefore instead of reaching B it reaches C, and its actual movement is from A to C.

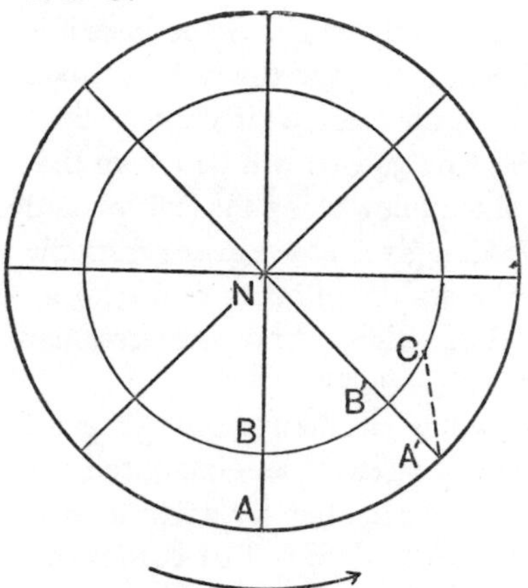

Fig. 3. Hadley's explanation of the deflection of a south wind.

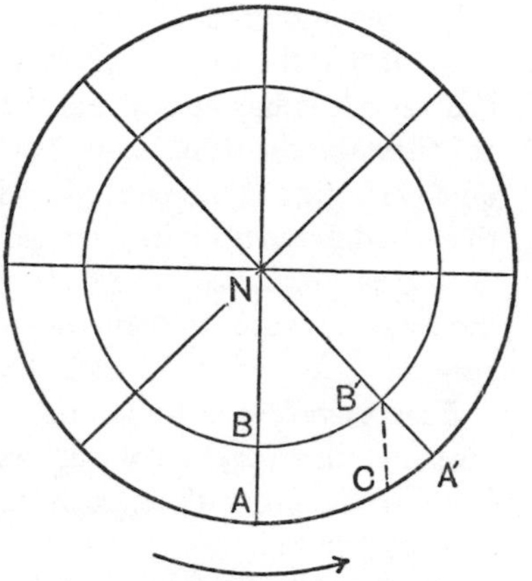

Fig. 4. Hadley's explanation of the deflection of a north wind.

But during this time the point A of the earth's surface has moved to A', and the point B to B'; and consequently the final positions of the starting point, of the point to which the particle was aimed, and of the particle itself, are A', B', and C. The apparent movement of the particle has been from A' to C and instead of moving as it was aimed, directly to the pole, its movement on the earth has been in a north-easterly direction.

If on the other hand we give a particle at B (fig. 4) an impulse which will carry it due south to A in three hours, it will move the distance BA in that direction and also the distance BB' eastward. It therefore reaches the point C, AC being equal to BB'. But in the three hours B has moved to B' and A to A'; and the final positions of the starting point, the point towards which the particle was aimed, and the particle itself, are B', A', and C. The movement of the particle on the earth has been in a south-westerly direction $B'C$, instead of due south BA.

In both cases the particle has been deflected to the right of its intended course. It can be shown in the same way that in the southern hemisphere there will be a deflection to the left.

Experimental illustration. It is easy to illustrate experimentally the apparent deflection of the course of a particle moving from the pole to the equator. Fix a circular piece of card upon the table by a pin passing through the centre. This may be taken to represent a view of the globe looking downwards on the pole. Turn the card round the axis formed by the pin and at the same time draw a pencil point from the pin in a straight line towards some other fixed point on the table, as indicated by the dotted lines in fig. 5. The line traced upon the card will be a curve similar to those in the figure. If the card is turned in the direction

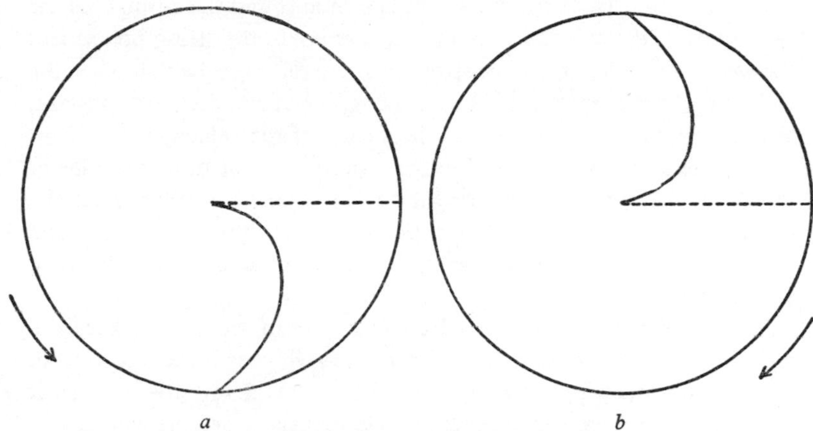

Fig. 5. Curve traced by a pencil on a rotating card.

shown by the arrow in fig. 5*a*, it represents a view of the globe looking down on the North Pole, and the curve will deviate towards the right. If the card is turned in the opposite direction (fig. 5*b*) it represents a view of the globe looking down on the South Pole and the deviation is towards the left.

It should be noted that this method cannot be used to illustrate the deflection of a particle moving from the equator towards the pole. On the earth such a particle, in addition to its poleward movement, has an eastward movement due to the earth's rotation. If, in our experiment, we draw a pencil line from the circumference of the rotating card towards its centre, the pencil does not share in the rotation, and a somewhat complex curve is produced which does not represent the movement of any wind upon the earth.

Incompleteness of Hadley's explanation. Hadley's explanation is not complete. According to the principle which he expounds, a wind which was nearly east or nearly west would suffer very little deflection. But observation shows that all winds, whatever their original direction may be, are equally affected, and, moreover, the deflection is always greater than his explanation would lead us to expect.

The effect of the earth's rotation has been more fully investigated by ater mathematicians. It depends upon the laws of centrifugal force, and the more important principles can be illustrated by a very simple experiment.

Centrifugal force. When a weight on the end of a string is swung round in a circle, the weight is continually attempting to fly off and accordingly exerts a pull upon the string. This pull is known as centrifugal force, and the faster the weight is swung round the stronger is the pull, until, if the velocity becomes great enough, the string breaks and the weight flies off. It may be stated as a general principle that when the weight and the length of the string (or radius of rotation) are constant, the centrifugal force increases as the square of the velocity.

Pass the end of the string through a short piece of tube, the edge of which should be rounded to prevent it from cutting the string. Hold the loose end of the string in the left hand and the tube in the right, and swing the weight round and round. It swings round the end of the tube as a centre.

When the weight has attained a steady rate of movement, keep the right hand still for a moment and pull the string with the left so as to shorten the swinging part. The weight is drawn inwards and, as it approaches the centre of rotation, its velocity increases. It will also be found that it pulls more strongly outwards—so strongly in fact, when the string becomes very short, that it is impossible to hold the hand steady. The centrifugal force is increased.

Repeat the experiment but, instead of pulling the string inwards, allow a little more to go out through the tube so as to lengthen the swinging part. The weight flies outwards and, as it recedes from the centre of rotation, its velocity decreases. It will be found, moreover, that the pull on the string diminishes, that is, the centrifugal force decreases.

These experiments show that when a body is rotating at a uniform speed round a centre, (1) if it is forced towards the centre its velocity increases and the centrifugal force also increases, (2) if it is forced, or allowed to fly, away from the centre, its velocity decreases and the centrifugal force also decreases.

Ferrel's explanation. Fig. 6 is a view of the globe from above the north pole, the circumference is the equator and the centre N is the pole. The axis of rotation passes through *N* at right angles to the paper; the direction of rotation is shown by the arrow. Anything that moves from the equator towards the pole is approaching the axis of rotation, as the weight did when the string was shortened. Anything that moves from the pole towards the equator is receding from the axis of rotation, as the weight did when the string was allowed to lengthen.

A particle at rest upon the earth at *A* is really moving round the axis at a rate of about 1000 miles an hour. If we attempt to force it directly towards *B* it approaches nearer to the axis of rotation and its eastward velocity becomes more than 1000 miles an hour. But *B* has an eastward

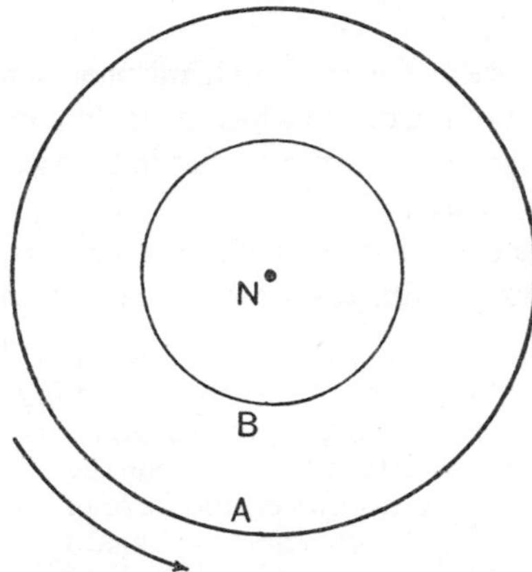

Fig. 6. Ferrel's explanation of the deflection of winds.

velocity less than 1000 miles an hour, and therefore the particle when it reaches the latitude of *B* is in front of *B*. It has been deflected to the right.

On the other hand a particle at rest in latitude 60° N. has a velocity round the axis of about 500 miles an hour. If we attempt to force it directly towards *A*, it recedes from the axis of rotation and its eastward velocity becomes less. But the eastward velocity of *A* is more than 500 miles an hour, and therefore when the particle reaches the latitude of *A* it is behind *A*. It has been deflected to the right.

These results are similar to those of Hadley, but calculation shows that the amount of the deflection is very much greater than he supposed.

Next we have to consider the case of an attempted movement in a due east or due west direction. A particle at rest at *B* in lat. 60° is moving round the axis in an eastward direction at a rate of 500 miles an hour. Give it an impulse towards the east. Its eastward movement is now increased and its rate of rotation becomes more than 500 miles an hour. Its centrifugal force is therefore also increased and it moves away from the axis of rotation towards the equator. Therefore instead of travelling due east it moves to the south of east. It is deflected to the right of its intended course.

Instead of attempting to move the particle eastward, give it an impulse towards the west. This is in opposition to its movement when at rest and its rate of rotation becomes less than 500 miles an hour. Because its rate of rotation is diminished, its centrifugal force decreases and accordingly it moves towards the axis, i.e. towards the pole. Instead of travelling due west it moves in a north-westerly direction. Again the deflection is to the right.

In all cases therefore in the northern hemisphere a moving particle is deflected to the right of the course which it would take if the earth were still. It can be shown in a similar way that in the southern hemisphere the deflection is to the left.

The following is a fuller statement of Ferrel's explanation of the effect of the earth's rotation on due east or due west movements.

If the rotating earth were a true sphere with a smooth and frictionless surface, no loose particle could remain at rest excepting at the poles or the equator. Fig. 7 is a section of the earth through the poles, *NS* being the axis of rotation. Every particle, such as *A*, upon the surface, moving with the earth, is acted upon by two forces, the force of gravity in the direction *AB* towards the centre, and the centrifugal force in the direction *AC* at right angles to the axis of rotation. The latter is a very small force compared with the former. If the earth is a true sphere, *AB* will be at right angles to the surface and can have no tendency to make the particle move in any direction. But the force *AC* is oblique to the surface. It is not enough to lift the particle, but it is clear that if there is no friction it will cause the particle to slide towards the equator.

At the pole there is no centrifugal force. At the equator the centrifugal force is at right angles to the surface and is directly opposed to the force of gravity. It therefore has no tendency to make the particle move on the surface and, because it is so small compared with gravity, its only effect is to diminish slightly the weight of the particle.

But the earth is not a sphere. A section through the poles is not a circle as in fig. 7 but an ellipse, as shown, with the ellipticity very greatly exaggerated, in fig. 8. In an ellipsoidal earth the force of gravity is not, in general, directed exactly towards the centre, but it is nearly so, and is not at right angles to the surface, except at the poles and the equator. Elsewhere it may be resolved into two components, one *AD* at right angles to the surface the other *AE* tangential. The former presses the particle against the surface, the latter tends to move it towards the pole.

The centrifugal force is at right angles to the axis, in the direction *AC*. It may be resolved into two components, one *AF* at right angles to the surface, the other *AG* tangential. The former makes the particle a little lighter than it would otherwise be, the latter tends to move it towards the equator.

When the particle is at rest on the rotating earth, the forces *AE* and *AG* must balance each other. If we now give it an eastward motion relatively to the earth, we are increasing the velocity of rotation which it

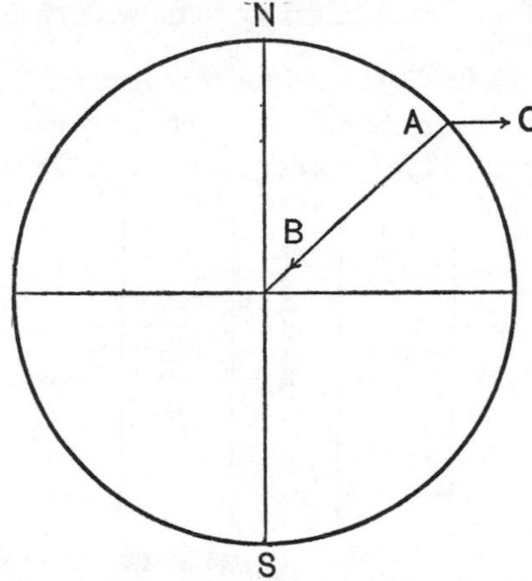

Fig. 7. Effect of centrifugal force upon a spherical earth.

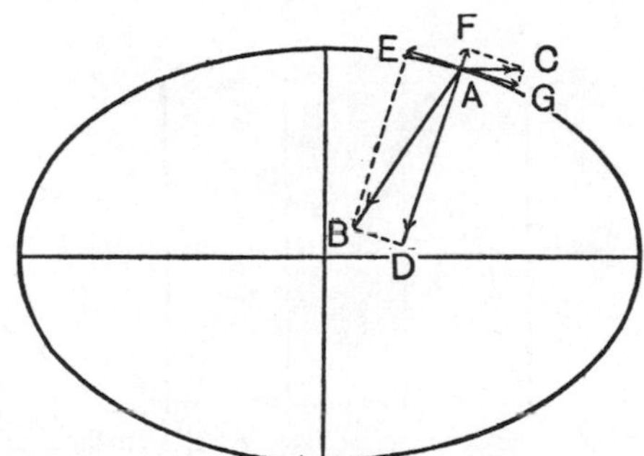

Fig. 8. Effect of centrifugal force upon an ellipsoidal earth.

already had. The centrifugal force *AC* increases, *AG* therefore increases and becomes greater than *AE*. The particle therefore slides towards the equator and instead of moving due east it moves to a point somewhat south of east.

If on the other hand we give the particle a motion westward, this is opposed to its direction of rotation. Its velocity round the axis becomes less. The centrifugal force decreases and the force *AG* therefore decreases and becomes less than *AE*. The particle therefore slides towards the pole and instead of moving due west it moves to a point somewhat north of west.

In both cases the deflection is to the right. In the southern hemisphere the deflection will be to the left.

The law of deflection of moving bodies on the surface of the rotating earth is often spoken of as Ferrel's law, because Ferrel was one of the earliest writers to develop it fully, particularly in its application to the winds; but he was not actually the first to enunciate the principle. The deflecting force causing an acceleration to one side or the other of the nitial direction of motion is called by some writers the Coriolis force.

Motion of air under balanced forces. Any small mass of air set in motion on the earth's surface has thus a tendency to be deflected to the right or left of its path. This tendency results from the action of a deflect-

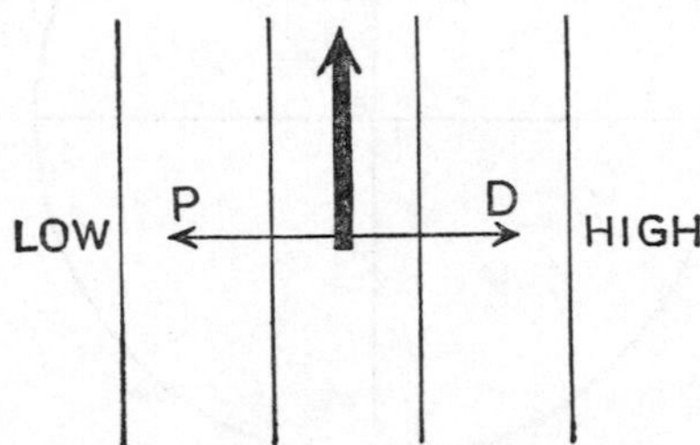

Fig. 9. Wind in relation to isobars. For steady motion the deflecting force *D*, acting at right angles to the direction of motion, must be equal and opposite to the pressure force *P*. Wind must blow along isobars. The closer the isobars, the stronger the wind.

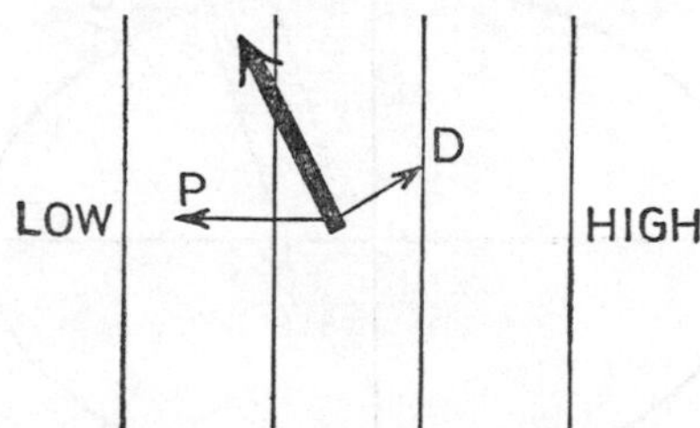

Fig. 10. Surface wind in relation to isobars. At the surface, wind speed is decreased owing to friction. Deflecting force *D* is then insufficient to balance the pressure *P*, and resultant movement of air is inward across the isobars.

ing force which is always acting at right angles to the direction of movement.

Any small mass of air is thus under the influence of a pressure force, causing it to tend to move directly towards lower pressure, that is, in a direction at right angles to the isobars. But if it moves, it is also under the influence of a deflecting force, which continually tries to accelerate the particle in a direction at right angles to its initial motion. A little consideration will show that if this small packet of air is to move steadily, the only way it can move is with the pressure force (*P*) and the deflecting force (*D*) acting in equal and opposite directions.

As *D* must always be at right angles to the direction of motion, the only possible path will be along the direction of the isobars as shown by the thick arrow.

This deflecting force can be shown to be proportional to the square of the velocity of movement and to the sine of the latitude. Hence, if the pressure force is large, i.e. if there is a steep pressure gradient as defined on p. 11, the deflecting force must be large to balance it. But the deflecting force will only be large if the velocity is large. Therefore, with a steep pressure gradient, represented by closely spaced isobars, there will be strong winds which, at no great height above the earth's surface, will blow very nearly along the isobars. It will be seen that Buys Ballot's law (p. 10) follows.

But it is to be remembered that the earth's surface is rough, i.e. there is friction. Woods, houses and other obstacles hinder the flow of the surface layers of air, i.e. decrease the speed of movement. The result of this is a decrease in the deflecting force (*D*); but the pressure force (*P*) remains the same. Hence a small mass of air at the surface tends to be drawn across the isobars at an angle. Even on the sea friction is appreciable and this angle is commonly about 10°; inland, over open level country, it approximates to 30°. At an altitude of 2000 feet, however, over the sea or level country, the flow of the air is for practical purposes along the isobars as in the first diagram above.

CHAPTER III

DISTRIBUTION OF PRESSURE AND THE CIRCULATION OF THE ATMOSPHERE

On a frictionless rotating earth, as a result of the balance of pressure and deflecting forces, the surface air-streams would tend to flow along the isobars, and in practice this state of affairs is broadly found to prevail at 2000 feet above the sea or low-level uniform plains. At the surface, however, the wind directions cross those of the isobars at an angle, as we have seen.

It is possible to calculate from the spacing of the isobars what the resultant wind speed should be. Again it is found that the actual wind speed at 2000 feet over the sea closely approaches that calculated from the pressure gradient. But at the surface the wind speed is less. No precise rule can be given, but it is not uncommon to find that with fresh or strong wind, the surface speed over the sea is of the order of two-thirds of that which prevails at 2000 feet. Over a completely open plain the ratio may be about a half; for obvious reasons it decreases more where there are many obstacles. Resultant irregularities in the speed of flow of the surface stream of air give the effect known as gustiness, so characteristic of the streets of towns on a windy day.

Almost any issue of the Daily Weather Report of the Meteorological Office giving a chart showing the distribution of pressure and wind, preferably for an hour towards the middle of the day, will corroborate this. However, at a few stations the wind, if light, may deviate from the isobars considerably more than the normal given above. The most common explanation of such exceptions is that the station is in a well-defined valley in mountainous or hilly country, where the surface flow of air is compelled to follow the trend of a valley rather than that of the isobars.

It is also interesting to try to correlate the isobars with the wind direction and speed at the surface, and that given, for example, by pilot-balloon ascents up to 3000 feet. This too can be done by making use of the data in the Daily Weather Report.

The origin of differences of pressure. The origin of the differences of pressure which give rise to the winds, and the consequent movement of air with varying characteristics over the earth's surface, now demand attention. The primary cause lies in the differences of temperature of the surface air. Suppose that a block of air, like a balloon, is resting on the ground. If for some reason, e.g. conduction of heat from the adjacent warm ground, such a block is warmed to a temperature above that of the surrounding air, it will rise, and on doing so will be replaced by an inflow of the neighbouring cooler air. If this in turn is heated, as for example over a hot sandy desert, the rising 'bubbles' of air are sufficiently frequent to be indicated by the barometer as a decrease of pressure over the heated area. It follows that a given volume of warm air is less dense, and therefore weighs less, than a similar volume of cold air. Hence, with the same pressure at the surface, pressure at the top of a warm air-column will be greater than at the top of a cold air-column of equal height. Air will therefore tend to flow from the top of the warm column towards the cold.

The reasons for such surface heating are more fully dealt with in ch. v. Here it suffices to accept the fact that the heat balance of the atmosphere is such that the total heat, i.e. the excess of the gains above the losses, received by the surface atmosphere directly or indirectly from the sun, is greater at the equator than at the poles.

It is very important to recognise that, although we ourselves feel the warmth of the sun as radiation which warms our bodies, the atmosphere where free from cloud is largely transparent to such radiation. Solar radiation warms the earth's surface, which in turn warms the air adjacent to it, mainly by conduction. The atmosphere, however, is not equally transparent to the radiation given out by the earth at night; even with clear skies much depends on the amount of water-vapour present in the air above. The gain of temperature during the day and loss at night are most marked in regions where the air is dry, as in the great deserts. The same phenomenon of a large daily range may frequently be observed in the British Isles, if the country happens to be covered in summer by an extensive anticyclone, in which the air is prevailingly dry for several thousand feet above the surface.

When the air has been warmed, it rises; as it rises, it expands. Provided that it is not saturated with water-vapour (a term explained in ch. VI), the result of its expansion is that it will fall off in temperature, following the laws of gases, by 5½° F. per 1000 feet of rise. It is common to find that air dropping in temperature at this rate reaches after a time a level at which it is no longer warmer than the surrounding air, even though it was considerably warmer at first. This is because the prevailing lapse-rate, or rate of decrease of the temperature of the air up to the tropopause (p. 5), is (allowing for all observations both by day and night) considerably less than 5½° per 1000 feet. Normally about 3·3°–3·5° may be expected in temperate latitudes. Rising air, therefore, does not necessarily ascend all the way to the tropopause; and from what has been said no air from the earth's surface can be expected to ascend beyond that level into the stratosphere, because above the tropopause the temperature of the air as a whole remains stationary or rises. A rising bubble of air, however, must continue to expand and cool; hence even if by virtue of its exceptional warmth it has come up all the way to the tropopause, a very slight ascent beyond will result in the rising air being colder than the environment; hence it cannot rise any farther. It is important to bear this in mind to account for the way in which the rising air from the tropics spreads out at a certain level towards the poles.

The general distribution of pressure. At the surface of the earth the predominance of heating in equatorial regions compared with the nocturnal cooling results in a well-developed permanent belt of lower pressure, which stands in contrast with the regions to north and south, and into which air tends to flow.

If the earth were entirely stationary, the surface pressure would be highest at the poles, where surface heating was least effective, and lowest at the equator. But the earth is rotating; hence the streams of air moving from polar regions towards the equator are deflected. Even on a rotating globe with a uniform surface, there would not be an uninterrupted flow of air at the surface from pole to equator, in the form of a north-east wind in the north, south-east in the south. Because of the friction between these great streams of air and the globe (cf. pp. 26–27) there is a tendency for the streams to be broken up into large eddies soon after leaving the polar regions. The centres of these eddies form areas of lower atmospheric pressure; this follows from a consideration of Buys Ballot's law (p. 10). In higher temperate latitudes over the oceans they are sufficiently frequent and persistent to render the *average* pressure taken over a long period slightly lower than that either to the north or the south.

Here it must suffice to say that the disturbances and irregularities in the surface flow arise not merely from the features of the surface, but also from the varying speed and manner of movement of air currents at higher levels which convey further complex stresses to the layers below (see pp. 23 and 104).

Between this belt of eddy-development as we may call it, and the equatorial low-pressure region, there is necessarily a region from which air-streams at the surface diverge, either poleward towards the persistent eddies, or equatorward as the trade-winds. This region of slightly higher pressure is generally found between lat. 30–35°; and the outward divergence of the surface air-streams means that descending air-currents from above prevail in the centre of the region. In ch. VI it will be shown that a normal result of this is that the sky within the region is almost free from cloud. In what has been called the eddy-region, the eddies themselves do not behave with the simplicity of those in water, because the characteristics of the air-streams drawn into them differ widely. Simple analogies must, therefore, not be pressed too far, since no full explanation of the complexities of the atmospheric circulation can yet be given.

Nevertheless, if we had a rotating earth with a uniform surface, a distribution of atmospheric pressure and resultant winds, somewhat like that shown in fig. 11, would develop. But in practice, as the maps show, this relatively simple scheme is only approached in the southern hemisphere. In the northern hemisphere the irregular distribution of land and sea produces a great exaggeration of the high-pressure region in winter over the continents, while the low-pressure systems become much more marked over the oceans. To some extent the converse obtains in summer: and further modifications arise from the fact that the region of greatest heating is not stationary at the equator throughout the year, but moves with the seasons.

The upper currents of the atmosphere move approximately in the manner shown in the diagram. Air spreading from high levels in the tropics descends in the high-pressure belts; some, however, continues towards the poles. Because of deflection (see p. 26) there is at very high

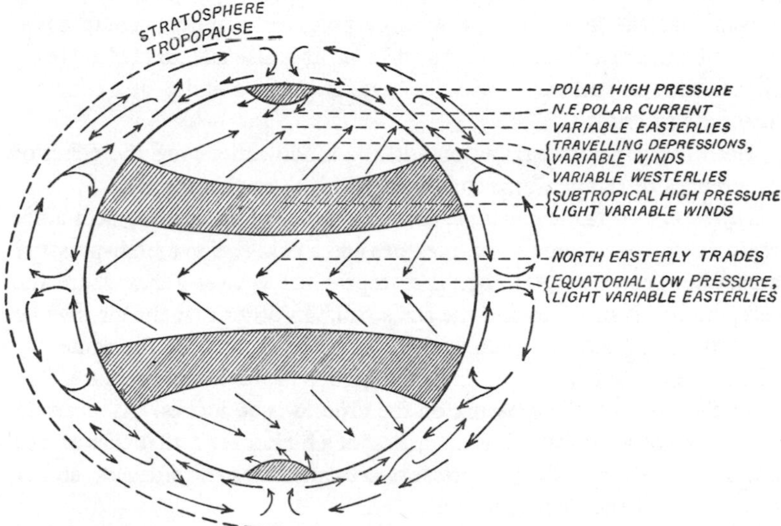

Fig. 11. Diagram of the general distribution of pressure and winds of the globe. The horizontal and vertical circulation are indicated by the arrows. High-pressure areas are shaded.

altitudes in temperate and polar latitudes an overwhelming preponderance of winds from westerly points. The conflict in temperate latitudes between the disturbed and variable surface air-streams which so often differ from each other in temperature and moisture content produces many important developments which are dealt with in a separate chapter (p. 104).

From this distribution of pressure it is easy to deduce the direction of the prevalent winds, remembering always that they blow from high pressure to low pressure but are deflected to the right in the northern hemisphere, to the left in the southern hemisphere.

Winds also blow from the tropical high pressure to the low pressures of the temperate regions. In the northern hemisphere they are south-westerly, in the southern hemisphere north-westerly. These are the westerlies. They are not so steady as the trade-winds, especially in the northern hemisphere, for in these regions cyclonic and associated disturbances are common.

Finally, from the high-pressures of the poles the winds blow outwards, from the north-east in the northern hemisphere and from the south-east in the southern hemisphere. The polar high pressure and the outflowing surface winds are better defined in the Antarctic regions than in the Arctic, but even there they do not extend very far from the pole.

A comparison of the diagram (fig. 11) with the map (map 1, p. 473) shows that the actual distribution of pressure is influenced to some extent by the distribution of land and sea. It is also affected by the position of the sun and varies with the seasons (maps 2 and 3, and compare also figs. 13 and 14).[1]

Both the general distribution and the modifications are the effect of differences of temperature combined with the earth's rotation.

Influence of temperature. In the absence of other influences a hot region tends to become a low-pressure and a cold region a high-pressure area. Suppose that *AB* (fig. 12*a*) represents a level plain where the temperature is uniform and the air is still. In order that the air may be still, the pressure at all points on the same level must be the same, for otherwise a wind will blow from the higher to the lower pressure.

In the diagram the pressure on the ground is 30 inches. At a certain height above the ground it is 29 inches; at a higher level 28 inches and so on. These surfaces of equal pressure are called isobaric surfaces, and as the air is still they must be level.

Suppose that a part *CD* of the plain (fig. 12 *b*) is heated and becomes hotter than the rest. The air in contact with it will be warmed and will expand, lifting the air above it. Consequently the isobaric surfaces above *CD* will be raised as in fig. 12*b*. The air, however, cannot remain in this condition. The pressure at *E* is now greater than at *F* and *G* on the same level, and accordingly the air will flow outwards from *E* to *F* and *G*.

When this happens, some of the air above *CD* is removed from there and is added to that above *A* and *B*. Consequently the pressure *on the ground* is no longer uniform. It becomes less than 30 inches on *CD* and more than 30 inches at *A* and *B*. The isobaric surface of 30 inches ceases

[1] Maps showing actual pressure distribution and frontal activity at the two solstices give a good idea of the way in which weather charts can broadly reflect the climatic zones of the earth, for it is important to remember that the climate of any one place is made up of innumerable weather situations continuously following one another. The moving fronts and depressions of the temperate regions produce the greatest and most rapid weather changes. The sub-tropical anticyclones and the low-pressure belt of the equatorial region remain relatively stationary.

to coincide with the ground but runs as in fig. 12*c*. Near the ground the isobaric surfaces will now be concave upwards while higher in the air they are concave downwards.

Because the pressure on the ground at *A* and *B* is now greater than at *CD*, there will be a surface wind from *A* and *B* inwards to *CD*.

The effect of heating *CD* is therefore to cause an outflowing current above and an inflowing current below; and on the ground-level to decrease the pressure on the heated part and increase the pressure on the cool part.

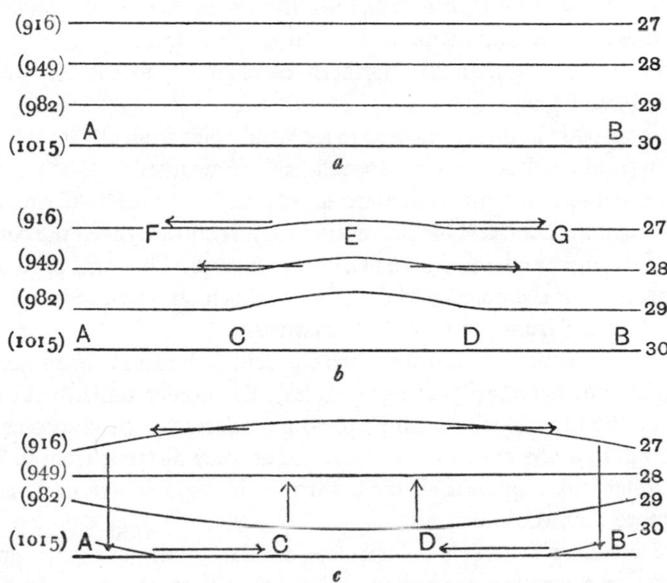

Fig. 12. Effect of heat upon pressure and winds. Approximate millibar equivalents shown.

Moreover, the air over *A* and *B* is pressed downwards by the addition of air above, and therefore sinks. The warmer and lighter air over *CD* is lifted upwards by the influx of the colder and denser air below and therefore rises. The upper currents will be cooled as they flow away from the source of heat, the lower currents will be warmed as they flow towards it; and consequently as long as the difference of temperature on the ground is maintained the circulation will be kept up.

It must not be supposed, however, that this circulation extends to the top of the atmosphere. When first *CD* is heated, only the layer of air in contact with it is warmed and expanded. But because the air is elastic this expansion does not at once lift the layers above. Its only effect for the moment is to compress the next layer. Thus it takes time to establish the circulation described. In a general way it may be said that the longer the difference of temperature is kept up, the higher in the atmosphere will the circulation extend.

According to the principle explained above, the lowest pressure at sea-level should be about the equator and the highest pressure at the poles, and there should be a gradual increase from the equator to the poles. The surface winds should blow from the poles to the equator and the upper winds from the equator to the poles.

Influence of the earth's rotation. But owing to the rotation of the earth these winds cannot maintain their original directions. They are deflected to the right in the northern hemisphere, to the left in the southern hemisphere.

If a large body of men is moving to a central point from all around, and those in front reach the centre about the same time, there will be a block. If those behind still move forward a very high pressure will soon be produced at the centre. This illustration represents fairly well the conditions of the upper currents on a non-rotating earth. They will produce a high pressure at the poles, and the effect of this high pressure is to cause under-currents from the poles to the equator.

But suppose that before they reach the centre the front ranks turn to the right (not necessarily at right angles), the hinder ranks will catch them up, and the block and high pressure will not be produced at the centre but in a ring around the centre and at some distance from it. The same thing will happen if all ranks turn to the right but those in front turn more than those behind.

The conditions now are somewhat similar to those of the upper currents on a rotating earth, flowing from the equator to the north pole. As they move northwards they are deflected to the right and instead of adding to the pressure at the pole, they produce a ring of high pressure between the equator and the pole. On the surface this high pressure will cause under-currents flowing both to the equator and to the pole.

This illustration will perhaps serve to show why, on a rotating earth, the principal high pressure is not at the pole. But the whole problem is one of great complexity and the mathematical theory of the general circulation of the atmosphere is still very imperfect.

Seasonal changes. If the sun were always vertical at the equator, the position of the high- and low-pressure belts would remain unchanged throughout the year. But in our summer the sun is above the Tropic of Cancer, in our winter above the Tropic of Capricorn. The pressure belts move with the apparent movement of the sun, but not to the same extent.

In the northern summer the equatorial low-pressure belt lies a few degrees north of the equator, in the southern summer a few degrees south.

But there is a greater change than this. In the northern winter the northern land-masses are far colder than the neighbouring seas and they therefore become areas of high pressure. The tropical high-pressure belt accordingly spreads northwards over the continents of America and Asia.

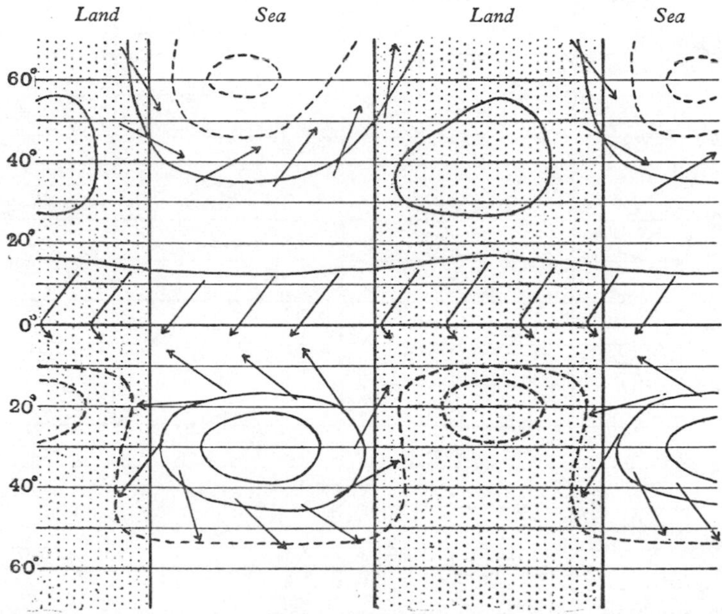

Fig. 13. Diagram of the distribution of pressure over land and sea in January. Isobars over 30 inches shown as continuous lines; isobars under 30 inches as broken lines.

At the same time it is the southern summer, and in the southern hemisphere the land-masses are much hotter than the sea. They become areas of low pressure and the southern tropical high-pressure belt is broken over South America, Africa, and Australia.

In the northern summer, which will be southern winter, the conditions are reversed. The high-pressure belt is interrupted over the northern continents but spreads outwards over the southern continents. Owing to the small extent of the latter the effect is much less marked than in the northern hemisphere.

These changes in the position and extent of the pressure belts are shown diagrammatically in figs. 13 and 14, in which the land and sea are supposed to stretch from north to south in alternate bands.

Since the continental masses alter the distribution of pressure to so great an extent they will have a corresponding effect upon the winds. The winds will always blow away from the high pressures but with the deflection proper to each hemisphere, and their directions are shown in the diagrams.

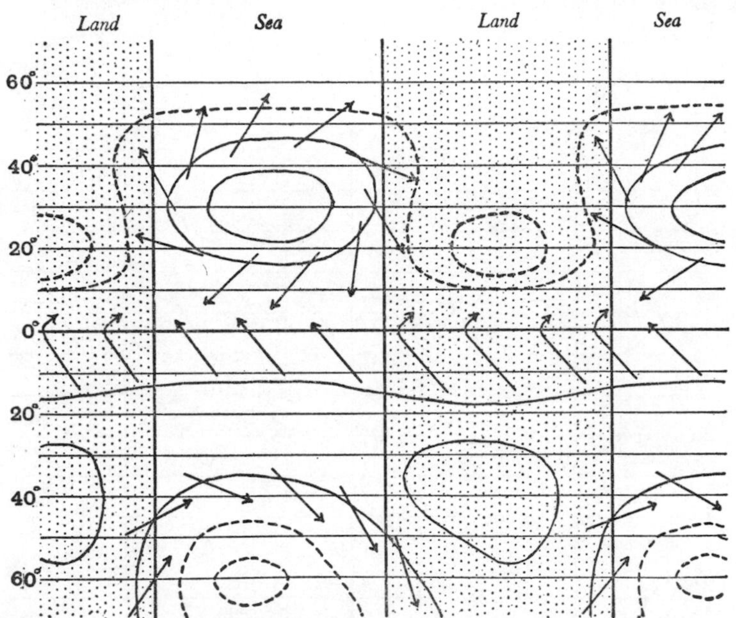

Fig. 14. Diagram of the distribution of pressure over land and sea in July. Isobars over 30 inches shown as continuous lines; isobars under 30 inches as broken lines.

Besides the change due to the migration of the belts from north to south and back again, the most notable seasonal variation is that upon the eastern margins of the continents. Here the winter winds are directed towards the equator, and the summer winds towards the pole. Their precise direction and their extent in latitude will depend upon the form of the continental mass. The change is actually most noticeable in south-eastern Asia, where it gives rise to the monsoons; but a similar effect is observable in the south-eastern part of the United States and elsewhere.

It will be seen from the diagrams that apart from the effect of the continents there would be somewhat similar seasonal variations of the wind near the equator, because the line of lowest pressure lies south of the equator in our winter, north of the equator in our summer. In our winter therefore the north-east trades are carried across the equator and are then deflected to the left. In our summer the south-east trades are carried north of the equator and are then deflected to the right. But if the globe were covered with water the effect would be limited to a narrow belt extending only a short distance on each side of the equator; and, since the deflecting force near to the equator is very small, the trade-winds when they cross the line would deviate but little from their original directions. This is seen to be the case in the middle of the Pacific, where there are no large land-masses to intensify the effect.

The two world pressure maps (January and July) should be studied and their characteristics carefully observed, as they illustrate at once the prevailing air-streams, summer and winter, and enable a first estimate of the climate of many parts of the world to be made.

LOCAL WINDS

The winds of the general circulation of the atmosphere, as described in the preceding pages, are the consequence of the decrease of temperature from the equator to the poles combined with the rotation of the earth. But there are also local winds due to local differences of temperature. In the strict sense of the term the monsoons are local winds, for they are caused by the interference of the continental masses with the general fall of temperature from the equator to the poles. But they are on so large a scale and cover so wide an area that in the ordinary sense of the word they can hardly be called local.

Land and sea breezes. The most familiar of the local winds are the land and sea breezes which at certain seasons and in certain regions blow day by day with the greatest regularity. Even in so variable a climate as that of England they are often felt during settled weather.

They are the result of the unequal heating of land and water. It is well known that when the sun's rays fall with equal intensity upon land and sea, the temperature of the land rises more quickly than that of the sea. But on the other hand, after the sun has set the land cools more quickly than the sea.

Consequently, during the day while the sun is shining, the land becomes a hot area compared with the sea. The circulation described on p. 25 is set up; an upper current of air flows from land to sea and on the surface a lower current from sea to land. The latter is the sea breeze. It does not begin to blow as soon as the sun has risen, for at night the land has become cooler than the sea. It is not till the sun has had time to raise the temperature of the land above that of the sea, that these currents start. Moreover, it has already been shown that the establishment of the circulation between cold and hot areas takes time. It begins on a very small scale and extends gradually, if the heating continues, both horizontally and vertically. On the coast the sea breeze often blows in the forenoon, while inland it may not be felt till a much later hour.

In the afternoon when the sun has sunk so low that the heat received from it is less than the heat lost by radiation, the sea breeze begins to die away, but it does not cease entirely until the temperature of the land has fallen to that of the sea.

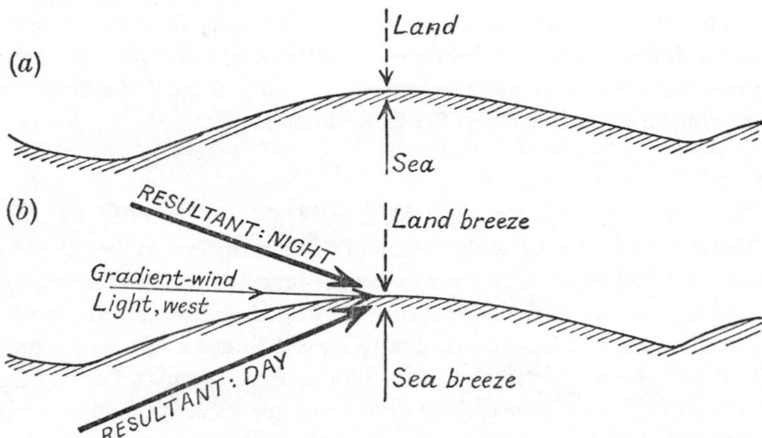

Fig. 15. Thermal effects: (*a*) under calm conditions; (*b*) land and sea breezes combining with a gradient-wind from west to east. The resultant wind backs seaward in the daytime and veers landward at night.

The land still continues to cool more rapidly than the sea, and consequently the sea becomes a hot area compared with the land. A reverse circulation is then set up; the upper currents flow from the sea towards the land, the lower currents from the land towards the sea. It is the latter that are felt on the surface of the ground, and they form the land breeze, which is experienced in the evening and at night.

The length of time during which either the land or the sea remains hotter than the other is only a few hours. Consequently, the height to which the circulation of air extends is not great. Observations with pilot balloons at Coney Island near New York showed that the sea breeze was felt only to an altitude of 500 or 600 feet.

Land and sea breezes can only be experienced when the sky is fairly free from cloud, for otherwise the sun will not warm the land to any great extent by day nor will much heat be lost by radiation at night. They are strongest when the diurnal range of temperature is greatest. In England they are seldom noticed except during the summer, for in the winter the sun has very little power, even at noon. Their strength is never very great and consequently they are easily overpowered by the winds due to other causes. Occasionally the land breeze is noticeable in winter when the land is snow-covered and the gradient wind is slight. Cooling of the surface air due to outward radiation on a clear night from snow-covered land is great; hence in the night hours the land breeze becomes more marked than usual.

The conditions favourable to the production of land and sea breezes are therefore a clear sky and the absence or feeble development of other winds. These are the characteristics of anticyclones, and land and sea breezes are accordingly most marked in anticyclonic areas, whether these are temporary or permanent. In fig. 15 the result of the combination of land and sea breeze effects with a light prevailing wind is shown. Such effects are very common on our coasts in summer.

Lake breezes. In the neighbourhood of large lakes, offshore and onshore breezes are sometimes produced in precisely the same way. They do not differ in any essential respect from land and sea breezes but, in correspondence with the comparatively small area of the water surface, they are usually weaker.

Mountain and valley winds. In mountainous regions, winds are often caused by the unequal temperature of the free air and of the air in contact with the mountain sides. But the way in which the difference is brought about will be more readily understood after the vertical distribution of temperature has been explained, and these winds will therefore be dealt with in the chapter on that subject.

CHAPTER IV

ISOBAR SHAPES AND PATTERNS

In a later chapter, it will be necessary to go more fully into the association between weather and pressure conditions, and the extent to which observed weather conditions can be related to the varying characteristics of the air-mass over the station. At this stage only the different shapes or patterns commonly assumed by the isobars when plotted on a map will be described. The six principal patterns are shown in the diagrams.

Depressions or lows. A depression is the name given to an area of low pressure surrounded by closed isobars. As a rule the isobars assume a more or less oval form, although any series of daily weather charts will show that these are not always similarly curved at the surface. The surface winds within the depression will tend to blow slightly across the isobars, i.e. spirally inward (p. 10). Hence there must always be a certain amount of convergence of the surface air-streams, leading to some ascent of air. It will be shown in ch. VII that the forced ascent of damp air, i.e. air containing a good deal of water-vapour in suspension, leads to cooling by expansion and therefore to the condensation of some of the vapour into the visible form of cloud, or even rain. Hence for this reason alone a low-pressure area tends, in general, to be characterised by the existence of a good deal of cloud unless it lies on an extremely dry area such as a desert. There are, however, more significant reasons for the formation of cloud and rain in depressions; these are given in ch. IX.

In temperate latitudes depressions may cover areas up to 2000 miles in diameter; but diameters of the order of 300–500 miles are more usual. Thus the circulation round a large depression centred, for example, over the Irish Sea would be likely to produce easterly winds as far north as Cape Wrath, and westerly winds in Cornwall and Brittany.

Inside the tropics pressure is in general rather lower than over their marginal regions. Sometimes a localised area of low pressure, some 50–200 miles in diameter, occurs in which the isobars are almost circular, and very closely spaced. In a tropical depression of this type exceedingly violent winds occur. The term cyclone is nowadays reserved for this type of disturbance, which is confined to certain parts of the tropical oceans at particular seasons of the year. Fortunately their passage over any one locality is rare.

The origin, movements and behaviour of lows are discussed later, in ch. IX.

Anticyclones or highs. An anticyclone is an area of high pressure with the pressure gradually decreasing outwards. The isobars therefore assume a more or less oval or circular form. So far as the distribution of pressure is concerned an anticyclone is the opposite of a depression or cyclone, and there is a corresponding contrast in the character of the weather associated with it (fig. 16*a*).

An anticyclone as a rule does not travel in any well-defined path. It may wander undecidedly in almost any direction: it may spread outwards on one side or another and may afterwards retreat; it may remain stationary for days with very little change. It disappears sometimes by drifting slowly away, sometimes by gradually diminishing in intensity.

But whatever changes take place, they are usually slow and never violent.

Winds. The isobars in an anticyclone are far apart, especially towards the middle, and the winds are therefore light. Near the centre there is a

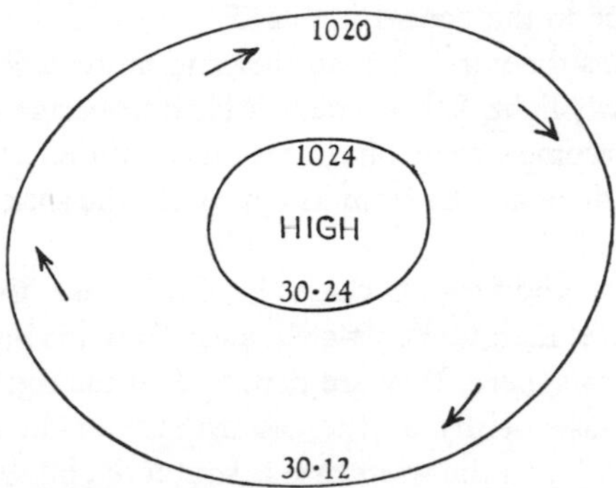

Fig. 16*a*. Isobars and surface winds in an anticyclone (northern hemisphere)

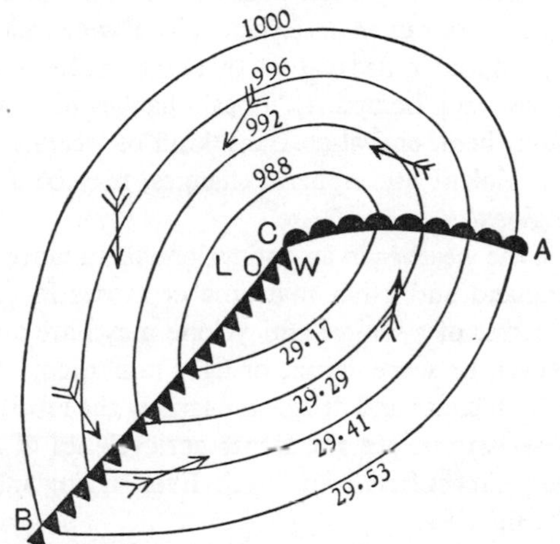

Fig. 16*b*. Isobars and surface winds in a depression (northern hemisphere). *AC*, *BC* represent the warm and cold fronts respectively. 'Fronts' signify the boundaries between air masses differing in character and origin, drawn into the circulation round the 'low'.

calm, or very light and variable airs. It is this stillness of the air that forms the primary characteristic of an anticyclone. It is in fact an almost motionless mass of air taking little part in the movements around it. It is analogous in some respects to the patches of smooth water which drift downstream amongst the swirls and eddies of a river in flood.

On account of the general stillness of the air local influences make themselves felt. Differences of temperature due to unequal heating of land and water or of mountain and plain produce local winds. Land and sea breezes, and mountain and valley winds often become noticeable; in a depression, on the other hand, they are completely overpowered by the strong winds due to the depression itself.

On the margins the winds are steadier and more definite in direction but are still usually light. When a depression approaches they increase in force and may become strong, but this is merely the effect of the steepening pressure gradient arising from its approach; the anticyclone does not always give way.

Apart from the modifications due to local influences the general direction of the winds is naturally outwards, away from the high pressure. In the northern hemisphere, they are deflected to the right by the earth's rotation, and consequently on the eastern side of the anticyclone the winds are northerly, on the western side southerly, on the northern side westerly and on the southern side easterly.

Weather. It has already been pointed out that, on account of the general stillness of the air in an anticyclone, local winds may be produced by local causes, and for similar reasons there may be local rains. Indeed, according to Shaw and Lempfert, 'Local changes of many kinds may take place within them, and almost any kind of weather, except those which represent violent atmospheric changes, may be associated with their central regions'.

Nevertheless, the weather in an anticyclone in summer is usually fair or fine. In England and other maritime countries in cool temperate latitudes the interior of a winter anticyclone may have an overcast sky and there may even be some drizzle or light rain, though the amount is usually small. Both cloud and drizzle are largely the result of the insular position of these islands. In the larger anticyclones of the globe the interior is usually almost free from cloud. Even in England this is often, if not generally, the case.

In the middle of such an anticyclone, without cloud and without wind, the weather experienced will depend largely upon the season. Although there is but little actual cloud, the atmosphere is not clear. The sky above is blue, but the horizon has the characteristically hazy appearance so often seen in settled fine weather. The absence of cloud permits the sun to shine brightly during the day, but at night there is free radiation and consequent loss of heat. In summer, therefore, the day is hot, but by sunset the temperature is falling rapidly. Even in the middle of summer it usually falls sufficiently to allow of the development of a surface inversion (see pp. 67, 108), and the formation of dew and mist in the early morning, but this disappears soon after sunrise.

In the late summer or early autumn, the mists and dews are more pronounced and may last for several hours after the sun has risen.

In winter the sun is never high and it is above the horizon for so short a time that it produces little warmth. The nights are longer, the loss of heat is greater, and often there is frost and fog. The fog may be so thick as to last throughout the following day.

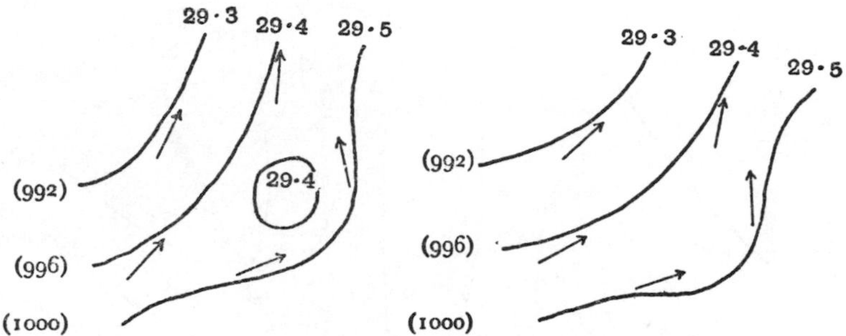

Fig. 17. Secondary depression with a centre of low pressure.

Fig. 18. Secondary depression without any definite low-pressure centre.

Millibar equivalents approximate.

In spite of the exceptions already noticed, due largely to local causes, the weather just described is that which is characteristic of the middle of an anticyclone. Towards the margins it varies. Although the winds are slight there is a general drift of the air, and the temperature depends largely on the source from which it comes. Thus on the eastern margin (in the northern hemisphere), the winds are northerly and the temperature is generally low for the time of the year. In winter it is likely to be frosty with perhaps some slight snow.

On the southern margin the winds are easterly. In England they come from the continent, which is hot in the summer and cold in the winter. Therefore, with us the temperature will be high in the summer; in winter it will be cold and often frosty. In the winter the sky is frequently overcast and 'black'.

The winds of the western margin are southerly, and this side of the anticyclone is usually warm.

On the northern margin the winds are westerly, coming to England from the Atlantic, which is relatively cool in summer and warm in winter. The temperature will be comparatively cool in summer, depending partly on distance from the sea; and in winter it will be comparatively warm.

Secondary depression. A secondary depression first appears on a chart as a mere bend in the isobars, usually towards the margin of a well-established low. Sometimes a more definite centre of low pressure develops in the middle (fig. 17), but more commonly the pressure decreases gradually towards the primary cyclone (fig. 18). The bend may cover a considerable area or it may be so small that the observing stations are not close enough to reveal its presence. But, unfortunately

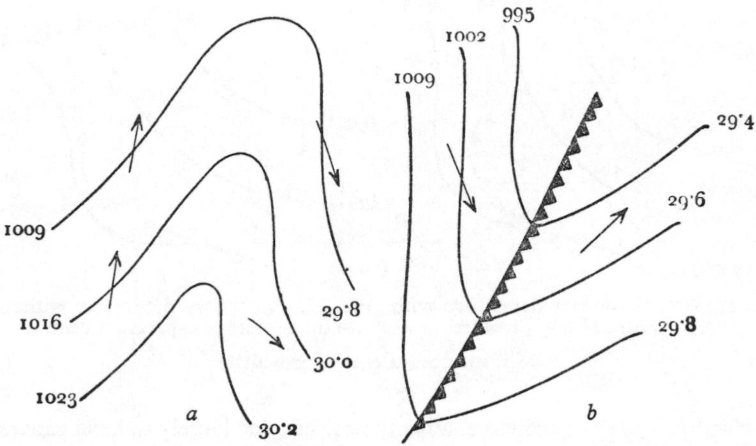

Fig. 19*a*. Isobars and winds in a wedge (northern hemisphere). *b*. Isobars and winds in a trough of low pressure or V-depression. At the cold front shown by the jagged line, cold air from the rear is undercutting the warmer air ahead.

for the forecaster, the effect upon the weather is often out of all proportion to the magnitude of the bend, and will be illustrated in ch. IX. A secondary depression may often develop on the polar front as a small wave: it may occasionally grow to become a major disturbance, or it may merely be a polar depression as described in ch. IX.

Wedge. A wedge is a triangular area of high pressure, with the pressure highest at the middle of the base and decreasing towards the point and sides. It is the region of high pressure between two depressions (fig. 19*a*).

Most depressions in north-western Europe pass to the north of England and the point of the wedge is accordingly directed northwards. But if the path of the depression lies to the south the wedge will point southwards.

The wedge necessarily moves with the depressions between which it lies. The line of highest pressures from the point to the middle of the base is called the crest, and the direction of movement is approximately at right angles to the crest.

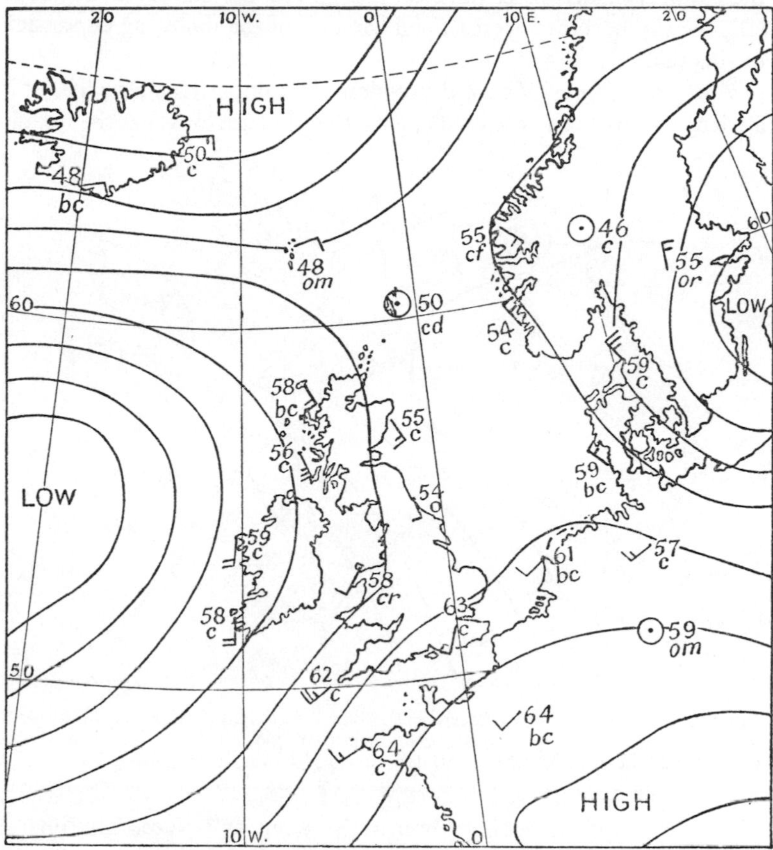

Fig. 20. Weather map showing a col over the North Sea.

The winds (in the northern hemisphere) will be as shown in the diagram. In the usual case, with the wedge pointing northwards, they will be northerly in the front half, southerly in the back half. The isobars are generally rather far apart and the winds are therefore light.

The front half of a wedge is characterised by a remarkable clearness of the atmosphere. The sky is cloudless and brilliantly blue. There is no haze and the horizon is sharp and clearly defined. The air is fresh and the barometer rising.

About the time of passage of the crest, however, the western sky grows milky, and through the thin white cirro-stratus clouds which produce this appearance the sun and moon may form halos, caused by the refraction of light passing through the minute ice crystals of which the cloud is made. After the crest has passed, the barometer begins to fall, the sky becomes overcast and the rain of the following depression begins (ch. IX).

V-depression. A V or V-depression is the opposite of a wedge. It is a triangular area of low pressure, with the pressure lowest at the middle

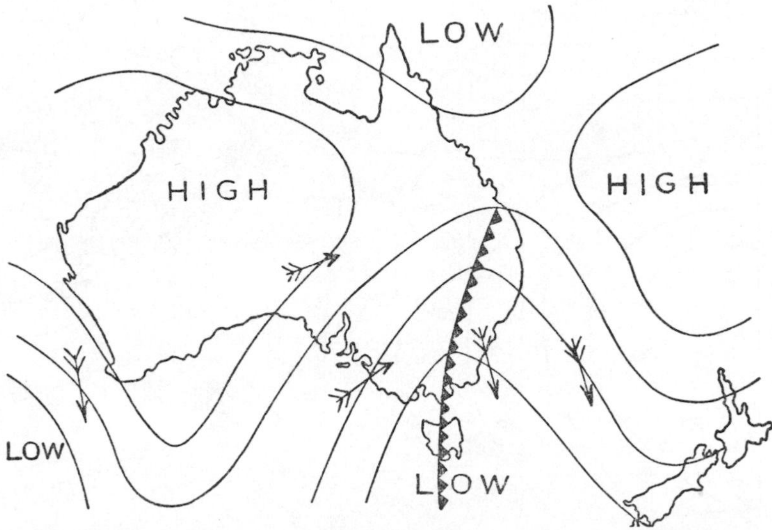

Fig. 21. Isobar patterns: southern hemisphere. At the cold front near Melbourne warm air from the tropics is being undercut by cool air from the ocean to the southward: the well-known 'southerly burster' of south-east Australia.

of the base and increasing towards the point and sides. The line of lowest pressures from the point to the middle of the base is called the trough, and the movement is usually at right angles to the trough in an easterly direction. The V, however, may point in almost any direction (fig. 19*b*).

In the case of a V-depression with its point directed southwards, the winds in the front half are southerly and in the back half northerly; they differ sharply in temperature and hence the boundary is generally shown as a cold front. The isobars are usually close together and the winds are strong. The trough of low pressure marked by the cold front is sometimes a line of violent squalls, often with thunderstorms, and as it passes there is a sudden shift in the direction of the wind, which may often be very dangerous to shipping.

The distribution of cloud and rain in a V-depression resembles that which may be expected on either side of a well-marked cold front. Ahead there is sometimes a milky sky, forming halos round the sun and moon. The front half is wet, with heavy and squally rain. At the trough the squalls attain their greatest violence and the wind shifts. Then the clouds begin to break, after a period of steady rain of variable but usually short duration. Finally the clouds disappear, leaving a bright sky and a cold fresh wind as at the back of a depression.

Col. The term col has been adopted for a formation such as that shown in fig. 20. It will be evident that the pattern of the isobars resembles that of contours on either side of a mountain saddle (or col). While the winds are light and variable, the slow-moving streams of air entering such a region from either side may differ a good deal from each other in temperature and in their content of water-vapour. Hence a col is usually characterised by variable weather, and in the summer light variable winds and scattered thunderstorms may be expected. In winter there may be patches of stagnant fog, or low cloud or drizzle may occur.

CHAPTER V

THE HORIZONTAL DISTRIBUTION OF TEMPERATURE

Measurement of temperature. Air temperature is measured by means of the thermometer. On the continent the Centigrade thermometer is usually employed, but in English-speaking countries the Fahrenheit thermometer is still used for most meteorological observations.

The temperature of a place is the temperature of the air at about 4 feet above the ground at that place. The temperature of the ground itself may be distinctly different.

It seems an easy matter to take the temperature of the air; but it is not so easy as it seems. If a thermometer is hung against the wall of a house it will be affected by the temperature of the wall as well as by that of the air. If it is hung from some support by a string, so that it is completely surrounded by free air, away from any buildings or trees, it will be heated by the direct rays of the sun, and even when the sun is not shining it will be influenced by radiation from the earth.

There are two ways in which the true temperature of the air may be obtained with considerable accuracy. The thermometer may be protected from all external radiation by a screen of some kind which allows free access to the air. The form of screen which is most commonly employed in England is known as Stevenson's. It is a kind of wooden box raised above the ground on posts. To protect the thermometer from the rays of the sun the roof is double, with an air-space between the two boards which form it. Radiation from the earth is intercepted by the floor, which may be double also. The sides are louvred, like Venetian shutters, thus keeping out the sun's rays while allowing the air to enter freely. The thermometer is supported on a frame inside, so that its bulb is near the middle, as far as possible from the roof and floor and sides.

Such a screen is not very portable and explorers generally use a sling thermometer. This is nothing more than a simple unmounted thermometer, like an ordinary chemical thermometer, with a piece of string tied to the ring at the upper end. By means of the string it is swung round and round at a moderate rate in the open air. In a minute or two it will attain the temperature of the air, even if the sun is shining. While swinging, it is brought continually into contact with fresh particles of air, and its temperature is therefore kept down very nearly to that of the air, in spite of the heating effect of the sun's rays. If the sun is very strong, the thermometer may be shaded with an umbrella while it is being swung and read.

Isotherms. The distribution of temperature is shown on maps by means of isotherms. An isotherm is a line along which the temperature is everywhere the same. The method of drawing them is the same as the method of drawing isobars.

Temperature as well as pressure varies with the altitude, though not so regularly. In a hilly district the isotherms often run nearly along the contour lines. If, therefore, we wish to consider the effects of other causes than altitude upon the distribution of temperature, the thermometer readings must be corrected for altitude just as the barometric readings are corrected in isobaric maps. Unfortunately the allowance to be made for altitude is less certain in the case of temperature and is undoubtedly influenced by the form of the ground. The average fall of temperature with increase of altitude is about 1° F. for 300 feet. If, then, the average of all temperature readings at a place 600 feet above sea-level stands at 52°, the mean temperature reduced to sea-level would be 54°.

In almost all isothermal maps the temperatures have been corrected for altitude; and in such maps an isotherm is a line along which the temperature, reduced to sea-level, is everywhere the same.

Sources of heat. There are two possible sources from which the warmth of the earth's surface may be derived. The first of these is the sun, the effects of which are evident to everyone. The second is the interior of the earth.

Seasonal variations of temperature are not felt below the ground to a greater depth than 60–80 feet, and beneath that limit mine-shafts and well-borings show that the temperature increases downwards. The rate of increase varies greatly in different places, and even at different depths in the same shaft; but a large series of observations gave an average rise of about 1° F. for each 64 feet of descent. If this rate is maintained the interior of the earth must be excessively hot; and in any case, since it is certainly hotter than the exterior, it must warm the surface to some extent. It is impossible to determine how great its influence may be, but since it must affect the poles as much as the equator it is evidently very small compared with that of the sun, and for practical purposes it may be neglected.

A certain minute amount of heat must also be received from the stars and, by reflection of the sun's heat, from the moon, but the quantity is so small that it is barely appreciable even by the most delicate instruments.

Consequently, the only source of heat that need be considered is the sun.

Insolation. It is convenient to have a term to express the amount of heat received from the sun and the term employed is insolation. The insolation for a day is the total amount of heat received from the sun during that day. The expression 'intensity of insolation' has nearly the same meaning as the common phrase 'strength of the sun' or 'strength of the sun's rays'; but it is used more definitely. If we say that at a certain time the intensity of insolation at one place is twice that at another, we mean that during equal very short periods of time the former place receives twice as much heat (per square foot or per square inch) as the latter.

Insolation on an airless and waterless globe. It the earth were a solid globe of uniform composition, without water and without an atmosphere, it would be a comparatively simple matter to calculate the effect of the sun's heat upon its surface.

If a beam of light in section one foot square falls vertically upon a plane horizontal surface, its light and heat will cover an area of one square foot (fig. 22*a*). But if the same beam falls obliquely its light and heat will be spread over a larger area (fig. 22*b*). For simplicity we may suppose that in both figures the sides of the beam are respectively parallel and perpendicular to the paper. In the former case the area illuminated will be a square, with each side one foot in length; in the latter it will be an oblong with a breadth a of one foot but with a length b greater than one foot, and its area will be b square feet. As the angle of altitude of the sun θ decreases, the length of b increases and the area of the oblong increases in the same proportion.

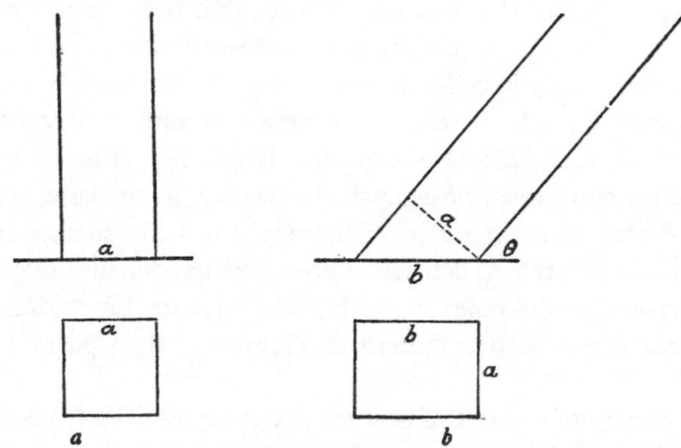

Fig. 22. Areas illuminated by vertical and inclined beams.

But since the total amount of heat received from the beam remains the same, the heat per square foot is evidently inversely proportional to the area illuminated; that is, the intensity of insolation is inversely proportional to b, or directly proportional to $\frac{1}{b}$.

In the upper part of fig. 22*b*, $\frac{a}{b} = \sin\theta$, and since the width a of the beam is 1 foot, $\frac{a}{b} = \frac{1}{b} = \sin\theta$. The intensity of insolation is therefore proportional to $\sin\theta$, that is, to the sine of the angle of altitude of the sun.

At the equinoxes the sun is vertical over the equator; elsewhere its altitude at noon is the complement of the latitude, and the intensity of insolation at noon is therefore proportional to the cosine of the latitude. Throughout the day, the altitude is greatest at the equator and decreases towards the poles.

Accordingly at the equinoxes the amount of heat received from the sun will be greatest at the equator and will decrease gradually to the poles.

At the summer solstice the sun is vertical over the Tropic of Cancer and it may be thought that the insolation will be greatest there. But a new factor is now introduced. At the equinoxes the day is 12 hours long and the night is 12 hours long all over the earth; but at the solstices the length of the day varies with the latitude, as shown in Table 2.

Table 2

Lat.	0°	10°	20°	30°	40°	50°	60°	66½°
	h. m.	h. m.	h. m.	h. m.	h. m.	h. m.	h. m.	h. m.
Longest day	12 0	12 35	13 13	13 56	14 51	16 9	18 30	24 0
Shortest day	12 0	11 25	10 47	10 4	9 9	7 51	5 30	0 0

Consequently, although at our summer solstice the sun will be hotter at the Tropic of Cancer than in lat. 60° N., it will not be above the horizon for so long a time. The length of the day more than compensates for the obliquity of the sun's rays and the amount of heat received during the day is greater in lat. 60° N. than at the tropic.

The calculation of the insolation at different latitudes in these circumstances is rather difficult, even on the assumption that the atmosphere has no influence; and only the results need be given here. Taking the insolation at the equator for 21 March as 1000, the insolation at various latitudes on 21 June is shown in Table 3.

Table 3

Latitude N.	0°	10°	20°	30°	40°	50°	60°	70°	80°	90°
Insolation on June 21	881	975	1045	1088	1107	1105	1093	1130	1184	1202

According to this table the insolation on 21 June is greatest at the North Pole, and in England it is greater than in the Sahara. Such results appear to be totally at variance with actual observations; but there are two points which should be borne in mind. In the first place the table gives the total amount of heat received during the day, which is quite a different thing from the temperature attained. Secondly, the table takes no account of the absorption of the sun's rays by the atmosphere. It applies to a globe without an atmosphere, or, in the case of the real earth, to the external surface of the atmosphere and not to the surface of the ground.

Influence of the atmosphere on insolation. Although the air seems so transparent, it does not allow the rays of the sun to pass through it without loss. Some of the light and heat is absorbed and does not reach the earth. The absorption appears to be due chiefly to the water-vapour and carbon dioxide in the air.

It is evident at once from fig. 23 that where the rays are oblique the length of their journey through the atmosphere is greater than where they are vertical. Consequently, the loss of heat is greater and their power at the earth's surface is less. The atmosphere in fact greatly increases the effect of obliquity, and the intensity of insolation does not vary with the sine of the altitude of the sun but much more rapidly.

It is difficult to determine how much of the heat is lost in this way, but in the case of vertical rays it is believed to amount to one-third of the total.

Since the atmosphere increases the effect of obliquity it increases also the effect of latitude; and taking the average temperature for the whole year, the poles are colder compared with the equator than they would be if there were no atmosphere.

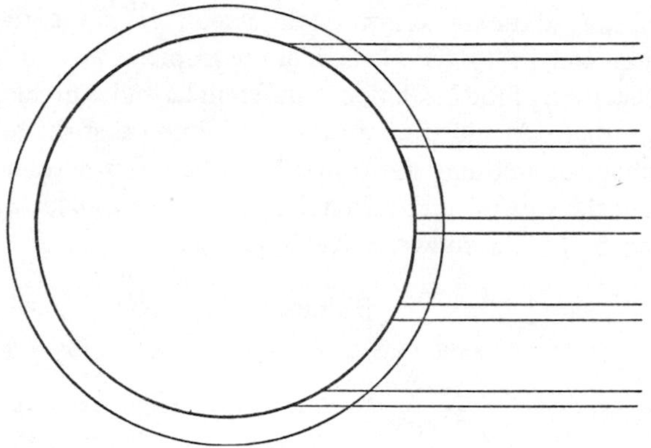

Fig. 23. Influence of the atmosphere on insolation.

Influence of land and water. Taking the whole year round, the amount of heat received from the sun is greatest at the equator and decreases gradually towards the poles. But the equator is not the hottest part of the globe. The thermal equator, or line of maximum temperature, lies for the most part north of the real equator.

The principal reason for this and other irregularities is that heat affects land and water differently, and therefore the distribution of temperature is greatly influenced by the distribution of the continents and oceans.

In general, the land-masses heat more quickly in the summer and cool more quickly in the winter than the seas; and there are several reasons for this difference between them:

(1) The specific heat of water is much greater than that of the solid earth. It takes nearly five times as much heat to raise the temperature of a pound of water 1°, as it does to raise the temperature of a pound of

sand 1°. On the other hand, while its temperature is falling 1°, the pound of water gives out nearly five times as much heat as the pound of sand.

The amount of the sun's heat received by a land-mass or a sea is affected by its area and not by its weight, and therefore it is the specific heat by volume rather than by weight that concerns us; and the difference in this is not quite so great. It requires about twice as much heat to raise the temperature of a cubic foot of water 1° as it does to raise the temperature of a cubic foot of sand 1°.

(2) The rays of the sun penetrate more deeply into water than into earth. The daily variations of temperature are not perceptible below a depth of about 3 feet in earth; in water they may sometimes be observed at 60 feet beneath the surface. The seasonal variations disappear at a depth of 60–80 feet in earth, of 300–600 feet in water.

Thus the sun's rays falling on water are engaged in heating a much larger volume of material than when they fall on land. The temperature reached is therefore not so high; but when the sun sets there is a larger quantity to cool and the cooling is slower.

(3) Water is mobile and land is not. When the sun's rays fall on land their effect is practically limited to the area on which they fall; in water, convection currents are set up and the heat is partly carried away. Consequently, when the sun's rays fall on water they warm not only the area on which they fall but also the surrounding parts.

(4) When the sun shines on water a considerable proportion of the heat is used in evaporating the water and not in raising its temperature. On dry land there is no such loss. In marshes and swamps a certain amount of heat will disappear in the same way.

(5) Much of the heat that falls upon the water is reflected and does not raise its temperature. Land surfaces are poor reflectors and but little heat is lost in this way.

(6) On the whole the sky is cloudier over the ocean than over the land. The clouds obstruct the rays of the sun, but they also hinder loss of heat by radiation. Their effect is therefore to retard both the heating and the cooling of the water.

All these causes tend to make the water heat more slowly than the land, and all excepting the fourth and the fifth make it cool more slowly.

Distribution of temperature in the British Isles. The difference between land and sea is very clearly shown by the distribution of temperature in the British Isles in summer and in winter (fig. 24).

In the July map it will be seen that the general direction of the isotherms is from east to west, but they bend northwards over the land, southwards over the sea. The highest temperature is in the neighbourhood of London. In the January map the general direction of the isotherms is roughly north and south, with the highest temperatures in the west; they bend southwards over the land, northwards over the sea.

In July the sun is high for a large part of the day, and the nights are short. More heat is received from the sun during the day than is lost at night by radiation, and the temperature is therefore rising, both on land and sea. It rises most rapidly in the south, where the sun is most powerful, and consequently the general direction of the isotherms is from east to west. But the temperature of the land rises more quickly than that of the sea and therefore the land becomes hotter than the sea in the same latitude. The highest temperature is not in the extreme south, because the coast is cooled by the waters of the English Channel; it is a little inland, about the neighbourhood of London. Moreover, although the general direction of the isotherms is from east to west, they bend towards the pole over the land, towards the equator over the sea.

In January the sun is always low, even in the middle of the day, and its rays accordingly have little power. The days are short and the nights are long. More heat is lost at night than is received by day, and both land and water are therefore cooling. But the water cools more slowly than the land, and by the month of January the temperature of the land is considerably less than that of the sea. So great is the difference and so weak are the sun's rays at this season that the Atlantic is now a more important source of heat than the sun. Consequently, the isotherms in January run roughly parallel to the Atlantic coast, and the warmest part of the British Isles is not the south, but the west. The Irish Sea and North Sea are also warmer than the neighbouring land and the isotherms accordingly bend towards the pole over the sea, towards the equator over the land.

In the British Isles, therefore, when the sun at noon is high up in the sky, the land is hotter than the sea and the isotherms bend equatorwards over the sea, polewards over the land; when the noonday sun is low, the land is cooler than the sea and the isotherms bend equatorwards over the land, polewards over the sea.

General distribution of temperature over the globe. This is a general principle and applies to the whole earth. Towards the equator, where the sun at noon is always high, the conditions are those of the English summer; towards the poles, where the sun is always low, the conditions are those of the English winter. Near the equator therefore the isotherms bend polewards over the land, equatorwards over the sea; towards the poles the bends are in the opposite directions. At some intermediate latitude, land and sea will be at about the same temperature

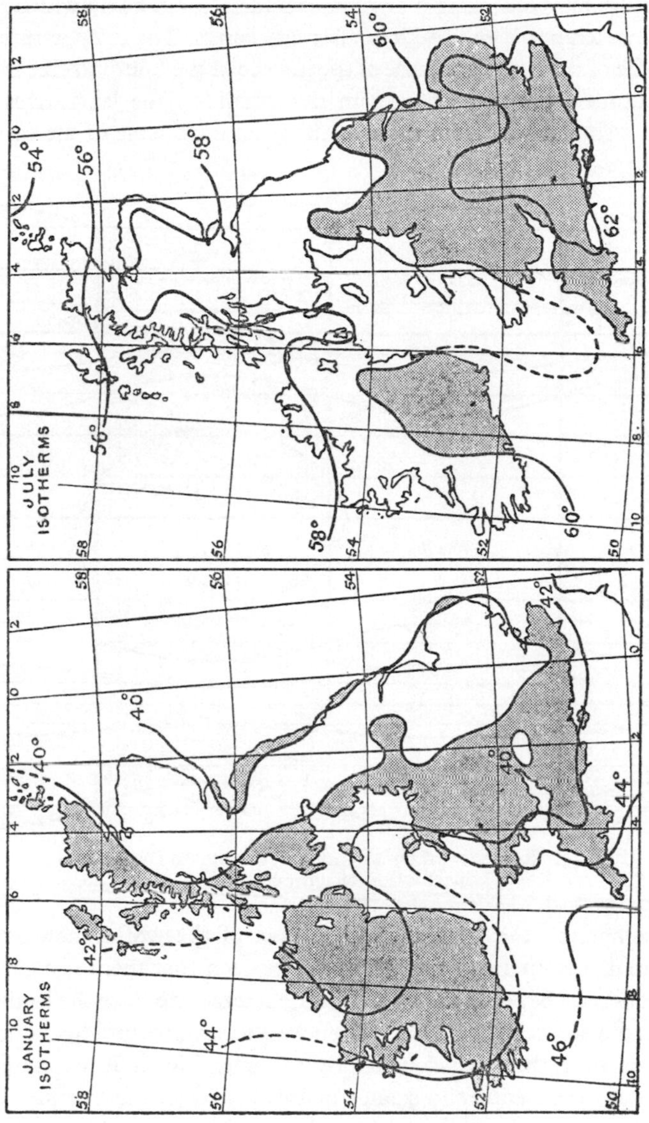

Fig. 24. Isotherms of the British Isles. Mean temperature for January and July.

and the isotherms will be nearly straight. The general distribution of temperature may accordingly be represented as in fig. 25, in which land and sea stretch north and south in alternate bands. The temperatures in the middle of the ocean are those of the middle of the South Pacific in the same latitudes; the temperatures in the middle of the land strips are taken in a similar way from those of the great continents of the eastern hemisphere.

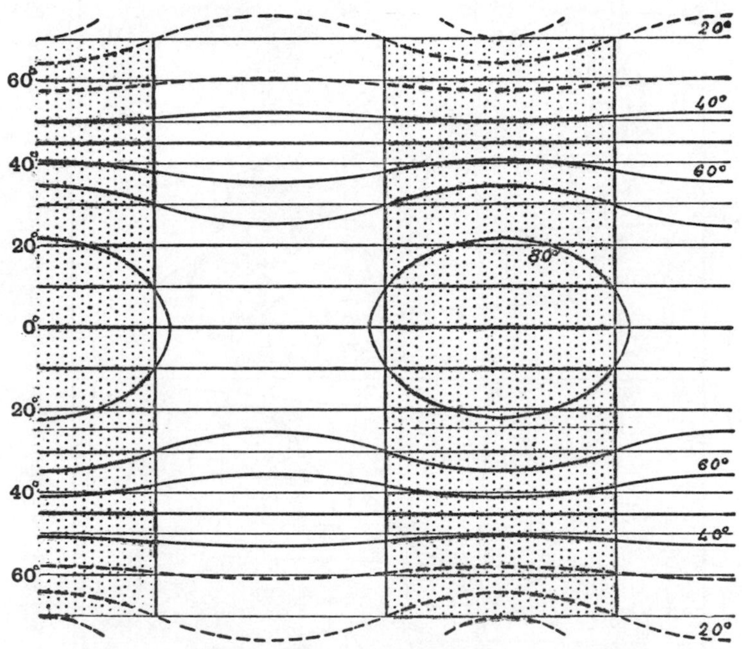

Fig. 25. Influence of continents and oceans on the general distribution of temperature.

On comparing this diagram with a map of the world showing the actual annual isotherms (map 4), it will be seen that there is a general correspondence between the two. If, for example, we trace the isotherm of 30° in the northern hemisphere from west to east, we find that it bends polewards over the Pacific, equatorwards over North America, polewards over the Atlantic and again equatorwards over the Eurasian continent. In the southern hemisphere the bends are much less marked, because the land-masses are narrow.

Near the equator on the other hand the isotherm of 80° in the northern hemisphere bends towards the equator over the Atlantic, towards the poles over America and Africa.

About lat. 45° N. the isotherm of 50° is comparatively little affected by the distribution of land and sea, and does not deviate far from the parallel of latitude, indicating that the difference of temperature between land and sea is small.

Effect of the prevalent winds. Thus the diagram represents very fairly the actual distribution of temperature over land and sea. But even if we allow for the difference in the form of the continents, it is not perfect. In the diagram the isotherms of the north temperate zone are farthest from the equator in the middle of the ocean and nearest in the middle of the land; in the map they are farthest on the western coasts of America and Europe, they are nearest close to the eastern coasts of America and Asia.

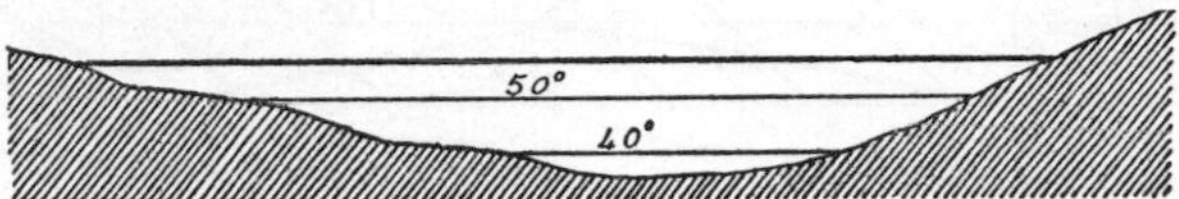

Fig. 26. Isotherms in a lake of still water.

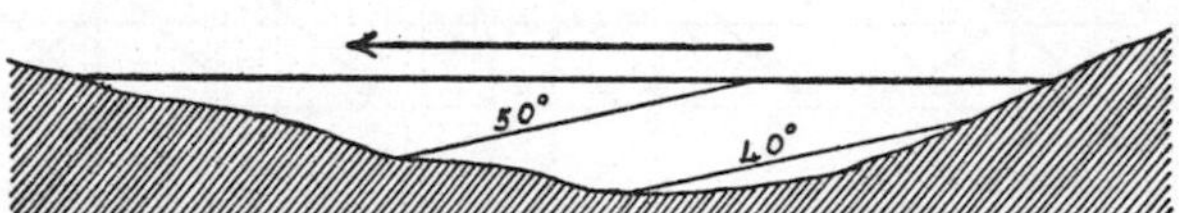

Fig. 27. Isotherms in a lake when a wind is blowing.

This is the effect of the prevalent winds. There are two ways in which the distribution of temperature is influenced by the winds. A wind is a movement of the air from one place to another and it therefore carries, as it were, the temperature of one place to another. Neither the interchange of air nor the transference of temperature is complete; but it is sufficient to be of great importance.

The winds also blow the surface layers of a body of water in the direction in which they themselves are travelling. Without winds the coldest and densest water would be at the bottom, the warmest and lightest at the top, and the isothermal surfaces in the water would be horizontal, as in fig. 26. When a wind blows in the direction of the arrow in fig. 27 the warm surface water is carried to the windward shore, colder water comes to the top on the leeward shore, and the isotherms are displaced as shown. The effect is to raise the temperature of the shore towards which the wind is blowing and to lower the temperature of the opposite shore.

North of lat. 40° N. the prevalent winds are from the south-west. They therefore blow the surface waters of the ocean towards the east, warming the western coasts of the continents and cooling their eastern coasts. Moreover, on the western coasts the south-west winds are coming from the warmer sea; on the eastern coasts they are coming from the colder interior of the land. Therefore in this way also they raise the temperature of the western coasts and lower the temperature of the eastern coasts.

If, then, we wish to alter the diagram (fig. 25) so as to show the effect of the winds, we must place the isotherm of 40° nearer to the equator on the eastern shore of the continent and farther away from it on the

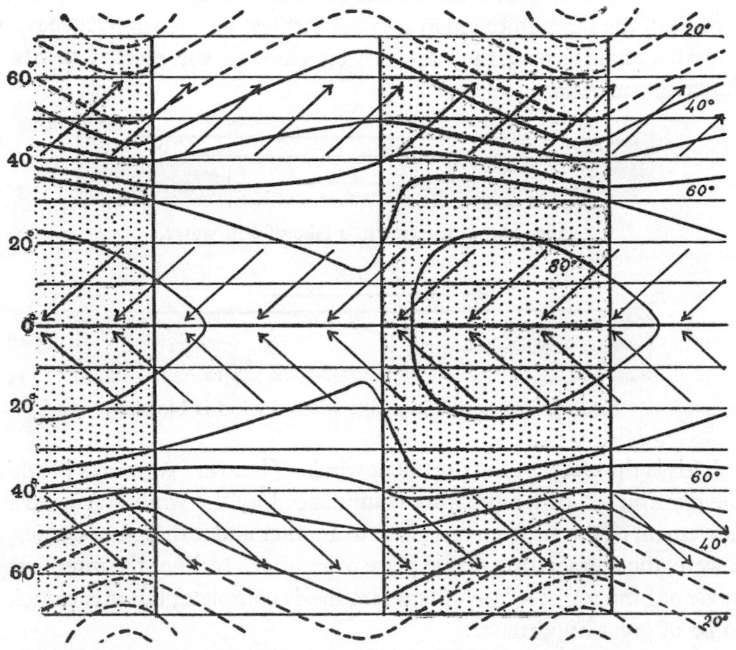

Fig. 28. Influence of the winds on the course of the isotherms.

western shore; and similarly with all the other isotherms within the region of the south-westerly winds. Moreover, since the western side of the continent is warmer than the east, the minimum temperature will be displaced eastward. The general result of these modifications is shown in fig. 28.

Between the tropics the prevalent winds are the trade-winds. There is not the great difference of temperature between land and sea that there is in temperate latitudes and consequently the direct effect of the winds is slight. But they blow the surface waters towards the west, warming the eastern shores of the continents, while the western shores are cooled by the upwelling of the colder water from below. Within the tropics generally the eastern shores of the continents are therefore warmer than they would be without the winds, the western shores are cooler. To make the proper alteration in the diagram (fig. 25) we must place the isotherms farther from the equator on the eastern coasts of the land-masses, nearer to the equator on the western coasts.

But because the prevalent winds on the western coasts blow from the land, the cooling effect is limited to a comparatively narrow strip close to the coast, and the isotherms accordingly take the form indicated in fig. 28.

This figure is now complete and shows diagrammatically the general distribution of temperature over land and sea when we take into account the effect of the prevalent winds. Comparison with the map of the actual isotherms discloses a very close agreement. The differences are due almost entirely to the form of the continental masses, and their effect upon the direction of the winds.

Seasonal variations. Both in the diagram (fig. 28) and the map (map 4) the isotherms are what are known as annual isotherms. They show the average temperature for the whole year of the places through which they pass. But isotherms may also be drawn showing the average temperatures for a month or any other period of time, and these will usually differ from the annual isotherms.

In the northern hemisphere generally, July is the hottest month and January the coldest, and the isotherms for July may therefore be taken as showing the general distribution of temperature in summer and the isotherms for January as showing the general distribution in winter (maps 5 and 6).

It will be seen at once that the seasons bring great changes not only in the actual temperature, but also in the distribution of temperature. The course of the July isotherms is very different from that of the January isotherms or of the annual isotherms.

The general nature of the changes, and the reason for the changes, will be most easily understood if we take the diagram of annual isotherms in fig. 25, and consider how it is likely to be modified in July.

In this diagram the part of the continent north of lat. 45° N. is colder than the sea. But in July it will not be so. It is then the northern summer and the northern continents will be warmer than the seas. The bends of the isotherms will therefore be reversed and will be directed southwards over the sea, northwards over the land. The lowest temperature will be found on the ocean and not on the land.

Within the tropics there will be comparatively little change. There the land is always warmer than the sea. In July this difference will be increased north of the equator and somewhat decreased south of the equator. The maximum temperature will be a little north of its position in the annual diagram.

In the southern hemisphere July is the middle of winter. Beyond the tropics the land will be colder than the sea. Even if we take the average temperatures for the year it is colder, as is shown in the diagram (fig. 25)

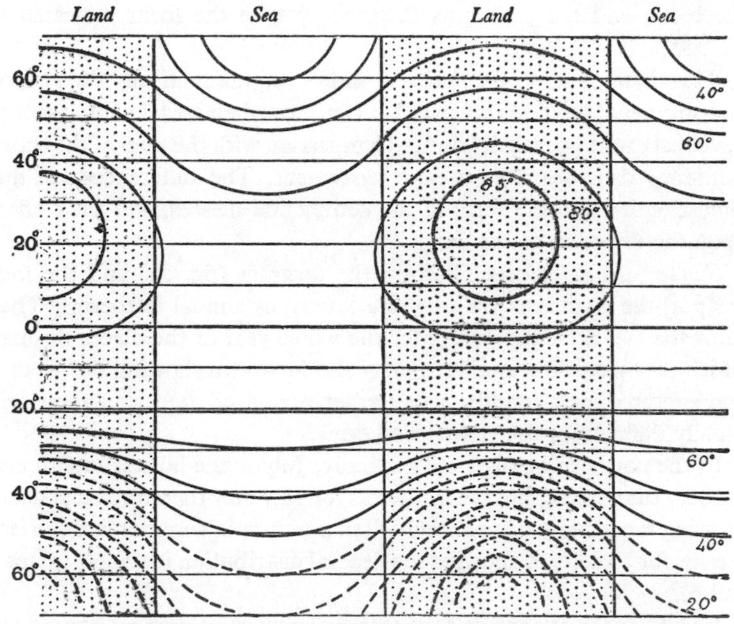

Fig. 29. Diagram of general distribution of temperature in July.

and map (map 4) of the annual isotherms. But in winter the difference is intensified and accordingly the bends in the isotherms will be in the same direction as in the annual diagram but will be more pronounced.

The effect of all these modifications is shown in fig. 29, which is a diagram of the isotherms for July, just as fig. 25 is a diagram of the annual isotherms.

It is hardly necessary to consider in detail the diagram for January (fig. 30). It is northern winter and the southern summer. The conditions of the two hemispheres are interchanged and the diagram is like that for July reversed. In fact, if a mirror stands along the northern (or southern) edge of the July diagram, the reflection in the mirror will be exactly like the diagram for January.

Range of temperature. The difference between the summer and the winter temperatures of any locality is known as the annual range of temperature at that locality. But the phrase will have different meanings according to the definition of the terms summer and winter temperatures.

Strictly speaking, the range is the difference between the highest and lowest temperatures ever experienced at the place in question. This is the absolute range of temperature. But the maximum and minimum will not be the same every year; and if we take their averages for a series of

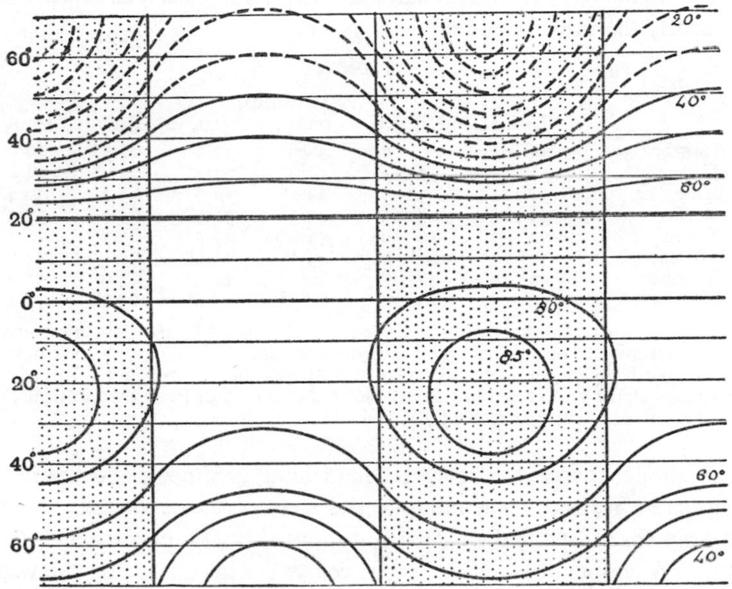

Fig. 30. Diagram of general distribution of temperature in January.

years, the difference may be called the mean annual extreme range, or simply the annual extreme range.

The maximum and minimum temperatures are exceptional and endure for a short time only. Perhaps a better idea of the difference between summer and winter is given by comparing the average temperatures of the hottest and the coldest months. The difference between these is the range of monthly mean temperatures, and it is this difference that is most commonly called the annual range or the mean annual range.

In the British Isles July is in most places the hottest month and January the coldest, so that the difference between the temperatures of these months is the annual range. In July the temperature is highest towards the south and decreases northwards; in January it is highest towards the west and decreases eastwards. It follows from this that the annual range is not everywhere the same. It is least towards the north-west, where the January temperature is high and the July temperature low; it is greatest towards the south-east where the January temperature is low and the July temperature high.

The increase of range towards the east is continued right across the continent of Europe and almost to the eastern shores of Asia. Table 4 gives the longitude, the mean annual temperature, the January and July temperatures, and the annual range of a number of places, all of which are in nearly the same latitude.

Table 4

	Lat. N.	Long. E.	Mean annual temp.	Jan.	July	Range
Cambridge	52° 13′	0° 6′	48·6°	37·6°	61·5°	23·9°
Utrecht	52° 6′	5° 11′	48·0°	34·2°	62·6°	28·4°
Hanover	52° 22′	9° 45′	47·1°	32·7°	63·1°	30·4°
Berlin	52° 30′	13° 23′	47·3°	31·3°	64·6°	33·3°
Posen	52° 25′	16° 56′	46·6°	29·3°	65·5°	36·2°
Warsaw	52° 13′	21° 0′	45·1°	25·9°	65·8°	39·9°
Tambov	52° 44′	41° 28′	40·8°	11·3°	68·9°	57·6°
Irkutsk	52° 16′	104° 19′	31·3°	−5·4°	65·1°	70·5°

It should be noted that Irkutsk stands at a considerably higher level than any of the other towns in the list. The mean temperatures apply to various periods before 1910. For the years 1906–35 Cambridge gave Jan. 39·5°, July 61·7°. A similar slight winter rise has been observed at the other European stations, but it does not affect the argument as a whole.

A similar increase in range is found in all continental masses in the temperate regions. Not only are the western coasts warmer (on the average for the year) than the eastern, but they also have a much more uniform temperature. The western coasts are influenced by the winds from the oceans and accordingly they share in the uniformity of temperature characteristic of large masses of water.

It is in north-eastern Siberia that the greatest ranges of temperature have been observed. The range of monthly means at Yakutsk amounts to 112·1°; the annual extreme range to 158·0°, and the absolute range (in thirty-two years) to 185·8°. Ranges almost as great as these have also been recorded in the north-western parts of Canada. In the British Isles the greatest range of monthly means is only about 26°; in the western part of Ireland it is about 15°.

In equatorial regions the range is very small. At Jaluit in the Marshall Islands the difference between the hottest and the coldest months is only 0·8°. Here the climate is influenced by the sea, but even at Equatorville on the Congo, in the middle of Africa, the difference is no more than 2·2°.

Towards the tropics, where the air is dry and the sky is clear, the range increases, but it is small compared with the ranges in eastern Siberia and Canada. It is in fact in the so-called Temperate Zone that the greatest extremes of temperature are experienced.

Construction of range-maps. In general, maps showing the range of temperature are drawn by plotting the observed ranges at different points and proceeding as in the case of isotherms. But if, for any area, January is everywhere the coldest month and July the hottest, it is possible from the isothermal maps for these months to construct a map of annual ranges. In fig. 31 the isotherms for July are shown as thin continuous lines, the isotherms for January as thin broken lines. Where the July isotherm of 60° crosses the January isotherm of 38°, the range is the difference between these temperatures, namely 22°. Similarly at every intersection the range can be at once determined. By drawing lines joining points where the range is the same, we obtain lines of equal range, or range-lines as they may be called. But these connecting lines are not necessarily straight, and there are certain rules which must be obeyed in drawing them.

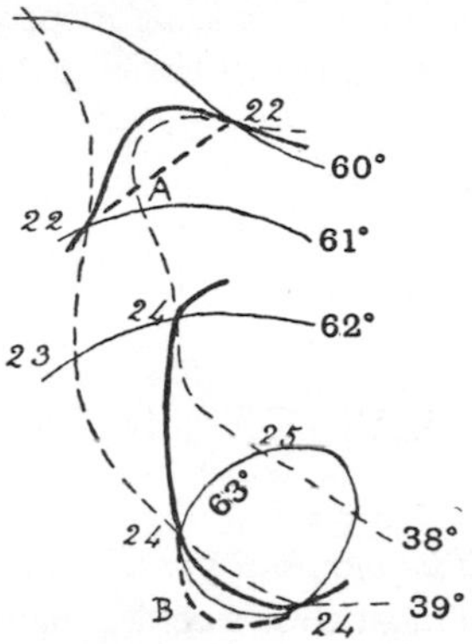

Fig. 31. Construction of range-maps.

The range-lines must not cross an isotherm except at the intersections. For example, the range-line for 22° must be drawn as shown by the heavy continuous line and not as indicated by the heavy broken line. It cannot cross the isotherm of 38° at *A*, for at that point the winter temperature is 38° and the summer temperature is more than 60°; the range is therefore more than 22°. The range-line for 22° can only cross the January isotherm of 38° at its intersection with the July isotherm of 60°.

The range-lines must cross *both* isotherms at the intersections. The range-line for 24° must not be continued in the direction shown by the heavy broken line at *B*, which crosses the January isotherm of 39° but only touches the July isotherm of 63°. It cannot lie at *B*, for there the January temperature is more than 39°, and the July temperature is less than 63°; the range is therefore less than 24°.

The map is divided into a number of spaces by the crossing of the January and July isotherms. In drawing the range-line in the manner described, two range-lines of different value must never lie in the same space. It is perhaps unnecessary to give the proof of this rule. It is useful sometimes towards the edge of the map, where there may be a doubt as to which way the range-line is to cross an intersection.

The range-lines of the British Isles obtained in this way from the isotherms for January and July agree very fairly with the observed annual ranges, because in most places January is the coldest month and July the hottest. Even in the case of large areas the method gives a good idea of the difference between winter and summer; but unless all parts of the area have the same month as their hottest and the same month as their coldest, it will not give the real annual range.

CHAPTER VI

VERTICAL DISTRIBUTION OF TEMPERATURE

The vertical gradient of temperature. On the top of a mountain it is almost always colder than at the foot. Similarly, in balloon ascents it is usually found that the higher the balloon rises the lower the temperature falls. It is only now and then that there is any exception to this rule, even for a short distance.

Yet on the top of a mountain the rays of the sun have passed through a smaller thickness of atmosphere than they have when they reach the foot; and consequently we might expect them to be more powerful and to produce a higher temperature. They really are more powerful. High up in the mountains, when the sun is shining, the face becomes sunburnt more quickly than on the plains; and in taking photographs the exposure required is distinctly less. But in spite of this the temperature of the air is lower. The only possible conclusion is that it is not the rays of the sun that warm the air.

The rate of fall of temperature with increase of height is called the vertical gradient of temperature, or simply the lapse-rate. It varies from time to time and from place to place, but by taking the mean of many series of observations it is found that on mountain slopes the average vertical rate of change is about 1° F. for each 300 feet of ascent. In the free air the average rate of decrease near the earth's surface is much the same.

Frequently it happens that for short distances there is an increase of temperature as we go upwards. The lapse-rate is then said to be negative, or inverted. But such inversions, as they are commonly called, do not often extend more than a few hundreds of feet. They are most common at the surface of the ground after clear nights (cf. pp. 34, 67).

The air is heated chiefly from below. Air is not readily warmed by radiant heat, that is, by the heat which radiates outwards from a hot body. A fire may feel hot to the face, while the intervening air is still quite cold. The radiant heat from the fire warms the face, but has comparatively little effect upon the air through which it passes. In the same way the rays of the sun may heat the earth, while they hardly affect the air through which they travel.

It is true that in passing through the entire thickness of the atmosphere a considerable proportion of the light and heat from the sun is absorbed and is in fact spent in raising the temperature of the atmosphere. The total amount of heat absorbed is large, but it is spread through so great a mass of air that the increase of temperature is small.

The air is not equally transparent to all radiant heat. It is less transparent to the infra-red rays than to those of the visible part of the spectrum. The former give heat without light, and are the only rays emitted by a body that is warm but not incandescent, such as the earth itself. Thus the air absorbs a larger proportion of the heat radiated out from the earth than of the heat which passes through it from the sun. For this reason the air is warmed by the earth rather than by the rays of the sun.

But there is another reason, and a more important one, why the air receives its heat principally from the earth. Although the air is comparatively little affected by radiant heat passing through it, it is warmed at once by actual contact with anything hotter than itself, and cooled by contact with anything colder.

Thus the air is but little affected by the direct rays of the sun. It is warmed to some extent by radiant heat from the earth and still more by contact with the earth. Therefore, it is warmed from below and it is natural that the temperature should decrease upwards.

Experimental illustration. A very simple experiment which may be made on any still and sunny day will show how little direct effect the rays of the sun have upon the temperature of the air. Hang a thermometer in the open air, freely exposed to the sun. The mercury rises and the thermometer soon shows a decidedly high temperature. Now swing the thermometer round and round, still in the open air and still in the sun. Its temperature at once falls, although it is just as much exposed to the sun's rays as before. The reason for the difference is that although the sun warms the thermometer it does not warm the air. The air therefore is colder than the thermometer, and when the thermometer is swung rapidly so as to bring it continually into contact with fresh air, its temperature falls to that of the air. When, on the other hand, the thermometer is hanging quietly, the sun warms the thermometer, and the thermometer warms the air immediately in contact with it.

If the day is windy, the experiment cannot be performed unless the thermometer is sheltered in some way from the wind, for the wind produces the same effect as the swinging of the thermometer. Even a gentle breeze is sufficient to cause a considerable fall in the temperature of the hanging thermometer. In order to protect it from the wind the thermometer may be hung in a flask, but in that case the experiment is not quite so satisfactory, for the hanging thermometer and the swinging thermometer are not then exposed in quite the same way to the rays of the sun.

The upward movement of changes of temperature. When the sun shines, the earth is heated and warms the air in contact with it. The heat spreads slowly upwards, partly by conduction from one layer of air to the next, partly by convection, the heated air rising and its place being taken by colder air from above. The earth being the principal source from which the air derives its heat, the temperature will decrease upwards.

If the sky remains clear after the sun has set, the earth rapidly loses heat by radiation and its surface becomes colder than the air. It cools the air in contact with it. The lowest layer of air then cools the next, and in turn each layer loses heat to the one below it and the cold spreads upwards. In this case the temperature upon the ground is low, and there is a partial reversal of the temperature gradient.

That this is the way in which the air is warmed and cooled is shown by the observations made on the Eiffel Tower. The Tower is 300 metres high (rather less than 1000 feet), and there are observing stations at the bottom, at the top, and at two or three intermediate heights. Table 5 shows the average temperature (in degrees Fahrenheit) at various hours of the day in the months of December and July, at the lowest and the highest stations:

Table 5

	a.m.						p.m.					
Midnight	2	4	6	8	10	Noon	2	4	6	8	10	Mean
December (lower station)												
33·8	33·4	33·1	32·9	32·7	35·2	37·9	39·0	37·6	36·0	35·1	34·2	35·1
December (upper station)												
34·5	34·3	33·8	33·8	33·4	34·0	35·2	36·0	35·6	35·2	35·1	34·9	34·7
July (lower station)												
58·1	57·0	55·6	57·7	63·3	67·8	70·2	71·1	70·2	68·2	63·7	60·6	63·7
July (upper station)												
59·2	57·7	56·5	56·8	58·3	61·2	63·9	65·1	65·5	64·4	62·2	60·8	61·0

These observations are shown graphically in fig. 32.

Both in December and in July the average temperature at the bottom of the Tower is higher than that at the top. The maximum is also higher at the bottom than at the top, but the minimum is lower. At an altitude of 1000 feet the temperature does not rise so high nor fall so low as on the ground; the range of temperature is less. In both months the temperature at the foot of the Tower is higher than that at the top as long as the sun is up and for some time afterwards; but in the early morning, when the ground has cooled, the temperature gradient is reversed.

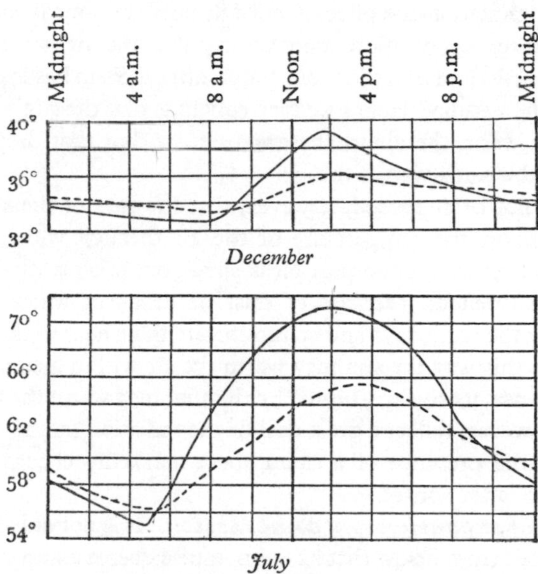

Fig. 32. Temperature changes at the Eiffel Tower. The continuous line shows the temperature at the foot of the Tower; the broken line that at the top of the Tower.

In December the minimum is reached at the lower station at 7.25 a.m., at the upper station at 7.55 a.m.; the maximum at the lower station occurs at 1.50 p.m., at the upper station about 2.30 p.m. In this month the sun rises about eight o'clock and sets about four. As soon as it is up the fall of temperature ceases and a rise begins. The temperature of the ground continues to increase until noon; but because the sun is low in the sky it rapidly loses its power, and in the afternoon the earth is losing more heat by radiation than it gains from the sun's rays. Therefore the ground itself is at its maximum shortly after mid-day. The effect of this is felt at once by the air at the lower station, which accordingly has its maximum about the same time. But the air at the upper station is warmed by conduction and convection from below, a process which takes time, and the maximum is therefore 40 minutes later.

In July, the minimum at the lower station occurs at 5.0 a.m., at the upper station at 5.55 a.m. The maximum at the lower station is reached about 2.0 p.m., and at the upper station at 3.0 p.m. In this month the sun remains high in the sky far into the afternoon. It is not till two o'clock or even later that the heat received from the sun's rays becomes less than the amount lost by radiation. The maximum of the ground itself and of the air at the lower station therefore occurs about this time. At the upper station the effect is not felt until an hour later.

These observations show quite clearly that the air is warmed from below upwards, and that the cooling also, after the sun has lost its power, begins at the bottom. Hence we may conclude that the sun's rays do not themselves warm the air to any great extent, but that they warm the earth and the earth warms the air.

It must not be supposed, however, that the rays of the sun have no influence upon the temperature of the air through which they pass. Their effect, indeed, upon pure air is small, but it is greatly increased if there are suspended particles of dust or drops of water. These are warmed by the sun's rays and communicate their heat to the surrounding air. In this way the sun may warm the air within a cloud; or if the cloud be dense, its surface, heated by the sun, may warm the air above it. Clouds, however, reflect a great deal of the radiation falling upon them; moreover, the presence of a cloud sheet markedly checks the fall of temperature after sunset.

Effects of expansion and compression. It is not only because the air is warmed from below that its temperature decreases upwards. There is another reason, depending upon the diminution of pressure in the same direction.

When air is compressed, without any heat being added to it, its temperature is raised. This is the chief reason why a bicycle-pump becomes warm when it is in use. No doubt the heating of the pump is due in part to the friction of the piston within the barrel; but if that were all it would be equally great when we move the piston backwards and forwards with the nozzle open to the air. Moreover, the heating of the pump when it is inflating a tyre is greatest near the nozzle. The friction is very little greater there, but the compression of the air is at its maximum.

When the air is allowed to expand by reduction of the pressure upon it, without any addition or subtraction of heat, its temperature falls.

At the earth's surface the pressure is greater than it is above. If the air is forced in any way to rise, it moves into a region of lower pressure; and it therefore expands and becomes cooler. If, on the other hand, the air above is forced to descend, it moves into a region of higher pressure; and it is therefore compressed and becomes hotter.

There are three principal ways in which the air may be forced to rise. It may be heated by contact with the warm earth. The heat will cause it to expand and become lighter. If it becomes lighter than the surrounding air it will rise like oil in water.

Or a wind may blow against a mountain side. In that case, even if the air is cold and heavy, it will be forced up the slope. Or warmer air may be forced to rise over the surface of colder, denser air (see pp. 109–112). Descent of the air is caused most frequently by cooling. If a mass of air is cooled so much as to be heavier than the surrounding air, it will sink.

In these ways there is a constant tendency for the lower layers of the atmosphere to become mixed with one another. Any air that falls is warmed by compression, any air that rises is cooled by expansion, and thus the average temperature increases downwards, and decreases upwards.

The vertical movements of the air are due chiefly, as we have seen, to the form of the ground and to the changes of temperature of the ground, and the influence of these does not extend indefinitely upwards. Above a certain altitude their effect becomes imperceptible, vertical movements cease, and beyond that limit the temperature no longer decreases upwards.

Stable and unstable equilibrium. When a wind blows against a mountain side it is mechanically forced to ascend. When it reaches the top it may continue to rise into the air or it may sink down the other side of the mountain. Which of these courses it takes will depend upon the vertical gradient of temperature, or lapse-rate.

The effect of the lapse-rate will be most easily understood if we take a special case as an example and, for simplicity, round numbers will be used throughout. The exact figures would be slightly, but only slightly, different from those given. Moreover, it will be assumed that the water vapour content of the air is such that the air is at no point saturated.

If we begin with dry air at a pressure of 30 inches and a temperature of 60°, and decrease the pressure upon it to 29 inches, then without any communication of heat to or from outside its temperature falls to 55°. If the pressure is further reduced to 28 inches, the temperature will fall to 50°. If we now increase the pressure to 29 inches, the temperature will rise again to 55°, and if to 30 inches the temperature will return to 60°. Air is said to expand *adiabatically* when there is no communication of heat to or from it.

Now suppose that a hill rises from sea-level to a height of 1800 feet, and that the pressure at the bottom is 30 inches and the temperature 60°. The pressure at a height of 900 feet will be 29 inches (using round numbers, as throughout the example) and at the top, or 1800 feet up, 28 inches. If the wind blows towards this hill, the air at the foot will be forced upwards, and when it reaches a height of 900 feet the pressure on it will be only 29 inches and its temperature will fall to 55°. When it reaches the top its pressure is reduced to 28 inches and its temperature to 50°.

These may or may not be the actual temperatures of the air at those heights. If they are, then the temperature of the air which has been forced upwards will always be the same as that of the air already at the

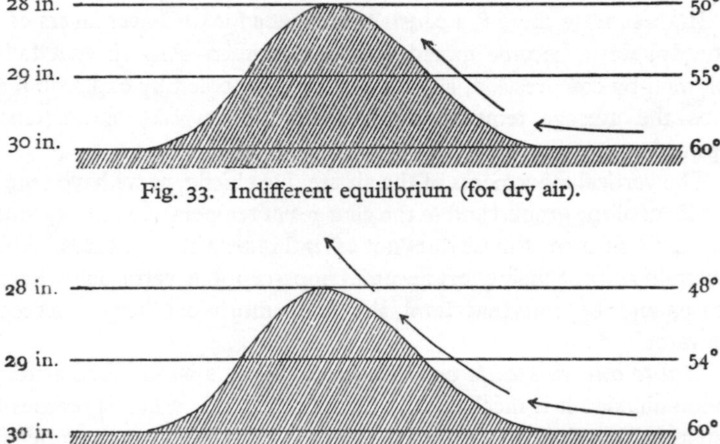

Fig. 33. Indifferent equilibrium (for dry air).

Fig. 34. Unstable equilibrium (for dry air).

same level and its density will therefore also be the same. If the wind ceases there will be no tendency for this air either to go on rising or to sink back. In such a case the air is said to be in a state of indifferent equilibrium. In this case the vertical gradient of temperature is 5° F. for 900 feet (fig. 33). This gradient is the dry adiabatic lapse-rate, or D.A.L.R.

But the temperature at 900 feet is not necessarily 55°. Suppose that the temperature at the foot is still 60°, at 900 feet 54°, and at 1800 feet 48° (fig. 34). The vertical gradient is now 6° F. for 900 feet. The pressures will be scarcely altered. If the wind blows towards the hill, the air at the foot will be forced upwards. At 900 feet its pressure is reduced to 29 inches, its temperature to 55°; at 1800 feet its pressure is 28 inches, its temperature 50°. Under these circumstances it will be observed that the temperature of the risen air is higher than that of the air already at the same level, and the risen air is therefore lighter than the air surrounding it. Accordingly, even if the wind ceases, this risen air continues to rise; and if the temperature gradient above the mountain top is the same, it will go on rising indefinitely. In this case the air is said to be in a state of unstable equilibrium. It may be left to the student to show that with this vertical gradient, if any mass of air is forced to descend, it will continue to descend even after the force has ceased to act.

Lastly, suppose that the temperature at the foot is 60°, at 900 feet 56°, and at 1800 feet 52° (fig. 35). The vertical gradient is 4° F. per 900 feet. When the wind blows towards the hill the air at the foot is forced upwards as before. At a height of 900 feet its pressure becomes 29 inches

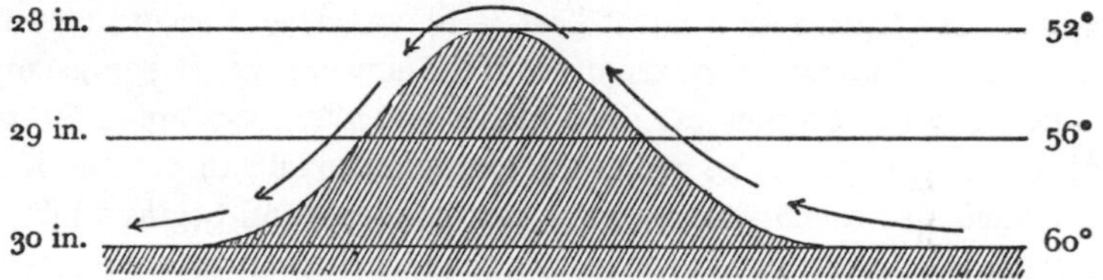

Fig. 35. Stable equilibrium (for dry air).

and its temperature 55°, at a height of 1800 feet its pressure is reduced to 28 inches and its temperature to 50°. In this case the air, after it has begun to rise, is always colder and therefore heavier than the air already at the same level. Therefore, if the wind ceases, it drops back again. If the wind continues to blow, it is carried to the top of the hill and falls down on the other side. The equilibrium is said to be stable. In such circumstances it may be shown in a similar way that if any mass of air is forced downwards it becomes hotter and lighter than the surrounding air, and therefore, when the force ceases to act, it rises again.

In a condition of indifferent equilibrium if any mass of air is forced either upwards or downwards it assumes the temperature of the surrounding air; and when the force ceases to act, it remains in the position to which it has been moved. In unstable equilibrium if any mass of air is forced upwards it becomes hotter than the surrounding air, and if the force ceases, it still continues to rise; if it is forced downwards it becomes colder than the surrounding air, and when the force ceases, it continues to fall. In stable equilibrium if any mass of air is forced upwards it becomes colder than the surrounding air, and when the force no longer acts, it falls back to its original level; if it is forced downwards it becomes hotter than the surrounding air, and when the force ceases to act, it rises again to the level from which it started.

In older texts the temperature gradient for indifferent equilibrium was often called the normal gradient. For unstable equilibrium the gradient is greater than the normal; for stable equilibrium it is less. It is now more common to describe this normal gradient as the adiabatic lapse-rate.

Effect of water-vapour. In the preceding example it was assumed that the air was free from water-vapour, and the gradient for indifferent equilibrium is in that case the dry adiabatic lapse-rate. If water-vapour be present, as it always is in fact, the conditions become more complicated. As long as the water remains in the form of vapour, the cooling caused by expansion continues at the dry adiabatic rate; but when the temperature falls below a certain point, condensation of the vapour begins. In condensation latent heat is liberated, and accordingly the temperature does not fall so rapidly as if the air were dry. If, for instance, we take dry air at a pressure of 30 inches and a temperature of 60° and reduce the pressure to 29 inches the temperature falls to 55°; but if the air contains so much water-vapour that condensation begins while the pressure is being reduced to 29 inches, then when the pressure is reached the temperature will be more than 55°—on account of the heat set free by the condensing vapour.

Thus the adiabatic lapse-rate, or gradient for indifferent equilibrium, is less for saturated air than for dry air; and with saturated air it varies according to the water content of the air.

The saturated adiabatic lapse-rate (S.A.L.R.) at a temperature of 85° F. is only 1° for every 500 feet, whereas at 20° it is 1° for every 250 feet; that for unsaturated or dry air is 1° for 185 feet approximately (nearly 5½° per 1000 feet).

Vertical gradient at great altitudes. The vertical gradient or lapse-rate near the earth's surface is far from constant and varies greatly even in the same locality. It generally approaches the adiabatic lapse-rate for dry air over the first 3000–4000 feet on a fine breezy afternoon. Air under such circumstances is turbulent as it flows over the surface; packets rising and falling rapidly imply that the adiabatic lapse-rate prevails, or very nearly so.

Above about 10,000 feet, the prevailing rate of fall of temperature in the atmosphere is nearly equal to the adiabatic lapse-rate for dry air, and it remains fairly constant to the tropopause at a height of about 33,000 feet (in England). Beyond that limit the temperature ceases to fall and is almost constant up to heights of the order of 40,000–50,000 feet. There are also indications of a slight increase of temperature upwards (cf. p. 4).

Thus over north-western Europe the part of the atmosphere accessible to observation may be divided into three layers according to the vertical gradient:

(1) A lower layer, from the ground level to about 10,000 feet, in which the lapse-rate is generally less than the adiabatic for dry air.

(2) A middle layer, from about 10,000 to 33,000 feet, in which the vertical gradient approaches the adiabatic for dry air.

(3) An upper layer, from 33,000 feet upwards, in which there is either no change with height, or a very small inverted lapse-rate.

The upper layer (p. 5) is known as the stratosphere. It is sometimes called the advective region of the atmosphere, while the air below it is called the troposphere or the convective region.

In the lower layer there is always water-vapour present, and (see ch. VII) the heavier types of cloud lie for the most part between 3000 and 10,000 feet, though rising currents may carry their summits to much greater altitudes; even in England the tops of cumulo-nimbus sometimes exceed 25,000 feet, and cirrus may be seen up to the tropopause. Within the stratosphere there is practically no water-vapour, and cloud is not observed.

We have already seen that wherever there are vertical movements of the air, the temperature must decrease upwards; and therefore the fact that there is no decrease in the stratosphere shows that vertical movements cease where it begins. The lower part of the atmosphere is disturbed by the differences of temperature on the surface of the earth. Ascending and descending currents are produced, but apparently the influence of the surface is not felt beyond a certain altitude. Just as the disturbance which produces land and sea breezes is very shallow, so we may expect that even the largest disturbances will have an upward limit.

The height of the tropopause, i.e. the base of the stratosphere, is not everywhere the same and, even at the same place, it is not constant. It tends to be lower over depressions and higher over anticyclones. It is clear that towards the equator its altitude is much greater than in more northern latitudes. In Europe it begins at a height of about 7 miles, near the equator at a height of 10 or 11 miles. Accordingly, in lower latitudes high cloud can be found to much greater heights than in England, and, for example, in the southern United States thunderstorm tops reach (occasionally) 40,000–50,000 feet.

The base of the stratosphere is sometimes very sharply defined, and the cessation of the lapse of temperature with height is sudden; but at other times the change is more gradual and the boundary is not so sharp. We may conclude that although the stratosphere is little affected by the disturbances below, yet at times their influence extends into its base.

Temperature on mountains. Over a plain, when the sun is shining, the temperature decreases upwards, because, as we have seen, the air receives most of its warmth from the earth. If the air is still, the isothermal surfaces will be horizontal, for otherwise there will be hotter and lighter air lying amidst heavier and denser air. The distribution of temperature will be similar to that shown in the right-hand part of fig. 36, where *AB* represents the surface of the plain, with a temperature of 60°.

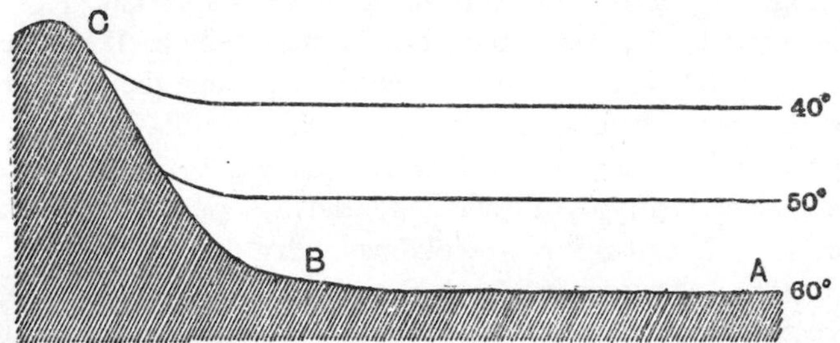

Fig. 36. Isothermal surfaces against a mountain side heated by the sun.

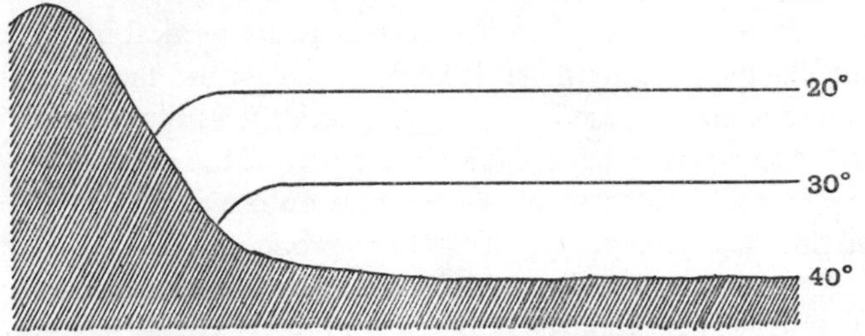

Fig. 37. Isothermal surfaces against a mountain side cooled by radiation.

But if a mountain, *BC*, rise from the plain, the mountain is warmed by the sun in the same way as the plain and becomes a source of heat to the air into which it penetrates. The air on the mountain side is warmed by contact with the mountain and becomes hotter than the air at the same level above the plain. The isothermal surfaces therefore rise towards the mountain, as shown in the diagram.

Since the air in contact with the mountain is warmer than the air at the same level outside, it is also lighter. Therefore it rises and the cooler air from outside flows towards the mountain. In this way, even though the mountain itself may be as hot as the plain, the air on the side and top of the mountain is kept cooler than the air that rests on the plain.

At night if radiation is unchecked, both the plain and the mountain grow cold and cool the air in contact with them. The isotherms will now bend down towards the mountain as shown in fig. 37. The air on the mountain side becomes colder and heavier than the free air at the same level above the plain. Accordingly it sinks downwards and the warmer air from outside flows towards the mountain.

Mountain and valley winds. It follows from this that, in still weather, when the sun is strong there will be a flow of air towards the mountain and up its slope; at night, if the sky is clear, there will be a flow of cold air down the mountain side. The flow is naturally concentrated into the valleys running up into the mountain; and accordingly in many mountain districts a wind blows up the valleys by day and down them by night. Such winds are often felt in the Alps, and in the Himalayas they are frequently very strong. In cloudy climates they are scarcely noticeable; and, like land and sea breezes, these local winds may be overpowered by winds due to other causes.

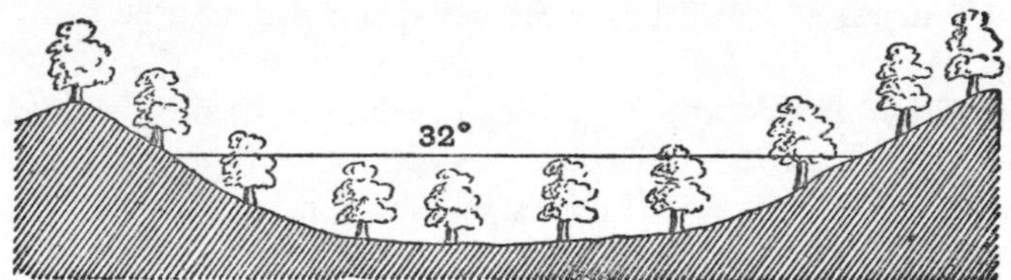

Fig. 38. Inversion of temperature.

Inversions of temperature. In winter the nights are long, and, if the sky be clear and the air still, the conditions illustrated in fig. 37 may be maintained for hours. Gradually the cold air collects in the hollows and valleys, and a very marked reversal of the temperature gradient, or inversion of temperature, is brought about (see fig. 49*a*).

A pool of cold air lies in the valley, on the mountain side above the pool the air is comparatively warm, and higher still the ordinary decrease of temperature with increase of altitude begins. Such inversions of temperature occur to a greater or less extent on every clear calm night. In mountain districts their effects become very well known, the valley floors being so often colder than the sides of the valley at a higher level.

Under such circumstances it may freeze in the valley while higher up there is no frost. Examples of this phenomenon occur every winter and spring and are of the utmost importance to fruit-growers. For example, on an evening towards the end of May in 1894, after the ash-trees were in leaf, the air was still and the sky was clear. At night cold currents flowed down the slopes in the manner described and the hollows were half-filled with air below the freezing-point, while the warmer and lighter air floated quietly upon the denser air beneath. The trees on the floors of the valleys were frost-bitten to their tops. On the slopes the leaves of the lower branches were affected, but the upper branches were untouched. The trees on the higher ground escaped the frost altogether (fig. 38).

Table 6

Average daily minima at (*a*) Malvern (377 ft.) and (*b*) Perdiswell near Worcester (94 ft.), 1926–1940:

	J	F	M	A	M	J	J	A	S	O	N	D
(*a*)	35·3	35·5	37·4	40·7	45·1	51·1	55·4	54·8	51·2	44·8	40·2	36·1
(*b*)	33·4	33·7	34·9	38·5	43·4	48·3	52·5	51·6	47·6	41·6	37·6	34·2

Many examples can be quoted of places on hillsides being less liable to frost than the valleys; Malvern, for instance, is noteworthy, compared with the Severn valley (Table 6). The development of autumn and winter morning fogs in English valley-bottoms when the air over a considerable depth is cooled below the dew-point may also be noted (cf. p. 80).

The Föhn. Besides the mountain and valley winds already described there is a wind of a very different type which blows from the mountains to the plains. In Switzerland it is called the Föhn, on the eastern side of the Rocky Mountains it is known as the Chinook, and similar winds with various local names are met with in other parts of the world. The special characteristic of these winds is their dryness and their high temperature.

If the barometric pressure on one side of a mountain chain is higher than on the other a wind will blow towards the chain from the higher pressure, and if the atmosphere is in a state of stable equilibrium it will descend the other side.

The wind will always contain a certain amount of water-vapour and if the mountain chain is high enough, some of the vapour will be condensed and will often be precipitated. Accordingly, the decrease of temperature as it ascends the mountains is less than if the air were dry, on account of the liberation of latent heat. On the other side as the air descends the pressure upon it increases and its temperature rises. Further, once over the crest and immediately descent begins compression starts and the temperature of the air rises above that at which it was saturated when it passed the crest. Hence from the summit downward the air will be unsaturated and the rise in temperature will be at the D.A.L.R.

An example similar to those already given will serve to make the matter clear. Suppose that the chain is 1800 feet high and that the wind starts towards it with a temperature of 60°. We have already seen that if it were dry air, its temperature when it reached the top would have fallen to 50°, owing to expansion. But if there is any condensation of vapour, the fall is less, and the temperature actually reached will be higher, for example 52°. In descending the other side the temperature increases. Since there is no further condensation the temperature throughout the descent will rise at the dry adiabatic rate (nearly 5½° per 1000 feet). When it reaches the level from which it started, its temperature will have risen 10°, and will be about 62°. It is hotter as well as drier than when it started.

If the air is saturated to begin with, so that condensation goes on all the way up the windward slope, the temperature at the top will be much higher than in the example given and the difference of temperature on the two sides will be far greater. In such a case the increase of temperature in descending the leeward slope is approximately twice the decrease in ascending the windward slope, so that with a mountain range 8000 feet high, places at the foot on the lee side may be 15° warmer than on the windward side.

Thus the Föhn is a decidedly warm wind for the season, and very dry, and if it comes in spring, it rapidly melts the snow in the valleys and on the slopes of the mountains. Much of the snow indeed disappears by direct evaporation into the warm dry air. In the instance of a range 8000 feet high a little consideration will show that close to the foot of the mountains the dew-point may be as much as 40° below the air temperature on the lee side; hence the vigorous evaporation.

Temperature of plateaux. A plateau differs from a mountain or a mountain chain in the fact that it is much broader. It is in fact a very much larger mass projecting into the atmosphere and it produces a greater effect upon the temperature of the air.

In fig. 39, *AB* represents the surface of a plain and *CD* the surface of a plateau rising above it. If both of these are equally exposed to the rays of the sun, the plateau will become as hot as the plain—possibly hotter, because the rays have a smaller thickness of the atmosphere to penetrate. Supposing that each of them is heated to a temperature of 70°, then each will tend to produce a vertical distribution of temperature such as is shown on the right-hand and the left-hand sides of the diagram respectively. On the slope *BC* the isothermal surfaces will bend upwards, as on the sides of a mountain in similar circumstances.

With such a distribution the air cannot be at rest, for the air at 60° above the plateau is on a level with the air at 30° above the plain; and in general the air above the plateau is hotter and lighter than the air at the same level above the plain. The effect is much the same as if the two were covered with liquids of different density: the plain, for example, with water, the plateau with oil. The denser fluid flows beneath the lighter and the lighter fluid flows over the denser.

Accordingly the cooler air from outside flows under the warmer air of the plateau, displacing it and forcing it to rise and at some higher level to overflow.

In consequence of the influx of cold air, the air on the plateau is kept cooler than it would otherwise be, especially near the edge. But the inflowing air is continually being warmed by the heat of the plateau itself, and the temperature still remains far higher than that of the air at the same level above the plain.

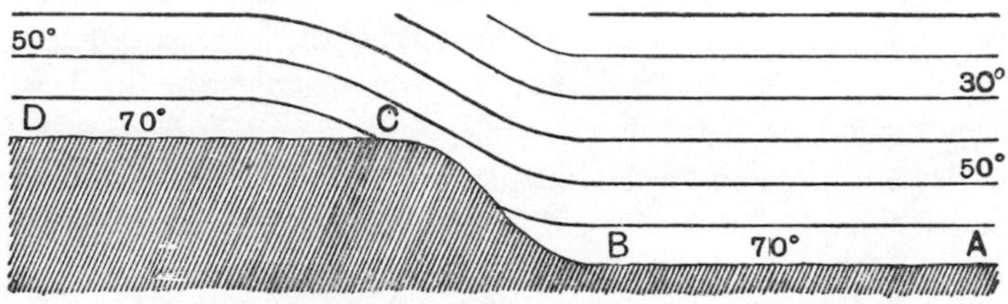

Fig. 39. Isothermal surfaces over plateau and plain.

The general form of the isothermal surfaces will therefore be as shown in fig. 39. But it is probable that at higher altitudes the bend above the edge of the plateau will gradually diminish.

In this diagram the plateau is comparatively low. The air on its surface has a temperature of 70°, the air at the same level above the plain has a temperature of 40°. The difference of density is the same as if both rested on a plain, one part of which was heated to 70° and the other part to 40°. If the plateau is high the difference will be far greater than can ever be caused by unequal heating of a plain; and accordingly the winds that flow inwards to a heated plateau are often stronger than those that flow towards a heated plain. Moreover, the air rising from a heated plateau soon finds itself in a very much cooler environment, and may then continue to rise to great heights; hence the well-known tendency of certain plateau-regions, when invaded by humid air, to produce violent thunderstorms. The South African veldt gives a good example.

CHAPTER VII

HUMIDITY OF THE ATMOSPHERE

Water-vapour in the air. Wherever air and water are in contact, there is always an interchange of particles between them. Particles of air pass into the water, particles of water pass into the air in the form of vapour. Therefore, there is always a certain amount of water-vapour present in the air and a certain amount of air present in the water. Some of the air in the water passes back again into the air and some of the vapour in the air passes back into the water.

If the amount of vapour present in the air is small, more particles of water will pass from the water into the air than from the air into the water, and the water gradually dries up or evaporates. But if the amount of vapour already in the air is large, then as many particles of vapour may pass from the air into the water as from the water into the air, and the water will not evaporate. In such a case the air is said to be saturated or in ordinary language to hold as much vapour as it can contain.

Even from the surface of snow or ice evaporation may take place. Sometimes during a long frost the snow that has previously fallen gradually disappears without melting.

The vapour in the air above the oceans is carried by the winds into the heart of the continents, and, even in the driest parts of the globe, the air is never absolutely dry. But the amount of vapour present varies greatly according to the place and the season.

It is a matter of common observation that in general evaporation is most rapid at a high temperature. Therefore, we may expect to find the greatest amount of vapour over the oceans near the equator and the smallest amount over the land in a cold region such as north-eastern Asia in winter.

The amount of water that can exist as vapour in a cubic foot of air has a definite limit, depending solely upon the temperature. When the limit is reached the air is said to be saturated, and if more vapour of water is forced into the space, the excess above the limit will condense into the liquid form. It is important to notice that the pressure of the air has no effect; more dry air could be pumped into the same space without producing any condensation.

Table 7 gives the number of grains of water in a cubic foot of saturated air at various temperatures. At 50° a cubic foot of saturated air contains

4·28 grains; it can take up no more. If its temperature be raised to 60° it will be able to contain 5·87 grains, that is, it will be able to take up 1·59 grains more than it actually holds. If on the other hand its temperature falls to 40°, it can only hold 3·09 grains, and therefore 1·19 grains will condense as water. For these figures to be exactly correct the air must be confined in a vessel, so that the change of temperature has no effect upon its volume.

Evidently therefore the feeling of wetness or dryness in the air does not depend only on the actual amount of vapour present. In the case described the same air, with the same amount of water in it, would feel dry at 60° and wet at 40°. At 60° a damp cloth hung in it would become drier, at 40° it would become wetter.

Table 7

Temp. Fahr.	30°	32°	40°	50°	60°	70°
Grains per cu. ft.	2·21	2·37	3·09	4·28	5·87	8·00

So far as the sensations or the formation of cloud and rain are concerned, it is not the actual amount of vapour present which is of importance, but the proportion of the actual amount to the maximum amount possible at the particular temperature. The air of the Sahara holds more vapour per cubic foot than the air of England on a wet day in winter, but because of the high temperature it is able to take up still more.

Absolute and relative humidity. In any particular case the actual amount of vapour in a cubic foot of air (or a litre, if metric measures are being used) is called the absolute humidity of the air in question; the proportion of this amount to the amount possible at the actual temperature of the air is called its relative humidity. If, for example, the temperature of the air is 50° and the amount of vapour is 2·14 grains per cubic foot, then the relative humidity is $\frac{2{\cdot}14}{4{\cdot}28}$ or 50 per cent, 4·28 grains per cubic foot being the maximum possible at this temperature.

Absolute humidity is often expressed in terms of the pressure exerted by the aqueous vapour present. The relative humidity is then the proportion of the actual vapour pressure to the vapour pressure in saturated air of the same temperature. This gives practically the same result for the relative humidity as when the weights of vapour per cubic foot are compared.

Dew-point. The quantity of water-vapour in the air can be determined chemically by passing a known volume of air through tubes containing calcium chloride or some other drying reagent, and noting the increase of weight. But the process is rather long, and some quicker method must be employed if daily observations are to be made. One of the simplest is the determination of the dew-point.

If the air is gradually cooled, it will at length reach the temperature at which it is saturated, and if it is cooled any further, condensation will take place. The temperature at which condensation begins, that is, the temperature of saturation, is called the dew-point.

Having determined the dew-point, reference to a table such as that on p. 72, but more complete, will give at once the amount of vapour present, or the absolute humidity. If, for example, the dew-point is 40°, then the air which has been tested contains 3·09 grains per cubic foot. It should perhaps be mentioned that in the original preparation of these tables, the amount of vapour present in saturated air at different temperatures was determined chemically.

The instruments employed for determining the dew-point are known as hygrometers. Various forms are described in elementary text-books of physics and as they are seldom used in meteorological observations, nothing further need be said about them here.

Wet and dry bulb thermometers. The humidity of the air is usually determined by the use of a pair of thermometers, the bulb of one of which is kept continually moist. Such a pair of thermometers is sometimes called a psychrometer.

Both thermometers are mounted on a stand, with their bulbs projecting beyond the mount, so as to be freely exposed to the air. One of the bulbs is left in this condition. Round the other muslin or cotton is loosely wrapped, wetted with water and kept constantly moist by allowing a few threads to dip into a little cup of water. The whole instrument should be placed inside a screen such as that described on p. 40.

The thermometer with the dry bulb gives the temperature of the air. If the air is completely saturated with vapour the reading of the wet bulb thermometer will be the same. But if the air is not saturated there will be evaporation from the moist cotton round the bulb; this evaporation will cool the bulb and the reading will be lower than that of the dry bulb thermometer. The more rapid the evaporation the greater the cooling will be; and consequently the drier the air, the greater is the difference between the two thermometers.

The relation between this difference and the relative humidity is somewhat complex. But tables have been constructed which give the relative humidity at once when the readings of the two thermometers are known.

It is, however, clear that the rate of evaporation from the cotton around the wet bulb will depend not only upon the relative humidity but also on the rapidity of the currents of air past the thermometer. If, for example, we blow the wet bulb with a pair of bellows, the mercury in the thermometer will fall.

Consequently this method of determining humidity is not entirely satisfactory, for even in a Stevenson screen the air currents will not always be the same.

A form of psychrometer has, however, been devised in which this difficulty is avoided. It is known as Assmann's psychrometer. The bulbs and the lower part of the stems of both thermometers are enclosed in wide metal tubes, which are open at the bottom. At the top the two bulbs unite into a single tube leading into a kind of reservoir which has an outlet to the air and in which there is a small ventilating fan operated by clockwork. In taking an observation the clockwork is wound and set going. It works the fan at the same rate and for the same length of time at every observation, and thus it always draws the same amount of air at the same rapidity past the bulbs of the thermometers. All observations are accordingly made under the same conditions so far as the movement of the air is concerned, and the results are much more reliable than in the ordinary form of psychrometer.

Condensation. When a mass of air is cooled below the dew-point, some of the vapour, as we have seen, condenses into the liquid or the solid form. In nature this condensation may take place in several different ways. The water produced may collect on solid objects as dew or hoar-frost; it may hang in the air in little drops, forming mist or fog or cloud; or it may fall as rain, snow, or hail.

Super-cooling of liquid drops and some consequences. Condensation at temperatures above the freezing-point will be into small liquid droplets of the order of $\frac{1}{500}$ inch in diameter. These, when present in large numbers, constitute the majority of clouds or fogs. It is important to recognise that, provided that a drop is small and remains undisturbed, it can be cooled many degrees below the freezing-point and yet remain liquid. On the other hand, when a cloud is composed of such supercooled drops some of the drops may be disturbed, for example by the passage of an aircraft, and they will immediately freeze. This is of common occurrence and results in the accumulation of ice on the leading edges and other projecting parts of the aircraft.

But the same phenomenon may frequently be observed in winter by anyone who walks or rides through a fog at a temperature below freezing-point; as he collides with the droplets, which are still liquid, they freeze. If such a fog is accompanied by a slight wind the drops freeze against the sides of all objects exposed to the wind, such as branches of trees and telephone wires. Such deposits are known as rime, and must be carefully distinguished from the hoar-frost (see below) which forms on surfaces exposed to the sky, such as lawns and roofs, where they are sufficiently cooled by radiation to a clear sky.

Rime-deposits become very conspicuous in the form of frost-feathers, projecting to windward of exposed objects, especially on British mountains in winter. The summits are frequently covered by low cloud at a temperature well below freezing-point, accompanied by strong wind. At the old Ben Nevis observatory such deposits on the masts supporting the various instruments have been known to attain a length of 5 feet.

It is as a result of this property of small water drops to remain liquid at temperatures below the freezing-point that the predominant component of the majority of clouds over England up to a level approaching 20,000 feet is still liquid drops rather than ice crystals. The average temperature of the air at 15,000 feet is not far from zero (Fahrenheit). Above 20,000 feet it may for all practical purposes be assumed that any cloud is composed of ice crystals throughout. Observation of the growth of a towering cumulus cloud on a summer day will show that the top retains the characteristic rounded and 'bubbly' form up to heights greater than 15,000 feet. But if the growth of cumulus cloud continues much beyond this, the top then generally acquires a fibrous appearance and the cloud becomes the cumulo-nimbus described in a later paragraph. The fibrous appearance begins when the super-cooling of the ascending cloud drops is so great, that, combined with the disturbance within the cloud, the drops can no longer remain liquid—they become ice crystals. The fibrous appearance arises from the sweeping out of the crystals by the wind and is analogous to that of much of the high cloud we call cirrus, which is also composed of ice (cf. also p. 87).

Condensation of water-vapour in air below the freezing-point results in the formation of minute ice crystals. Accordingly, if in a vigorous ascending current of vapour-laden air condensation begins at a temperature above the freezing-point, and the air which is now saturated with vapour continues to ascend, at some higher level the freezing-point will be reached and ice crystals will begin to form among the super-cooled water drops which are being carried upward from below. These ice crystals have a tendency to aggregate, and form snowflakes which may become large enough to fall. Frequently, therefore, in winter or on high mountains in summer, snow may fall from a cloud, although the cloud itself is still largely composed of the very small super-cooled liquid drops.

The characteristic droplets which go to form cloud are very much smaller than those forming drizzle or rain; the small drops forming drizzle drift rather than fall downward and average $\frac{1}{100}$–$\frac{1}{50}$ inch in diameter. Raindrops vary from about $\frac{1}{25}$–$\frac{1}{5}$ inch; they very rarely attain greater size and then are so unstable that they break up almost at once. The process by which cloud droplets aggregate into the larger drops we call drizzle or rain, depends on several physical factors of some complexity; it is clearly necessary, however, for considerable turbulence to exist in the lower parts of the cloud in order that aggregation may be encouraged. In a later chapter it will be shown that all clouds from which heavy precipitation may be expected, whether of rain, snow, or hail, satisfy this requirement. On the other hand, not all turbulent clouds give rain; in order that raindrops can be formed it has been shown that, in cooler latitudes, some ice crystals should in general be present in the cloud.

Dew and hoar-frost. Dew and hoar-frost are the effect of condensation not in the air itself but upon the surface of solid bodies exposed to the air. If the temperature of the air is higher than the dew-point, and a cold object at a low enough temperature is brought into the air, then the cold object cools the air in contact with it below the dew-point and causes condensation, but there is no condensation in the rest of the air. The water formed settles upon the cold object and is known as dew. If the dew-point is below the freezing-point, the vapour will condense as spicules of ice and not as drops of water, forming hoar-frost instead of dew.

For the natural formation of dew there must be water-vapour in the air and the temperature of the grass or of other objects on the ground must fall below the dew-point. The greater the amount of vapour present and the lower the temperature of the ground the more abundant will be the dew.

It is essential that the air should be still or nearly so, for if the wind is strong there is too much mixing of the air and none of it remains in contact with the ground long enough to be cooled to the dew-point—unless indeed the whole mass of air is already near that temperature.

A warm day favours the production of dew during the following night; for a warm day assists evaporation and therefore tends to increase the amount of vapour present. At night the ground must be cold, but it must not owe its coolness to a cold wind, for it is indispensable that the ground or grass should be colder than the air. It must be cooled by radiation. Consequently, the conditions most favourable to the formation of dew are calm weather and a clear sky, allowing the ready access of the sun's rays by day, and free radiation by night.

These are the conditions characteristic of anticyclones and of the fronts of wedges; and it is accordingly, when these types of pressure distribution prevail, that dew, and also hoar-frost, most frequently occur.

It was Dr Wells, in the year 1818, who first gave a satisfactory explanation of the formation of dew; and since his time until about seventy years ago, it was believed that the vapour which condenses into dew was already in the air at sundown. But in 1885 Dr John Aitken, a Scottish meteorologist, published a number of observations which show that this view is not quite correct.

He cut a turf out of his lawn and fitted it into an iron tray so that it could be removed or replaced at will. On an evening when dew was likely to form, the turf was taken out and weighed and then put back into its place in the lawn. After a heavy dew had been deposited and the turf was wet, it was again removed and weighed. In spite of the dew upon it, it weighed less than before, showing that the turf had lost more water to the air than it had gained by condensation.

He also made shallow boxes or trays of tin-plate, about 3 inches deep; and rested them upside down upon the ground, so that the bottom was about 3 inches above the surface. Dew was deposited profusely upon the inside of the trays, while on the outside there was little or none. Similarly it may be noticed that when a stone lies loose upon the ground there is often a far more copious deposit of dew upon its lower than upon its upper surface.

These experiments seem to prove that the vapour which forms the dew largely rises from the ground. In such a climate as ours the earth is always more or less moist, and this moisture is continually evaporating and passing upwards into the air. Grass and other plants assist the process considerably. They draw up the moisture through their roots and transpire it through their leaves. The warmer the earth is, the more rapid will be the stream of vapour from the earth into the air. As long as the air is warm and unsaturated and the surface of the ground is also warm, the moisture will still remain as vapour in the air. But loss of heat by radiation at night cools the blades of grass and also the actual surface of the ground (while the earth beneath still remains warm), and the vapour condenses upon them as dew. Plants, in removing moisture from the ground, cannot always rid themselves of excess moisture through evaporation from their leaves. The result is that droplets of water are exuded on to the leaves from the plants themselves—a process known as guttation. This happens under cloches or in cold-frames where radiational cooling is negligible and ordinary dew does not form.

When the earth beneath the surface is cold, evaporation takes place more slowly and the vapour rises much less freely. There is, accordingly, less vapour in the air immediately above the ground, and the grass must cool to a much lower temperature before the dew-point is reached. In such circumstances the dew-point is likely to be lower than 32° F., and hoar-frost will be formed instead of dew.

From what has been already said, it will be evident that dew is most likely to be abundant when the earth beneath the surface is warm, but the surface itself is cold. This is the reason for the heavy dews of early autumn. The earth is still hot from the summers' sun, but the nights are long enough for the grass and the surface of the ground to become very cold by radiation, if the sky is clear. In spring the earth for some distance below the surface is still cold after the winter's frosts, and gives off vapour much more slowly.

Mist or fog. In the formation of dew the air is cooled where it is in contact with something colder than itself, the rest of the air remaining comparatively warm; and condensation takes place upon the surface of the cold object. But if the air is cooled throughout, condensation takes place within the air itself. Small drops of water are formed, which may float in the air for a considerable time, and a fog or mist is produced or, higher in the atmosphere, a cloud.

It may be expected that the drops of water would fall as soon as they are formed. They actually do fall, except when an upward current of air prevents them, but they are very small and owing to the resistance of the air their fall is very slow. The smaller the size of the drop the greater, compared with its weight, is the resistance of the air.

The weight of a uniform sphere is proportional to its volume and increases with the cube of the radius. The laws which govern the resistance of the air are complex. Experimentally it has been shown that at high velocities the resistance to a sphere increases nearly with the square of the radius. At low velocities the rate of increase is less. Therefore, the larger the drop the greater is the weight compared with the resistance, and the smaller the drop the smaller is the weight compared with the resistance. A large drop therefore falls rapidly, a small drop slowly. Falling water-drops larger than about 5 mm. ($\frac{1}{5}$ inch) in diameter are, however, unstable; they soon break up into smaller drops. A drop of this size falls through the air with a terminal velocity of about 18 m.p.h. (25 feet per second). Hence the observed fact that no rain will fall when the vertical current exceeds this value.

There are several ways in which air near the ground may be cooled throughout its mass.

Air may be cooled by mixing it with colder air, but the amount of condensation brought about in this way cannot be great, for while the warm air is cooled, the cold air is warmed and is therefore able to hold more vapour.

From Table 7 on p. 72, it appears that:

1 cu.ft. of saturated air at 60° contains 5·87 grains of water-vapour.
1 cu.ft. of saturated air at 40° contains 3·09 grains of water-vapour.

The result of mixing, if there were no condensation, would be practically

2 cu.ft. of air at 50° containing 8·96 grains of water-vapour.

But on looking at the table it will be seen that 2 cu.ft. of air at 50° cannot contain more than 8·56 grains. The extra 0·40 grain will be condensed. The figures are approximate only, because in the process of condensation latent heat will be given out, and the final temperature of the mixture will be a little more than 50° and its volume a little more than 2 cu.ft. But the calculation shows that when two masses of saturated air at different temperatures are mixed, there is condensation of vapour, but although the amount condensed is small, it is observed as fog.

It appears, therefore, that mixing is not likely to produce a really heavy fog, although as a process leading to the condensation of water-vapour along the boundary between two moist air currents differing in temperature, it must not be overlooked, either on the ground or (as cloud) at higher levels in the atmosphere.

There is another way in which a fog or mist may be formed. Instead of cooling the air we may add to it more water-vapour, and if we add more than enough to saturate the air, condensation of the surplus vapour will take place. This is what happens above a hot bath in a cold room. More vapour passes from the water to the air than the air can contain, and some of it condenses into little drops of water and becomes visible to us as steam.

The conditions are precisely similar when the air is cold and the earth is warm and moist or, at sea, the water is warm. The vapour rising from the warm earth or sea, like that from the hot bath, is partially condensed and forms a fog. We can frequently observe steaming from the surface of unfrozen rivers and lakes in winter, but the rising patches of saturated air are quickly swept away and mixed with the drier air above. Steam fog accordingly is rarely of any significance except in extreme cases, e.g. when open water is found in high polar latitudes in winter. It has been called Arctic Smoke.

Radiation fog. Air may be cooled more effectively as a result of radiation. In the first place the surface of the earth cools rapidly by outward radiation on a clear evening. The air adjacent to the ground is also cooled, though the cooling may be slight if there is a strong wind, which will carry away the patches of cool air close to the ground and replace them by warmer air. In quiet conditions, however, a layer of air many feet thick is cooled; the process is probably assisted by the very slight surface air movements resulting from the small local differences of temperature between different types of vegetation and soil, arising from their different rates of radiation.

Moreover, in undulating country the high ground at first radiates a little more freely, and accordingly a small patch of air adjacent to each hilltop is cooled below the temperature of the air at the same level away from the hill. These slightly cooler patches of air, being heavier than the neighbouring air, tend to flow downward, and so fill up the neighbouring hollows and valleys. This process takes place widely; shallow downhill surface trickles of cool air about sunset can, for example, be recognised on very small hills by noticing the drift of cigarette smoke, or even better by the downhill drift of bonfire smoke which can often be seen lingering in hollows in sheets and wisps. The same process has been observed, even in Chiltern valleys, to produce perceptible local evening breezes. On a larger scale the down-flowing winds, of great strength, which blow from time to time in the Greenland fiords, arise because the high snow-covered interior of the ice-cap is an extremely good radiator. Gravitational streams of air of this kind are called katabatic winds. In Greenland the surface air on the ice-cap may at times be more than 50° colder than the air at the same level over the adjacent seas.

In this country valleys, large and small, soon become ponds of cold air which has slid down from surrounding higher ground on winter evenings. Such a pond of air itself loses heat by outward radiation. When the ground is already damp the cold air flowing downward cannot take up much moisture and requires but little further cooling to reach saturation-point. Hence, we find that fog begins to accumulate in valley-bottoms, particularly over open patches of damp ground and coarse marshy vegetation. Moreover, mixing takes place between the various trickles of almost saturated air, which differ but slightly in temperature, and the air above. Consequently, after a clear late autumn night following a period of damp weather, most of the midland river valleys will be covered with radiation fog to a considerable depth, sometimes as much as 500 feet (pl. 2*b*).

Shallow radiation fog, once formed, will soon dissipate as the sun gains power. Summer morning valley mists are common in the early hours, but they do not last. The deeper radiation fogs of the longer nights of autumn are more resistant, and may last through the next day and increase in depth on the following night. This arises from the fact that the effect of the sun is less powerful in autumn, and its rays cannot penetrate the fog to warm the ground and the air above it sufficiently for the moisture to be absorbed.

It is evident, therefore, that hilltops above 500 feet frequently project above all but the worst radiation fogs, a fact well known to dwellers on the North Downs who have to travel into London or other parts of the Thames valley in winter.

The unpleasant brownish-yellow pea-soup fog of our great cities results from the accumulation within the fog of vast numbers of smoke particles, frequently containing sulphur in various compounds. The pool of colder air in which the fog has formed is overlain by air at a higher temperature, i.e. an inversion exists. Accordingly, if a mass of cold air below the inversion is caused to rise, it will at once find itself in a warmer environment and will sink back. In short, the atmosphere is in stable equilibrium. Under such conditions the smoke and other products of combustion are trapped and can only spread horizontally. A pilot flying above the fog in clear air with a blue sky can see nothing of the ground beneath him although his horizontal visibility may be many miles.

Extensive radiation fogs formed over land may drift with a light wind into adjacent areas. The winter fogs in the estuaries of the Thames and Mersey are generally caused in this way. If the wind becomes stronger, the colder layers near the surface mix with the warmer and drier air above, and the fog soon disappears.

In recent years it has been observed that winter fogs are not quite so dense at street level in the middle of a big city as they are in parks and open spaces. This is attributed mainly to the slight but perceptible warming in the neighbourhood of large heated buildings. Outside the London area, for example, there may sometimes be thick, white fog while in the centre of the city itself it is relatively clear. The heat from buildings, underground stations and other sources is sometimes sufficient to prevent a dense fog at the surface, but a thick black pall of smoke may hang overhead when an inversion is present with little or no wind to diffuse it.

Radiation fogs are common throughout western Europe especially in autumn, and some continental cities situated in valley-basins—Prague, for example—have an unenviable reputation for them.

Advection fog. Another effective method of cooling large masses of air at the earth's surface below the dew-point takes place when an extensive stream of warm moist air moves over a decidedly cooler region, e.g. a cold ocean current, a snow-covered land surface, or a land from which the snow has only recently melted. Advection fog is often known as movement fog since, unlike radiation fog, it is associated with large-scale movement of air. If such a fog follows several days' cold weather in winter it is usually the precursor of a general thaw.

To give an example: nearly saturated air from sub-tropical areas may arrive on a south-westerly wind at the Isles of Scilly with a temperature of 50° F. If the country has previously had a snowfall then the passage of this air northwards will be rapidly cooled by the snow which, so long as it stays in a thawing state, remains at a temperature of 32° F. The air will, therefore, give up its moisture rapidly over the snow-covered countryside, so that it is possible to have fog in such conditions even with a strong wind blowing.

The classic example of warm moist air passing over a cold sea is provided by the Atlantic fogs off Newfoundland. The boundary between the warm surface-waters of the Gulf Stream Drift and the Labrador Current lies not far to the south and south-east of Newfoundland and it will be evident that almost always when a light wind blows from between south-west and east the requisite conditions are fulfilled. The surface air picks up moisture from the warmer waters to the south, and then flows over a surface which is often 20° cooler. Persistent fogs develop; whilst they may occur at any period of the year, they tend to be more frequent in early summer, when the melt-waters from the winter pack-ice off Labrador combine with the icebergs from Greenland to render the water particularly chilly in comparison with the rapidly warming continent to the south-west.

Similar conditions—warm moist air flowing gently over a cooler sea—are frequent in British waters. Early summer coastal fogs are frequent in Cornwall when a light warm south wind is blowing. The surface air is soon nearly saturated as it crosses the Channel, and its movement over waters which are often colder near England leads to the formation of fog. Similar processes explain the development of coastal fogs, known as sea-fret, or in eastern Scotland as haar, on the North Sea coast. They, too, are most frequent in May and early June, because at that season the coldest waters generally lie off our north-east coasts. A map showing the isotherms for the month of May clearly illustrates the effect of the neighbouring cool sea on the temperature of our north-east coasts. (For the effect of winds on advection fogs, see p. 108).

By international agreement the term fog is used in weather reports for a condition of atmospheric obscurity in which objects at a distance of 1 km. (1100 yards) are not visible. It may be added that in some parts of the world such a condition arises from causes other than the presence of moisture, notably the dust fogs of the deserts and their border regions in West Africa, which are associated with strong winds, such as the Harmattan, at certain seasons.

The characteristic hill fog of the British Isles is simply low stratiform cloud, and is considered under that heading in a later paragraph.

Effect of dust particles. Some degree of heating and cooling of the air may be brought about by heating and cooling of the dust particles within the air. They are solid, and are readily warmed by the rays of the sun, and easily lose heat by radiation at night, like the ground itself. But they also play another part in the condensation of vapour, especially those which are hygroscopic, that is, have an affinity for water. Such particles include the minute particles of salt which are left in the air after the evaporation of spray.

It was shown by Aitken that if the air in a flask is suddenly cooled throughout its mass the mode in which condensation takes place depends upon whether the air is dusty or free from dust. The sudden cooling is brought about by reducing the pressure in the flask by means of an air-pump and thus causing expansion. If the air is full of particles of dust, condensation takes place upon these particles and little drops of water are formed throughout the air, and the flask is filled with fog. If the number of particles is less, fewer drops are formed, but they are larger. If the air is entirely free from dust, condensation takes place only on the sides of the flask. For some time it was believed that dust particles were absolutely essential to the formation of mist, cloud, or rain.

It has since been proved, however, by Professor C. T. R. Wilson that under certain conditions condensation can take place upon the ions of the air itself; but the temperature must be lowered considerably below the normal saturation point before such condensation begins.

Clouds. In mountainous districts clouds often cover the tops of the mountains, and if we climb up till we reach the clouds we find that they are precisely similar to the fogs of the lower ground. A cloud in fact is a fog formed high up in the atmosphere. Like a fog it can be produced only by the cooling of the air *en masse*, and this cooling may be brought about in several ways.

Stratiform or layer clouds. (Pls. 1 and 2.) Clouds of this type like fog, may form by the mixing of moist air currents differing slightly in temperature. There are often currents of air flowing in various directions at different heights in the atmosphere, and at the surface of contact between two currents there will be a certain amount of mixing. If the temperatures are not the same there may be condensation. A cloud formed in this way will usually be a thin sheet, with a current in one direction above it and a current in a different direction below it. The surface of contact may be thrown into waves, like the surface of a river when a wind is blowing. Owing to the low density of air the waves will probably be much higher than water-waves, and, on account of the lower temperature and pressure, condensation will be greatest at their crests. The cloud itself will therefore be influenced by the waves and may appear as long bars stretching across the sky. Or there may be two sets of waves crossing each other, and the sheet will be broken into rounded patches with pools of blue between.

Stratus cloud may also form when a moist layer itself loses heat by radiation.

Stratiform clouds, especially near the surface, may arise in another way which goes far to explain much of the characteristic low cloud. If a stream of air is moving vigorously over a moist surface it picks up moisture; but at the same time its flow due to friction is turbulent. Small masses of air are continually rising off the surface and being replaced by others descending to it, and with moderate or fresh breezes such turbulence may extend upward to 2000 or 3000 feet. But every small packet of moist air which is being swept up from the surface expands as it rises and is cooled at the normal rate for unsaturated air (*c.* $5\frac{1}{2}°$ per 1000 feet). By the time it has risen through 2000 feet it is quite likely, therefore, to have been cooled to its dew-point, and cloud will therefore be formed somewhere towards the top of the layer of air in which the surface turbulence occurs. Cloud produced in this way may form an almost unbroken sheet of stratus or strato-cumulus, especially in the cooler months when less moisture is required to saturate the air—i.e. cloud-base is reached at a lower level.

The conditions for the formation of cloud of this type are best established when the air at higher levels is relatively warm. Suppose a stream of warm air is reaching us in winter from, say, Madeira. As it approaches Britain its lower layers cool because the sea-surface temperatures gradually decrease. At some higher level, however, the air is still warm; hence between the surface air and that above there is an inversion. Under these circumstances turbulence will carry masses of moist air up to but not beyond the inversion, and the characteristic sky of a dull mild day, with a fresh south-west wind, results—a nearly continuous stratus or strato-cumulus cover at about 2000 feet.

When a dry and rather warm east wind reaches our shores across the North Sea in spring, the upper layers remain warm but the lower layer is cooled; again stratus or strato-cumulus cloud commonly forms below the boundary of the inversion. Similarly, a west wind in summer, blowing over the relatively cool Atlantic, may give extensive patches of similar cloud, often broken into waves or rolls.

The terms stratus and strato-cumulus are reserved for low clouds, the base of which lies below 7000 feet. The higher level layer clouds, comprising alto-stratus, alto-cumulus, cirro-stratus and cirro-cumulus, generally indicate the existence of a boundary layer along which the upper and lower streams of air are moving with differing direction and speed. Alto-cumulus and cirro-cumulus, for example, represent the results of the partial break-up of a sheet formed by the crossing of two sets of air currents. In British practice the distinction between 'alto' and 'cirro' clouds lies in the fact that the first are clouds of medium height the base of which lies above 7000 but below 20,000 feet, and are predominantly composed of small liquid drops; whereas the base of the latter lies above 20,000 feet and they are composed of ice crystals. In polar regions, however, such clouds may be found at lower levels. It may be added here that, under conditions of very exceptional cooling, surface fogs may also be composed of ice crystals rather than water drops. This is known, for instance, in Arctic Canada at times when winter temperatures fall unusually low.

Another type of cloud which is partly associated, on account of its origin, with the stratiform clouds is that known as nimbo-stratus—the large, low and shapeless cloud of great extent from which steady and persistent rain or snow falls. Its characteristics are described more fully in ch. IX. Clouds which give rain, as distinguished from drizzle, are those in which there is considerable turbulence: this in turn is associated with the aggregation of numerous smaller droplets to form rain. In stratus and strato-cumulus there is much less vertical motion and disturbance, so that, if some slight precipitation does occur, it is merely in the form of drizzle.

Clouds of great vertical extent (pl. 3). Neither surface turbulence nor mixture can, however, produce the great masses of cloud which are often seen in an English sky. These are due for the most part to rising currents of air. As the air ascends the pressure upon it is reduced and it expands; and accordingly throughout its whole mass the temperature falls. At a certain height the dew-point is reached and condensation begins. Clouds formed in this way, therefore, have a nearly level base. But if the air continues to rise, condensation will still go on and the cloud may tower upwards to an altitude of many thousand feet. Usually it seems to be made of a number of globular masses merged together, and presents some resemblance to the steam from a locomotive. It is in fact an ascending column of vapour, the upper part of which is rendered visible by condensation.

Such clouds as these are called cumulus clouds. Their apparent shape will vary according to their position in the sky. When they are near the horizon both their flat bases and their rounded tops are visible. When they are near the zenith they will be seen from below; their tops will be hidden, and only their bases will be visible, and the outline may be quite irregular.

The strength of the winds frequently increases upwards and therefore the top of a cumulus cloud often leans to one side or another, generally forwards, i.e. in the direction in which the cloud is travelling. If the upper currents are very strong it may be drawn out like the trail of steam from an express train at full speed.

The small detached cumulus clouds of fine summer weather show little vertical development (pl. 4). This generally implies that the air at higher levels is relatively warm, so that by the time the rising and expanding bubbles of air from below reach these levels they are cooler than their environment and can rise no further. Cumulus growing to very great heights is a characteristic feature of unsettled weather.

If the top of the cumulus reaches so high that the temperature of the rising air is sufficiently reduced, spicules of ice may be formed instead of drops of water. The top loses its rounded outline and hairlike streamers spring out from it. When this happens rain or hail generally falls from the base of the cloud, and the cloud is distinguished as cumulo-nimbus (pl. 3 *b*). The height at which ice first appears is variable and dependent upon the level of freezing. Consequently, the lower the freezing-level, the greater the likelihood of precipitation. In winter, precipitation will fall readily from low, small cumulus but in summer a great height of cumulus development is often reached before anything falls out of the cloud.

At other times the rising current to which the cloud is due seems suddenly to cease, or perhaps it meets a horizontal current blowing across it. The top of the cloud spreads outwards in a horizontal sheet, and while the lower part may be a typical cumulus the top is stratiform. Occasionally the rising current does not entirely cease where the outward spreading begins, and the top of the cumulus breaks through the horizontal sheet.

Owing to the effects of perspective a stratiform cloud which is at a comparatively low level, may seem to cross or rest upon the top of a more distant cumulus cloud, and the two together may present a deceptive resemblance to the form above described. But if they are watched for some time their relative positions will usually alter and it will become obvious that the two clouds are distinct from one another.

Medium and high clouds (pl. 4). On account of the upward decrease of temperature the greater part of the water-vapour is condensed at comparatively low altitudes, and above 7000 feet the amount of vapour present is usually small, except where the rising current of a cumulus cloud carries the vapour to greater heights. But even at an altitude of 6 or 7 miles there is frequently enough water-vapour to lead to saturation and formation of cloud. The intermediate 'alto' clouds have already been mentioned; they are layer clouds characteristic of the region between 7000 and 20,000 feet.

If from any cause the small amount of vapour present at great altitudes (above 20,000 feet in England) is condensed, the cloud which is produced will not consist of water but of little crystals of ice. It will be thin, and the light of the sun or even of the moon will pass through it with very little loss.

Clouds of this kind are known as cirrus clouds. By day they are almost uniformly white, never showing more than the faintest trace of shade; but at sunset they may be brilliantly coloured. Often they consist of a small white clot with streamers hanging downwards. Sometimes the streamers are drawn out into long horizontal threads, owing to strong currents in the upper air: and not uncommonly the cloud takes the form of a feather with the web stripped from one side. Immediately in front of a cyclone the cirrus clouds become so abundant as to form a thin continuous sheet, giving the sky a somewhat milky look and causing halos round the sun and moon (see p. 38). A sheet of high cloud of this kind is known as cirro-stratus (pl. 1*b*). The halo is the result of refraction of the rays of light which pass through the ice-crystals; these behave as prisms, and accordingly a well-developed halo exhibits the colours of the spectrum.

International nomenclature of clouds. The variety of form amongst clouds is infinite and the names given above are not always sufficient for descriptive purposes. There are, for instance, varieties of cirrus differing greatly from one another in their general appearance, and there are also clouds which are intermediate in character between the principal types.

In order to introduce uniformity into the nomenclature the International Meteorological Committee held at Uppsala in 1894 decided upon a classification of clouds for international use, and an 'International Cloud Atlas' was issued with figures of the principal varieties.

Some amendments have since been made, and in the latest (1932) international scheme the following types of cloud are distinguished:

1. *Cirrus.* Detached clouds of delicate and fibrous appearance, without shadows, often of a silky appearance, generally white in colour.

2. *Cirro-cumulus.* A cirriform layer or patch composed of very small globular masses or white flakes without shadows, which are arranged in groups or lines or more often in ripples resembling those of the sand of the seashore.

3. *Cirro-stratus.* A thin, whitish veil which does not blur the outlines of the sun or moon, but gives rise to halos.

4. *Alto-cumulus.* A layer (or patches) composed of laminae or rather flattened globular masses, the smallest elements of the regularly arranged layer being fairly small and thin, with or without shadows.

5. *Alto-stratus.* Striated or fibrous veil, more or less grey or bluish in colour.

6. *Strato-cumulus.* A layer or patches composed of globular masses or rolls. The smallest of the regularly arranged elements are fairly large they are soft and grey, with darker parts.

7. *Stratus.* A uniform layer of cloud, resembling fog, but not resting on the ground.

8. *Nimbo-stratus.* A low amorphous and rainy layer, of a dark grey colour and nearly uniform.

9. *Cumulus.* Thick clouds with vertical development: the upper surface is dome-shaped and exhibits rounded protuberances, while the base is nearly horizontal.

10. *Cumulo-nimbus* (thunder-cloud, shower-cloud). Heavy masses of cloud, with great vertical development, the cumuliform summits of which rise in the form of mountains or towers, the upper parts having a fibrous texture and often spreading out in the shape of an anvil.

The ten principal types of cloud can also be classified as shown in table 8.

Table 8

High clouds. Base > 20,000 feet	Medium clouds. Base > 7000, < 20,000 feet	Low clouds. Base < 7000 feet	Clouds of great vertical extent. Base frequently < 2000 feet. Summits may exceed 25,000 feet
Cirrus—Ci	Alto-stratus—A St	Strato-cumulus—St Cu	Cumulus—Cu
Cirro-stratus—Ci St	Alto-cumulus—A Cu	Stratus—St	Cumulo-nimbus—Cu Nb
Cirro-cumulus—Ci Cu		Nimbo-stratus—Nb St	

CHAPTER VIII

PRECIPITATION

If the condensation in a cloud goes sufficiently far, the little drops of water may coalesce into larger ones, which fall as drizzle or rain, depending to a large extent on the degree of vertical motion within the cloud. If the dew-point is low enough, the vapour condenses into minute crystals of ice instead of drops of water, and these may unite and form flakes of snow. An ordinary flake of snow, such as we usually see in England, consists of a large number of small ice-crystals clotted together, and such flakes are most readily formed when the temperature is not too low and the crystals of ice are more or less wet. In very cold weather the ice-crystals usually remain separate.

Another form in which the condensed vapour may fall is hail. Hailstones are essentially the result of the freezing of raindrops. In a cumulo-nimbus cloud the vertical currents are so violent that a raindrop formed in the lower part of the cloud may be carried up to a level at which it freezes, and on the outside of the pellet thus formed there may collect other ice-crystals from the upper part of the cloud. The pellet then falls, and may partially melt, but another strong vertical gust carries it up once more, and the process may be repeated many times. Large hailstones are therefore found which show, when cut, a concentric structure of clear and opaque layers of ice. Since the vertical currents due to surface heating are more vigorous in warmer countries, the cumulo-nimbus or thunder clouds there attain a greater height and the largest hailstones come from tropical or sub-tropical countries, especially plateau-lands, e.g. South Africa (cf. ch. VI). In temperate lands hailstones attain a much larger size in summer. The soft hail of winter, consisting of small pellets, falls after raindrops are carried only slightly above the level of their formation. This commonly occurs when shower clouds, brought by a wind of average temperature, say 42° at sea-level, arrive on our coasts; the slight uplift as the air rides over the land is often enough to carry some of the raindrops just sufficiently upward for them to freeze. Soft hail is, therefore, fairly frequent in cool showery weather in winter.

It is relevant to add here a reference to the electrical disturbance which accompanies large cumulo-nimbus clouds. It is clear that more than one process operates in a well-developed cumulo-nimbus to give various parts of the cloud large and very different degrees of electric charge. It has been shown, for example, that the breaking-up of large raindrops in the lower part of the cloud leaves a charge on the surrounding air; and another source of static electricity may be sought in frictional effects among the ice-crystals above. Certainly, observation leads to the view that the presence of ice-crystals is essential for the large-scale sparking which we call lightning to occur. A great proportion of such discharges occur between different parts of the cloud; some are directly to the earth. The confused disturbance set up by the passage of the spark reaches our ears as the sound we call thunder.

Rain-gauge. The total amount of water that falls on any given area, whether in the form of rain or snow or hail, is known as the precipitation, or more commonly (though not quite correctly) as the rainfall. It is measured by means of a rain-gauge, which in principle is simply a funnel leading into a vessel of some kind to contain the rain that falls upon the funnel. The area of the opening of the funnel is known and by measuring the amount of water collected in the vessel beneath, we know how much has fallen on that area.

There are, however, several precautions which must be taken in order to ensure an accurate result. If the gauge projects well above the ground, windy weather gives rise to eddies round the gauge which tend to carry some of the rain drops, which would otherwise fall within the gauge, outside the rim. Consequently a rain-gauge close to the ground always collects more water than a similar gauge set at a height of three or four feet. The standard height adopted in England is 1 foot. It follows that for purposes of comparison rain gauges placed on roofs are almost useless.

Some of the water that falls on the inside of the funnel splashes outwards and is lost. To prevent this loss as far as possible, the sides of the funnel should be vertical for 2 or 3 inches at the top.

When the precipitation takes the form of snow, the funnel may be choked and filled before the storm has ceased. To lessen this danger the upper vertical-sided part of the funnel should be made fairly deep. In order to melt the snow a measured quantity of warm water may be poured into the funnel when the observation is being made, and this quantity must be subtracted from the total in the collecting vessel. It is, however, only seldom that snow can be accurately measured in this way. Snow often comes with a strong wind and blows across the rain-gauge. No really satisfactory method has yet been devised to measure snowfall with wind. On a quiet sheltered surface one foot is said to be the equivalent to one inch of rain if it is newly fallen and uncompressed. Here we are up against the problem of drifted snow, for it is impossible to separate newly fallen snow from blown snow which has been removed from one place and deposited in another.

In English-speaking countries the amount of rainfall is usually expressed in inches. It may be said, for example, that at a certain place an inch of rain has fallen during the day. The meaning is that if all the rain that fell during that day had stayed where it fell, it would have covered the ground to a depth of an inch.

A rain-gauge is therefore usually provided with a measuring-glass specially graduated to suit the funnel. If the area of the opening of the funnel is 16 square inches, it needs 16 cubic inches to cover that area to a depth of 1 inch. Accordingly, the measuring-glass will be graduated so that a volume of 16 cubic inches is marked as 1 inch. The graduations are not cubic inches but depths on an area equal to that of the funnel opening.

In the plains of England a rainfall of an inch in a day is exceptional, in the more mountainous parts it is not uncommon. But even in the plains much heavier falls are occasionally experienced. On 26 August 1912, more than eight inches fell in twenty-four hours near Norwich. On 28 June 1917, and again on 18 August 1927, over 9 inches fell in the plain of Somerset and, near Lynmouth on 15 August 1952, just over 9 inches were recorded. By far the heaviest rainfall measured for any one day in Britain was 11 inches at Black Down, Dorset, while nearby at Weymouth 7·2 inches fell. All this fell between 4.30 p.m. on 18 July 1956, and 2.0 a.m. the next morning. (See ch. XVI, pt. III.)

In the east of England the average rainfall for the whole year amounts to about 25 inches; in the plains of the west it may be as much as 30 or 40; in the mountains it is very much more. Close to Sty Head in Cumberland the average annual rainfall is 185 inches, and for long this ranked as the wettest place in the British Isles from which records were obtained. But in recent years more rain-gauges have been set up amongst the mountains and greater rainfalls have been observed. From the evidence from neighbouring gauges it is estimated that the summit of Snowdon receives an average of just over 200 inches.

Outside the British Isles much greater extremes are met with. At Aden there may be no rain at all for two or three years. At Cherrapunji in Assam the annual rainfall is about 460 inches.

General distribution of rainfall. Rain is due to the cooling, *en masse*, of air which contains water-vapour. Apart from local and temporary conditions there are two principal methods by which this cooling may be brought about. The air may flow to colder latitudes or it may rise to greater altitudes where both temperature and pressure are less. In either case there will be a tendency to produce rain. Warm air impelled towards colder latitudes commonly causes rain when it meets and rides over the colder air-masses lying in its path or it may be precipitated as drizzle or form fog by advection over colder surfaces.

Where, on the other hand, the air is flowing to warmer latitudes or where it is descending, it will in general be able to take up more vapour and, in the ordinary sense of the word, it will be dry.

In the diagram of the general distribution of pressure on p. 23 it will be seen that the earth is surrounded by a series of belts, of high pressure and low pressure alternately, parallel to the equator. The winds blow into each low pressure and out from each high pressure, and these winds are permanent. Since the low-pressure belts are also permanent it is evident that the winds which blow into them must escape upwards; and since the high-pressure areas are permanent, the air which blows outwards must be replaced by air from above. Therefore, towards the middle of the low-pressure areas the air must be rising, towards the middle of the high-pressure areas the air must be sinking.

Where the air is rising and where the winds are blowing towards the poles the climate will on *a priori* grounds tend to be wet; where the air is sinking and where the winds are blowing towards the equator the climate

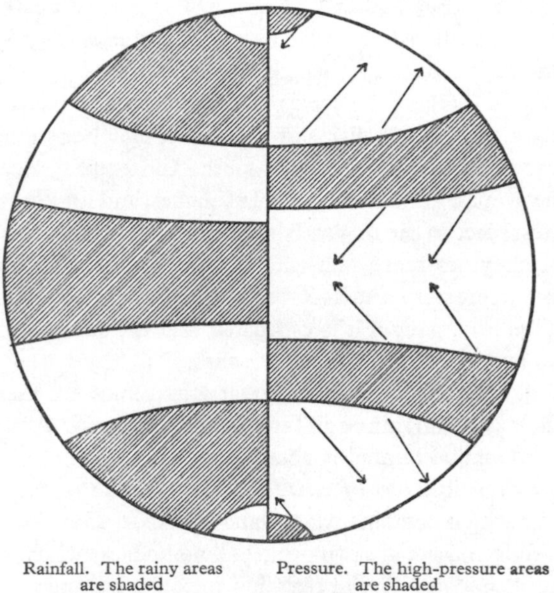

Rainfall. The rainy areas are shaded   Pressure. The high-pressure areas are shaded

Fig. 40. Relation of rainfall to pressure.

will be dry. Thus we may divide the globe into a series of alternate dry and wet belts corresponding with the general distribution of pressure and the permanent winds (fig. 40). Such a division is necessarily diagrammatic. There is no sharp line in nature between the belts, and there are modifications due to the distribution of land and sea and to the seasons; but the diagram represents very nearly the probable distribution of rainfall on a globe covered with water.

It should perhaps be noted that in the diagram the dry belts are made wider than the high-pressure belts, because on the equatorward margins of the high pressures the winds blow towards the equator and are therefore dry.

The greatest rainfall will be in the middle of the equatorial low pressure, for there the rising air is most heavily charged with vapour.

Influence of land and sea and of the winds. In general the rainfall will be heavier over the sea than over the land, because there the supply of vapour is greater; and consequently if land and sea stretched from north to south in alternate bands, the general distribution of rainfall might be a little more accurately represented as in fig. 41.

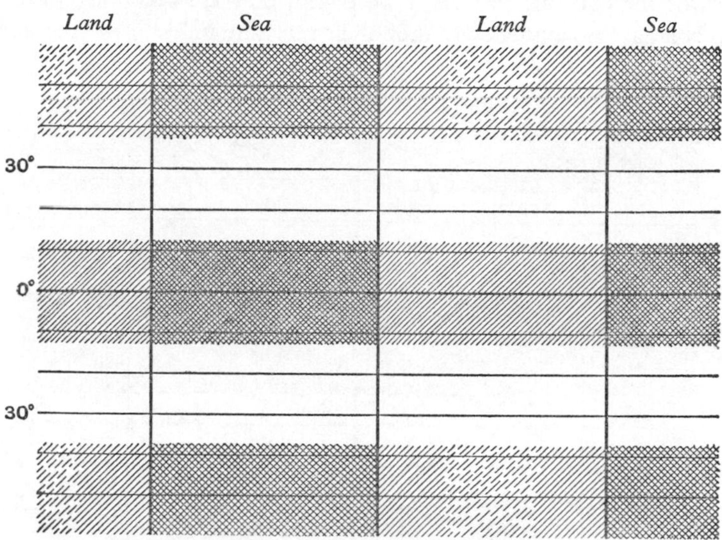

Fig. 41. Influence of land and sea on rainfall. In each belt the depth of the shading indicates roughly the amount of rain.

In this diagram the rainfall is represented as greater over the sea than on the land. In the temperate rain-belt the rain is caused mainly by cyclonic depressions and is considerably greater near the coast than in the interior of the continents. In the equatorial belt the rain is caused chiefly by convectional ascent of air, and there is no very marked difference between the rainfall of the coast and that of the interior. In all belts the amount of rain decreases gradually towards the edges of the belt; but to avoid complication no attempt is made to show this in the diagram.

A very marked effect, however, is produced by the winds. In temperate latitudes the prevalent winds are westerly. They bring the moisture of the ocean over the western margin of the continents, and they to a certain extent take the dryness of the continent over the margin of the sea that washes its eastern shores. They shift, in fact, the whole band as shown in fig. 41 a little to the east as in fig. 42. Accordingly in these latitudes the western coasts of the continents have an oceanic rainfall, the interior and eastern coasts have a continental rainfall. The change from the oceanic to the continental rainfall will be gradual, since the winds will gradually lose their moisture as they proceed inland.

Within the tropics the trade-winds carry vapour from the oceans over the eastern margins of the continents. But because they are blowing towards the equator, as well as westward, they are becoming warmer and will have no tendency to drop their moisture unless they are forced

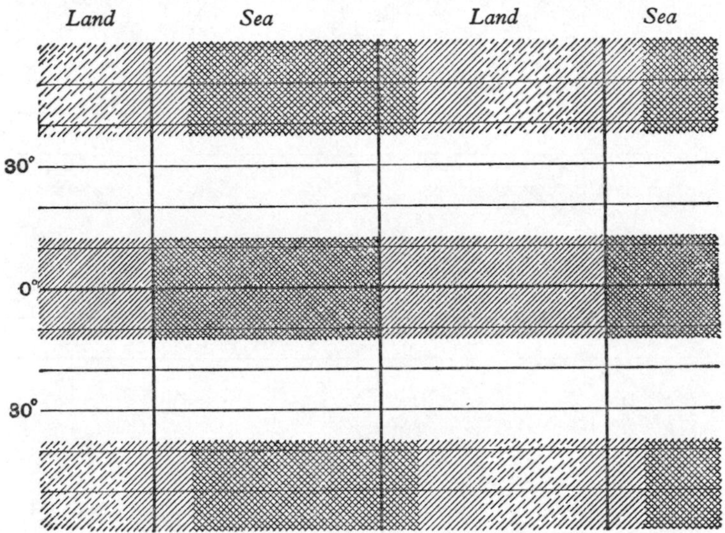

Fig. 42. Influence of winds on rainfall.

upwards by rising ground. Their effect, therefore, will depend largely upon the configuration of the land. In favourable circumstances they make the eastern margin of the continents within the tropics wetter than the western, but they will not necessarily do so.

The general distribution of rainfall over land and sea, allowing for the influence of the winds but neglecting that of altitude and of seasonal variations, will be as shown in fig. 42.

Seasonal variations due to the migration of the rain-belts. As the year advances the position of the sun with respect to the earth is changed. There is a corresponding movement of the high- and low-pressure belts and along with these the wet and dry belts travel north and south. The extent of the migration varies in different parts of the world, but roughly it may be put at about 8° on each side of their mean positions. Thus in the northern summer the middle of the equatorial rain-belt reaches 8° N., in the northern winter it has moved to 8° S. In consequence of these movements some parts of the world are in a rain-belt during one season and in a dry belt during another.

The approximate positions of the wet and dry belts over the oceans at the equinoxes and the solstices are shown diagrammatically in fig. 43.

From these diagrams it is easily seen that any place between 30° and 40° north or south of the equator will be in the temperate rain-belt in the

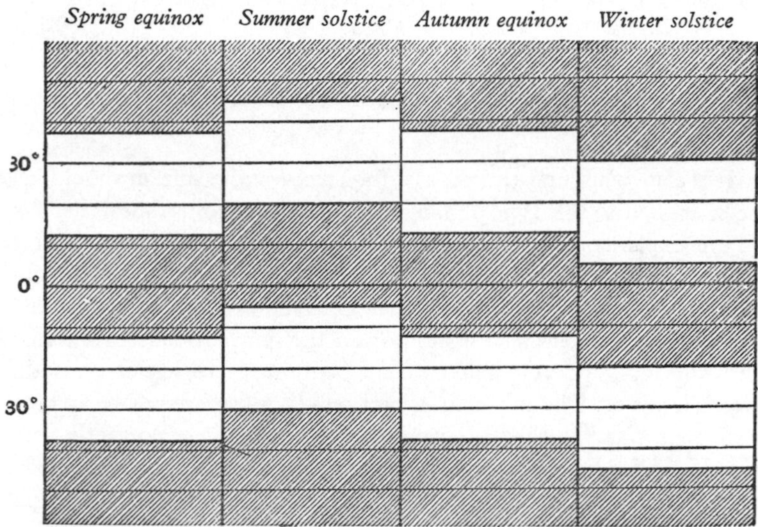

Fig. 43. Migration of rain-belts.

winter and in the tropical dry belt in the summer, and it will accordingly have a wet winter and a dry summer. This is the characteristic climate of a large part of the Mediterranean, and is accordingly often spoken of as the Mediterranean type of climate. For a reason which will be explained later it is not met with on the eastern coasts of the continental masses, but only upon their western sides. The Mediterranean itself, California, a part of Chile, the south-western corner of Africa, the south-western corner of Australia, and a small part of South Australia, all have their principal rains in the winter, that is, the colder half-year; while their summers are nearly dry.

Since their is no definite boundary between the wet and dry belts the limits of the Mediterranean climate are not sharply defined. There is a gradual transition from the more variable climate of the temperate rain-belt to the winter rains and summer droughts of the typical Mediterranean climate.

This is clearly brought out by Table 9, in which the percentage of the total annual rainfall that falls during each season is given for several localities in the western half of the Spanish peninsula.

Table 9

	Latitude N.	Spring March–May	Summer June–Aug.	Autumn Sept.–Nov.	Winter Dec.–Feb.
Oviedo	43° 28′	29·4	17·1	27·6	25·9
Guarda	40° 23′	31·2	8·0	30·3	30·5
Lisbon	38° 42′	30·3	3·4	28·0	38·3
San Fernando	36° 28′	29·0	2·3	29·0	39·7

Southwards the proportion of summer rain diminishes and the proportion of winter rain increases.

It is somewhat unfortunate that the term Mediterranean should have been applied to this type of climate; for in the Mediterranean itself the simple explanation given above is quite inadequate and the origin of the winter rains is much more complex. A glance at the map of the distribution of barometric pressure in January will show that the Mediterranean area lies on the southern instead of on the northern side of the high-pressure belt, and very seldom comes within the region of the south-westerly winds. The prevalent winter winds in fact are northerly rather than southerly. In the western part of the basin these northerly winds may be looked upon as the south-westerly winds of the Atlantic deflected round the subsidiary anticyclone which covers Spain. But a large proportion of the Mediterranean rainfall is the result of low-pressure systems developed within the Mediterranean Sea itself, independently of the temperate belt of low pressure (ch. IX).

On the oceanic coast of California or Portugal, however, the seasonal distribution of rainfall can be attributed much more clearly to the migration of the rain-belts in the manner described.

Places near the southern margin of the tropical dry belts, between latitudes 5° and 20°, north or south, will, on the other hand, be in the dry belt during the winter, while in the summer they will lie within the equatorial rain-belt. Therefore, their winters will be dry and their summers wet.

In the middle of all the belts the seasonal changes will be slight. The equator is always in the rain-belt and hence the rain is almost equally liable to fall throughout the year. In the greater part of the temperate regions there will also be rain at all seasons of the year. In the middle of the dry belts there will be practically constant drought.

Seasonal variations due to the distribution of land and sea. Hitherto we have imagined the wet and dry areas as continuous zones passing completely round the globe. But it has already been pointed out that, owing to the presence of the continental masses, the form of the high-pressure areas alters with the seasons; and there is a corresponding change in the distribution of rain.

Figs. 13 and 14 show diagrammatically the distribution of pressure in winter and in summer, and the directions of the winds due to such a distribution are indicated by arrows.

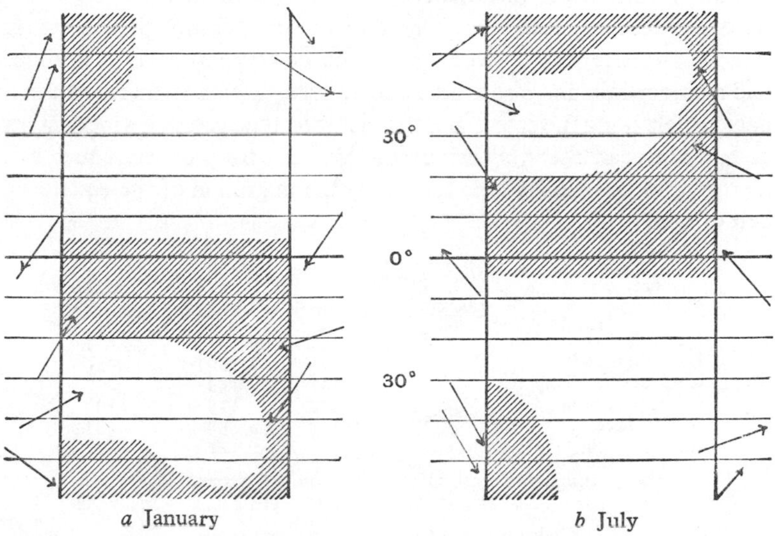

Fig. 44. Diagrams of the seasonal distribution of rainfall on a continent.

In our winter it will be observed that on the western coasts of the land, north of lat. 30° N. the prevailing winds are south-westerly. They blow from sea to land, and away from the equator. Therefore, at this season the western coasts are wet, even down to the latitude of the Mediterranean. On the eastern coasts the winds are northerly and blow from land to sea; and therefore in winter the lands adjacent to these coasts are dry and cold (fig. 44*a*). This is why the Mediterranean type of climate with its freedom from severe frost is not found in the same latitude on the eastern coasts, although on the coasts themselves and especially on islands lying nearby, winter precipitation in middle latitudes is not lacking, because of the formation of depressions along the region where the cold air from inland meets the warmer air over the unfrozen sea. This will be explained more fully in ch. IX.

In our summer the high pressure lies a little farther north, but is broken by the land-masses, which are now low-pressure areas. On the western coasts there are still south-westerly winds, but they do not extend so far south. About lat. 30–40° N., the winds are more or less northerly, and though they come from the sea they are moving into a warmer area. Therefore they are dry and we get the summer drought of the Mediterranean type of climate. On the eastern coasts, the winds in the same latitudes are southerly and blow from sea to land. Therefore they bring rain (fig. 44*b*).

Thus on the western coasts between 30° and 40° north or south we have the Mediterranean type of climate with summer drought and winter rain; on the eastern coasts we have the monsoon type with winter drought and summer rain and also a little winter precipitation farther north in a narrow belt along the coast. But the monsoon type covers a wider extent in latitude than the Mediterranean type and towards the equator it merges into the similar type caused by the migration of the equatorial belt of rain.

Table 10

	Spring	Summer	Autumn	Winter
Ireland	21*	24	27	28†
East England	19*	28	30†	23
Central Germany	23	34†	23	20*
Central Russia	22	37†	25	16*
West Siberia	13*	42†	32	13*
East Siberia	12	58†	21	9*

(Autumn and winter rainfall increases on the extreme east coast and in Japan: cf. pp. 112–114.)

* Minimum. † Maximum.

In the temperate zone outside lat. 40° N. the prevalent winds on the western coasts are from the south-west throughout the year and therefore there is rain at all seasons; but the maximum is in the winter, because then the gradient for westerly winds is steepest. Expressed otherwise, deep and active depressions are then the most frequent. On the eastern coasts the winter winds are more or less northerly, blowing from land to sea, and the rainfall is therefore small except in a narrow belt adjacent to the coast. In the summer the winds tend to blow inwards from the sea, and bring a little rain. The interior of the land-mass is a high-pressure area in winter and is dry, in summer it is a low-pressure area, and most of its rain, accordingly, falls during that season.

Thus in these latitudes, from about 40°–60° or 70°, the western coasts of the continents have rain all the year round, with a maximum in winter, or late autumn; the interiors and eastern coasts have their heaviest rainfall in the summer, but even then the amount is smaller, because of the high proportion of winds which have travelled so far overland.

Table 10 gives the percentage of the total annual rainfall that falls during each season, and shows the change as we cross the Eurasian continent from west to east.

The tropical dry regions. Because of the seasonal changes in the distribution of rain, the dry regions of the tropics do not form a continuous belt around the globe or even across the land. On the western coasts they correspond fairly closely with the normal position of the dry belt as shown in fig. 41. But the eastern coasts in the same latitude belong to the monsoon area and have heavy summer rains. Therefore on the western side of the continents the deserts extend to the sea, but on the eastern side they end before the coasts are reached. Towards the east, however, they tend to spread away from the equator, because in temperate latitudes the rainfall becomes very small in the interior of the continents.

The general form which the dry regions tend to assume will be understood from the diagrams, figs. 44*a* and *b*. In fig. 44*a* the area of the January rainfall in a continent extending from north to south is shown diagrammatically. Considering only the northern hemisphere it will be seen that the equatorial rain-belt extends to 5° N. On the western coast the rainfall due to the westerly winds reaches southwards to 30° N. The interior and eastern coasts, as already explained, are dry.

In July (fig. 44*b*) the equatorial rain-belt extends to lat. 20° N. The temperate rain-belt reaches southwards only to 45° N., but it now stretches right across the continent, decreasing, however, in amount towards the east. On the eastern coast are the monsoon rains produced by the winds blowing inwards from the sea. These rains reach northwards as far as the temperate rain-belt and thus the whole of the eastern coast is wet.

In fig. 45 both the January and the July rainfall are shown, and it will be seen that the area which is dry in both months touches the western coast between latitudes 20° and 30° N. It expands inwards and northwards but nowhere reaches the eastern coast.

Owing to the irregular outline of the continents and to the influence of mountain chains the actual dry areas of the globe are not precisely of this form. But the map of annual rainfall (map 7) shows that in the great land-masses of the northern hemisphere and also in Australia, a region with a rainfall of less than 10 inches touches the western coasts about latitudes 20° to 30°, expands inwards, especially on the side away from the equator, and does not reach the eastern coasts.

Influence of altitude upon precipitation. Half the water-vapour in the atmosphere lies below an altitude of 6500 feet, three-quarters lies below 13,000 feet. Therefore a high mountain chain is a very effective barrier to the passage of vapour, and accordingly we find that most of the great ranges of the globe separate regions which differ from each other in climate. On the west of the Canadian Rockies and Coast Ranges lies

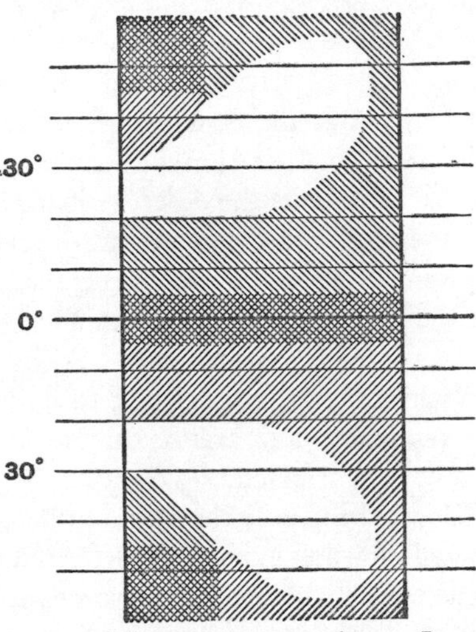

Fig. 45. Diagram of wet and dry areas on a continent. January rainfall indicated by shading inclined downwards from right to left; July rainfall by shading inclined downwards from left to right.

coastal British Columbia with its heavy rains and equable temperature, on the east are the plains of Saskatchewan with a low rainfall and great extremes of temperature. On the north of the Atlas Mountains lies Morocco, on the south the Sahara Desert, the one with a climate approaching the true Mediterranean type, the other sun-baked and virtually rainless throughout the year.

But the influence of a mountain chain on rainfall is not due entirely to the fact that it rises like a ridge above a sea of vapour. Not only does it obstruct the easy passage of vapour from one side to the other, but it tends to cause the condensation of vapour on each side. For whenever a wind blows to the mountain chain it is forced upwards. The air expands and is cooled, and if it reaches a sufficient height, some of the vapour in it will condense, forming clouds and rain. Hence almost every mountain or mountain range has a greater amount of cloud and a heavier rainfall than the plains from which it rises. Even in the midst of the Sahara the ranges of Asben and Tibesti have regular seasonal rains.

If the mountain range is high the greater part of the vapour will be condensed on the windward side, and on the leeward side the rainfall will be small. It is chiefly for this reason that the west side of the British Isles is so much wetter than the east. In the southern half of France, which is also under the influence of the south-west winds, the heaviest rainfall is not on the west, but towards the east where the land is higher. If the mountain range is low the rainfall on its leeward slope may be almost as great as on the windward side.

Precipitation caused or intensified by the presence of high ground is called orographic, and it may be noted that while the hilly districts of

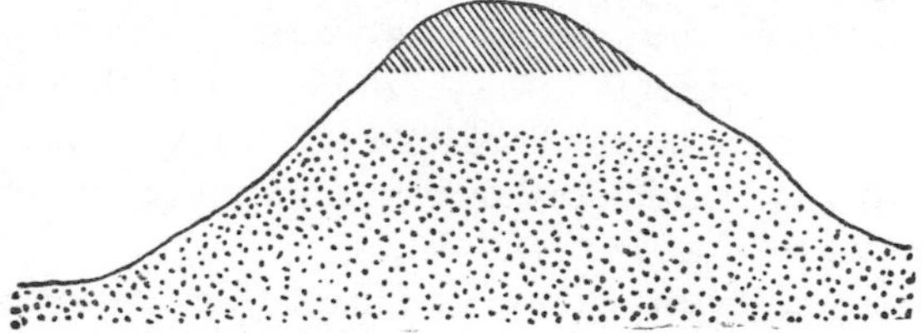

Fig. 46. Diagram of climate and vegetation zones in the Thian Shan. Obliquely shaded area: summer rains, grass. Unshaded area: winter snows, trees. Dotted area: dry, barren.

western Britain receive on an average far more rainfall, it is the hilly eastern districts which receive in general more snowfall. Heavy snowfalls are most often associated with a strong cold surface wind from an easterly direction. Hence eastern Scotland, the eastern slopes of the Pennines, and other hills near the North Sea experience as a rule heavier falls of snow than the country farther west under the lee of the hills.

When the mountain range is very high, condensation will not necessarily continue to its summits. As the air ascends and is cooled, condensation will begin at a certain level, depending to a large extent upon the amount of vapour originally present. But as the air goes on rising, the quantity of vapour in it decreases. Sooner or later, as the air continues to rise, the amount condensed will begin to decrease, and finally condensation may entirely cease before the top of the range is reached. On a high mountain chain therefore there is a zone of maximum condensation, and this is usually far below the summits. Its altitude varies, chiefly according to the temperature and the amount of vapour present in the prevalent winds. On the Himalayas it is about 4000 feet above sea-level, but alters with the seasons. On our own mountains the rainfall is so variable that no definite statement is possible.

A curious instance of the influence of this zone of maximum condensation is given by Hann. In the Thian Shan, which rises from the arid plateau of Central Asia, the winter snows fall between the altitudes of 8000 and 10,000 feet. Below 8000 feet the range is dry and bare. Above 10,000 feet there is little condensation in winter, but in summer there are abundant rains. The zone of winter snows is also a belt of trees; above it, in the region of the summer rains, there is grass but no trees. The inhabitants move upwards in the winter, taking their flocks above the snows into the grassy belt (fig. 46).

The snow-line. When the temperature is low the condensed vapour may fall not as rain but as snow, and the snow stays where it falls instead of running off like water. In polar regions the precipitation is in the form of snow throughout the greater part of the year. From the poles towards the equator the season during which the temperature is cold enough for snow decreases in length, and in general the annual fall of snow decreases, until about 40° from the equator it practically ceases at sea-level. At greater altitudes, however, snow continues to fall even to the equator itself.

Snow which has fallen on the ground may be removed in several ways. It may be blown away by the wind, it may slip down a mountain side as a snow-slide or an avalanche; it may be carried away slowly in the form of a glacier; it may evaporate; or it may melt. But if it is not removed in some way it will stay where it fell, and every year will add to the thickness of the deposit.

Where the annual fall of snow equals or exceeds the amount removed in the year, the ground will be covered by a permanent layer of snow; where it is less the ground will be free from snow for a part of the year. In high polar latitudes the covering of snow is permanent even at sea-level, in lower latitudes it is only on the mountains that snow lasts throughout the year.

The lower limit of permanent snow upon the mountains is called the snow-line. It is not a sharp and definite line, for towards its lower edge the carpet of snow is ragged and irregular. Holes and rents appear, through which the bare gound shows. The covering becomes patchy, and downwards the patches grow smaller and more scattered until at length they disappear entirely.

The snow-line is at sea-level about 80° N. and 70° S. and from there it rises, somewhat irregularly, to the equator.

The altitude of the snow-line is necessarily influenced by the temperature, and in general the higher the temperature at sea-level the higher also will be the temperature of the air above and the greater the altitude of the snow-line. Therefore, there is a general rise of the snow-line towards the equator.

But the height of the snow-line does not depend entirely upon the temperature. It is influenced by the amount of snow that falls, and also by the form of the ground, for upon the latter will depend, in part, the amount of snow that stays. On a steep mountain slope much of the snow slides down in avalanches; on a gentle slope most of it must lie until it melts. In the latter case the snow-line will be lower than in the former.

The snow-line is the level where the amount of snow melted in the year is just equal to the amount which would otherwise collect. In a dry region therefore it will be higher than in a wet one, if the temperature, slope of the hill sides, etc. are the same in both cases. Even if the dry region is the cooler of the two, its snow-line may still be higher. The

Fig. 47. Snow-line on the Himalayas.

Himalayas form a striking and well-known example. The snow-line on the northern slopes is at an altitude of about 18,000 feet, on the southern slopes at about 16,000 feet, although the southern slopes are naturally the hotter. But the difference in temperature is more than compensated by the difference in the annual snowfall. The vapour brought by the south-west monsoon is mostly condensed on the southern side of the range, and comparatively little passes to the north.

The Himalayas are not a single chain, but a series of parallel chains, and although it is true of the range as a whole that the snow-line is higher on the north than on the south, yet with the individual chains the reverse is the case. This is shown diagrammatically in fig. 47.

On each chain the precipitation is approximately equal on both sides, the sun is stronger on the southern side and therefore the snow-line slopes down from south to north. But the precipitation on the southernmost chain is greater than that on the next and accordingly its snow-line is lower. In the same way the snow-line of each chain is lower than that of the chain north of it. Thus, although in each chain the snow-line slants down from south to north, yet taking the range as a whole, the snow-line is higher on the northern side than on the southern, and the general slope, indicated in the figure by a broken line, is from north to south.

CHAPTER IX

THE MINOR CIRCULATIONS OF THE ATMOSPHERE AND ASSOCIATED WEATHER

In ch. II there is a general account of some characteristic patterns assumed by isobars. A more detailed discussion of these minor features of the atmospheric circulation is, however, necessary. In ch. III it was shown that the general circulation of the atmosphere over a rotating earth can be sufficiently explained for our purpose if it is borne in mind (*a*) that there is a tendency for pressure belts to be established in certain areas (see fig. 11); (*b*) that these pressure belts become greatly distorted in winter and summer, especially in the northern hemisphere, owing to the different degree of heating of extensive land and sea surfaces. Account must also be taken of the cooling due to the special qualities of ice and snow surfaces. Snow not only reflects more than four-fifths of the radiation falling upon it from the sun or sky; it is also an excellent radiator, and on a clear calm night the air temperature over a snow-covered plain will always fall lower than it would if there were no snow present. Hence the surface air over the interior of the great northern continents becomes very cold and dense in winter, and the barometer readings are correspondingly high as the January isobars show.

The southern hemisphere is considerably less broken up by land masses in high temperate latitudes, and its chief source of cold air, the snow-covered Antarctic plateau with the adjacent ice-covered seas, is nearly symmetrical about the pole. Accordingly the arrangement of high- and low-pressure belts shows a very fair resemblance to the theoretical arrangement on a uniform rotating globe.

Moreover, at levels above about 25,000 feet, and poleward of lat. 35°, there is a preponderance of winds from westerly points, whatever the direction of the winds may be at lower levels.

The atmosphere varies in density not only on account of changes in temperature, but also on account of changes in the moisture content. Air with a high relative humidity is less dense at the same temperature than air which is drier. Moreover, when two air-streams meet, the less dense stream will always tend to override the denser; and the overriding or undercutting by air-streams plays a very large part in the day-to-day behaviour of the atmosphere. This is especially marked in the regions where the great eddies (p. 22) are dominant.

Indeed, on a globe with a completely uniform surface an atmosphere devoid of water-vapour would no doubt give a system resembling the simple series of eddies in higher latitudes. Correspondingly in this region average pressures would be lower than on either the poleward

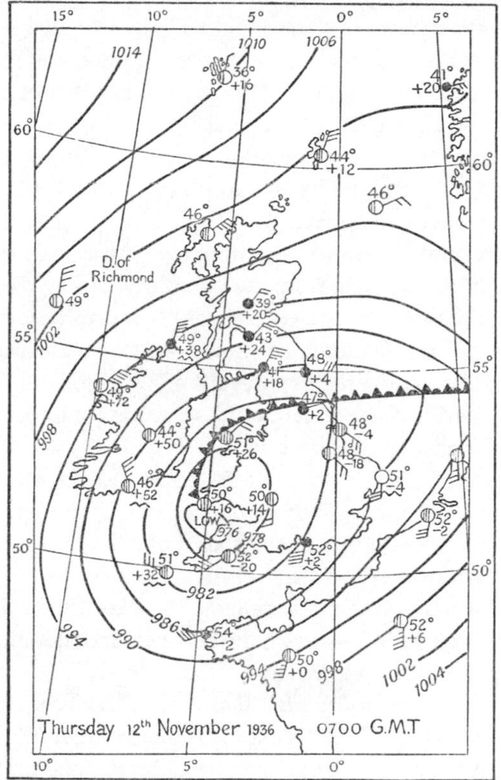

Fig. 48. Weather map showing a typical depression in which the principal front over England has become an occlusion. The figures below the temperatures at each station indicate the barometric tendency, or movement of the barometer in tenths of a millibar, during the past 3 hours. Occlusions are defined on pp. 114–15.

flank or that towards the tropics, as in fig. 11. But the earth displays a number of irregularities which in turn lead to very variable development in extent, direction, and speed of movement of the eddies already described, not only from season to season but also from year to year. Hence, it becomes desirable to adopt a more practical working view of the behaviour of the air based on observation, especially in the depressions so characteristic of higher latitudes. While the simple scheme of the distribution of precipitation given in the previous chapter is generally applicable, what appear at first to be departures from this scheme are soon met when the subject has been further pursued—for example with regard to the distribution of seasonal rainfall in the eastern United States. But by adopting a clearer idea of the behaviour of the air, particularly in depressions, an explanation is at once afforded of apparent departures, and their ultimate cause may be sought in the irregular disposition of land and sea surfaces and mountain barriers. Routes and speed of travel vary so much that in Britain, for example, the character of the individual months can vary a great deal from year to year.

Polar and tropical air-streams: the polar front. It has already been shown that air making its way southward from the Arctic regions, or northward from the Antarctic, is deflected by the earth's rotation. At the same time, however, tropical air making its way poleward, either at high levels or at the surface, from the poleward flank of the sub-tropical belt of higher pressure, gives a general south-west to west current over a broad belt of the temperate zone (north-west to west in the southern hemisphere). The same direction prevails at high levels all the way to the poles; the outflowing north-east or south-east current is relatively shallow (commonly less than 10,000 feet).

Now these two currents, the one of polar and the other of tropical origin, moving over the surface might apparently flow smoothly along beside each other without difficulty or impediment on a frictionless earth; but in practice something very different occurs. The boundary between the two types of air is called the polar front. In the North Atlantic it is often found somewhere between Ireland and Greenland, but may oscillate over a wide range of latitude.

Characteristics of polar air. If the boundary between air of polar and tropical origin in the North Atlantic is plotted daily, it will be noticed that it frequently develops kinks or waves, Air of polar origin is moving from the cool surfaces and icy seas, over which it has acquired its chill, towards warmer regions. If it flows over the oceans it is usual to find that the air temperature in a polar current is slightly below that of the sea surface over which it is flowing. Moreover, the warming takes place at the base of the current of air, and hence air of polar origin flowing over an open sea is very liable to become unstable. Masses of the warmed surface air begin and continue to rise on the slightest provocation; moisture from the sea surface is carried upward and forms cumulus or even cumulo-nimbus cloud. Such events are very characteristic of polar air reaching the British Isles, especially in winter when the difference of temperature between the air at its source, and the warm Atlantic over which it travels, its greater than in summer. Sharp showers are also to be expected; the stormy winter sky and the lashing showers associated with a winter north-wester will be familiar to British readers, especially those living near the Atlantic coasts. In extreme cases, when very cold polar outbursts occur, usually accompanied by strong winds or gales, the warming of the surface layers by comparison with the cold air above is so marked that cumulo-nimbus develops in the rapidly ascending currents. This process explains the occasional outbreak of winter thunderstorms in exceptionally stormy weather at a season when solar heating is negligible.

Characteristics of tropical air. Air of tropical origin behaves differently. Over the Atlantic it starts from a warm source and steadily moves over cooler waters on its way poleward. Hence, after a time, the surface layers of air are slightly cooled by comparison with the temperature of the overlying layers. This produces a condition of stability, accompanied as a rule by a greater or less degree of inversion. Consequently, if a small mass of air is displaced upward from the surface, it will quickly find itself surrounded by warmer air, and so will tend to return towards the position from which it was displaced.

It is readily seen that the further cooling of air already moist from its passage over the sea will eventually lead to condensation. Hence, in cases where the sea surface becomes very cold, extensive advection fog develops (p. 81).

It is important to recognise that if the warm, moist air current is moving more vigorously, i.e. when moderate to strong winds prevail, low stratus cloud rather than surface fog is likely to develop. The turbulence resulting from the friction of the air moving over the sea means that small packets of humid air are continually being carried up a little from the surface, while others are brought down. If this process is in action the expansion of the rising packets leads to cooling, and so the coolest air, in which condensation is effected, is not now at the surface of the sea, but somewhat above. In other words, an inversion develops, not at the sea surface, but some distance above it. Observation of the behaviour of coastal fogs around the British Isles shows this frequently. If the air is calm or nearly so, the fog lies on the surface of the sea. If a light breeze arises the base of the fog may be lifted 200 or 300 feet above the sea; headlands and capes are still enshrouded, but objects can be seen along the beach a mile or more distant. With stronger winds cloud-base may rise to 1500 feet or more. The widespread low cloud characteristically associated with mild and windy winter weather in western Europe is thus explained, especially when it is recalled that the position of these islands, somewhat to the south of the track followed by the

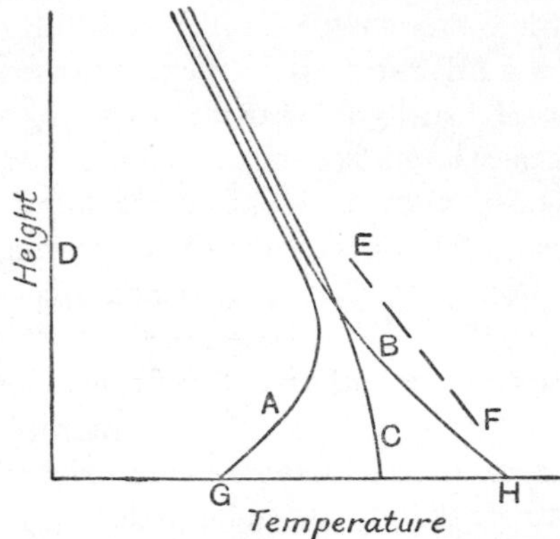

Fig. 49 (*a*). The diurnal variation in stability over the land on a fine day. *A*, early morning: stable; *B*, early afternoon: unstable; *C*, evening: stable. Over level lowlands a normal height for *D* is 3000 feet. Parallels to the line *EF* are dry adiabatics for rising air. *GH* represents the diurnal range of temperature at the surface.

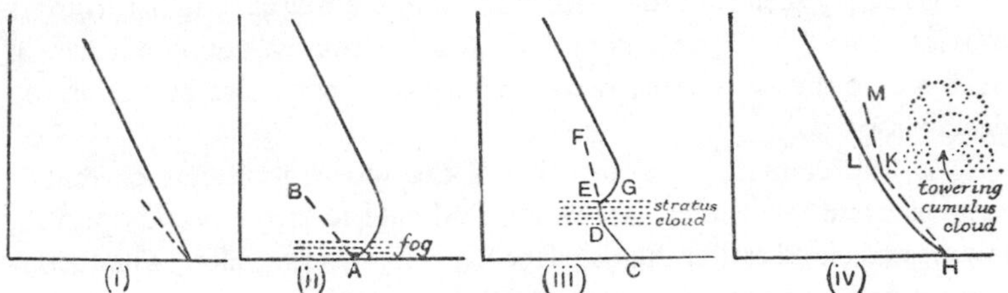

Fig. 49 (*b*). The effect on the stability when air moves over cooler and warmer surfaces.

(i) Lapse-rate in original air. Adiabatics shown - - - - - -.

(ii) After moving gently over a cooler surface: for example, tropical air approaching England. Fog at surface: the lowest layer of the humid air-stream is cooled below the dew-point.

(iii) If air moves briskly over a cooler surface, the lapse-rate for a short distance above is the dry adiabatic, as masses of air are continually moving up and down close to the surface. Moisture from *C* is carried up to *D* and stratus cloud forms. No surface air rises above *E* as it must fall off in temperature along *EF*; as the temperature of the environment is given by *G* such cooler air if it rises must at once fall back.

(iv) If air moves over a warmer surface it becomes unstable. Rising packets of air reaching condensation level at *K* will still be warmer than the environment given by *L*, and cumulus cloud will form; the fall of temperature in the rising air will then be given by *KM*, the saturated adiabatic, and the air will continue to rise, giving towering cumulus.

majority of depressions, ensures that strong winds from between south and west frequently occur and fulfil the conditions described above.

The processes at work can be explained with the aid of figs. 49 (*a*) and (*b*), which illustrate the characteristic lapse-rate of temperature in the surface layers, associated with the movement of polar and tropical air over an extensive sea surface.

In practice very slight differences in sea and air temperatures are enough to initiate these developments, and further complications arise from the irregularities of the earth's surface. Polar air is frequently unstable and in winter produces vigorous convectional showers on the west coast of Britain. But the same air, moving eastward over a snow-covered Germany, may become so cooled and sufficiently stable in its surface layers as to give considerable inland fog. Hence, in deciding what a mass of air is likely to do from day to day account must not only be taken of its origin, but also of the details of the course it has followed and the degree to which its characteristics may change as it moves from sea to land and vice versa. Indeed, the surface temperature of the air is not a sufficient guide to its behaviour, especially when it has moved for some distance over a continental land-mass. Local heating or cooling by day or night may have affected the surface layers up to several thousand feet. Consequently, the meteorologist often classifies the types of air by comparing the observations of temperature and humidity several thousand feet above the surface.

Inland waters and seas like the Great Lakes of North America also modify the behaviour of the air. In Ontario polar air approaching from the north-west in the early winter is very cold, dry, and clear after its long land travel; but on the American shores of the lakes the result of the passage of the cold air over the unfrozen lakes is seen in towering cumulus clouds and showers.

Depressions and the polar front. Observations of the behaviour of the atmosphere in the neighbourhood of the polar front have revealed that a great many of the depressions in temperate latitudes develop along it. This is shown by careful plotting of barometric readings and is particularly noticeable in winter to the south of Greenland or south-west of Iceland.

Frontal depressions appear to originate in the following manner:

On the earth's surface where there is considerable friction, the air at the boundary between a cold and warm air-stream is often unstable. In fig. 50 the lines represent the isobars, and the air is assumed to flow along, or nearly along them; if a small mass of air rises, it produces a small area of lower pressure which may be represented as in (*b*). Some of the air must then endeavour to follow the isobars round such a low, however small it may be.

But if this occurs, the warmer air from the south side will ride forward over the colder air to the eastward of the initial low; and the colder air from the northern side will displace some of the warmer air on the west side. Thus if the boundary between the two types of air is now plotted the result will be that shown in (*c*).

It is evident, however, that such a boundary is not a vertical wall which has been kinked, but a sloping surface intersecting the earth along

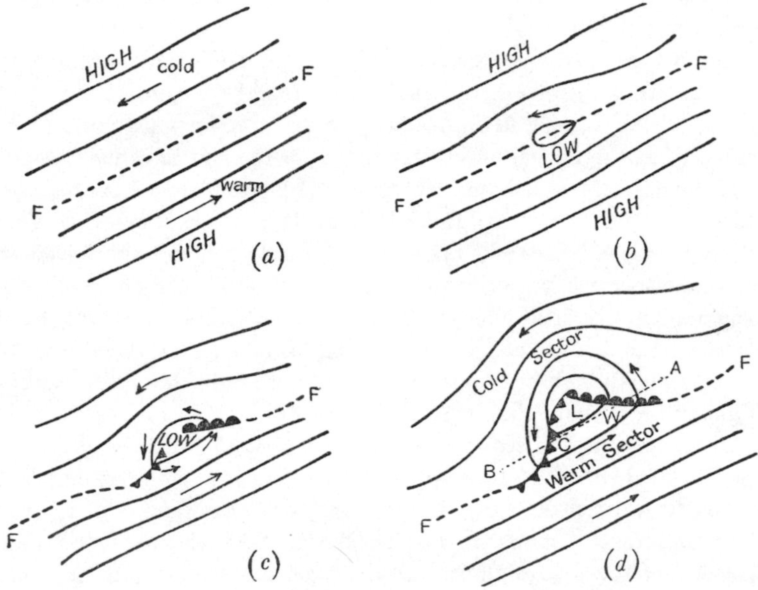

Fig. 50. Formation of a depression on a front.

the line shown on the map. In diagram (*c*) conventional representation distinguishes the cold front, where the cold air is advancing, from the warm front, where a tongue of warm air is riding over some of the cold surface beneath.

At this stage it is evident that a column of air just to the east of the centre of the low will be a little lighter as a result of the displacement of some of the cold air by warmer air advancing above. Therefore, once the kink or wave has been initiated barometric pressure begins to fall noticeably a little eastward of the initial centre. The depression deepens, the pressure gradient increases, more air flows in vigorously from either side, and the lively Atlantic low (or for that matter Aleutian, or Antarctic low) is fully developed. At this stage in a sector (diagram *d*) towards the north-east of the centre, large masses of warm, moist air are continually advancing and being uplifted. Continuous formation of dense low cloud takes place, accompanied by the persistent growth and aggregation of the cloud droplets, producing heavy rainfall (or snowfall if the temperature is low enough). This dense, low cloud is the nimbo-stratus shown in the vertical sections through a well-developed low in fig. 51*b*. Beyond the nimbo-stratus the warm air overriding the cold layer at still greater heights gives first alto-stratus, then cirro-stratus and even outlying fragments of cirrus. Accordingly, if the barometer begins to fall and part or all of a solar or lunar halo is observed (indicating the presence of cirro-stratus overspreading the sky), a depression is almost certainly approaching, and nimbo-stratus with rain (or snow, if the air is cold enough) will follow in a few hours. In a typical Atlantic low the sky will begin to cloud over with thin cirro-stratus at about 30,000 feet some 300 miles ahead of the warm front.

At the cold front, however, there is a region in which warm air is being uplifted by cold air advancing beneath it. This, then, is another region of cloud and rain, but generally quite narrow. The cloud, resulting from the rapidly rising moist air, is commonly of the cumulo-nimbus type. The passage of the front across a station is generally marked by a sharp fall of temperature and a heavy shower of rain or sometimes of hail. Perhaps there may be lightning and thunder, and there is always a well-marked change in the surface-wind direction.

Thus a warm sector, associated with continuous precipitation, and a belt of squally showers may be distinguished. In other parts of the earth the type and extent of cloud round a well-developed low depends largely on the course followed by the air. In north-western Europe the air in a warm sector is usually moist after its long sea passage: the sky is overcast at sea, but as the air moves inland in summer the greater warmth of the land may lead to increased convection and the development of the cumulus type of cloud. In winter overcast skies, with stratus or strato-cumulus, are commonly observed. The rear of the depression is marked by clear skies and fresh and bracing atmosphere. Sometimes, however, cumulus clouds and more local showers develop. When a depression is centred well inland over a continent even the warm sector may have relatively clear skies; and behind the cold front there is practically no cloud at all in the dry, clear air.

The moist air in the warm sector of a depression off north-western Europe normally gives heavy and continuous rain over any mountain region lying in its path. A great part of the rainfall of our western mountain districts, and of western Norway, can be attributed to the fact that they are so often beset by the south to south-west winds in the warm sector of depressions situated between Iceland, Scotland, and Norway.

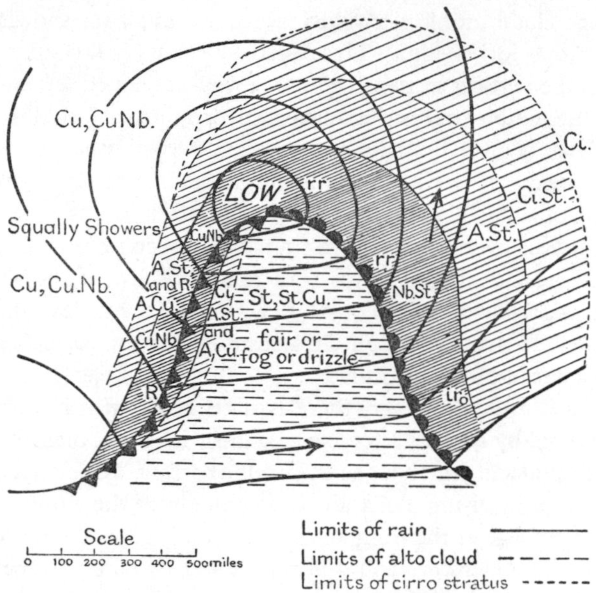

Fig. 51 (*a*). Cloud and weather in a warm-sector depression.

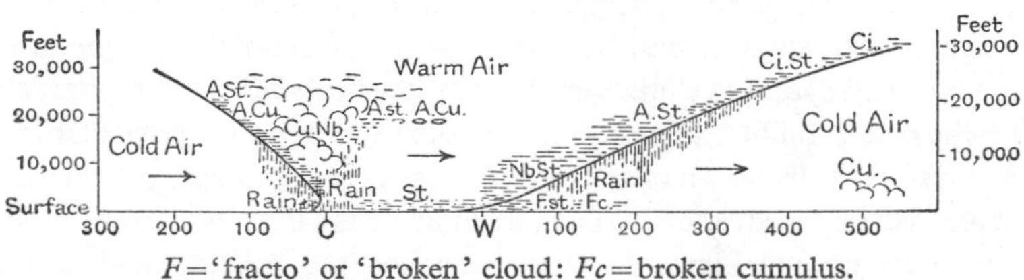

F='fracto' or 'broken' cloud: *Fc*=broken cumulus.

Fig. 51 (*b*). Vertical section through the warm sector of a depression.

Movement of depressions. Frontal depressions may move in any direction, but almost invariably there is an eastward component in their direction of travel. If the trend of the polar front runs west-east, the continued ascent of warm moist air east of the centre leads to a decrease of pressure on that side. When the pressures are plotted on a succession of weather maps, this fact appears as a steady eastward movement of the centre of the low. It is found that if a depression remains stationary, it usually fills up, that is, the difference between the pressures at the centre and at the margin decreases, and after two or three days no depression remains. Depressions also tend to move round, rather than across, well-developed anticyclones. In winter many Atlantic lows fill up in the North Sea, or move north-eastward along the Baltic or Norwegian coasts; few penetrate far into the continent during the period when the Siberian high is strongly developed.

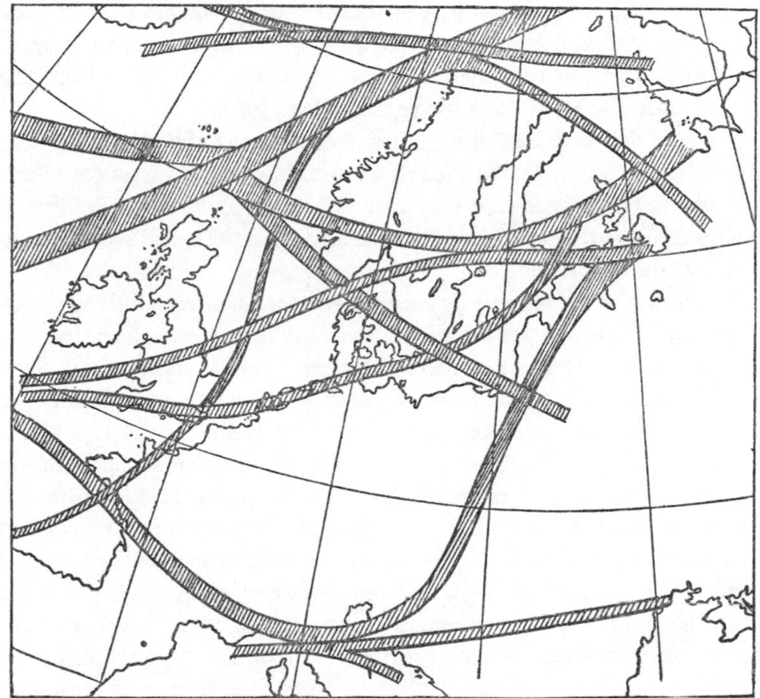

Fig. 52. Generalised tracks of depressions in Western Europe.

In the Mediterranean (cf. ch. VIII) there is throughout the winter a marked contrast in temperature between the warm air over the sea and the cold air over Europe. Hence frontal depressions are engendered; they frequently develop in the north-western Mediterranean, or even in the Adriatic, and may retain sufficient energy to carry rain as far eastward as Iraq or north-western India, where the light cool-season rains play an important part in agriculture.

Depressions frequently develop and travel along the east coast of the United States in winter. They also arise in the Japan Sea, and, on an enormous scale, all round the margins of the Antarctic. Those which form between the cold continental air and the warmer oceanic air off the east coasts of continents in middle latitudes give a certain amount of winter precipitation over the adjacent coasts and islands (see ch. VIII). A great part of the winter precipitation of New England, the Maritime Provinces of Canada, and Japan is thus derived.

Since the maintenance of active depressions depends on their being able to draw in freely a supply of warm moist air, they show a marked tendency in the winter months to follow tracks over the sea. If they move over land at any season they tend to avoid high mountain ranges, or to cross them at their narrowest point; many depressions from the Pacific cross the Rockies in the region of lat. 50° N.

Pressure at the centre of a deep winter low over the North Atlantic may fall to 960 mb. (28·35 inches) or even lower; but pressures below 940 mb. (27·76 inches) are very rare. Their direction of movement is closely associated with the trend of the isobars in the warm sector, while this is at the surface.

Influence of upper winds on movement. Daily analysis of upper winds and pressures are issued by the Meteorological Office, but the study of these, in relation to meteorological events, is complicated. One of the chief factors which controls the movement of depressions is the circulation in the upper air, above 8000 feet or so. In the two hemispheres north and south of the sub-tropical pressure belts, there are westerly upper air-streams circulating round the poles. These streams are not parallel to lines of latitude but undulate in troughs and ridges and flow along upper pressure surfaces in the same way as does the gradient wind. Depressions will follow the course of these upper winds which are nearly always in the same direction as those indicated by the trend of the isobars in warm sectors (see previous paragraph). Upper winds are, therefore, extremely valuable to the weather forecaster in determining the direction of movement of disturbances.

Processes leading to extinction: occlusions. Frontal depressions rarely retain their energy for more than a few days, as a study of daily weather charts soon shows. It is found that, as the low moves eastwards, the cold front gradually advances relative to the warm front and finally overtakes it.

When this happens, the depression is said to be occluded; in other words the merging of the fronts is called an occlusion. At first the warm air above the occlusion continues to rise and thus to give rain; but as the system travels on the changes of temperature and of wind direction at the surface are far less noticeable than those associated with a cold front.

In theory, there should be no change of temperature at all in the surface air; but in practice, the cold air, which has travelled on a long track round the low, generally differs a little from that which it meets. In England a rise or fall of two or three degrees may occur as the occlusion passes, whereas a well-marked cold front may give a fall of fifteen degrees, and often very much more in America.

When a depression has become occluded, it generally fills up rapidly. The life of a normal Atlantic low, from the first kink traceable on the polar front to the last feebly revolving mass of cold air with a little cloud

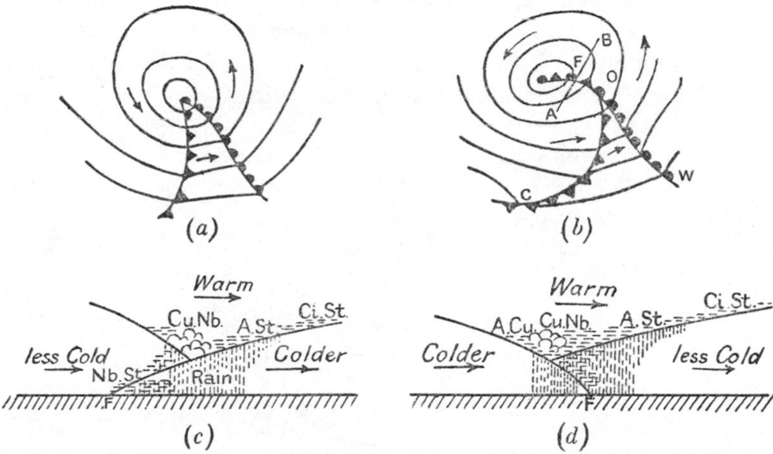

Fig. 53. Diagrams (*a*, *b*) and sections (*c*, *d*) to illustrate the formation of an occlusion. Sections (*c*, *d*) are taken along the line AB in (*b*). (*c*) Warm occlusion, where the surface air after coming round the low is a little warmer than that which it has overtaken. (*d*) Cold occlusion, in which the surface air coming round the low is somewhat colder than that which it overtakes. As a rule the associated belt of rain in (*c*) is broader than in (*d*).

remaining above, is commonly about six days. The majority of the fronts crossing Britain in association with Atlantic depressions are more or less occluded, and it is accordingly not unusual to find that depressions fill up as they move towards northern Norway or the Baltic.

Prevailing winds in relation to the passage of depressions. It will now be evident that the predominant wind direction at any place in the temperate zone depends largely on the frequency with which depressions pass, and whether they do so to the north or south of the place in question.

Southern Iceland, for example, experiences a high proportion of easterly winds. In Great Britain the majority of days have wind from points between south and west; winds from between north and east are commonest in the spring months (April–May), when depressions often follow tracks to the south of the British Isles, and a large anticyclone remains persistently over Scandinavia or the neighbouring seas.

The remarks in ch. VIII about the dominant oceanic winds bringing rain are approximately correct, but many of the wettest days, even in southern England, occur with a light or moderate easterly wind *at the surface*. This results from the passage over the rainy area of a vigorous depression the centre of which moves eastward across France or up the English Channel. Such systems have ultimately acquired at higher levels their moisture from the ocean, and move eastward from it. But not all winds blowing directly from the ocean give rain, neither must the surface wind always blow directly from the ocean for rain to occur; a matter which is readily confirmed by observation.

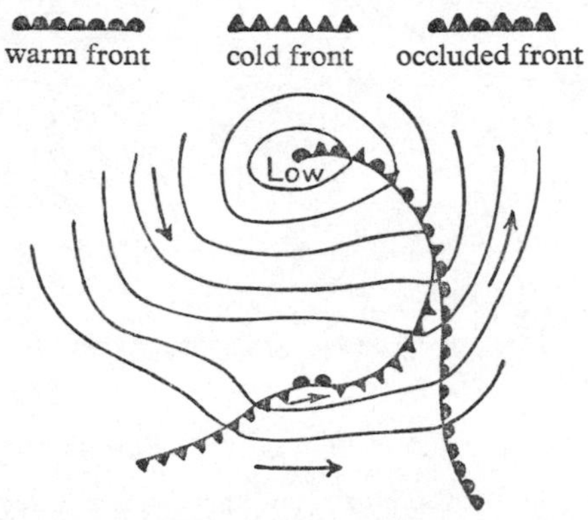

Fig. 54. Initial stage of a secondary depression forming on a cold front. Note that the primary is already partly occluded, i.e. the cold air coming round the depression has overtaken that which lies ahead in the region south-east of the principal centre.

Secondary depressions. The boundary represented by the cold front of an active low is often well marked, and frequently it is found that a further fall of pressure occurs on it, causing the formation of a secondary depression (see also fig. 54). This first appears as a kink or wave, and is usually on the cold front of the primary, as shown above.

If the chart indicates that the barometer is falling a little in the region of the cold front while elsewhere it is steady or rising there is reason for interest. If, for example, there is a deep primary low to the north of Scotland, a secondary may develop off southern Ireland and move rapidly eastward up the Channel. It will give easterly winds and continuous precipitation all along the south coast of England. Farther north cool westerly winds and showers will occur associated with the sweep of the polar air round the primary, and no doubt these would also have occurred in southern England if a secondary had not developed.

When a vigorous secondary has developed, the primary low fills up. Sometimes additional secondaries develop in the rear of the first; and occasionally a whole series of such depressions can be seen on the weather maps covering the Atlantic. The occasional winter rains off the coast of Africa to the south of Morocco, or off Lower California, can frequently be attributed to the approach of a secondary formed on the cold front behind a primary which has already moved on a southerly track.

Frontal development and air-masses. Polar and tropical air-masses have been distinguished; but it is important to note that each type may be further modified. Air-masses can be classified on the basis of (i) their source-region from which they acquire their original character, and (ii) their route of travel. In Britain certain principal types of air-masses are recognised and named, of which the characteristics can be summarised.

Maritime tropical air originates from the region of the Azores high and approaches us over a gradually cooling sea. It is warm, humid, and stable in its lower layers; at all seasons as has been shown it gives much low cloud near our coasts. In summer the low cloud often dissipates after the air has flowed inland, and towards eastern England heavy cumulus builds up; the surface air is humid and relaxing. In winter temperatures well over 50° are common.

Maritime polar air originates from the region of Labrador or south Greenland and travels towards us over a warmer sea. It therefore tends to be unstable, especially in winter, and gives showers. It is by far the commonest type of air to reach us. It gives morning surface temperatures of about 40–45° in January and 60–65° in July. Much depends on whether the air has crossed the Atlantic by a longer or a shorter route. In the former case it approaches our coast as a south-west wind and is almost as mild, cloudy, and humid as tropical air in winter. In the latter case it is cooler and more bracing.

Maritime arctic air is simply that which comes by the quickest route from the Arctic, north of Iceland. In winter it reaches us as a biting north wind, and even after a thousand miles of open sea crossing it may still have a surface temperature close to the freezing-point. After crossing the open sea it is very unstable, and gives brisk showers of snow and hail, especially on coasts and hills exposed to the northward as in Cleveland, the Lammermuirs, and north Norfolk. It is this type of air which brings wintry showers and frost occasionally in May, and can prove so damaging to fruit crops.

Continental air, whatever its origin, is generally much drier. In summer continental tropical air occasionally reaches us in the form of a hot dry south-east wind from the region of the east Mediterranean; it may give afternoon temperatures of over 90° in London. The term

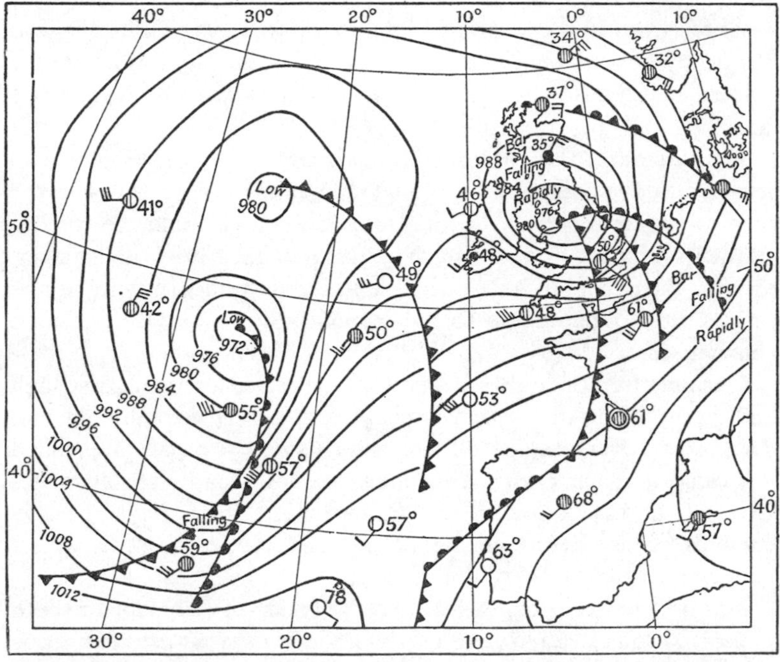

Fig. 55. Complex frontal depression over Northern England, 16 March 1947, with further Atlantic depressions approaching from the west. South of the centre this depression gave one of the greatest gales on record in the East Midlands, while heavy snow fell in the Highlands of Scotland.

'continental arctic' is reserved for the bitterly cold air stream which reaches us from time to time in winter, flowing round a big Scandinavian anticyclone and originating somewhere in north Russia or the Arctic Seas beyond. It is very cold and often brings much cloud; as the result of its passage across the North Sea, it is frequently 10° or 15° warmer on the Yorkshire coast than in Denmark, but the moisture picked up in the surface layers gives it a peculiarly raw and unpleasant sting. Where it crosses the greater breadth of the North Sea, the resultant warming often leads as before to instability and frequent snow showers in eastern Scotland.

Between any two of these air-masses, or even within them, fronts often exist and develop. Along these one air-mass undercuts the other, giving more or less cloud and rain. By the time that a large depression from the Atlantic has reached us, it is often found that in addition to the original warm and cold fronts with which it began, two or three minor fronts have developed; these represent the boundaries between the slightly differing types of air which have been drawn in to the system.

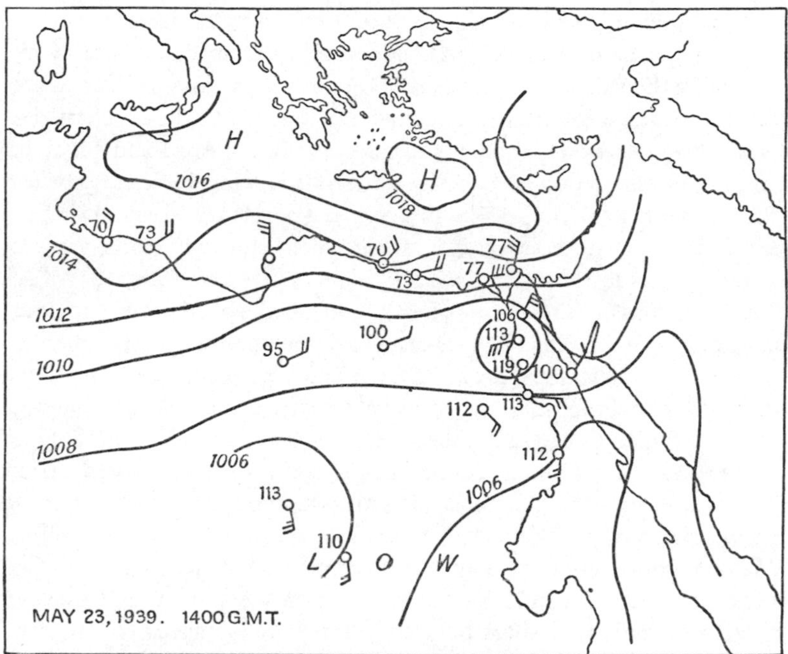

Fig. 56. 'Khamsin' depression originating in the Sahara and moving north-east. Temperature 109° at Cairo, May 1939.

Forecasting is now largely a matter of recognising the various air masses, the fronts between them, the type of cloud that may be expected, and whether the air-masses and fronts concerned are moving quickly or slowly.

The rate at which further modification of an air-mass takes place depends not only on its speed of movement but also on the nature of the track it follows—whether it be over mountainous land, ice-covered sea, or warm, humid, sunlit plains. This is but a brief introduction to a large subject. With the aid of the illustration (fig. 55), showing a complex depression with several fronts, the student will at once see why the behaviour of the air especially off north-western Europe in a large depression is often considerably more varied than our simple initial theory would demand. Eleswhere in the world, while the general results of the circulation described in the earlier chapters hold, the details from season to season and day to day should be studied with regard to the characteristics of the air masses invading the region.

Thermal depressions. Not all depressions are frontal. The warming of large and more or less quiet masses of air lying on the earth's surface is often associated with a fall of pressure sufficient to be noticeable on the barometer. When this occurs a gentle circulation of air following the isobars round the region of lower pressure is likely to be set up. The best example of a thermal low can be seen in the charts for India (fig. 57), which show the mean pressure for April and July. In summer pressure over the Iberian peninsula is often sufficiently below that over the adjacent seas to give rise to a gentle circulation bringing light south-east to east breezes to Barcelona, and light north-west to north breezes to the Atlantic coast.

Circulations of this kind are often initiated in the hot deserts, and since all the air within them is dry, cloud and rain cannot be expected unless at a later stage moist air is drawn in from another region. In India these conditions begin in June, when moist air with a much longer journey over the Indian Ocean to the southward, begins to be drawn in. Similar low-pressure areas which develop in the south-western United States give at first hot, dry, and damaging south-westerly winds; as they move eastward, however, they begin to draw in moist air from the Gulf of Mexico, and eventually they may become frontal depressions giving beneficial rain. Thermal lows developing in the Sahara and moving north-eastwards give short but very uncomfortable spells of hot, dry, southerly wind in Egypt—the Khamsin (fig. 56).

In summer in Europe from time to time light and irregular winds and a feeble pressure gradient may prevail for a few days. In such cases small thermal lows are liable to develop, and if the ground is moist and the upper winds cool they are generally associated with widespread thunderstorms. Thermal depressions are common over France in summer and when the general air-stream is southerly they are carried across the Channel to England, bringing thunderstorms with them. Storms of this kind are often severe in southern England but they gradually die out in their passage northwards, giving only a prolonged period of thundery rain in the midlands and north. Storms of this sort affected southern England on 18 July 1956 and brought about the Weymouth floods mentioned in ch. XVI, pt. III.

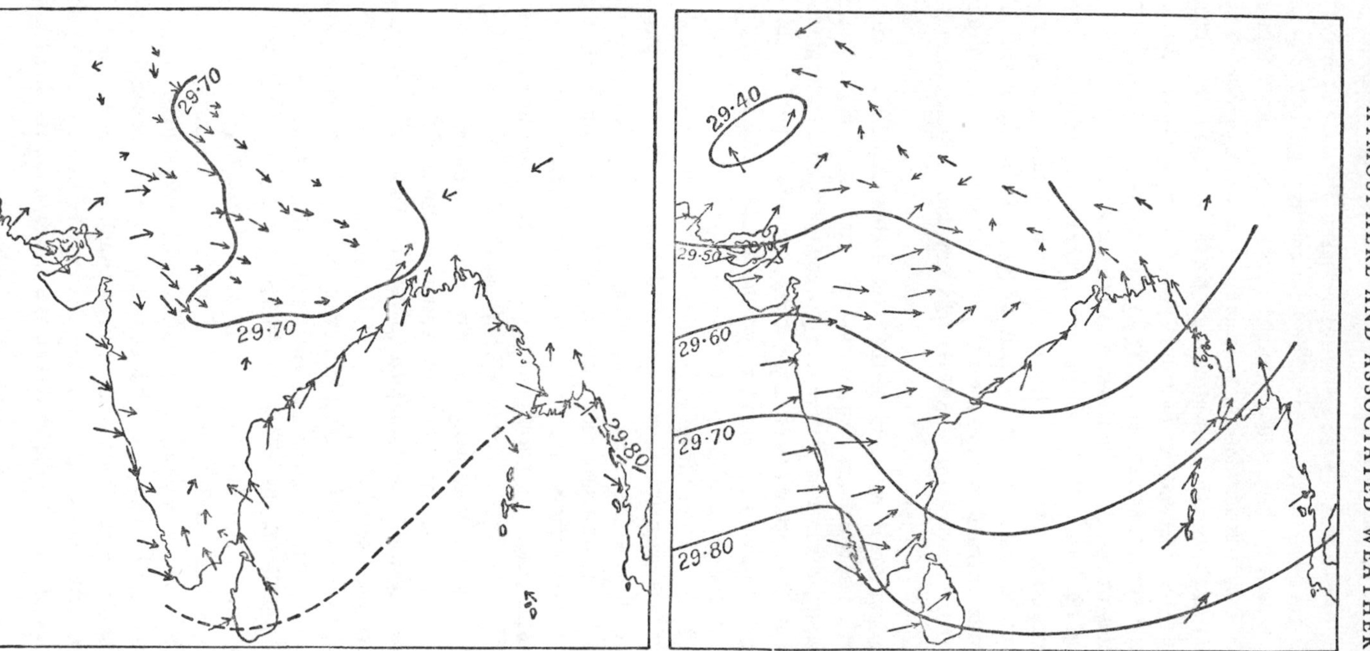

(*a*) Isobars and winds for India, April.

(*b*) Isobars and winds for India, July.

Fig. 57. Development of the low pressure over north-west India: (*a*) before the monsoon; (*b*) after the arrival of the monsoon.

Polar depressions. These are also thermal in a sense but are of a different origin from those described in the previous paragraph. As has already been stated, when cold air from the polar regions moves rapidly southwards into warmer latitudes, instability is set up. Sometimes eddies form in this general air-stream giving rise to small non-frontal depressions, which are a type of secondary depression. These are carried along in the general stream and may in winter give periods of continuous snow in an otherwise showery Arctic air-flow.

Tropical cyclones. By far the greater number of depressions originating in temperate latitudes are frontal in origin. Nearer the equator, especially under conditions of stagnant air (i.e. very light and variable surface winds) thermal causes appear to preponderate; but it is not to be forgotten that one type of depression may develop or merge into the other.

Special mention is required of the violent disturbances known as tropical cyclones, which are characteristic of certain parts of the oceans. They are really whirlwinds of large area (50–200 miles in diameter). On a weather map they appear as a closely-packed series of concentric isobars, for in spite of their small diameter pressure at the centre is very low, frequently under 960 mb. (28·35 inches).

The great majority occur towards the end of the hot season in either hemisphere, and are first observed between 6° and 15° from the equator. Their route of travel lies round the southern and western borders of the great subtropical highs; and they rarely retain their characteristic energy more than 30° from the equator. The speed of travel of the whole system, westward and poleward, varies but is commonly of the order of 10–15 m.p.h. If a tropical cyclone moves over the land, it immediately loses its energy and as a slow-moving low-pressure system merely gives cloud and rain. Hence the damage and devastation resulting from the extremely violent winds are confined to certain coasts and groups of islands in tropical seas.

The season and circumstances of development point to an origin in the stagnant moist air of the Doldrums at the time of year when this region of calms lies farthest from the equator. The absence of these disturbances in the South Atlantic is attributed to the fact that in this ocean the belt of calms never moves farther south than the region of the equator itself. It is probable that the initial stage may often be sought in convection—in the strong currents of rising moist air ascending from small tropical islands. Under special circumstances which are not fully understood, but may be related to the existence of fronts between different types of air at higher levels in the atmosphere, the local low-pressure area thus established develops and deepens. The winds follow the isobars and blow with great strength round the centre, converging a little at the surface, and cause a steady ascent of the almost saturated surface air. This leads to the formation of heavy cloud and torrential rain. If a tropical cyclone 100 miles in diameter moves from east to west directly across a station at an average speed of 10 m.p.h., the station will experience (in the northern hemisphere) about five hours of extremely strong northerly winds, and later a similar period of southerly

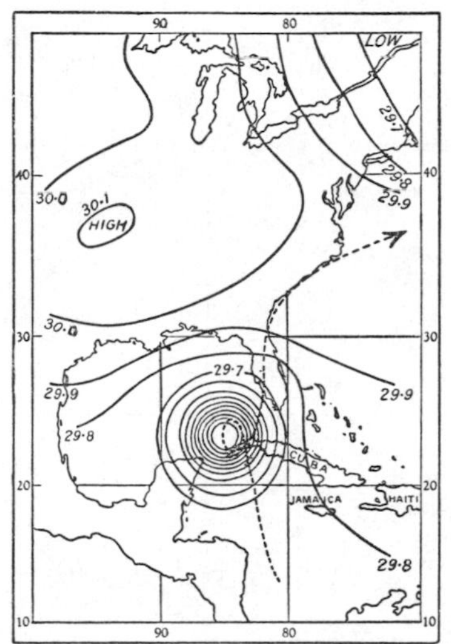

Fig. 58. Isobars in a tropical cyclone (hurricane) off Cuba.

winds. In the centre of a tropical cyclone, a small area of descending air, clear skies, and little wind, is often reported; this is known as the eye of the storm.

Frequency and distribution. From what has been said it will be evident that tropical cyclones, locally called typhoons, can be expected to develop over the seas east of the Philippine Islands and to move westward and then northward among these islands and on to the China coasts. On an average between 20 and 25 yearly are reported from some part of this large area; the great majority occur from June to October. In the West Indies, Caribbean, and Gulf of Mexico, where they are called hurricanes, they occur mainly from August to October and vary greatly in number from year to year—four or five is an average. Some occur to the west of Mexico. In the southern Indian Ocean, perhaps six may be reported annually, mainly from January to April. They may cause

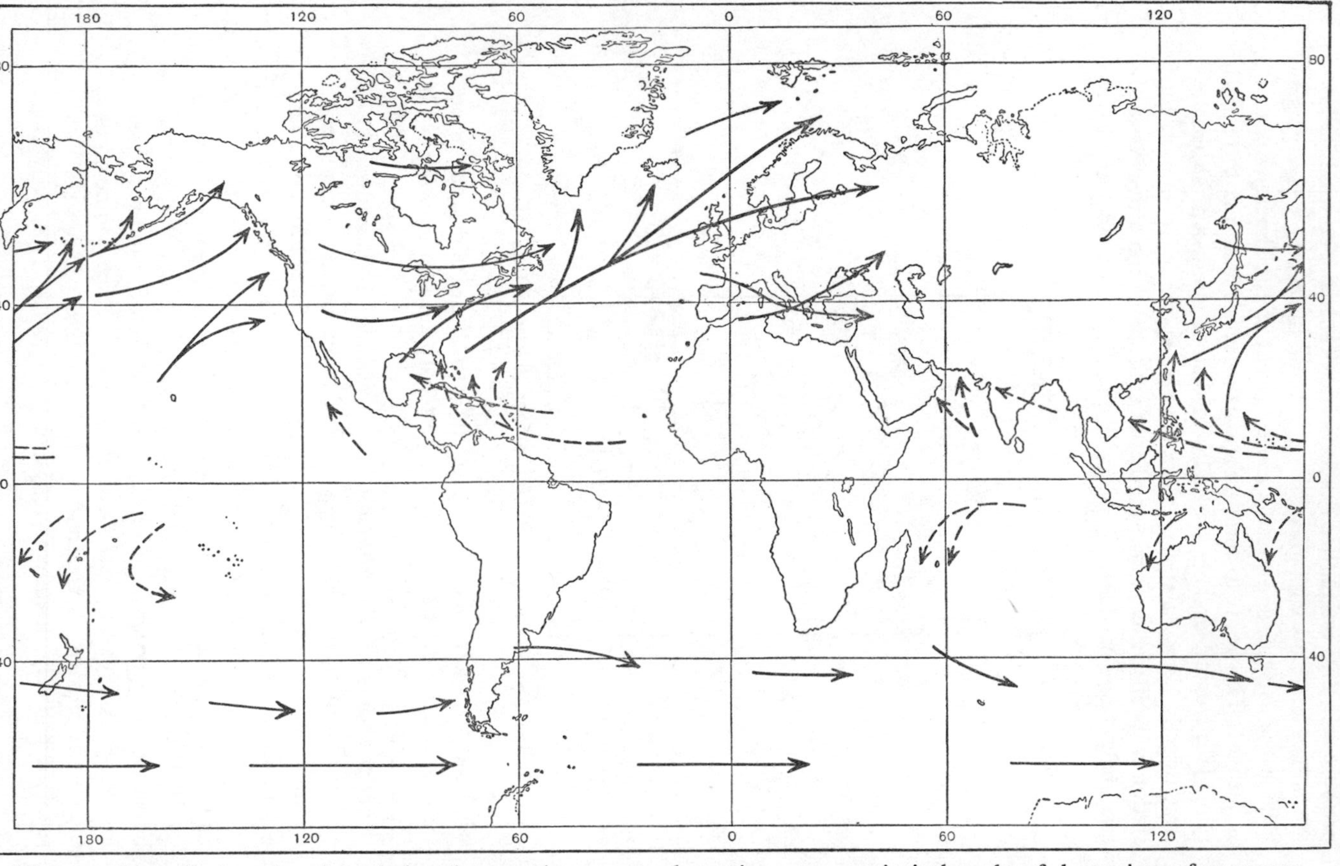

Fig. 59. Generalised tracks of tropical cyclones and temperate depressions. ——, principal tracks of depressions of temperate latitudes; - - - -, principal tracks of tropical cyclones.

damage in Mauritius and northern Madagascar. A few occur off the north-east of Australia.

Lastly, disturbances of a similar kind develop over the Bay of Bengal, either during the relatively calm hot weather (April to May) before the onset of the monsoon in June; or at the end of the monsoon in October. Not all of them attain the violence of typhoons. Moreover, the behaviour of all tropical cyclones is somewhat erratic in that their route of travel is not always regular, and a cyclone which appears to be decreasing in intensity may sometimes be rejuvenated as it moves onwards. From their diameter, frequency, and rather erratic behaviour it will be evident that many tropical islands and coasts may be fortunate enough to escape serious damage over many years.

On occasions when a tropical cyclone reaches higher latitudes, e.g. on the coast of the United States or southern Japan, it generally decreases in intensity and may pick up the polar front and become rejuvenated as a normal depression in temperate latitudes.

Tropical cyclones must not be confused with tornadoes. Tornadoes are extremely intense local whirls of very small extent, affecting areas from a few yards to a quarter of a mile in diameter, and occur inland when exceptionally violent convection is set up. They are associated with severe outbreaks of thunderstorms, notably in the south-central United States, and occasionally elsewhere. Small tornadoes have occurred on a number of occasions in association with thundery weather in England. Even within the United States, the number of tornadoes occurring in a year is small (of the order of fifty) and fortunately only small areas are affected by these most violent of all atmospheric disturbances.

PART II

THE OCEAN

CHAPTER I

THE OCEANS

General distribution of land and sea. If we look at a globe, with our eyes half shut so as to obscure all details, we shall see in the western hemisphere a large triangle of land, with its base in the north, against the Arctic Ocean, and its point in the south. In the eastern hemisphere the land is also widest towards the north, but instead of tapering southwards into a single point, it ends in two, the Cape of Good Hope and the island of Tasmania. It is like two triangles which have become united at their bases; and, as in the western hemisphere, the bases lie against the Arctic Ocean and the points are directed southwards.

Besides these three triangles, stretching from north to south, there is a fourth land-mass of smaller size, with its centre about the South Pole.

Between these three triangular masses of land lie three still larger triangles of sea. But, necessarily, these are turned the other way. They are wide towards the south, where they unite with one another, and they taper towards the north. In the western hemisphere is the Pacific, ending northwards at the Behring Straits. In the eastern hemisphere are the Atlantic and Indian Oceans. The former is fairly wide even at the Arctic Circle, the latter is completely closed towards the north by the union of the land-masses between which it lies.

There is still another area of sea, the Arctic Ocean, round about the North Pole.

The triangles, both of land and sea, are very irregular, but nevertheless it will be seen that there is a certain symmetry in the arrangement of the continents and oceans.

Although there is no known explanation of this symmetry it is still worth while to call attention to the suggestion put forward in 1875 by Lowthian Green. If a solid tetrahedron is placed in the midst of a globe of water, not sufficient to cover it (fig. 60), the points and parts of the sides and edges will project above the water. They will form triangular masses of land, and between them, on the faces of the tetrahedron, will lie areas of water.[1] If one of the points of the tetrahedron is placed at the South Pole and the other three symmetrically around the North Pole, the

[1] It should be observed that if the tetrahedron has plane faces the water areas will be circles, more or less complete according to the extent of the projecting land-masses.

arrangement of land and sea will be somewhat similar to that on the earth. There will be three triangles of land with their bases in the north and their points towards the south, and also a fourth mass at the South Pole. There will be three areas of water which will unite with one another towards the south and narrow towards the north, and also a fourth area at the North Pole. The exact shapes of the land and the sea will depend upon the relative sizes of the globe of water and the solid tetrahedron.

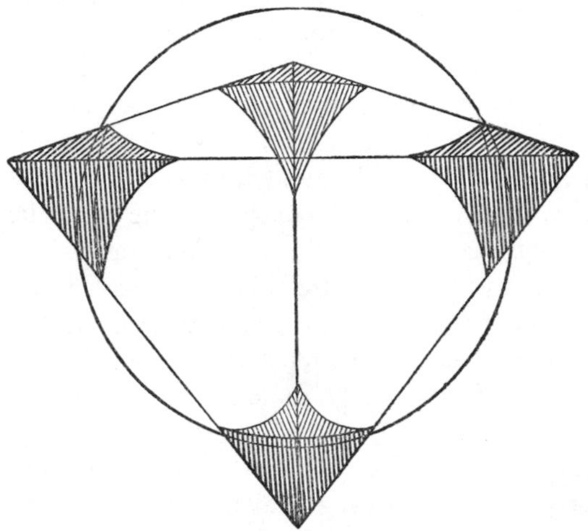

Fig. 60. A tetrahedron placed symmetrically in a globe.

Area and depth of the ocean. A glance at a terrestrial globe is sufficient to show that the area of the oceans is far greater than that of the land. According to the earlier estimates of Wagner water covers 71·7 per cent of the globe, land occupies 28·3 per cent. More recently Krümmel has given the figures as, water 70·8 per cent, land 29·2 per cent; these figures still hold good.

The chief reason for minor differences between estimates is our imperfect knowledge of the polar regions, both in the north and in the south. But the differences are small, and in round numbers we may take the percentages as, water 71; land 29.

Attempts have also been made to determine the average height of the land and the average depth of the ocean, and also the proportion of land of various altitudes and the proportion of ocean floor at various depths. These estimates are necessarily even more uncertain than those of the relative areas of land and water. Sir John Murray's figures are shown in Table 11.

Table 11

LAND

Height (feet)	Area (million sq. miles)	Percentage of whole globe
over 12000	2	1
6000–12000	4	2
3000– 6000	10	5
600– 3000	26	13
0– 600	15	8
	57	29

SEA

Depth (feet)	Area (million sq. miles)	Percentage of whole globe
0– 600	10	5
600– 3000	7	3
3000– 6000	5	2
6000–12000	27	15
12000–18000	81	41
over 18000	10	5
	140	71

The hypsographic curve. If we take the figures in this table, and draw a diagram in which areas are represented by lengths along a horizontal line, and the heights and depths, measured from sea-level, are represented by vertical distances from this line we obtain a curve, as shown in fig. 61.

The hypsographic curve represents in some respects the average form of the surface of the solid globe if the surface of the sea be considered as level; but the heights and depths are very greatly exaggerated.

Sometimes the proportions of land at various altitudes and of ocean at various depths are expressed as a frequency curve. It is easy to combine these methods on the same diagram as is done in fig. 61, which also shows that the mean elevation of the land is *c.* 2750 feet, and the mean depth of the ocean is *c.* 12,400 feet.

From this diagram it will be seen that the ocean floor may be divided into four parts:

(1) The continental shelf lying next to the land, and sloping very gently from the shore. It extends to a depth of about 100 fathoms.

(2) The continental slope immediately outside the continental shelf, and sloping more steeply. It must not be forgotten that owing to the exaggeration of the vertical heights in the diagram, the angle of slope is also greatly exaggerated. The continental slope extends from about 100 fathoms to about 2000 fathoms.

(3) The deep-sea plain; a broad and nearly level area forming by far the greater part of the ocean floor. Its depth varies from about 2000 to 3000 fathoms but its slopes are always very gentle.

(4) The deeps; the deepest parts of the ocean, forming depressions in the floor, relatively small in area, and with comparatively steep sides.

In all the oceans these different parts can be readily recognised, although they may differ in proportions. In the Atlantic, for example,

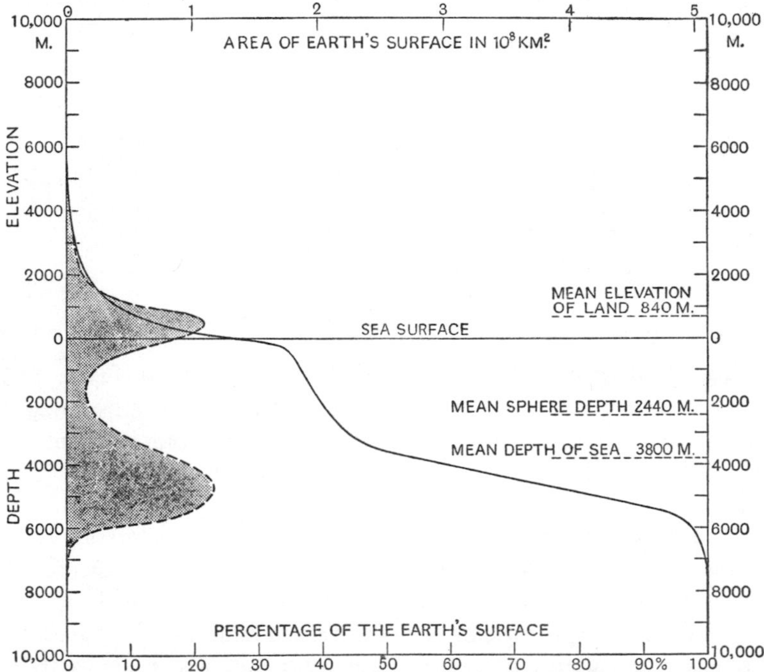

Fig. 61. Hypsographic and frequency curves. ——, *hypsographic curve*. Area above any given level of elevation or depth. - - - -, *frequency curve*. Frequency distribution of elevations and depths.

the continental shelf is generally wider than in the Pacific. In all the oceans the greater part of the floor is formed by the deep-sea plain; and at various places in the plain are the deeper depressions known as deeps. They are not at a rule in the middle of the oceans but rather towards the margins.

The continental shelf and slope. The continental shelf is the zone around a continent, extending from the line of permanent immersion to the depths at which there is a marked increase of slope to greater depths. Conventionally its edge is taken at 100 fathoms (or 200 metres), but it may be between 65 and 300 fathoms. Its width varies greatly. Off the coast of Ireland it stretches westward for a distance of 50 miles or more and off Siberia it reaches a maximum width of 800 miles; but it may be only a few miles wide, or it may even be absent altogether. The angle of slope is also variable and is usually least where the shelf is widest. West of Ireland it is less than one degree, and it is seldom more than two or three.

Seawards the continental shelf usually ends somewhat abruptly, and there is a relatively rapid increase in depth beyond its outer margin. It is here that the continental slope begins, and the slope is really the edge of the shelf.

The angle of the continental slope varies far more than that of the shelf. Off Ireland, it is only about 5°; but off the coast of Spain it is much steeper and near Cape Toriñana it is in one place as much as 36°, a steep angle even for a mountain side. Recent measurements suggest that the average inclination of the continental slope off mountainous coasts is about $3\frac{1}{2}$°, whereas off well-drained coastal plains it is about 2°.

The origin of the continental shelf is still uncertain. In the hypsographic diagram it appears as a direct continuation of the surface of the land beneath the level of the sea; there is no change of angle where the water begins. Many writers accordingly, especially in America, hold that the continents really end at the outer margin of the shelf; that at some former time the sea reached only to the top of the continental slope and for some reason (see also pp. 211, 212) it has since overflowed the edges of the continents.

In support of this view there is the undoubted fact that many river-valleys are continued beneath the sea, across the continental shelf, and open on the continental slope.

According to this view the continental shelf was formed either by a rise in the level of the sea or a fall in the level of the land. Since the shelf is almost continuous around the shores of the Atlantic, the movement must have affected half the globe, and it must have been remarkably uniform in amount. Unless there has been an increase in the quantity of water in the ocean it is difficult to understand how a change of level so widespread and regular could be brought about.

There are, however, other ways in which a ledge may be formed upon the margin of a continent. If the relative level of land and sea remains unaltered, the waves and currents will gradually wear away the edge of the land, cutting a notch in the original profile, as shown in fig. 62. The side *AB* of the notch will form a cliff, and the floor *BC* will be a gentle slope, reaching from high-water mark to the depth where waves and currents cease to erode. The breadth of the platform will depend upon the resistance of the rocks, the strength of the waves and currents, and the length of time during which the level of land and sea remains unchanged.

Shelves of this kind exist round Iceland and the Faroe Islands. On the coast of Norway a similar wave-cut platform has been lifted above the sea. But a shelf produced by erosion alone can hardly be more than a narrow fringe. The motion of the water due to a passing wave decreases very rapidly downwards and is scarcely felt at a depth of 100 feet; and even currents seem to have little or no erosive action beyond 600 feet. Moreover, as the width of the platform increases, the force of the waves

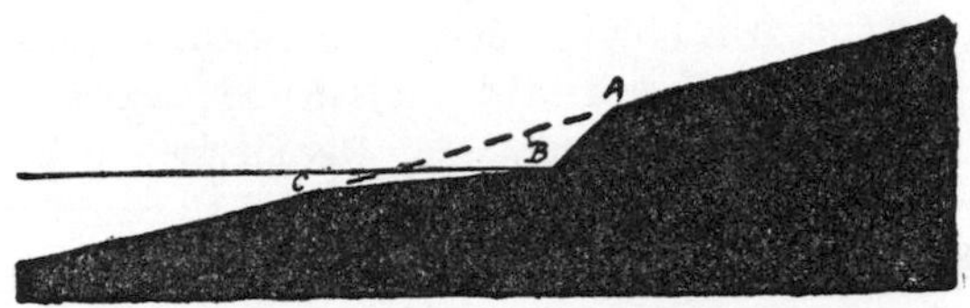

Fig. 62. Shelf cut by the sea.

at its shoreward margin diminishes, and at length they cease effectively to wear away the cliff (see p. 257). On the other hand glacial erosion has undoubtedly played a large part in the formation of shelves surrounding glaciated countries. These shelves often show characteristics—basins and troughs—resembling terrestrial features produced by ice. Moraines may sometimes form banks on them, and it is reasonable to assume that such deposits have often been modified by current or wave-erosion. F. P. Shepard (*Submarine Geology*, 1948) concludes that 'The most clear-cut history of shelf-development is found around the glaciated areas. The shelves in these places appear to have been greatly deepened, especially on the inside, by the movement of glaciers...across them. The glacial erosion of the continental margins may have also considerably widened the shelves in the glaciated areas.'

A shelf may also be formed by deposition (fig. 63). The surface of the land is worn by rain and rivers and its edge by the waves of the sea. The broken material thus produced is laid down beneath the water, but always near the land. Off the mouth of the Amazon it is said that the sea is sometimes discoloured by mud at a distance of 300 miles. But even the largest rivers must deposit most of their burden near the shore. Waves and currents may bear it a little farther, but their action is slight except in shallow water. Consequently the material derived from the land accumulates as a submarine terrace upon the margins of the continents.

The edge of the terrace is the limit beyond which waves and currents cease to be effective, and within that limit the material collects and is distributed along the shore.

This limit, however, is not permanent, for as the terrace is built up and the water becomes shallower, the action of the transporting agents becomes more effective and they are able to carry the material farther than before. The terrace therefore grows gradually outwards by addition at its edge, in the same fashion as a railway embankment or the tip-heaps of a quarry.

Delta growth is locally also an important factor in the formation of the shelf. The rate at which some deltas grow outwards is known, and geophysical investigations have shown that, for instance, in the Mississippi

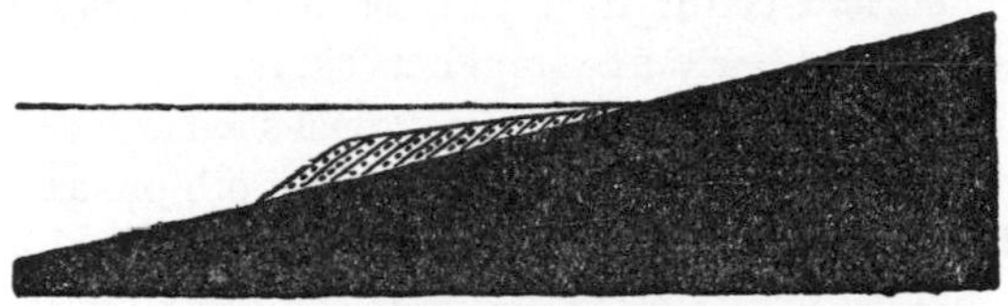

Fig. 63. Shelf formed by deposition.

delta, there is also a great thickness of deposits. Delta deposits may be swept along the coast by current action.

In the north Atlantic the great width of the continental shelf may be due in part to deposition around the margins of the great ice-sheets which, in geologically recent times, covered the north of Europe and the north of America.

According to this explanation the continental shelf and slope are formed by deposits brought from the land. The shelf is the surface of the deposit, smoothed and redistributed by waves and currents; the slope is the edge of the deposit, too deep to be thus affected.

The action of currents in general is said to cease at about 600 feet beneath the surface and this may be one reason why the edge of the shelf is usually found at about this depth.[1]

Shepard also suggests that in some cases a combination of erosion and deposition may have produced wide shelves. Imagine a shelf fringed by island arcs like that off part of eastern Asia; suppose also that in past times the islands were worn down by erosion and then drowned. Ideal conditions would exist for the accumulation of sediments within an enclosed basin, and the resulting shelf would be mainly one of deposition, but bordered by a rim of solid rock. The filling of the enclosed basins may well have been partly deltaic.

[1] Further work on this matter is needed.

It was argued that the valleys which cross the shelf are not, according to this view, submerged valleys of erosion, but have been built up beneath the sea by the deposits brought down by rivers. When a rapid river enters the sea, its current continues outwards for some distance from the land. The current will be swiftest in the middle, while at the sides it will be retarded by friction with the water of the sea. Consequently, the material which it carries will be laid down chiefly at the sides and in the middle there will be but little deposition. Thus the river will form a channel on the shelf, not by excavating its bed but by building up the sides; and if the process continues long enough it may carry the channel right across the shelf. It is, however, evident that if the currents which sweep along the shore are stronger than the river, no such channel can be formed. The current of the river must be strong enough to keep the middle of its channel fairly free from deposition.

It should perhaps be added that a marginal shelf will seldom be due either to erosion alone or to deposition alone. Both processes go on together and the shelf will be the result of their combined action. Recent geophysical work on the origin of continental shelves suggests that they are in part gigantic prism-shaped accumulations of sediments reaching perhaps several thousand metres in thickness.

Mention has already been made of rivers which traverse the shelf. Some of the rivers debouch low down, or even at the foot of, the continental slope, thus producing deep and long submarine canyons. F. P. Shepard writes 'We can state that many of the canyons extend down steep slopes to a depth of at least a mile, but that there is now no justification for saying that these canyons go to depths of as much as 2 miles.' (*Submarine Geology*, 1948, p. 235.) Fig. 64 shows the sea-bed contours of the area of the Monterey Canyon, one of the best known in the world. The axis of the canyon winds, and its head is almost on the beach. After a course of about 50 miles it enters, at about 1500 fathoms, a trough of different character from the inner one—the inner V-shape giving place to a much flatter cross-section. There are many tributaries, a characteristic of many other canyons: granite was found at 500 fathoms, and Pliocene sediments at lesser depths. From the floor of the canyon were dredged sand and silt, and in places coarse gravel. Many other canyons have much in common with Monterey Canyon, which is not alone in affording evidence of dated sedimentary rocks.

Submarine canyons are found in many parts of the world, and their origin, not yet explained, has given rise to various hypotheses. Since so many of them closely resemble features like the Grand Canyon of Colorado, it is but natural that their origin as subaerial valleys has been considered. Their winding nature, steep sides, general form, and tributaries all support such a view, but unfortunately it implies shifts of sea-level, or of the land, of many thousands of feet. Moreover, canyons are not limited to unstable coasts, and since Tertiary rocks are found in

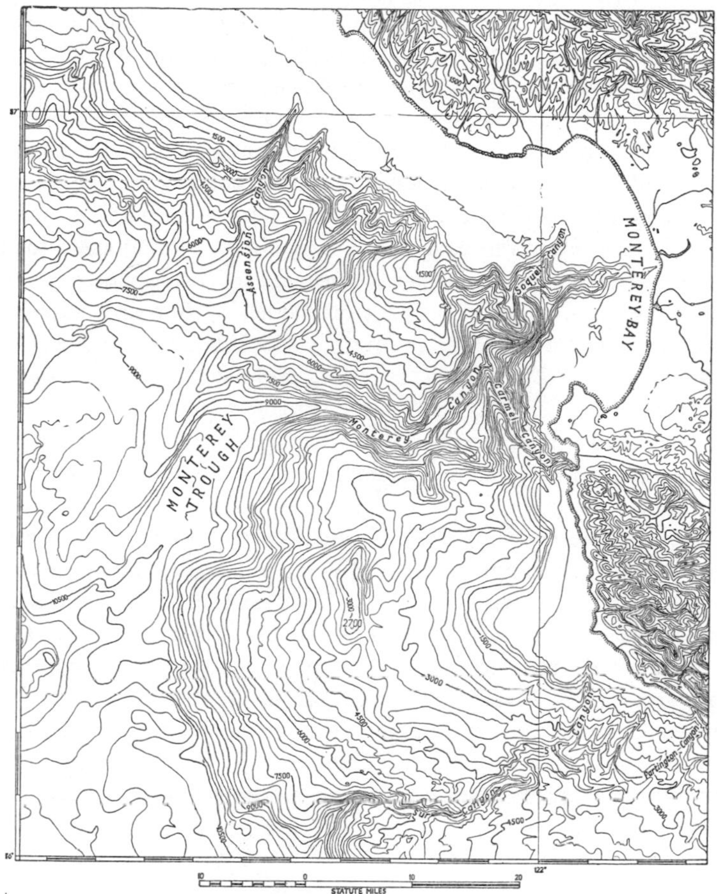

Fig. 64. Submarine canyons in Monterey Bay.

them, a subaerial hypothesis suggests also a recent origin. It is true that sea-level has fluctuated in association with the waxing and waning of the ice-sheets of the Quaternary period, but the usual estimates of these oscillations do not exceed about 300 feet, and are, therefore, quite inadequate to explain canyons of more than 5000 feet deep. Strong partisans of the glacial view sometimes argue that the ice-caps may have been far larger than usually assumed, and that consequently changes of sea-level were greater. However, there is little, if any, evidence, apart from the canyons themselves, to support this view.

The investigation of submarine canyons proves that in some places they are cut in solid rock. Both sedimentary and igneous rocks have been found *in situ*. This finding, and the fact that sediments do not necessarily become finer with distance from the shore and in deeper water, are opposed to the simple depositional view of the origin of the continental slope and shelf. The suggestion has therefore been made that the slope is produced by the down-warping of a former peneplain. This view is not, however, easy to prove. Moreover, the general straightness of the shelves is not suggestive of down-warping, and simple down-warping of continental materials might well bring them to the same levels as the heavier submarine materials of the deep oceans. This view is not supported by geophysical evidence. Shepard, therefore, tentatively suggests a fault-scarp origin, which is in consonance with the known seismicity of the slopes, as well as of the features of the slopes—their straightness and the fact that they are often bordered by trenches. Whatever their origin, modifications have taken place as a result of sedimentation and the submarine landslides which are known to occur on the slopes.

Other hypotheses about their origin include density currents, submarine spring sapping, submarine mudflows, and tsunamis (earthquake waves). It is doubtful if any of these is likely to be of more than local significance.

The deep-sea plain. By far the greater part of the floor of the ocean is formed by the deep-sea plain. It is certainly not a level surface and its depth accordingly is variable; but the slopes are usually so slight that they would be quite imperceptible to the eye. However, the far greater number of soundings obtained in recent years by the echo method have shown that while slopes are not steep, the deep-sea plain is a region of more varied topography than was formerly supposed.

The deep-sea plain is for the most part entirely free from the sediments brought down by rivers, but its surface is not formed of solid rock. A large part is covered by a kind of fine mud or ooze consisting of the shells and tests of minute animals and plants which during life float on the surface of the water. In the deeper parts there is a red clay, which appears to have been formed chiefly from the fine ash thrown out by volcanoes and carried out to sea by the wind.

The deeps. The deeps are depressions in the ocean floor still deeper than the deep-sea plain. Their sides are fairly steep and their area is generally small. They do not usually lie in the middle of the oceans, but towards the margins or along the outer side of island arcs. Most of them are found near coasts where volcanoes are still active and earthquakes common. There are many, for example, around the shores of the Pacific, and there is one close to the West Indies.

The Atlantic Ocean. The Atlantic Ocean is rather irregular in outline. It is very wide towards the south where it opens into the Antarctic

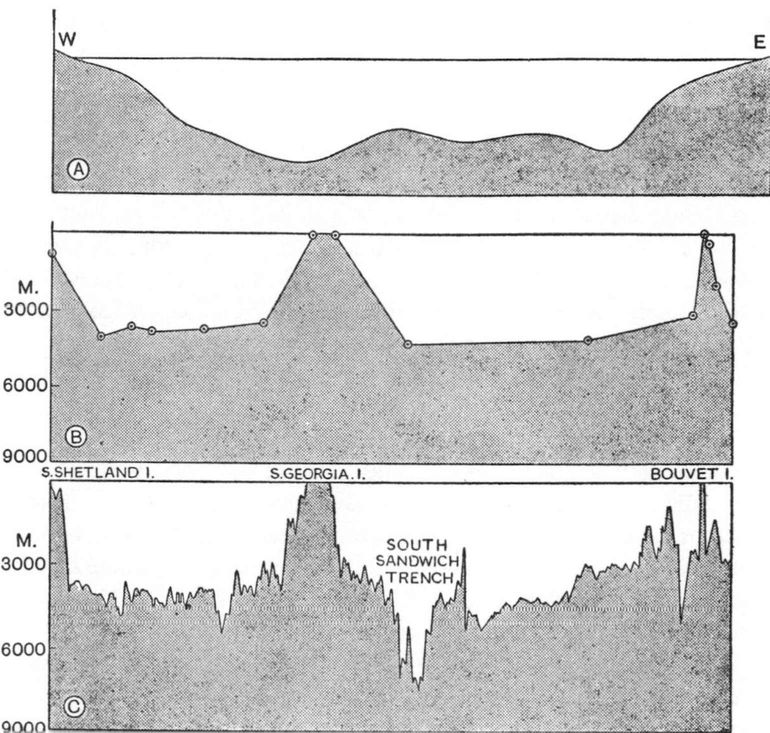

Fig. 65. Sections across Atlantic Ocean. *A*, diagrammatic section of the Atlantic Ocean; *B*, profile of S. Atlantic based on wire soundings; *C*, same profile based on 1300 sonic soundings.

Ocean, but narrows towards the equator between Africa and South America; it widens out between Africa and North America, and again narrows rapidly northwards. But it is not closed towards the north and communicates with the Arctic Ocean by a fairly wide opening, which however corresponds in places with the Wyville-Thompson Ridge, the true boundary between the Atlantic and the Arctic Oceans.

On the borders of the Atlantic there are a number of seas which are more or less completely separated from the main ocean. In the north are

Baffin Bay and Hudson Bay on the western side and the North Sea and the Baltic on the eastern side. All of these are shallow. Nearer to the equator are the Gulf of Mexico and the Caribbean Sea on the west and the Mediterranean on the east. All of these are deep.

The average depth of the Atlantic Ocean is rather more than 2 miles. The greatest depth which has been satisfactorily measured is 4561 fathoms in the Blake Deep, north of Porto Rico.

The continental shelf is generally well marked and is particularly wide in the North Atlantic, both on the eastern and the western coasts.

The deep-sea plain presents the usual characters; but it is not uniform in depth. Both from east and west it rises gradually towards the middle, forming a long and gentle undulation which divides the ocean longitudinally into two deeper basins. Except near the equator where it is cut by the Romanche trench the crest of the rise is generally less than 2000 fathoms deep, and upon it stand the Azores, Ascension, Tristan da Cunha, and one or two other islands. It is known in the North Atlantic as the Dolphin Rise, in the South Atlantic as the Challenger Rise; and it is often called the Atlantic Rise. It lies about half-way between the eastern and the western coasts, following the curves of the coasts with considerable fidelity.

Throughout the greater part of its extent the slopes on both sides of the Atlantic Rise are very gentle. But close to the equator the western side falls steeply to the Romanche Deep where a sounding of 4030 fathoms has been obtained. The only other deep with soundings of more than 4000 fathoms is the Blake Deep already mentioned. There are also two important transverse ridges, the Walfisch (Walvis) Ridge which runs from the neighbourhood of Tristan da Cunha (37° S.) to the African coast in lat. 20° S., and the Rio Grande Ridge which runs westward from the Atlantic Rise between lat. 30° and 35° S. The former is continuous at 3500 fathoms, the latter almost continuous at 4000 fathoms. Both have a profound effect on the deep-water circulation of the east and west basins.

Special characteristics of the Atlantic Ocean are then the well-marked continental shelf, the rise in the middle, the general absence of deeps, and the transverse ridges. Diagrammatically therefore the general form of the section is as shown in fig. 65 *A*, but it should be clearly understood that the figure is only a diagram, vertical heights are greatly exaggerated, and accordingly all slopes are very much steeper than in nature.

The Pacific Ocean. The Pacific Ocean is more regular in outline than the Atlantic and is roughly triangular in shape. At the base of the triangle it is open to the Antarctic Ocean, at the apex it is almost closed, communicating with the Arctic Ocean only by the narrow and shallow Behring Strait. But the sides are not straight and the greatest width is not at the base but about the equator.

As in the case of the Atlantic there are a number of seas upon its margin which are more or less completely cut off from the main body of water. Most of them are upon the western side of the ocean. In the north there are the Sea of Okhotsk, the Sea of Japan and the Yellow Sea, all of which are comparatively shallow. Nearer to the equator are the China Sea, the Celebes Sea and a number of others amongst the islands of the Malay Archipelago. Most of these in their deepest parts are as deep as the ocean itself. It should also be noted that much of the area between the Philippines, New Guinea, the Java-Sumatra arc, and the Asiatic continent is mainly a submerged platform covered by about 200 metres of water. The bottom topography is intricate, and islands and volcanoes are often arranged in loops which may enclose deeper basins. Between Borneo and the mainland the old subaerial relief may be traced on detailed charts.

The average depth of the Pacific is about 2½ miles. The greatest depths measured occur in the Philippine Deep off the island of Mindanao, where some soundings of over 10,000 metres (5468 fathoms) have recently been obtained, including one of 10,793 metres (5902 fathoms).

If we exclude the marginal seas on the Asiatic coast the continental shelf throughout the Pacific is either narrow or completely absent, and the edges fall almost uninterruptedly to the level of the deep-sea plain.

There is no continuous dividing ridge as in the Atlantic Ocean, but the surface of the plain rises up into a number of isolated curvilinear plateaux, on which stand the island arcs which are so characteristic a feature of the Pacific, especially of its southern and western portions. Recent work on the Pacific Ocean has revealed a very extensive plateau-like area which extends from central America south and westwards to meet Antarctica in the longitudes of New Zealand. This ridge, or system of ridges, is continuous at depths of less than 4000 metres, and separates the main central area of the ocean from the basins bordering South America and the Antarctic continent. There is also a region in the west Pacific, made up of several smaller ridges, which extends from Japan to the Antarctic, and apart from breaks in 11° N., 10° S. and 53° S. is continuous at depths of less than 4000 metres.

Most of the deeps form narrow trough-shaped depressions along the margins of the ocean. Amongst them are the Tuscarora Deep off Japan, the Atacama Deep along the coast of South America and many others. There are also deeps along the edges of some of the plateaux already mentioned. One of these stretches from the Tonga Islands nearly to New Zealand.

Thus the characteristic features of the Pacific Ocean are the feeble development of the continental shelf and the absence of any continuous dividing rise, the presence of numerous deeps along the margins and of isolated plateaux rising from the deep-sea plain. Some of these characters are shown diagrammatically in fig. 66 in which, as in the section of the Atlantic, vertical heights are greatly exaggerated. In this diagram one of the marginal seas of the north-eastern Asiatic coast is also shown. It will be seen that these seas occupy the position of the continental shelf, but they probably owe their origin to a different cause.

Fig. 66. Diagrammatic section of the Pacific Ocean.

The Indian Ocean. This ocean is smaller than the Atlantic, and there are fewer adjacent seas cut off by islands. It is regular in form. One of its most characteristic features is the series of curving ridges in the north-west. Of these the Carlsberg Ridge is the best known, and runs, roughly, between Sokotra and the Maldives. Nearly at right angles to this is the Kerguelen-Gaussberg Ridge which runs between India and Antarctica, and sends out a branch which reaches Madagascar.

The eastern part of the Indian Ocean, near Australia, is, in general, the deepest area, and it is only along the arc of the East Indian Archipelago that the deeps, so characteristic of the Pacific Ocean, enter into the anatomy of the Indian Ocean.

The Arctic Ocean. Recent Soviet work in the Arctic has revolutionised our knowledge of the polar seas. The Arctic Ocean is divided into two deep basins by a great ridge which extends from the Novo Sibirskie Islands almost across the pole to Greenland and Ellesmere Land. The ridge in places rises to within 1000 m. of the surface, has steep slopes, spurs, and saddles in which the depths are 1500–1600 metres. Some profound deeps have also been found: 5220 + metres in approximately 86° N. and 40° E.; approximately 4000 metres in 85° N. and between 160° E. and 90° W.; and another of 3820 metres to the north of the Beaufort and Chukchi Seas. The continental shelf has also been more exactly defined; to the north of the Behring Strait it almost reaches 80° N. It has been suggested by the Russians that the Ocean as we now see it is a recent formation, having been formed within the last 100,000 years. (*Izvestia Akademii Nauk.* S.S.S.R. no. 5, Sept.–Oct. 1954.)

CHAPTER II

SALINITY, TEMPERATURE, AND DENSITY. CONVERGENCES AND DIVERGENCES. WATER-MASSES

Composition of sea-water. Sea-water is always salt, but the degree of saltness is not everywhere the same. In the North Sea, for example, the percentage of salt is less than in the midst of the Atlantic; in the Baltic it is very much less. In the Mediterranean, on the other hand, the proportion of salt is considerably greater than in any part of the open ocean.

The saltness is due mainly to chloride of sodium; but other salts are also present. On the average in 1000 grams of sea-water there are 35 grams of dissolved solids; and according to Dittmar these solids are constituted as shown in Table 12.

Table 12

Sodium chloride ($NaCl$)	27·213
Magnesium chloride ($MgCl_2$)	3·807
Magnesium sulphate ($MgSO_4$)	1·658
Calcium sulphate ($CaSO_4$)	1·260
Potassium sulphate (K_2SO_4)	0·863
Calcium carbonate ($CaCO_3$)	0·123
Magnesium bromide ($MgBr_2$)	0·076
	35·000

It is known now, however, that in a solution such salts will to a large extent be dissociated into their separate constituents. But the analyses imply that if a mixture of the salts in the proportions indicated were dissolved in the proper amount of water, the solution would be similar in composition to sea-water.

Besides the salts mentioned in the table many other substances are also found, but in such minute quantities that for most purposes they may be disregarded.

Although the total amount of dissolved solids in 1000 grams of sea-water varies in different parts of the ocean, the proportion of the different constituents to one another remains almost unaltered. If, for instance, the amount of sodium chloride is less than 27·213 then all the other constituents will be reduced in the same proportion.

The degree of salinity is usually expressed in parts per thousand. Thus the average salinity as given above is said to be 35 or, as it is often written, 35‰.

Specific gravity. The density or specific gravity of sea-water depends partly on its salinity and partly on its temperature. At freezing-point water of the average composition given above, with a salinity of 35, has a specific gravity of 1·028. But as the temperature rises the water expands and the density decreases; and it is quite possible for water of low salinity and low temperature to be denser than water of high salinity and high temperature.

Origin of salt in the sea. The salt in the sea is no doubt derived in part from rivers. River-water always holds a certain amount of material in solution and most of this is carried into the sea. It is estimated that each year the rivers contribute a tiny fraction, $5{\cdot}4 \times 10^{-8}$, of the total dissolved solids in the ocean.

If this were the way in which the sea originally became salt, sea-water would be only a concentrated river-water. But it is by no means clear that the whole of the salt has come from rivers. There is a considerable difference between the salts in sea-water and those in average river-water. In the former by far the greater part consists of chlorides, especially chloride of sodium; in the latter the most abundant compounds are carbonates, especially carbonate of lime (calcium). Considering the very subordinate part played in sea-water by carbonate of lime, it appears at first sight improbable that sea-water could be produced by any concentration of the water of existing rivers. But this objection is not decisive. A very large number of animals which live in the sea, such as molluscs, corals, etc., form their shells or skeletons of carbonate of lime which they abstract from the water. Therefore the carbonate of lime brought into the sea is continually being used up, while the sodium chloride is left behind.

Possibly the difference in the relative abundance of carbonates and chlorides in sea- and river-water may be accounted for in this way; but there are other differences also. In the water of rivers, to judge from actual analyses, the sulphates exceed the chlorides and the proportion of potassium to sodium is very much greater than in the water of the sea.

The composition of river-water, however, varies greatly; and most of the rivers of the world have not yet been chemically examined. The analyses which have been made certainly suggest either that the salts of the sea have not been derived entirely from rivers or that in past times the composition of river-water must have been very different. But until a much larger series of analyses is available, from rivers in all parts of the globe, it is unsafe to assume that the average composition of river-water is even approximately known.

Distribution of salinity. The variations in the salinity of the surface waters of the ocean are due mainly to three causes. They depend upon the supply of fresh water and upon the rapidity of evaporation, and upon changes due to mixing. The influence of these causes is clearly shown in the map of the oceans, Fig. 67, in which isohalines, or lines of equal salinity, have been drawn. The map shows the salinity of the surface waters only. At a depth of 1000 fathoms, or even 100 fathoms, the isohalines would be very different.

The greatest proportion of salt is found in two areas which lie about the tropics of Cancer and Capricorn. From these regions the salinity decreases both towards the equator and towards the poles.

The high salinity at the tropics is due to the rapidity of evaporation beneath the clear skies and brilliant sun of the tropical anticyclones and the trade-wind region. The vapour which is formed is carried away by the winds and condenses elsewhere.

At the equator the heavy equatorial rains dilute the surface waters and the cloudiness of the region somewhat retards evaporation. About the mouths of the Niger and the Congo the salinity is particularly low, on account of the volume of fresh water poured out upon the surface by these rivers. Since fresh water is lighter than salt water (of the same temperature) the water of rivers may float for some time upon the sea before complete mixture takes place.

Towards the poles at certain seasons water that is almost fresh is supplied by the melting of the ice, and accordingly the salinity of the surface is low. For reasons which will be explained later this less saline water tends to flow especially along the eastern margins of the continents. As it moves towards the equator it encounters water of increasing salinity but also of increasing temperature. At first it floats upon the surface, but farther on the difference of temperature more than compensates for the difference of salinity; the cold polar water finds itself amongst water this is more saline but, on account of its high temperature, less dense than itself, and accordingly it sinks beneath.

Partially enclosed seas. Seas like the Mediterranean and the Baltic, which communicate with the ocean only by narrow straits, show much greater differences in salinity.

In the Mediterranean at the Straits of Gibralter the salinity is about 36·5, but it increases eastwards and on the Syrian coast it exceeds 39. At

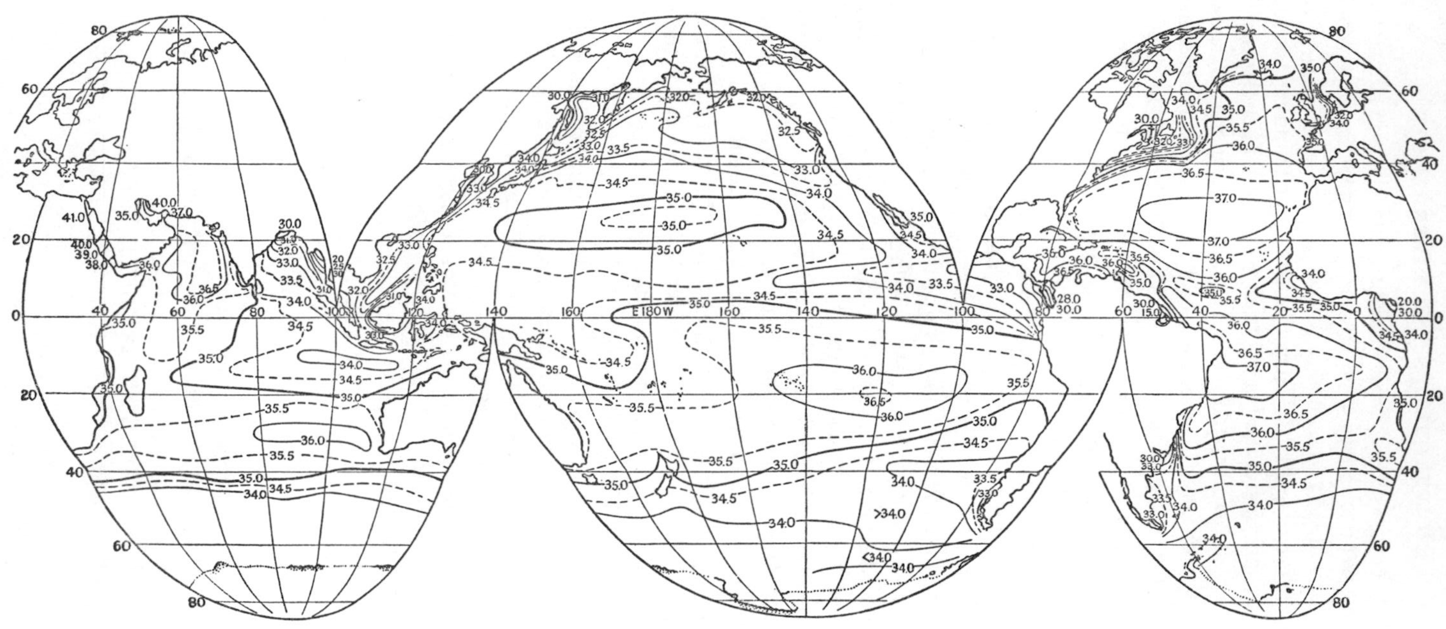

Fig. 67. Surface salinity of the oceans in northern summer.

the southern end of the Red Sea the salinity is about 36·5, but it rises towards the Gulf of Suez, where it is more than 41. These are examples of seas with a higher salinity than any part of the open ocean.

In the Black Sea, on the other hand, the surface salinity over the greater part is only 18 or 18·5, and in the Sea of Azov it is considerably less. In the Baltic the salinity at the entrance varies considerably and is influenced, among other things, by the direction of the winds and perhaps by the difference between the atmospheric pressure inside and outside the sea. With low pressure inside and high outside there is usually a current from the Baltic, which is then higher. The converse also is true. About the island of Rügen the salinity is only 7 or 8, and it decreases northwards. At the heads of the Gulfs of Bothnia and Finland it is often less than 2, and in spring the water is practically fresh.

The salinity of these seas, like that of the open ocean itself, depends upon the relation between the supply of fresh water and the loss by evaporation which does not remove the salts.

In the Mediterranean and the Red Sea the evaporation is great and the rainfall small. The Red Sea is practically without rivers. The Mediterranean receives the waters of the Rhone, the Po and other rivers, but the total amount is small compared with the area of the sea.

In the Black Sea evaporation is less than in the Mediterranean, and many large rivers such as the Danube, the Dniester, the Dnieper, and the Don bring a much larger supply of fresh water in proportion to the size of the sea.

In the Baltic also, which lies in a colder region, evaporation is comparatively slow. A large amount of fresh water is received from the numerous rivers of Sweden and northern Russia, especially during the melting of the snow in spring and early summer.

Inland seas and lakes. In a lake which has an outlet there is no tendency for the water to be more saline than that of the rivers which flow into it, for the salt which they bring is carried away by the river that flows out. Absence of an outlet implies that evaporation is at least equal to the supply, for otherwise the depression would fill up until the water overflowed. In such cases there is no escape for the salts brought in by the rivers which enter the lake, and the water must gradually grow more and more saline. The degree of salinity will depend in part upon the length of time that the lake has existed without an outlet.

Even in the same lake, however, there may be considerable variations. In the northern part of the Caspian the salinity is less than 14, while in the shallow Gulf of Karabugas, which is connected with the rest of the Caspian only by a narrow and shallow opening, the salinity reaches 170.

In this gulf evaporation is rapid and there is a constant inward stream of water from the Caspian to make up for the loss.

The Dead Sea is the saltest of the larger lakes, the salinity reaching 237·5, but even this is exceeded by some of the smaller lakes in the dry regions of the globe.

In most of these inland seas and lakes the composition of the dissolved salts is not the same as in ordinary sea-water. Sodium chloride is usually, though not always, abundant; but other constituents play a more important part than in the oceans.

Temperature of the surface layers. The factors controlling sea surface temperatures are more complex than those for salinity. Table 13 gives average figures for the temperatures of the surface water in different latitudes of the northern and southern hemispheres. It will be seen that everywhere temperatures are highest a little to the north of the equator, a fact probably related to the atmospheric circulation. This 'oceanic' thermal equator, like its 'atmospheric' relation, shifts with the season, but only locally transgresses into the southern hemisphere. The table also shows that latitude for latitude temperatures are higher in the northern hemisphere; this is probably due to the more efficient circulation of water between the temperate and polar regions in the southern hemisphere; in the northern hemisphere such movements are restricted by the narrowness of the communicating channels and by submarine ridges.

Table 13

North latitude (degrees)	Atlantic Ocean	Indian Ocean	Pacific Ocean	South latitude (degrees)	Atlantic Ocean	Indian Ocean	Pacific Ocean
70–60	5·60	—	—	70–60	−1·30	−1·50	−1·30
60–50	8·66	—	5·74	60–50	1·76	1·63	5·00
50–40	13·16	—	9·99	50–40	8·68	8·67	11·16
40–30	20·40	—	18·62	40–30	16·90	17·00	16·98
30–20	24·16	26·14	23·38	30–20	21·20	22·53	21·53
20–10	25·81	27·23	26·42	20–10	23·16	25·85	25·11
10– 0	26·66	27·88	27·20	10– 0	25·18	27·41	26·01

(Temperatures in degrees Centigrade)

There is also a considerable annual variation in surface temperature which is controlled by the varying radiation received during the year, by the nature of the ocean currents, and also by the wind. Naturally the variation will differ greatly with locality. For example, the annual temperature range is greater in the North Atlantic and North Pacific than it is in the southern oceans. This is mainly because in winter cold winds often blow from the interior of continents to the oceans, and so lower winter temperatures.

A little below the surface there are four important factors which govern the variation of temperature: (1) the quantity of heat absorbed, (2) conduction effects, (3) changes due to currents associated with the horizontal movement of water masses, and (4) vertical motion and its effects. The time has not yet come when this matter can be treated generally, but investigations in Monterey Bay, California, indicate that the variations throughout the year are due to changes in currents, to upwelling, to conduction of heat, and to the seasonal variation of atmospheric temperature. On the other hand, observations made in the Kuroshio, south of Japan, suggest that heating and cooling of the surface are transmitted downwards by conduction, so causing a subsurface variation.

There is also a daily variation of surface-water temperatures which will vary with locality and season, but is primarily caused by the amount of cloudiness and velocity of the wind. As on the land, clear anticyclonic conditions favour a greater range, and strong winds cause a good deal of mixing of the surface layers, thus evening out the temperature and reducing the range. For the subsurface layers we have very little information. In general it may be assumed that the stratification of the water will control the depth to which diurnal variation takes place. The *Meteor* expedition found in some tropical stations that the variation at 50 metres was $<2/10$ that of the surface, and that the maximum was about $6\frac{1}{2}$ hours later. These observations were made where the homogeneous surface layer was some 70 metres thick.

Temperature and salinity govern the density of sea-water, and clearly any processes which alter these two factors also alter the density. Generally, increase of temperature, rainfall and other forms of precipitation, river-water, and melting ice all decrease density, whereas decrease of temperature and evaporation increase it. If the surface density becomes greater than that of the water beneath, vertical currents will arise, which under favourable circumstances, may penetrate to the ocean floor. On the other hand, as will appear later, the downward penetration may be much less, and the heavier water will then spread out horizontally at some intermediate level.

Within the tropics the temperature of the surface waters is always high, and even in the areas of high salinities the densities still remain low. In consequence the convection currents do not descend very far, and (see p. 185) only a shallow layer is involved. In higher latitudes where temperatures are less and for this reason densities increase, precipitation is often copious and so prevents very deeply descending currents. Because of these factors the water that actually reaches the deeps of the oceans is formed only in two ways: first by water of high salinity which, after having been carried polewards by currents, is cooled and so sinks, and secondly, by the freezing of highly saline water. The north-eastward flowing waters of the Gulf Stream Drift illustrate the first process very well, because as a result of their saltness, and because they mix with the cold polar water, sink down to the bottom. The second process obtains around the Antarctic continent where locally the precipitation is low, and the winter freezing produces water of high density which slides down the continental slope to the bottom of the ocean. Whilst sinking this water mixes with other water of rather higher temperature and salinity, and hence finally attains a temperature slightly above freezing-point. It is because the deep oceanic waters are produced in these ways that they are so cold.

Convergences and divergences. In considering oceanic circulation, in its widest application, convergences are of the utmost importance. A convergence will take place at the meeting of two converging currents, and necessarily there will also be a sinking of water. The Antarctic convergence is the most marked (see fig. 68). Water of fairly low salinity but low temperature sinks there because its density is relatively high. This is the origin of the Antarctic intermediate water which travels horizontally over the deep water at depths between 800 and 1200 metres. Largely on account of the different configuration of the North Atlantic, there is no very marked Arctic convergence, but it is better developed in the North Pacific. There is a second important convergence, the sub-tropical convergence, between sub-Antarctic and sub-tropical waters, and possibly a third, not well defined, between sub-tropical and tropical waters. Both seem to be more variable in position than the Antarctic convergence. Since the sub-tropical convergence is situated in latitudes where the temperature and salinity are decreasing rapidly polewards it is often marked by very large differences in both temperature and salinity. The tropical convergence is of a more fragmentary nature. Both occur in areas where converging currents are present.

It is obvious that to counterbalance water that has sunk at the convergences there must be rising water ascending in areas of diverging currents (divergences). These divergences are not so regular in their occurrence as the convergences, but the effect is seen most clearly in the upwelling that takes place on the west coasts of continents. This is largely the result of offshore winds, and the rising water is of greater density and lower temperature than that which it replaces. There is also some upwelling of deep water around Antarctica, but especially off that sector facing the Atlantic Ocean.

Before leaving this matter, it is important to note that where, as through the Straits of Gibraltar, dense water spills over a sill from a neighbouring sea, it may add considerably to an intermediate layer of like density in the open ocean.

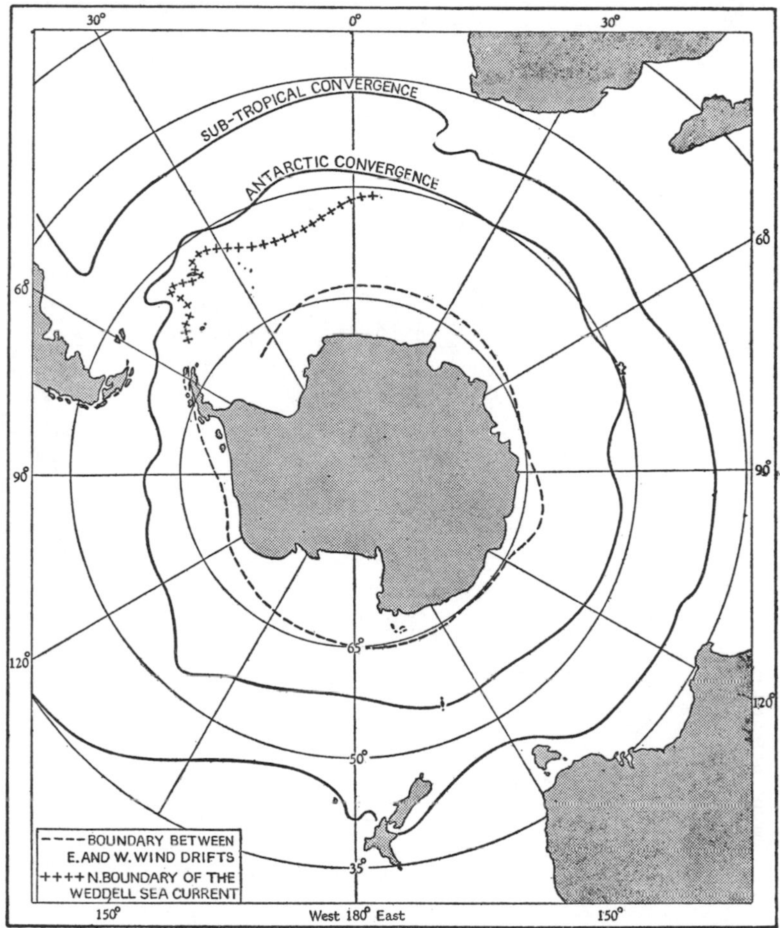

Fig. 68. The Antarctic and sub-tropical convergences.

Water-masses. It will now be clear that in any vertical column taken through the open oceans water of different densities and different origins will be encountered. These various types of water had their origin somewhere or another at the surface, descended at a convergence, and later travelled horizontally at different depths. How these general conditions are modified in the actual oceans is yet to be discussed.

On the whole there is a fairly close relationship between the distribution of temperature and salinity. In colder areas the temperature is low from top to bottom, and the cold waters that sink in those areas carry low temperatures far from their place of origin. In warm temperate and tropical areas there is a warmer surface layer of no great thickness: it is

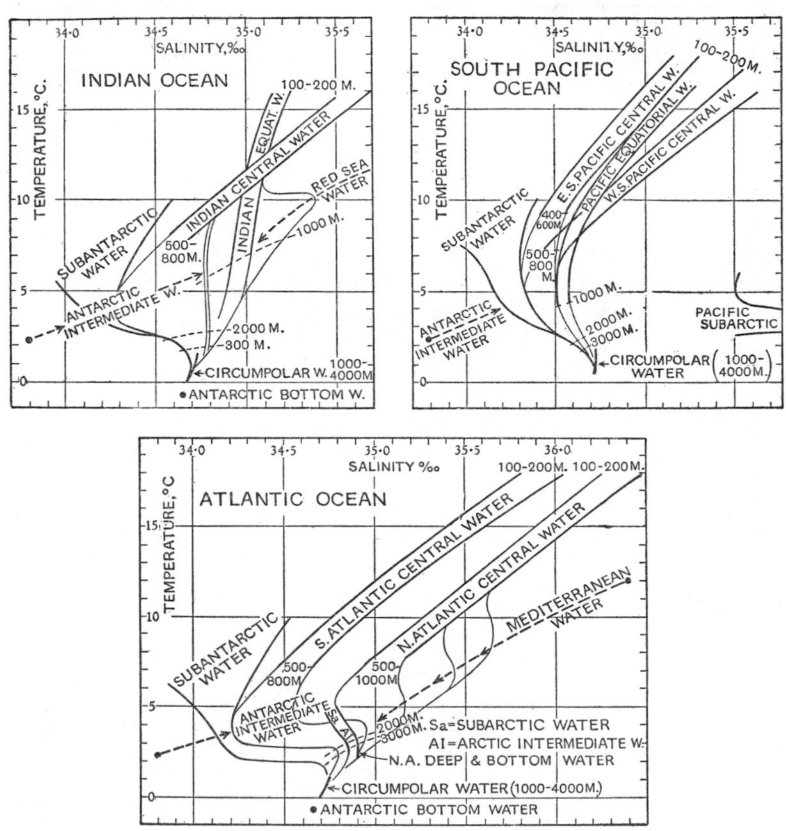

Fig. 69. Temperature-salinity relations of oceanic water-masses.

separated by a marked discontinuity layer from the cold and deep water below. This separation has given rise to an analogy with the atmosphere. Defant has called the upper and warmer layers of the hotter parts of the world the troposphere; the stratosphere includes the vast mass of cold and deep water reaching to the bottom of the oceans. Whilst the distinction between troposphere and stratosphere is of some use, it must not be pushed too far and the comparison with the atmosphere is by no means complete.

In modern oceanography it is easy to classify masses of water if we know their salinity and temperature characteristics. Since various combinations of these two factors will give similar densities, it is important to realise that density by itself is insufficient as a basis of differentiation. Helland-Hansen first drew attention to this matter and introduced a temperature-salinity (*T-S*) diagram (fig. 69). Strictly this cannot include the actual surface water because variations of one sort or another are there too serious. However, if, in any part of the ocean, subsurface salinities and temperatures are plotted on a graph, it is found that the points usually conform fairly closely to a curve—the *T-S* curve. These values of salinity and temperature vary with depth, so that if also the depths of the observations are shown on the curves, we have a clear indication of the temperature-salinity conditions at any depth. The resulting curves may be simple, almost straight lines, or complex. The differences are the result of mixing of two or more bodies of water of unlike characteristics. It must, however, be remembered that *originally* the water bodies obtained their individuality when in contact with the atmosphere.

This conception of water-masses is extremely important in modern oceanographic work. It will, therefore, be convenient first of all to call attention to the main characteristics and places of origin of the more significant of these masses (see fig. 70). The Antarctic bottom water originates near Antarctica, especially in the Weddell Sea: on the continental shelf it has a salinity of *c.* 34·62‰ and a temperature of *c.* −1·9° C. Because it is denser than the circumpolar waters it sinks and to some extent mixes with these waters so that finally the Antarctic bottom water has a salinity of *c.* 34·66‰ and a temperature of *c.* −0·4° C. Other slight modifications take place as it spreads northwards on the ocean floor.

In the North Atlantic *deep* and *bottom* water have their origin in the Labrador Sea and between Iceland and Greenland. There is some variation in the *T-S* characteristics from year to year because a good deal of mixing takes place owing to juxtaposition of surface currents. The water sinking to more than 1000 metres has a temperature between 2·8 and 3·3° C. and a salinity from 34·90 to 34·96‰.

The Antarctic convergence is the sinking place of the Antarctic intermediate water: the descending water has a salinity of *c.* 33·8‰, and a temperature of *c.* 2·2° C. There is some further mixing with adjacent water after sinking has taken place. In the North Atlantic the corresponding intermediate water sinks at a less marked convergence in the Labrador Sea. In the North Pacific intermediate water is formed in the

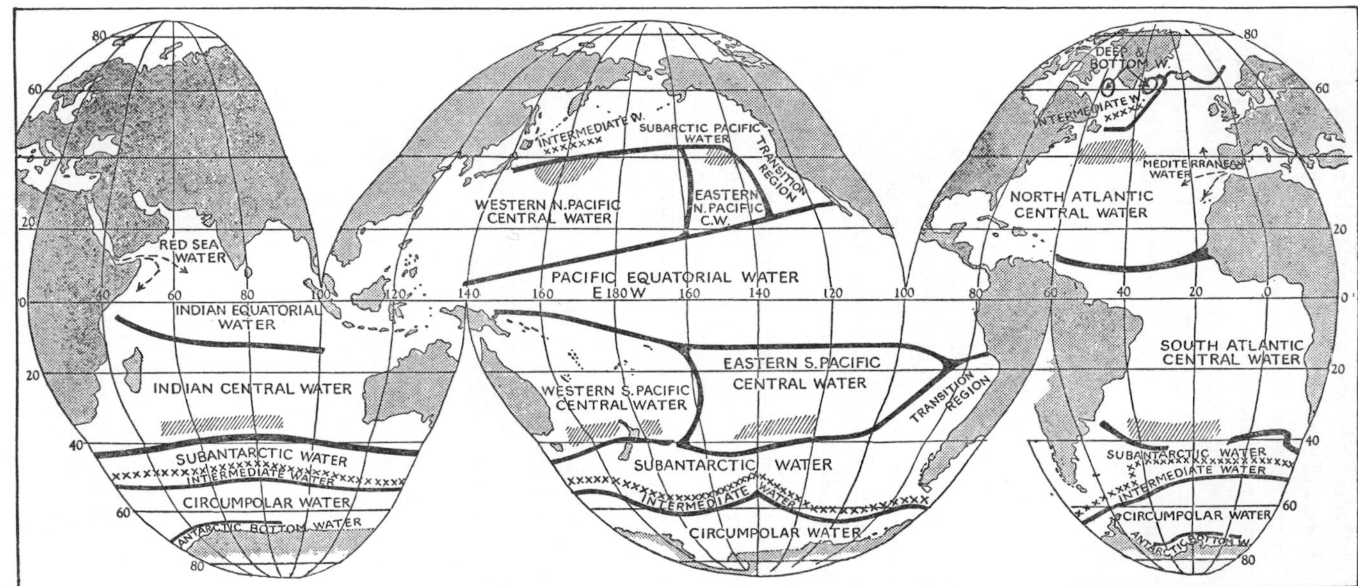

Fig. 70. Approximate boundaries of the upper water-masses of the oceans. Shaded areas indicate the regions in which the central water-masses are formed, and crosses show the lines along which the Antarctic and Arctic intermediate waters sink.

north-eastern part of that ocean round about the parallel of 40° N., but in spreading this water is considerably adulterated, and so loses a good deal of its original nature.

Sinking also takes place at the sub-tropical convergences between 35 and 40° N. and S. of the equator. These are far less well defined than the convergences nearer the poles. Clearly in these areas temperature and salinity both decrease with increase of latitude, and so density increases in the same direction. It is in these places that the central water-masses of the different oceans are formed.

Some oceans also receive a considerable amount of water from adjacent seas. The denser deep water of the Mediterranean (13·0–13·6° C.; 38·4–38·7‰) flows out over the Gibraltar sill and spreads over large areas beneath the Antarctic intermediate water. There is a similar efflux through the Straits of Bab-el-Mandeb: Red Sea water (21·5–22° C.; 40·5–41‰) spreads in the Indian Ocean but to a far less extent.

Subsurface mixing also accounts for certain water masses. The Antarctic circumpolar water mass is really a mixture of, first Atlantic deep water and Antarctic bottom water, and secondly very little Mediterranean water and some Antarctic intermediate water. The sub-Antarctic water lies between the Antarctic and southern sub-tropical convergences and is transitional in type. The sub-Arctic water masses are somewhat similar, and due to mixing, winter cooling and heavy rainfall. These north and south masses in the Pacific Ocean work towards the equator off the American coasts and in doing so suffer changes due to evaporation and increase of temperature. In the Pacific and Indian Oceans there are also equatorial water masses: there is no corresponding feature in the Atlantic.

In general there is some similarity between the oceans, but the Atlantic and Pacific also show marked differences—a point that can be appreciated if fig. 70 is studied. All the central water-masses are thin, the greatest thickness being only 900 metres in the Sargasso Sea. In the Pacific 200–300 metres covers them. These, together with the equatorial water-masses, are covered by a layer 100–200 metres thick in which *T-S* characteristics vary much from place to place. This surface layer, the whole of the central water-masses, and the *upper* parts of the equatorial water-masses form the troposphere (see p. 152). It will be appreciated that the various types of water around the Antarctic continent tend to maintain their peculiar characteristics round the world; on the other hand, the much more local origin of the corresponding northern waters introduces marked differences.

CHAPTER III

WAVES AND TIDES

Movements of the ocean. The water of the ocean is never still. It is blown into waves by the wind, it rises and falls with the tides, and in many places there are definite currents either permanently in one direction or changing with the tide or with the season.

WAVES

When water is thrown into waves its surface takes the form shown, in section, in fig. 71.[1] The waves travel in some definite direction, but a cork thrown into the water does not travel with the waves. It moves up

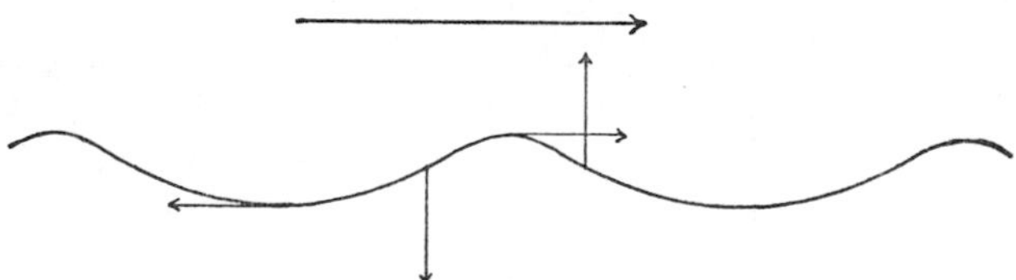

Fig. 71. Profile of ordinary waves. The long arrow shows the direction of movement of the waves; the short arrows show the direction of movement of particles at different points of the wave.

and down, to and fro, but unless it is blown by the wind or carried by a current it returns to the same position with each wave and does not permanently leave its place. The cork must move with the water on which it floats, and thus it is clear that although the wave travels forward the particles of water do not.

The highest part of the wave is called the crest, the lowest the trough; the distance from crest to crest, or from trough to trough, is called the length of the wave and the vertical height of the crest above the trough is the height or amplitude.

In *deep* water the motion of the particles is circular at all depths. At the crest the movement of the particles is forward, at the middle of the hinder slope it is downward, in the trough backward, and at the middle of the front slope upward.

The wave is felt beneath the surface, but in shallow water the amount

[1] The profile of an ordinary wave in water is approximately a trochoid. It is similar to the curve traced by a marked point on a carriage-wheel when the carriage travels in a straight line on a level road, but compared with this curve it is inverted in position.

of movement diminishes rapidly downwards. The up and down movement decreases more quickly than the movement to and fro and thus beneath the surface the motion of the particles becomes elliptical. At a depth equal to the length of the wave the extent of the movement is only about $\frac{1}{500}$th of the extent at the surface. Consequently, waves have very little effect excepting near the surface, and even in the stormiest seas the disturbance is confined to a shallow layer of the water.

Our natural impressions of the height of waves are greatly exaggerated. When a wave dashes against a cliff the water may be thrown up 100 or 200 feet or even more; but it is no longer part of the wave. On board ship an approaching wave seems higher than it is, because the ship is on the slope of the preceding wave and is heeling towards the one that is approaching. The highest wave actually measured by Scoresby was 43½ feet, and it is probable that in the open ocean the height of waves formed by the wind seldom exceeds 50 feet.

Speed of waves. The speed of waves depends partly upon their length and partly upon the depth of the water.

When the water is shallow relatively to the length of the wave, the velocity depends on the depth alone and is proportional to the square root of the depth.

When, on the other hand, the water is deep relatively to the length of the wave, the velocity depends on the length alone and is proportional to the square root of the length.

If the water is neither shallow nor deep, relatively to the length of the wave, the velocity is affected both by the depth and the length. Roughly speaking, we may say that if the depth of the water is greater than half the length of the wave the velocity depends chiefly on the length; if the depth of the water is less than half the length of the wave, the velocity depends chiefly on the depth.

Consequently, in the open ocean the speed of a wind-wave depends upon its length, but on a shelving shore it depends upon the depth of the water.

It is for this reason that on a sandy beach the crests of the waves are nearly parallel to the shore whatever the direction of the wind may be.

On such a shore the depth of the water gradually increases outwards. In the open sea the crests of the waves are at right angles to the wind, as shown by the lines *AB*, *CD* (fig. 72). But as they approach the coast the end *E* of the wave *CDE* will be in shallow water before the end *C*, and will accordingly travel more slowly. Consequently, the wave gradually turns until its crest is nearly parallel to the shore.[1]

[1] The important effect of waves breaking obliquely on the beach on the movement of beach material is discussed on p. 253.

If the coast is steep and the water is deep to the foot of the cliffs, the waves will not be retarded as they approach and will keep their original direction.

Breaking of waves. When a wave approaches a shelving shore it keeps its form as a wave until it is near the land and then the top falls forward and the wave breaks. This, like the turning of the wave, is due in part to the fact that the wave travels more slowly as the water becomes shallower. The front of the wave is in shallower water than the back and therefore moves more slowly. The back gains upon it and the front

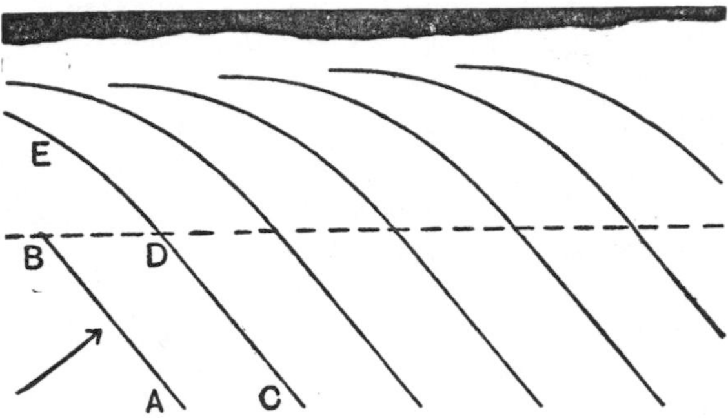

Fig. 72. Waves approaching a shelving shore. The arrow indicates the direction of the wind. The broken line marks the position where the water becomes shallow enough to affect the speed of the waves.

becomes steeper, until in fact the crest is practically unsupported in front, and then, because of the forward movement of the particles at the top of the wave, the crest falls forward.[1]

When the water is deep close up to the shore, the waves, if they break at all, break in a different fashion. They appear to throw themselves against the cliff and the water dashes up the face of the cliff, sometimes to a very great height.

TIDES

From the earliest times it has no doubt been known to dwellers on the coasts of tidal seas that there is some connection between the tides and the moon. The tides are highest when the moon is either new or full, and at full moon the interval between the time of high tide and the time when the moon is on the meridian is approximately constant for each locality. But the interval is not everywhere the same. In some places it is one hour, in others two and so on, and, moreover, even at the same place it varies to some extent. It is easy, therefore, to see that there is

[1] Compare p. 252/3: the two views differ because the matter is not fully resolved.

some connection between the tides and the moon, but it is not easy to see what that connection is.

The cause of the connection was not understood until the time of Newton. Gravitation is a mutual attraction which exists between all particles of matter in the universe. The earth attracts the moon and the moon attracts the earth. The moon attracts every particle of matter in the earth. The amount of the attraction varies inversely as the square of the distance, and the moon, therefore, attracts the part of the earth, which is nearest to it more strongly than the parts which are farthest away.

The equilibrium theory. The diameter of the earth is about 8000 miles. Consequently, the side of the earth facing the moon is 4000 miles nearer to the moon than the centre, and 8000 miles nearer than the opposite side. The moon, therefore, attracts the near side of the earth more strongly than it attracts the centre, and the far side less strongly.

Let us assume for the moment that the earth is surrounded by the liquid ocean, and that the waters yield and are heaped up beneath the moon. On the other side the attraction is less than at the centre and the waters being less attracted than the solid earth bulge outwards on the side away from the moon.

There is a difficulty in appreciating this explanation of the bulge upon the side opposite to the moon. The earth does not approach the moon and, therefore, we naturally look upon it as fixed in position with regard to the moon, and we imagine the moon as revolving round it. If this were so it would mean that the solid earth did not yield at all to the attraction of the moon. In that case there would be a bulging of the waters on the side facing the moon but none on the opposite side.

But, apart from its revolution round the sun, the earth is not fixed in position and it yields to the attraction of the moon. The moon does not revolve around the earth, but both earth and moon revolve around their common centre of gravity. Owing to the much greater mass of the earth this common centre is situated about 1000 miles beneath the surface of the earth. The relative positions of the earth and moon at different stages in a complete revolution are shown in fig. 73, in which the common centre of gravity, *G*, is a fixed point, which does not alter its position. When the moon is at *a* the earth is at *A*; when the moon is at *b* the earth is at *B*; and when the moon is at *c*, the earth is at *C*. In this diagram, if the mutual attraction were suddenly to cease, the earth and moon would fly off in the direction of the arrows (i.e. the direction in which they were actually moving at the time) and would separate from one another. But their mutual attraction draws them together, with the result that they do not separate but revolve around the centre *G*. Thus although they do not actually approach one another they are continually yielding to each other's attraction and do not follow the course which they would otherwise take. When it is once clearly understood that the earth is yielding to the attraction of the moon it is easy to see that the solid earth will yield more than the water which is on the side away from the moon, and, therefore, on that side the waters will bulge outwards, as well as on the side facing the moon.

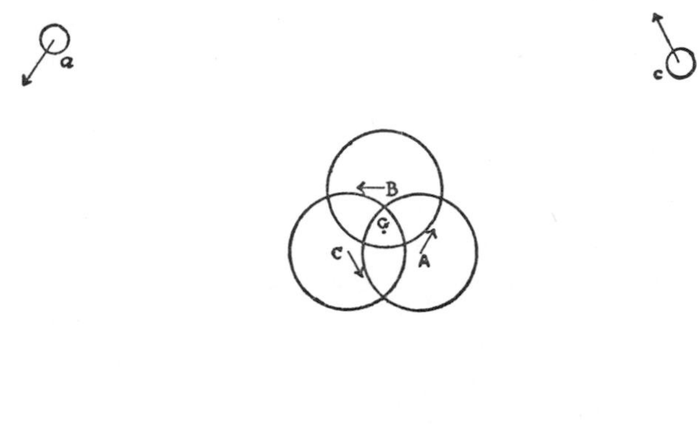

Fig. 73. Relative movements of the earth and the moon.

We may also look at the question in a slightly different way. Take a lath or a strip of thick cardboard and fix it to a blackboard by means of a drawing pin *G*, round which it is free to turn (fig. 74). The pin should be much nearer to one end than to the other. At the end of the longer arm fasten a small card disc to represent the moon. Take a larger disc to represent the earth and by means of a drawing-pin through its centre fix it to the shorter arm of the lath in such a way that its edge overlaps the pin *G*. The disc representing the earth should be free to turn round the drawing-pin through its own centre.

Such a model as this will show very well the relative movements of the earth and the moon. The common centre of gravity is represented by the pin *G*, round which both discs can revolve; and the disc representing the earth can rotate about its own centre.[1]

[1] This illustration must not be pushed too far. Since the moon's orbit is elliptical (see p. 166) the lath joining earth and moon must be allowed a fair amount of elasticity!

It is important to remember that although the earth *revolves* around the common centre of gravity it does not *rotate* about that point. Its rotation is round its own axis, and has nothing to do with the revolution round *G*, or with the production of the tides. If, therefore, we wish to consider the effect of the movement of the earth round the common centre of gravity we must put aside its rotation round its own axis and make it move round *G* without rotating. To assist in doing this it is well

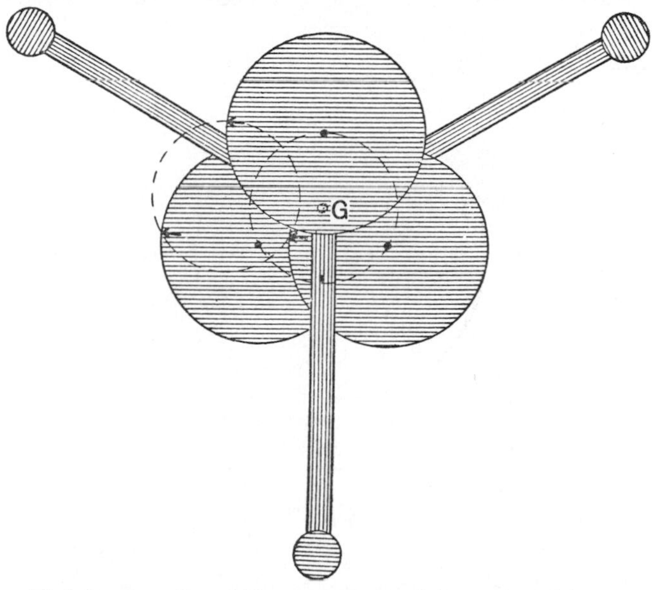

Fig. 74. Model to show the relative movements of the earth and the moon. The model is shown in three positions of a complete revolution. The broken circles are the circles described by the centre of the large disc and by the point of the arrow marked upon its edge, when the large disc is not allowed to rotate on its own axis.

to draw an arrow at the edge of the disc representing the earth and to remember that this arrow must always point in the same direction.

Take hold of the large disk, and without allowing it to turn on its own axis, make it move round the pin *G*. The lath will swing round and the smaller disc with it; and the movements of the two discs will be similar to those of the earth and the moon.

Next, while doing this, hold a piece of chalk against the edge of the large disc in such a way as to touch the board. As we make the revolution the chalk will draw a circle.

Repeat the experiment with the chalk at other points on the edge of the larger disc, or passed through a hole in the disc. It will be found that it always draws a circle, and that all these circles are equal in size and are described in the same direction; but they are round different centres. Moreover, if two chalks are used at the same time it will be found that they are always at corresponding positions in their circles at the same moment.

Thus, putting aside its rotation round its own axis, every part of the earth during a lunar month describes a circle, and all these circles are of the same size and are described in the same direction. In every part, therefore, centrifugal force is developed and it is everywhere of the same amount. Moreover, since all parts of the earth are at corresponding

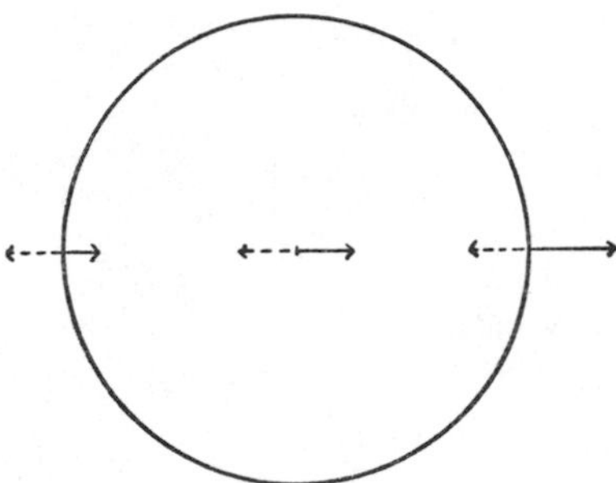

Fig. 75. Tide-producing force of the moon. The moon is supposed to lie to the right of the diagram. The solid arrows represent the attractive force of the moon; the dotted arrows represent the centrifugal force.

points of their circles at the same time the centrifugal force is everywhere in the same direction. At the centre of the earth, which describes its circle round the point *G*, it is easy to see that the centrifugal force is directed away from the moon; and everywhere else it will be parallel.

Accordingly at all points of the earth there are two forces—an attractive force directed towards the moon and a centrifugal force directed away from the moon. The latter is everywhere the same, but the former is greatest on the side facing the moon.

Since the earth and moon neither approach nor recede from each other, it is evident that at the centre of the earth the centrifugal force is just equal to the attractive force. On the side nearest the moon the attractive force is greater than at the centre, and is therefore greater than the centrifugal force; and there is accordingly a surplus force pulling the waters towards the moon. On the side farthest from the moon the attractive force is less than at the centre, and is therefore less than the centrifugal force; and there is a surplus force directed from the moon. Thus the bulging of the water beneath the moon is due to the excess of the attractive force above the centrifugal force, the bulging on the other side is due to the excess of the centrifugal force above the attractive force (fig. 75).

In this way, according to the equilibrium theory, the moon causes the water to be drawn towards the part of the earth facing it and also towards the opposite side, and thus produces high tide (fig. 76). But the water has been drawn *away* from the other parts of the earth, and about half-way between the two high tides the sea is below its normal level and there is low tide. As the earth rotates on its axis every meridian comes in turn beneath each of the high tides and each of the low tides, and accordingly there are in most places two high tides and two low tides in the day.

It must not be supposed that this explanation means that when the moon is over a given place, it pulls the water away from the earth, where-as on the opposite side of the earth it pulls the earth away from the water. To begin with, high water does not occur when the moon is directly

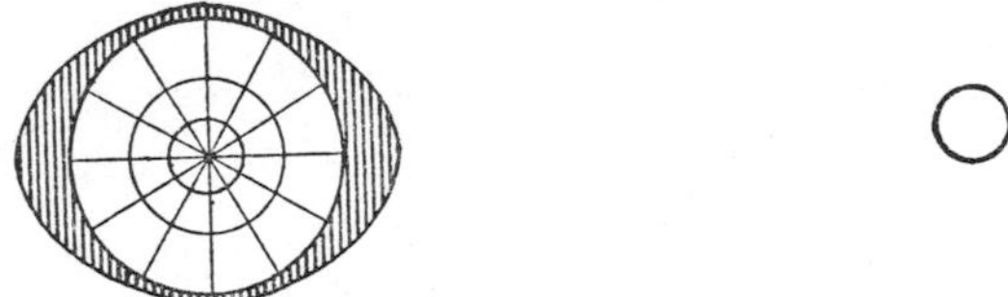

Fig. 76. Tidal effect of the moon.

overhead: it may occur any time before or after the moon's meridian passage. Secondly, when the moon is directly overhead it could only pull the water away from the earth if its pull were greater than that of the earth—and this is evidently not the case. The correct explanation of this apparent contradiction is that between P_4 and P_1 and P_2 and P_1 there is a horizontal component of the moon's attraction. It is this that sets the water in motion and causes the bulge. A similar effect occurs between P_4 and P_3 and between P_2 and P_3, causing the bulge at P_3, where the force is again vertical (fig. 78).

But while the earth is rotating on its own axis the moon is moving in the same direction round the centre of gravity of the earth and moon. Consequently, after the earth has made a complete rotation it has still to turn a little farther before it brings the same meridian again beneath the moon (fig. 77). Therefore high tide each day is later than it was the day before. The difference is roughly about fifty minutes, but it is sometimes more and sometimes less.

So far it has been assumed that the sun, earth, and moon are in, or nearly in, one plane. With respect to the earth's equator, however, both sun and moon appear to move north and south. The sun is to the north in the summer, to the south in winter: the moon crosses the equator twice a lunar month. The varying distance of these bodies from the equator is called declination. When the moon is at or near maximum declination the tides are no longer symmetrical about the equator, and relative to a given parallel of latitude there will be one high water higher than usual and one lower. When the moon is at zero declination the tides will once again be symmetrical about the equator (see fig. 78).

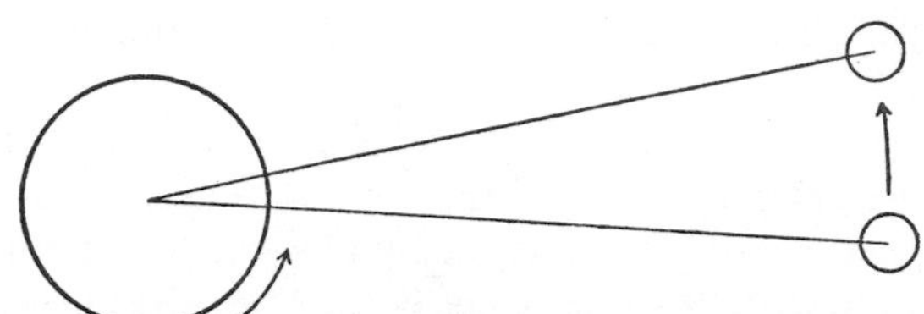

Fig. 77. The daily change in the time of high tide.

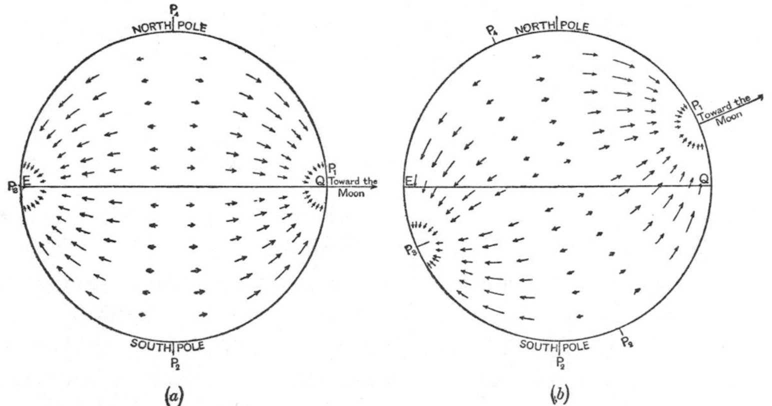

Fig. 78. Distribution of tidal forces. Moon (*a*) on equator, and (*b*) north of equator.

Effect of the sun's attraction. The moon is not the only heavenly body that draws the waters of the ocean towards it. The sun also produces a very distinct effect. But although the attraction exerted by the sun is far greater than that of the moon its influence upon the tides is less. For the tides are not determined by the amount of the attractive force, but by the *difference* in the attraction at the centre of the earth on the one hand and at the near side and the far side of the earth on the other hand. The centre of the moon is about 240,000 miles from the centre of the earth, or 236,000 miles from the nearer side. Its attractive force on the near side is to its attractive force at the centre in the proportion of $240{,}000^2$ to $236{,}000^2$, or nearly 31 to 30. The difference, which is the tide-producing force, is one-thirtieth of the force exerted by the moon at the centre of the earth.

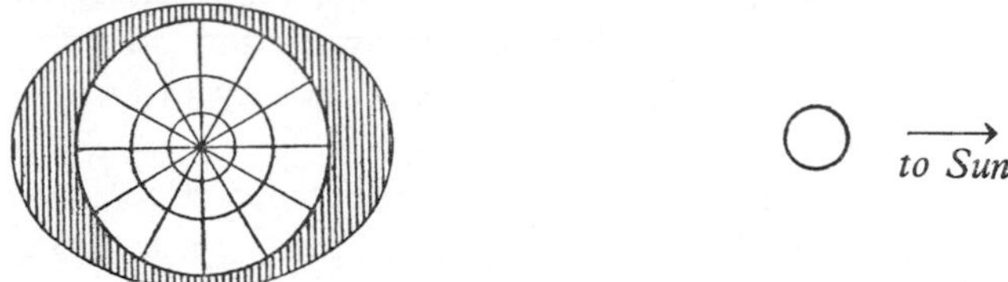

Fig. 79 (*a*). Spring tides (at new moon).

The distance of the sun is about 93,000,000 miles, and its attractive force on the nearer side of the earth is to its attractive force at the centre in the proportion of $93{,}000{,}000^2$ to $92{,}996{,}000^2$ or about 1,000,086 to 1,000,000. The difference, or tide-producing force is, $\frac{86}{1{,}000{,}000}$ of the attractive force of the *sun* at the centre of the earth. The mass of the sun is about 25,500,000 times that of the moon, but owing to its much greater distance its attractive force at the centre of the earth is only about 169 times that of the moon. Its tide-producing force is accordingly $\frac{86 \times 169}{1{,}000{,}000}$ of the attractive force of the *moon* at the centre of the earth. It will be found that this is about four-ninths of the tide-producing force of the moon, as given in the preceding paragraph.

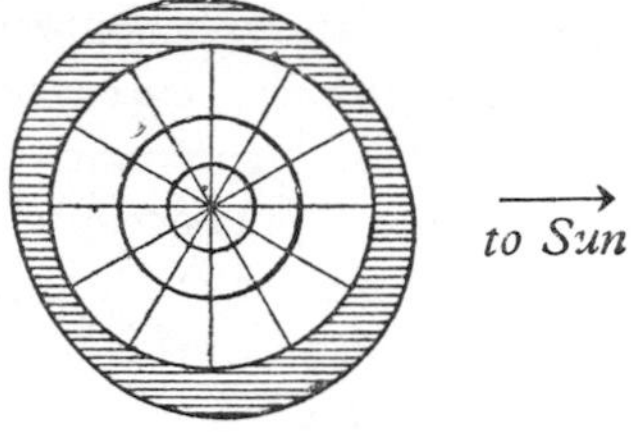

Fig. 79 (*b*). Neap tides.

In fact, the *tide-raising* force of a heavenly body varies as the inverse cube, and not as the inverse square of the distance from the earth.

Thus the tides are caused chiefly by the moon, but the sun has sufficient effect to modify them.

Spring and neap tides. When the earth, the sun and the moon are almost in the same straight line, which is nearly the case at full moon and at new moon, the tide-producing force due to the sun is nearly coincident with that due to the moon. The tides are, therefore, greater than usual, the high tide is higher and the low tide lower, and they are known as spring tides.

When, however, the moon as seen from the earth, is 90° from the sun, as it is at the half-moons, the tide-producing forces of the sun and moon are acting at right angles to one another, and consequently there is a smaller difference than usual between high water and low water. High tide is lower and low tide higher than usual, and they are known as neap tides.

There is another factor which should be borne in mind. The moon's orbit is elliptical so it follows that at times the moon is nearer to the earth than at others. When the distance is at a minimum the moon is said to be in perigee, and when at a maximum in apogee. Since the tide-producing force varies inversely as the cube of the distance, tides are some 20 per cent above average when the moon is in perigee and about the same amount below when in apogee.

There are longer-period variations, including the times when the earth is in perihelion and aphelion, but these need not concern this discussion.

The progressive wave theory: influence of the continental masses. From the preceding account it might be inferred that at each place high tide should occur when the moon is on the meridian; and all places in the same longitude should have their high tide at the same time. But reference to an almanack will show that this is not the case. Liverpool and Leith are both about three degrees west of Greenwich but there is a difference of three hours or more in the time of high water.

Anomalies are due chiefly to two causes. In the first place it should be observed that in a globe completely surrounded by water the tides, as shown in figs. 79 (*a*) and (*b*), have the form of waves, the high tides being the crests and the low tides the troughs. The length of the wave is the distance from crest to crest, and in any given latitude this is half the circumference of the globe at that latitude. The tidal wave, like other waves, tends to travel round the earth at its own proper rate, independently of the sun and moon. Since the length of the wave, excepting close to the poles, is very great compared with the depth of the ocean, the rate depends on the depth of the water (see p. 157); and near the equator it is less than the rate at which the sun and moon appear to travel in their daily course. It is easy to see that this difference between the natural rate of the wave and the rate forced upon it by the sun and moon will introduce complications, but these complications are too intricate to be considered here.

The movement of the tidal wave is also greatly influenced by the continental and other land-masses. If the globe were completely surrounded

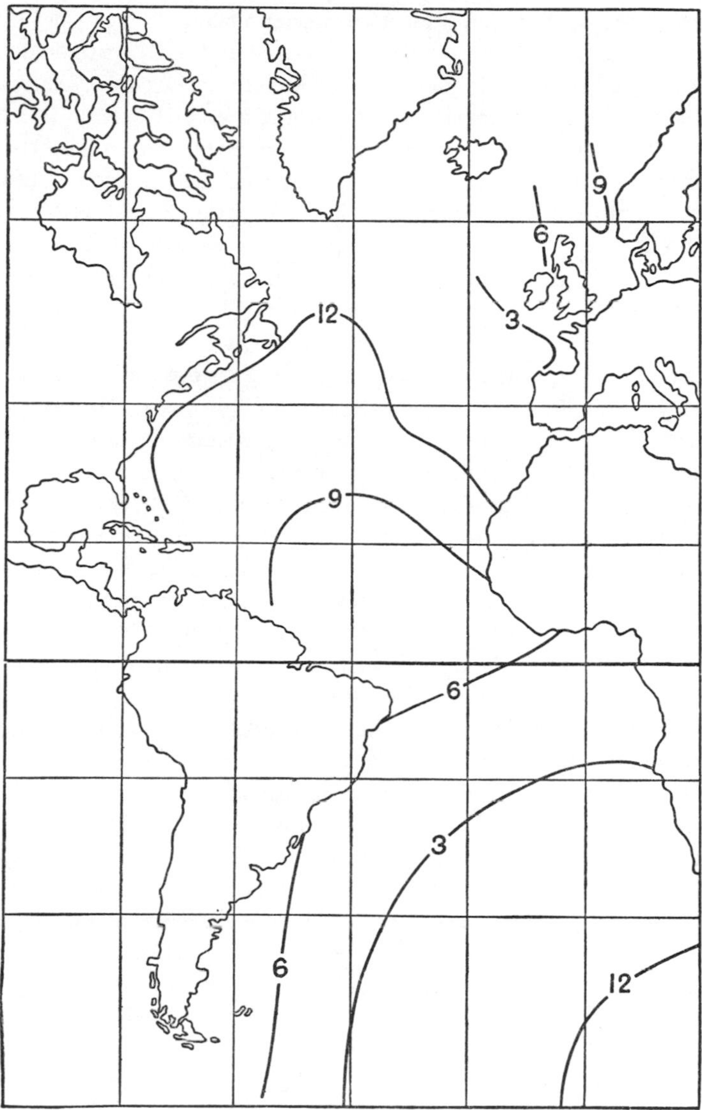

Fig. 80. Co-tidal lines of the Atlantic Ocean, based on the theory of a progressive wave.

by water the tide would travel smoothly round from east to west. But the great land-masses stretch from north to south and prevent its progress. Since in the Antarctic Ocean there is an open and unobstructed course, it was argued that it is only in this southern sea that the tides are free to follow the moon and travel round the world from east to west, like two long but very low waves. As the wave passes the opening of the Atlantic it sets up a branch wave which travels up the Atlantic from south to north. Similar branch waves are formed in the Pacific and Indian Oceans.

The general course of the tidal wave, according to the progressive wave theory, in the Atlantic is shown in fig. 80 by means of co-tidal lines. A co-tidal line is a line drawn through places which have their high tide at the same time, and the numbers placed against the lines indicate the Greenwich time of high tide on the days of full moon. However, the information for drawing co-tidal lines is even now almost limited to coastal waters, and when the progressive wave theory was current it is fair to say that the lines represented little more than enlightened guess-work based on what is now known to be an erroneous assumption.

From this map and from theory it appears that the Atlantic tidal wave travels more rapidly in the deep water of mid-ocean than in the shallower water along the shore, and the crest becomes curved. As it passes northward the convexity of the curve increases, and when it reaches Europe the trend of the wave is from north to south and the wave approaches from the west. On the opposite side of the ocean the trend is also nearly north and south, but the wave approaches the coast from the east.

The tide accordingly was supposed to reach the British Isles from the west and its course within our seas is shown by co-tidal lines in fig. 81. The wave is supposed to have divided into two parts when it met Ireland. The northern part sent a small off-shoot into the Irish Sea, but the main wave travelled round the north of Scotland and gave rise to a wave passing from north to south along the eastern coast of Great Britain. The southern part of the wave from the Atlantic was again divided by the Cornish peninsula, one branch going up the Irish Sea and Bristol Channel and the other up the English Channel.

If progressive waves entered a sea with two or more entrances, various anomalies and complications in the tides were sometimes apparently easily but nevertheless falsely explained. The best-known example of this kind is the stretch of water between the Isle of Wight and the mainland, which was assumed to be reached by tidal waves travelling up both the Spithead and the Solent. If, on the other hand, at any place the high tide due to the tidal wave from one end coincided with the low tide due

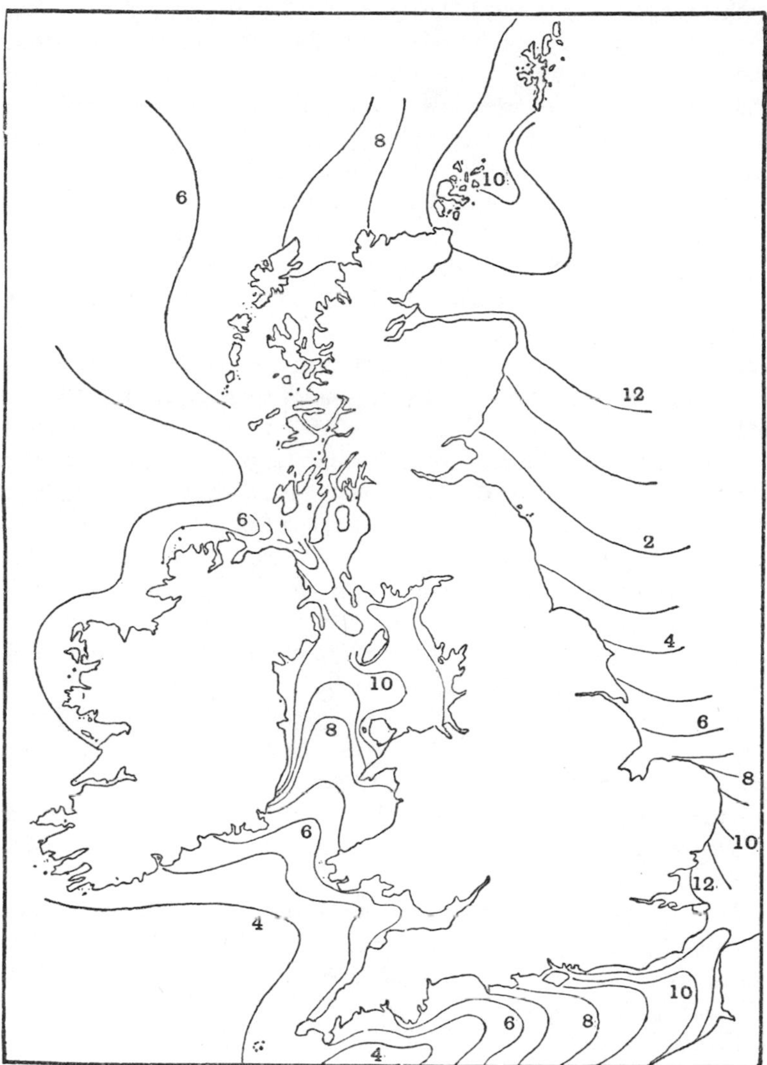

Fig. 81. Co-tidal lines of the British Seas according to the progressive wave theory.

to the tidal wave from the other end, the two were thought to neutralise each other more or less completely and there was no tide at all.

From the co-tidal maps it will be evident that it was supposed that the speed of the tidal wave was much greater in the open ocean than in shallow seas. In mid-Atlantic its velocity reached 600 or 700 miles an hour, on the east coast of England about forty. The length of the wave, which on the map is the distance from any of the co-tidal lines to the next line marked with the same number, was great compared with the depth of the ocean, and therefore, as we have seen on p. 157, the velocity varied as the square root of the depth.

The stationary wave theory. The amount of tidal knowledge has increased rapidly in recent years, and it is now no longer possible to accept the apparently simple explanations of many of the phenomena at first sight adequately dealt with by the progressive wave theory. According to that hypothesis the tide travelled round the southern ocean and sent waves travelling northwards along the Pacific, Indian, and Atlantic Oceans. Consequently in any one ocean the age of the tide[1] became later the farther north the wave travelled. But, apart from local differences in narrow gulfs or estuaries, the age of the tide on the western side of the Atlantic varies very little between Cape Horn and Cape Farewell. Moreover, the type of tide (p. 175) commonly experienced is not the same everywhere. In the Atlantic the semi-diurnal tides with a very small daily inequality contrast, for example, with the tides on the Californian coast which show a marked diurnal inequality, or with those at Tahiti where high water occurs regularly about noon and mid-night, with a range of less than a foot. Clearly the tides are here following the sun and not the moon. Moreover, it is reasonable to suppose that bodies of water of the size of the Indian, Atlantic, and Pacific Oceans are able to produce their own tides.

Modern work on tides replaces a world phenomenon by regional or even local phenomena, and instead of assuming a progressive wave either for the world or for an individual ocean a stationary wave is postulated. This idea is simple and is easily illustrated. If a fairly shallow rectangular tank is partly filled with water it is quite easy to set the water in it rocking so that it is high at one end and low at the other. It is not difficult to produce a rocking (fig. 82*a*, *b*) in which the water is high in the middle at the same time that it is low at both ends. In the first case there is one

[1] It is found that the tide does not immediately follow variations in the moon's position relative to the sun and earth. The maximum rise and fall at springs, for example, is not precisely at new and full moon. There is also a lag in the maximum noted at perigee of up to $1\frac{1}{2}$ days. This retardation in tidal response is called the age of the tide and usually is assumed to be due to friction.

line—a nodal line—about which the water oscillates; in the other case two. Further complications can be visualised. The period of oscillation is given by a simple formula, $T=\frac{2L}{\sqrt{gh}}$, where L is the length of the tank, h the depth of the water, and g the acceleration of gravity. This implies that each and every body of water has a definite and natural period of oscillation which depends upon the length of the body and the depth of the water.

If an experiment is made with a tank in a laboratory it will soon be found that if one tries to quicken or diminish the period of the oscillation

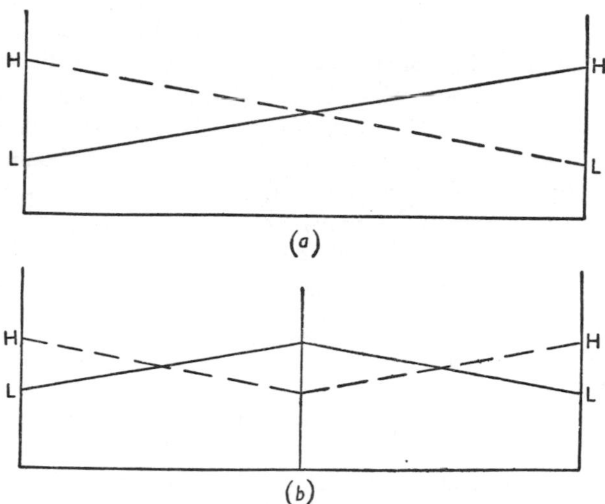

Fig. 82. (*a*) Uninodal, and (*b*) binodal oscillating systems.

confusion is apt to occur. Once the natural period is attained, it needs but the slightest effort to maintain it.

What, then, are the periodic forces in nature which can set parts of the oceans oscillating in this fashion? They are, in fact, the tide-producing forces of the sun and moon which have already been described. There are four main ones: the sun appears to move round the earth in 24 hours, but the solar forces repeat themselves every 12 hours. Consequently, solar tides are repeated at the same time each day. The moon's period of revolution is 24 hours 50 minutes, and the half-periods are 12 hours 25 minutes. Hence the solar tides may be a little before or after the lunar tide, and so the combined tide varies a little in time. The idea underlying the stationary wave theory is that there are in the oceans bodies of water the periods of oscillation of which correspond exactly or approximately to these periods, and that the stationary waves are best developed in those parts of the oceans corresponding most closely to the period of the tide-producing force.

Fig. 83 shows the oscillating systems for the semi-diurnal tide-producing forces as conceived by Harris in the early years of this century. In the tank experiments the width of the tank did not matter; hence the width of the oceanic oscillating areas is of no significance. The systems shown in fig. 83 are drawn according to mathematical and physical principles which cannot be discussed here. It must, however, be emphasised that there is no general acceptance of the areas shown in this figure. The roman figures indicate in lunar hours the time of high water after the moon's transit of the Greenwich meridian. The areas often overlap. The nodal lines are shown by chain dots. The parts of the ocean left unshaded are those in which because of their size and depth the tide-producing forces can produce but little tide. This means that the effective tides in these areas are the direct result of those in neighbouring areas.

If this is compared with fig. 80 a vast difference is seen. In the North Atlantic a nodal line runs north-eastward from the Lesser Antilles, and the American coast between Florida and Newfoundland is at one end of an oscillating system. This conforms with the known facts that along that coast the age of the tide is almost contemporaneous throughout, and near the Lesser Antilles the range of the tide is extremely small. Incidentally it is only on islands such as these, or even more isolated ones, that we can obtain any direct measurement of the tidal rise and fall of the open ocean. It has already been remarked that at Tahiti the tides follow the sun and high water is at midnight and midday. Fig. 83 shows this island close to a nodal line for the semi-diurnal tides, implying that at Tahiti these tides are small. The actual tide, therefore, is a solar one of a 12-hour period. Another refinement, touched on in more detail on p. 176, must now be considered, namely the rotation of the earth. The effect of this is to give a gyratory motion to the rocking of the standing wave which may now swing round a point, called an amphidromic point, rather than oscillate about a nodal line. Clearly this modifies the scheme shown in fig. 83 very considerably, and it is in fact premature to try to show a world map of this type. The difficulties experienced in working out the tides in small seas like the North Sea are amazingly intricate, and at present, knowledge relevant to this problem in the Indian and Pacific Oceans does not exist. The North Atlantic is better known, and fig. 84, after Sterneck, gives a picture of a modern view. It will be seen to stand in strong contrast to the old progressive wave theory and also to Harris's very generalised world scheme.

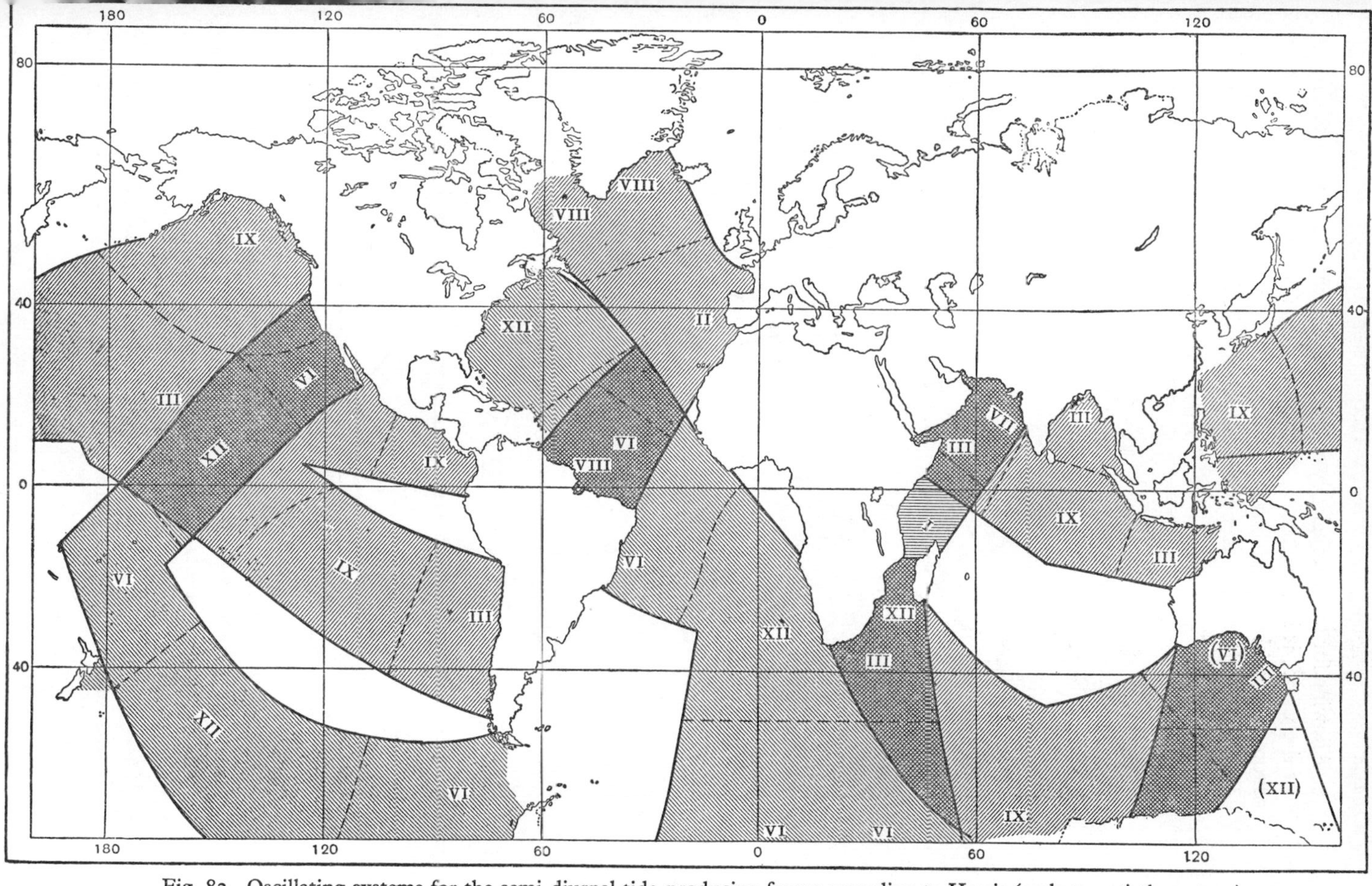

Fig. 83. Oscillating systems for the semi-diurnal tide-producing forces according to Harris (early twentieth century).

Allowing for the insufficiency of knowledge of the tides in many parts of the world, it is clear that in this theory there is the basis of a much more reasonable approach to the problem. Under the progressive wave theory difficulties and exceptions had either to be explained by the over-

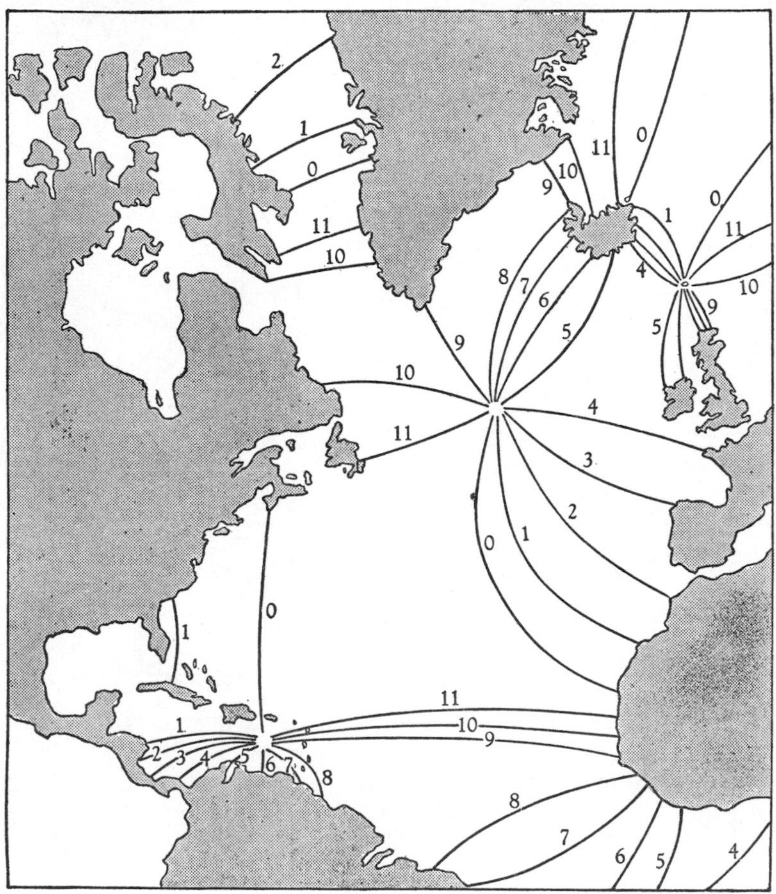

Fig. 84. Co-tidal lines of the Atlantic Ocean according to Sterneck (1920).

lapping of waves from different directions or ignored. There was no reasonable explanation of the fact that the type of tide varies with locality. In the stationary wave theory the assumption that certain areas or portions of the oceans are of such shape and size as to respond to one or other of the lunar or solar forces is a great step forward, as is also the elimination of a world phenomenon. This can, perhaps, be best illustrated by an account of modern views concerning tidal phenomena around the coasts of the British Isles. But before doing so a brief account of the types of tide will be helpful.

Types of tide. In and around the British Isles, and generally in the Atlantic Ocean the rise and fall of the water takes place twice daily, and on a tide-gauge record the resulting curve is of the type shown in fig. 85*b*. In the Gulf of Mexico, around the Philippine Islands and a few other places there is a daily tide, one in which there is but one high and one low water in a lunar day (fig. 85*a*). In the mixed type all tides are included which have two high and two low waters in a day, but which

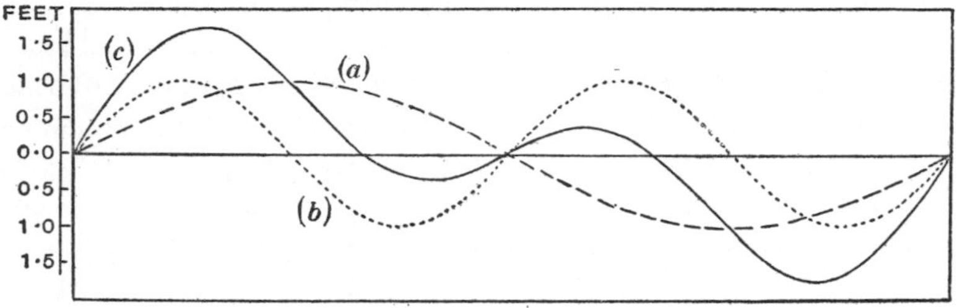

Fig. 85. Types of tide.

nevertheless show a marked difference between morning and afternoon tides, or a marked diurnal inequality. There are many ways in which this may be shown: they include (1) those containing the diurnal inequality mainly in the high waters, (2) those containing the diurnal inequality mainly in the low waters, and (3) those which show it partly in the high and partly in the low waters.

This mixed type of tide is the result of a combination of the daily and semi-daily types. In fig. 85 let the chain-dotted line represent the daily tide and the dotted line the semi-daily tide. Let them coincide at mean water and have the same range. The continuous curve is the algebraic sum of the other two, and represents the actual mixed tide; it shows inequality in both high and low waters. It is clear that all kinds of combination are possible, since the phases and ranges may differ considerably. Hence many variations in the nature of the curve for mixed tides are possible.

The mixed tide arises from a combination of the daily and semi-daily types, and the semi-daily types tend to occur in those areas where there is little or no daily tide, and vice versa.

The actual tide-producing forces (p. 162) are distributed regularly over the earth's surface. Semi-daily forces are greatest at the equator and least at the poles; daily forces show the converse. Actual configuration of the ocean and sea basins severely modifies this, however, and, in practice, there is really no relation to latitude. In fact it is found that the semi-daily type is prevalent in the Atlantic Ocean, the mixed type in the Indian and Pacific Oceans, and the daily type, as already noted, in certain special areas.

Tides in British seas. In seas like the Irish Sea, English Channel, and North Sea intensive tidal investigations have been made, and accurate data concerning the relations between tidal streams and surface gradients obtained. From this material it is possible to draw co-tidal charts with considerable accuracy, and the important point to note is that the co-tidals so drawn do not depend on any preconceived hypothesis, but are based upon observations made both at sea and on the coast, and also on well-established mathematical principles. The chart (fig. 86) is the outcome of these investigations, and the most cursory glance shows a complete change from the old views represented in fig. 81.

Before examining the chart in more detail one general point needs some explanation. It will be seen, for example, that in the North Sea the co-tidal lines meet in points which are called amphidromic points. Underlying the present scheme is the stationary wave theory, but modified in one important respect. Suppose a rocking is started in a given basin; naturally it is subject to the deflective effects occasioned by the rotation of the earth, and instead of a simple swinging we have also a gyratory motion set up about the nodal line which becomes an amphidromic point.

In the North Sea the local tides result from oscillations travelling in from the Atlantic round the north of Scotland.[1] Because of the shape, size, and depth of the North Sea three nodal lines occur as indicated in fig. 87. Between any two lines high (or low) water will occur simultaneously, and the maximum range will be half-way between any pair of lines, and in crossing any line one passes from an area of high (or low) water to one of low (or high) water. If now the effects of gyration are added, forces are brought into being which deflect the tidal currents to the right (see p. 16) and so at certain hours gradients would occur along the nodal lines. In other words, there will be oscillations along the nodal lines, but at some point on any given line the water level will remain constant. This will be the amphidromic point, around which the tidal

[1] On any largely land-locked body of water, such as the North Sea, Black Sea, Gulf of Mexico, or a large estuary, the moon has a direct tide-raising action. In addition there may be forced oscillations like those described for the North Sea. These are nearly always far more important than is the direct action of the moon. which for small bodies of water may really be disregarded. In large ocean basins the direct action is very important, and is enhanced when there is approximate resonance.

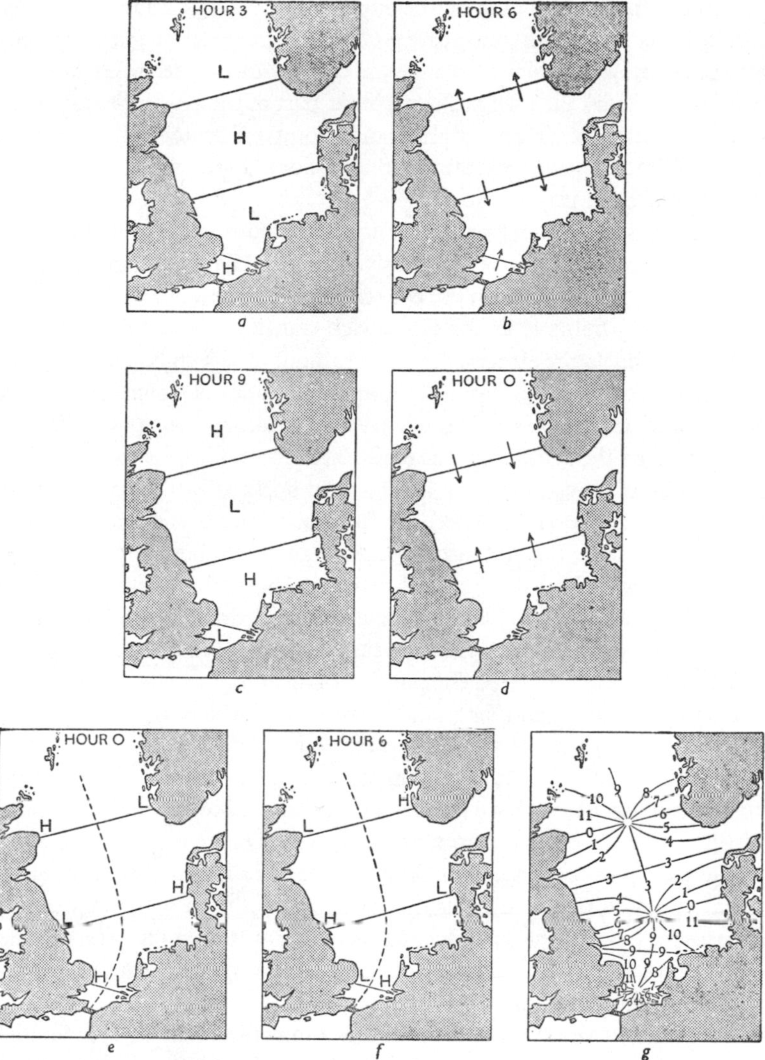

Fig. 87. Tides in the North Sea. *a–d*, four successive phases of standing oscillation, in absence of gyration; *e–f*, first and second phases of standing oscillation, modified by gyration; *g*, co-tidal lines deduced from particular phases of standing oscillation, modified by gyration.

oscillation turns in an anti-clockwise direction, and produces the effects illustrated in fig. 86. One of the effects of friction is a loss of energy which in its turn has a diminishing effect on the range of the tides, and also produces a difference between the eastern and western shores. This is most markedly the case in the northern part of the North Sea; there is some doubt whether an amphidromic point exists off south-western Norway; it may be degenerate, i.e. the co-tidals appear to radiate from a point some little way inland.

In the Irish Sea water enters by north and south channels, and once again local tidal conditions are greatly influenced by the Atlantic. It is a fact that the tidal streams in the two entrance channels reach a maximum at about eight hours after the Greenwich transit of the moon, and since in both channels the streams begin to run out at eleven hours it follows that at about this time there is a maximum amount of water in the Irish Sea basin. In this sea again we have a standing oscillation which is influenced by the rotation of the earth. The effect of this is to produce at hour eight an elevation of the water on the north Wales coast relative to that on south Scotland. There are further complications, but the final result is that high water is rather earlier than eleven hours on the Welsh coast, and rather later on the Scottish coast. The probable position of the amphidromic point in the North Channel, and the one, which may be degenerate, near the coast of south-east Ireland are indicated on fig. 86. It is to be remembered that the position of an amphidromic point is controlled by the depth and form of the basin, and if the basin is irregular it is impossible to assume simple explanations.

Finally, we may glance at the English Channel. Instead of the arcuate co-tidals of fig. 81, we have lines often bending in the opposite direction. If there were a barrier across the Straits of Dover the Atlantic tides would set up in the Channel a fairly simple standing oscillation about a nodal line running southwards from the region of the Isle of Wight. The gyroscopic forces do not produce a true amphidromic point here, but the converging of the co-tidal lines near the Isle of Wight suggests a degenerate amphidromic point.

Southampton tides. The old explanation of the four tides at Southampton given on p. 168 is completely false. It is based on the view that two waves, travelling up the Solent and up the Spithead, act quite independently and therefore give separate high waters. Since the laws governing the combination of waves are the same, no matter what may be their periods, it follows that two tidal waves of the same period will combine and make a tide of the same period. This means that in a given time, the combined or resultant tide has the same number of high or low waters as each constituent tide. In other words, double high or double low waters are not the outcome of two combined normal oscillations.

Unfortunately, no simple or even complete explanation exists for the tidal phenomena at Southampton. Some idea of the problem can, however, be given. In fig. 88 curve *a* shows double high waters; let it be represented as closely as possible by the simple harmonic curve *b*, which is so drawn that it is symmetrical with respect to high water, low water, and mean sea-level. The curve *c* is obtained by taking the differences of the ordinates of the other two curves, and it shows a quarter-daily

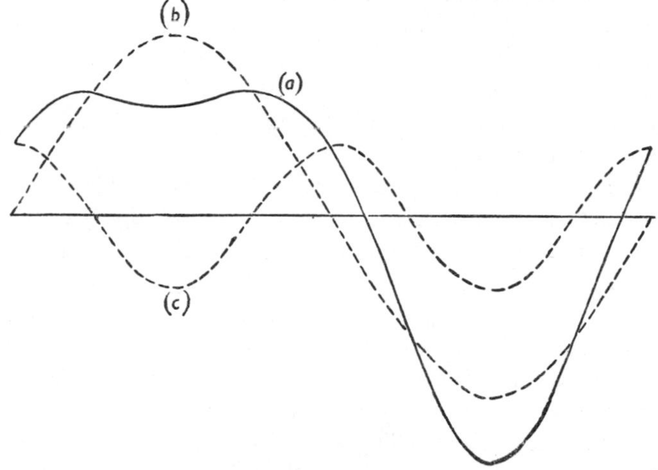

Fig. 88. Illustration of a particular type of double high water, showing partial tides.

oscillation. In other words curve *a* can be regarded as a combined semi-daily and quarter-daily curve. It will be noticed that curve *c* has a trough nearly at the same time as the high water on curve *b*. This is important. Their phase relationships as well as their amplitudes must also be correct. To produce double high or low waters the amplitude of a quarter-daily tide should at least equal one-quarter that of a semi-daily tide. A similar type of reasoning applies to one-sixth daily tides, and possibly to even smaller periods.

'If the quarter-diurnal tide has a suitable phase relationship with the semi-diurnal tide, but has not a sufficiently large amplitude actually to produce double high waters it will tend to produce a marked flattening out of the high-water curve and in the limiting case there will be a pronounced stand of tide. Now it is evident that if the curve is much flattened out over an interval of time comparable with, say, half the period of the sixth-diurnal tide, then this latter tide will be revealed at once by its oscillations about the approximately steady state on which it is superposed. Further, any short-period tide will be readily revealed under these conditions.

'Hence double high waters may not be due to any single species of shallow-water tide but to the combined effects of several species. What is essential to the phenomenon is firstly that *one* of the shallow-water tides (not necessarily even the quarter-diurnal tide) must have the right phase relationship and a sufficiently large amplitude to give a short stand and the next higher species will then tend to produce the double tide.'[1]

Even a detailed analysis of the tides at Southampton is of little help; if sixth-daily tides are considered the curve at high water is flattened. Further, if eighth-daily tides are carefully interpolated they tend, but actually just fail, to produce a double high water. In this unsatisfactory state the matter must be left. Enough has been said to show that the subject is one of great complexity, and that the old-fashioned explanations are entirely inadequate.

Tides in estuaries and rivers. In the lower parts of rivers and other similar indentations of the coast the tidal phenomena are directly due to the tides of the sea or ocean into which they run. Hence, the nature of river tides depends upon those in the adjacent sea. On the other hand, as the tidal impulse moves up a river it takes on certain definite features so that it is quite appropriate to speak of river tides. Since the river slopes down to the sea the tide has to work against gravity, and this naturally shortens the period of rise and increases the period of fall of the tide. Because the river is also bringing water down to the sea and, as it were, opposing the tide, the rise and fall of the tide are similarly affected for this reason also. The latter factor, however, is a fluctuating one and necessarily varies with the amount of water brought down by the river; in other words it varies seasonally.

Characteristically, the tidal curve which may be almost or even actually symmetrical near the mouth of the river, becomes more and more asymmetrical as the tidal wave progresses upstream. The front (i.e. the interval between low water and high water) steepens and the back (i.e. the period between high water and the next low water) lengthens. In some rivers, especially those which are funnel-shaped or which contain extensive shoals of mud or sand, the steepening of the front of the curve is so sudden that it becomes vertical for at least a part of the rise. This phenomenon is called a bore, and in a bore the water moves bodily forward as a wall of tumbling waters. In the Severn the bore at spring tides is often 3 or 4 feet high. In the Tsien-tang-kiang in China it may be 12 feet.

[1] *Admiralty Manual of Tides*, 1941, p. 222.

Tides in bays and gulfs. As in rivers, the nature of the tides in bays and gulfs depends entirely on those in the open sea into which the bays open. But there are two types of tidal behaviour in such inlets. In most cases the tide enters as a progressive wave which travels to the head of the bay so that, as in a river, high water becomes later with increasing distance from the mouth. Because the bottom of the bay probably has a fairly continuous seaward slope, much energy has to be used in overcoming friction, so that the height of the tide often decreases as it progresses up the bay. It may be remarked that, although we are so far dealing with progressive waves, these are nevertheless caused in the first place by stationary waves in the open sea.

On the other hand, in certain gulfs and straits it is found that the time of the tide is very similar throughout. In Long Island Sound at a distance of 75 miles from its entrance the difference in time of tide is half an hour. If the tide behaved as a progressive wave, the difference in time of high water at the mouth and a point 75 miles distant from it would be about 2½ hours. Long Island Sound has an overall length of nearly 90 miles; its average depth is 65 feet; its natural period of oscillation 11½ hours. In other words its own period of oscillation so closely corresponds with the semi-diurnal period of the adjoining ocean that a stationary wave oscillation, with a node near the mouth of the Sound, is set up. The same kind of thing takes place in the Bay of Fundy, at the head of which, in Noel Bay, the tidal range is about 50 feet at spring tides. The natural period of the bay is about 11½ hours, and once again a stationary wave is set up. It should, however, be added that the very great range is not wholly due to a standing oscillation, but partly to the great decrease in the cross-section of the bay in its upper parts.

Tidal currents. We have seen that in an estuary or inlet the tide may be either of the progressive wave type or of the stationary wave type. In the former, the wave approximates to the cosine curve and as in an ordinary wind wave the forward motion is in the upper parts, or crest, of the wave, and the backward motion in the trough. Put into other words, this is equivalent to saying that in progressive wave movement the currents are at a maximum at high and low water. Since progressive wave movement generally prevails in inlets it clearly follows that as the tide is rising during the first half of the flood and falling during the second half, the often assumed synonymity of flood of current with rise of tide is not wholly true. The same holds good for the false assumption that ebb is synonymous with fall.

If, however, there is stationary wave motion in the inlet or strait, it is obvious that both the horizontal and vertical motion cease, at any rate in theory, at the same time. In other words, the slack of the current comes at the times of high and low water, and the strength of the current midway between those times. In actual fact there may be some departures from this because usually a certain amount of progressive wave motion is also involved.

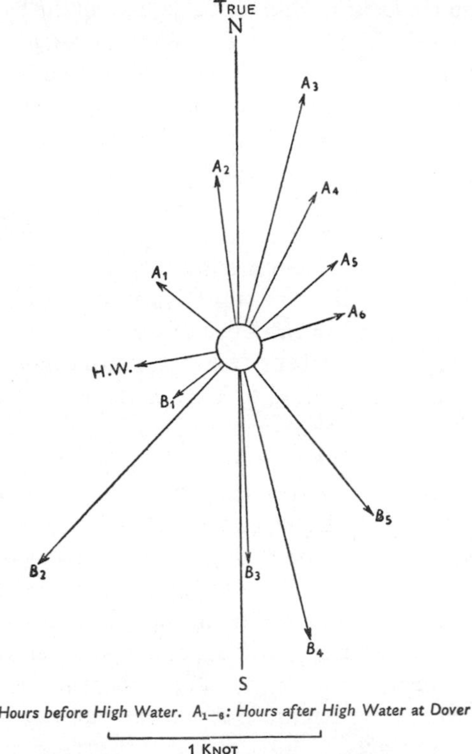

B_{1-6}: Hours before High Water. A_{1-6}: Hours after High Water at Dover

1 KNOT

Fig. 89. Strength and direction of tidal streams near Seven Stones light vessel, 50° 3′ N., 6° 4′ W.

Offshore tidal currents. There is no space to deal with these currents in any detail, but a brief account is desirable. If from a vessel anchored a mile or two offshore a series of readings is taken with a weighted float that indicates the water motion as distinct from any wind effects, it will be found that the current is always flowing, but that its direction is constantly changing. Fig. 89 shows the strength and direction of the tidal currents at Seven Stones light vessel off Land's End.

If a long series of observations is made at any one place the mean strength of the current in different directions can be found, and a smooth curve passed through the extremities of the 'arms'. Current curves of this sort vary a good deal in shape, partly with the varying declination of the moon, partly with locality and other factors. Nearer inshore the ellipse becomes very eccentric and close to the beach the currents, on an open coast, are usually found to flow parallel to the beach, but reversing in direction with the state of the tide. Off part of the Norfolk coast near Brancaster the water flows eastwards for about 2½–3 hours following high water. After a slack period of about ½ hour, the water then runs westwards for 2–2½ hours before the next high water. The speed of these currents is greater at spring than at neap tides.

These currents close inshore and in shallow water may have great transporting power. If their velocity is sufficiently great they may move material directly. What is more often noticed is that in shallow water incoming waves stir up material on the bottom and this is then moved laterally in a saltatory fashion by the tidal current (see ch. IV).

The cause of diurnal tides. The tidal force exerted by the moon reaches a maximum twice a lunar day, and that of the sun twice a solar day. When the moon's declination is such that it is overhead some way north or south of the equator, then in a given latitude one of the daily maxima of the lunar tidal force is greater than the other. The same is also true of the weaker tidal force of the sun. This produces the diurnal inequality in the tides (see p. 164), an effect not confined to any particular ocean, and which disappears when the moon or sun is overhead at the equator. It follows, therefore, that the diurnal tide which is, at all states of the moon and sun, much more important in the Pacific than in the Atlantic cannot be due to this cause. Its real cause, like that of the quarter-daily and lesser tides that may help to account for such anomalies as the double tide at Southampton, is *resonance*.

Any body of water has its own natural period of oscillation according to its length and depth (see p. 171). A body of water such as that of the Bay of Fundy, the natural period of which approximates to that of the lunar tidal force, oscillates readily, and with a great tidal range, when it receives its semi-daily impulse from the waters of the Atlantic. But if a body of water has a natural period, perhaps half that of the lunar tides, it also has a tendency to rock for the same reason, but with a smaller amplitude. In a still lesser degree this is also true of water bodies with a period one-quarter or one-eighth of that of the tidal forces. Thus, even with a semi-daily tidal force, certain bodies of water, especially if they are partially confined by sea-coasts or submerged banks, will oscillate daily, quarter-daily, or eighth-daily. Presumably in the Pacific there must be many water bodies with a natural period of about a day, and it is for this reason that a daily tide occurs widely in that ocean.

CHAPTER IV

OCEANIC CIRCULATION

Ocean currents may be divided into (*a*) those due to the distribution of density in the ocean waters, (*b*) those due to wind, and (*c*) tidal currents. The third class does not concern us in this chapter. Whereas it is easy to divide currents into these three classes, it is by no means as simple to say of any one current that it is the result of one cause; density differences, for example, often work in with wind effects. In general, the important currents including the Gulf Stream, the Kuroshio, and the North and South Equatorial Currents belong in part to the first class. However, it will be better to take the oceans in turn and examine their surface movements.

The Atlantic Ocean. The North Equatorial Current lies in the area of the north-east trade-winds and flows from east to west. To the west of the ocean it is joined by a branch of the South Equatorial Current which brings with it water of different type. Some of the combined current enters the Caribbean Sea, and the remainder passes outside the West Indian Islands. The Gulf Stream system is really the continuation of these currents. This system can be divided into (1) the Florida Current, which includes all the northward travelling water from the Straits of Florida to Cape Hatteras; (2) the Gulf Stream which is the name properly applied to the current between Cape Hatteras and the Grand Banks in about long. 45° W., and (3) the North Atlantic Current eastwards from the Grand Banks. This part often breaks up into branches and is masked by local wind movement and is often referred to as the North Atlantic Drift. The Gulf Stream water finally disappears in the Irminger Current which flows westward along the south coast of Iceland, and the Norwegian Current which eventually reaches the Polar Sea.

The current through the Straits of Florida derives its energy from the difference of sea-level between the Gulf of Mexico and the Atlantic; since this difference of level is probably due to the trade-winds, it follows that the energy of the Florida Current is primarily due to the circulation of the atmosphere. Eastwards of the Straits, this current is joined by that part of the North Equatorial Current flowing outside the Antilles. Since most of this area is not more than some 800 metres deep the current is fairly shallow. The Gulf Stream proper is a well-defined and also a narrow current well beyond the continental shelf. It separates the

Sargasso Sea to the right from the shallow coastal and rather deeper slope waters to the left. Assuming that there is no motion at a depth of 2000 metres it is estimated that off Chesapeake Bay the Gulf Stream transports between 74 and 93 million m.^{3} sec. The surface velocities are also high, reaching 120 cm./sec. in lat. 30° N., long. 73° W., and 140 cm./sec., in lat. 38° N., long. 69° W.

The well-defined nature of the Gulf Stream disappears completely in the North Atlantic Current, some of the branches of which turn south while others turn east across the Atlantic Ridge and then south between Spain and the Azores. Whirls are also sent off into the Bay of Biscay. In this region there are no very clear currents, but there is a general southward movement of the water, some of which runs on the surface into the Mediterranean, but most eventually joins the North Equatorial Current.

That part of the Gulf Stream system which flows into the Arctic along the coast of Norway is called the Norwegian Current; on its western side there are many whirls which may be either stationary or shifting. Still farther north this current splits, one branch running into the Barents Sea and the other toward the Svalbard archipelago. Along the east coast of Greenland there is a southward-flowing current, composed of water of low temperature and low salinity; most of this runs through Denmark Strait, but a small branch turns south-eastwards to become the East Iceland Arctic Current which eventually becomes involved with the whirls already mentioned to the west of the Norwegian Current.

In the Labrador Sea the West Greenland Current flows northwards along the Greenland coast whereas the Labrador Current runs southwards on the mainland coast. Near Davis Strait part of the former current turns to join the Labrador Current, while the rest continues into Baffin Bay. Between these two main currents is an area of eddies, about which little is known. The outflowing cold Labrador Current sooner or later sinks and its waters have considerable significance in the deeper circulation of the Atlantic.

In the equatorial regions of the Atlantic there is a strong discontinuity below a depth of 50–150 metres. It is in this area that the Equatorial Counter Current, flowing eastwards, is developed. This current is the direct result of the slope produced by the north-east and south-east trade-winds continually carrying water to the American side. It has been shown that the slope is about 4 cm. per 1000 km. It must be borne in mind that this counter current exists entirely above the discontinuity, and so involves but a thin layer of surface water. It is best developed in the northern summer.

South of the equator there is another closed system of currents. Flowing northwards along the African coast is the Benguela Current. The prevailing winds, southerly and south-easterly, carry the surface layers away from the coast and cause an upwelling of colder water, but only from moderate depths. As it approaches the equator the Benguela Current diverges more and more from the coast and becomes in fact the northern part of the South Equatorial Current. As has been pointed out, this current bifurcates and some of its water crosses the equator into the North Atlantic. The remainder turns southwards along the Brazil coast as the Brazil Current. But farther south the Falkland Current, of low temperature and low salinity, flows northwards to about lat. 30° S. The circulation is completed by the westerly winds carrying the South Atlantic Current to the east. This is a shallow current and is wholly above the Antarctic intermediate water. The movement of this and other deeper water is described below. Hence, both in the North and in the South Atlantic there are anticyclonic current systems, and in the North Atlantic the Sargasso Sea is thus enclosed. In this sea is found, often in great quantities, the floating weed *Sargassum*. There is no foundation for the belief that the amount and thickness of the weed can hinder a ship, but a schooner, the *Fanny Wolston*, left derelict in the northern part of the Sargasso Sea in 1891, seems to have circled the whole region in about three years. There is no similar phenomenon in the other oceans, and Krümmel regards the weed-beds of the West Indies (the ultimate source of the weed), the strong currents around those islands, and the Gulf Stream as a combination of circumstances more favourable to the accumulation of weed than occurs elsewhere on the globe.

The Pacific Ocean. Here again there is north of the equator a North Equatorial Current which is added to (see fig. 90) by water from the California Current and also by both eastern and western North Pacific water. As far as is known it is a broad and fairly deep current, which towards the western margin of the ocean throws off branches to north and south. There is a marked bifurcation of the current into north and south streams off the Philippine Islands. The branch which flows northwards soon becomes part of the Kuroshio (the Gulf Stream of the Pacific). The Kuroshio *sensu stricto* is the current running from Formosa to about lat. 35° N. It is continued directly as a warm current known as the Kuroshio Extension which can be traced to about long. 160° E., whence it is continued as the North Pacific Current to long. 150° W., near to which it sends branches to the south. The Tsushima Current is also a part of the Kuroshio and is the warm current which runs into the Japan Sea along the west coast of Japan. The swirl or eddy to the east

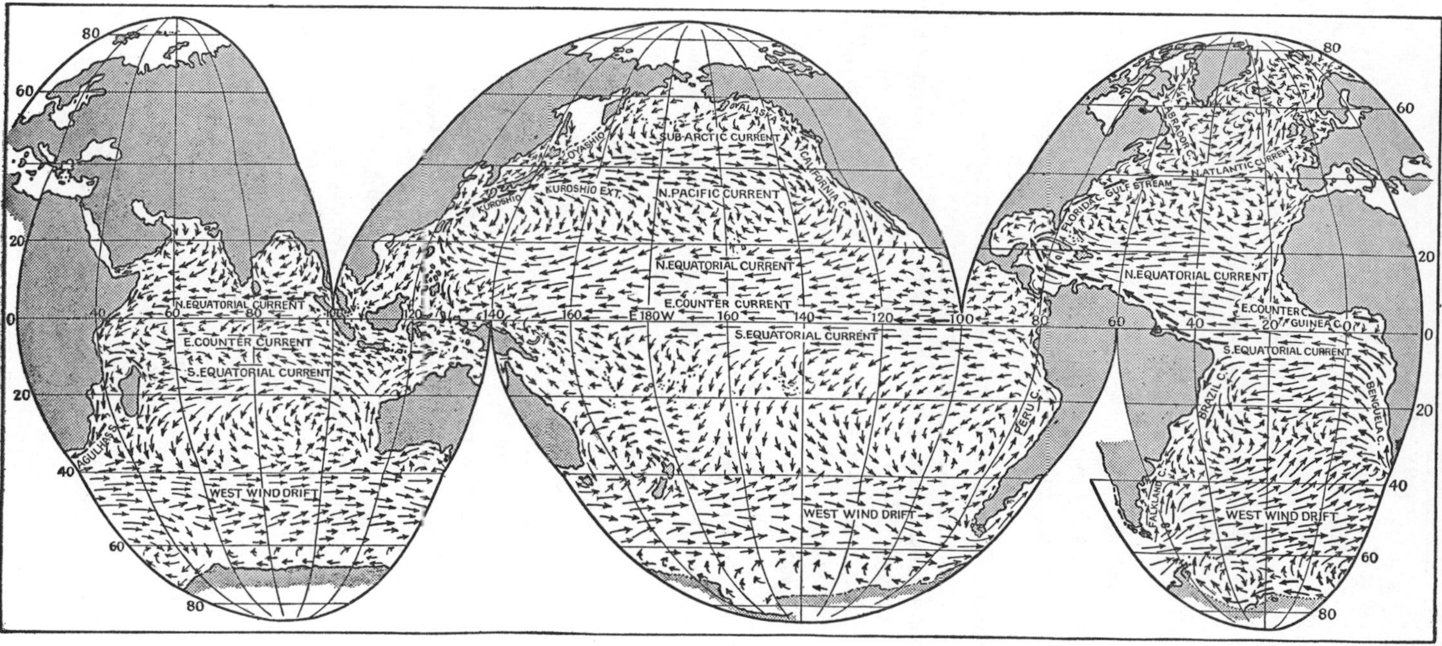

Fig. 90. Surface currents of the oceans in February–March.

and south-east of the Kuroshio is called the Kuroshio Counter Current. The parallel between the Kuroshio system and the Gulf Stream system is evident, but it is interesting to note that, whereas the temperature of the Kuroshio water and that of the Florida Current are much the same, the Florida Current is 1·5‰ more salt (36·50‰ as against 35·00‰).

To the north of the Kuroshio system is the Aleutian or Sub-Arctic Current also flowing eastwards. This water appears to be a mixture of Kuroshio water and Oyashio, the cold current flowing southwards along Kamchatka and then turning eastwards. Before the American coast is reached the Aleutian Current divides: one branch turns north-westwards as the Alaska Current which, coming from the south, is therefore relatively warm, and the other follows the American coast to become part of the California Current which may be compared to the Peru Current (below). In spring and early summer north-north-west winds prevail off California and these aid greatly in the upwelling which goes on until July. It has recently been found that this upwelling takes place more particularly in certain localities (e.g. 35° N. and 41° N.) from which cold water streams oceanwards. Between these localities warmer water moves coastwards. The result is a series of swirls. In any case the upwelling water only comes from depths of about 200 metres. During the season of upwelling there is a subsurface (i.e. below 200 metres) current of equatorial water flowing along the coast. When the upwelling has ceased in July the normal pattern of currents is soon re-established and a surface counter current (the Davidson Current,) flowing northwards, is formed, and this is additional to the subsurface counter current which still exists. Hence, the main difference is that when upwelling takes place, the surface counter current disappears.

The best-known current in the South Pacific is the Peru Current; the part close inshore is now usually called the Peru Coastal Current, and that farther westwards the Peru Oceanic Current. Both have their origin where the eastward moving Sub-Antarctic water turns north along the Chilean coast. In the Coastal Current upwelling is important, and is brought about mainly by the south and south-easterly winds. The upwelling is not equally strong everywhere, possibly because of swirls of water which would cause upwelling water to move oceanwards on one side of a swirl, and relatively warmer oceanic water to move inwards on the other side. The outer boundary of the Oceanic Current is ill-defined; in lat. 35° S. it is about 550 miles from the coast.

There are some interesting seasonal changes in the Peru Coastal Current. In the *northern* summer it extends beyond the equator and generally converges with the Equatorial Counter Current (q.v.); but in winter this current is displaced somewhat to the south, and some of its water, warm, but of low salinity, flows southwards along the Ecuador coast. It is called El Niño, and normally it extends only a few degrees to the south of the equator. Every now and again, however, it may reach to about lat. 12° S. and in doing so has disastrous consequences. Fish and plankton are destroyed in countless numbers, and in this way food for the guano-producing birds is lost. It is also accompanied by a southward migration of the rain-belt and great floods are produced in normally semi-arid or arid districts.

When they finally leave the coast the waters of the Peru Current join the South Equatorial Current, which is analogous to the current of the same name in the Atlantic Ocean. Little is known about the other currents in the South Pacific Ocean, though there appears to be a southward movement in the open ocean to the west of the Peru Current—900 km. or more from the coast. In the western half of the ocean there is greater uncertainty. Older maps are often over-simplified in the matter of currents, and the comparison of current maps of different dates of the west part of the South Pacific will illustrate this point very well. The West Wind Drift, between approximately lat. 40° and 50° S., is mentioned in the section on the Southern Ocean.

In the equatorial parts of the Pacific there is an eastward flowing counter current between the North and South Equatorial Currents. It is very marked in the Pacific and is noted all the year round. It is always situated to the north of the equator, but is farthest north in the northern summer. Like its counterpart in the Atlantic, it appears to be due to the piling up of water in the west of the ocean. It is curious that this current should be more marked than in the Atlantic since the Pacific has no continuous western barrier. To the north of New Guinea the South Equatorial Current follows the *north* coast of that island and so converges with the North Equatorial Current in about lat. 5° N., the birthplace of the counter current. On the other hand from December to February the North Equatorial Current sends a powerful branch southwards from the Philippines to New Guinea and another branch, the counter current, towards the east. There are also variations of some magnitude on the American coast: the most important point is that for much of the year the Equatorial Counter Current is most marked between lat. 5° and 6° N., and most of its water is diverted north-westwards. Other local changes in this region are associated with changes in wind direction.

The Indian Ocean. In the southern part of the Indian Ocean there is a circulation closely resembling that in the South Atlantic. The South Equatorial Current flows from east to west north of lat. 20° S.: it reaches its highest velocity during the northern summer when the south-west monsoon is really a direct continuation across the equator of the south-east trades. There is also at this season some reinforcement by water from the Pacific Ocean travelling westwards to the north of Australia. On reaching the African side of the ocean the South Equatorial Current turns southwards to form the powerful Agulhas Current, which, as a matter of fact, does not extend more than 100 km. outwards from the coast. About the latitude of the extreme south of Africa the current turns eastward to form part of the West Wind Drift which traverses the whole ocean. In the southern summer some of this current seems to turn northwards before reaching Australia and (see fig. 90) is added to by a current flowing westwards along the south coast of Australia. In winter a greater part of the current passes south of Australia. Most of the older charts of the Indian Ocean indicate that the current bifurcates sharply off Cape Leeuwin, but more recent work shows that there is no strong northward current along the west coast. The coastal currents are described as weak and variable with a tendency to the south in winter and to the north in summer.

In the northern part of the Indian Ocean there is a complete reversal of currents between winter and summer as a result of the alternating monsoon winds. When the monsoon is blowing from Asia, the North Equatorial Current is best developed, and consequently there is then an Equatorial Counter Current situated about lat. 7° S. During the period of the south-west monsoon, especially in August and September, a current flows from west to east, completely obliterating the North Equatorial Current. Since this current starts from about 10° south of the equator it follows, as suggested above, that a good deal of South Equatorial water crosses the equator and also that along the African coast, particularly that of Somaliland, a good deal of upwelling takes place. There is no Counter Equatorial Current at this time of year.

The Southern Ocean. This ocean is in one sense a part of each of the other three oceans. The West Wind Drift is continuous right round the globe, but suffers some deflection due to the continents and also some seasonal variations. The Falkland Current is a branch of it: there is a corresponding northward current along the eastern side of the southern island of New Zealand. Strictly, the Circumpolar Current which is close to the Antarctic convergence should be distinguished from the rest of the West Wind Drift of the sub-Antarctic Region. It can easily be maintained that, e.g. in the Pacific, the northern part of this drift is solely a Pacific phenomenon. In short, there is no rigid northern boundary to the Southern Ocean (see fig. 68).

Immediately adjacent to the continent of Antarctica, the flow of water is locally to the west, especially in the region of the Weddell Sea. This is due to outblowing winds, and the deflection to the left characteristic of the southern hemisphere. Between the eastward and westward flowing currents there will be a divergence which lies close to the continent and is clearly indicated by the high temperature and high salinity of water at 100 metres depth. The occurrence of the sub-tropical and Antarctic convergences and the divergence close to the continent implies complex transverse water movements which are superimposed on the general eastward flow. Sections made in these waters seem to indicate that between lat. 45° and 63° S. deep water climbs from about −3000 to −200 metres, and presumably adds to the actual surface layer which is otherwise too salt to originate in a region of high rainfall and abundant melting of ice. Since much water is deflected northwards of the circumpolar winds a southward flow of deep water is necessary to maintain a balance. In the Weddell Sea, in particular, there is a downward streaming of very cold water to the ocean floor.

There is further sinking at the Antarctic convergence, but here water of relatively low temperature and low salinity is involved. Most of this goes to form the Antarctic intermediate water which changes somewhat as a result of mixing. It is, nevertheless, easily traced in all the oceans (see below) despite lack of precise upper and lower boundaries.

Whilst this is a rather oversimplified statement of the actual conditions, it suffices to show that there is a much more complicated movement of the mass of water in the Southern Ocean than a timeless circumpolar revolution. Since water travels northward from this region both on the surface and at the bottom, and since there is an indrawing of water at intermediate levels there must be some renewal of water even if the process is very slow.

The circulation of the sub-surface waters of the oceans. Enough has been said already to indicate that temperature and salinity relations are sufficient to allow of the identification of water masses below the surface. To these should, for the present purpose, be added oxygen content. This is usually high near the surface, but small in water that has sunk to the bottom and so given time for marine organisms to use the oxygen.

All the water circulating within the oceans must at one time have been surface water and has sunk down and then spread laterally. As has been pointed out the main areas of descending water are in the sub-Arctic and Antarctic regions, especially those of the Atlantic Ocean, and there is also no small contribution of dense water from the Mediterranean and Red

Seas. It will be appreciated that there are still very large gaps in our knowledge of this subject, and so far our information is most comprehensive for the Atlantic Ocean. North Atlantic deep and bottom water

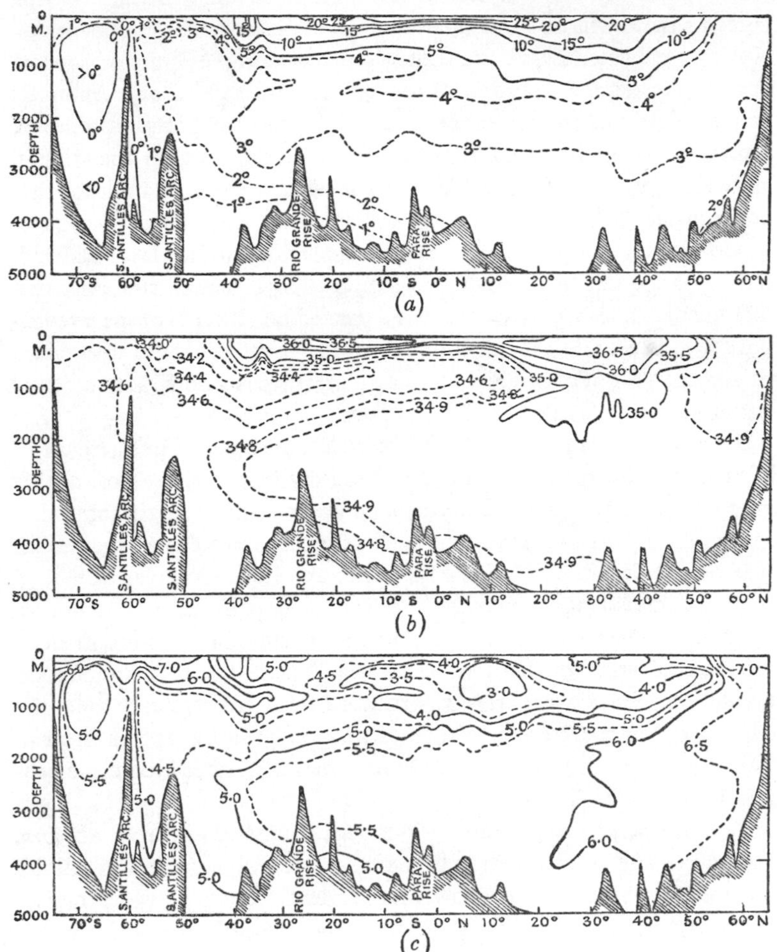

Fig. 91. Vertical sections of the West Atlantic Ocean showing the distribution of (*a*) temperature, (*b*) salinity, and (*c*) oxygen.

both travel to the south, and the outflow from the Mediterranean adds to the upper part of the deep water. The oxygen content of both deep and bottom waters decreases with increase of distance from their place of origin. The Antarctic bottom water flows along the floor of the ocean northwards, but the bottom topography favours a greater penetration (to about lat. 35° N.) in the western basin of the Atlantic. This Antarctic bottom water is overlain by the North Atlantic deep water, which, in its turn, keeps below the Antarctic intermediate water: the deep water is of higher salinity and also usually of higher temperature than those waters between which it flows.

There also appears to be a kind of local circulation working in with the major one. Observations show that much Antarctic bottom and intermediate water returns to that continent after mixing to some extent with the southward-moving deep water of North Atlantic origin. The resulting water is less salt and of less temperature than the North Atlantic deep water, but it is a most important component of the water circulating round the Antarctic continent.

Since the Indian Ocean has no Arctic area, there is clearly a much less noticeable southward movement of deep water; what there is appears to be mainly of Red Sea origin. In the southern part of the ocean, Antarctic intermediate and bottom water can both be recognised. The deep water between these two is, at least partly, from the Atlantic Ocean. There may be a circulation near the Antarctic similar to that in the South Atlantic.

The circumpolar circulation implies that waters from both the Atlantic and Indian Oceans reach the Pacific: mixing, however, has taken place and their salinities in the New Zealand area are considerably less than at their places of origin. Moreover, observations show that round about lat. 40° S. in the Pacific, the greatest salinities are near the bottom, and not in the deep water as in the other oceans. It is suggested that there is a northward movement, as in the other oceans, of the intermediate and bottom water, and a southward flow of deep water. In addition there is the west-to-east flow, which means that some of the deep water of the South Pacific is from the Atlantic and Indian Oceans and has been much diluted by mixing, so losing its salinity maximum.

In the North Pacific there is no formation of deep water. This means that the deeper parts of the North Pacific contain water similar to that in the corresponding northern parts of the South Pacific. What little is known about the exchange of deep water across the equator in this ocean suggests a slight northward motion on the west of the Pacific and possibly a very slow return flow on the east. The fact remains that the deep water of the whole Pacific is extremely uniform in character.

CHAPTER V

DEPOSITS ON THE OCEAN FLOOR

Terrigenous and pelagic deposits. Excepting near a rugged coast the bed of the sea is seldom formed of solid rock. The rock which no doubt exists beneath is usually covered by a layer of loose material which has been deposited upon the ocean floor.

There is a broad and general distinction between the deposits of the continental shelf and slope on the one hand and those of the deep-sea plain and the deeps on the other. The former consist mainly of material derived from the land, and are therefore often called terrigenous deposits; the latter, known as pelagic deposits, are formed to a large extent of the shells and skeletons of animals and plants which when alive float on the surface of the water.

But the distinction is not absolute. The deposits of the continental shelf and slope are not entirely of terrigenous origin; and the pelagic deposits are not entirely composed of the remains of animals and plants. The former include, for example, shell-banks and coral reefs; whilst amongst the pelagic deposits one of the most widespread types consists chiefly of the products of volcanic eruptions.

Moreover, there is no sharp line of demarcation. Pelagic deposits may extend far up the continental slope, and in seas that are free from sediment they are occasionally found even at depths of 200 fathoms.

Pelagic deposits, formed of the remains of floating animals and plants, are probably accumulating all over the ocean. Near the continental masses they are completely masked by the much greater amount of material which is brought down from the land, but where the proportion of terrigenous matter decreases the pelagic deposits begin to show.

Thus near the continents the deposits are mainly of terrigenous origin; away from the continents, even on the ridges and plateaux which rise nearly to the surface of the water, pelagic deposits predominate.

In the shallow waters of the continental shelf and slope both animals and plants flourish abundantly upon the bed of the sea and their remains are added to the material derived from the land. They sometimes constitute, in fact, the greater part of the deposit; but such deposits must be distinguished from the true pelagic deposits formed of the remains of animals and plants which float upon the surface.

The larger fragments thrown out from volcanoes fall mostly on or near the land. When, however, they are of the nature of pumice, they may float for days and may be drifted into the open ocean before they become waterlogged and sink. The finer products of an eruption, known as volcanic dust, may be blown thousands of miles by the wind. It is said that at the eruption of Krakatoa in 1883 much of the dust was carried three times round the globe before it fell. No part of the ocean, therefore, is beyond the reach of material of this kind, and volcanic dust is found even at the greatest depths.

The finer particles of soil from a desert are also sometimes blown far out to sea. In higher latitudes icebergs may carry sand and mud and even boulders into the deep ocean and on melting drop their burden on its floor. In these ways terrigenous material may be mingled with the pelagic deposits proper to mid-ocean, but only the volcanic dust occurs in any considerable quantity.

In general, therefore, the deposits on the continental shelf and slope consist mainly of:

(1) Material derived from the wear and tear of the land.

(2) The remains of animals and plants that live on the bed of the sea.

(3) Volcanic material.

The deposits on the deep-sea plain and in the deeps are formed chiefly of:

(1) The remains of animals and plants that float on the surface of the water.

(2) Volcanic material.

If, however, at any part of the continental shelf or slope there is a deficiency in the supply of the normal material, the pelagic type of deposit will appear.

DEPOSITS OF THE CONTINENTAL SHELF AND SLOPE

Material derived from the wearing of the land. By far the greater part of the deposits on the continental shelf and slope consists of material brought down from the land by rivers or worn from its edge by the sea. The larger fragments are laid down close to the shore, for it is only in shallow water that the waves and currents have power to move them; but the finer particles may be borne a considerable distance out to sea, and the more minute they are the farther they can be carried. Thus to a certain extent the material is sorted according to size. The large blocks which have fallen from the cliffs are often too heavy to be moved at all, and they remain where they fell, until they are further broken up. Smaller boulders and pebbles form shingle-banks, usually between tide-marks, where the waves break violently, and being continually washed to and fro they are worn smooth and round and are gradually reduced in size. Sand is more easily transported and accordingly extends beyond low-water mark, often, indeed, to the edge of the continental shelf. The finest material, which may be grouped under the general name of mud, is carried still farther and covers a large part of the shelf and of the slope beyond. Thus from the shore outwards there is a gradual decrease in the coarseness of the deposit. But the distance to which it travels is not determined entirely by the size of the fragments; it depends also on the strength of the waves and currents, and since this is variable, the sorting of the material is not complete.[1] Only a very small proportion, however, even of the finest particles, is ever carried beyond the continental slope.

It often happens that the strongest currents run parallel to the coast. In that case much of the fine material derived from the land is not carried outwards but is drifted along the shore. Therefore, the sand and mud brought down by a river is not always deposited at the river's mouth; it may travel along the coast for miles and find a resting-place in some quiet bay. It is on account of this lateral drifting of the land-derived material that there is no very striking increase in the width of the terrigenous deposit opposite the mouths of rivers.

The *sand* that is derived from the wearing of the land may contain fragments of any of the rocks or minerals which help to form the land. But some of these are soft and are quickly ground to powder, producing mud instead of sand; others are easily decomposed and the product of the decomposition is usually friable; others again occur only in small quantities or are only locally abundant, and it is only here and there that they form any considerable proportion of the sand. Thus it comes about that by far the greater part of an ordinary sand is made of grains of quartz; for quartz is one of the most abundant constituents of the earth's crust, one of the hardest and most resistant, and one of those least liable to chemical change.

The *muds* are of finer texture than the sands. They consist to a large extent of minute particles of various rock-forming minerals, quartz again being the most abundant; but there is also, as a rule, a considerable quantity of impalpable clayey matter, the proportion of which increases with the distance from the land.

Blue Mud is by far the most widely spread type, but Red Mud is found in the Yellow Sea and off the coast of Brazil. In both the colour

[1] It is now known that the deposits on the continental shelf are seldom arranged with any regularity. Whilst in theory an outward decreasing size of particles and fragments is to be expected, it must be realised that with the lower sea-levels during the Ice Age, the shelf deposits would be resorted, so that at the present time little if any definite arrangement remains.

is due to compounds of iron, but in the Red Mud the iron is in a more highly oxidised condition.

Green Mud is found in some localities, especially on the continental slope off rocky coasts where no large rivers enter the sea. The colour is due to grains of a mineral called glauconite. Glauconite is a silicate of iron and it seems to be formed only in the presence of decaying organic matter. It often fills the chambers of the shells of Foraminifera, and when the shell dissolves, the casts of glauconite are left as little, rounded grains. Where the accumulation of mud is rapid, the proportion of glauconite is too small to affect its general colour; but where the supply of mud is less the glauconite grains are relatively more abundant. Glauconite may also occur in sands in sufficient quantity to give them a greenish colour. Where warm and cold currents alternately invade each other's territory glauconite is sometimes associated with phosphatic nodules, which are derived from organic matter.

Organic deposits. On many parts of the continental shelf both animals and plants live and grow in multitudes, and their shells and skeletons may form the greater part of the deposit. On our own coasts, for example, there are oyster-banks and mussel-beds; in warmer seas corals and calcareous algae flourish luxuriantly. The shells and skeletons may be broken up by the waves, forming sands and muds which differ from the ordinary terrigenous deposits in the fact that they consist almost entirely of carbonate of lime.

It is in the West Indian seas that such organic deposits reach their greatest development. The Bahamas are formed almost entirely of shells and coral sands blown up by the wind, and sands and muds of similar constitution cover the bed of the surrounding sea and are also found extensively in the Gulf of Mexico and the Caribbean Sea.

Volcanic deposits. In volcanic regions the deposits of the continental shelf and slope consist chiefly of fragments thrown out during eruptions, and are not derived to so great an extent as usual from the wearing away of the land. There is the same sorting and distribution of the material, but there is a difference in its composition. Volcanic sands, for example, consist of fragments of lava, instead of grains of quartz.

The various deposits laid down in the waters of the continental shelf and slope in past geological times form the bulk of the sedimentary rocks described in pt. III, ch. I. Sands, for example, are indurated by pressure caused partly by the weight of the accumulating deposit, perhaps even more by pressure produced when the sea floor on which they rest is raised up or folded as a result of earth movements. Similarly muds may become mudstones, or even slate as a result of intense pressure. Shales may be formed in tidal flats where, either between tides, or during neap tides, the surface dries in part before the next tide or the next spring tides bring about the deposition of new material. Pebble beds become conglomerates, and sedimentary rocks may be cemented by calcite or silica introduced in solution at some stage in the evolution of the rock. Limestones may be wholly or largely organic, or partly formed by the erosion of former limestone rocks. Many rocks are mixed; an argillaceous limestone, for example, implies that during deposition much mud was deposited at the same time as the limestone accumulated.

DEPOSITS OF THE DEEP-SEA PLAIN AND OF THE DEEPS

With the exception of the finer sorts of volcanic dust very little terrigenous material is carried beyond the foot of the continental slope, and the deep-sea plain is covered for the most part by pelagic deposits. Even on the slope itself, wherever the supply of terrigenous mud is deficient the deposit becomes more or less pelagic in type.

The pelagic deposits consist in part of the remains of animals and plants which float on the surface of the sea and in part of volcanic dust brought by the wind. On account of the low temperature of the water and for other reasons also the number of animals and plants which actually live at the bottom of the deeper parts of the ocean is comparatively small, and their remains help but little in the formation of the deposit.

When first brought up to the surface most of the pelagic deposits are in the form of a liquid mud, which is commonly spoken of as ooze. When dried the ooze becomes a fine grained and powdery mass, partly amorphous and partly made of little shells, sometimes visible to the naked eye and sometimes of microscopic size.

These shells belong to several different kinds of organisms, and the ooze is named after the predominant type. In some the shell is made of carbonate of lime, in others of silica, and the ooze accordingly may be either calcareous or siliceous.

Besides the organic oozes, formed of the remains of animals and plants, there is another type of deposit, known as Red Clay, which consists mainly of inorganic material and which is apparently of volcanic origin.

The pelagic deposits may therefore be classified as follows:

Organic	Calcareous	Pteropod ooze Globigerina ooze
	Siliceous	Radiolarian ooze Diatom ooze
Inorganic		Red Clay

Pteropod ooze. In this the shells of a certain class of floating molluscs, known as Pteropods, form the most conspicuous constituent. These shells are always thin and fragile and are often more or less conical in shape. They may be a quarter of an inch or half an inch in length and they are always formed of carbonate of lime.

Pteropod ooze occurs chiefly on the ridges and plateaux which rise from the deep-sea plain, where the water is comparatively shallow but at the same time distant from any continental mass. It is found, for example, at several places on the mid-Atlantic ridge. It is most typically developed at depths of about 800–1000 fathoms, but is often met with in shallower waters and it may extend downwards to about 1800 fathoms.

Pteropods flourish most abundantly where the surface water is warm and the annual range of temperature small, and the deposit is therefore found mostly within or near the tropics. But it is not very widely spread and it is principally in the Atlantic Ocean that it occurs.

Globigerina ooze. Globigerina ooze is made up chiefly of the calcareous shells of Foraminifera, *Globigerina* and its near relatives being the most abundant and widely distributed genera. These shells are always small, commonly about the size of the head of an ordinary pin, but often smaller and sometimes larger.

This is the most widespread type of ooze in the Atlantic and Indian Oceans and covers also a large area of the South Pacific. In general it is a deposit of either warm or temperate seas: between Greenland and Norway it spreads beyond the Arctic Circle, but here, the temperature of the surface waters is far above the average for the latitude.

It is at depths ranging from 1500 to 2000 fathoms that Globigerina ooze is most abundantly and most characteristically developed. But where it is not masked by too great an accumulation of terrigenous material it may be found in waters much shallower than this. Its lower limit varies. As the depth increases it gradually disappears, giving place to Red Clay. Occasionally it has been found even below 3000 fathoms, but it does not occur in the actual deeps.

Diatom ooze. Diatoms belong to the vegetable kingdom and are in general of microscopic size. Their skeletons or frustules are made of silica. They flourish principally in the colder seas.

This type of ooze is found chiefly at depths varying from 600 to 2000 fathoms, but it may extend even to 4000 fathoms. It forms a broad belt in the Southern Ocean outside the terrigenous deposits of the Antarctic continent and a narrower band on the northern border of the Pacific Ocean.

Radiolarian ooze. The *Radiolaria* are minute organisms belonging to the same great division of the animal kingdom as the Foraminifera. Their shells or skeletons, however, are made of silica instead of carbonate of lime, and are characterised by their remarkable openwork structure, forming a kind of lattice supporting the body of the animal rather than enclosing it.

Radiolarian ooze occurs only in deep waters, and is seldom found at depths less than 2000 fathoms. It extends downwards to 5000 fathoms or more and is accordingly met with in the deeps as well as on the deep-sea plain. It is confined to tropical seas and occurs chiefly in the Pacific Ocean and to a very much smaller extent in the Indian Ocean, but is not known in the Atlantic, although *Radiolaria* are often found alongside the predominating *Globigerina* and allies.

Distribution of the organic oozes. The distribution of the organic oozes is governed partly by the depth of the ocean, partly by the productivity of the surface water. The calcareous oozes are never found in the deepest parts of the ocean. At these great depths the carbonate of lime is dissolved, either in falling or soon after it reaches the bottom. Consequently, although Pteropods and *Globigerina* live at the surface and are not affected by the depth of the water beneath, their shells form no deposit in the deeps. The shells of Pteropods are thinner and more easily dissolved than those of *Globigerina* (*sensu lato*), and therefore Pteropod ooze does not extend downwards so far as Globigerina ooze. Pteropods, moreover, or at least the shell-bearing Pteropods, do not flourish to any great extent except in water that is warm, while *Globigerina* lives also in colder seas but dislikes the turbidity of shallow seas near the mouths of muddy rivers. For these reasons Pteropod ooze is limited to tropical and sub-tropical regions, while *Globigerina* ooze spreads over both tropical and temperate seas.

Siliceous material is not so easily dissolved and the siliceous oozes, therefore, extend to greater depths than the calcareous deposits. But they can only occur where the organisms that form them live in abundance in the surface waters. *Radiolaria* flourish principally in the warmer seas and diatoms in the colder waters. Consequently, Radiolarian ooze occurs within the tropics, Diatom ooze within and near the polar seas. Even in warm waters, however, *Radiolaria* are generally less abundant than Foraminifera, and it is accordingly only in deep water, where the foraminiferal shells are dissolved, that the proportion of Radiolarian remains rises sufficiently high to form a true Radiolarian ooze.

Red Clay. Red Clay is the most widely spread of all the pelagic deposits. In composition it is a true clay, consisting mainly of hydrated silicate of aluminium, coloured by oxide of iron. It is not found above 2000 fathoms but it is the characteristic deposit of the deeper parts of the ocean. It covers more than half of the Pacific Ocean, and also large areas of the Indian and Atlantic Oceans, extending downwards to the greatest depths observed.

The Red Clay is apparently formed at least in part by the decomposition of the volcanic material which is carried out to sea, either as pumice floating on the waves or as dust blown by the winds. Such material falls all over the ocean floor, but excepting near volcanic regions the supply is small and the rate of accumulation is extremely slow.

The calcareous oozes are deposited much more rapidly, and where the water is not too deep they conceal except locally the comparatively small amount of volcanic material that falls with them. If, however, Globigerina or Pteropod ooze is treated with dilute hydrochloric acid, the carbonate of lime is dissolved and the material left is very like Red Clay; the volcanic matter is there, but it is small in amount compared with the carbonate of lime. At great depths in the ocean a similar process goes on; the carbonate of lime is dissolved and nothing but Red Clay is left. At intermediate depths there is a gradual passage from Globigerina ooze to Red Clay.

Since silica is not so easily dissolved, the siliceous oozes may extend even into the deeps, and Radiolarian ooze has been found beyond 5000 fathoms. Whether the deposit formed is a Radiolarian ooze or a Red Clay depends not so much on the depth of the water but rather on the abundance of *Radiolaria* at the surface.

The extreme slowness of the deposition of Red Clay in mid-ocean is shown by the fact that sharks' teeth and ear-bones of whales, sometimes of extinct species, are frequently brought up in dredging and soundings in the Red Clay areas. They have lain so long that the remainder of the skeletons has been dissolved, and in the case of the extinct species they must have been there for many thousands of years; yet, at the most, they have been barely covered by the deposit. Moreover, spherules of iron and other minerals like the dust that sometimes falls upon the earth in meteoric showers have also been found. There is no reason to suppose that this dust falls more abundantly on the ocean than on the land. But on the land it is lost in the mass of other material; in the Red Clay area it is buried very slowly and forms a much larger proportion of the whole deposit.

Coring the ooze. It has recently been possible to take samples of the deep-sea oozes by means of coring tubes let over the side of research vessels at the end of long hawsers worked by winches. Up to about

60 feet of ooze have in some places been so obtained, each sample being about 2 inches in diameter.

The modern device to obtain cores of this length is a simple tube with a piston inside. When two counter weights suspended a little below the end of the tube touch the bottom, tension slackens and a catch is released above the corer, allowing the tube to fall under a weight of about 8 tons into the ooze; the piston up the centre is held in position and allows hydrostatic pressure to force the ooze up the tube. A valve at the bottom of the tube prevents the ooze slipping out as the apparatus is being hauled up to the ship.

The *Globigerina* content of many of the cores has been analysed biologically and as a result it is now possible to trace into the past the variations of temperature which must have taken place in the surface layers of the waters where these Foraminifera used to live, each species having a definite tolerance to temperature limits. The validity of this method has been confirmed by recent work with oxygen isotopes which can give a clue to the past temperatures by testing the oxygen content in the shell substance of the Foraminifera. The rate of productivity can also be used in this respect, for the shells of these minute organisms secrete more carbonate of lime in warm waters than they do in cold. The carbonate content of core-samples is, therefore, a further reflection of temperature conditions of surface waters. It is estimated by radioactive methods that the rate of accumulation of Globigerina ooze is $2\frac{1}{2}$ cm. per 1000 years, so a time scale can be given to climatic variations.

Cores also tell us much about the history of ocean deposits from their mineral content, volcanic ash particles, and the accumulation of sands and pebbles at great depths. These often indicate submarine movement and deep currents.

It has been found, too, that some of the oozes in different parts of the world have been stirred up by bottom-living organisms such as holothurians (sea-cucumbers). These organisms burrow into the surface of the ooze, feeding on decaying organic matter, so that the true sedimentation of the ooze becomes mixed up; it is then impossible to use such material in cores as an indicator of true chronology and steady deposition.

CHAPTER VI

CORAL REEFS AND ISLANDS

In many parts of the tropical seas coral grows in such profusion that it forms rocky reefs, often of great size, rising up to the surface of the water. Such reefs may fringe the shores of land that is not made of coral or they may form islands far removed from any other kind of land. Excepting where earth movements have taken place it is seldom that a coral island rises more than 10 or 20 feet above the level of high tide, and even this height is reached only by the heaps of broken coral and coral sand thrown by the waves upon the reef. The living coral does not grow above water, scarcely indeed above low-water mark, and it is only where there has been elevation of the land that the reef itself stands up above the waves (cf. pl. 5*b*).

Coral reefs and islands are not made entirely of corals. Other organisms play a very considerable part in their formation. Calcareous algae are often at least as important as the corals themselves, and much of the deposit consists of the shells of Foraminifera, Molluscs, Echinoderms, and other creatures.

The coral is formed by animals which are very like the sea anemones of our own coast. Some of them live apart, each on its own little cup of coral; but in the true reef-builders the individuals or polyps have budded off from earlier ones so that the carbonate of lime stems or skeletons of the polyps are attached in a branching form to produce colonies. The coral is deposited at the base of each individual, as internal skeletal material on the sides and as vertical supporting plates within the flesh of each polyp. The polyp continues to grow upwards upon newly deposited basal plates.

Distribution of coral reefs. Coral reefs belong to the warmer seas and are almost entirely confined to the zone between lat. 30° N. and 30° S. In the Bermudas in lat. 32° N. there are reefs which are partly made of coral, but calcareous algae and other organisms take a larger share than usual in their formation.

The coral animal or polyp lays eggs—or rather ejects them into the sea. When these hatch the young live freely in the sea among the plankton for some three or four days, some only a few hours. If by some good fortune any one individual happens to find a resting place on stone or other coral or algae it will survive, but the great majority of the young perish in the open ocean, unable to find a resting place to start a new colony, or drift beyond the lower limit of temperature tolerance. In this precarious manner coral has, through the ages, gradually spread at the mercy of ocean currents to form reefs in widely separated localities.

Calcareous algae are also prolific in coral reefs. These organisms are primitive plants which secrete carbonate of lime and the two chief genera living today in sea-water are *Lithophyllum* and *Lithothamnion.* Many live in lime-rich fresh-water streams and assist in the formation of tufa; large numbers are marine and may be found encrusting rocks in many parts of the world, but it is in the warm, tropical seas that they thrive best, and it is therefore not surprising that these live among the corals and assist in the construction of the reef. The carbonate secreted by these organisms often incorporates broken corals, foraminiferal and mollusc shells filling in to some extent the interspaces in coral colonies.

Even within the zone from 30° N. to 30° S. true coral reefs are unknown on the western shores of the continents. Masses of coral may occur but they do not form typical reefs on the western coast of either America, Africa, or Australia, although on the eastern sides of all these continents there are regions where reefs abound. It is the zone of the trade-winds and the western side is the leeward side, where there is an upwelling of cold water. Probably this is the principal cause of the absence of reefs; but it can scarcely be the sole one, for near the equator, even on these shores, the surface water is warm enough for corals.

Coral reefs are especially numerous in the Pacific and Indian Oceans. In the Atlantic they are abundant in the West Indian seas and are also found off the coast of Brazil, but the only reefs in mid-Atlantic are those of the Bermudas.

The largest of all coral reefs are the Great Barrier Reefs of Australia, which extend along the coast of Queensland for more than a thousand miles. The 'Barrier' is composed of myriads of reefs of all sizes spread over a coastal platform. In the north the Outer Barrier is about 80 miles from the mainland: the distance decreases to the south as far as Cape Melville from which point the inner edge of the Barrier is only seven miles. Still farther south the distance increases, and south of Cairns it is no longer even approximately continuous, but splits up into a wide band of discontinuous reefs, and in the far south the so-called Barrier runs seaward of the Capricorn Channel, and the Bunker and Capricorn Islands are the most southerly coral islands on the Queensland coast. They are a series of individual reefs, some of which are crowned with an island. Although usually marked on maps as part of the Barrier, they are totally unlike the real Barrier which only begins north of Trinity opening off Cairns.

There are corals even in the northern seas and in deep waters, but they do not there form masses of any great size. Red coral, used for necklaces, consists of tree-like branching species of the genus *Corallium*. One of these inhabits the Mediterranean, and the waters around the Cape Verde Islands. It lives in fairly deep water. Other species of considerable value are found in Japanese waters, and another is found off Timor Island. While these 'precious' corals are not reef-builders, there is no reason to suppose that species do not live on reefs. The real reef-builders require a surface temperature that does not fall more than a degree or two below 70° F., and they do not grow freely at greater depths than 30 fathoms, though scattered colonies may spread downwards to 50 fathoms. Moreover, they are quickly killed by any deposition of sediment,[1] and therefore they are found only where the sea is clear, and never where a river brings down mud from the land.

It is easy, accordingly, to understand why coral reefs are practically confined to the zone between 30° N. and 30° S., and why, within that zone, they favour the eastern shores of the land-masses. But there are thousands of coral reefs in mid-ocean, rising, to all appearances, directly from the floor of the deep-sea, and it is not easy to prove how the foundations of these reefs were built, at depths far below those in which the corals can live. This is a problem concerning which there are still great differences of opinion.

Structure of coral reefs. Three kinds of coral reef are generally recognised as more or less distinct—namely, fringing reefs, barrier reefs, and atolls.

A fringing reef is one that lies close to the shore of some continent or island. Its surface forms a rough and uneven platform around the coast, about the level of low water, and its outer edge slopes downwards into the sea. Between the coral platform and the land there is sometimes a shallow channel or lagoon which is filled with water even at low tide (fig. 92).

When the lagoon is wide and deep and the reef lies at a distance from the shore and rises from deep water it is called a barrier reef (fig. 93).

An atoll is a reef in the form of a ring or horseshore with a lagoon in the centre (fig. 94). Sometimes there is a small island in the middle of the lagoon and the reef is really a barrier reef around it. But in the true atoll there is no central island, only a ring-shaped reef enclosing a lagoon.

[1] Care must be taken in this matter. Corals can clean themselves very effectively, and a slow but more or less continuous supply of sediment is far less destructive than a sudden influx. Many of the Australian waters where coral thrives luxuriantly are at least as 'dirty' as those of the English Channel.

There are reefs which are never uncovered even at the lowest tides, and their jagged crests hidden beneath the waves are a serious danger to passing ships. But as a rule, when circumstances are favourable, a coral reef grows both upwards and outwards until it reaches low-water level. Its upward growth then ceases, but it may still continue to spread outwards. Therefore, whether it is a fringing reef, a barrier reef or an atoll, the top of the reef is a rugged and uneven flat which at low tide is just awash. It is traversed by fissures, especially near its margin, through which the sea advances and retreats as the waves break over its outer edge. The outer edge itself is often slightly raised, forming a low rim, which is made of calcareous algae rather than of coral.

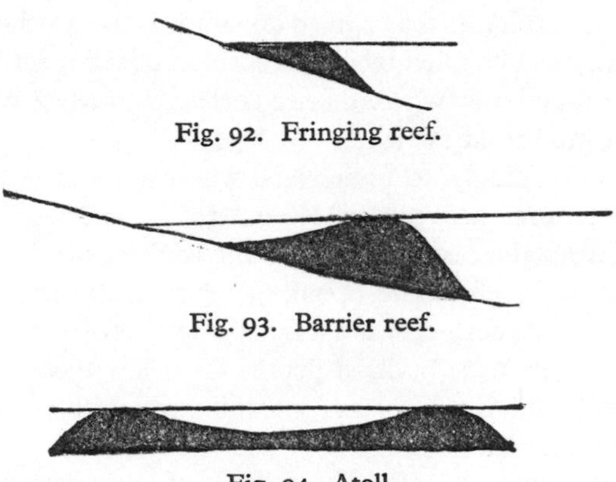

Fig. 92. Fringing reef.

Fig. 93. Barrier reef.

Fig. 94. Atoll.

The seaward face of the reef is steep and compact, but at the top it is usually rounded or bevelled, so that for some 20 or 30 fathoms the slope is moderate (fig. 95*b*). Perhaps the growth of coral is most luxuriant some distance beneath the surface, and in any case the deeper colonies are less liable to be torn off by the waves. At greater depths the angle of slope may be 40 or 50 degrees or even more.

Towards the lagoon the flat may slope gently beneath the water, or it may end in a sort of step of no great depth. But often the shore of the lagoon is sandy and the reef itself is completely concealed. In the lagoon the water usually deepens very slowly except at the step already mentioned, and even in the deepest lagoons soundings of more than 50 fathoms are rare. Coral heads may rise from the floor of the lagoon.

On the reef-flat the coral is often dead. In the lagoon there will be living corals, and calcareous algae and Foraminifera are abundant. But the reef-building types of coral thrive better on the seaward face of the reef, where there is less sediment and the supply of food is ample. On the other hand it is clear that the more fragile forms cannot exist on the exposed side of a reef. The growth of a reef is therefore mainly outwards. In some cases the lagoon appears to be filling up, in others it is deepening.

Fig. 95 (*a*). Generalised section of a low wooded island (island reef) within the Great Barrier Reefs of Queensland. *A*, low-water spring tides; *B*, coral heads; *C*, Cay; *D*, beach-rock; *E*, mangroves; *F*, dunes; *G*, high conglomerate platform; *J*, low conglomerate platform; *H*, Avicennia (mangrove); *L*, rampart; *M*, windward pavement of coral rock; *P*, coral head. (See pl. 5*a*).

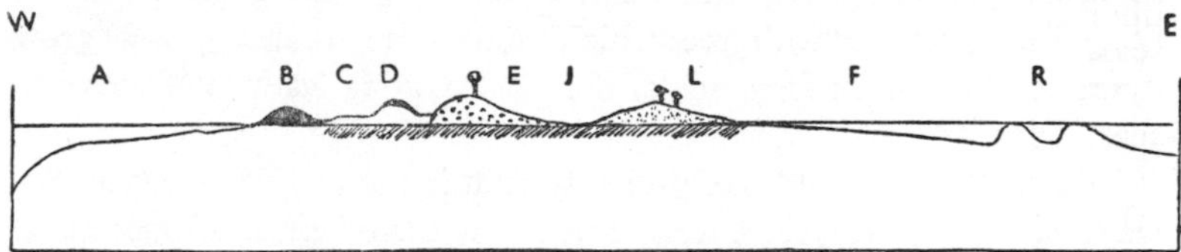

Fig. 95 (*b*). Diagrammatic section through the rim of Funafuti atoll. *A*, constantly submerged portion of the reef; *B*, Nullipore rim; *C*, reef flat of coral rock; *D*, ledge of coral rock; *E*, seaward (outer) ridge; *F*, lagoon floor; *J*, central flat of islet; *L*, lagoon mound; *R*, growing reefs of lagoon.

Coral islands. Some little distance within the outer edge of the reef flat there is a zone of boulders, consisting of masses of broken coral thrown up by the sea and sometimes standing above the water even at high tide. If the reef is narrow the boulder zone may border the lagoon; the smaller fragments, forming coral sand, find no resting-place upon the flat, excepting in the hollows, and are swept across into the lagoon or backwards into the sea. But if the reef is wide, the waves are unable to wash the sand across and it collects in mounds behind the boulder zone, forming islands which rest upon the coral flat. Sand from the lagoon may also be added to these mounds, if the direction of the wind is favourable. Foraminifera often form a large proportion of the sand, in addition to the fragments of coral and calcareous algae. The whole is easily consolidated by percolating water, which dissolves and re-deposits carbonate of lime, cementing the particles together. In this way beach-rock or beach conglomerate is formed. There is no completely comprehensive explanation of this phenomenon: more commonly it occurs on the windward side of islands and always within the extreme tidal range. On the other hand it is often in patches and seldom continuous for long distances. The finer varieties resemble paving stones; the coarser may be very rough indeed. It is fairly stable, and it is common to find old lines of beach-rock from inside of which the uncemented sand or boulders have been washed away. Sometimes the rock or conglomerate is definitely in steps, indicating slight changes of level.

Many coral islands are nothing more than mounds of sand, resting upon a reef-flat. In that case they may be several miles in length and may even be of considerable breadth, but they are always low. When, however, there has been elevation of the land, the reef itself may be raised above the sea, and the island may attain an altitude of several hundred feet.

In the course of time seeds brought by winds and currents, or carried by birds, will establish themselves, and may clothe the island with a luxuriant growth of vegetation almost to the water's edge. The low-lying islands covered with trees which from a little distance seem to grow upon the water itself form one of the most striking features of the coral seas.

Whilst all coral islands are probably built in the way described above, there is, nevertheless, considerable variety in their form and appearance. If the reef on which the islands are forming is annular, sooner or later a fairly continuous island—or a line of islands—carrying trees and shrubs will enclose the lagoon, thus producing the typical atoll. Any part of an atoll island may have originated as a cay, a simple flat heap of sand. Simple cays often occur on isolated reefs in shallower waters. The small cays outside Kingston Harbour, Jamaica, or those in the Bay of Batavia, Java, are mainly of this type. They are common, too, along the Queensland coast where, also, another type of coral island occurs. In the steamer channel, between the outer barrier and the mainland, there are many isolated reefs of all shapes and sizes. On many of them a true cay, partly surrounded by beach-rock and carrying land plants and trees, is found near the leeward side. On the windward side of the reef there are ridges of coral shingle piled up by the waves, and enclosing mangroves which often make a dense wood 40–50 feet high and covering several acres. (See fig. 95*a* and pl. 5*a*.) It is not uncommon to find that the shingle ridges have been cemented very hard, and indicate, under certain circumstances, slight changes of sea-level. They can be correlated with raised beaches on the mainland.

Mode of formation of coral reefs. A fringing reef is formed by corals, with the help of other calcareous organisms, growing upon the floor of the shallow seas around a continent or island. The corals spread outwards from the shore to a depth of about 30 fathoms, but beyond that depth there are practically none. The coral masses grow upwards until they reach low-water level, and thus a platform is formed, which ends within the position of the original 30-fathom line, and the edge of the platform rises from about that depth. The outer corals grow more freely than those which are closer to the shore, probably because they are more favourably situated for receiving supplies of food from the sea, because they are less liable to be covered by sediment, and also because of oxygenated water. Consequently, the outer part of the reef may reach the surface first and a shallow channel or lagoon may be left between the platform and the land.

So much is generally agreed; but in barrier reefs and atolls the outer side of the reef rises from depths where no reef-building corals live. Various explanations have been suggested to explain this, but the problem is still not solved completely. The theories and ideas advanced may be treated conveniently under four main headings: first, the Darwin-Dana hypothesis of subsidence put forward in the 1840's; secondly, the non-subsidence views associated with Murray, Semper, Agassiz, and others; thirdly, the glacial control hypothesis put forward by Daly; and finally the more general application of the significance of the physiography of the shores around which reefs exist. Davis was the first to emphasise this matter which has now been recognised as of great importance.

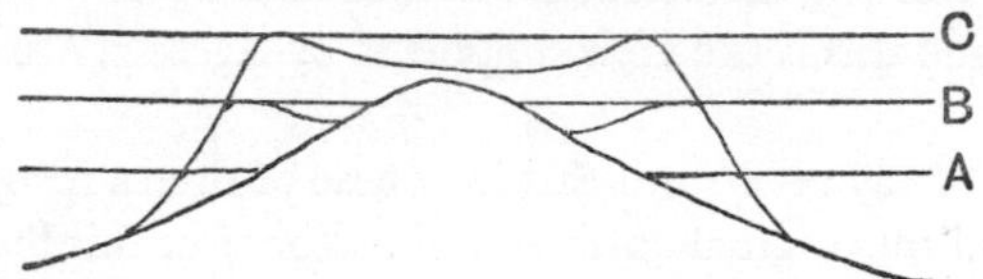

Fig. 96. Darwin's theory of the formation of atolls. *A*, *B*, *C*, represent the level of the sea at successive stages in the growth of the reef.

The Darwin-Dana hypothesis. The theory of subsidence was first proposed by Darwin.[1] He supposes that all reefs begin as fringing reefs around a continent or island (fig. 96). As long as the relative level of land and sea remains unchanged, the reef will continue as a fringing reef. But if the land and sea floor subside[2] so that the reef sinks beneath the water, the corals will again begin to grow upwards. The growth, as already

[1] Independently Dana put forward extremely similar views at almost the same time; it is fairer that the hypothesis should be known by the joint names.

[2] The same effects will be produced by a rise in the level of the sea. It is very difficult and often impossible to distinguish locally between sinking of the land and rising of the sea, and in the following account the term subsidence must be understood to apply to both.

explained, is most vigorous at the outer edge of the reef, while nearer to the shore it is extremely slow. Accordingly, it will often happen that only the outer part of the reef can keep pace with the subsidence, and the inner part is flooded by the sea, thus forming a lagoon between the reef platform and the land. As the subsidence goes on, the width and depth of the lagoon increase and the reef becomes a barrier reef. If the reef is round an island the island may at length be entirely submerged, and nothing will be left but a ring of reef enclosing a lagoon.

According to this view, barrier reefs and atolls can occur only where there has been subsidence, and every atoll marks the position of a former island. Moreover, the sea outside an atoll will usually be deep, for the subsidence must have been sufficient to submerge the central island.

Non-subsidence theories. If atolls and barrier reefs rising from deep water do not owe their formation to subsidence in the manner described by Darwin, an alternative is that their bases were not built by living coral; and this is the view supported by Agassiz, Murray, Semper and others.

Sir John Murray points out that in course of time a fringing reef may spread beyond the original 30-fathom line; for after this limit is reached fragments of coral, both large and small, will accumulate at the foot of the reef, and upon the pile of talus the corals will continue to grow outwards. In this way, without any subsidence the reef may extend into deep water; but only the upper 30 fathoms will be built by living coral; in deeper water the foundations will consist of the debris from the reef, cemented together by the action of the water.

As the reef grows outwards the inner corals die, and Murray believes that the dead coral is slowly dissolved. Thus a lagoon is hollowed out between the rim of the reef and the shore, and the fringing reef is gradually converted into a barrier reef.

Atolls, according to Murray's view, are formed on the tops of plateaux and hills which rise from the sea floor to depths at which reef-building corals live. Colonies of corals will establish themselves and grow both upwards and outwards, many colonies perhaps uniting into a single mass of reef. In any such mass the outer corals will grow most freely and will reach the surface first, forming a ring or atoll enclosing a lagoon. When the reef has reached this stage, or even at an earlier period, the living coral is practically confined to its seaward face and the interior of the reef is dead. The lagoon, it was argued, but not proved, will be enlarged and deepened by solution of the dead coral, while the outward growth will still go on. The ring of coral will open out more widely and the size of the atoll will increase with age.

Murray's theory requires a very large number of submarine hills or plateaux, all of them reaching to about the same level; their tops must all have been some 15–30 fathoms below the surface of the water. Such a remarkable coincidence in height needs explanation, and Murray suggests two ways in which it may be brought about, even if the original heights were different.

Most islands in mid-ocean, except the coral islands themselves, are of volcanic origin, and he believes that the elevations on the ocean floor were mainly volcanic. Many of them rose above the sea, and many still stand above the waves; but since volcanoes are often nothing more than piles of fragments thrown out during eruptions, many would be quickly worn away by the sea, till only a shoal was left to mark the site. This has actually happened in the case of one or two new volcanic islands which have appeared and disappeared during the last hundred years.

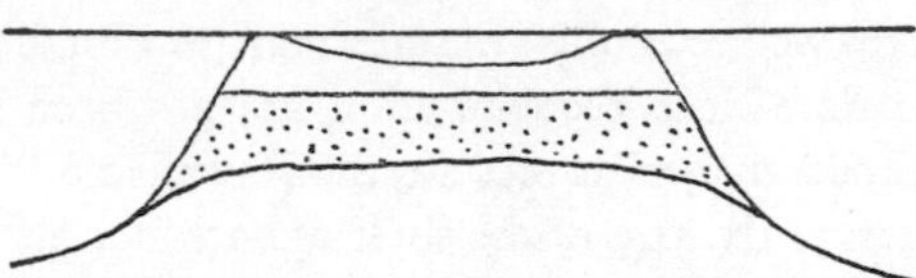

Fig. 97. Murray's theory of the formation of atolls. The dotted portion represents pelagic and other deposits,[1] reaching upwards to the level of coral growth.

Other hills may not originally have reached the 30-fathom line. Pelagic deposits, it was assumed, would accumulate upon them more quickly than in the deeper sea around because there would be less solution of the carbonate of lime.[2] In time their summits would be raised to the level at which shells and deep-sea corals live; and finally they would reach the depth where reef-building corals can begin to grow (fig. 97).

In these two ways, by the wearing away of hills which stood above the sea and by deposition upon those which lay too deep beneath the surface, a sufficient number of elevations may be produced on which reef-building corals can live.

Daly's glacial control theory. This theory was first published in 1915 after a visit by Daly to the Hawaiian Islands where he was struck by the narrowness of the reefs. He also noticed traces of former glaciation on the mountains of the islands. That there might be some

[1] It is difficult, if not impossible, to see how soft pelagic oozes accumulating in the manner Murray supposed could stand at the steep angle characteristic of the outer slopes of coral reefs.

[2] It will be noticed that Murray allowed solution at great depths and in lagoons, but seems to have assumed that there was little or none at or near the summits of convenient submarine mountains.

connection between reef growth and the temperature of the water was thus suggested to him. Since the present temperature of Hawaiian waters in winter is only just sufficient for coral growth, it is undoubtedly correct to assume that during the Ice Age it was far too cold, hence any pre-glacial reefs would have been killed. Moreover, it is now generally accepted that, whatever view may be taken about the precise number of major advances and retreats of the ice-caps during the Pleistocene, the level of the sea fell, perhaps as much as 200–300 feet, during the times of maximum glaciation, and rose again in warmer times. The combination of cold water and a low sea-level would not only kill reefs, but would also lead to the formation of platforms and benches at a level now well below that of the existing sea-surface. Daly, however, believed that the major benching was completed in the Tertiary period, and that only minor trimming took place during the low-sea levels of the Ice Age (see his *The Changing World of the Ice Age*, p. 247). When conditions ameliorated corals might well recolonise the area and grow on the newly formed shelves. If the time since recolonisation has not been long then it is reasonable to expect that, as at present, the Hawaiian reefs might well be out of proportion to the size of the shelf upon which they rest.

The drop in temperature as well as the fall in water-level must have been world wide, but there is good reason to believe that in equatorial areas the lower temperatures did not fall below that required for coral growth; only near the limits of coral growth (i.e. the marginal belts) was this the case. Near the equator, therefore, we may suppose that the fall of water-level temporarily exposed reefs which, on the death of the coral and other organisms, were soon eroded away. On the other hand there was always plenty of growing coral about sea-level so that there need not have been much, if any, active platform-making in these seas as in the marginal belts.

This theory does not, by itself, imply any great vertical movements like those invoked by Darwin and Dana. Nor is any excessive amount of erosion implied—usually not more than may on reasonable grounds be expected to have occurred. At this stage only two other points need mention: first that Daly recognised the possibility of local tectonic movements, and second that it is now quite clear that whatever may be the final solution of the coral reef problem, it is impossible to omit from it the significance of Pleistocene fluctuations of sea-level.

The significance of coastal physiography. Just before the war of 1914–18 Davis became interested in the coral reef problem, and although he has not put forward any particular hypothesis that may be linked with his name, he has, nevertheless, given us a new outlook. It is true that

Dana and others had, rather incidentally, called attention to drowned valleys, but no one had really focused attention on the true meaning of the physiography of the coastlines within a barrier reef. It is not easy to compress this subject into one or two paragraphs, but particular attention may be called to two points. Drowned valleys or embayed coastlines imply a change of level of either land or sea. But it is true also that in Daly's theory a post-glacial rise of sea-level will imply the occurrence of drowned valleys, but only to a depth not exceeding about 300 feet as a maximum. If it can be proved that drowned valleys of *subaerial origin* exist within barrier reefs to considerably greater depths than this, then we have good evidence of subsidence. On the other hand, great care must be taken in this matter since it may happen that a given valley has subsided several hundreds of feet, but soundings only reveal water less than, perhaps, 200 feet deep because sediment has filled up the lower part of the valley. To prove this is not always easy, but accurate charts are clearly necessary, and if they suggest steep-sided and flat-floored submerged valleys, there is *prima facie* reason for supposing that sedimentation has taken place. The whole of the topography must, however, be carefully considered.

The other important matter concerns cliffs. This subject is also closely linked with Daly's theory, according to which it is clear that if platforms were cut at low levels during the Ice Age, cliffs were obviously formed as well. Hence cliffs wholly or partly drowned and existing behind reefs should be characteristic of the more marginal coral areas. In those parts of the world where coral growth was continuous, although sea-level fluctuated, the reefs would have protected the land within and, apart from any minor nipping by lagoon waves, cliffs should be absent.

Davis also laid stress upon two other points—the uncomformable contacts of reefs with their foundations, and the disposal of detritus eroded away from reef-encircled islands. Both these points, together with those mentioned above, were used by him in supporting the subsidence theory of coral reefs. They will not be discussed further here, because they appear to be mainly of academic interest and of considerably less importance than drowned valleys and cliffing.

Discussion of the evidence. In the limited space that is here available it is impossible to do more than indicate a few of the arguments that have been advanced in support of these theories.

The evidence is strong that some atolls and barrier reefs have been formed in areas of subsidence. The coast of Queensland within the Great Barrier Reefs shows the drowned valleys and outlying islands characteristic of a sinking land. In many ring-shaped reefs with a central island, the island has a similar indented coast-line, and it is evident that a little further depression would convert the reef into an atoll. But clearly the submergence must be shown to be greater than that implied in the glacial control theory if actual subsidence has taken place.

It is equally clear that other atolls have been formed without subsidence. Darwin himself recognised that in shallow seas the natural outward growth of coral masses would lead to the formation of ring-shaped reefs, and he thought that the atolls and barrier-like reefs of the West Indian seas grew in this fashion upon banks of sediment accumulated by currents. But he distinguished between these and the deep-rooted reefs of the Indian and Pacific Oceans, which he believed to have a solid foundation of coral.

Even in the Pacific, however, many atolls are found in areas where there is no evidence of subsidence, and where, on the contrary, there is definite proof of elevation. In the Pelew Islands, and in many other island groups of the Pacific, there are coral reefs which have been raised above the sea, pointing clearly to elevation of the land; and yet in the same groups there may be atolls. Moreover, atolls are sometimes found in water of no great depth, rising from a plateau and not apparently from sunken peaks.

According to Darwin's view barrier reefs and the reefs of atolls must be of very considerable thickness, often 2000 feet or more. According to Murray's view only the upper 30 fathoms (or less than 200 feet) of such reefs is made of coral which has grown in place. It has been observed that in many raised reefs the thickness of coral is not more than 200 feet, and it has even been maintained, though on very insufficient evidence, that this thickness is scarcely ever exceeded. There are several examples of atolls which have been raised above the sea, and in those which have been examined the depth of the coral deposits is less than 200 feet. Santa Anna, in the Solomon Islands, and probably Christmas Island, south of Java, are instances.

On Murray's hypothesis the steepness of the external slope of many reefs is somewhat difficult to explain. It is easy to understand that a mass built up solidly of growing coral may have almost perpendicular walls, but according to him it is only the upper 30 fathoms of a reef that are formed in this way. The lower part consists of pelagic deposits, the shells and skeletons of animals and plants which live on the floor of the sea below 30 fathoms, and the talus of the reef. It is, in fact, an accumulation of fragments; and it is difficult to believe that any such accumulation can have an external slope even approximating to 75°. Yet slopes as steep as this or even steeper are met with on the seaward faces of coral reefs at depths far greater than 30 fathoms. It is possible, however, that calcareous algae or other sedentary organisms might form a solid deposit—that, in fact, reef-builders other than corals may grow in deep waters.

The depth of the lagoon in many reefs is also not very satisfactorily accounted for by Murray's explanation. The reef is supposed to be built upon a platform which has been lowered by erosion or raised by deposition to a depth of 30 fathoms. Therefore the natural depth of the lagoon should be less than 30 fathoms; but it frequently exceeds 40 or even 50 or more fathoms. Murray ascribes the deepening to solution of dead coral by the water of the sea; but in order that the depth may reach 40 fathoms, not only must the whole thickness of coral in the lagoon have been removed, but also 10 fathoms of the foundation on which the corals built. This foundation was in general either volcanic or formed by deposition in the sea, and there seems to be no reason why it should be dissolved more easily by the water of the lagoon than by that of the open ocean. It may be argued that deposition went on more rapidly in the open sea than in the lagoon, and so exceeded the rate of solution; but the evidence on this point is somewhat conflicting. Observations indicate that in some atolls the lagoon is filling up, in others it may be growing deeper.

The destruction of dead coral, which undoubtedly goes on, has also been attributed largely to boring animals and plants, and the hollowing of the lagoon to the action of currents as well as of solution.

Daly's views imply stability: he argued that there are a number of submarine mountains and banks which as a result of the Pleistocene benching were cut down to a level on which corals could build when temperature and other conditions became suitable. There are clear resemblances to Murray's theory in this, and he also argued similarly about the depth of lagoons being accordant with the premised low sea-level. But the argument based on similarity of depth goes against Daly even more than against Murray. Moreover, since many submarine banks are often very wide (e.g. the Macclesfield Bank is 55 km. wide and depths of 55 and 60 fathoms are found on it) it is not easy to assume that they were benched to this level even in Tertiary times. It is also to be remembered that, whereas at first sight flat lagoon floors are favoured by Daly's hypothesis, this argument would be stronger if true rock platforms were proved. It is, however, likely that many lagoon floors owe their flatness, and their height, very largely to sedimentation.

Cliffing has been already referred to. It is clear that oscillations of sea-level must be taken into account in any theory, and it is in this respect that Daly's theory makes its greatest contribution. The main outlines of Davis's arguments have already been given. Since many drowned valleys of far greater depths than the assumed Pleistocene sea-level movements have been demonstrated, the net result of the physiographical argument has been to favour Darwin's views on subsidence in many places. However, it is clear that no one theory need be comprehensive: we may, so far as our knowledge goes at present, reasonably assume subsidence for parts of the Pacific and Indian Oceans while we know that other parts have remained stationary or have risen. In any case we do not yet know why or how sinking to great depths can have taken place.

In view of all these inconclusive arguments it might be thought that bores put down through reefs would demonstrate their nature. According to Murray's view only the upper 30 fathoms should consist of coral, and this should rest either directly upon a foundation of volcanic rock, upon a talus of broken coral, or upon an accumulation of pelagic and other organic remains of a different type from the reef-building corals. According to Darwin's theory, the corals and other reef-building organisms should extend far below 30 fathoms and should rest directly upon the flanks of the peak round which the atoll was formed.

In 1904 the atoll of Funafuti in the Ellice group in the South Pacific was selected, and after several attempts a boring was put down to a depth of 1114½ feet. Much of the material passed through, especially in the upper part of the boring, was not sufficiently consolidated to withstand the action of the borer and came up in fragments. About one-third, however, was firm enough to yield a solid core. The detailed examination of the material showed that the whole was made up mainly of Foraminifera, corals, and calcareous algae, and the same types extended from the top to the bottom. Reef-building corals were found throughout. Even in the lower part of the boring they appeared to be in the position of growth, but this conclusion is open to doubt owing to the imperfect state of preservation of the coral remains. In addition the rocks passed through were nearly all dolomitised, and it has been shown that dolomite is formed in shallow water. So far as the evidence goes, therefore, it is decidedly in favour of Darwin's theory. It is possible that the lower part of the reef may be made of talus, but there is nothing to support this view; and there were no traces of any other kind of deposit, such as Murray's theory demands.

Two borings were put down in the lagoon, where the depth of the water at low tide was 101 feet. One of the borings reached 113 feet and the other 144 feet below the floor of the lagoon, and at these depths they met solid limestone too hard to be penetrated by the apparatus used.

In each the upper 70 feet was made chiefly of fragments of calcareous algae and was similar in general character to the deposit now forming in the lagoon.

The Funafuti boring is still a subject for debate. T. F. Grimsdale (*Occasional Papers*, Challenger Society, 1952) discusses the significance of a foraminifer, *Cycloclypeus*, in the cores of the bore. After a careful consideration of the evidence, he comes to the conclusion that

The reef core cum lagoonal deposits encountered between 1114·5 feet and 771 feet represent accumulation during a period in which coral growth was able to keep pace with sea-level, though towards the end of the period an accelerated rise of sea-level caused a recession of the reef-margin to such an extent that the site later to be pierced by the boring was occupied by talus slope. The acceleration was followed by a period of very slow rise or even a stillstand, which eventually permitted the reef to grow seawards again until the site of boring was again occupied by reef rock (represented by the levels at 560 feet and above in the boring). Slow or intermittent rise of sea-level continued until the present day.

Other bores have been put down on the Great Barrier Reefs. That on Michaelmas Cay gave unexpected results. There were a few feet of solid material, below which came some 400 feet of loosely coherent coralline material, and finally quartz sand with Foraminifera. A later bore was put down on Heron Island, at the southern end of the reefs. Here again results were rather similar: below 500 feet the bore passed through quartz-foraminiferal sands, above 500 feet mainly through reef forming materials. It is suggested that the evidence implies subsidence of at least 60 fathoms.

In 1947 five bores, one reaching 2556 feet, were put down on Bikini atoll. The records are interesting, but certainly do not prove any theory. From the surface to just below high-tide level unconsolidated sand and gravel occurred. This was followed by two feet of bedded calcareous sandstones and conglomerate. Then followed 65–75 feet of reef limestone, only in part consolidated. From this layer to a depth of 425 feet there was a zone of porous, poorly cemented, white or creamy coralliferous limestone with algae and other fossils. Between 425 and 725 feet the material passed through graded from a white, poorly consolidated limestone to a tan-coloured and very porous fossiliferous sand. The rock between 725 and 1100 feet was sandy and poorly consolidated and contained shallow-water Foraminifera, corals, and shells. There was a thin layer of fairly firm limestone between 1100 and 1135 feet, and thence to the bottom at 2556 feet was a medium to fine calcareous sand with few identifiable fossils. So far as is known there is very little magnesium carbonate present. (See *Science*, **107**, 1948, 51.)

Whilst, then, the general evidence to be derived from bores may be in favour of subsidence, it cannot be said that the arguments are unequivocally in favour of any theory so far put forward.

General conclusions. Owing to the conflicting nature of the evidence it is difficult to draw any general conclusions, excepting that atolls and barrier reefs may be formed in various ways. Some have grown in areas of subsidence, others in regions where no depression has taken place.

There is no proof that the majority of atolls surround submerged islands. On any extensive shoal a number of ring-shaped reefs may be formed by the outward growth of coral masses; and if the shoal is slowly depressed each of these may continue to grow upwards, finally becoming an atoll rising from the floor of the deep sea.

There is but little evidence that the accumulation of pelagic deposits has done much to raise the summits of submarine elevations to the level of coral growth. *Globigerina* limestones and similar deposits have been found at the base of raised coral reefs; and in the Solomon Islands a reef has been described resting upon a material very like the Red Clay of the deeps. But this is evidence of elevation of the sea floor by earth-movement rather than by deposition. It can hardly be maintained that any deposition of oceanic Red Clay could raise the floor of the sea to the level at which reef-building corals live.

It may be added that there is no sufficient proof that in lagoons generally the deepening due to solution and erosion is greater than the shallowing due to deposition.

PART III

THE LAND

CHAPTER I

MATERIALS OF THE EARTH'S CRUST

In the ordinary sense of the word the term rock implies something which is hard and resistant, but by the geologist the meaning of the word is extended so as to include all the solid material of the earth's crust,[1] whether it is hard like granite, soft like clay or uncompacted like gravel.

There are many different kinds of rock, but the different kinds are not sharply distinguished from one another. A rock is not a definite chemical compound but is usually a mixture of various minerals. A limestone is made up chiefly of carbonate of lime, and a clay consists mainly of silicate of alumina; but many limestones contain a large proportion of clay, and many clays contain a large proportion of carbonate of lime.

Rocks may be divided into two main classes according to their mode of origin, and these two classes are known respectively as igneous and sedimentary. A third class may be added consisting of rocks which have been so greatly altered, by heat or pressure or by both combined, that their original characters are completely lost. Such rocks are known as metamorphic.

The igneous rocks have at one time been molten and have solidified from the molten condition. In many of them the various minerals have crystallised separately and the rock is a mass of large or small crystals interlocking with one another. Such rocks are called crystalline.

The sedimentary rocks have been laid down by rivers or other agents, or they are formed of the shells and skeletons of animals or plants. They consist for the most part of fragments, such as grains of sand or pieces of shell, usually bound together by some cementing material. Generally, owing to their mode of formation, they are deposited in layers known as beds or strata, and hence are often spoken of as stratified.

Igneous rocks. Igneous rocks have at one time been molten in the interior of the earth. Sometimes the molten material has been poured out upon the surface of the earth, as in volcanoes. Sometimes it has

[1] The term 'earth's crust' requires a little explanation. It appears to have originated when it was believed that the interior of the earth was molten, and it was applied to the outer solid crust resting upon the liquid interior. There is now a considerable amount of evidence that the interior of the earth is not liquid; but its condition must be very different from that of the exterior, and the term earth's crust is still employed to denote the outer part of the solid earth, in which the rocks are more or less similar to those at the surface.

solidified deep down beneath the surface, sometimes in the channels which connected the molten reservoirs with the exterior.

In the interior the cooling is necessarily slow, allowing time for the crystallisation of the different minerals, and a rock which has solidified deep down in the earth is always completely crystalline. Such rocks are called plutonic rocks, and granite is a good example (fig. 98).

The molten material sometimes finds its way to the surface through clefts, or it may melt a passage for itself; and it may solidify on the way. It will then form vertical walls or dykes cutting through the beds; or more

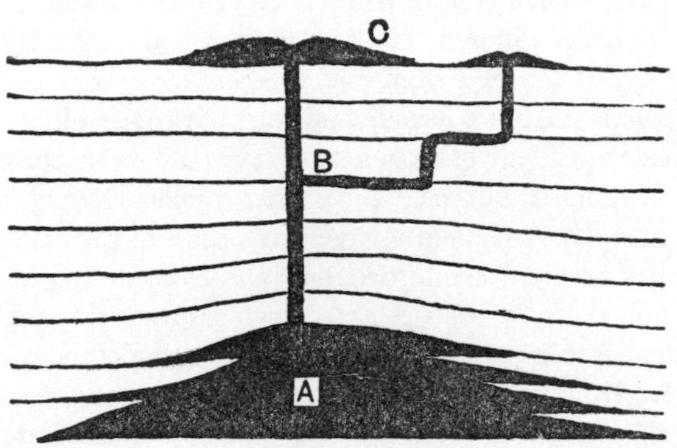

Fig. 98. Igneous rocks. *A*, plutonic rocks; *B*, dyke rocks; *C*, volcanic rocks, or lava.

or less horizontal sheets, or cylindrical necks. In these the cooling is more rapid than in the great masses below, and the rocks are sometimes less completely crystalline than the plutonic rocks, and the crystals are small. They are often spoken of as dyke rocks.

When the molten rock escapes upon the surface it is known as lava. A stream of lava may flow for miles, but naturally it will cool and solidify more quickly than in the interior of the earth. The different minerals composing it have less time to crystallise. Many lavas, indeed, are not crystalline at all, but resemble glass. Obsidian is a good example. In other lavas the crystals are too small to be visible to the unaided eye; but sometimes they are of moderate size.

Sedimentary rocks. The sedimentary rocks are commonly divided into four classes according to their composition, as follows:

Arenaceous rocks, e.g. sandstone, grit.
Argillaceous rocks, e.g. clay, shale.
Calcareous rocks, e.g. limestone.
Carbonaceous rocks, e.g. coal, lignite.

A rock which is made of pebbles of other rock, like a consolidated gravel, is called a conglomerate. A rock which is made of angular fragments of considerable size is called a breccia. Such rocks hardly come into any of the four classes given above.

Arenaceous, or sandy, rocks are usually composed chiefly of grains of quartz; but fragments of other minerals are commonly found in them, and may even form the bulk of the material.

Argillaceous, or clayey, rocks are typically made of clay, a hydrated silicate of alumina. But very fine particles of other minerals may form a deposit which in ordinary language would be called a mud or clay. There are, for example, calcareous muds, consisting chiefly of minute particles of carbonate of lime.

Calcareous rocks or limestones consist mainly of the shells or skeletons of animals or plants, and are formed of carbonate of lime. Deposits of carbonate of lime are sometimes produced when water containing a large proportion of that mineral evaporates, leaving a film of carbonate of lime where it stood or flowed. It is in this way that petrifying springs apparently convert objects into stone. They cover them with layer after layer of carbonate of lime. Deposits of carbonate of lime formed in this manner are called travertine or calcareous tufa.

Carbonaceous rocks usually consist of the remains of plants, converted, apparently by heat and pressure, into coal. Lignite is a similar kind of deposit in which the change has not been so complete.

Metamorphic rocks. In some regions, owing to heat, pressure, or the movements to which they have been subjected, both igneous and sedimentary rocks may be so greatly altered that they entirely lose their original character. They are then called metamorphic. A metamorphic rock is usually crystalline, but differs from an ordinary igneous rock in the fact that the different minerals are generally arranged in layers. Metamorphic rocks often form the central axis of a great mountain chain.

Folding and faulting. When first deposited the stratified rocks are usually laid down in almost horizontal beds or strata; but subsequently, owing to movements of the earth's crust, they are often tilted out of their original position.

When a bed is not horizontal but has been inclined, the direction of maximum slope is called the dip, and the angle which the dip makes with the horizontal is called the angle of dip. A line on the surface of the bed at right angles to the dip is called the strike (fig. 99).

If a bed is inclined and the ground does not slope at the same angle, the edge of the bed will come out on the surface in a more or less regular band, which is called the outcrop.

Often the beds, which were originally horizontal, are bent into a series of folds, as in fig. 100. The arches of the folds are called anticlines and the troughs synclines.

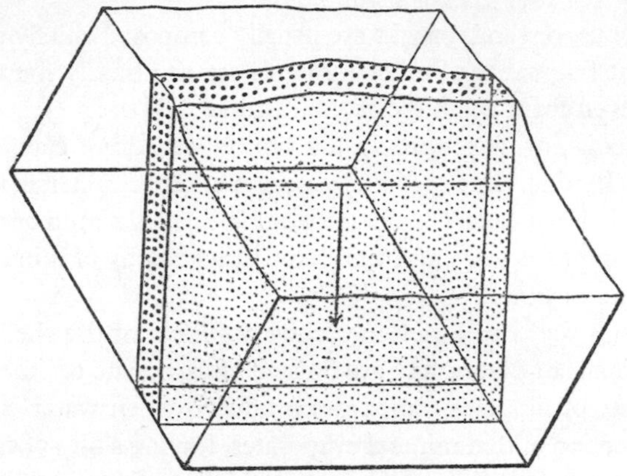

Fig. 99. Dip, strike, and outcrop. The dip is shown by the arrow; the strike by the broken line; the outcrop is the exposed edge of the bed on the upper surface of the block.

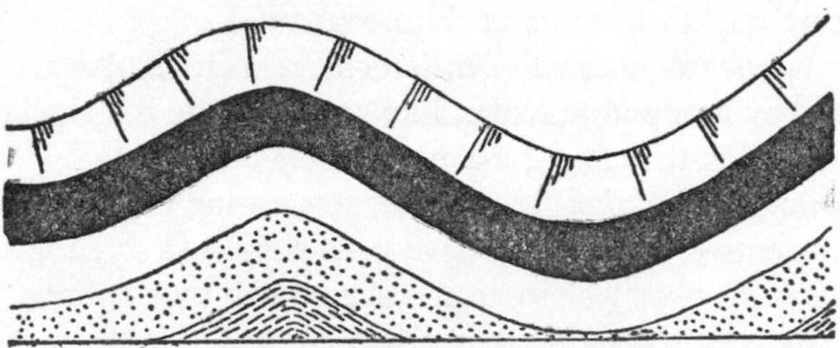

Fig. 100. Anticline and syncline.

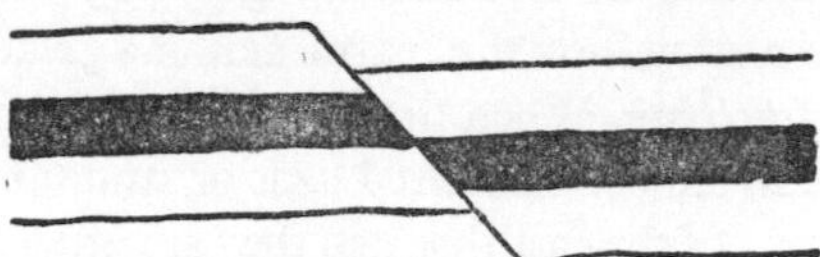

Fig. 101. Fault.

Sometimes the strata break instead of folding, and on one side of the break the beds are dropped, relatively to those on the other side. Such a fracture is called a fault (fig. 101).

When the fault is nearly horizontal and the beds above it have been pushed forward over those below, the fault is called a thrust-plane (fig. 113).

Joints. Most rocks, whether igneous or sedimentary, break more easily in some directions than in others. Many kinds of stratified rock split readily along the bedding, that is to say, between the layers or beds of which they are composed; but usually they will also break fairly easily along two sets of planes which are at right angles to the bedding. These planes of weakness are known as joints and exert a considerable influence upon the forms of crags and cliffs where the rock is exposed to the weather (pls. 6*a*, 7*a*). Most commonly one set of joints is parallel to the dip of the beds and another set is parallel to the strike.

In igneous rocks the form of the joints varies. Basalt, as in the Giant's Causeway, often breaks into a series of hexagonal columns, and there are also often transverse joints across the columns (pl. 7*b*). In granites the joints frequently make the rock break into rectangular blocks which on exposure to the weather become rounded, producing the characteristic forms of the tors of Devonshire and Cornwall (pl. 7*a*).

Cleavage. The presence of joints will cause a mass of rock to break into blocks of various shapes and sizes. But some kinds of rock, which have been subjected to great pressure, also split or cleave easily into thin sheets or slabs. Occasionally, the direction of cleavage is parallel to the stratification, but more often it is inclined at an angle to the bedding. Cleavage-planes are different in their nature and origin from joint-planes. Ordinary roofing slate is a rock in which the cleavage is well developed. Such rocks have often lost all tendency to split along the bedding.

CHAPTER II

EARTH MOVEMENTS

ELEVATION AND SUBSIDENCE

Changes of level. On many coasts there are legends of invasions by the sea and stories of ancient towns which now lie beneath the waters. When these legends have any real foundation, the invasion has usually been due to the wearing away of the land by the waves, but in some cases there is evidence of an actual change of level. Either the land has sunk or the sea has risen.

Occasionally, on the other hand, a town that was once upon the coast is now some distance from the sea and the land has evidently grown outwards. Generally this is due to deposition of material in the sea, but sometimes it is the effect of an actual elevation of the land relative to the sea. Both loss and gain of the land are well illustrated by the fate of Winchelsea, near the Sussex–Kent border. The old town, after being threatened for some time, was finally lost to the sea in the great storm of 1287. The new town was built by Edward I on a spur of high ground about two miles to the west of the original site. But the estuary on which it relied as a port steadily silted up, as so many others of the southern and eastern coasts of Britain have done since Roman times. Nearby, in Dungeness, slight variations in the height of the beach-ridges which form the foreland may reflect changes of the relative level of land and sea.

These changes of level are usually attributed to upward or downward movements of the land, but an alteration in the level of the sea would produce a similar result. There is, however, one important difference. The surface of the sea is nearly but not absolutely level. On continental coasts near great mountain ranges it is slightly raised by the attraction of the land-masses. It is also influenced by active mountain building which alters the attraction of gravity, as in the East Indies today. Changes in the level of the sea of 10 or 20 feet or more, however, must be world-wide.

Movement of the land, on the other hand, is not likely to be uniform, some parts will rise or fall more than others, and, especially in volcanic areas, there may be a rise in one place and a fall in another.

It is, however, often very difficult to determine to which cause the change of level is due, and on this account some observers speak of an elevation of the land relative to the sea as a negative movement, and a depression of the land relative to the sea as a positive movement, whether the cause is an actual movement of the land or an alteration in the level of the sea. In the following pages, however, the terms elevation and subsidence (or depression) will be used with their ordinary significance, meaning elevation and subsidence relative to the level of the sea.

Changes of level may be either sudden or gradual. Sudden changes take place only during earthquakes. On the sea coast their effect is conspicuous, even if they are small in amount, and they have accordingly often been noticed. Sir Charles Lyell in his *Principles of Geology* describes many examples. In the New Zealand earthquake of 1855, an upheaval amounting to 9 feet was recorded. After the Chilean earthquake of 1822 the coast for a long distance is said to have stood 3 or 4 feet higher than before.

Some most conspicuous coastal changes occurred in the Alaska earthquake of 1899. Fig. 102, based on a survey by Tarr and Martin, shows that in the region of Yakutat Bay the movement was mainly one of uplift.

There had been a long interval of quiescence before the earthquake, and beaches and benches had been formed. As a result of the earthquake they were lifted up, as much as 40 feet in places. The upward movement is also shown by caves raised above wave-level and, more conspicuously, by dead barnacles.

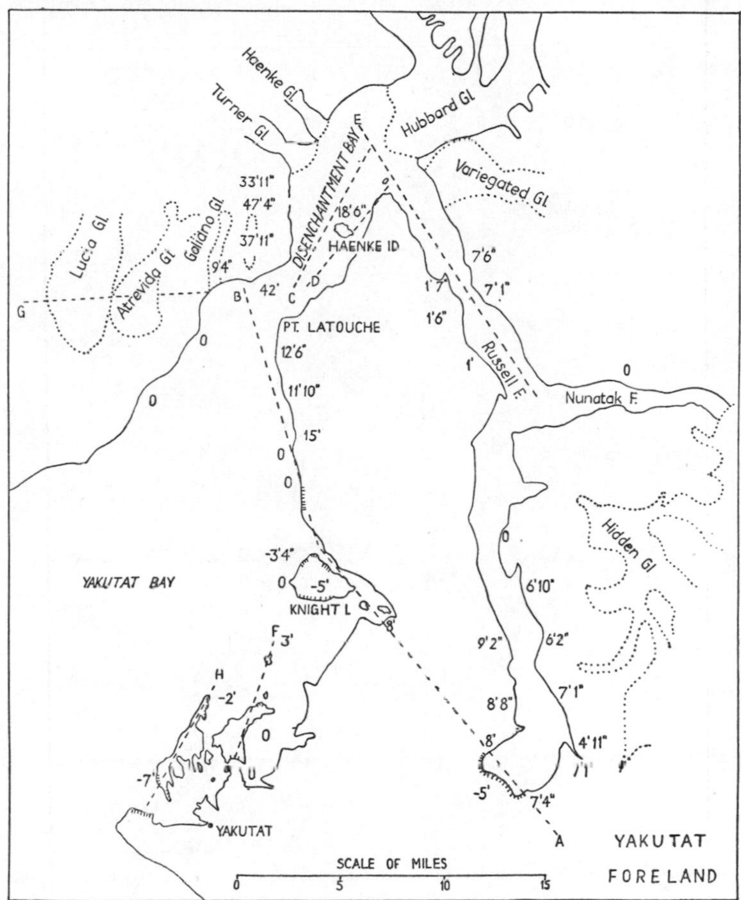

Fig. 102. Yakutat Bay after the Alaska earthquake of 1899. Movement of the land is shown in feet.

Inland such changes are not so easily observed; during the Japanese earthquake of 28 October 1891, a fracture of the surface occurred and on one side of the fracture the ground sank 20 feet relative to the other side.

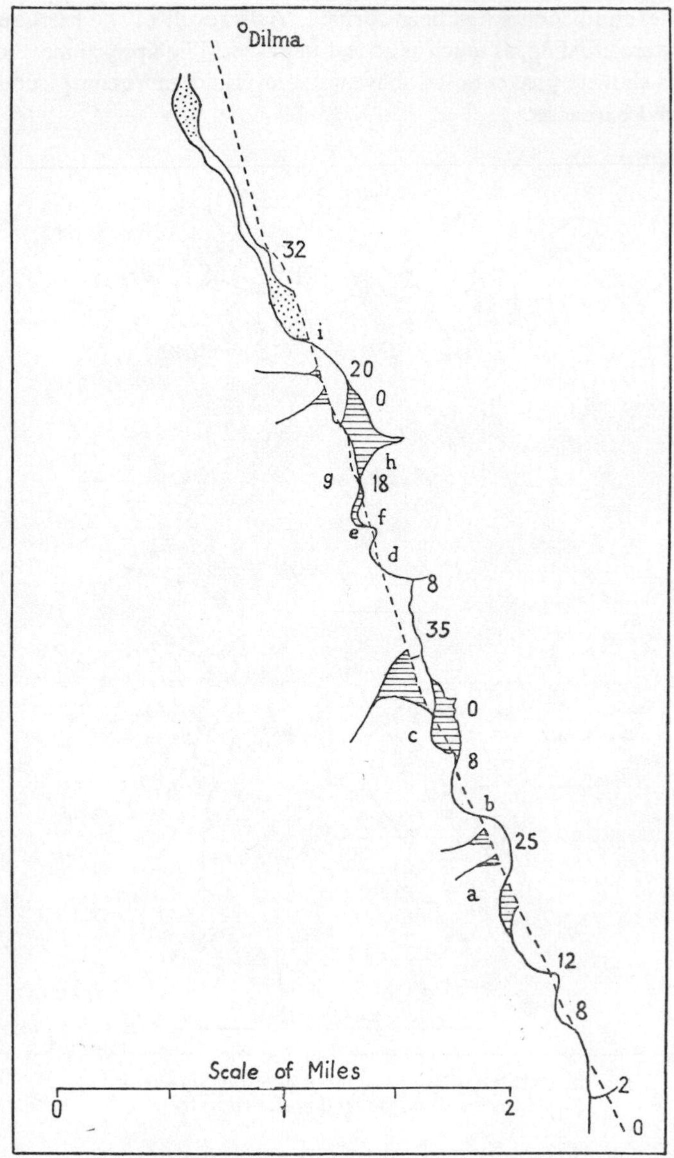

Fig. 103. The Chedrang Valley in Assam, showing the fault caused by the earthquake of 1897.

The Assam earthquake of 1897 affords an example both of the movement of land and of the formation of small lakes. Fig. 103 is a sketch-map of the Chedrang Valley; the dotted line shows the line of the fault which crosses the stream several times. The numbers indicate the upward throw in feet of the east side of the fault. When the river crossed the fault from east to west a small waterfall was formed; where it crossed from west to east small pools or lakes were formed. The large pool at *c* is situated at a point where the natural slope of the ground was reversed.

A gradual change is much more difficult to prove. It might be thought an easy matter to make a mark upon a sea-cliff and to measure the height of this above the surface of the water. But on our own coasts, for instance, the level of the sea is continually fluctuating. It varies not only with the tides but also with the direction and strength of the winds, and a long series of observations is necessary to determine the mean sea-level. In the Baltic the difficulties are not so great, on account of the absence of tides and the number of sheltered inlets. In the early part of the eighteenth century Celsius came to the conclusion that the waters of the Baltic were slowly falling; but several objections to his views were advanced by other writers. It was pointed out, for example, that the lower part of the town of Danzig still lay at the level of the sea and had done so since A.D. 1000. The interest aroused by these discussions led to the placing of marks upon the rocks, indicating the level of the water on a calm day, and these marks have since been examined from time to time. The observations have shown conclusively that there has been a change in the relative level of land and sea; but since the change varies from place to place, it has been due to movement of the land rather than of the water. At Stockholm, the land has risen at the rate of about 18½ inches in a century; farther north at twice that rate, and in southern Sweden only about half as fast. In the last few years there has been no change at Stockholm, but this is attributed to the sea rising at the same rate as the land.

In the Baltic the gradual elevation of the land has thus been shown by actual observation and measurement; but in most cases changes of level can only be proved by inference. One of the most famous examples is that of the Temple of Serapis at Pozzuoli near Naples (fig. 104). The pavement of the building is now a little below high water and upon it three of the original pillars are still standing. Below the present

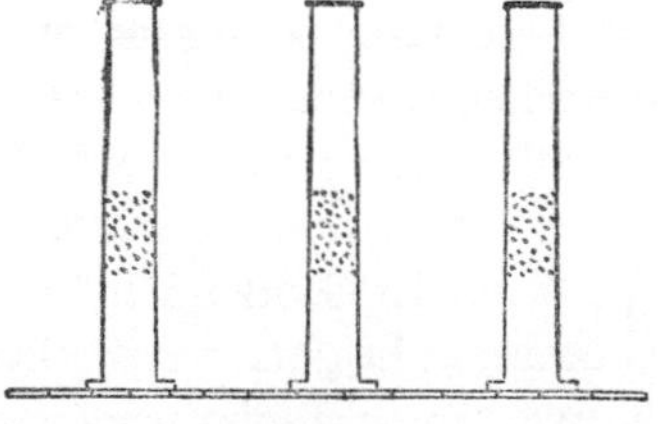

Fig. 104. The Temple of Serapis.

pavement excavations have shown that there is an older one, at a depth of about 5 feet. The pillars are smooth up to a height of 12 feet, and the next 9 feet are pierced by numerous holes bored by a species of shell-fish which does not live above high-water mark. The upper part of the pillars is free from perforations.

When the first pavement was constructed, the land, presumably, stood at least 5 feet above its present level. When the holes were bored the land had sunk, and the second pavement was submerged to a depth of 21 feet. To account for the absence of holes in the lower part of the pillars, it is supposed that the building had been previously buried to a depth of 12 feet by volcanic ash thrown out during some eruption of Vesuvius.

Thus the remains point to an oscillation of the land of at least 26 feet, from 5 feet above the present level to 21 feet below it.

Geological evidence of elevation. Besides the evidence afforded by the works of man, the sea itself often leaves indications of its former position. But it is important to distinguish between the effect of deposition and the effect of elevation, for either may lead to an apparent retreat of the sea. In Romney Marsh and in the Wash, for example, the land is gaining on the sea, but this is due simply to the deposition of sand, mud, and gravel swept along the coast by waves, and to a lesser extent brought by currents. Similarly, owing to the advance of the delta of the Po into the Adriatic, the town of Adria, which was a port in ancient times, is now 14 miles from the sea. In such cases as these, the new land is always low-lying and is formed of mud and sand and other similar deposits, often with a high organic content, owing to accumulation of coastal swamps and salt marshes.

There are, however, various kinds of evidence which prove that in some parts of the world the sea stood higher or the land lower than it does now.

Above the present beach and beyond the reach of the waves in the greatest storms there is sometimes a kind of terrace which may or may not be covered with sand or gravel like the seashore (fig. 105). If, as often happens, sea-shells are found within the sand, it is clear that at one time the terrace was the actual beach and the land must since have risen. Raised sea-beaches of this kind are found in many parts of Great Britain (pl. 8*a*). In Scotland there are sometimes two or three, one above another, at heights varying from 25 to 100 feet. Many of the fiords of Norway show similar terraces up to a height of at least 600 feet.

Behind the present shoreline and above the level of the highest tides there is occasionally a line of cliff, sometimes with caves hollowed out at its base (pl. 8*b*). At one time the cliff marked the limit of the tides, and its present position is due to elevation. It must be not assumed, however, that every sea-cliff that is not touched by the waves has been raised. Sometimes it is simply the accumulation of beach material at its base that prevents the sea from reaching it.

The shells of animals such as barnacles, which live in the sea but fix themselves to rocks, are sometimes found attached at heights which are not now reached by the water. In such cases the land must have risen, relative to the sea. Similar reasoning applies to the various kinds of boring shells such as those in the pillars of the Temple of Serapis.

Reef-building corals cannot stand exposure to the sun and air for more than a few hours. When, therefore, a coral reef is found above the sea, it is clear proof of a change of level. There are many examples of raised coral reefs in the Pacific and Indian Oceans and also in the West Indies.

Elevation of the land is sometimes indicated by the form of the coast.

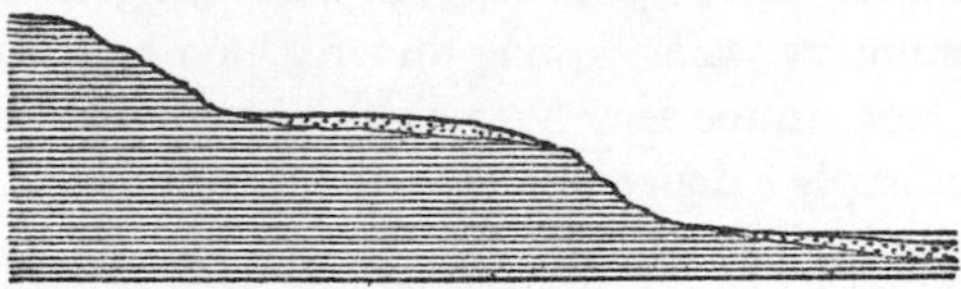

Fig. 105. Raised sea-beach.

A widespread elevation will raise a part of the continental shelf above the sea, and the land will, accordingly, be fringed by a coastal plain. The outline will be smooth and free from indentations, and behind the coastal plain there will usually be a sudden rise or even a cliff, marking the former position of the shoreline. This subject will be discussed more fully in a subsequent chapter.

Geological evidence of subsidence. Subsidence is in general more difficult to detect and prove than elevation, because the evidence of the former position of the sea is destroyed or hidden. The old sea-beaches and the old sea-cliffs sink beneath the waves and are lost to sight. It is, moreover, often difficult to distinguish between the effects of subsidence and those of erosion. The sea may cover the site of a former town, but this in itself is no proof of subsidence. It is often due to the wearing away of the land by the waves. This is the case, for example, at Cromer, Dunwich, and other places upon the East Anglian coast, where the sites of the old towns now lie beneath the water.

Upon our own coasts one of the most cogent arguments in favour of recent subsidence is the presence of submerged forests and accumulations of peat or leaf-mould at or below low-water mark. Only the stumps of the trees are left, but in some places these are in the position of growth and afford clear evidence that the forests or woods were invaded by the sea. Submerged forests are found along the shores of Devon and Cornwall and in other parts of Great Britain, and important sections have been exposed during the construction of docks at Barry (Glam.) and elsewhere. In these sections several peat or forest layers may be found one below the other, and separated by marine clays. They prove not only that subsidence has occurred, but also that it was intermittent. Peat dredged from the Dogger Bank implies that at one time the bank and much of the North Sea floor was a swampy plain. In brief, the evidence of the many peat beds excavated, and of the peat dredgings, indicate that sea-level was about 200 feet lower in relation to ordnance datum in early post-glacial times than it is now.

It is, however, possible for peaty and other accumulations of vegetable material to be formed below the level of the sea in a lagoon cut off from the open water. It has also been suggested that the gradual removal of a sandy substratum by water flowing underground may cause a growing wood to sink beneath the sea. Such a subsidence would be purely local and would not imply a depression of the land as a whole. Depression or elevation of the land must be demonstrated from the careful and full analysis of the evidence from several places.

According to Darwin's theory of coral reefs, both barrier reefs and atolls are evidence of subsidence; but this theory is not universally accepted. The question has already been discussed (ch. VI, pt. II). Recently flat-topped table mounts (guyots) in the Pacific have yielded reef corals and Foraminifera of Cretaceous age. These mounts are now sunk below the sea surface at a depth of about 1700 metres.

As a rule the most conclusive proof of subsidence is afforded by the form of the coast. Whenever a land-mass sinks, the sea will enter the valleys, forming inlets which will frequently branch inwards. A stream or river will usually flow into the head of each inlet, and each inlet will be the direct continuation of a valley in the land. The indented outline produced in this way is well shown on the Cornish and Essex coasts, and elsewhere. The whole subject of the effects of elevation and subsidence on the form of the coastline is dealt with in a later chapter. (See also p. 211.)

NATURE OF EARTH MOVEMENTS

It has been shown in the preceding pages that the surface of the solid earth is not still. Even within the last few hundred years the Scandinavian peninsula has risen perceptibly, the Temple of Serapis has sunk and risen again and similar changes have gone on in other parts of the world.[1] In course of time such movements, if continued, must produce very great effects upon the continents and oceans; and geology shows that many parts which are now land were once beneath the sea. Many of the rocks which now form part of the land contain the remains of marine animals and were evidently deposited beneath the sea. In the chalk of southern England there are sea-urchins; in the limestone of Derbyshire corals and shells are abundant. In the Alps and the Himalayas beds with marine fossils are found even on the topmost peaks.

The stratified rocks which form so much of the surface of the globe were originally laid down horizontally or nearly so, and for the most part beneath the sea. They serve, therefore, as an index of the nature of the movements which have taken place. These movements are of two kinds, which may be distinguished as vertical (or radial) and horizontal (or tangential), according to the principal direction of the movement. In vertical movements there is a simple elevation or depression of a large area of the earth's crust, the beds remaining nearly horizontal. The effect is to form plateaux or to raise a large mass of land above the sea, and this type of movement is accordingly known as plateau-building or continent-building or epeirogenic.

Horizontal movements are due to forces in the earth's crust acting more or less tangentially to the surface. The originally horizontal strata are compressed from side to side, with the result that they crumple or fold. The crumpling takes place where the crust of the earth is weakest. This is usually in a zone where much recent sediment has accumulated and depressed the underlying harder rocks into deeper and hotter parts of the crust where they lose much of their strength. The effect of the crumpling is to raise up a narrow belt of folded strata, forming a mountain chain. This type of movement is known as mountain-building or orogenic.

Vertical movements. The general characteristic of these movements is that there is no crumpling of the strata, which for the most part remain horizontal; but as will be seen in the accompanying diagrams, the beds may in places be tilted even into a vertical position.

Sometimes a part of the earth's crust is raised in the form of a broad flat arch, or depressed in the form of a wide and shallow basin. The strata will be scarcely disturbed but will have a very slight dip towards or from the centre (fig. 106). Such a movement may cause the elevation of a continent, or if it produces a depression beneath the ocean, it will lower the level of the sea and cause an apparent rise of the surrounding land.

[1] There is every reason for thinking that movements of this type are still proceeding. South-eastern England is sinking very slowly.

Sometimes the boundary between the elevated and the depressed areas is very sharply marked, and we have then the form shown in fig. 107. The strata are in general horizontal, but at the edges of the areas which have been raised or depressed they may be almost vertical.

In many cases the beds have been unable to stand the amount of bending required, and they have accordingly fractured. Large blocks have been raised, and others depressed, relative to each other, and these blocks are bounded by faults (fig. 108). Frequently, there is a certain

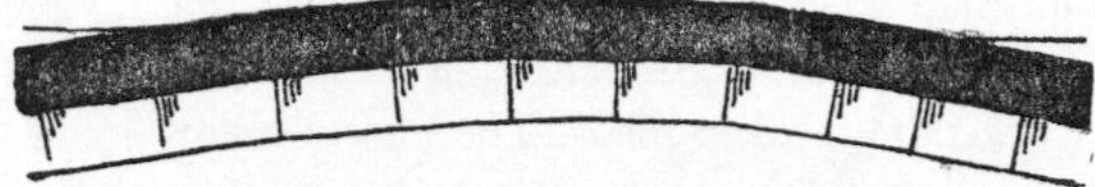

Fig. 106. Vertical movement with gentle bending.

Fig. 107. Vertical movement with local abrupt bending.

Fig. 108. Vertical movement accompanied by faulting.

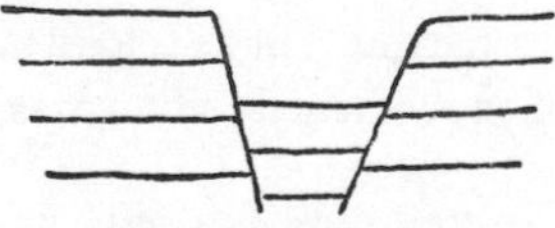

Fig. 109. Rift-valley.

amount of tilting of the blocks and the strata are no longer horizontal, but they are not crumpled. This type of movement is widespread in the Great Basin of the United States, and in Iceland (cf. pl. 12*b*).

Occasionally a strip of country is let down between two faults and a long and narrow depression is formed (fig. 109). Such a depression, produced directly by earth movements and not, like most valleys, by erosion, is often called a rift-valley. The Jordan flows in a valley of this type. Parts of the Rift Valley of Africa are now thought to result from the forcing down of a central block along reverse faults caused by fracturing of the strata under horizontal pressure (fig. 110).

In the examples given above the strata were approximately horizontal until the earth movements occurred. But the same type of movement sometimes affects areas which had been previously folded, e.g. the block-faulting on either side of the Middle Rhine which occurred concurrently with the folding of the Alps.

Horizontal movements. These are characterised by the crumpling or folding of the strata, but there is great variety in the forms and structures produced. If the amount of compression is small, the beds may be thrown into a series of simple arches and troughs (fig. 111). This is the case in a considerable part of the Jura Mountains.

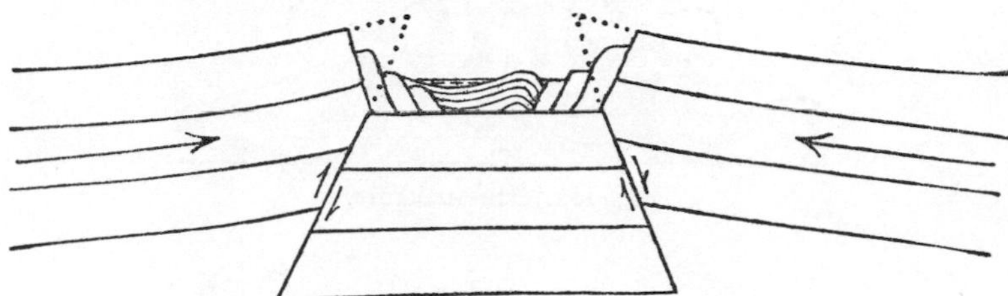

Fig. 110. Rift-valley due to compression.

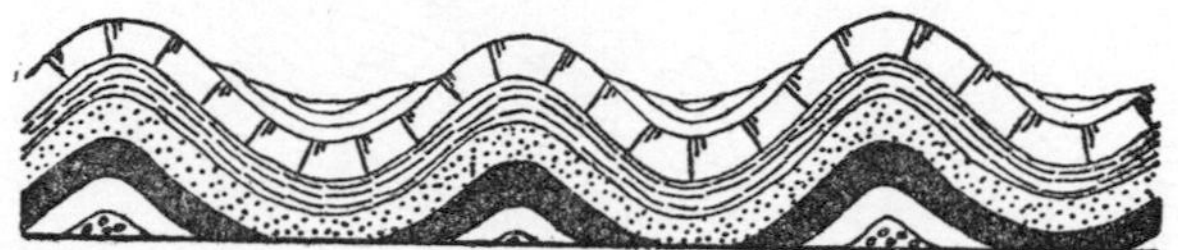

Fig. 111. Folding of the Jura type.

When the compression is greater the centre of the folded belt is raised and the marginal folds lean outwards. The structure may become that shown in fig. 112, and because the beds in general dip inwards from both sides, it is called fan-structure. During the process of folding, which is always slow, the whole is subject to denudation, and the outer parts of the folds are worn away as they are produced.

Sometimes the lateral compression causes the crust to fracture, and one side is pushed over the other, crumpling in the process. This is well shown in the Ardennes (fig. 113), which are the remains of an ancient mountain chain, now very greatly denuded so that its internal structure is exposed. In this case, moreover, our knowledge of the structure is increased by the borings which have been put down for coal.

The structure of the Alps has been more fully investigated than that of any other major mountain range. The western Alps, in particular, have been subjected to very intensive folding. They were compressed between two rigid masses, one to the south, now partly buried beneath the sediments of the Po Basin, and the other to the north and now represented by the Central Plateau, the Vosges, and Black Forest. The great curve of the western Alps results from the disposition of these old rigid masses.

The cross-section shown in fig. 114 runs north-west to south-east through Monte Rosa. The arrangement of the folds is deduced from the evidence of the remnants which have not been removed by erosion. The

Fig. 112. Fan-structure.

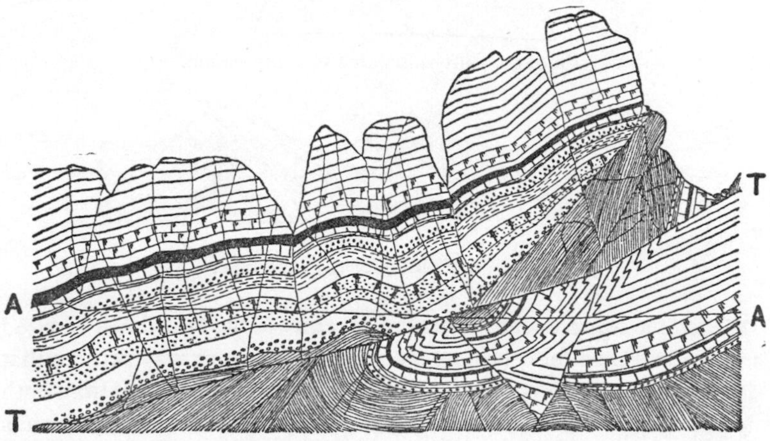

Fig. 113. Section of the Ardennes and the Belgian coalfield. *AA*, the present surface of the ground. The rocks above this line have been removed by denudation. *TT*, the great thrust-plane. The mass of rock above *TT* has been pushed forward over the mass below.

mechanism of the folding is still far from clear, because it is difficult to imagine how the thrusts were transmitted for tens of miles through the relatively yielding strata, especially if, as is suggested, some of the underlying folds pushed forward into beds previously folded. It may be that the folded sediments were compressed between the jaws of a vice, i.e. the rigid masses to the north and south, and bulged upwards. When the slope of the sides of the bulge exceeded about 15° the beds may have broken away and started slipping downhill, thus forming an overfold. Renewed pressure caused further bulging and led to the formation of a second overfold, and so the process continued until the whole complex series was produced (fig. 115).

This explanation has two chief advantages. The distance the rigid masses would have to move would not be as great as that necessitated by pulling them apart until all the folds were unravelled, and the enormous

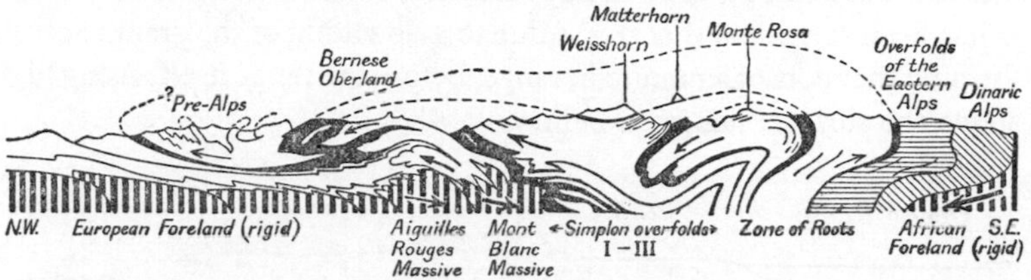

Fig. 114. Section through the overfolds of the western Alps.

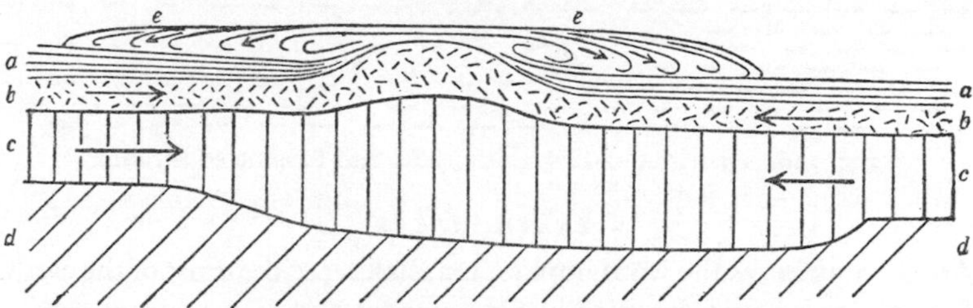

Fig. 115. Final stage in the formation of symmetrical overfolds in a mountain range by crustal shortening. *aa*, sediments; *bb*, granite layer; *cc*, intermediate layer; *dd*, lower layer; *ee*, folded sediments.

mass of material marked by broken lines in fig. 114 would not have to be removed by erosion, the folds never having been continuous over the top. There is insufficient evidence of the enormous deposits that one would expect to find if this quantity had really been removed since the period of folding. Some authorities think that the compressional forces result from the shrinking, due to cooling, of the layers beneath the crust, and so do not favour very large movements of the rigid masses of the earth's crust. Others consider that even masses of continental size can move great distances very slowly.

Whatever divergent views might be held concerning continental drift and the causes of mountain building, the reason mountains stand high above plateaux and plains, and the latter high above the floors of the oceans is now generally agreed. The higher masses have roots of relatively light material projecting down into the heavier layers below. The deeper and bulkier the root, the higher the land-mass will stand (fig. 116), on much the same principle as icebergs of different thickness float high or low in the water. The continental masses are probably composed of granitic rocks with a density of about 2·65, and the ocean floors and deeper rocks, probably of a basaltic nature, have a density of about 3·0.

In the East Indies south of Sumatra and Java pendulum observations reveal an extensive strip where the value of gravity is less than normal, as if an unusually thick mass of light material exists beneath the sea-floor. It has been suggested that this is due to a downfold of the granitic crust, forming the roots of a mountain range, before the range itself, rising high above the surface, has been built.

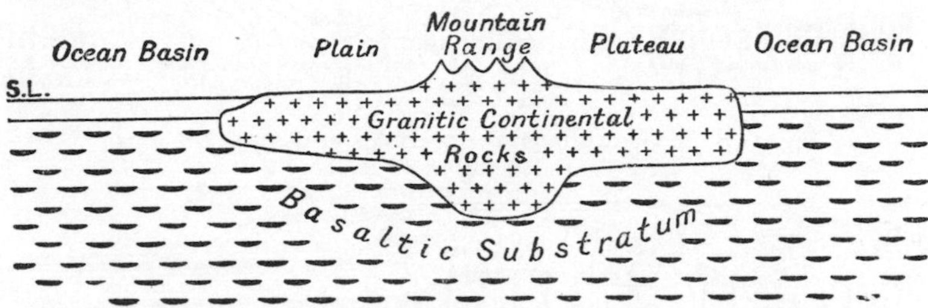

Fig. 116. Distribution of granitic rocks and basaltic substratum.

EARTHQUAKES

An earthquake, as the word implies, is a shaking of the crust of the earth. Sometimes it is accompanied by a permanent elevation or depression of the ground; but often no lasting effect is visible at the surface except the damage done by the shaking.

In many cases earthquakes are undoubtedly closely connected with the earth movements of the types already described, and seem to result from the fracturing of rigid beds of rock within the earth's crust. They are most frequent where there is evidence of recent folding or faulting and where it is probable that the movements have not yet ceased. In the Japanese earthquake of 28 October 1891, and in the San Francisco earthquake of 18 April 1906, visible faults were formed at the surface of the ground, but these may have been the consequence rather than the cause of the earthquakes. The actual movements to which earthquakes are due are probably more deeply seated, but not so deep that the rocks would yield by folding to the stresses within the crust.

Earthquakes, however, are not always caused by folding or faulting. They are sometimes the result of volcanic explosions. They are common in most volcanic districts; and eruptions are often preceded or accompanied by earthquakes.

Whatever the cause may be an earthquake is a vibration of the crust of the earth. Sometimes actual waves are seen to travel along the ground, like waves on the surface of a sheet of water. More often the waves are too long and too low to be visible to the eye, but the rocking of the ground may be felt as they pass. Buildings sway to and fro and fissures sometimes open in the ground and again close up.

The earthquake usually originates some miles beneath the surface, and from the origin or seismic focus the vibrations spread in all directions (fig. 117). They reach the surface first at the point immediately above the origin and this point is called the epicentre. It is at the epicentre that the shock of the earthquake is first experienced, and on the ground it seems to spread outwards as waves spread from a stone thrown into a pool of water.

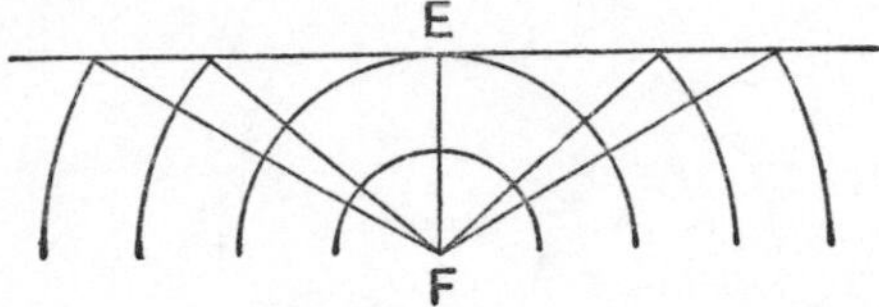

Fig. 117. Seismic focus (*F*), epicentre (*E*), and waves radiating from the focus of an earthquake. The diagram represents conditions near the epicentre.

If the time of arrival of the earthquake is observed at a number of different places it is usually possible to determine the position of the epicentre. Lines, called homoseismal lines, are drawn through places which were affected by the earthquake at the same moment. These lines are generally elliptical in shape, and the middle of the ellipse is the epicentre. The actual place of origin of the earthquake is below the epicentre.

Observations of the time of an earthquake, however, are seldom very accurate, and other methods are therefore usually employed. As the vibrations spread outwards from the origin their intensity diminishes. Far away from the centre the movement may be sufficient to displace ornaments on brackets or shelves but not to injure buildings. Nearer to the centre tall chimneys may be overthrown while houses are but little affected. Nearer still the shock may be so great that not even the most solidly constructed buildings remain standing.[1] By classifying the damage in this way it is possible to draw lines through places which have suffered equally, and such lines are known as isoseismal lines (fig. 118). Isoseismal lines are often very irregular in form, because the damage depends in part upon the nature of the foundations on which the buildings rest, as well as upon their distance from the origin. Nevertheless, if

[1] Ferro-concrete buildings often stand up to violent earthquake shocks remarkably well.

a number of the isoseismal lines can be drawn, it is usually possible to determine approximately the position of the epicentre.

It might be expected that the greatest amount of damage would be at the epicentre itself, but this is not always the case. At the epicentre the intensity of the movement is at its maximum, but it is here an up and down movement, which does less injury to buildings than a shake from side to side. The greatest damage is done where the earthquake wave

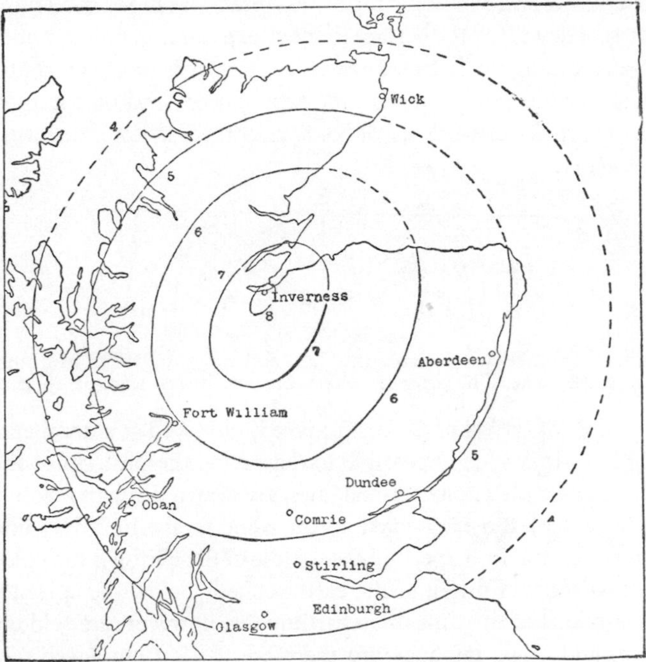

Fig. 118. Isoseismal lines of the Inverness earthquake of 1901.

emerges obliquely, but is still near enough to the origin to retain a considerable proportion of its energy.

In recent years it has been shown that in an earthquake at least three distinct kinds of vibrations or waves are set up. There are longitudinal, primary, or *P*, waves, like those of sound in air, in which the particles move to and fro in the direction in which the wave is travelling. There are transverse, secondary, or *S*, waves, like the waves which run along a rope which is fastened at one end, stretched fairly taut, and shaken at the other end. In such waves the particles move to and fro at right angles to the path of the wave. Finally, there are the surface, or *L*, waves, which travel along the ground like waves on a sheet of water. In these the motion of the particles is also transverse, but they differ from the transverse waves in the body of the earth.

Close to the epicentre all these waves reach the observer so nearly together that they are not readily distinguished. Farther away there is an interval of time between them, which increases with the distance from the origin. The waves which pass directly through the earth reach the place of observation before the surface waves, partly because their path is shorter and partly because they move more rapidly (fig. 119). Consequently, at a considerable distance from the epicentre there are as a rule at least three distinct sets of disturbances, the first two due to the longi-

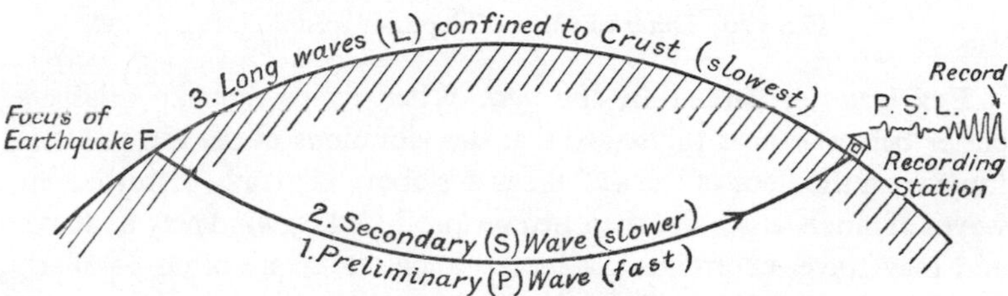

Fig. 119. Paths of waves from a distant earthquake, and record at recording station. Focus and epicentre not distinguished on this scale.

tudinal and transverse waves which travel below the surface; and the greater the interval between these disturbances, the greater is the distance of the origin.

Instruments are now made of such extreme delicacy that they will record the vibrations due to an earthquake on the opposite side of the globe, and thus it is possible to say, from observations made in England, that an earthquake has occurred 1000 or 2000 or, it may be, as much as 8000 or 9000 miles away. The distance of the origin can be given, approximately, and even, with certain forms of instrument, the direction in which it lies.

Depth of origin. It is a comparatively easy matter to find the epicentre of an earthquake, but it is difficult to determine the depth of the centre or origin.

At one time it was supposed that cracks in buildings served as an indication of the angle of emergence of the earthquake wave. It was assumed that they were formed at right angles to the path of the vibrations, and in that case observations at two or three points suitably placed would be sufficient to determine the position of origin (fig. 120). But the results obtained were often not concordant, and there can be no doubt that the structure of the building and other circumstances have a considerable influence upon the direction of the cracks.

Other methods have been tried, but none is completely satisfactory. There is little doubt, however, that the depth of the origin is always small compared with the diameter of the globe, and usually does not exceed 30 miles (but see p. 247).

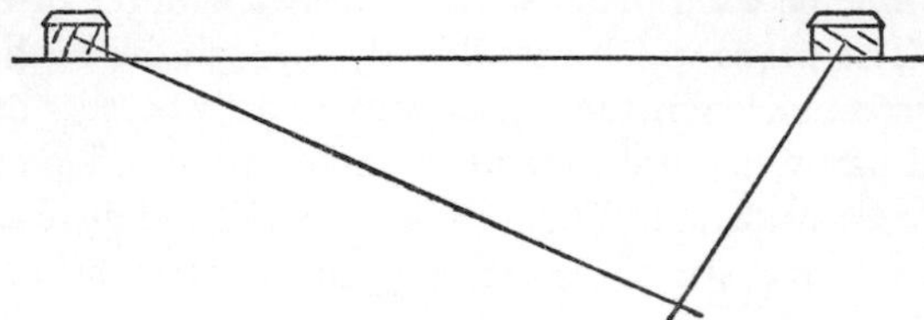

Fig. 120. Determination of depth of seismic focus.

Earthquake waves in the sea. When an earthquake originates either below or near the sea so that the vibrations of the crust are still intense on the floor of the sea, the water above is greatly disturbed and waves of much larger size than are ever produced by wind may be started and may travel enormous distances. Such waves are often popularly, but quite incorrectly, spoken of as tidal waves. They are properly called tsunamis.

In many of the great earthquakes of the past more loss of life has been caused by these sea-waves flooding low-lying coasts than by the earthquake itself.

Distribution of earthquakes. In some parts of the world, such as Japan, there is hardly a day without an earthquake of greater or less intensity; but there are large areas also in which earthquakes are extremely rare. The principal earthquake regions are shown in fig. 121. In most of them there is geological evidence of recent earth movements; and in many, but not all, there are numerous active volcanoes.

From the point of view of the geographer, the physiographical effects of earthquakes are of great interest. Reference (pp. 227–228) has already been made to the shoreline changes produced by the Alaska earthquake, and the effects of the Assam earthquake in the Chedrang Valley. Many other instances could be given, but it will suffice to call attention to the movements of the land in the San Francisco earthquake of 1906, and of their relation to earlier effects along the San Andreas fault, and to the great changes in the sea-bed as a result of the disastrous earthquake at Tokio in 1923.

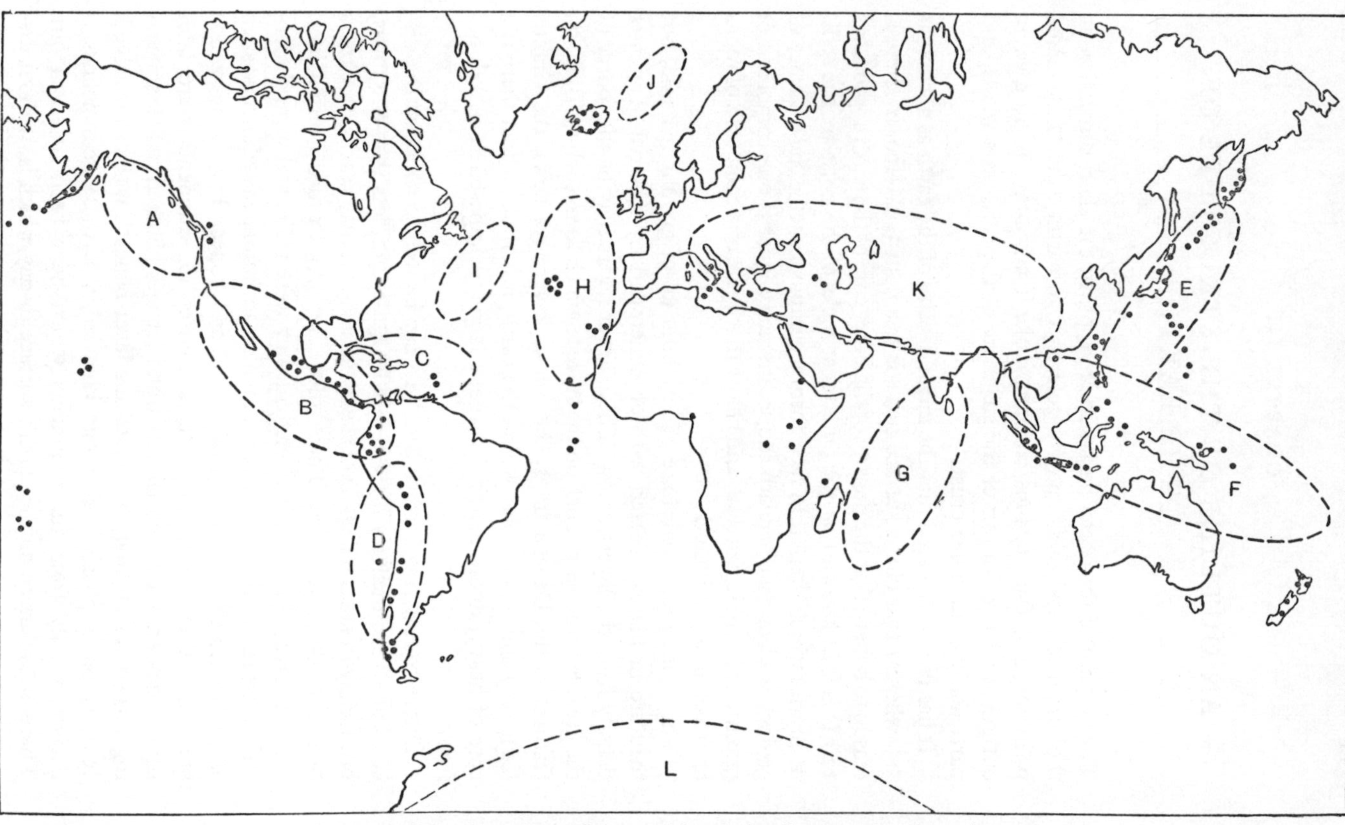

Fig. 121. Seismic regions of the world and distribution of active volcanoes.

CHAPTER III

AN OUTLINE OF THE STRUCTURE OF THE EARTH

The account of the ocean basins in ch. I, pt. II, the short discussion on the origin of coral reefs and the reference to earthquakes and related phenomena in the previous chapter, make it advantageous to give an outline of what is known of the structure of the earth as a whole, and particularly of its outer crust.

It has been calculated that the mean density of the earth as a whole is 5·5, whereas that of the surface rocks is less than 3. Moreover, there is reason to believe that the density of the inner core of the earth approaches 12. It is well known that the outermost rocks of the crust are the sedimentaries which do not, in fact, form a complete shell. The evidence of geology is clear that beneath the sedimentary layer is one composed of granitic or gneissic material, and below that again one composed of rocks approximating to basalt.

The continental masses are mainly built up of granitic material, but they are in places injected with or penetrated by material of greater density from the layers below. These lower layers may be the source of the great basaltic extrusions on the surface which form such well-known features as the Deccan traps, the Snake River lava flows, the Giant's Causeway and others. Far within the earth, it is thought that there is a core of heavy, dense material perhaps largely composed of nickel and iron.

Before considering further detail, it may be well to note that the discontinuous sedimentary layer is usually quite thin, less than two miles, but locally in areas which have slowly subsided it may reach a thickness of twenty or more miles. These subsiding areas, called geosynclines, seem to have been much longer than they were wide, and were characterised by relatively shallow seas in which accumulated sediments, such as are formed on the continental shelves and slopes. For reasons which are not yet explained these thick masses of sediments were later squeezed out to form our major mountain ranges. Sometimes the squeezing was so violent that the crystalline layer beneath was also involved. It must be emphasised that our knowledge of these geosynclines is derived wholly from the sediments which have been squeezed out. There is no feature on the earth's surface to-day which is, without dispute, a modern geosyncline. Certain of the East Indian troughs and island lines are often regarded as partially squeezed out geosynclines, and the Indo-Gangetic plain and the Persian Gulf have been given as other examples.

There is general agreement that the earth is made up of shells of increasing density. The great Austrian geologist Suess postulated a tripartite arrangement for the earth. He ignored the discontinuous sedimentary layer, and his first shell is the granitic, which he called Sial or Sal, the word Sial being made up of Si (silicon) and Al (aluminium), the chemical symbols of the two commonest elements in this layer, the specific gravity of which lies between 2·75 and 2·90. His second shell he called Sima (Si, and Ma, for magnesium). This, with a specific gravity varying between 2·90 and 4·75, he considered to be a much thicker layer than the Sial. His third shell formed the core of the earth composed of dense heavy material which he called Nife (Ni, nickel; Fe, iron). It is only recently that more exact knowledge has been obtained, especially as a result of careful records and observations of earthquake waves. It was stated on p. 239 that when an earthquake takes place waves of three main types are set up. They start from the origin or focus of the quake, and, at first, they are not clearly differentiated. If, however, a record of a typical shock, taken at a considerable distance from the origin, be examined (see fig. 119), the three phases of motion are distinct. First, there are the preliminary tremors (*P*), followed by a second phase (*S*) which usually begins with a marked increase in amplitude over the first phase. Both these phases may show sudden reinforcements. The waves of the second phase usually merge fairly gradually into the longer period waves (*L*) with greater and more regular amplitude of the third phase. Finally, there is a tail or coda which records the gradual dying away of the shock.

When it was realised that these three phases corresponded with particular types of wave a great advance was made. Both the *P* and *S* waves travel through the earth from the focus to the observing station. The *L* waves are those that travel along the surface. Further research has established the fact that the *P* and *S* waves travel along curved paths, the convexities of which are directed towards the centre of the earth. Moreover, it has also been discovered that the *P* and *S* waves are themselves subdivisible into what are called P^* and *Pg* and S^* and *Sg* waves. It is essential to realise that all the different waves travel with distinct velocities which are controlled by, and consequently give information about, the nature of the crustal layers through which they pass. Whilst it is abundantly clear that the seismic evidence also indicates inward increasing densities of the various layers, it cannot be said that there is precise agreement as to their exact nature. It is, however, clear that the Sial-Sima scheme is not sufficient: there may be several layers in the earth's crust, as distinct from the core. It may, therefore, be best to speak of (1) the discontinuous sedimentary layer, (2) the outer layer, which all agree is granitic, (3) the intermediate layer which may be of the nature of tachylite or diorite, and (4) the lower layer consisting of high-density rocks like dunite, peridotite, or eclogite. However, a good deal of uncertainty remains about these inner layers, which may yet be further subdivided.

Distant earthquakes also give some information about the central core of the earth. The *S* waves are not transmitted by a liquid, and it is interesting that they do not appear around the anticentre (the diametrically opposite point to the epicentre). This suggests that the inner core of the earth, a core of radius at least half that of the earth as a whole, is of liquid iron, but under the enormous pressures there obtaining, liquid must not be interpreted in the ordinary surface sense.

Apart from the difficulty of agreeing on the actual nature of the rocks composing these various layers of the crust, there is also considerable disagreement as to their thickness. The following figures are only indicative of the presumed order of thickness under a continent—outer layer 10–15 km., intermediate layer 20–30 km., lower layer reaching to the core at about 2900 km.

Implicit in any modern investigations into the nature of the earth's crust is the doctrine of isostasy which states that, wherever equilibrium exists on the earth's surface, equal mass must underlie equal surface areas. We have seen that the lighter rocks form the outer crust, and if we think of a large land-mass of continental dimensions, the average height of which is two to three miles above that of the mean depth of the surrounding oceans, we must also assume that in order to compensate for its greater mean height, there must be a downward penetration of the lighter material well below the level of the ocean floor in order that unit areas beneath continents and oceans may remain in stable equilibrium. The same view holds for great mountain chains: excess of material on the surface must be counter-balanced by deep penetrations of their roots. On the other hand, it is important to remember that only large areas or masses should be envisaged; the crust has sufficient strength of itself to bear the weight of individual mountains or small land-masses (fig. 116).

In short we may think of the outer crust resting on or floating in a denser substratum, but the word floating must not be taken to mean that the substratum, whatever its exact nature may be, is actually fluid. In principle the relation of outer crust to substratum is similar to that of ice to water: the relative densities of ice and water are such that ice floats about nine-tenths submerged. If, for example, we take the average density of the continental rocks as 2·67, and that of the substratum, which for general purposes we may tentatively take as the intermediate layer, as 3·0,[1] it is easy to show that the relation of submerged to emerged parts is about eight to one. If the *relative* amounts of emerged and submerged parts are borne in mind, no matter what the exact arithmetical ratio may

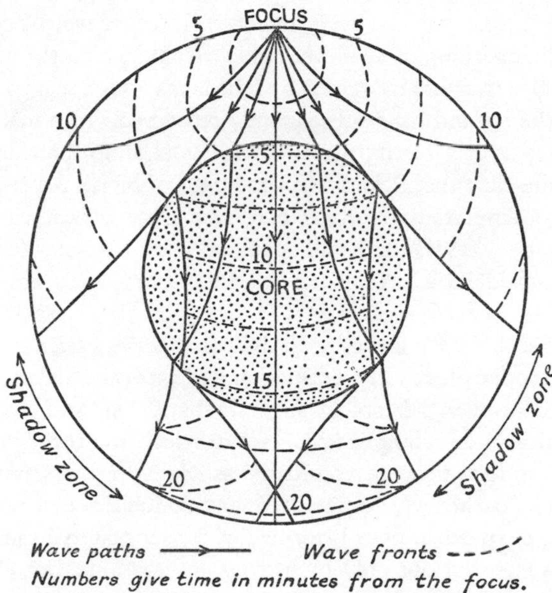

Fig. 122. Wave-fronts and paths of waves in distant earthquake.

be, it will be clear that under great thicknesses of surface rocks, or where they have been folded and refolded into mountain chains, there the downward penetrations will be greater than elsewhere. On the other hand, under the oceans there is reason to think that the substratum is higher. Clearly the waters of the oceans represent a great deficiency in mass, and it is found that if observations are made with a pendulum around the shores of a continent, the plumb-bob is very often attracted *to* the ocean. This can only mean that the sub-oceanic rocks are denser than those forming the mass of the continent. The significance of this point is considered below.

[1] Any suggestion of the precise nature of the rock in the substratum is deliberately omitted. In any case the example is over-simplified.

Clearly, if this idea of flotation is valid, it follows that if certain areas of the globe are heavily weighted they should sink downward and displace the layers beneath. It has been noted in ch. VI, pt. II, that the level of the oceans fluctuated considerably in the Ice Age. The most probable reason for this is that in the periods of intense cold great ice-caps formed, and were naturally fed by moisture derived in the first place from the oceans. But if some of the known main centres of glaciation are carefully examined very interesting phenomena are found, including many raised shorelines which are usually so disposed that the highest occur in the area where the ice was originally thickest. In other words, quite apart from the fluctuations of sea-level, which would be world wide, there have been also warping movements of the lands which sagged under the weight of the ice and have subsequently recovered. As a matter of fact this recovery is still taking place: careful tidal and other observations make it quite clear that Scandinavia and parts of North America are still rising. In a similar way sinking may take place beneath a huge and growing delta, whereas there will at any rate be a tendency for the areas suffering considerable erosion to rise, since such areas are becoming lighter.

The whole subject is one of great difficulty, and is easier to appreciate if we revert to the older views of Suess and think of the Sial as floating on the Sima. However, seismology suggests that the structure of the crust is a good deal more complicated. Nevertheless, the theory of isostasy holds, and, in fact, must be considered as having passed from the stage of theory to that of fact, despite the many difficulties that remain.

That the deep ocean floor is formed of denser material than the continents is suggested not only by gravity observations, but also by the speed of transmission of earthquake waves, which is usually appreciably higher in the sub-oceanic areas. Geographically there is a clear distinction between the Pacific and Atlantic Oceans. The former is almost encircled by mountains folded parallel with the ocean margin. Some times these mountains may be partly submerged as off eastern Asia, elsewhere they may be incorporated in the continents as in South America. Encircling mountains are absent from the Atlantic which is more characteristically bordered by plateaux or even, as in Brittany, south-western Ireland, Maine, and elsewhere, by mountain chains which run transversely out into the ocean. Some other differences have been noted in ch. I, pt. II. This distinction between Atlantic and Pacific is fundamental. It should be borne in mind that most of the Indian Ocean and some of the Arctic Ocean belongs to the Atlantic type.

Reference to fig. 61 shows that there are two levels of major significance, the one close to present sea-level, the other about 5 kilometres below it. This in itself is sufficient to enable us to distinguish true oceans from shallow seas under which the continental structures extend. Further study leads finally to a separation of the deep Pacific basin from the rest of the globe. What is this deep Pacific basin? Suess recognised a line in the west Pacific separating two very different types of structure. This line is now often called the Andesite[1] line, because to the west of it the younger eruptive rocks are mainly andesitic, whereas to the east of it they are mainly basaltic, although the exact details of structure are not clear. Nevertheless, the line is a very significant structural boundary. To the west of it all the structures, including the island arcs, are truly continental, or formed of continental rocks. To the east of it the islands are volcanic; they are often in chains but it is not clear whether they are folded.

The true boundary of the Pacific is partly shown in fig. 123: to the north it is continued along the Japanese Islands, Kamchatka, the Aleutian Islands to North America. Thence onwards the separation of structure is not so clear, and the seismic evidence suggests quite strongly that in the south-eastern part of the Pacific Ocean there are vast areas possessing a continental structure. This region does not reach as far northwards as to include Easter Island. The southern boundary is uncertain, but probably lies near Antarctica.

There are a few other areas which have a Pacific type of structure; the West Indian arc is the best example, another may be the deep basin of the Arctic Ocean.

Not only is the Pacific area rimmed by arc-like chains usually folded towards the ocean, but its margin is also a zone of great seismic activity, and it is significant that deep focus earthquakes (300–700 km. beneath the surface) appear to be limited to this belt. Their epicentres are always on the surrounding continental structures, and their alignment is not always associated with the boundary of the ocean. The evidence of earthquake waves again makes a very clear distinction between the true Pacific and the surrounding regions: the rigidity of the Pacific rocks is higher.

This stands in marked contrast to the Atlantic Ocean. Earthquake waves passing through the floor of that ocean strongly suggest that it is underlain by a considerable thickness of continental rocks, and also emphasise that there is really no structural significance at all in the margin of the Atlantic basin as there is in the Pacific. It has, in fact, been

[1] Andesite is a fine-grained igneous rock, usually a lava, of intermediate composition, and has plagioclase as the dominant felspar. Named after the Andes Mountains.

suggested that much of the sub-Atlantic structure is composed of downwarped pre-Cambrian and Palaeozoic rocks similar to those of the surrounding continents. There are many epicentres associated with the mid-Atlantic ridge, especially north of the equator. This ridge may be a line of present tectonic activity.

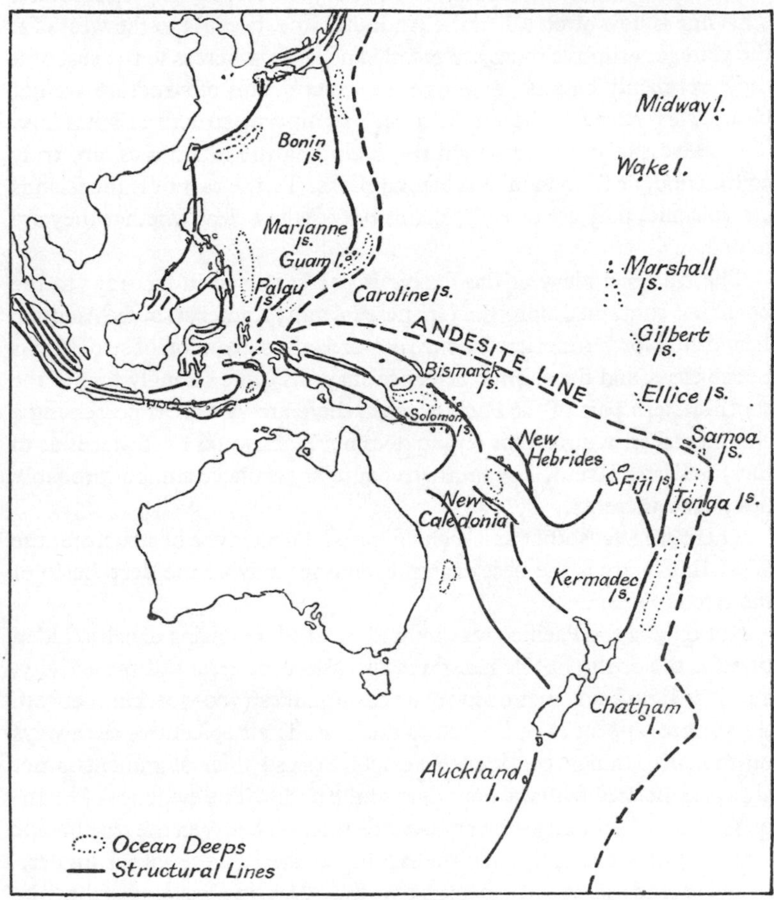

Fig. 123. Structural map of the south-west Pacific Ocean.

The Indian Ocean is similar to the Atlantic, except for the north-eastern margin along the Malay Peninsula and East Indian arc. Apart from this area, the data derived from earthquakes all indicate the presence of continental structures.

In short, it seems that the surface of the earth is divided into two distinctly different structural areas. The one includes the major basin of the Pacific Ocean and possibly a very few other regions, the other comprises the rest of the earth's surface including the continents with their shallow seas and lakes, and also the Atlantic Ocean and considerable regions on the margin of the Pacific itself.

Ocean basins, continents, and mountain chains are perhaps the major features of the globe. Naturally, their origins have given rise to much speculation, but it is essential to realise that there is no explanation of their origin which in any sense can be regarded as even partially complete. In general, theories fall into two main groups, the one group depending upon the notion of a contracting globe and the other, and in some ways more modern view, envisages the possibility of continental masses moving laterally over or through the 'substratum'—whatever that word may signify in any particular theory. It is natural that speculation of this sort should arise. We are confronted with great and easily visible folding in mountain ranges, with the fact that various forms of life are scattered over vast areas separated by wide oceans over which it is difficult if not impossible to suppose they passed unless at some stage in the earth's history there was a land connection, and again with the traces in many widely separated parts of the southern continents of an Ice Age which was nearly contemporaneous with the formation of our northern coal deposits.

It is not possible to explain these things yet, but it is easy to see that the idea of moving continents will make a great appeal. Unfortunately, there is no known cause adequate to produce movement. But if such movement is assumed, it is comparatively easy to explain many but by no means all distributions of extinct and living organisms on the assumption that the now widely separated lands in which they are found were once contiguous. Others would argue that since continental movement is impossible, there may have been land connections formerly existing between areas now separated by oceans. But we have seen that isostasy is more than a theory: if, as we have very good reason to believe, the outer crustal rocks are of lighter material than those beneath, it is difficult to see how a land connection across a deep ocean can disappear, even if, as it is sometimes assumed, rocks can flatten and spread out. There is no difficulty in accounting for former connections between, say, the British Isles and the continent, but this is a vastly different matter from a trans-Atlantic connection.

It is, however, essential to keep an open mind. Because the various suggestions made to explain moving continents are known to be inadequate, it does not follow that the continents have not moved; perhaps a sufficiently powerful force will yet be discovered. Contraction theories necessarily imply a fair amount of tangential pressure which must result in lateral movement, and it has been argued that this tangential pressure is inadequate to account for the crustal shortening observed. But we must not too readily assume that great folding in mountain chains is as indicative of great crustal shortening as it is sometimes taken to be. Many of the estimates made of folding in mountain ranges may well be too great, because they are often based on the assumption that overthrust masses now separated from their place of origin by erosion were once continuous. That this may have been so is not disproved, but it is also possible that such masses, at a certain stage in the squeezing-out process, broke away and slid forward under their own weight. If this is so, it is obvious that the actual shortening may be very much less than the apparent shortening as a result of compression (see p. 237 and fig. 115).

Because of uncertainties of this nature, to say nothing of the many others concerning mountain building, and because of the wide range of opinion possible concerning the structure of the earth's crust and of the forces involved, a discussion of earth theories is out of the question in the limited space available. Moreover, their proper appreciation depends on a knowledge of geology and other sciences not relevant to the subject-matter of this book.

CHAPTER IV

SHORELINES

The shape and character of a coast are determined partly by the movements of elevation and depression which have affected the earth's crust, partly by the action of the sea and other denuding agencies. They depend also to a large extent upon the nature of the materials which form the land.

The action of waves. Waves are usually the most important agent modifying a coastline. Tides are also effective first because they raise and lower the plane of action of the waves, and secondly because of the currents associated with them. The direction of flow of tidal currents alternates, and so they may lose much of their effectiveness as agents of longshore drift. In narrow entrances to lagoons and in places where tidal races form close inshore, the influence of tidal currents is great. Currents due to winds are usually too weak, where they actually make contact with the shore, to have any direct influence. On the other hand, tidal and possibly other currents close inshore often carry in saltatory fashion great amounts of fine material which has been stirred up by the waves. This is a most important process and can often be readily observed by anyone bathing on a gently shelving, sandy beach where small waves are running.

The movement of water particles in a simple wave in deep water has been discussed on p. 156. It is convenient at this point to consider what happens when the waves enter shallow water and break on beaches.

As waves enter shallow water their speed is reduced and so they become more closely packed; the orbital motion becomes elliptical, the

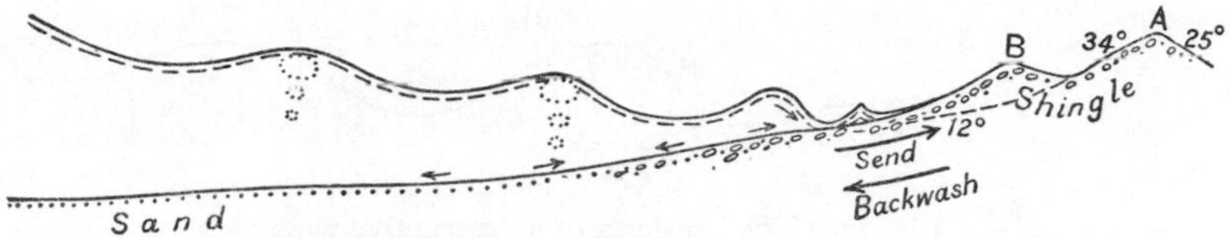

Fig. 124. Motion of water particles in waves before and after breaking, and the building of beach ridges.

major axes of the ellipses being horizontal (fig. 124); the crests become steeper and higher, and the troughs flatter. Finally the crests hollow out, curve over, and break. The reason for this is not entirely clear, but may be attributed to the fact that there is insufficient water to form the complete wave crest into which the wave energy can be transmitted. As the crests steepen the forward movement on the bottom increases in speed and the return movement under the troughs becomes slower. The total distance moved by the water particles each way may still be the same, the slow return movement taking the water just as far as the short, sharp forward movement.

Landwards of the breaker the water alternately advances and retreats up and down the beach as the *send* (or *swash*) and *backwash*.

The to and fro motion of the water particles actually touching the seabed just seawards of the breaking waves is important in moving the sand and pebbles. The quicker landward thrust under the crest is more effective in moving bed material than the slower return movement. Thus material is pushed landwards until the slope is such that as much material is carried seawards down the slope by the weak return currents as is driven up the slope by the more powerful shoreward thrusts. This is called the slope of equilibrium.

The movement of the water landwards of the breakers is best seen on a fairly steeply sloping shingle beach. The send from the breakers is weakened by gravity, friction, and loss of water by percolation. The backwash returns directly downhill and is continuously weakened by friction. Water percolating out again from the pebbles may slightly help the backwash. Thus the equilibrium slope of the beach is steepest near the land where the backwash is small in volume and low in velocity.

The evolution of the beach gradient is not quite as simple as this, because waves of different height and length produce different profiles of equilibrium, and the level of wave action is constantly changing in tidal waters. Consequently, a shingle beach, which can be modified far more quickly than a sandy beach, is in a constant state of flux.

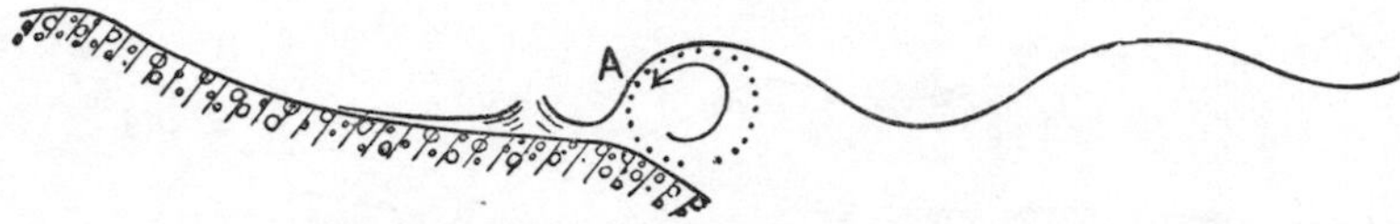

Fig. 125. The breaking of a destructive wave.

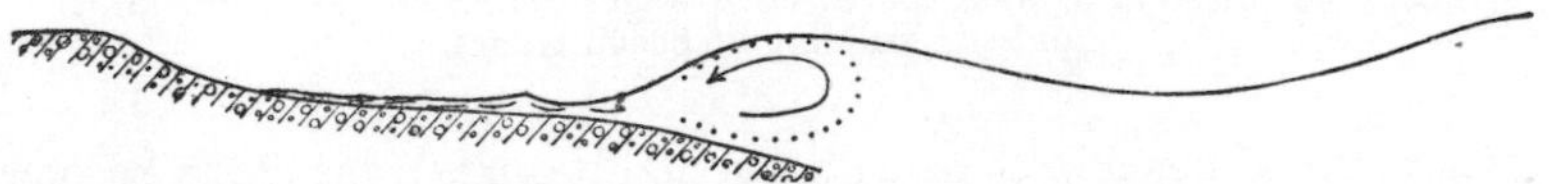

Fig. 126. The breaking of a constructive wave.

Waves caused by local winds vary greatly, but they are generally high in proportion to their length. The orbital velocity is great, but the rate of advance low, because the latter is proportional to the wave-length. Since the plunge is nearly vertical (fig. 125), much energy is lost in the bounce and still more in the eddies or rollers as they travel up the beach in the send. Although the send is therefore weak it nevertheless carries a large volume of water up the beach, which returns as a relatively powerful backwash. This meets the next oncoming send and reduces its effect. Consequently, these waves tend to drag material down the beach and might be termed *destructive waves*.

As waves move away from a storm centre the ratio of their length to height increases, and the smaller waves die down sooner. Thus is produced the long ground-swell from a distant storm. These waves, if they are not too large, build up the beach and might be termed *constructive waves*[1] (fig. 126). Their rate of travel is fast and they have a low orbital velocity. The backwash of one wave has usually returned before the suc-

[1] Destructive waves, about 3 feet high on breaking, have a frequency of 12 to 14 a minute. Constructive waves of the same height break with a frequency of 6 to 8 a minute.

ceeding wave breaks. The quickly moving wave seems to transfer all its energy into a swift send which rushes much farther up the beach than that from a shorter destructive wave of similar height. The orbital velocity, too, seems to end abruptly at the breaking-point. Moreover, the backwash is much weakened by friction in its long run down the foreshore.

These two types of waves can be produced in the laboratory, and it can then be seen that the destructive and constructive actions also take place seawards of the breaker line. The steep destructive waves build a bar below water-level just seawards of the breaker line. The flatter constructive waves produce a simpler profile without a bar.

Storm waves are short in proportion to their height, and on account of their size are extremely destructive. A single great storm in 1852 removed 4½ million tons of shingle from Chesil Beach, most of which was returned in a few days, probably by the long constructive waves of the ground-swell succeeding the storm. But small waves, whatever their type, return shingle to a beach after a storm.

Although storm waves are mainly destructive they can, nevertheless, throw shingle over the top of the beach and so build a new ridge[1] (*A*, fig. 124). Smaller ridges, such as *B*, represent the work of lesser storms. The profile of a sandy beach is different and always less steep. If the tidal range is small the profile between tide-marks may resemble a flatter version of that shown in fig. 126. In particular the steepening at the upper limit of wave-action is less. The top of the beach does not rise so high and unless capped by substantial dunes it presents a less formidable barrier against storm waves which sweep right over it. If the tidal range is great, half a mile or more of sand may be exposed between tide marks. The profile of such a beach is usually slightly wavy.

Wave refraction. In shallow water the rate of wave advance depends on the depth of water.[2] A wave (*aa*, fig. 127) close to an indented shoreline travels fastest in the deep water opposite the bays, and so on approaching the shore it curves as indicated in the figure. This produces two important results. The energy of a wave is transmitted in a direction perpendicular to the front and so a greater proportion of energy is concentrated on the headlands than on the bays. Also the waves strike the sides of headlands and bays at an angle and this causes the sand and pebbles to drift alongshore.

[1] The beach profile between tide-marks might slope seawards at about 12°, increasing gradually to 34° near the crest. The shingle washed over the landward side comes to rest on a slope of about 25°.

[2] If the depth (h) is less than one-sixth of the wave-length, then $c = 2gh$ (where c is the velocity and g gravity).

On any open foreshore the winds may cause the waves to approach the beach obliquely. When the waves break the send will also move obliquely up the beach, and will carry loose material with it. But the backwash will return directly down the steepest slope, and it too will carry sand and pebbles with it (*a*, fig. 128). A similar action occurs on a lesser scale seawards of the breakers and results in a movement along a saw-tooth path (*b*). It follows, then, that if oblique waves act on a beach for some time the shingle and sand which come within their reach are moved sideways along the beach. This process is called longshore or beach drifting and is of great significance.

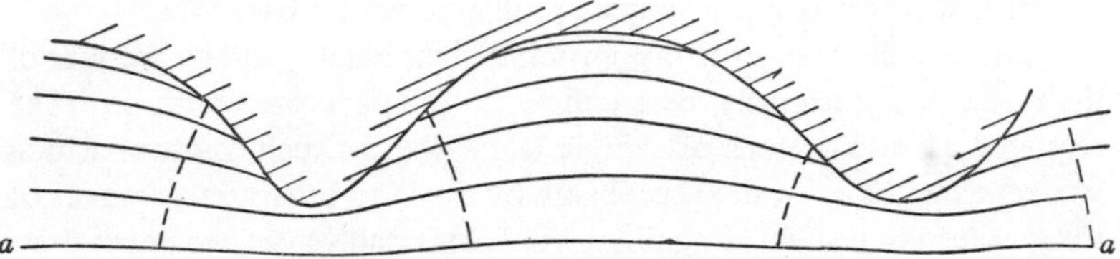

Fig. 127. Wave refraction off an indented shoreline.

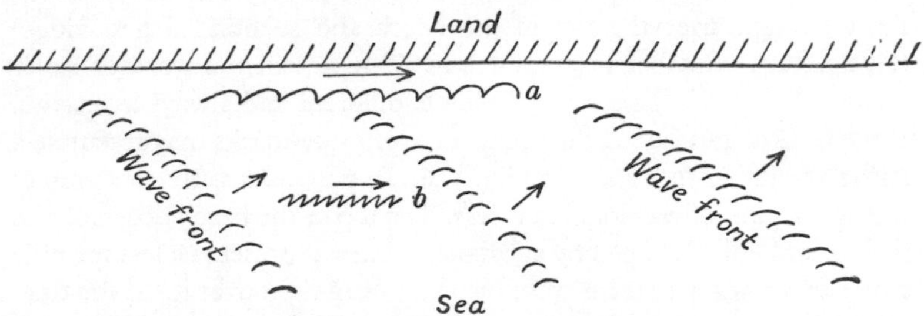

Fig. 128. Longshore drift by oblique waves. *a*, landward, and *b*, seaward, of the breaker line.

Distinction must here be made between prevalent and dominant waves. Prevalent waves are those which are most commonly seen on a beach. The word does not so much refer to their size as to the frequency of their occurrence and the direction from which they come. Dominant waves are those which may have an effect on the beach out of all proportion to the time during which they act. On many parts of our western coasts waves from west or south-west are to be expected: in calm weather they do not have any great effect, although over a period of time their collective effect may be considerable. In a storm there may be powerful waves from the same direction which may cause great changes in a single tide. These waves could be called dominant. On our eastern coasts the dominant waves come in from the north and east, and there, as elsewhere, are closely related to the fetch of open water off any particular stretch of coast.

The longshore drift of material is usually due to the action of the prevalent waves, for they are incessantly at work and, near the water line, are usually well able to move sand and shingle. This beach drifting is clearly shown at many seaside towns where groynes have been thrown out to protect the cliffs and promenades. A groyne is a wall of wood, stone, or concrete, built seawards, usually at right angles to the shore. The sand and shingle drifting along the shore are piled against one side of the groyne. On the other side, where there is no heaping up, the beach is lower until the effect of the next groyne begins to be felt. The object of the groynes is to prevent the loose material from travelling onwards and thus to cause the accumulation of a beach which will prevent the waves from reaching the cliffs.

Such beach drifting is halted at the heads of bays where the wave fronts are parallel with the shoreline, and so the send and backwash move directly up and down the beach. The drift is also halted at river mouths where the deeper water and the river's current impede the longshore movement. If the coast curves gently landwards waves swing round and continue to carry the material forwards, but at a reduced rate because the waves lose much of their power in swinging round the bend.

Any stretch of shore from which material is being removed quicker than it is being supplied suffers erosion, and conversely any stretch of shore to which material is brought in greater quantities than it is removed, e.g. when longshore drift is reduced in speed or halted, becomes a zone of deposition.

Development of the cliff and wave-cut platform. The waves of the sea continually breaking upon the shore gradually wear away the land, whether its margin is a shelving beach or a steep and rocky cliff. If the coast consists of loose material, the waves themselves may wash away the fragments; but if it is formed of firm and solid rock their action is indirect. The pebbles and boulders that they throw against a cliff serve as battering-rams and the face of the cliff is slowly broken up, especially at its base (pls. 6*b*, 10*a*). Most rocks, moreover, are fissured and the fissures are filled with air. When the wave rises against a rock or cliff, the air is compressed. By this alternate compression and subsequent expansion the fissures are enlarged and masses of rock are slowly broken off.

Caves, which are invariably located at lines of weakness such as faults or major joints, are cut partly by the compression and expansion of air in a fissure, when its mouth is closed by water. Caves sometimes cut through a narrow headland and produce an arch. If the arch subsequently collapses a stack is left which, in turn, will itself succumb to the attack of the waves. Blowholes also have formed in a similar way (frontispiece).

Waves acting on a newly submerged land surface will first cut a nick at *a* (fig. 129). This is the embryo cliff and platform. The waves are most destructive near high-water mark but as they try to undercut the cliff the overhanging parts collapse. The debris produced in this way is steadily worn down in size and carried seawards or alongshore to be deposited elsewhere. Continued erosion causes the cliff to grow in height[1] and the gently inclined wave-cut platform to increase in width (profile *bb*).

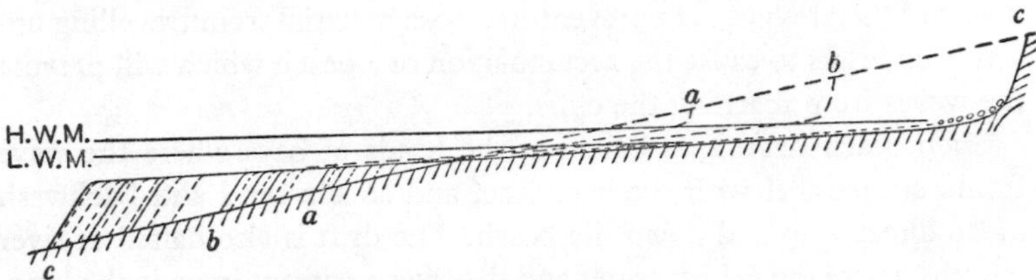

Fig. 129. The development of the shore profile.

If the rock is limestone solution plays a part. The intricate details of the Carboniferous Limestone coast west of Tenby are by no means wholly the result of wave erosion, but to waves acting upon rocks already greatly affected by subaerial and subterranean denudation.

At stage (*cc*) the shallower water offshore reduces the power of the waves which reach the cliff and the fallen debris remains longer at the foot of the cliff and forms a beach. A thin cover of gravel or sand extends seawards concealing the wave-cut platform. The slope of the cliff depends a great deal upon the relative rates of marine and subaerial erosion: if the latter is for some reason more rapid the slope will decrease and vice versa.

The form of the cliff is also greatly affected by the stratification and jointing of the rock, for it is along the planes of bedding and along the joints that rocks usually break most readily. If the beds dip seawards and the joints landwards, large blocks of rock will easily be detached and will fall upon the beach, and the cliff will rise in a series of overhanging steps (fig. 130). If on the other hand the beds dip landwards and the joints seawards, the blocks, even when loosened, will not fall until they are actually undermined. Erosion at the base in this case is less effective and the face of the cliff will usually slope towards the sea (fig. 131). If

[1] This assumes that the land slopes towards the sea. It is worth remarking here that exaggerated notions of cliff erosion are common. The configuration of the land, as well as the nature of the rocks, must be considered.

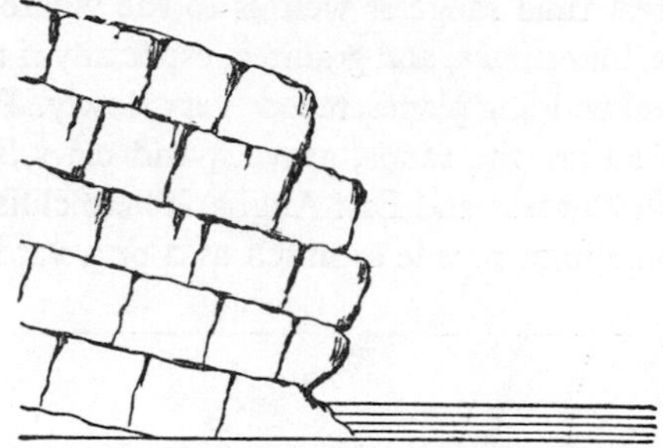

Fig. 130. Erosion of cliff (beds dipping seawards). (Cf. pl. 6*a*.)

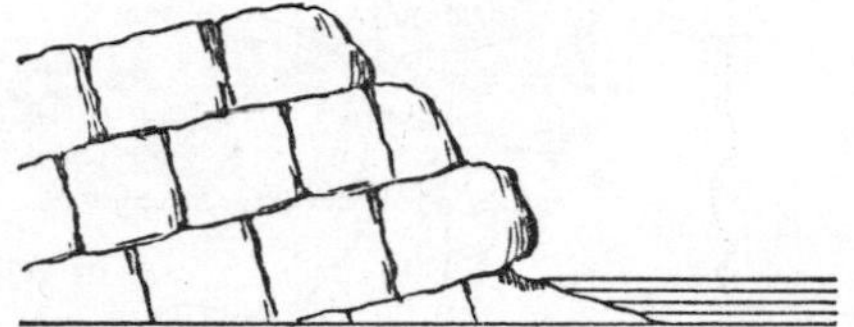

Fig. 131. Erosion of cliff (beds dipping landwards).

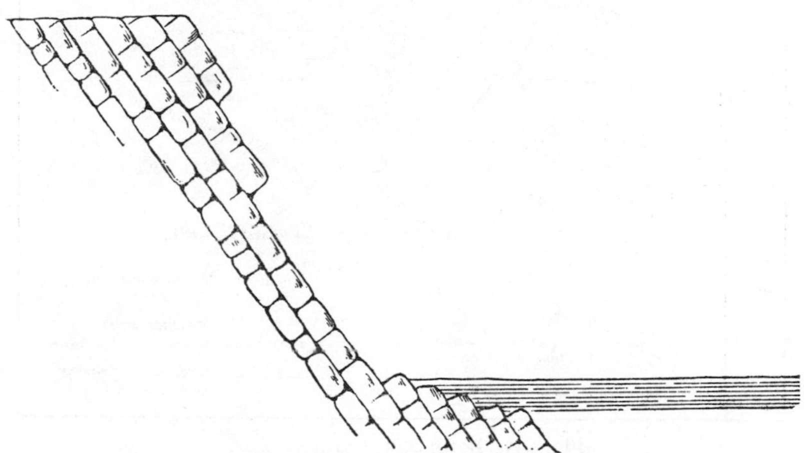

Fig. 132. Erosion of cliff (beds dipping steeply seawards).

the beds dip steeply seawards the blocks slip down the bedding planes which may form a smooth cliff face very resistant to wave erosion (fig. 132).

In the Liassic cliffs of south Glamorgan, where thin limestone bands alternate with weaker shale beds, cliff recession is relatively rapid (pl. 9*a*). The shore platform is a quarter-mile or more wide, but this is related to the great tidal range as well as to the vigorous wave attack. Hard sandstones, limestones, and granites, especially if they are massive with few joints and bedding planes, recede very slowly. Perhaps the most easily eroded of all are the sands, gravels, and clays like those in the glacial cliffs of Holderness and East Anglia. There cliffs a hundred feet or more high sometimes recede as much as 2 or 3 yards a year.

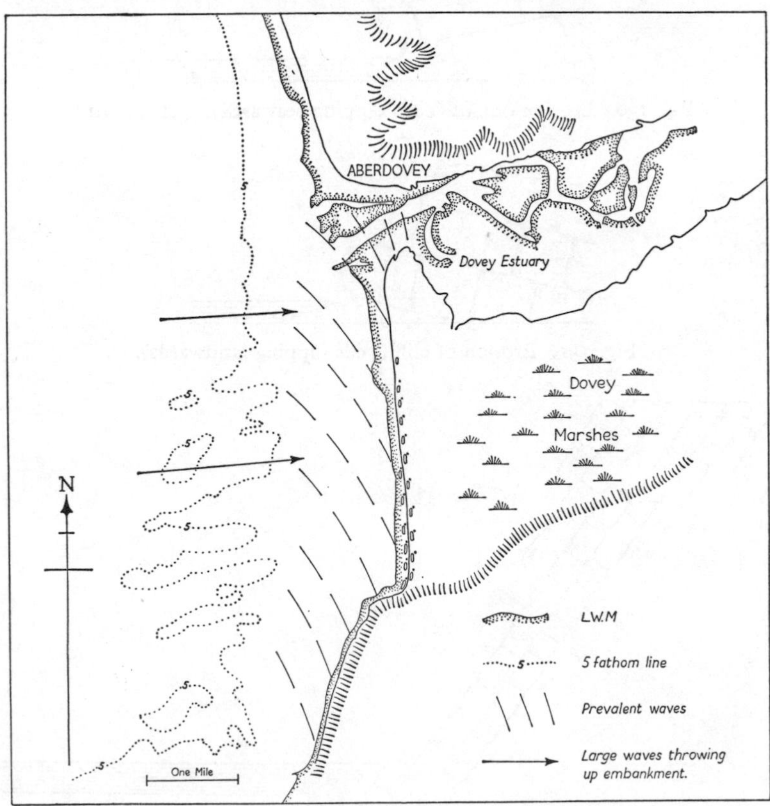

Fig. 133. Borth Spit, Cardigan Bay.

Shore features of deposition. Perhaps the most interesting of all coastal features are the shingle and sandspits, forelands and embankments of which many fine examples occur round the shores of Britain. They produce some of the most striking changes in the coastline resulting from the action of the sea.

First let us consider a simple spit formed at a bend in the shoreline caused by an estuary. Borth spit (fig. 133) in Cardigan Bay is a good example. It extends four miles from south to north, almost crossing the mouth of the Dovey estuary. Extensive salt marshes have formed in the sheltered waters behind it, and it has been largely responsible for the silting of the estuary. The prevalent south-westerly waves drift both sand and shingle from south to north, and large waves coming from a direction slightly south of west have thrown this material up into an

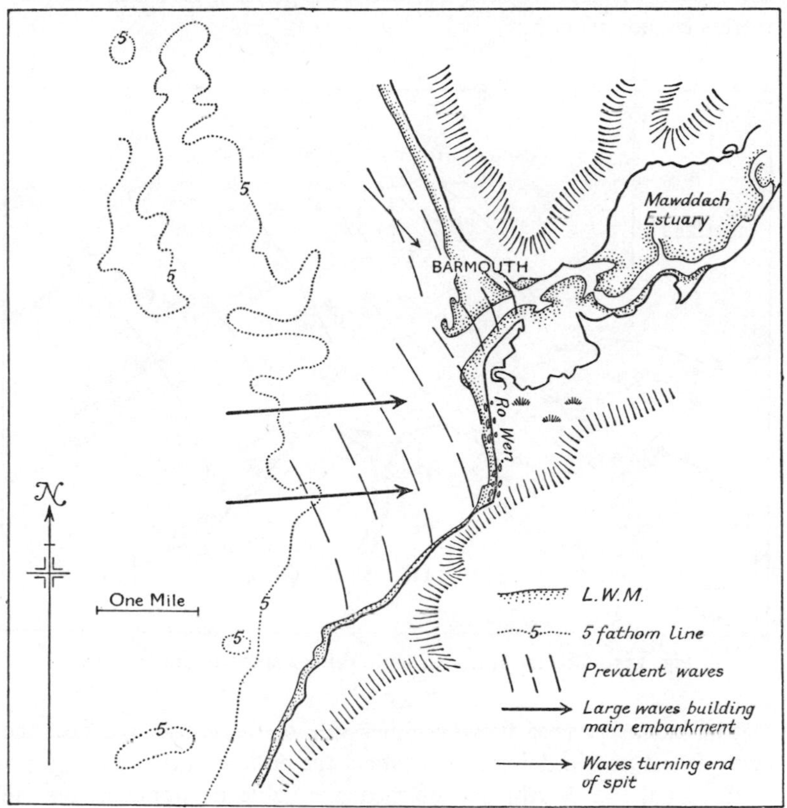

Fig. 134. Ro Wen, Cardigan Bay.

embankment—the sand on the lower foreshore and the shingle at and above high-water mark. Dunes have formed on top of the shingle particularly at the northern end, where extensive sand flats dry out at low water and supply the sand which drifts landwards until caught by the marram grass of the dunes.

Ten miles to the north is the Mawddach estuary, the entrance to which is almost crossed by Ro Wen (fig. 134 and pl. 9*a*), a sand and shingle spit smaller, but in one respect more complicated than Borth spit. Ro Wen, after extending northwards for two miles, turns abruptly to the north-east, continues in this direction for another mile and then ends only a few hundred yards from the opposite shore. This turned end of the spit is probably built by occasional severe storm waves from the north-west. These, whilst not powerful enough to turn the whole spit, are able to drive back the less massive free end to a position in which westerly storms cannot affect it.

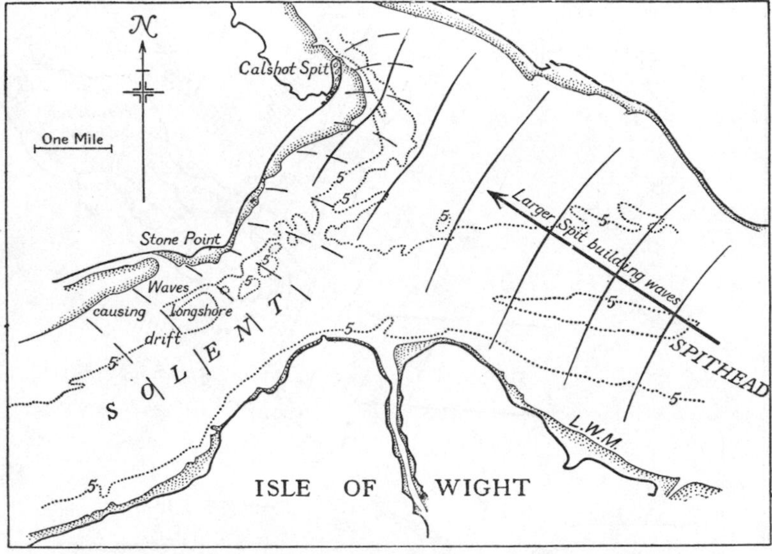

Fig. 135. Calshot Spit. A simple shingle spit without laterals.

The extensive sand flats on either side of the entrance deflect the wave-fronts and in doing so may affect the outline of the spit.

Ro Wen, like Borth, has afforded a suitable environment for the development of salt marshes, the older parts of which have been reclaimed.

A further example of a simple spit is Calshot spit (fig. 135) at the entrance to Southampton Water. Shingle is continuous at the foot of the cliffs from Stone Point to the spit, but it becomes more abundant as the spit is approached. Finally, the beach merges into an embankment which continues independently where the cliff line turns northwards into Southampton Water. The lower foreshore off the spit is fairly wide, especially at the eastern end, and consists of mixed sand and pebbles.

Again there are saltings in the sheltered water to the lee of the spit, and the most abundant plant is *Spartina townsendii*, which thrives on soft mud that is covered by salt water for much of the time.

South-westerly waves drift material to the spit and the far larger south-easterly waves travelling along Spithead from the open Channel throw this material up into an embankment. The slight curve of the spit

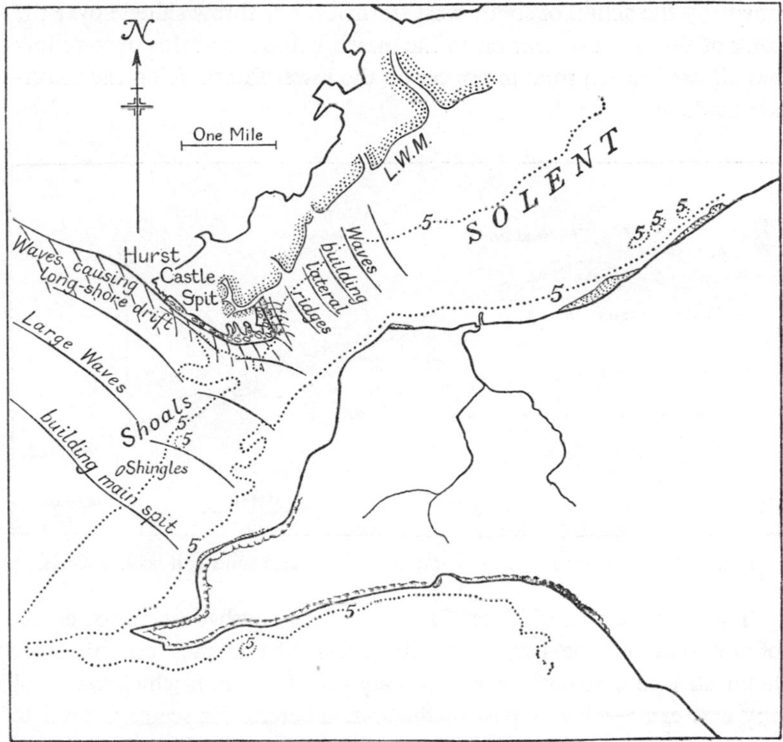

Fig. 136. Hurst Castle Spit. A shingle spit with parallel laterals. The dotted area between the coast and L.W.M. is mainly *Spartina* marsh.

may be due to the deflection of the large wave-fronts by the extensive shallows off the bend.

Hurst Castle spit (fig. 136 and pl. 9*b*) resembles Calshot spit in its relationship to the mainland. The shingle in front of the low cliffs of Christchurch Bay becomes more plentiful towards the east, and eventually merges into the embankment forming the spit. The lower foreshore is in the main sandy, and just opposite the first bend shoals extend south-westwards for more than a mile and include the Shingles which are exposed even at high water. These shoals deflect the large waves, and so may indirectly be the cause of the first bend in the spit.

A series of lateral ridges join the main spit at a sharp angle. Each series consists of parallel shingle ridges and represents a stage in the growth of the spit. The westernmost lateral marks the end of the spit at an early stage and the easternmost one is still forming to-day. As the end of the spit grew eastwards the main ridge was pushed north-eastwards by the action of south-west storms. They throw shingle over the back of the embankment on to the marsh behind, and this over-rolling has allowed marsh mud to appear on the lower foreshore on the south-west side of the bank.

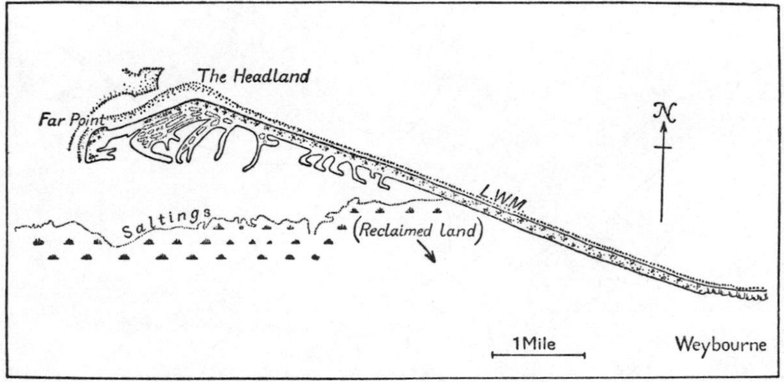

Fig. 137. Blakeney Point. A complex shingle and sand spit with laterals.

The main portion of Hurst Castle spit faces south-west, the direction of approach of the largest storm waves. The laterals on the other hand all face east-north-east, the only direction from which waves of any size can reach this part of the spit. Therefore it seems natural to attribute the direction both of the main spit and of the laterals to that of the waves which built them. The absence of laterals from Calshot and Borth spits may be due to the fact that these spits are sheltered from waves which approach the end of the spit obliquely.

To the west of Sheringham on the north Norfolk coast, the shingle below the cliffs grows more abundant and eventually merges into the embankment forming Blakeney Point (fig. 137). The old cliffed coast-line runs east-west but the spit leaves this line and runs in a west-north-west direction. The main shingle ridge remains very massive when traced in this same direction. The spit continues thus for about 6 miles: at first it lies in front of reclaimed marshes and later in front of saltings and lagoons. About half-way along appear the earliest lateral ridges. These are short whereas the newer ones farther west are long and narrow. They nearly all leave the main spit almost at right angles. When the easternmost ones formed the end of the spit the main embankment was seawards of its present position. During the later westward growth, marked by the various laterals, the bank retreated landwards so that the oldest laterals are now much shortened. The wide spacing of the laterals may be due to the relatively rapid westward advance of the spit which was growing into fairly shallow water. The shingle of which Blakeney beach is formed is very ill-sorted and varies greatly in size.

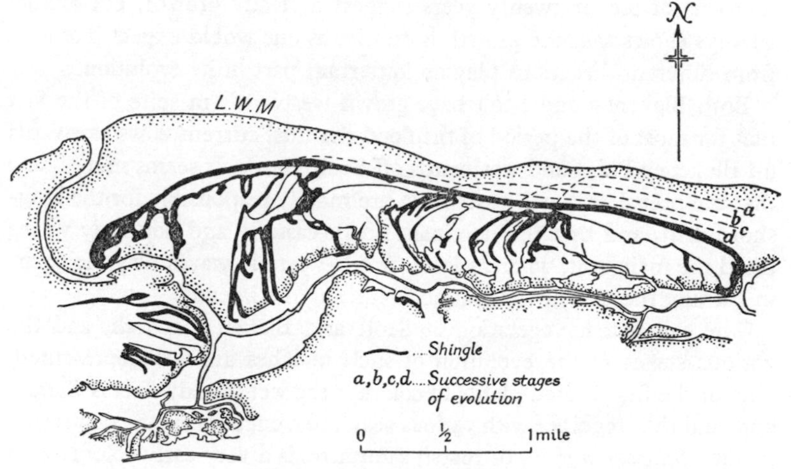

Fig. 138. Scolt Head Island.

Off the Headland the amount of sand on the foreshore is great and this may materially have assisted the waves to maintain the north-north-east facing direction of the spit for so great a distance. These extensive flats have also supplied sand for the dunes which conceal the shingle ridges in this neighbourhood (pl. 19*b*).

As in the case of Hurst Castle spit the direction of the main spit may be largely due to the action of the dominant waves, and that of the laterals to other lesser waves approaching the end of the spit obliquely. On an open coast, such as that of north Norfolk, quite large waves can approach the end of the spit from a variety of directions, and this might explain why the laterals at Blakeney are not so consistent in direction as those at Hurst.

Scolt Head Island (fig. 138) has been more closely studied and mapped than any other such coastal form in this country. Its recent evolution is, therefore, fairly well known. It possesses many of the features of a complex sand and shingle spit but it is not joined to the mainland. Early writers considered that it once continued across the present site of Burnham Harbour entrance, but it is now thought that this gap is not new. The lower foreshore is sandy throughout its length and dunes cover most of the shingle ridges. Like Blakeney, the western laterals are usually longer than the eastern ones and the reason again seems to be the landward movement of the spit in the course of its development, a movement that has been authenticated by the mapping. The western end has fluctuated a good deal in the last one hundred years. Maps made at intervals of ten or twenty years suggest a steady growth, but annual surveys shows that the growth is erratic, as one would expect if storms from different directions play an important part in its evolution.

Both Blakeney and Scolt have grown westwards in spite of the fact that for most of the period of the flood the tidal current flows eastwards off Blakeney Point and westwards off Scolt Head. It seems more likely that the prevalent north-east waves are mainly responsible for the longshore drift, and that the dominant north-easterly and northerly waves build the main spit, whereas lesser north-westerly waves play their part in turning the end of the spit and building the laterals.

The salt-marsh vegetation at Scolt and Blakeney is rich, and the various stages in the evolution of such marshes are well represented. One of the first rooted plants to colonise the wet muddy flats is *Zostera* spp. and this, together with various seaweeds, encourages the deposition of silt. *Salicornia* spp., or marsh samphire, is a very early coloniser on firmer ground. It is followed by a succession of plants including sea aster, sea pink and sea lavender, and various grasses (e.g. *Puccinellia maritima*) which spread over large areas of marsh. During this upgrowth of the marsh branching and meandering creeks are developed, and in eastern England are commonly fringed by *Halimione portulacoides* which often spreads over wide areas. Fine sediment and blown sand combine with the vegetation to build up the level of the marshes (almost 1 cm. a year under favourable conditions) until they are covered by only the highest tides. At this stage plants such as *Glaux maritima* and *Juncus maritimus* or sea rush flourish, and the marshes afford some pasturage for sheep and are ready for reclamation. All that is necessary for final reclamation is to build an embankment to keep out the high spring tides and to construct sluices and drains to let the land-water drain seawards but prevent the entrance of salt water at high tide.

Orford Ness (fig. 139) consists almost entirely of shingle and is remarkable for the distance it has deflected the River Alde southwards.

It is also instructive as an example of the transition from a shingle spit to a shingle foreland. *A*, *B* and *C* (fig. 139) are widely spaced groups of laterals formed when the young spit was growing southwards. As the end approached the site of the present Ness the rate of southerly extension seems to have been reduced, and the laterals were piled one

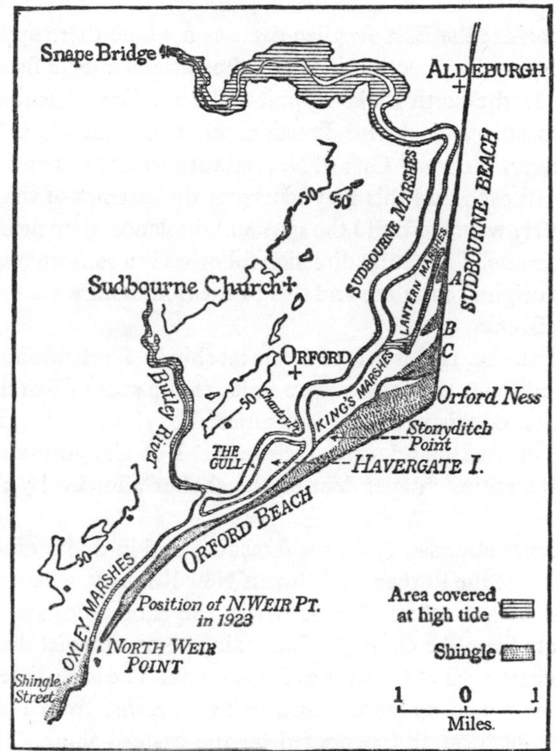

Fig. 139. Orford Ness. A shingle spit which has developed into a cuspate foreland.

against the other. Many shingle ridges end at Stonyditch Point, and it was almost certainly at this time that Orford developed as an important medieval port. The long tapering part of the spit south of Stonyditch Point seems to have developed since the time of Henry II. The spit is a good example of a cuspate foreland, and as it lengthened it deflected not only the Alde but also the Butley stream farther and farther south-west. On the landward side of the river's mouth are vast expanses of shingle forming Shingle Street. This material is nearly all the wastage of the spit, large masses of which are from time to time cut off in storms. In 1897, for example, the spit was shortened by a mile in this way.

Both the dominant and prevalent waves come from a direction somewhat north of east, and it is significant that the zone of deposition is to the lee of the Ness where the prevalent waves, which are responsible for the longshore drift, have lost some of their energy after swinging round the Ness.

If we consider the East Anglian coast as a whole there appears to be some system in the direction in which the various coastal features leave the shore. In the north Blakeney spit and Scolt Head Island turn away from the coast in a clockwise direction, whereas southwards Yarmouth spit, Lowestoft Ness and Orford Ness all turn away in an anti-clockwise direction. In each case this may represent the attempt of the dominant north-easterly waves to build the spits and forelands more nearly parallel with their fronts. The actual direction followed is a compromise between that of the original coastline and that of the dominant wave-fronts some distance offshore.

Dungeness (fig. 140) is one of the finest shingle forelands in the world. It has added more than 100 square miles to the area of Britain. Only a small portion of this new land is composed of shingle, the greater part consisting of marshland now reclaimed. But the formation of the marshes was entirely dependent on the shelter afforded by the shingle ridges.

Sand occurs abundantly on the foreshore and in dunes on either side of the mouth of the Rother, and also off New Romney, where the Rother debouched before 1287. But elsewhere the shore consists of shingle, mainly flints from the chalk, but including some material derived from the south coast even as far west as Devonshire. The longshore drift is to the north-east, and material is still being removed from the southern shore of Dungeness and deposited on the eastern shore. This results from the weakening of the prevalent south-westerly waves as they round the Ness, for they are unable to drift as much material northwards from the Ness as they bring to it from the west.

The early evolution of Dungeness is, of course, a matter of speculation, but the following seems to be the sequence of events as far as they are at present known. In Neolithic times, when the sea-level was lower than at present and forests were growing on land now submerged beneath the sea, a spit grew nearly across the bay now occupied by Romney Marsh. Some parts of this ancient spit running through Lydd and New Romney are still preserved. As sea-level rose and submerged the forests, this spit or bar appears to have been broken through near *A*

The loose end was then swung round to *B*, *C*, etc., by the dominant south-westerly or southerly storm waves. But as the bend thus formed grew sharper, the eastern shore became more sheltered from the prevalent south-west waves and so the speed of drift was there reduced. This gave rise to deposition and the building of a fine series of ridges forming the extensive shingle foreland of to-day. These ridges were thrown up by waves approaching Dungeness from the east. Thus the very characteristic outline of Dungeness is due to its being subjected, in the main, to

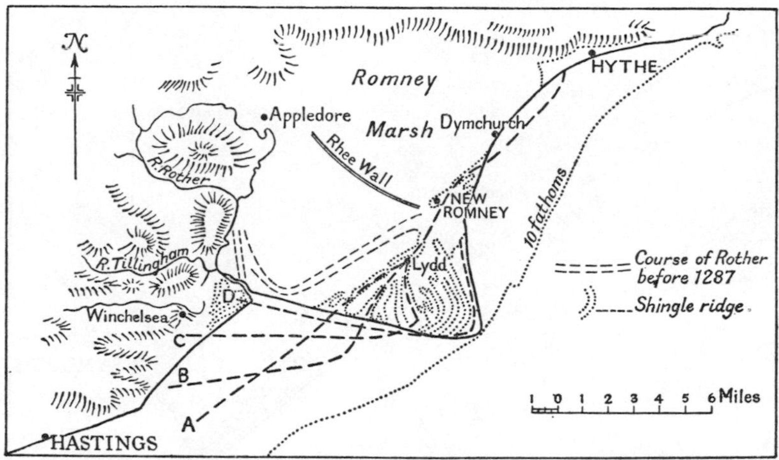

Fig. 140. Dungeness: a cuspate shingle foreland which protects extensive areas of reclaimed marsh. *A*, *B*, *C*, *D*, indicate suggested stages in the evolution of the foreland.

two distinct sets of waves—the largest from the south-south-west moulding the southern shore, and the next largest from the east-north-east moulding the eastern shore.

The Chesil Beach (fig. 141) is unique in these islands, and perhaps in the world. It consists of one major ridge which starts abruptly at the south-east side of Bridport Harbour breakwaters and extends 16 miles to Portland: southwards from Abbotsbury it leaves the land and encloses the Fleet. The surface shingle is remarkably graded; near Bridport it is about the size of a pea or hazelnut, and near Portland about the size and shape of a potato. Moreover, the height and width of the beach increases steadily to the south-east. It rises 19 feet above high water at Bridport, 23 feet at Abbotsbury and 43 feet near Portland. Many have investigated its problems, but there is no comprehensive explanation of them. The beach is fed at both ends, and the pebbles are nearly all flints. Some

Portland Stone, however, travels northwards and far-travelled rocks are not uncommon, probably derived from the raised beaches and river gravels of the south coast. In fact the beach must have originated somewhat to the south-west of its present position and may consist mainly of the hard residue of land now eroded from West Bay.

The beach is almost at right angles to the dominant and prevalent winds and waves acting upon it, and so it forms a cul-de-sac to any

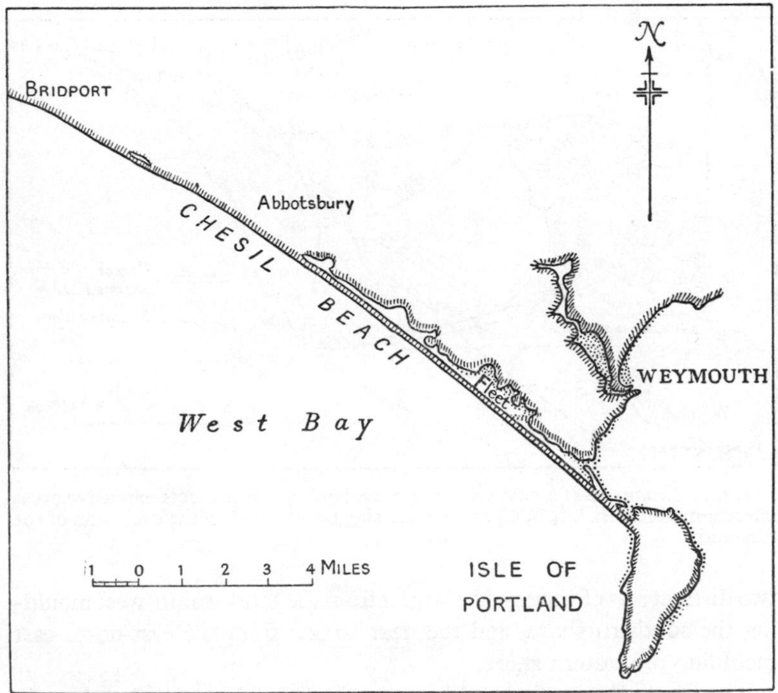

Fig. 141. Chesil Beach. A great shingle embankment.

material added to it. Since occasional storms even now overtop the beach, it is adjusted to existing conditions of wind, tide, and waves. Its great height at the Portland end is a measure of the power of the Atlantic storm waves which strike this shore head-on during south-westerly gales.

There is no doubt that wave action is the most important factor in its formation, and it is easy to see that waves caused by the predominant winds from between west and south-west will cause an eastward drift of beach material. Winds from the south and east generate smaller waves in confined waters of the Channel and these, acting intermittently over a long period, have tended to return only the smaller shingle westwards. Nevertheless the perfect grading and the regular increase of the beach in height and width are not yet fully explained. Detailed and prolonged observation on various parts of the beach are essential preliminaries before any dogmatic statement can be made.

One of the great difficulties in the investigation of shingle and sand beaches is to discover precisely how the beaches are fed. Lateral drift may be apparent, but it is often supposed that new materials come from seaward. Quite recently some experiments with radioactive pebbles have been made—one off Scolt Head Island, and the other at the south end of Orford Ness. The former has shown that it is possible to trace the movement of stones in water up to 20 or 25 feet deep. Further experiments are required, but unfortunately they are very expensive. Some conclusive investigations on the movement of mud were made in the Thames Estuary. (See *Geographical Journal*, 122 (1956), 343.)

TYPES OF COASTS

Shores formed by depression. When a large area of the earth's crust is slowly depressed and a long-established continent quietly subsides, the sea spreads over the edge of the land and enters the river valleys. The coastline will then become irregular, and its form will depend upon the character of the flooded land.

Coastline of subsided lowland region. If the land is low-lying and consists of soft rocks the valleys will be broad and shallow and often meandering. A very slight depression of the land will cause the sea to spread up the valleys and the coastline will become excessively winding. On account of the gentle slopes of the flooded land the shores will be low and often there will be salt marshes which are covered at high tide and uncovered when the tide is low. In Essex and the southern part of Suffolk much of the coast is of this character. The sea has spread far up the valleys of the Orwell, the Stour, the Blackwater and other rivers, and the shore is low and often marshy (fig. 142).

A coast of this kind, however, seldom maintains its character for long. Because the rocks are soft the sea quickly wears away the prominent points, and the material thus produced together with the deposits brought down by the rivers gradually fill up the estuaries.

Longshore drift will supply sand and shingle for spits to be formed across the mouths of the irregular inlets, cutting them off from the open sea and converting them into lagoons or backwaters. In the course of time deposits fill these backwaters and they pass first into marshes and later into low-lying flats. At this stage they will be suitable for grazing and ready for reclamation.

The various stages in the straightening of the shoreline are well shown on the coast between the Thames and the Wash. In Essex and the south of Suffolk the sea has evidently entered the valleys of the rivers and the outline of the land is very irregular. Prominent points such as the Naze

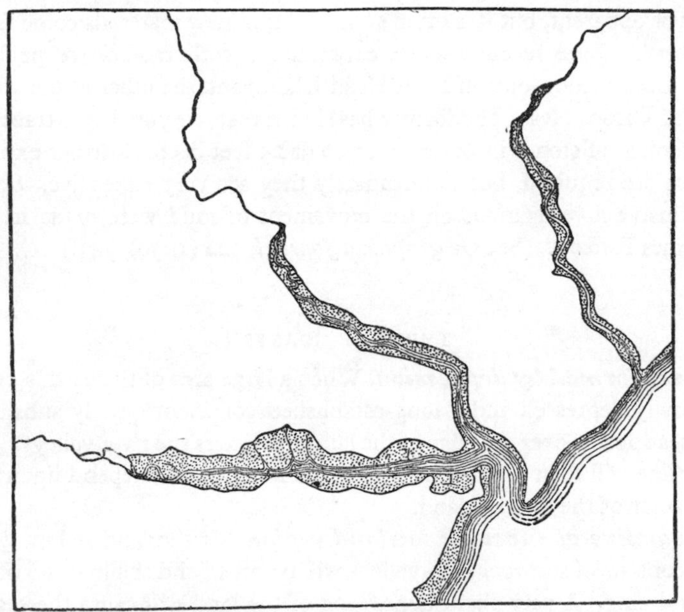

Fig. 142. Mouths of the Deben, Orwell, and Stour.
The dotted areas are uncovered at low water.

are gradually being worn away, while at Landguard Point near Felixstowe there is a well-formed shingle spit across the mouths of the Orwell and the Stour. Farther north the spits are more fully developed, as in the case of the Alde: all the irregular inlets have been cut off from the sea and the coast is smooth. Some of the backwaters have been completely filled up, but in several cases the process is not complete and a partially filled lagoon like Breydon Water is characteristic of this part of the country.

Coastline of subsided highland region. If the land is high and rises abruptly from the sea, and the rocks are hard, the valleys will usually be narrow and deep. They will not as a rule meander, but there will be branches or tributary valleys. When such a region is depressed the new coastline will be deeply indented. The flooded entrances of the valleys will become long and narrow gulfs, often branching inwards. The hilltops near the old sea margin may be completely surrounded by water and form groups of islands fringing the shore of the mainland. The coast will everywhere be steep and rocky and there will be little or no beach. In Norway and the west of Scotland this type of coast is beautifully shown. The coast of Cornwall affords a simpler example, but the hinterland is rather low.

The characteristic features of such a coast may long remain unaltered by the sea. Owing to the hardness of the rocks even the most exposed points offer great resistance to the waves and the amount of fragmental material produced is comparatively small. Partly for this reason and partly on account of the steepness of the seaward slope there is either no beach or the beach is very narrow. Little loose material is available to form spits of sand or shingle, excepting where moraines, gravel fans, or deltas occur. Consequently, the general character of the coast changes much more slowly than where the land is low-lying and is composed of softer beds. Nevertheless, even the hardest rocks give way in time; the promontories are gradually worn back, the re-entrants are filled with deposits brought down by the rivers, and at last the irregularities of the coastline may disappear.

In spite of the small amount of beach material, longshore drift may help to smooth the outline of the coast, distributing river deposits along the shore, or bringing material from some other region where the rocks are soft.

Coastline of subsided mountain range. If the subsiding coast is formed by a range of mountains similar to the Alps, the sea will enter the longitudinal valleys between the individual chains which constitute the range. The higher hills of the outer chains will be represented by lines of islands off the mainland and the valleys will form narrow gulfs almost parallel with the general direction of the shoreline. The Dalmatian coast is one of the best examples of this type.

The theoretical evolution of a coastline formed by depression may possibly be represented in these diagrams of W. M. Davis (figs. 143, 144).

Shores formed by elevation. A continental area is usually surrounded by a continental shelf. The shelf is smooth and slopes gently outwards, and generally it is covered by mud, sand, and other soft materials. If the land is raised bodily, a part of this shelf is exposed to view and forms a fringe of low-lying and often marshy ground around

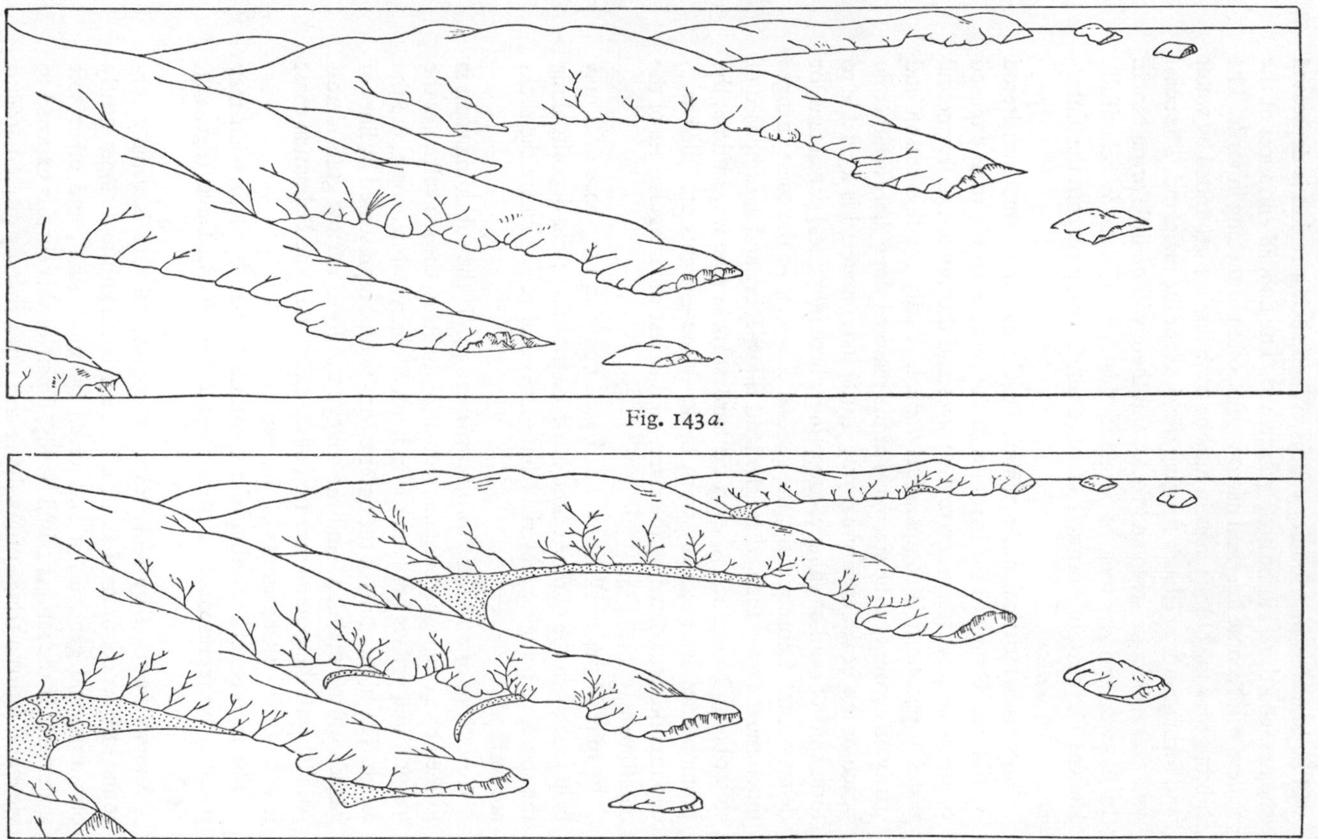

Fig. 143*a*.

Fig. 143*b*. Early stages in the evolution of a submerged coastline.

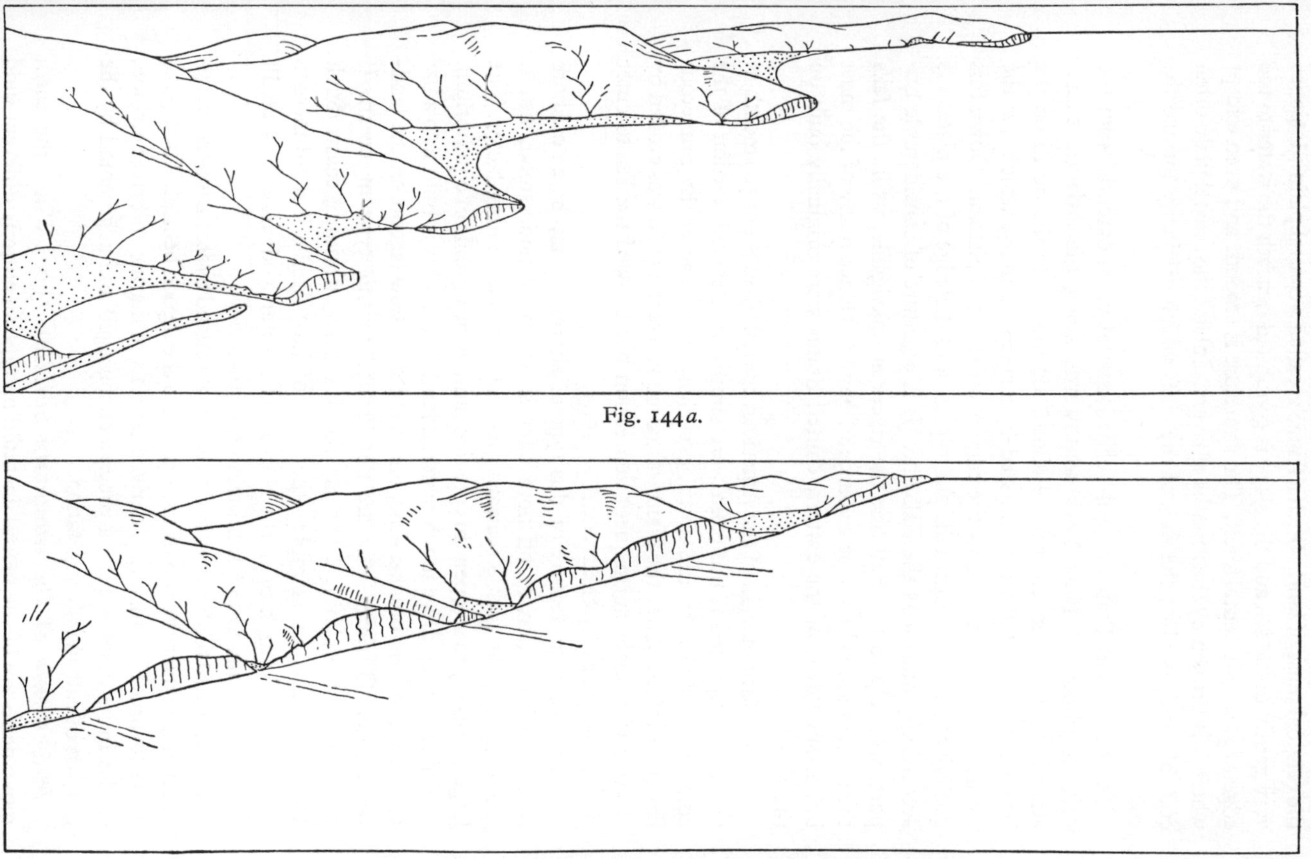

Fig. 144a.

Fig. 144b. Later stages in the evolution of a submerged coastline.

the original mass of land. Such a fringe is called a coastal plain. It slopes very gently to the sea and the slope is continued beneath the water to the edge of the continental shelf. The shoreline is smooth and even except where it is broken by the mouths of rivers. Inland the coastal plain often ends abruptly against the foot of the cliffs which originally formed the coast.

In the United States a well-defined coastal plain extends from the neighbourhood of New York southwards along the Atlantic shore, attaining a width in Georgia of about 100 miles. In the north on the landward side the plain is bounded by a steep declivity, which was the former coastline and is now the edge of an elevated plateau. Down this declivity the rivers form falls and rapids, and the edge of the plateau is accordingly known as the Fall-line. It is a feature of considerable importance. Up to the Fall-line the rivers are navigable, while the falls themselves are valuable as a source of power. Hence many of the most important towns of the eastern United States were originally built on the Fall-line.

The seaward margin of the American coastal plain is not so smooth as might be expected if the plain were simply an elevated portion of the continental shelf. In the north, especially, it is marked by numerous irregular inlets. After the plain was raised above the sea it was eroded by rivers and a slight subsequent depression has allowed the sea to enter the valleys worn by the rivers.

A characteristic feature of this type of shoreline may be an offshore bar. The formation of offshore bars is not fully understood, but it is agreed that the gentle seaward gradient is a determining factor. The large waves try to steepen this gradient and form a profile of equilibrium. In doing so they drive much material landwards. This is built into a bar shoreward of the breaker-line, enclosing a shallow lagoon on the landward side. Offshore bars are not limited to this type of coast. If conditions are suitable a bar can be built on a subsiding coast. Scolt Head Island is an example—the coast of East Anglia is a submerged coast, but off much of north Norfolk the water is shallow as a result of the accumulation of sand and other materials.

Once formed the bar may be driven slowly inland by storm waves sweeping material over the top of the bank into the lagoon behind. The lagoon also silts up. Fine material, derived both from marine and river erosion, settles in its quiet waters, a process encouraged and augmented by the growth of salt-marsh vegetation.

Movements of the mountain-building type. When the earth movements are of the mountain-building type an entirely different kind of coast may be produced. Such movements have often taken place near the margin of a continental mass and they may result in the elevation of a mountain range beneath the sea. The higher parts of the range will form chains of islands outside the coast of the mainland. The West Indies and the festoons of islands off the eastern coast of Asia have been formed in this way. It must not be supposed, however, that in such cases the original coast of the mainland remains unaltered, for the elevation of a mountain chain is often accompanied by the sinking of large blocks of the earth's crust, especially on the inner side of the mountain arc. The Sea of Japan and the other bordering seas of the east of Asia appear to owe their origin in part to this cause.

Coasts formed by faults. When the earth's crust collapses like a breaking arch, blocks of the crust sink downwards and other blocks perhaps are raised. If the falling blocks subside beneath the sea and the upstanding blocks remain land, the coast will coincide with the fracture or fault. In plan such faults are usually straight or gently curved, in section they are nearly vertical. The coast will, therefore, be nearly straight and very steep, the land rising abruptly from the sea.

The western coast of India from Bombay southwards is a good example. There is reason to believe that the land mass of India once extended much farther towards the west, but in geologically recent times the western extension sank beneath the sea. The coast has since been modified by denudation, but it is still remarkably straight and abrupt.

CHAPTER V

DELTAS AND ESTUARIES

When a river enters the sea its current slackens and finally ceases and its load is deposited upon the floor of the sea. The coarser and heavier material is laid down first and the finer and lighter material is carried farther out; but eventually the whole must fall. Off the mouth of the Amazon the sea is sometimes discoloured by mud to a distance of 100 or 200 miles, but even this is only a small fraction of the total width of the ocean; and in general the river deposits are confined to a comparatively narrow belt near the coast.

If there are tides or currents in the sea where the river enters, some of the material brought down by the river may be carried farther out or may be drifted along the coast and laid down many miles away. The tides and currents may be sufficiently strong to prevent any considerable deposition, and the mouth of the river will then be kept open and will form an estuary.

If on the other hand the sea itself is still, the river will deposit its burden near its mouth and will form a delta.

Accordingly deltas are sometimes regarded as characteristic of nearly tideless seas, and estuaries of seas in which the tides are great.[1]

Estuaries. According to the derivation of the word an estuary is the tidal portion of a river, but the term is usually confined to rivers that have a single mouth, and it is applied more particularly when the mouth is V-shaped and widest near the sea. The mouths of the Thames and the Severn for example are typical estuaries; the Hugli, although it is tidal, would hardly be called an estuary, because it is only one of the branches of the Ganges.

Since a river naturally tends to deposit its burden at its mouth, an estuary cannot be permanent unless the deposit is removed by some other agent, and, the material being fine, the removal is usually the work of the tide. The river is dammed by the rising tide at its mouth, and its current may even be reversed for some distance upwards; but when the tide is falling the pent-up water escapes and the current is increased beyond its normal strength. The tide in fact flushes the river's mouth and helps to keep it free from sediment. The permanently discoloured waters in the upper Bristol Channel well illustrate this action (see p. 180).

The funnel-like shape of a typical estuary usually occurs in regions where there is other evidence of subsidence. The sea has flooded the river valleys and the shape of the estuaries has been preserved, rather than actually made, by the action of the tides.

DELTAS

Deltas are formed when the deposits of a river are not removed by longshore drift, or by tidal or other currents, and they are especially characteristic therefore of tideless seas. Even where the tides are great, however, a river may build a delta if it brings down more material than can be carried away; but such a delta will usually be irregular in shape, as for example that of the Rhine.

Deposition of coarse material. The normal form of a delta depends

[1] Foulness and adjacent islands are deltaic in nature, but nevertheless part of the Thames estuary. The Rhine delta is also rather exceptional in that it is in a sea where the tidal range is considerable.

to a large extent upon the nature of the river's burden. The coarser material that is rolled along the bed is dropped immediately at the river's mouth, where the current slackens, and it forms a bank upon the floor of the sea. The deposit will be greatest where the supply of material is greatest; and this will be where the current is strongest, which is usually near the middle of the river. The sand and pebbles are swept along the bank and are tipped over its end and sides, and the bank grows outwards like a railway embankment in course of construction. But as the bank increases in height and length it obstructs the current more and more, until it becomes easier for the stream to divide and flow to each side. Each branch will then begin to form a new bank of its own. In time these branches will again divide and subdivide and so the deposit grows outwards in the form of a fan. The surface of the fan slopes gently seaward and is marked by irregular branching channels. The outer edge has a steeper slope, corresponding with the angle at which the material that is tipped over it comes to rest. The process of formation may often be watched upon the sea shore when a little stream runs down the sand into a quiet pool.

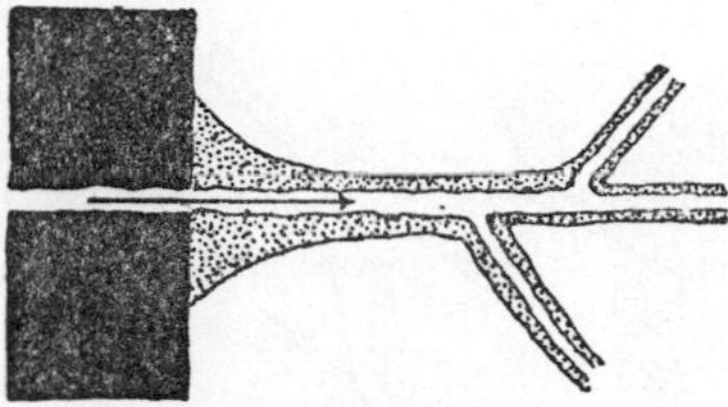

Fig. 145. Diagram of mud-delta.

Obviously the river can never raise any part of the delta above its own flood level, but the deposits formed during floods may at normal times stand above the water level, and the branches of the river may then be confined to definite channels. Vegetation may grow upon the higher parts and in course of time the gradual accumulation of vegetable matter may even raise the surface above the level of the floods.

Deposition of suspended material. Most large and long-established rivers, however, drop the coarser part of their burden far inland, and it is only the finer silt that reaches the sea. Most of this is carried in suspension and the mode of deposition is not quite the same as in the case of the material that is rolled along the bed.

One of the reasons for the difference is the peculiar action of salt water upon suspended mud. If pure and finely levigated clay is shaken up with fresh water and is then allowed to stand, the water will remain muddy for many hours. But if a few drops of brine are added, the clay settles rapidly and the water clears. With calcareous or siliceous muds the effect of the brine is much less marked or is even absent altogether. In most rivers, however, a large proportion of the silt consists of clay; and accordingly the mixture of the fresh water of the river with the salt water of the sea assists deposition.

When a river enters the sea its current is continued outwards for some distance and the mud is carried with it. In the middle of the current the speed is at its greatest and the water at its freshest, and deposition is comparatively slow; towards the edges, where the velocity is retarded and the fresh water mixes with the sea, the silt falls much more quickly. This action is further aided by the tendency of suspended sediment to

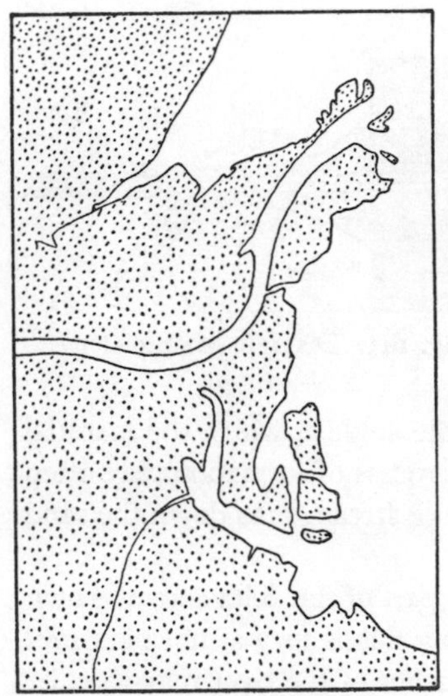

Fig. 146. Delta of the Dee at the south-western end of Bala Lake.

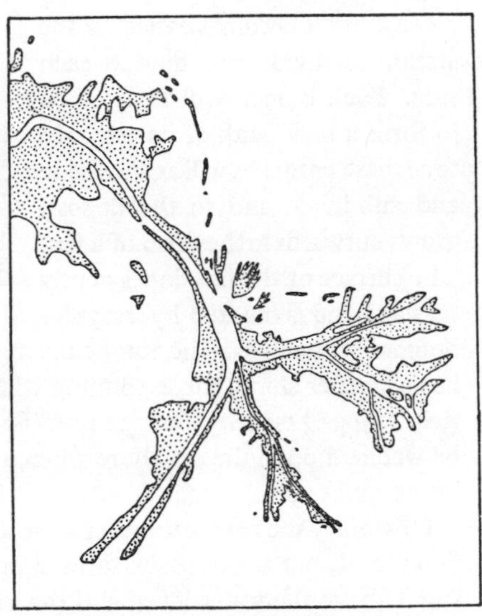

Fig. 147. The terminal portion of the Mississippi delta.

disperse outwards from zones of high concentration to zones of clearer water. Deposition is therefore most rapid at the margins of the current and on each side a muddy bank is built beneath the sea (fig. 145). In course of time these banks are raised to the flood level, and when the river is at its normal height they stand above the water as natural embankments running out to sea. The river no longer mixes with the sea until it escapes beyond the embankments. Its current therefore reaches outwards still farther than before, and it proceeds to extend its embankments seawards.

The river now runs in a channel upon a muddy tongue projecting out to sea. In floods it may break through its bank at some weak spot and a branch of the current will escape through the breach. This branch will build embankments of its own and thus the original tongue-like delta becomes forked. On a small scale the commencement of the forking may be seen in the delta of the Dee where it enters the southern end of Bala Lake (fig. 146 and see pl. 10*b*).

By the repetition of the process a branching delta like that of the Mississippi may be developed. For many miles the Mississippi flows out into the Gulf of Mexico upon a tongue of alluvial deposit. Towards the extremity of the delta it divides and subdivides and each branch runs between narrow branches of mud (fig. 147).

The major branches of the river will usually diverge from one another, but it may happen that two subsidiary branches meet. Their embankments will then unite, enclosing a lagoon, which may be gradually filled up by deposits formed during floods, perhaps assisted by growing vegetation.

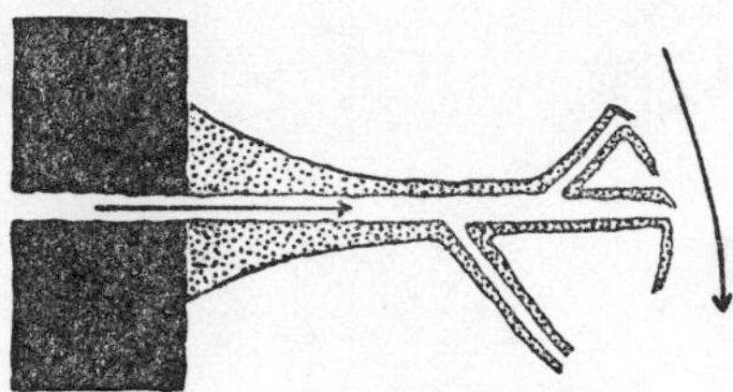

Fig. 148. Effect of currents upon the form of a mud-delta.

It is only at the surface that a muddy delta assumes the branching form described. Beneath the sea its shape is different. The embankments are not vertical walls but, being made of mud, their outer slopes are very gentle. Consequently, at a very small depth they become confluent with one another and the branches are no longer separate. The deposit spreads far beyond the embankments and upon the sea floor it forms a tongue which perhaps may be irregularly lobed. The slopes are everywhere extremely gentle and the embankments are only the highest and visible portions of the delta.

A branching delta can only be constructed where the river is free from external interference. If there is active longshore drift the shape is liable to be greatly modified, for the mud will no longer be distributed by the river alone. If longshore drift crosses the mouths of the river, as in fig. 148, the mud will be deflected to one side. Banks or spits of mud will be formed across the interspaces between the branches and in time may convert them into lagoons. This has happened, for instance, in the Nile (fig. 149). Both the Rosetta and the Damietta branches have built out tongues of land; but in this part of the Mediterranean a current flows from west to east and the mud brought down by the river is swept towards the east. In consequence of this a spit of land has been built eastwards from the Rosetta branch, enclosing Borollos Lake; and another spit from the Damietta mouth shuts off Lake Menzala. Other smaller lagoons have also been formed in a similar way. It is in fact to this current that the delta of the Nile owes its present smooth and regular outline.

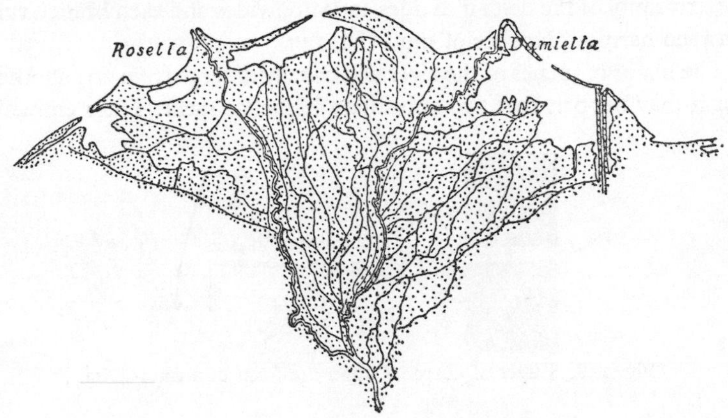

Fig. 149. Delta of the Nile.

The foregoing discussion of the nature of deltas has only by implication touched on their internal structure. Three sets of beds may theoretically be distinguished—bottom-set, fore-set, and top-set. The bottom-set beds are formed of fine material which is carried some way out to sea and settles slowly as a carpet on the sea-bed. The fore-set beds form the bulk of the delta and grow seawards in much the same way as does a tip-heap. They extend over the bottom-set beds and, in turn, as their upper surface grows seawards, are overlain by the thin top-set beds. Since the river distributaries work over all the circumference of the delta, the various sets of beds grow forwards at irregular and varying rates, and are modified in the ways described earlier.

R. J. Russell shows that these beds are not found in the Mississippi delta (*Geological Bulletin No.* 8, 1936, *Dept. of Conservation, Louisiana Geological Survey*). He makes the interesting point that evidence of coastal down-warping is shown in many deltas by the depressions on either side: the lakes east and west of the Nile, the Zuyder Zee and the Zealand estuaries on the Rhine, the Etang de Berre and the lagoons near Montpellier on the Rhone are examples. There are several other lines of evidence indicating actual subsidence of the Mississippi delta.

CHAPTER VI

EARTH SCULPTURE

General nature of the processes of earth sculpture. The main features of the land-masses are determined primarily by the movements of elevation and depression already described. But as soon as a part of the earth's crust is raised above the ocean it is exposed to various agencies which tend to modify its form. Its margins are worn by the sea, its surface by rivers and other agents; the material removed from one place is laid down in another; and thus the form of the land is slowly changed by the two processes of wearing away or denudation and laying down or deposition. The modifications produced on the surface are often spoken of collectively as land sculpture or earth sculpture.

Under the influence of atmospheric changes many kinds of rock seem to decay and even the hardest are slowly broken up. The process is known as weathering, because it is, in fact, due to the weather. The general result is to produce a layer of loose material resting upon the solid and unaltered rock. It is in this way that much of the soil has been formed.

The loose material produced by weathering is gradually carried downwards, a process known as transport. It may be washed down a slope by rain, it may be rolled by a river along its bed, or it may even slide downwards under the action of gravity alone. But however it travels it wears the surface over which it moves, and this wearing action of moving material is called corrasion.

From time to time the transported material finds a temporary resting-place and is laid down, sometimes in the sea, sometimes on the land. If it is deposited in the sea it may alter the shape of the coastline, if on the land it will change the form of the surface.

There is still another process by which the land is worn away. Water, and especially water which contains carbon dioxide, has a very considerable solvent action upon the earth's crust. Pure rock-salt is readily and completely soluble; pure limestone is dissolved more slowly but with equal completeness. In the case of most rocks, however, it is only some of the constituents that are dissolved, while the rest remain behind, and this is one of the principal causes of weathering.

Earth sculpture therefore is the effect of denudation and deposition, and the processes of denudation may be grouped under the heads of weathering, transport with its accompanying corrasion, and solution.

Weathering. Dry air has very little chemical effect upon the materials of the earth's crust, but few rocks can stand indefinite exposure if the air be moist. Either they gradually decay, which means that some of their constituents are decomposed, or they break up without any chemical change. The decay will go on even when the water is entirely in the form of vapour, but it proceeds more rapidly and vigorously when the vapour condenses as rain or dew. The condensed vapour will not be pure water, but will always contain gases dissolved from the atmosphere, and of these oxygen and carbon dioxide are the most important aids in weathering.

Some of the chemical changes are due to the oxygen of the air, which in the presence of moisture acts powerfully upon many minerals, especially those containing iron. Basalt, for example, when exposed to the air, becomes covered with a brown crust, consisting largely of oxide of iron.

But water containing carbon dioxide appears to be the chief agent of disintegration. It dissolves carbonate of lime with comparative ease, and in course of time a limestone may be entirely removed except the clay and other insoluble matter which it usually contains. In many sandstones, the grains of sand are cemented together with carbonate of lime. This may be dissolved and the rock will then fall to pieces.

Water containing carbon dioxide acts also on other minerals. It decomposes felspar, carrying away some of its constituents in solution and leaving the rest in the form of clay. A granite may accordingly become a mass of clay with quartz and mica scattered through it. Instead of being a firm and solid rock it will then be loose and friable, and will easily be washed away.

The longer the rain water is kept in contact with the rock the more rapid will be the disintegration. If the rock is free from pores and cracks, and its surface smooth, the rain will run off and will have little chance of causing any chemical change, e.g. many glacially smoothed surfaces of gabbro in the Cuillin Hills, Skye, have remained unaltered since glacial times. But if the surface is rough and there are crevices into which the water can penetrate, it will have a longer time to produce its effects. A polished slab of granite standing vertically will resist the weather longer than a rough block lying horizontally.

The surface soil may both aid and hinder the process of decay. It acts as a sponge and keeps the rock beneath it moist after the rain has ceased. Lichens and mosses produce a similar effect and beneath a patch of moss the stone is sometimes more decayed than on the exposed surfaces. On the other hand both soil and moss impede the removal of the decayed material and so prevent the exposure of a fresh surface to the action of the weather.

Weathering due to moist air or to clinging drops of water tends to round the corners and edges of rocks and to produce convex surfaces. If we imagine a large cube of rock as made up of a number of little cubes fitted closely together, it is evident that a little cube in the middle of the side of the large cube will expose only one of its faces to the atmosphere, at an edge of the main cube it will expose two faces and at one of the corners it will expose three faces. Therefore, the weathering is most rapid at the corners of the large cube, less rapid at the edges, and least rapid on the faces; and the cube becomes rounded like a cube of sugar dropped into a glass of water.

Of all the various kinds of rock the least liable to chemical change are those consisting chiefly or wholly of silica. In its crystalline form of quartz, silica is practically unaffected by water even when the water contains carbon dioxide or the acids produced by decaying vegetation. In its non-crystalline form it is soluble, but only to a very slight extent.

But even the most resistant rocks are gradually disintegrated. Changes of temperature, causing alternate expansion and contraction of the rock itself, will break up the surface. In desert regions this is one of the most important processes of denudation; but in temperate climates a much more powerful influence is frost. No rock is absolutely impervious to water, and when the water in the pores or crevices is frozen, it expands and exerts great pressure upon the walls of the space in which it is confined. By alternate thawing and freezing the cracks are gradually enlarged and the rock is broken up. Frost action is the most powerful disintegrating agent in nature. The screes or heaps of broken rock at the foot of crags in our hilly districts are due chiefly to this cause (pl. 11 *a*, *b*).

Effects of running water. Weathering is largely the effect of standing water, that is to say, of water which rests in hollows or cracks or which has soaked into the soil or rock. It breaks up the surface but does not remove the loose material, and if no other causes came into play, the layer of broken or decayed rock would increase in depth till the covering was sufficiently thick to protect the underlying rock from further action. Gravity alone will cause some of this material to fall to a lower level, but without the aid of water its effects are largely neutralised by friction.

When rain falls it assists the action of gravity in two ways. It acts as a lubricant, enabling the broken fragments to slide more easily upon one another. This is clearly illustrated by the tips or waste-heaps of a slate-quarry. When the useless material from the quarry is thrown down the sides of the heaps in fine weather it quickly comes to rest, and as long as the weather remains dry there is little further disturbance. But when rain falls the heaps become wet, pieces of rock which were at rest begin to slide downward and the movement usually continues until the heaps become dry again. In this way rain helps the downward movement even of the large masses of rock.

On smaller fragments the effects of rain are greater, for its own velocity as it runs down a slope enables it to carry mud and to roll down grains of sand or even little pebbles. As none of the ordinary agents of transport in a climate such as ours, excepting the wind, carries particles upwards, the effect of each shower is added to that of the previous one and consequently the soil gradually travels downhill.

Grass and trees, by preventing the free flow of the water and by binding the loose particles together, serve as a protection to the soil; and on a gentle grass-covered or wooded slope, the movement will be slow and may be imperceptible. The direct influence of rain is greatest in a hilly district where the slopes are steep and where there is little vegetation. In such circumstances the effect of a single storm of rain may be conspicuous.

When rain falls upon the ground, some of it is evaporated, some sinks into the earth and some runs over the surface. The portion which sinks in is not lost, but sooner or later, in most cases at least, it reappears, usually in a spring, and helps to form a stream. The part which runs over the surface may flow for a time as a sheet of water, but it will presently form little funnels and these will join into larger streams and eventually the water will find its way into a river. There is therefore no hard and fast line between the work of rain and the work of rivers. The work done before the water has been concentrated into definite channels, and even the work done in a channel which is only temporarily occupied during a rainstorm, may be called the work of rain. The work done by a more or less permanent flow of water down a definite channel may be called the work of a stream or river.

Valley slopes. The effects of rainwash and soil-creep on the evolution of slopes above the level of direct stream-action is not fully understood. In humid regions, valley-side slopes are commonly convex upwards at the top, uniform in the middle portions, and concave upwards where they join the valley floor. The upper convex slope may result from the rounding of the initial angle where the steep slope formed by the headward recession of tributary streams meets a gently sloping plateau surface. It may be the outcome of the increasing power of rainfall run-off, since this increases, on relatively impermeable ground, with distance from the watershed. During heavy rains surface run-off, whether unconcentrated as a sheet, or more or less concentrated into runnels, at a certain distance from the watershed acquires sufficient volume and velocity to overcome the resistance of the soil and vegetation, thus starting erosion. The severest downpours, which rarely occur, cause erosion to begin near the watershed and to continue downslope to stream-level. Lesser downpours cannot start erosion until the accumulating run-off reaches farther from the watershed. Thus ground farther from the watershed is lowered by erosion more than that nearer the watershed. In this way a convex profile may form. The concave profile below, if it is not inherited from past glacial action, may result from processes akin to those responsible for the curve of water erosion (see p. 299).

CHAPTER VII

UNDERGROUND WATER

The origin of underground water. Rain falling on dry ground has first to moisten the soil before any water can sink or percolate downwards even through a highly permeable bedrock. If the rock is impermeable then once the overlying soil has absorbed its share of rainwater the excess runs off to join a stream. The humus layer forming the top few inches of grassland soils can hold 60 or 70 per cent of moisture, and the subsoil can hold 40 per cent, an amount very similar to the capacity of chalk and other light permeable rocks. This moisture is held in the pore spaces and can only be released by evaporation even though the water-table is far below. The water-table is the level of saturation below which pores, joints, and fissures are full of water. This is the level to which water will rise in a well. It fluctuates with the season, most under the hill-tops and least near the springs. Above the water-table water occurs only in the pore spaces.

In the late winter and spring the soil is normally moistened to capacity, but in summer the soil moisture evaporates, and is absorbed by the growing plants, so that by the autumn the top layers of the soil might be dry to a depth of two or three feet. In summer light or moderate rainfall is wholly evaporated from the surface layer of the soil, or absorbed by plants. Only heavy and continuous summer rainfall is sufficient to allow for evaporation, to re-moisten the soil, and then to provide a surplus that sinks to the water-table. The first task of the autumn rainfall is to remoisten the top few feet of soil. Once this is done almost all of the subsequent winter rainfall percolates to the water-table, or, if the strata are impermeable, runs off to streams.

Thus for the supply of springs and streams summer rainfall is of little consequence, but winter rainfall is all important. Autumn rainfall may seem to have little or no effect in raising the level of the water in wells or of increasing the flow of springs and streams, but nevertheless it plays an essential part. If it is lacking the early winter rainfall is absorbed in the upper layers of the soil so that the rise in the water-table, and the increase in the flow of springs, are delayed until late in the winter. During a very dry spell, as in 1933–4 and again in 1942–3, the winter rainfall failed to saturate the soil and the water-table, springs, and streams remained unreplenished, the small outflow depending solely on underground storage.

The annual evaporation-loss from the land surface in south-eastern England varies between 14 and 16 inches, and it is close to this value in other parts of the country. This is surprisingly near to the evaporation from an open reservoir. The variation in the height of the water-table and in the flow of streams is controlled by the seasonal variation of evaporation and not by that of rainfall. It can, therefore, be readily understood why the western and northern parts of the country, with rainfall varying from 40 to 100 inches a year, according to height above sea-level and exposure to the rain-bearing winds, are well suited for water supply. In the south-east, where the rainfall may only exceed the evaporation-loss by as little as 8 inches on the average, and much less in a dry year, conditions are very different.

In warmer and drier parts of the world the potential evaporation-loss from land surfaces is far greater, often exceeding 60 inches if the ground is continually moist, but unless there is irrigation, the moisture generally gives out long before this amount has been lost to the air.

Chalk is a well-jointed rock which allows water to percolate through it readily. Even a rock like granite, which in itself is practically impervious, often has open joints reaching down to a considerable depth, along which the water can penetrate. Clay, although it is porous and can absorb water, is almost impervious and does not let water pass through it. A bed of clay generally forms a very effective barrier to the movement of the water underground.

There is reason to believe that water is often produced by chemical changes in the heated interior of the earth, and in volcanic districts and elsewhere this water may rise to the surface. But in a country such as ours underground water is almost entirely rain which has percolated from above.

This underground water is the source from which springs and wells draw their supplies, and a simple case will serve as an illustration.

Level of saturation. Fig. 150 represents a hill formed of a horizontal bed of clay capped by a layer of porous sandstone. When rain falls, it percolates through the sandstone, but cannot penetrate the clay. If the rain is long continued, all the pores of the sandstone may be filled with water and the bed of sandstone will be saturated. When the rain ceases the sandstone holds the water like a sponge, but like a sponge it allows it to trickle out slowly at its base and sides. The water therefore will issue from the hillside at the junction of the clay and sandstone, forming a spring or a series of springs. But as the water at the base of the sandstone oozes out, the water at the top sinks slowly downwards, and the

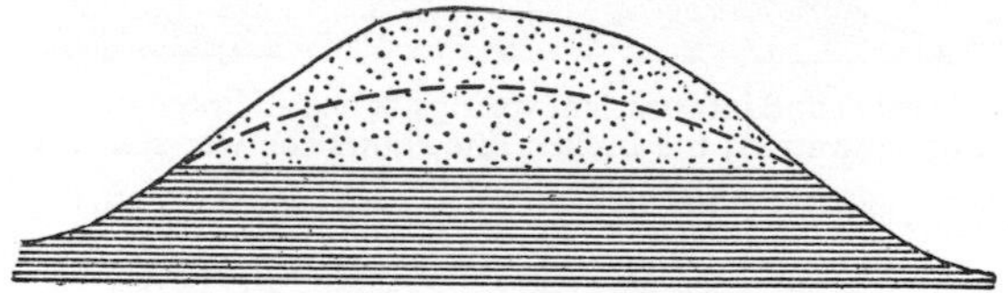

Fig. 150. Level of saturation.

sandstone dries from the top downwards. The sandstone near the outlet is drained most easily, and accordingly the surface of the water in the sandstone takes the form shown by the broken line in the figure. Below this line the sandstone is still saturated, immediately above the line it is damp, and higher up the cracks and cavities are dry, but the finer pore spaces still hold water.

If the weather remains dry the level of saturation will still continue to fall, until there is not sufficient pressure to force the water outwards, and the springs will then dry up. But if the layer of sandstone is sufficiently extensive the supply of water will last until the next rainfall percolates through from above and raises the level of saturation again.

In this way the level of saturation is continually varying according to the weather. In a dry season it falls, in a wet season it rises. But far the most important change is the steady fall in late summer and autumn followed by the quicker rise in winter and early spring. Usually there is a limit below which it never sinks and this is called the permanent level of saturation. There will also be a limit above which it never rises. This may be the surface of the ground itself, but more usually it lies some distance beneath. In the particular case illustrated in fig. 150 the water can escape so freely at the sides of the hill that, even in the wettest seasons, it is not likely that the whole of the sandstone will be saturated.

The fluctuations in the level of saturation cause corresponding fluctuations in the supply of water in wells and springs.

If a well is sunk to the wet-season level but not to the permanent level of saturation, it will have water in it in a wet season but not in a dry one. If it reaches the permanent level there will always be water in the well.

In fig. 151, in which the cap of sandstone slants to the left, the springs on the left slope of the hill will be permanent because they lie below the level of permanent saturation; the springs on the right slope will flow

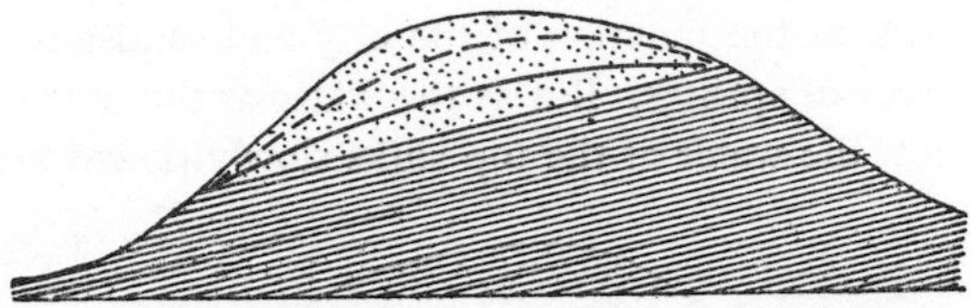

Fig. 151. Permanent and intermittent springs. The full line shows the permanent level of saturation; the broken line shows the wet-season level.

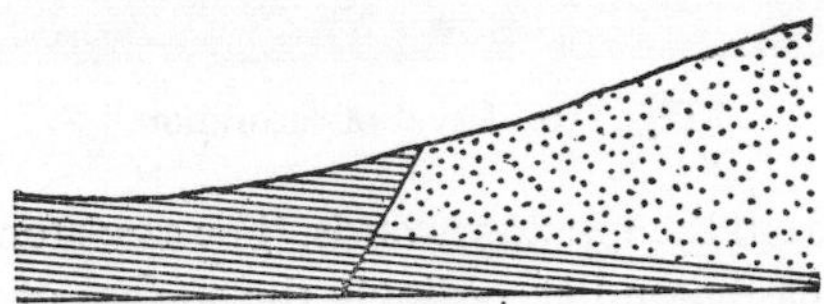

Fig. 152. Springs due to a fault.

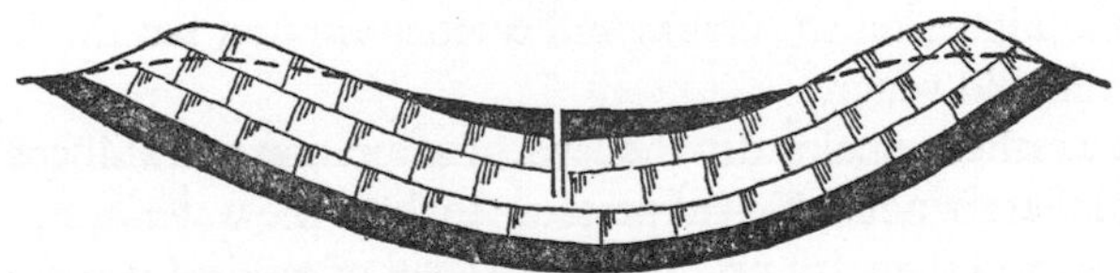

Fig. 153. Artesian well.

only during a wet season and are called intermittent springs. They lie above the level of permanent saturation but below the wet-season level.

Springs are usually at the junction of a pervious bed with an impervious one. It may be that the pervious bed lies on the impervious one as in the examples already given; but the two beds may be brought into contact by a fault as in fig. 152. In such a case as this there will be a spring or a line of springs at the fault, because this is the lowest point at which the water in the pervious bed can escape.

Artesian wells. If a porous bed like chalk, lying between two beds of clay, is bent into the form of a basin as in the London district (fig. 153) the rain falling on the outcrop of the chalk will sink downwards. There is no escape for it below, and the chalk will therefore be saturated with water to the rim of the basin. The level of saturation is shown by the broken lines. There will be springs around the edge, but only the water above the edge can escape. If a well is sunk through the upper layer of clay into the chalk, the water in the chalk will flow into the well. If the chalk offered no resistance to its movement it would tend to rise to the level of the rim of the basin; but the chalk is an obstruction and it does not therefore rise so high. If, however, the level of saturation at the outcrop of the chalk is sufficiently far above the well, the water in the well will rise above the ground and flow out over the surface or even form a fountain. Such a well as this is called an artesian well.

Conditions favourable to the formation of artesian wells may be produced by faulting. If, as a result of a fault, porous beds are brought against impervious beds, the water contained in the former may rise up the fault plane, and issue as springs. On a smaller scale pockets of sands and gravels in glacial deposits may act as local reservoirs of water, and if conditions are favourable the water will rise up in bores put down to the water-bearing deposits.

Underground water in limestone districts. The water which percolates through the rocks dissolves some of their constituents. In most cases the amount dissolved is small, the water is soon saturated, or holds as much as it can, and no further solution takes place. But ordinary rainwater, containing carbon dioxide absorbed from the air, can dissolve an appreciable quantity of carbonate of lime. In passing through a bed of limestone or chalk, therefore, the percolating water removes a small amount of material in solution, and the effects, acting over a long period, are often of great importance.

The water naturally takes the easiest route and flows through cracks, where they are present, rather than through the smaller pores and openings. The cracks, which are usually along joint-planes, are gradually enlarged by solution and become still easier channels than before (pl. 13*b*). Gradually the water concentrates in these channels, and in a limestone the underground water often forms streams of considerable size (fig. 154).

A crack at the surface may in time be enlarged so much that it forms a wide opening sinking deeply into the ground. Such openings are known as swallow-holes and are common in limestone districts. Occasionally a surface stream of considerable size falls into a swallow-hole and disappears. Gaping Ghyll on the side of Ingleborough is a well-known example.

The channels beneath the surface are often widened to so great an extent that they form a series of caverns running for miles into the ground. In Derbyshire and other limestone districts such caves are common.

The roof and floor of the cave are frequently covered with stalactites and stalagmites. A stalactite is a column of carbonate of lime hanging downwards from the roof. The water which trickles through the cracks in the ceiling contains carbonate of lime in solution. While a drop is hanging, it partly evaporates and leaves a little carbonate of lime behind. The next drop leaves a little more and so a small lump is formed and gradually grows downwards, the water tending to trickle down its side and hang in drops at the lower end.

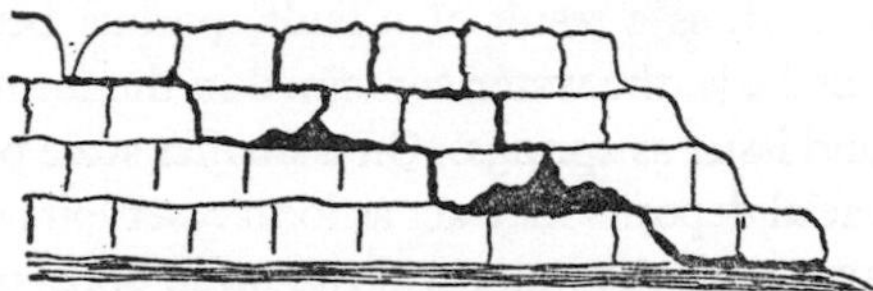

Fig. 154. Underground streams and caverns in limestone.

Stalagmites are similar lumps formed on the floor of the cave by the water that falls from above. Naturally they grow upwards instead of downwards and they are usually shorter and thicker than the stalactites. Often a stalagmite is produced by the water that drips from a stalactite, and sometimes the stalagmite and stalactite meet, forming a complete pillar from the floor to the roof of the cave.

The water that trickles down the side of the cave or over the bottom deposits its carbonate of lime in layers encrusting the walls and floor. This deposit is also often known as stalagmite.

Caverns in limestone are usually developed along the joints, and often therefore they are long compared with their width. If the roof falls in, the cavern is then converted into an open gorge, or perhaps simply an irregular cavity in the ground.

By no means are all gorges in limestone country produced in this way or even by rivers originating in the limestone area. In some cases they have been cut by rivers superimposed (see p. 323) from a covering of impermeable beds that once overlay the limestone. Some of the magnificent gorges in the Causses of central France are, at least in part, of this nature. In the karst areas of the Adriatic earth movements in addition to the ordinary processes of erosion and solutions have played an important role in the production of the present topography. Large low-lying areas, poljes (=plains), are often situated in faulted basins. In all limestone districts careful consideration must be given to the possibility of there having been former covers of other rocks, or of glacial deposits. The vagaries of the hydrological systems in relation to the structure of the limestones may often be best explained in this way.

Although chalk is carbonate of lime, caverns and underground channels are not formed in chalk to so great an extent as, for example, in the limestones of the Pennines. The reason appears to be that the jointing in chalk is much closer and so the water follows numerous small channels, instead of being confined to a few major joint-planes. For rather similar reasons gorges are rare in chalk districts, but steep valley sides are common. The gaps through the Chilterns, which are probably partly due to superimposition, illustrate this very well.

Special characters of limestone districts. Since a large proportion of the rainfall sinks immediately into the rocks and runs in channels underground, limestone districts usually have a special character of their own.

The higher land is always dry. Few streams flow upon its surface and even these may suddenly sink into the ground and disappear. Lower down the slopes the stream may reappear as suddenly from an opening in the rocks.

The valleys are often narrow, and their sides are usually steep, frequently forming precipitous cliffs; for limestone is a firm and compact rock, and, though it is readily dissolved, it resists mechanical erosion by the weather. Moreover, since the rain sinks so quickly into the rock, it has but little time to wear away the surface. Most limestones, too, have well-marked joints and the faces of the cliffs are therefore abrupt and cleanly cut (pl. 13*a*).

The carbonate of lime is carried away in solution and only the insoluble impurities are left to form a covering to the rock. Therefore the soil is usually thin, and limestone districts are often very bare, excepting in the valleys, where the soil may collect to a greater thickness.

These are the general features of the karst type of country, so named from the Karst district of Yugoslavia where they are developed to an exaggerated extent. They may also be seen in the Pennines and other parts of England, but they are not there so strongly marked.

Chalk districts show some of these characters, but not all. Chalk is made of carbonate of lime, but it differs from an ordinary limestone in several respects. It is softer and more porous, and generally it is not so strongly jointed. Chalk hills are as dry as limestone hills, and the soil upon them is often as thin; but because the rock is soft and easily worn away, the valleys are wide and open and show no crags upon their sides. Except on the coast, where the sea eats continually into its base, chalk seldom forms precipitous cliffs.

One of the most characteristic features of chalk scenery is the dry valley. On the relatively gentle dip slopes they start in the high ground as normal river valleys, and as they follow the slope the various tributaries unite and the valleys sink deeper. In plan they closely resemble a normal river system. In cross-section they maintain the characteristically rounded chalk outlines, especially where the steep uniform slopes curve over to merge with the plateau surface. On the steeper scarp slopes they are deeply incised and frequently begin abruptly.[1] Springs often occur where they merge into the plains.

The former type probably originated in peri-glacial conditions.[2] The subsoil froze in winter and became impermeable so that the melting snows and the spring and early summer precipitation ran off on the surface. Even now after a severe winter (e.g. 1941), surface run-off occurs in the dry valleys of the chalk. Some of the deeper-cut and shorter scarp valleys may be connected with the action of springs sapping headwards into the scarp when the water-table was higher than to-day.

CHAPTER VIII

RIVERS

It is evident to the most casual observation that a river does three kinds of work. It wears away its banks and bed; this is erosion. It carries the material brought into it by rain or by its own erosive action; this is transport. It drops this material, sometimes on its own bed, sometimes in a lake, sometimes in the sea, but always at a lower level than the point at which the material was received; this is deposition.

So far as the form of the land is concerned the erosive action is on the whole the most important, but the erosion depends to a large extent upon the material transported, and transport and erosion cannot be considered altogether independently.

[1] Sometimes the abrupt angle where the chalk plateau meets the steep slope of the dry valleys is due to early upland cultivation.

[2] Peri-glacial conditions existed when great ice-masses were near to, but did not envelop, the area.

Transport. Some of the material carried by a river is in solution, the rest consists of solid fragments of various sizes and shapes. Pieces of wood may float upon the surface. The smallest particles of rock sink very slowly and for most of their journey remain suspended in the water. The larger fragments are rolled along the bed and those of intermediate size move by hopping or saltation; by knocking against one another they become rounded and are formed into pebbles; by rubbing against the banks and bed they wear away the channel of the stream.

The size of the pebbles that a river can move depends upon the velocity of the current. It depends also to a considerable extent upon the shape and material of the pebbles. If, however, the pebbles are all spherical and of the same density, then the diameter of the pebbles that a river can just move varies as the square of its velocity, and their volume as the sixth power of the velocity. But this does not mean that the total load increases as the sixth power of the velocity.

The solid material carried by a river is called its load. Often the term is used to include also the material in solution, but this in fact forms part of the transporting agent itself; and for the present at least it will be more convenient to restrict the term to the solid fragments which float upon the surface, or are carried wholly or partly in suspension, or are rolled along the bed.

The transporting power of a river evidently depends upon its velocity and its volume or discharge, and on the grade or calibre of the load. For it is much easier to carry a load of fine material than an equal mass of coarse material. G. K. Gilbert's experiments with artificial stream channels showed, however, that adding fine material enabled a greater quantity of coarse material to be carried. The increased mobility of the coarse material is due to the finer particles smoothing the surface and enabling the larger particles to roll or slide more readily than they can over a more irregular surface formed only of their own kind. The presence of the coarse material may also encourage turbulence which greatly aids the movement of bed material by stirring up the bed. The upward movement of eddying motion may lift the bed material temporarily into the zone of quicker moving water (see fig. 155) where it will be carried a little downstream before it again falls to the bed. Turbulence plays a very important part in the transport of material by rivers and streams. As the discharge of a stream increases (i.e. during floods), its transporting power increases at a greater rate than the discharge, but friction with the bottom and sides increases only slightly with discharge, thus leaving all the more energy available for transport. A rapid stream can carry more material and can carry fragments of larger size than a slow one. Any stream without change of gradient or discharge can carry a greater amount of fine material than of coarse.

It is often stated that for any particular river or part of a river (assumed to have a constant velocity and volume) there is a limit to the oad that it can bear, and when this limit is reached the load is called the full or maximum load of the river. But without some further qualification the statement is not strictly correct, for as long as the water near the bed is moving faster than about one-third foot per second, it is capable of carrying a greater load, provided that the material is reduced to a sufficient degree of fineness. The effect of adding more material to the load of a river is to reduce the velocity of the current, for much energy is lost in impelling the solid particles forwards. The decrease of velocity

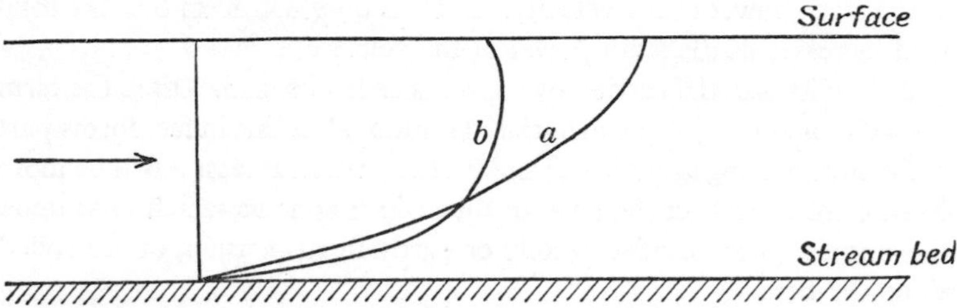

Fig. 155. Distribution of velocity with depth for *a*, laminar, and *b*, turbulent or more normal stream flow. The curves are superimposed to aid comparison. The velocities in turbulent streams are usually much greater than those in which the flow is laminar.

diminishes the size of the pebbles or boulders that the river can move. If, in its former load, there were any pebbles or particles which it cannot move with its diminished speed, these pebbles will be dropped, but if they were broken up sufficiently small, the river would still be able to move them and they would still remain a part of its load.

Thus the full load of a river depends not only on the velocity and volume of the river but also, and to a very important extent, upon the size, and the mixture of sizes, of the particles constituting the load.

Further complications are introduced by the fact that, owing to friction with its channel, the velocity of a river becomes greatly reduced as the bottom and sides are approached (fig. 155). But still it remains substantially true that there is a fairly definite limit to the possible load; and when this limit is reached, any further addition to the river's burden involves the dropping of an equivalent portion of the original load.

If there is an abundance of very fine material available the load may reach a 50 per cent concentration by weight, but for higher concentrations, the physical properties of the fluid changes abruptly and a mud-flow results. Sufficient fine material for such concentrations would rarely accumulate in normal stream beds without being washed away. But in arid regions, dry channels may collect enough wind-blown material to produce something resembling a short-lived mud-flow, when the streams just start to flow. Concentrations of this nature with fine material exist in the mud-flows or debris-slides found in peri-glacial areas when the spring thaw saturates the surface layers, and on our own mountain-sides when torrential rain falls (see ch. XVI).

Erosion. The erosion which a river accomplishes is of two kinds, chemical and mechanical. It may dissolve the rocks over which it flows, if they are of a suitable nature. This is chemical erosion or solution. It may break off fragments from its bed and banks. This is mechanical erosion or corrasion. In most cases the corrasion is far greater than the solution, and it is accordingly with the corrasion that we are chiefly concerned.

Corrasion may be vertical or lateral. Vertical corrasion is corrasion of the bed of the river, deepening its channel. Lateral corrasion is corrasion of the banks, and leaves the bed untouched.

Clear water does very little corrasion of solid rock; but, if swiftly moving, it can displace large blocks of highly jointed rock which have been loosened by chemical or other means. Also if the banks and bed are made of loose material, a stream of clear water becomes an effective corrasive agent. The greater part of the corrasion done by a river is due, especially in massive beds with few joints or bedding planes, to the pebbles and sand that it rolls along its bed.

In order to see how the corrasion and the load interact upon one another, it will be convenient to assume at first that all the particles which form the load and which the river breaks off from its banks and bed are of the same material and the same size. There will then be a definite limit to the load that the river can carry.

In these circumstances, when the river has no load, it does little or no corrasion. When it has a full load it corrades its banks and bed; but, because it already carries as much as it can, for every particle that it breaks off it must drop one of those that it was carrying. Deposition will then be equal to corrasion, and the vertical corrasion is ineffective, but lateral corrasion might continue on the outside of a bend and deposition on the inside.

Thus with no load there is little corrasion, with a full load corrasion is equalled by deposition. Therefore, there is some intermediate load for which the effective corrasion is at its maximum.

A similar law holds good even if the material that forms the load is of various degrees of fineness. The full load is not then such a definite quantity; but the effective corrasion will still increase with the load up to a certain point; and beyond that point it will decrease as the load increases, and will finally cease. This is a fundamental principle of river erosion.

The velocity required to pick up loose material from a stream-bed is distinctly greater than that required simply to keep it moving and this, in turn, is greater than that which occurs when deposition prevails. The disparity between the velocity necessary for erosion and the velocity necessary for transport is large in the case of fine clay particles owing to their power of cohesion. A velocity of about 4 feet per second is required to pick up these fine particles, and this is sufficient to pick up pebbles of about an inch in diameter. The grade of material most easily picked up is 0·004 to 0·02 inches in diameter, that is, the grade of a fine sand or silt.

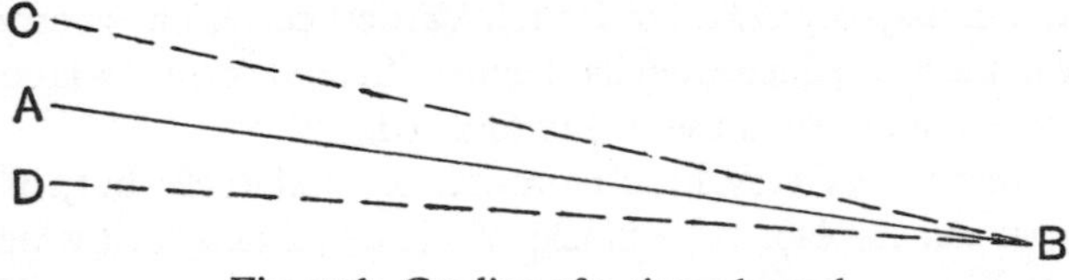

Fig. 156. Grading of a river-channel.

Grading of the river-channel. If we consider a single reach or portion of a river, in which it may be assumed that the slope of the bed and the velocity and volume of the stream are uniform, the effect of the load will become evident. For simplicity it will again be convenient to suppose that the particles of the load and the particles which the river breaks off are all of the same size and material.

The load that enters the reach depends upon what has happened above, and not in any way upon the reach itself. It may therefore be exactly the full load for the velocity and volume of the river in the reach or it may be more or less than this.

If the load that enters the reach is just the full load for the river in the reach, there will be no corrasion and no deposition, or, to be more exact, corrasion and deposition will be equal. The slope of the bed will remain unaltered and this part of the river is said to be graded (*AB* in fig. 156).

If the load that enters the reach is more than this full load, the river will be unable to carry the whole of it and the surplus material will be deposited at the head of the reach. The slope of the bed will accordingly be increased, and the velocity of the stream in the reach will therefore also be increased. This will go on until the velocity is just sufficient to enable the river to carry the load that enters the reach. In such a case the river is said to be aggrading its bed to *CB*.

If the load that enters the reach is somewhat less than the full load, the river will wear away its bed more than its deposits. In doing so it adds to its load. Accordingly the effective corrasion will be greatest at the head of the reach and will diminish downwards as the load increases. The slope of the bed, and with it the velocity of the stream, will be decreased; and this will go on until the velocity is just sufficient to enable the river to carry the load that enters the reach. In this case the river is said to be de-grading its bed to *DB*.

Thus throughout its course the river is continually engaged in adjusting the slope of each part of its channel to the load which enters that part.

If the load consists of particles of various sizes, the river tends to adjust the slope of the reach to the size of the largest particles that enter the reach in sufficient quantity. If the velocity in the reach is just enough to enable it to roll these particles along its bed, they will pass through. If the velocity in the reach is not sufficient to move them, they will be deposited at the head of the reach, increasing the slope. If, on the other hand, the velocity is more than is required to move the largest particles, there will be corrasion until the slope and velocity are sufficiently reduced.

Even in a single reach, however, the volume and velocity are not constant, and both are considerably increased during a flood. If most of the material enters the reach only during floods, and consists of boulders or pebbles so large that the river can move them during a flood but not in its normal state, the slope will be adjusted to the flood conditions, and at other times the water will be practically clear and will have scarcely any effect either of transport or corrasion. This is often the case with mountain streams.

If, on the other hand, a large part of the material that enters the reach is sufficiently fine to be moved by the river in its normal condition, the slope will in general be adjusted to this normal condition and the river will never be free from moving sediment excepting perhaps during a drought. This is usually the case in the lower part of a river's course.

Curve of water-erosion. We may next consider the effect of these principles upon the general slope of the river from its source to the sea. Suppose that a river starts upon a slope *AB* (fig. 157) which is uniform from the watershed to the sea and consists of rock of the same hardness throughout. Suppose that the water-table *EC* intersects the surface at *C*, and that as a result of evenly distributed rainfall the stream gains in volume at a uniform rate as it flows from *C* to *B*. Assume further that the slope and flood discharge are such that the stream can accomplish some erosion at its source, and that the sea removes material from *B* as quickly as it is brought down by the river.

Downstream, as the discharge increases, the stream's power to erode and transport increases at a faster rate than the discharge. Also some of the material gained near the source wears down as it travels seawards, and being then finer in calibre is more easily carried, so that still more of the river's energy becomes available for erosion. Thus a curve *CD*, perhaps slightly convex upwards in the first instance, is produced. Erosion prevails along this stretch so the details of the slope are determined

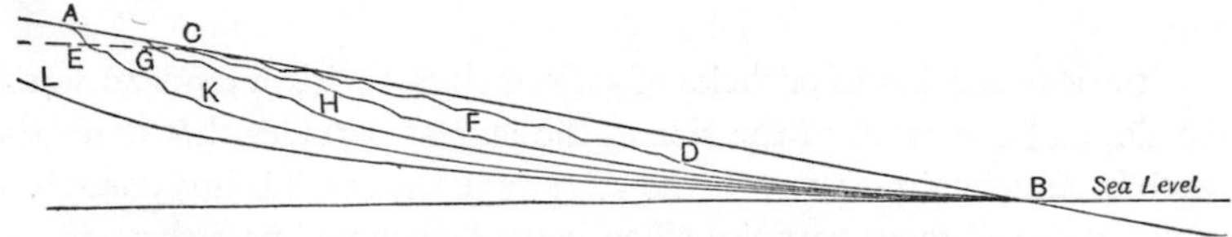

Fig. 157. Successive stages (idealised) in the evolution of the curve of water-erosion.

mainly by the nature of the rock outcropping at the surface. The curve *CD* is therefore represented by a slightly zigzag line to draw attention to this fact which would certainly modify, and might well overrule, any tendency to form a convex curve.

At *D* the stream first feels the effect of the base-level. From *D* to *B* the curve is such that the river, when in flood, can just carry its solid load to the sea—i.e. it is graded. This curve flattens downstream, sea-level acting as a hinge, owing both to continued comminution of the load and to increasing discharge. Thus it is the influence of a base-level of erosion that turns what might develop into a curve convex upwards, into the familiar concave curve.

Continued erosion results in the graded portion retreating upstream to *F*, for erosion must always end at the point from which the slope downstream is just sufficient for the river to carry its solid load to the sea. The source would also recede slightly, tapping the water-table a little farther back along the line *CE*. As this recession would probably be less than that of point *F*, the slope *CF* would be steeper and shorter than *CD*. Erosion and adjustment continue to the stage *GHB* by which time a steep slope—representing the angle of rest of the material—develops above the source *G*, down which material moves due to weathering and soil creep. *EKB* represents a still later stage. The steep slope *AE* above the source has increased in length as the source recedes into the mountain side where the water-table is deeper. Owing to the more rapid drainage by the river, and to the decrease in the amount of high ground, the water-table (and so the source) would, in all probability, have fallen below the original level *E*.

A further change would probably take place. The somewhat abrupt angle at *A* would become rounded. For soil creep down the steep slope *AE* would remove superficial material from the neighbourhood of *A* quicker than it would be supplied down the gentler slope above *A*. Thus the bedrock at *A* would always tend to be exposed and to suffer severe weathering. Frost shattering would be particularly effective at moderate altitudes in temperate latitudes. The consequent lowering at this point

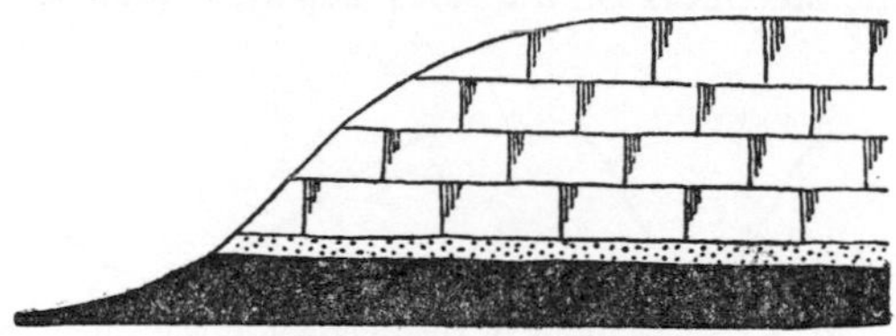

Fig. 158. Form of chalk hills.

would cause the slopes above *A* to increase, and those below to decrease, thus leading to a rounding of the angle. This rounded form would be fairly stable, for it would give rise to a more uniform rate of soil creep which would allow an unbroken mantle of waste to cover and help preserve the underlying rock.

The chalk hills of south-eastern England often show very clearly the change of curve at the level of the springs. The chalk itself is very permeable and beneath it there is locally a bed of permeable sandstone called the Upper Greensand, but the latter rests upon an impervious bed of clay. A large proportion of the rain that falls upon the chalk sinks into the rock instead of running over the surface. But it cannot pass through the clay and therefore escapes on the side of the hill at the junction of the Greensand and the clay, forming a line of springs. Below this level the hill slope is usually concave but above the springs the slope is convex. The form of the lower slope is due to running water, the form of the upper part of the hill is due to solution of the chalk (fig. 158. See note p. 455).

Development of the river-valley. As the curve of water erosion develops, the difference between the upper and lower parts of a river's course becomes more and more clearly defined. In the former corrasion increases and exceeds deposition, in the latter deposition increases and at length exceeds corrasion. In the upper part of its course, therefore, the river tends to deepen its channel and this part is accordingly often known as the valley tract. In the lower part the river spreads out the material that it carries, and tends to form plains, and this part is often called the plain tract. Owing to the gradual flattening of the lower part of the curve the plain tract spreads slowly up the stream and the extent of the valley tract diminishes.

Valley tract. In the upper part of the river's course corrasion is greater than deposition. The river, therefore, deepens its channel and forms a valley. If the river were the only agent concerned the sides of the valley would be vertical. But while the river is cutting downwards, rain and frost and other agencies wear away the sides and the valley becomes V-shaped. The steepness of the sides depends upon the rate of this

Fig. 159. Cross-sections of river-valley in the valley tract.

lateral wearing as compared with the rate of deepening. If the rocks in which the valley is cut are hard and resistant—or pervious so that rain-water sinks in causing little weathering—the sides will be steep and the V will be narrow. If the rocks are soft and easily worn away, the valley will form a wide and open V. The steepness of the sides is also influenced by the amount of rain. If there is but little rain, the sides of the valley will be steep, even though the rocks may be comparatively soft. If, on the other hand, the rainfall is heavy, the slope of the sides will be gentle unless the rocks are very resistant (fig. 159).

It is partly on account of the dryness of the climate that the walls of the Colorado cañon are so nearly vertical and the cañon itself so narrow.

Plain tract. In the lower part of a river's course, the river is graded and uses all its energy in transporting its load. Consequently, the valley is not deepened and there is no vertical corrasion. But the river can still wear away its banks and lateral corrasion still goes on. The corrasion will be balanced, or more than balanced, by deposition in some other part of the bed, and this may result in a shifting of the channel (pl. 11 *a*).

If for any reason one part of the bank is more easily worn away than the rest, the course of the river will become slightly curved, and when once a curve is formed the river tends to accentuate it. In fig. 160 the flow of the river is shown by the arrows. The current is directed towards the concave side of the bend at *A*, but a bottom return current moves towards the inside of the bend. It is this that moves bed material towards the inside of the bend, where it comes to rest. Consequently, the bank will be worn away at *A* while at *B* there will be deposition, and the bend will become more pronounced, as shown by the dotted lines.

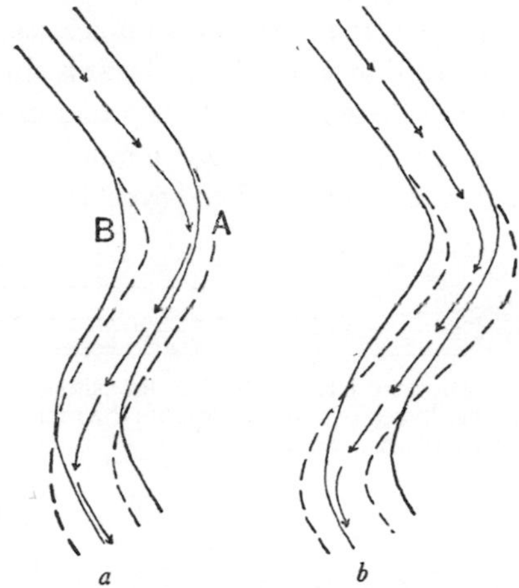

Fig. 160. Stages in the development of meanders.

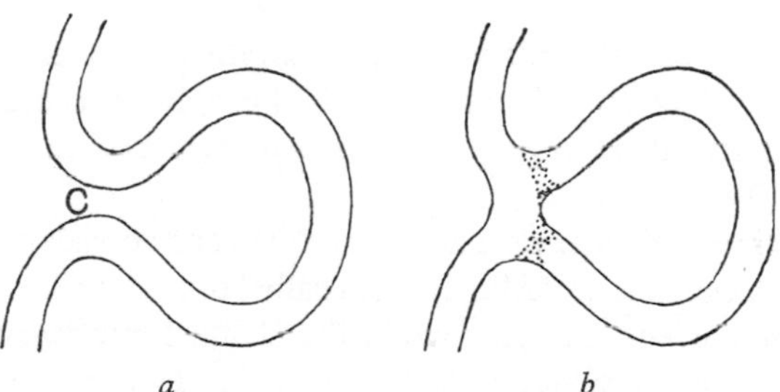

Fig. 161. Formation of ox-bow lakes.

Such curves in the course of a river are known as meanders. The same process will still go on until the meander forms almost a complete circle as in fig. 161 *a*. At length the river will cut through the narrow neck at *C* and its course will again become almost straight. The former meander will remain as a backwater for some time; but the entrances to it will gradually be silted up (fig. 161 *b*), because the current now goes by the shortest route and in the meander the water is still. The backwater will be completely cut off from the main channel and will form what is known as an ox-bow lake. Such lakes are very common at the sides of the Mississippi, and of the Middle Rhine.

The concave bank of a meander is continually being cut into by the river and is therefore steep; the convex bank is formed by deposition by the river itself and consequently slopes gently downwards to the water. Fig. 162 shows a typical section across the river in a meander.

Since, in the plain tract, the river is continually corrading laterally, forming meanders and cutting them off, its course is always changing. It swings, as it were, from side to side and thus produces a nearly level flat of considerable width. The limits of its lateral movements are marked by rising ground on each side of the broad and even floor through which the

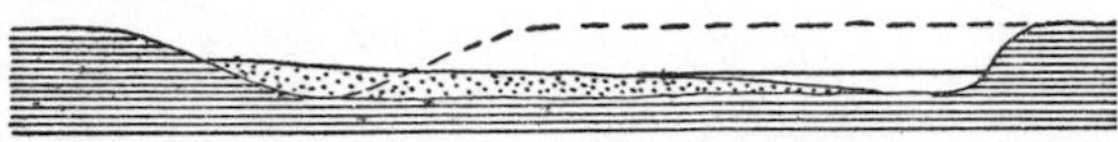

Fig. 162. Section across a meander. The broken line shows the original position of the river-channel. The dotted portion represents the material deposited by the river on the convex bank of the meander.

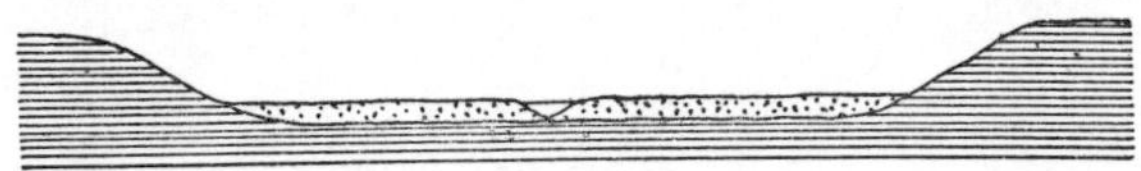

Fig. 163. Section of river-valley in the plain tract.

river meanders, and the valley therefore has the form shown in fig. 163. The channel of the river is cut within the floor, but because there is no vertical corrasion it is sunk but little beneath the level of the surrounding flats.

In flood time the water rises above its banks and spreads over the floor of the valley, which is accordingly often called the flood-plain. When this happens the current is strong within the channel but over the flooded area the water is practically still. Much mud is deposited at the margin of the current, because there the speed is slackened; and a bank of mud is therefore formed on the edge of the channel (fig. 164). When the flood falls the water in the channel subsides, the water on the flooded plain partly escapes into the river and partly sinks into the ground; but the mud deposited at the edge of the channel remains, raising the river-banks above the level of the plain. The river, if it is aggrading its course, begins to deposit in its proper channel, raising the level of its bed.[1] Consequently, although the banks are higher than before, their height above

[1] Aggradation may be due to the seaward extension of the delta, to a rise in sea-level, or to an increase in load.

the *bed* may be no greater and the river will not be less liable to overflow. If this goes on from year to year the banks may be raised to a considerable height and the bed of the river may lie above the level of the surrounding plain (fig. 165).

The natural embankments which a river forms in this way for itself, improved and strengthened artificially, are known on the Mississippi and elsewhere as levees.

Examples of rivers which have raised themselves above the surrounding country are to be met with in many low-lying districts. In the Fenland many of the present rivers are above the level of the land around. The wastage of the peat exaggerates this effect, and changes of level are noticeable over a period of a few years. Houses in the peat fens often have several steps in front of their doors, although when they were built the level of the doorstep conformed approximately with that of the

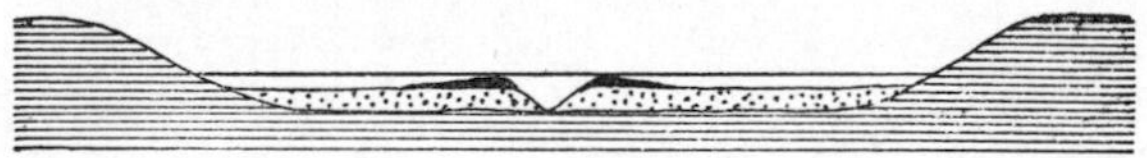

Fig. 164. Formation of natural embankments (shown black) during floods.

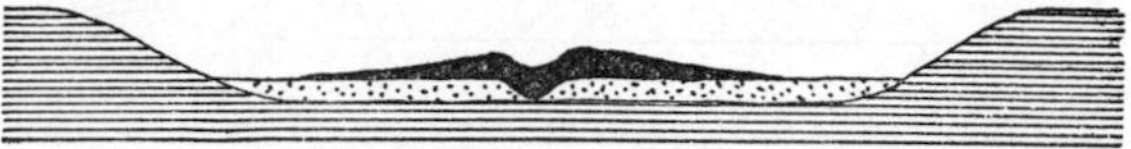

Fig. 165. River-bed raised by deposition above the level of the flood-plain.

ground. Some lines of railway can be seen to go 'uphill' over a bridge crossing a fenland dyke or drain, and culverts across these drains have sometimes to be reinforced downwards.

Traces of *former* rivers are found in the Fenland. Banks or ridges of silt, called roddons, wind through parts of the fens. They are in pairs, and represent the levees of ancient rivers. They are built in the manner described above but their elevation has been accentuated by peat shrinkage and wastage. Nearer the Wash, in the silt fens, similar levees are found which mark the courses of tidal creeks like those of a modern salt marsh. In the lower part of its course the Po is above the plain of Lombardy; and for hundreds of miles the channel of the Hoang-Ho stands high above the plain through which it flows.

But in all such cases, unless the natural embankments are strengthened artificially and are continually repaired, the river will not keep to a definite channel. In floods it is always liable to break its banks, to overspread the surrounding country and to forsake its old course for a new one. This has happened several times with the Hoang-Ho. At one time it flowed into the Yellow Sea; but in the year 1852 it broke its banks, flooded an area of thousands of square miles, drowning, it is estimated, nearly a million people, and took a new course into the Gulf of Pe-chi-li. The distance between its old mouth and its new one is nearly 300 miles. On several other occasions the Hoang-Ho has caused similar disastrous floods and has changed its course.

Influence of differences of hardness upon the development of river-channels. In the account of the development of the curve of water-erosion it is assumed that the slope on which the river starts is made throughout of rock of uniform hardness. If, as is usually the case, it consists partly of soft beds and partly of hard beds, the form of the curve will be modified.

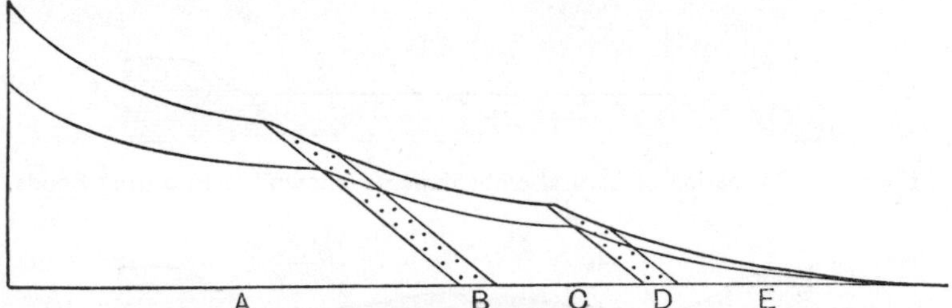

Fig. 166. Influences of differences of hardness on the development of the curve of water-erosion.

Suppose, for example, that upon the slope two beds crop out which are harder than the rest (fig. 166). The river tries to form the curve of water-erosion, but because the beds *B* and *D* are hard, they are corraded less rapidly than they would be if they were as soft as the rest, and they act as temporary base-levels. The curve is therefore bulged up at the outcrops of these beds and becomes three separate curves instead of a single simple one.

Except for small inequalities the bed of a river must everywhere slope towards the sea. Therefore the soft bed *A* cannot be eroded below the level of the outcrop of the hard bed *B*. But since the soft rocks are more easily worn away, the slope of the river above the outcrop of each hard band decreases while the section crossing the hard outcrop grows steeper. Over the soft beds the current will now be slow; over the hard beds there will be waterfalls or rapids. The increased speed of the river at the hard beds will, to some extent at least, compensate for their extra resistance, and the curves will gradually be cut downwards as shown in fig. 166. The steeper sections across the hard outcrops are ungraded, and if the river picks up extra load the gradient on the soft bed below a hard outcrop will be steeper than that immediately above. As this new material decreases in size the curve will flatten, and similar changes of gradient may also occur at the next hard outcrop. As the slope near the sea diminishes, the area of deposition spreads upwards, and in time the hard beds will be buried beneath the material laid down by the river and will cease to show. But as long as a hard bed is in a part of the river where corrasion exceeds deposition, there will be rapids through it and a smoother reach above.

Moreover, since the harder beds will also offer more resistance to the weather, the sides of the valley will be steeper than in the softer beds. In the latter the valleys open out, in the former the river often flows through narrow and rocky gorges.

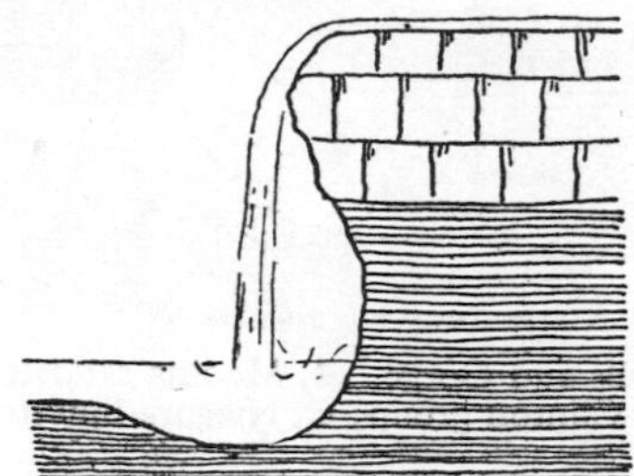

Fig. 167. Waterfall in horizontal strata.

Waterfalls. If a hard bed dips gently down the stream as in fig. 166 the river passing over it will generally form rapids rather than waterfalls. But if the hard bed is horizontal, or dips gently up the stream, the river will wear away the softer rocks beneath it, the hard bed will overhang and a waterfall will be produced (fig. 167). The falling water will continue to undermine the hard bed, and from time to time blocks of the latter will be broken off and the waterfall will gradually recede upstream. This is what has happened in the case of the Niagara Falls. The top of the fall is formed of limestone, which rests upon a bed of shale. The fall was once at the front edge of the plateau shown in fig. 168. It has gradually cut backward in the manner described, to its present position, and it is still receding. Below the fall is the gorge which the fall has cut, and the sides of the gorge consist of limestone above and shale and sandstone below. The backward erosion of the waterfall is comparatively rapid, because it depends upon the erosion of the soft rock at its base. The erosion of the sides of the valley below the fall is slow; it is due to the action of rain and other weathering agencies, and the hard rock above protects the softer rock beneath. Therefore the valley below the fall has steep sides and forms a gorge.

Whenever a waterfall cuts backwards there will usually be a gorge below it, for the backward erosion is generally rapid compared with the lateral erosion of the sides of the valley (pl. 12*a*). But there are cases in which there is scarcely any backward erosion at all. If a hard bed, or an

Fig. 168. Niagara Falls and Gorge. *A*, Medina sandstone; *B*, Niagara shale and Clinton group; *C*, Niagara limestone.

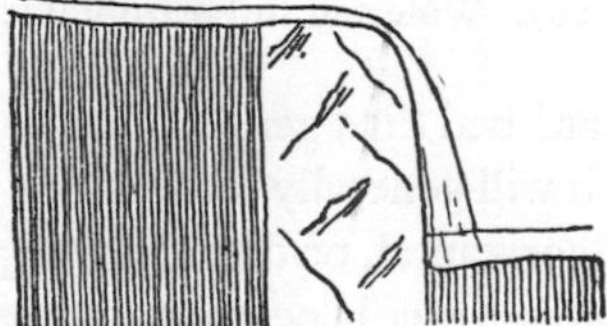

Fig. 169. Waterfall over a vertical hard bed.

igneous dyke, runs vertically across the river, the soft rock on the downstream side will be rapidly worn away and a waterfall will be formed (fig. 169). But little or no undermining of the hard bed is possible. The river will gradually cut its channel deeper, both in the hard and the soft rock, and the waterfall will not alter its position.

Rejuvenation. A river in its plain tract has ceased to corrade its bed, and as the curve of water-erosion becomes more and more developed the plain tract extends farther and farther up the stream. In a long-established river, which may be a mature river, vertical corrasion is accordingly limited to the tributary streams which form its headwaters and throughout the main part of its course the river meanders through the plain that it has formed by lateral corrasion and deposition.

After this stage is reached, it sometimes happens that the volume or velocity of the river is in some way increased. The rainfall may become greater, earth movements or a fall in sea-level may lead to a greater slope along the river's course. Vertical corrasion will begin again and the river is said to be rejuvenated.

The channel will be deepened, and the flood-plain will now become a flat alluvial tract considerably above the level of the river and out of reach of the greatest flood. It will form a kind of platform overlooking the river, and such a platform is called a river-terrace (fig. 170, see also pl. 10*b*).

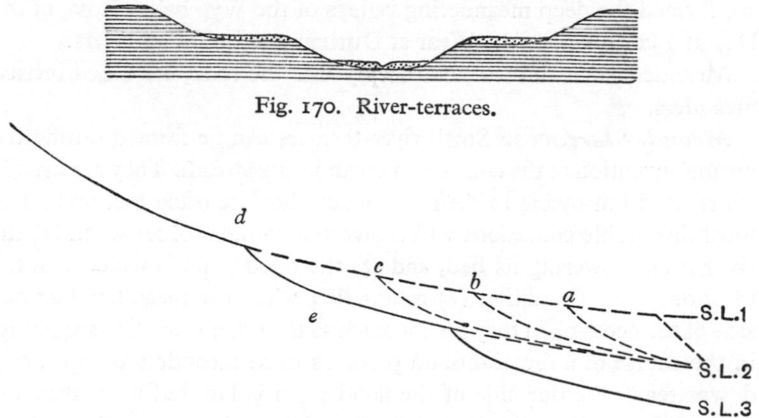

Fig. 170. River-terraces.

Fig. 171. Long profile of a river that has been rejuvenated by two successive falls in sea-level.

After equilibrium is restored and vertical corrasion ceases, the river will again corrade laterally and form a new flood-plain at a lower level than the old one. Possibly for some reason vertical corrasion may begin again and in this way a series of river-terraces may be formed one above another. The long profile of such a valley which has been twice rejuvenated will resemble that shown in fig. 171. When sea-level falls from 1 to 2 the offshore slope, which is assumed to be steeper than the lower course of the graded river, is raised above the sea. Erosion starts afresh down this slope which steadily retreats upstream through stages *a*, *b*, *c*, *d*. As it does so the break of slope or nick point remains distinct. But the steep slope *de* becomes shorter, because the gradient from *e* to the sea must remain steeper than the corresponding slope previous to rejuvenation, since extra load has now to be carried. So rejuvenation terraces may gradually approach each other upstream but will only coalesce at a nick point.

Much work has been done in recent years in attempts to plot and interpret rejuvenated profiles, and to deduce past changes of sea-level. The difficult question is the gradient of the part of the curve which has been removed by erosion—the broken lines in fig. 171. When remnants of the old course occur as terraces on the valley sides these are of much assistance in reconstructing these lost parts of the profiles.

If the rejuvenation of a river is sufficient, the vertical corrasion may become so effective that the lateral corrasion is relatively unimportant. The river will then sink its channel deeply into the ground while still preserving all the turns and windings of its original course. In this way are formed the deep meandering valleys of the Wye below Ross, of the Dee at Llangollen, of the Wear at Durham, and of other rivers.

Meanders such as these, cut deeply into the rock, are called incised meanders.

Meander terraces. Small river-terraces can be formed during the normal evolution of the course of a meandering stream. They are usually short-lived but owing to their frequency they are often met with. The most favourable conditions which give rise to them occur when (1) the river is still lowering its bed, and (2) the flood-plain is wider than the meander belt. Condition (2) means that when the meanders hug one side of the flood-plain they do not reach to the other side. Consequently, in the course of a few thousand years, as these meanders sweep slowly downstream, the one side of the flood-plain is lowered more than the other. When eventually the meanders swing across to the other side of the valley the river undercuts the old flood-plain, forming terraces. If the river is free to swing from side to side the terraces will be short-lived, but if this lateral swinging is restricted by a hard outcrop or in some other way, then a series of terraces may develop (fig. 172). It follows that the river must be slowly cutting downwards at the same time, hence a common condition necessary for the formation of a series of meander terraces occurs when part of a river-valley above a hard outcrop was filled with boulder clay in the Ice Age. The slow re-excavation of this material, governed in its downward rate of cutting by the hard outcrop, gives rise to sweeping meanders above.

Peneplanation. Earlier in this chapter it was shown that in every part of its course a river attempts to adjust the slope of its channel so that the velocity of the current is just sufficient to enable it to carry the load that enters that part. When this condition is attained, corrasion and deposition are equal and the river is said to be graded.

It is possible for the adjustment in a single reach to be perfect; but if any load is brought into this reach it implies that above the reach corrasion is greater than deposition and that the adjustment there is not complete. It is conceivable that in time the channel might be graded throughout. Everywhere corrasion would then be equal to deposition, no load would pass from any part of the channel into the part below and the river would cease to carry any material downwards. But it is evident that this condition cannot be reached until the velocity of the river is so low that it is unable to move even the loose particles on its banks and bed. Until this condition is reached there must be some corrasion.

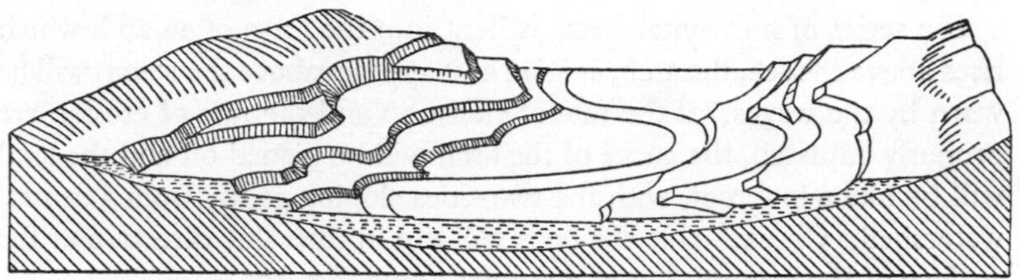

Fig. 172. Series of meander terraces.

It is the same with running water generally, even when it is not confined to definite channels, but flows as a sheet, as sometimes happens during a thunderstorm.

Running water, therefore, wears away the land until it has produced a slope so gentle that its velocity down the slope is not sufficient to move the particles produced by weathering or corrasion. Any projection above this slope will be eroded, any depression below it will be filled up by deposition.

Owing to earth movements, variations in the rainfall, and other causes, such a condition is never actually attained; but erosion by rain and rivers often produces an approximation to it. The surface of the ground will then be nearly a plane surface and is called a peneplane. Often the harder rocks, not yet completely worn down, still stand up as hills in the midst of the plain, like islands in the sea. But, given time, they too would be eroded and reduced to the common level.

Crickmay considers that the most likely way in which large areas can be reduced to a plain, close to sea-level, is by the widening and merging of the flood-plains of adjacent rivers.

CHAPTER IX

DEVELOPMENT OF RIVER-SYSTEMS

General principles. Up to the present we have considered only the changes that a single river produces in its own valley. But there may be many rivers upon the same slope and it often happens that the growth of one affects the development of others. It is with the changes which are thus produced that we are now concerned.

If a series of horizontal strata is bent into the form of an arch which rises above the sea, the arch, as soon as it appears above the water, will be worn by the waves. If the rate of elevation and the rate of erosion are properly adjusted, the curve of the arch will be planed off and the land will be like a low roof, with the two sides sloping gently from a central watershed. On each side the beds will dip in the same direction as the surface of the ground, but at a steeper angle (fig. 173).

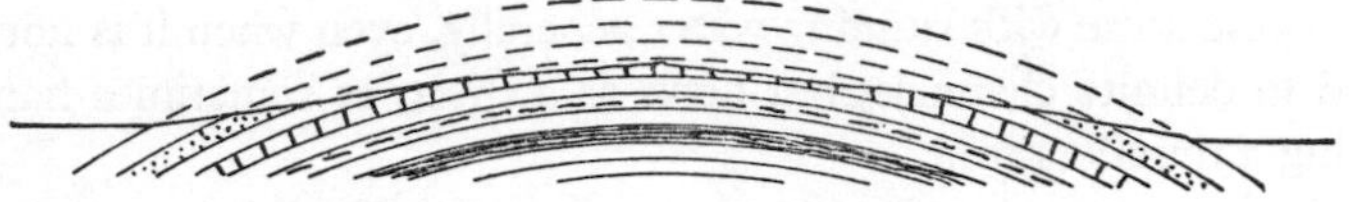

Fig. 173. A denuded anticline.

Upon each slope a system of rivers will be developed, and since the direction of the rivers is determined directly by the uplift which raised the arch, the rivers are said to be consequent on the uplift, and the whole forms a consequent drainage system.

The rivers will begin to flow almost as soon as the land appears above the sea; but in order to show how they develop it will be simpler to suppose that the slope is completely formed before the rivers start.

Suppose that in the manner described an uplift produces a region sloping directly and uniformly from a straight watershed to the sea and that the outcrops of two hard beds run parallel to the watershed, the beds dipping in the same direction as the slope but at a steeper angle. Fig. 174 shows a plan and section of a part of such a region. For the present we need not consider what happens on the other side of the watershed.

Upon this slope a number of parallel rivers will be developed, flowing directly from the watershed to the sea. These rivers are the immediate consequence of the uplift and are therefore known as consequent rivers.

As soon as the consequent rivers have excavated their valleys, water will enter these valleys from the sides, and tributaries will accordingly be formed, flowing more or less at right angles to the main streams. Such a direction is practically *along* the original slope, and is therefore impossible until the valleys of the consequent rivers have been carved out. The tributaries are accordingly called subsequent rivers—they are formed after the consequent rivers (fig. 175).

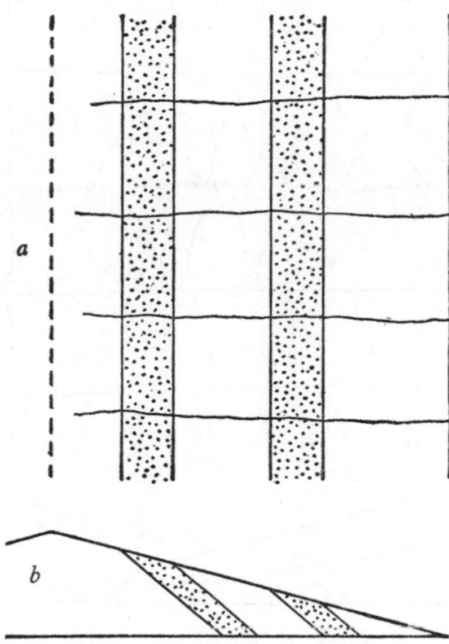

Fig. 174. Development of a river-system: first stage. *a*, plan; *b*, section.

If the consequent streams flow in the direction of the dip, they are equivalent to dip streams, and if the subsequent streams follow the strike they may be referred to as strike streams. But a consequent need not follow the dip. It may, for example, follow the axis of a synclinal valley which slopes gradually to the sea. It will then be parallel with the strike but is, nevertheless, a consequent, since it is a consequence of the formation of the terrain. The small streams flowing from the ridges and joining it at right angles are also consequent on the uplift. Similarly, subsequent and strike are not necessarily synonymous terms. If dip and strike are used, as they should be, in strict relation to the geology, and consequent and subsequent in relation to time or evolution, no confusion need arise.

Because the soft beds are more easily eroded than the hard ones, the tributary valleys will be formed in the soft beds, and the subsequent streams will flow along the outcrops of these beds. The hard beds, away from the actual channels of the consequent streams, will not be directly affected by river-erosion and will therefore stand up as ridges overlooking the valleys of the subsequent streams. A section along the channel of a consequent stream is shown in fig. 175*b*, while fig. 175*c* is a section

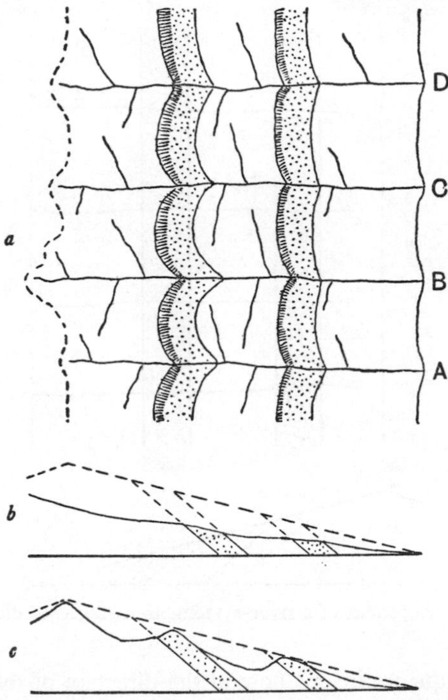

Fig. 175. Development of a river-system: second stage. *a*, plan; *b*, section along a consequent stream; *c*, section between two consequent streams.

parallel to a consequent stream, but not along it. The projecting edge of a hard bed is called an escarpment.

From fig. 175*c* it will be seen that as the subsequent stream deepens its valley, a slope of soft rock will be formed beneath the edge of the hard bed and this slope will gradually grow steeper. The soft foundation on which the hard bed rests is weakened; the edge of the bed breaks into blocks which slide slowly or rapidly down the slope in front; and the escarpment gradually recedes.

Both the consequent and the subsequent streams will cut backwards at their heads. The former will eat into the main watershed, the latter into the watersheds between the consequent streams. If, as will usually be the case, one of the consequent rivers, *B*, is larger, swifter, or finds a line of weakness through the hard bed nearer the sea, it will erode its valley more deeply. Its tributaries will therefore have a steeper fall than the tributaries of the other consequent streams, and the erosion at their heads will be more rapid. In time their valleys will be cut back into the valley of the neighbouring consequent river, and the headwaters of the latter will find their way into the larger river *B* (fig. 176). This process is known as beheading or river-capture.

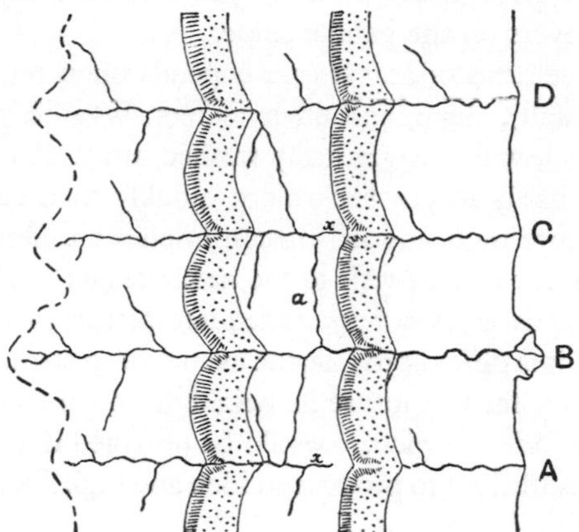

Fig. 176. Development of a river-system: third stage.

The lower part of the beheaded river, fed by the tributaries below the point of capture, will continue as a stream of diminished size as in the case of *D*. Before long, however, the increased erosion of the subsequent stream *a*, strengthened by its capture of the headwaters of *C* and *D*, will lower the level of the soft bed in which it flows, to so great an extent that all the water on its own side of the escarpment will run into it. In the figure this has already happened in the case of the rivers *A* and *C*. *Obsequent* streams, or streams flowing in the opposite direction to the consequent rivers, have been formed at *x*, *x*, in the original valleys of the beheaded rivers. The lower parts of *A* and *C* now begin on the other side of the escarpment and the gaps through which they originally flowed have become dry, forming what are known as wind-gaps. The valleys of the diminished streams *A* and *C* were made for a larger flow of water. They seem too large for their present streams and are accordingly often termed misfits.

If there is no interference by earth movements or other causes, the largest of the original consequent rivers may capture in turn the headwaters of all the rest. The tributaries which effect the capture may become considerably larger than the original consequent river into which they flow, and the latter may be by comparison an almost insignificant stream down to its junction with its tributaries.

A consequent river may even capture the headwaters of a river on the other side of the main watershed. If the slopes on the two sides of the watershed are unequal, the erosion at the heads of the rivers will be more rapid on the steeper side. The valleys on this side will gradually eat their way backwards through the watershed, and in time will tap the upper waters of the rivers on the gentler slope.

Erosion at the head of any stream depends upon rock type, climate (especially rainfall), slope, and other factors. Weathering leads to the formation of soil, which is gradually washed away. A river rising on a steep slope is likely to cut back more quickly than one on a gentler slope, and capture by headward erosion implies a difference in level of the streams concerned. A visit to the headstreams of rivers in normal weather conditions gives a very inadequate picture; little seems to be happening and it is difficult to imagine even a steep stream cutting backwards sufficiently far to capture its neighbour on the other side of the divide. A very different picture would be obtained if a visit were made during a storm sufficient to produce sudden and high floods. (See ch. XVI, pt. III.)

If the rocks of the divide are all impervious, capture cannot take place until the pirate stream has cut back through the divide to a level below that of the *extreme flood-level* of the stream it is about to capture. Once this level is attained, the floods in the captured stream will aid in its own diversion. If there are pervious rocks in the divide, it is probable that the capturing stream will draw off some of the ground water supply of the higher level stream. If this is the case, the flow of the lower stream will be increased and that of the upper decreased. But such a process will not be of much significance unless the rocks are soluble or very pervious. In limestones, for example, the interconnecting joint-systems are much more effective in this respect than the solubility of the rock. The process can take place in well-jointed rocks, even if they are not soluble. In certain sandstones it is aided if, in addition to passing freely through the joint-system, the water has also softened the sandstones. Allied to this is the possibility that the pirate stream may appreciably lower the water-table and so increase its own flow and decrease that of the stream it is about to capture. Variations of this process are legion, and may be conspicuous in unconsolidated and mixed deposits such as some of those resulting from glaciation. Nevertheless, capture is primarily a surface phenomenon, although it may be aided by any of these factors. (I. B. Crosby, *Journal of Geology*, **45**, 1937, 465.)

Capture can also take place laterally, when it is called planation capture or interscission. If two rivers in their lower courses flow roughly parallel to one another in flat country, through which they meander, it is possible that in their lateral wanderings they may draw so close to one another that either as a result of simple meander swinging, or perhaps during floods, they may unite.

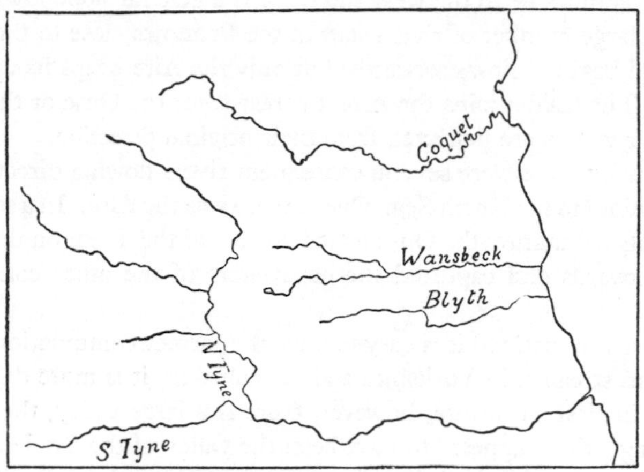

Fig. 177. The rivers of Northumberland.

The rivers of Northumberland. The rivers of Northumberland afford a good example of the development of a river-system in the manner described (fig. 177).

To the west lie the Cheviots and the Pennines, forming the watershed between the North and the Irish Seas; and from the watershed there is a general slope towards the east. Upon this slope flow the Coquet, the Wansbeck, the Blyth, and the Tyne. The Coquet and the branch of the Tyne known as the South Tyne rise near the watershed and flow directly to the sea. But the Wansbeck and the Blyth have their sources on the middle of the general slope.

The Tyne receives a tributary from the north, called the North Tyne, and on its western side the North Tyne receives tributaries coming straight down from the watershed. One of these tributaries if it continued its course would enter the valley of the Wansbeck, another would flow into the Blyth.

Originally the four rivers, the Coquet, the Wansbeck, the Blyth, and the Tyne, probably flowed straight from the watershed to the sea. The Tyne was the largest of these rivers and its tributary, the North Tyne, cut backwards until it had captured the headwaters of the Blyth and the Wansbeck. It has not yet reached the Coquet, but in time this river too may be beheaded.

The Humber. The Humber is really the mouth of the Aire, but the tributaries, the Ouse on the north and the Trent on the south, are now more important than the Aire.

The Pennines lie to the west and there is a general slope towards the east. A large number of rivers start in the Pennines close to the watershed and begin to flow eastwards; but only the Aire keeps its course to the sea. The Calder joins the Aire, the rest enter the Ouse or the Trent and their waters are deflected from their original direction.

Originally there were several consequent rivers flowing directly from the Pennines to the North Sea. One of these was the Aire. In a soft band of rock its tributaries, the Ouse on the north and the Trent on the south, cut backwards and captured the headwaters of the other consequent streams.

In Northumberland it is easy to trace the former continuations of the beheaded streams, in Yorkshire and Lincolnshire it is more difficult to do so. In East Yorkshire, however, there is a large valley, the Vale of Pickering, which appears to have been the valley of the Swale and Ure when those rivers flowed directly to the sea. The present Witham was probably the continuation of one of the original consequent streams in the south. It now rises in low ground and flows through a gap in Lincoln Edge; and it is said that during floods some of the water of the upper Trent still finds its way into the Witham.

The rivers of the Weald. The Weald (fig. 178*a*) lies between the North Downs and the South Downs.

The Downs and Salisbury Plain are formed by the outcrop of the chalk, which is comparatively hard and therefore forms high ground with an escarpment overlooking the Weald. More important than hardness is the ability of the chalk to let surface water percolate through it and so leave it free from erosion by surface streams.

In the middle of the Weald there is an upland area, formed by the outcrop of a series of sandstones much broken up by faults, and between this and the escarpment of the chalk is a broad depression, divided into two parts by the Greensand escarpment. On a map the depression is

U-shaped, with the bend of the U lying against the chalk to the west and the open end of the U against the sea. This depression is hollowed out in beds of clay.

Some of the rivers rise in the central area of high land, others in the depression itself; but almost all have cut their valleys through the Downs, although the Downs are higher than the sources of the river.

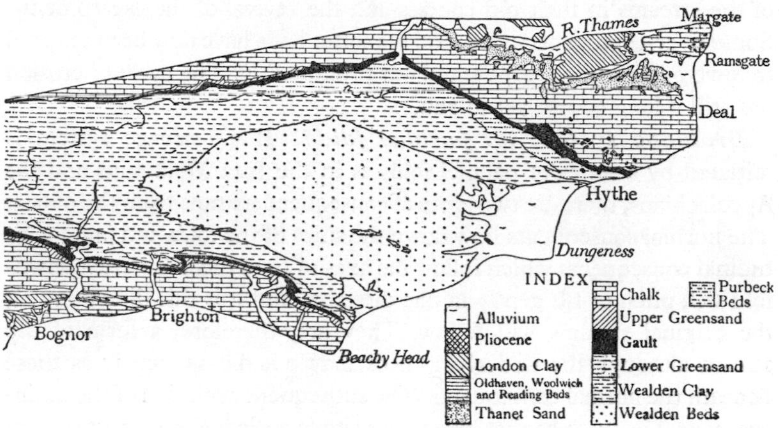

Fig. 178 (*a*). Geological map of the Weald.

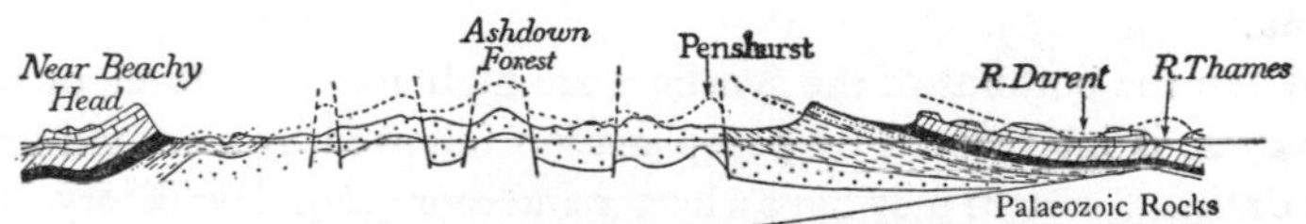

Fig. 178 (*b*). Section of the Weald.

At first sight it is difficult to understand how a river can cut its way through hills which are higher than its source; but the difficulty is explained by the geological structure. Fig. 178*b* is a section across the Weald from north to south. From this it is evident that the beds are in the form of a complicated arch or elongated dome. The rivers rose near the top of the arch and flowed towards the north and south. Gradually these rivers and their tributaries removed the higher beds from the whole of the central area, exposing those beneath. In course of time the number of consequent streams was probably largely reduced and the growth of subsequent streams increased. Erosion continued until the area was almost reduced to a peneplane.

The record was interrupted at this stage by the submergence of the northern and southern parts of the area beneath the Pliocene sea. The surface was trimmed by wave action and a thin sheet of sand and shingle was laid down. This sea did not extend over the central tracts and its incursion hardly affects the general course of landform development.

The next important event was the elevation of the whole area by about 600–800 feet. The main result of this uplift was to cause the re-incision of the streams in their old courses and the revival of the escarpments. Some river-capture occurred, and the softer beds have now been reduced to lowlands but the scarps stand out prominently. The cycle of erosion has still a long course yet to run.

Drainage system on parallel folds. If a drainage system is initiated by a series of parallel folds as in the Jura Mountains and the Appalachians, there are two types of consequent streams from the outset. The normal consequents flow down the sides of the folds and join longitudinal consequents which follow the axes of the synclines. Each downfold will pitch or tilt gently in one direction and it is this direction that the original streams will follow. They are, therefore, a form of dip stream although the underlying beds may not dip as steeply as those beneath the normal consequents. The subsequent evolution of the drainage system is much as that given for a single anticlinal axis, and is summarised in fig. 179. The nature of the divides separating the river-valleys depends on the dip as well as on the hardness of the different strata.

When the bottoms of the synclines are high above sea-level, or when the cycle is interrupted by peneplanation followed by a second uplift, the drainage system may have a longer and more complex history. First the anticlines are eroded down to the level of the synclines (see fig. 180). Then, after a second uplift or as a result of river-capture, a new cycle of erosion begins. This time valleys will probably develop along the axes of the anticlines, because folding permanently weakens rocks in anticlines, and encourages the breaking up of the rocks by weathering. Thus valleys will form in the old anticlines leaving the synclines as ridges. This arrangement of anticlinal valleys and synclinal mountains is most frequent in fairly old folded mountains such as the Appalachians. The beds forming the summit of Snowdon also lie in a syncline.

During this stage, if a very hard stratum is exposed it resists erosion, and after an intervening period of peneplanation or a change in the river pattern by some agency such as capture, the rivers might return to the synclines (fig. 182). This drainage pattern might be termed re-consequent or resequent drainage.

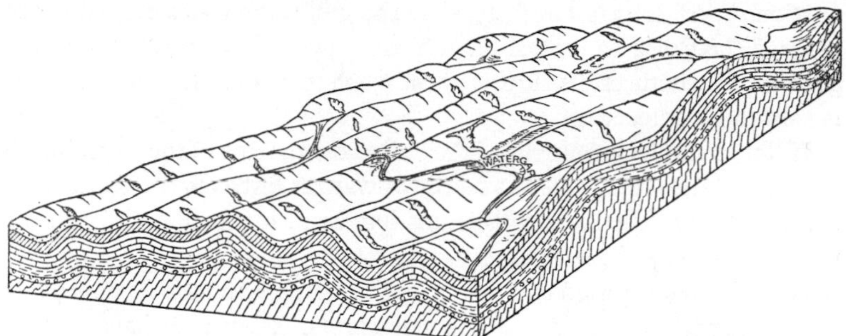

Fig. 179. Initiation of a drainage system on a series of parallel folds.

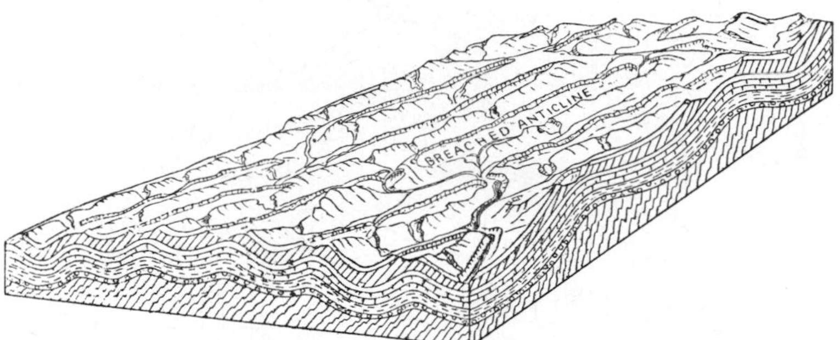

Fig. 180. Middle stage in evolution of drainage system on parallel folds.

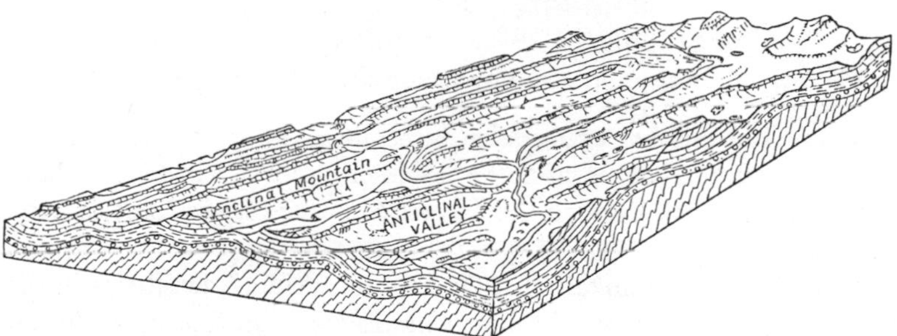

Fig. 181. Advanced stage in evolution of drainage system on parallel folds.

Antecedent drainage. In the cases already described the river-system or system of drainage is mainly the result of the earth movements to which the tilting of the surface and of the beds is due. It is therefore called consequent drainage, and in such drainage the direction of the rivers is closely related to the geological structure.

But it may happen that earth movements occur after the drainage system is established, and if the earth movements take place so slowly that erosion proceeds as fast or faster than the uplift, the rivers may continue to keep their original courses and in time may show no relation to the geological structures developed by the earth movements. Such drainage is said to be antecedent.

If, for example, an anticline is raised across the line of the river, but so slowly that the river erodes its bed downward as fast as the anticline rises, the direction of the river will be unaltered and it will flow through the ridge formed by the anticline.

It has been suggested that this is why the Indus and the Brahmaputra break through the chain of the Himalayas. They may have existed before the elevation of the chain and have simply kept their original

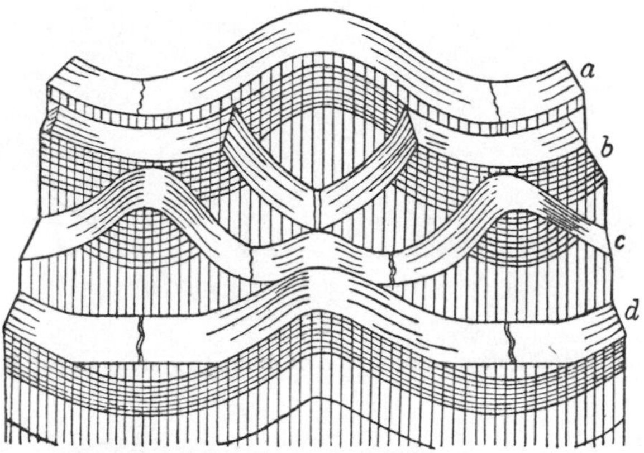

Fig. 182. *a*, consequent; *b* and *c*, subsequent; and *d*, resequent drainage.

courses. But another explanation is possible. They may have begun upon the southern slopes, after the mountains were raised, and may have cut their way back through the watershed in the manner described on p. 300.

It might appear unlikely that the greatest range of mountains in the world failed to start a completely new drainage system. The upper Indus, and the Brahmaputra for most of its course, lie closely parallel with the Himalayas—the Brahmaputra both to the north and to the south. This would be an unusual coincidence if the rivers were there before the ranges were formed. Nevertheless it is unwise to speculate on the origin of the drainage in an area about which so little is known, but in a fairly recent paper Wager analyses the Arun River and supports the antecedent theory.

It is in fact very difficult to prove a case of antecedent drainage. Usually some other explanation is also possible.

Superimposed drainage. There is another way in which the direction of the rivers may become independent of the geological structure of the country through which they flow. The courses of the rivers may be determined by an uplift and may be related in the usual manner to the structure. But in time their valleys may be cut down into an older series of rocks which have been affected by an earlier system of folding quite independent of the later movements to which the rivers are due.

This is the case in the Lake District. The older rocks which form the greater part of the region were thrown into a series of folds running from east-north-east to west-south-west, the oldest rocks of all appearing in the northern part of the area. The rivers rise near the middle of the Lake District and radiate outwards in all directions, quite independently of the

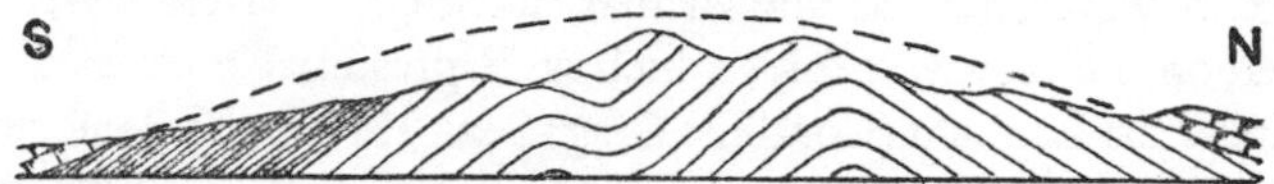

Fig. 183. Section of the Lake District. The broken line represents the base of the later beds which once covered the whole district but which are now left only round its edge.

arrangement of the beds on which they flow. But the older rocks of the Lake District are completely surrounded by a ring of later beds. Originally these later beds covered the whole area, forming a dome with its centre about the present position of Helvellyn (fig. 183). The rivers started near the top of the dome and flowed outwards in all directions. Erosion has gradually removed the later beds and exposed the older folded rocks beneath. The courses of the rivers were determined by the dome-like form of the later beds upon which they began to flow, and as they cut their valleys downwards they have kept, in general, to their original directions, in spite of the different structure of the rocks into which they cut.

Such a system of drainage as this is said to be superimposed, superinduced or epigenetic. It has been imposed upon the district not by the rocks which now form the region, but by the younger beds which once spread over them.

Superimposition is probably of far wider application in Britain than the reference to the Lake District may suggest. There is little doubt that at one time the Jurassic and Cretaceous beds spread much farther to the north and west than they do at present, and the Trias may have capped much of what is now Wales. If our river systems originated during the Miocene, it is possible that they did so on the chalk when it extended far beyond its present limits. These original rivers may have flowed radially from a centre in Snowdonia to South Wales, and across the Midlands to the London Area. In so doing, it is argued, they would have developed tributaries running into the main consequent streams trending south-west and north-east. In course of time, as the chalk cover was worn away, the streams cut down to the older rocks, and the subsequents became, in general, strike streams in the softer rocks and extended at the expense of the original consequents. In this way some authorities have seen in outline the beginnings of rivers such as the Warwickshire Avon and those flowing to the Wash, as well as the origin of some of the gaps in the Jurassic and chalk escarpments. More recently Linton has advanced the view that the original river system of north and south Britain possessed an east-west rather than a north-west to south-east trend. In Wessex, however, he has shown that north-south rivers were superimposed on the east-west folds which were presumably covered by the deposits of the Lenham (Coralline Crag) Sea. He has also demonstrated how the rivers in Wessex can be correlated with those in the Weald (p. 318).

There is not yet by any means complete agreement about the way or ways in which all our rivers came into being, and many objections can be raised against any single hypothesis. Sissons, for example, in southern Yorkshire, has cogently argued that the rivers there may well be built up by integration of small streams draining surfaces of erosion, and George, in the Southern Uplands, questions the reconstruction suggested by Linton since the summit-levels do not seem to lie on an easterly falling surface.

That these differences of opinion exist is all to the good; in any branch of physiography we should continually question hypotheses and examine them in the light of new facts as they become known. The *principles* outlined in this chapter are probably correct and unlikely to be modified; the river-systems need more study, and in view of recent work may have to be considered as part of a whole rather than as isolated phenomena.

In concluding this chapter, reference may be made once more to peneplanation (see p. 310) and to the numerous erosion-surfaces, best called upland plains, which occur throughout Britain and other lands. The term 'upland plain' does not imply any particular mode of origin. Traces of several of these surfaces are often found in the same locality, thus producing a staircase effect. The older and higher surfaces are usually so much dissected that but few and widely separated traces remain. This makes their interpretation difficult and provokes criticism of the view that they once formed a connected surface. Surfaces have been claimed at 1800 feet in the Highlands of Scotland, and a 3000-foot level may correspond with the Highland summits. The lowest levels are much less equivocal; that near Tenby at about 180 feet is a good example. An extensive and well-authenticated surface at about 400 feet stretches over most of southern England, and is probably part of the series comprising the Pliocene surfaces of the Downs and the Boyne Hill (100 feet) and lower terraces of the Thames. All these surfaces are in one sense part of the same sequence as the raised beaches and submerged forests if we assume that they are in some manner to be associated with either falling sea-level or rises of the land.

These upland surfaces exist, even if the explanations of their origin are still uncertain. They are usually assumed to be late Tertiary, probably Pliocene, in age. They are for the most part sub-aerial in origin, although their lower parts may be partly the work of marine erosion. Little is known about their effect on, or relation to, the rivers of this country, but their sub-aerial origin implies that river-action has played a major part in their evolution. They need far more study. If they represent a fall of sea-level, in stages, in relation to the land, all scenery, coastal as well as inland, must be examined with this in view; and it follows that the history and evolution of our river-systems and that of the upland-surfaces are so closely intermingled that they cannot be differentiated.

The following articles deal with recent work on this subject:

GEORGE, T. N., British Tertiary Landscape Evolution. *Science Progress*, 1955.

JONES, O. T., *Quarterly Journal Geological Society*, 1952 (Anniversary Address).

LAKE, P., The Rivers of Wales and their connection with the Thames. *Science Progress*, 1934.

LINTON, D. L., Midland Drainage. *British Association for the Advancement of Science*, 1951.

LINTON, D. L., The Origin of the Wessex Rivers. *Scottish Geographical Magazine*, 1932.

SISSONS, J. B., The Erosion Surfaces and Drainage Systems of South-West Yorkshire. *Proceedings of the Yorkshire Geological Society*, 1954.

WOOLDRIDGE, S. W., Upland Surfaces. *British Association for the Advancement of Science*, 1950 (Presidential Address.)

CHAPTER X

RIVER RÉGIMES

Definition of régime. Régime signifies the totality of phenomena relating to the alimentation of rivers and streams, and their variations in outflow. The volume of water in a river may vary much in the course of a year. The relations of discharge to weather, soil conditions, relief, rock-structure, and vegetation are as interesting as they are intricate, and present to the geographer many problems both of practical and theoretical interest. Hydrology, in fact, is in many ways an important link between the physical and human sides of geography.

Measurement of the discharge of rivers. Before discussing the factors governing the régime of a river, let us glance at the problem of measuring the rate and volume of flow. Except in particular circumstances—e.g. a lock or weir when the river is enclosed within an artificial bed—it is impossible to measure the flow with complete accuracy, but there are various ways in which an approximate value may be obtained. The simplest, and often the most practicable way, is to select a stretch of river which for 200 or 300 yards is straight and unencumbered with obstacles. By means of a boat and a sounding line or pole, make a careful cross-section of the river at a suitable place. It may be convenient to make two such cross-sections, 5–50 yards apart, according to the speed of flow: then by means of floats observe the rate of surface-flow of the river over a measured stretch—which may well be the distance between the two surveyed sections. Greater accuracy is possible if several floats are used so that the rate of flow can be obtained near the banks as well as in mid-stream. The floats themselves should be such that they are as little as possible influenced by wind or other extraneous factors—e.g. something that will float so that only a small part of it remains above the surface is best. Having obtained the times taken by the floats to travel between the two stations, and, if necessary, averaged them, all that is required is to multiply the speed (in, say, feet per minute), by the area of the cross-section in square feet, in order to determine the volume passing that particular cross-section in a minute. This method assumes that the flow of the river is the same at any depth. In fact, in any stream, the friction with the bottom and sides slackens the flow, which is in consequence faster near the centre line. There is no fixed relationship between the surface and the mean speed of a river, but in most cases the mean speed lies between 0·7 and 0·9 of the surface speed. The difference is least in shallow mountain streams, and greatest in the deep, slower flowing rivers of the plains.

Better results may be obtained if a sensitive current meter is used. The principle is the same, but the meter will measure the superficial speed as well as the speed at any depth at which it can be held.

Where there is a weir of rectangular cross-section much greater refinement is possible. If the length of the weir or sill is measured, and if also the difference in level between the top (assumed smooth) of the sill and the surface of the water immediately before it falls over the sill is known, a comparatively simple formula gives the discharge (Q) under normal conditions:

$$Q = mLh\sqrt{2gh}.$$

(L = length of sill; h = difference in level between top of sill and water level; g = acceleration of gravity; m = a variable coefficient, but for which the value 0·425 can be assumed for most cases.[1])

There are more precise formulae, but since they are only applicable in particular conditions they need no elaboration here. The geographer is far more likely to have to improvise under field conditions, and if time presses he will have to be satisfied with but a rough transverse section of a river and the minimum number of measurements of the speed at which it is flowing.

Geological factors influencing discharge. The outflow of a river represents only a proportion of the total amount of precipitation falling on the river basin. The effect of evaporation is often great, and naturally varies much with temperature and so with the season of the year. No small part of the rainfall percolates into the ground to reappear as springs, the fluctuations of which often reflect the variation in the amount of rainfall some weeks or even months earlier. Of the moisture which percolates into the ground, a proportion is returned again to the atmosphere by the transpiration of plants. The local and general gradients of the country also have a marked effect on the outflow; other things being equal more water will go directly to the streams in steep country than in low-lying plains.

The evolution of the longitudinal profile of rivers has been discussed in ch. VIII, pt. III, and needs no elaboration here. On the other hand, the transverse section of a river is of considerable significance in the present context. Distinction must be made between the low-water bed, which

[1] A V-notch is more sensitive at times of minimum flow than a rectangular shaped weir, but in both cases the water must fall freely over the weir into the river below. (Another formula must be adopted for the V-section.)

may be narrow and confined within alluvial banks, and the flood bed which may be far wider. In hilly and steep country the two may be the same, except that in floods the water level rises higher, but on account of the steep and rocky sides of the valley is unable to spread laterally. Lakes, especially if of any size, in the course of a river nullify extreme conditions of either flood or low water because they can store flood water and release it gradually.

The plan of a river basin depends on various factors, especially on the structure of the country, and the nature of the rocks. In an earlier chapter examples illustrating this matter have been given. Here, for example, it is relevant to draw attention to the contrast between the numerous brooks and streams in a predominantly clay area, as distinct from the more widely spaced rivers of a region composed of chalk or limestone. Moreover, the plan of a trunk river and its tributaries may have profound effects on floods. If many minor streams in an area of impermeable rocks receive an excess of rainfall at the same time, the floods in the major stream may be serious. The altitude and the orientation of the relief also influence flooding. In general, the greater the relief and the more the hill or mountain ranges lie athwart the rain-bearing winds, the greater the chance of heavy outflows.

The relative permeability of rocks is of the utmost importance. Crystalline rocks—granites, gneisses, schists—and also clays, marls, and certain other rocks are usually classed as impermeable. This may often be the case if the rocks outcrop without any soil or detrital cover. A piece of granite is certainly impermeable, but a granite outcrop is nearly always traversed by joints, and in humid climates its outer surface is much decayed so that sometimes for a considerable depth it may behave like a porous and permeable rock. This is true, *caeteris paribus*, of all crystalline rocks. Certain sedimentary rocks are impermeable in the sense that they do not allow the percolation of much or any water through them, but they are often largely saturated with water. Moreover, their surfaces are probably weathered, often cultivated, and in most regions largely or wholly covered with vegetation. All these factors to some extent encourage the percolation of water, and so prevent, or at least modify considerably, the run-off.

The more truly permeable rocks, including sandstones and limestones, allow the penetration of water, not so much through the mass of the rock itself, but through the numerous clefts and joints which penetrate the rock, often to considerable depths. Heavy rain falling on such rocks may have little or no effect on the surface, but will directly feed the springs (see p. 289) which may suddenly increase greatly in volume. If, on the other hand, the water finds its way to large underground reservoirs, the effects may be relatively small. The nature of karst erosion and the general effects of percolating water have been described in ch. VII, pt. III.

These considerations serve to emphasize the danger of using such terms as permeable, impermeable, pervious, or impervious without carefully examining the region in question. Even a thin clay cover over limestone may completely prevent the development of karst features. In equatorial and other humid regions weathering frequently produces a thick layer of detrital waste (p. 363). While this in itself may be porous, it may nevertheless act as a relatively impermeable layer above permeable rocks. Well-grassed or forested slopes, even in steep country, can hold a great deal of moisture, much of which is returned to the atmosphere by plant transpiration. If the vegetation cover is destroyed, the effects of heavy rainfall may be catastrophic. The results of soil erosion in many parts of the world are too well known to need further emphasis. Not only do the trees and other vegetation disappear, but so also does the detritus, and the rain falling on the bare rock flows directly into the streams, which immediately rise and so lead to serious flooding. The remedy, often a very long term one, depends on reafforestation, but this may be extremely difficult if not impossible if all the superficial deposits have been lost.

Although our interpretation of régime emphasises seasonal variations of discharge, long-term effects should not be overlooked. Fig. 184 illustrates some examples from the United States. The great difference in the run-off per unit area of basin between 24·34 inches in the Tennessee and 1·21 inches in the Red River shows the influence of climate on discharge. Moreover, the variability of discharge from year to year is greatest (*a*) when the run-off is least, since rainfall in semi-arid areas is uncertain and (*b*) where rainfall and evaporation are almost equal, so that a small change in either may produce a big effect in the rivers. The slight reduction noticeable in all four examples shown on fig. 184 is partly due to the withdrawal of river water for irrigation purposes.

Meteorological factors and their relation to river flow. The main meteorological factors influencing the régimes of rivers are temperature, the annual precipitation, its distribution throughout the year, and its nature—e.g. snow, and type of rainfall (evenly distributed, torrential but occasional, etc.). Temperature varies mainly with latitude and altitude, and also with the season of the year. It is a factor of great importance since it very largely controls the amount and rate of evaporation, and evaporation may often have far more decisive effects on outflow than does rainfall.

The seasonal and regional distribution of rain throughout the world has already been considered in the first part of this book. Here attention must be given to the variations in the total annual rainfall that may take place in any region, and also to the different climatic regions which produce rainfall maxima at different times of the year—the Monsoon type,

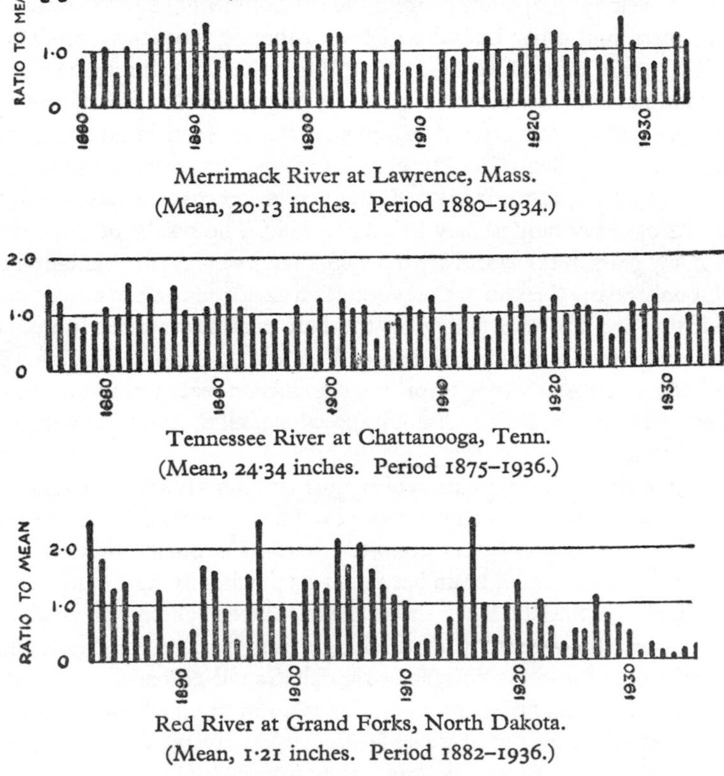

Merrimack River at Lawrence, Mass.
(Mean, 20·13 inches. Period 1880–1934.)

Tennessee River at Chattanooga, Tenn.
(Mean, 24·34 inches. Period 1875–1936.)

Red River at Grand Forks, North Dakota.
(Mean, 1·21 inches. Period 1882–1936.)

Columbia River at the Dalles, Oregon.
(Mean, 11·44 inches. Period 1879–1936.)

Fig. 184. Long period records of run-off in depth in inches over the drainage areas above the river-measurement stations. (0 = no flow; 1·0 = average flow; 2·0 = twice average flow.)

West European type, Mediterranean type, etc. These must be considered in relation to relief and rain-bearing winds. With increase of both latitude and altitude a greater proportion of the precipitation falls as snow, which in its turn leads to the formation of glaciers and ice caps. In temperate climates with high mountains the early summer melting of the winter snows has a profound effect on the rivers, as also does the spring melting of the snows on the great plains of Russia.

Estimates of summer run-off in the eastern parts of the United States and in the western Alps are, to an increasing extent, being based on estimates of winter snowfall. Snow surveys are carried out by direct measurement of snow depths in places chosen for their known reliability for indicating average snow depth over large areas. The density of the snow is also sampled. These surveys are required for hydro-electric and irrigation purposes, but also afford valuable data for flood warnings. The difficulties, however, in accurately measuring snow-depth are discussed on p. 90.

In examining the régime of a river attention must be given to the nature of its basin in relation to rocks and rock-structure, position and orientation with respect to wind and rainfall, altitude, and plant cover. Many rivers with relatively short courses and situated wholly within one climatic area usually show a simple régime, with one period of high water in the year. Others, which are longer and joined by tributaries draining areas of differing climates may have a complicated outflow, or perhaps the variation in the tributaries may be such as to give the main stream, in its lower course, a simple régime.

Types of régime: Pardé's classification. Pardé has given a useful working classification. He distinguishes three main types: simple régimes in which there are, in the course of a year, two hydrological seasons—one of high and one of low water; complex régimes of the first degree, a class which includes rivers with two or more principal and distinct sources of supply; and complex régimes of the second degree, a category comprising those water courses which like the previous type may have two distinct sources of supply in their upper parts, or even a simple régime, whereas further downstream they come more and more under the influence of a variety of factors, some of which may cancel one another because they have opposed effects.

Simple régimes. The first type includes streams fed by glaciers, those influenced by snow melting whether in mountains or plains, those whose main source of supply is oceanic rainfall, and the tropical rainfall type (fig. 185).

When a river rises in a glacier, the period of high water is in the summer when melting is at a maximum. There will also be a diurnal variation, since the melting is most rapid in the early afternoon. Variations will also depend upon altitude, since melting is likely to take place earlier in the season at lower altitudes, thus causing an earlier high-water period. In winter the flow is at a minimum and, largely depending on local factors, there is a gradual increase in late spring and early summer, and a corresponding decrease in late summer and early autumn.

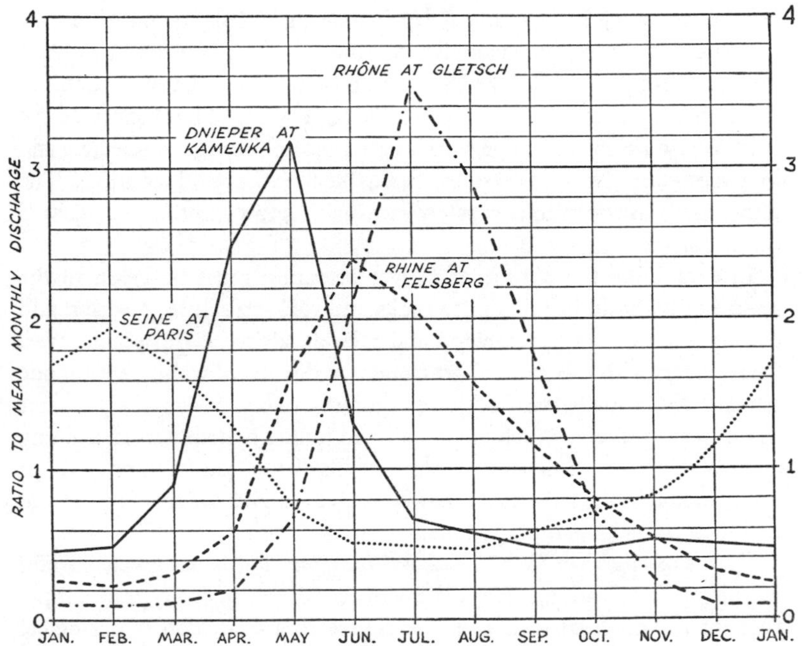

Fig. 185. Simple régimes. . . . ., evaporation-controlled régime with uniform oceanic rainfall; ——, snowfall-controlled régime in the plains; - - - - - -, snowfall-controlled régime in the mountains; - · - · - ·, glacial régime.

Rivers depending for their supply mainly on oceanic rainfall—and in this class are included almost all the rivers of the British Isles and France—show a very different régime (fig. 186). The winter half-year is the time of high water, and often the maxima are in February or March. This winter high water is by no means the direct result of great rainfall at that time. The outflows are, in fact, primarily controlled by temperature which controls the far greater rate of evaporation in summer, even if the rainfall is considerable (fig. 186). Moreover, these streams are often fed by springs, the outflow of which is related to percolation. Because of the slow rates of percolation and seepage, variations in their outflow may be delayed many weeks relative to the variation in rainfall.

The monsoon type of climate also produces summer high water. Despite the considerable evaporation at that time, the falls of rain are so great that rainfall alone controls the outflow. In long rivers, where the

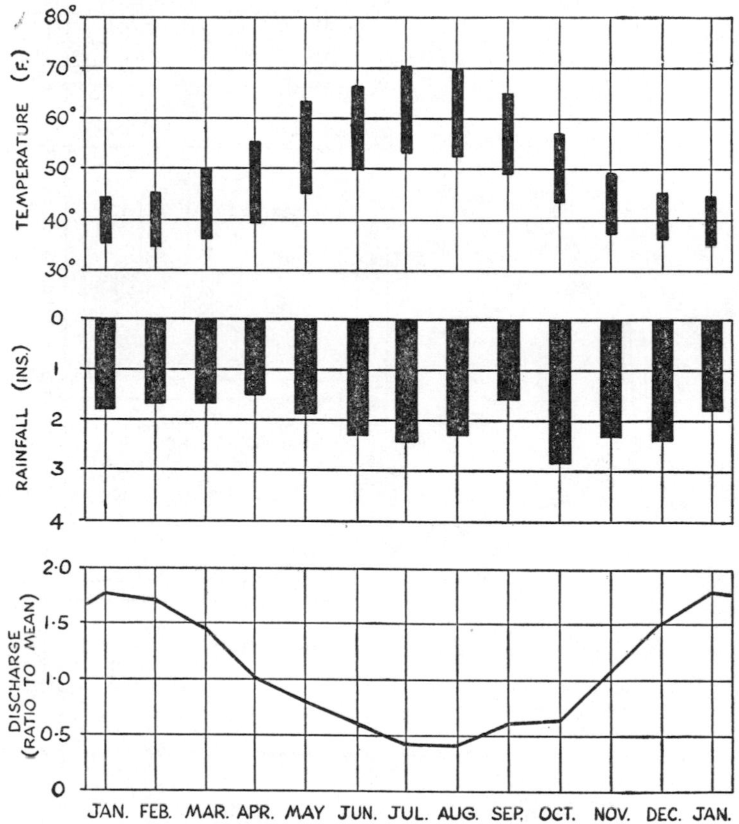

Fig. 186. Monthly temperature and rainfall at Oxford: mean monthly discharge of the Thames at Teddington. In the top diagram the bars show the range between the mean monthly maximum and minimum temperatures.

source of supply is in a climatic region very different from that of the lower parts, there may be great losses due to evaporation. The Nile (fig. 187) and Niger illustrate this very well. There is also a marked dry season in monsoon countries, and at that time the rate of evaporation is also high. In consequence the dry-season flow may fall very low, or even cease altogether.

In mountain areas of temperate latitudes where a good deal of snow, as distinct from glacier-ice, accumulates on the high ground, there is produced a régime in which the maximum occurs usually in early summer, probably June; whereas in the colder parts of the year, the flow may still

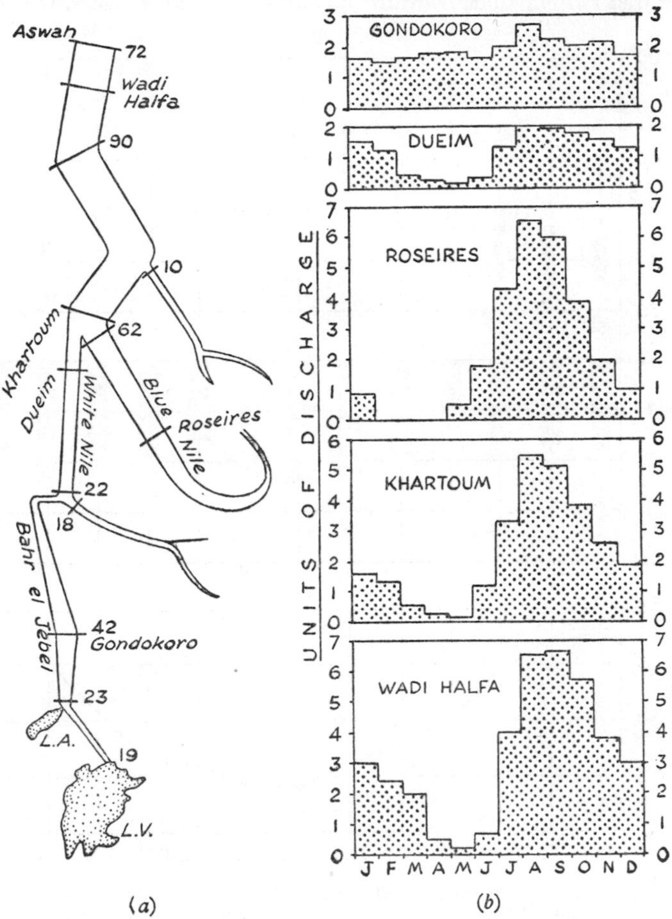

Fig. 187. Discharge and régime of the Nile. (*a*) Mean annual discharge in Km³ (after Pietsch). (*b*) Monthly discharge. (After Lyons.)

be considerable. Rivers of this type resemble those fed by glaciers as well as those fed by oceanic rains. They differ, however, from the great rivers of the Eurasiatic and North American temperate and polar plains. In the U.S.S.R., for example, the winter snows melt in April or May, or even later farther north. Hence in late spring there are severe floods in those rivers which flow slowly northwards and are augmented by the progressively later snow melting in the lower parts of these basins. Rivers of this type also show a minimum flow in late summer as a result of evaporation. This minimum can in some cases fall below that of winter.

Régimes of the first degree of complexity. In the second major class are included rivers in which, for example, there is a spring flood due to melting snow, and later in the year another period of high water. Such a stream therefore shows two distinct maxima and two distinct minima (fig. 188). Examples occur in the pre-Alps and in the Pyrenees. Usually the earlier period of high water is the more pronounced, but in the southern Alps the second is almost equally important, and follows from

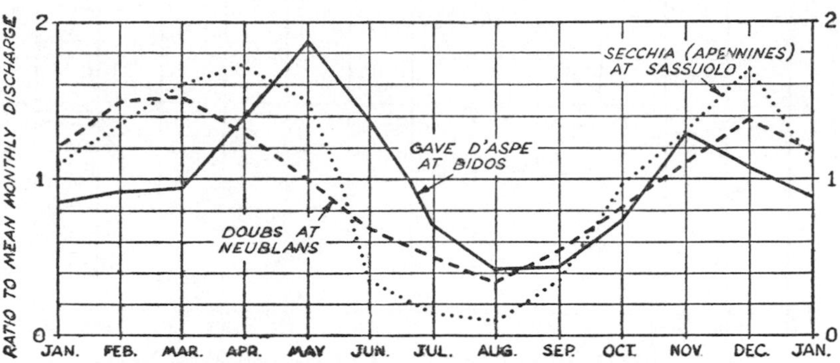

Fig. 188. Complex I régimes. - - - - - -, combined snow and oceanic rainfall régime; ——, combined snow and Mediterranean rainfall régime; . . . . . ., combined snow and Pyrenean rainfall régime.

the violent Mediterranean storms. Another comparatively simple régime of this type occurs near the equator. There the rate of evaporation scarcely varies throughout the year, but the double rainfall maximum produces two periods of relatively high discharge. The reader will realise that the spacing of these two periods varies somewhat with distance from the equator. There are many other ways in which two maxima may be produced, including a combination of early spring snow-melting and continental rains in summer or, as in the Jura mountains, where there is a maximum in April as a result of snow-melting, a marked low-water period in summer because of evaporation, and a high-water period in December produced by relatively heavy rains and low evaporation.

Régimes of the second degree of complexity. The third group is far more complex, and in general applies to the major rivers of the world. Since their basins may cover many hundreds of thousands of square miles, it follows that different parts of the main stream, to say nothing of the major tributaries, may be in quite distinct climatic regions. The Rhine is in its upper parts a river fed by a glacier, but in its lower parts is a river draining uplands and plains and fed by long tributaries from east and west (fig. 189). The Danube rises near the Black Forest and much of its course is in a continental climate, but some of its tributaries are subject to a strong Alpine and others to Mediterranean influences. The régime of the Rhône is complex because some of its tributaries rise in

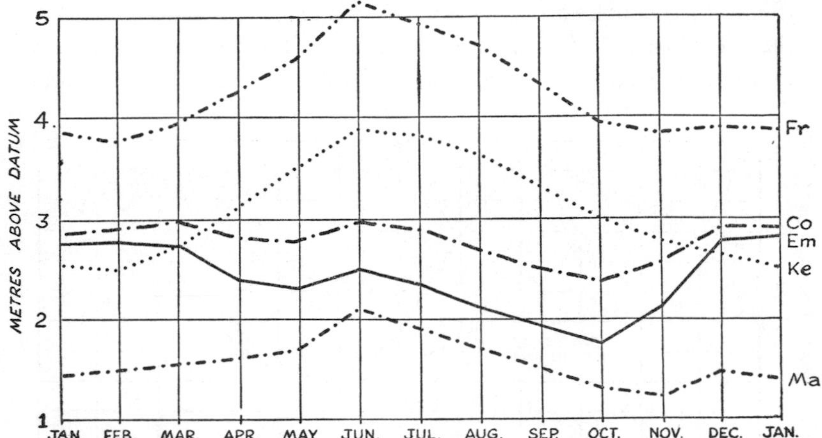

Fig. 189. Complex II régime. The Rhine. Five observation stations are shown. Kehl (Ke), opposite Strasbourg, shows the simple ice and snow régime after the Rhine has left Lake Constance and its Swiss course. Frankenthal (Fr), below the junction of the Neckar, still shows the early summer maximum, with another high-water stage in December. At Mainz (Ma) the December maximum is distinct, and that of June is maintained. Thus, the early winter run-off from the Main and other streams is making itself felt. At Coblenz (Co) the early and later winter run-off is evident, and the summer maximum is far less pronounced. At Emmerich (Em) near the Dutch frontier, the winter effects greatly predominate, but the summer maximum can still be recognised.

glaciers, some are of the oceanic pluvial type, and some belong to the Mediterranean region. Thus we find a simple maximum in July at Lyon, two at Givors in March and December, two at Valence in June and December, and two at Beaucaire in May and November. The régime of the Nile is complex. In its course it traverses the equatorial belt with two maxima, the tropical belt with a summer maximum, and an arid desert. Moreover, the régime is much modified by the Victoria and Albert Nyanzas which nullify extreme conditions, and also by the influence of the Blue Nile with its tropical flood from Abyssinia (fig. 187).

River régimes in the British Isles. A word may be added about the rivers in these islands. Even rivers of the length of the Shannon,

Severn, and Thames are short compared with the major rivers of France, and most of our rivers are very small indeed. All, however, show a marked low-water period in summer. A period of sixteen years of observations (1921–36) shows a minimum in July and a maximum in January for the Severn at Bewdley. For the Thames at Teddington (1883–1917 and 1925–34) the corresponding months are August and January, and for the Shannon at Killaloe (1893–1934) July and January. The Aberdeenshire Dee shows a late autumn and early winter maximum and a marked but lesser high-water period in early spring. If this river may be taken as typical of others in north-eastern Scotland, it suggests that the early snow-melting has a profound effect. In these islands, however, there is also to be noted a marked seasonal variability, and unless a period of observation covering thirty or more years is available, there is relatively little value to be attached to average conditions. The reason for this uncertainty is chiefly the great irregularity of our climate. Evaporation, here as elsewhere, plays a very important part, and is largely responsible for summer low waters, although, in many of our smaller rivers, a heavy storm may, and often does, produce a severe summer flood. The Shannon is noteworthy for its extreme minima. This is partly due to limestones, through which it flows for considerable distances, forming low ground, so that the water with which they are impregnated is subject to evaporation, and partly to the extensive peat mosses acting in much the same way. It is, however, far from certain that these two reasons are a sufficient explanation.

The extreme importance of water-power and of water-resources in general needs no emphasis. But the success of hydroelectric schemes, to say nothing of navigational and other interests, depends ultimately on a comprehensive knowledge of river régimes. Also important are the incidence of floods and the accuracy with which warnings can be given of their approach. In mountainous countries the catastrophes that can follow from a temporary dam, produced by a landslip or by the sudden draining of impounded water through the crevasses of a glacier, are but two examples of the importance of making careful hydrological surveys. The study of rivers, whether from the physical or the human point of view, is always a matter of prime geographical importance.

REFERENCES

MEINZER, O. E. (Editor). *Physics of the Earth:* vol. IX, Hydrology. McGraw-Hill, 1942.

MEYER, A. F., *The Elements of Hydrology*. John Wiley, 1928.

PARDÉ, M., *Fleuves et Rivières*. Armand Colin, 1947.

CHAPTER XI

SNOW AND ICE

Frost and snow. When water enters a narrow cleft in a rock and afterwards freezes, its expansion on changing into ice tends to widen the cleft. If this happens often, a part of the rock may be broken off. The consequence is that in mountain districts projecting crags are gradually broken up, and the fragments are scattered on the mountain side, often forming screes (pl. 11).

This kind of action goes on only in places where the temperature is sometimes below the freezing-point and sometimes above, and the more rapid the alternation the more rapid is the disintegration of the rock. Where, on the other hand, the temperature is always above freezing-point the water never becomes ice, and where it is always below freezing-point the ice never becomes water. It is accordingly on the borders of the polar regions and towards the tops of mountains in other parts of the world that the effect is greatest, and it is there so marked that in some places it is almost impossible to find a projecting point of rock firm enough to afford a hold in climbing.

Snow itself as it lies upon the ground is neither a disintegrating nor a corrasive agent. It may protect the rocks beneath. It is a bad conductor of heat, and acts as a blanket, preserving the ground from changes of temperature. As it begins to melt in the spring, however, moisture soaks through to the ground and in the night this freezes near the edges and where the snow is thin. This thaw-freeze process continues until the snow disappears. Downhill movement of comminuted material is aided because snow that lasts late into the summer kills the vegetation and keeps the soil bare.

This downhill movement or creep leads to a general smoothing of the contours, and rocks projecting through the mantle of debris tend to be rounded off.

If the snow lasts longer in one place than another, as when a greater thickness of snow accumulates in a slight hollow or on a ledge, the comminution by thaw-freeze and the downhill movement act over a longer period. The material is broken up until it is fine enough to be removed by the smallest runnels from the melting snow. In this way the hollow is slightly enlarged each year and eats back into the hillside. A larger snow-drift collects the next year and so the process continues. In time the hollow grows until it can contain enough snow to last through the summer. The next stage is that in which the lower layers turn into ice, and as this increases in thickness movement begins and we have a little glacier. Many ledges, benches, and irregularities in the topography, which appear quite unrelated to present streams, in countries which were once glaciated, no doubt owe their origin to snow-patch erosion or nivation in glacial and peri-glacial times.

The change from snow to ice is assisted by rain and moisture from the summer thaw sinking through the snow and freezing in the lower layers. Quite a thin snow patch, provided that it lasts through the summer, can have ice beneath. The change from snow to ice in a glacier takes place in much the same way though pressure greatly aids the compacting of the ice crystals in this case.

The percolating melt-water produces a rather unexpected and important result. It keeps the whole glacier at 0° C.[1] even though the mean annual temperature of the air may be several degrees below freezing. Spring and early summer melt-water, percolating downwards through the compacted snow or névé on the upper parts of a glacier, freezes and gives out 80 calories per cubic centimetre. This amount of heat quickly raises the temperature of the upper layers of the glacier to the freezing-point although they may have fallen well below 0° C. in the winter.

In the summer the snow melts even on the top of a high mountain, but above the snow-line the total loss by melting and evaporation during the year is less than the amount that falls. If there were no other means of escape the thickness of the snow would accordingly increase indefinitely. But the snow is got rid of in two other ways. If the slope of the ground is sufficiently steep, when the snow becomes deep its own weight makes it slide down rapidly as an avalanche.

Glaciers. If the slope is less the sliding still takes place, but slowly and in a different way. A thicker accumulation of snow can be formed on such a slope. This changes into a kind of granular ice by pressure and by the process of melting and re-freezing, and the whole begins to flow slowly down the hill. As in the case of water, the flow is naturally concentrated in the valleys; and from the snow-fields high up in the mountains tongues of moving ice flow slowly down the valleys as glaciers.

A glacier may extend far below the snow-line. At its origin the supply of ice is comparatively rapid and the melting slow, the glacier is broad and deep, and its section concave upwards, since most snow collects on

[1] A pressure of 500 feet of ice lowers the freezing-point by $\frac{1}{10}$° C. so the ice deep down in a glacier has to be fractionally below 0° C. If it is not, a little melting occurs and the latent heat drawn from the surrounding ice soon cools it down sufficiently for it to remain in the solid state.

the sides of the glacier from the hill slopes above, and also because of faster movement in the mid-parts. As it flows downwards it encounters higher and higher temperatures, and the supply of ice diminishes because some of it has melted higher up. The glacier therefore dwindles in size until it reaches the limit where the supply of ice from above is just equalled by the melting, and there the glacier ends. Glaciers accordingly are usually tongue-shaped, broadest above and narrowest below. A glacier moves most rapidly in the middle, where also the supply of ice is likely to be greatest. Consequently the termination of the glacier is convex.

Rate of movement. The movement of a glacier is most rapid in the middle because at the sides and bottom it is retarded by friction against

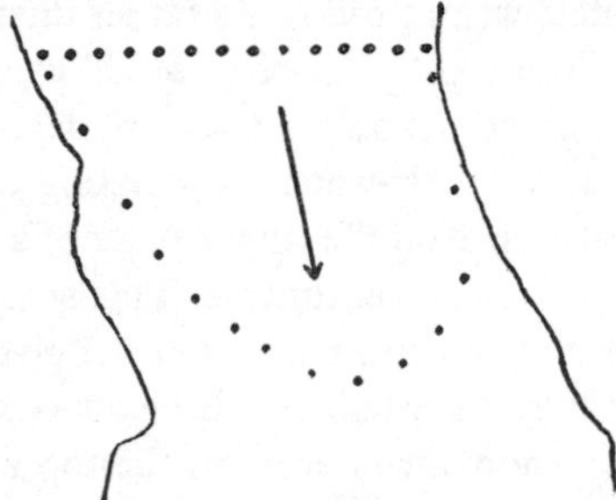

Fig. 190. Movement of a glacier. The small circles indicate the original position of the stakes; the black dots indicate their position after the lapse of a few years.

its bed.[1] If a row of stakes is driven in a straight line across a glacier, they will travel downwards with the glacier; but in the course of a year or two the row will become curved, with the convexity facing downwards (fig. 190).

In the Mer de Glace, J. D. Forbes found that in summer and autumn the rate of movement was 20–27 inches per day near the centre, 13–19½ inches near the side. In Greenland the motion is often much more rapid and in one place a rate of 100 feet per day has been observed.

Crevasses and ice-falls. If the valley of the glacier is uniform in width and has a smooth and regular floor, the surface of the ice is usually even and unbroken. But if the slope of the floor changes, or the valley becomes contracted, the rate of movement is no longer uniform and the

[1] Recent work suggests that only the upper 200 feet thick layer of a glacier consists of fairly rigid ice. At greater depths stress differences may cause the ice to change its state and become more plastic. This lower plastic ice may, on occasions, move faster than the overlying rigid ice. There is need for further investigation in this subject.

surface becomes broken and irregular, just as a stream becomes rough in similar circumstances. If, for example, the slope increases as in fig. 191 the glacier moves more rapidly on the steeper part, and where the change of slope begins, a vertical crack or crevasse forms across it. Down the steep slope the ice is greatly broken, forming what is known as an ice-fall (pl. 15*a*). At the foot, where the slope again decreases, the rate of movement diminishes and the cracks begin to close up.

Crevasses formed in this way are transverse to the glacier, and since they move more rapidly in the middle than at the sides, they become curved like the row of stakes in fig. 190.

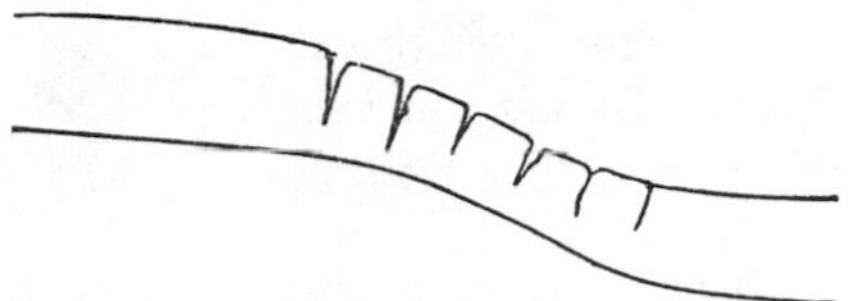

Fig. 191. Formation of crevasses and ice-falls.

But crevasses are not always transverse. If the valley suddenly widens, the glacier in spreading out may develop cracks which are more or less longitudinal in direction.

Even the difference between the velocity in the middle and the velocity at the sides tends to produce cracks. It is evident from fig. 190. that as the row of stakes moves downwards and becomes curved the distance between the stakes increase, especially at the sides. The ice is stretched along the line of stakes, and cracks may be formed across the line obliquely to the course of the glacier.

Moraines. The crags which overlook the glacier are broken up by frost and other agencies and blocks of rock fall from them on to the ice below, and are slowly carried downwards. From every projecting bluff accordingly a stream of blocks stretches down the side of the glacier, and these streams of broken rock uniting with one another form the lateral moraines, one upon each side (fig. 192 and pl. 15*a*). When two glaciers meet, a lateral moraine of one glacier unites with a lateral moraine of the other forming a medial moraine. If other tributary glaciers join them subsequently, there may be several medial moraines (fig. 193).

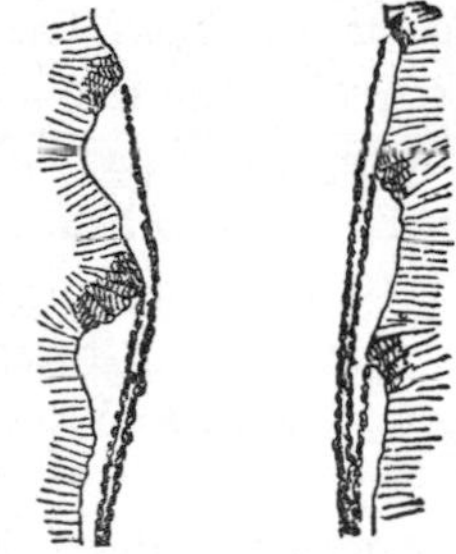

Fig. 192. Lateral moraines.

A block of rock resting on a glacier protects the ice beneath it, while all around the surface may be melted by the sun. The block will then stand on a pedestal of ice; but the pedestal itself will slowly melt and sooner or later the block will fall to one side or another. In a similar way the material of the moraines is slowly spread out and sometimes covers almost the whole width of the glacier. This occurs most frequently in the lower parts of a glacier since there the melting of the ice causes the proportion of morainic material to increase. Sometimes the end is so thickly covered that it is difficult to tell where the glacier ends and the terminal moraine begins. Small stones which can be warmed all through by the sun melt their way into the glacier, thus forming small pits.

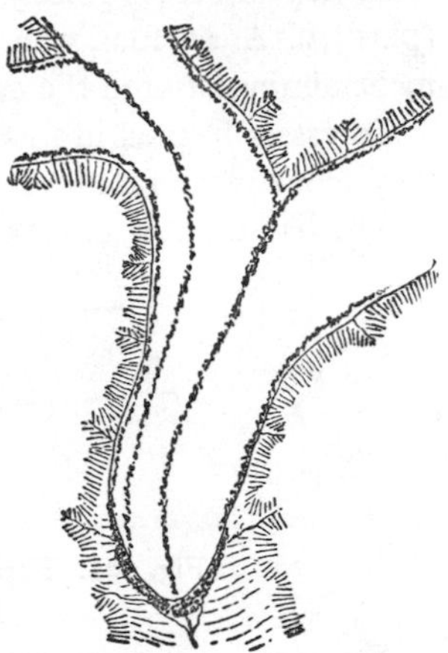

Fig. 193. Lateral, medial, and terminal moraines.

When the superficial material is distributed in patches it protects the underlying ice from the sun and often a series of cones and ridges are formed thinly covered by debris.

When a glacier melts at its termination, all this material is dropped and a mound is formed, called the terminal moraine. It stretches across the valley like a dam, and since the end of the glacier is rounded it is usually crescentic in shape.

The boulders which fall upon the glacier do not all travel downwards on its surface. Often they are engulfed in the crevasses which open beneath them, and they finish their journey either in the middle of the ice or at its base. The streams formed by the melting of the surface also frequently fall into a crevasse, carrying with them the finer material of the superficial moraines. Moreover, the moving ice itself breaks off fragments from its bed. Thus a glacier carries a great deal of material in its midst and at its base and sides as well as on its surface.

The material frozen into the sides and base of the glacier is dragged along by the movement of the ice and rasps the sides and floor of the valley. The finer material acts like sandpaper, smoothing and rounding the surface of the rocks over which it rubs; but the larger fragments cut deep grooves. The fragments themselves are ground down in the process and consequently the boulders carried in the foot of the ice show smoothed or even polished faces, marked by scratches or striations. Sometimes only one side is affected, but in the course of its journey downwards a boulder will usually turn over more than once and several surfaces will be ground down. A glacial boulder, however, is not rounded like a pebble in a river. The ice into which it is frozen prevents it from turning freely. Usually it is dragged along with its longer axis parallel to the direction of movement; the ends are left comparatively rough, the angles are rounded off, and the sides are smoothed, but with the scratches more or less parallel to its length.

At the end of the glacier all this material is set free by the melting of the ice. Some of it is added to the terminal moraine, some is carried away by the glacier stream. There is always a stream flowing from the end of the melting glacier. Generally it emerges from a tunnel beneath the ice. It represents the surface melting which has taken place over the whole of the glacier in summer and over the lower parts even in winter. Very small quantities of ice are melted by heat from the interior of the earth, and also by pressure.

In addition to boulders, the glacier stream is abundantly charged with fine mud and rock flour, produced by the grinding action of the boulders at the bottom and sides of the glacier. For this reason glacier streams are very milky in appearance.

Piedmont glaciers. In the Alps the glaciers terminate before they reach the foot of the mountains. But in colder climates they may flow out over the plains beneath. Sometimes several glaciers unite at the base of a mountain range and form an extensive sheet of ice over the low-lying ground. Such a sheet is called a piedmont glacier.

The width of a piedmont glacier is usually greater than the united widths of the glaciers which form it, and the rate of movement is therefore slow, for the same reason that a river slackens when its channel widens. Sometimes indeed the movement practically ceases; and trees have time to grow upon the moraines that cover the surface of the motionless ice.

The Malaspina glacier in Alaska is one of the best-known examples of a piedmont glacier.

Ice-sheets. When the winter snowfall is sufficiently in excess of the loss by melting during the summer, the snow may accumulate to so great an extent as to bury plains and mountains indiscriminately. There will not then be separate glaciers, each in its own valley, but one continuous sheet of snow and ice, which will flow outwards from its highest point.

This is the case in Greenland, which is almost completely covered by such a sheet. Near the edge the peaks of some of the buried mountains pierce the covering, and close to the sea the ice divides into separate streams with rocky ridges between. But in the interior there is nothing visible but snow and ice.

The greater part of the ice-sheet is free from moraines because no rock rises above its surface, but towards its margins, where projecting peaks[1] appear, moraines are formed in the usual way.

The Antarctic land-mass is also covered by an ice-sheet; but owing to the greater irregularity of the surface and probably in part to the smaller snowfall, the higher hills are not completely buried (pl. 16*a*).

Icebergs. When a glacier enters the sea the ice floats upon the water, and the end of the glacier is buoyed up. It is accordingly easily broken by the waves, and the mass of ice floats off. Occasionally the glacier reaches a cliff overlooking the sea. The ice will still move on, and at intervals the overhanging part will break and fall (pl. 16*b*).

It is in these ways that icebergs are formed. Since the specific gravity of ice is about eight-ninths of that of sea-water, about eight-ninths of the iceberg is below the water and only one-ninth above.

Icebergs bear away with them the boulders and mud carried by the glacier, and when they melt they deposit the material upon the bed of the sea. The Newfoundland banks have probably been formed partly in this way.

Characteristic features of a glaciated region. The Alpine glaciers were once more extensive than they are at present, and even in the last hundred years they have sometimes advanced and sometimes retreated. In recent decades, the great majority of the world's glaciers have retreated markedly. The parts of the valleys which have been beneath the moving ice show certain peculiar features which are easily recognised and which are evidently due to the action of the glacier. Similar features are to be seen in our mountain districts, proving that glaciers once occupied the valleys.

The heads of the valleys, instead of being funnel-shaped like a steep river valley, are rounded and flat-floored resembling a round-backed arm-chair. These cirques[2] are usually perched high up the mountain side, and streams flowing from them plunge down as falls and rapids into the main valley below.

The best way to study glacial action is to visit countries where glaciers exist today. Evidence from such areas suggests that the head-wall of a cirque (fig. 194) is shattered mainly by the freezing of water in cracks in the rock. This water is derived partly from spring, summer, and autumn precipitation on the head-wall, and partly from the melting of much of the winter snow that accumulates in the sheltered angle between

[1] These peaks are called nunatakr.

[2] Cirque is the French term and is widely used. In Wales cwm is used, in Scotland corrie, and in central Europe kar.

the head-wall and the surface of the glacier. Freezing occurs readily where the head-wall is exposed to atmospheric changes of temperature, and where melt-water penetrates to rock which has been chilled by the winter's cold. Glaciers many hundreds of feet thick may insulate the bedrock against such falls of temperature, and head-wall erosion at such depths must depend on other factors incompletely understood. Direct plucking by the ice, helped by the grinding of boulders incorporated in the ice, may be effective if the rock is weakened by joints. Stresses present in rocks such as granites may assist in this all-important initial cracking of the rocks to enable frost-shattering and plucking to proceed. When layers overlying such rocks are removed by any form of erosion

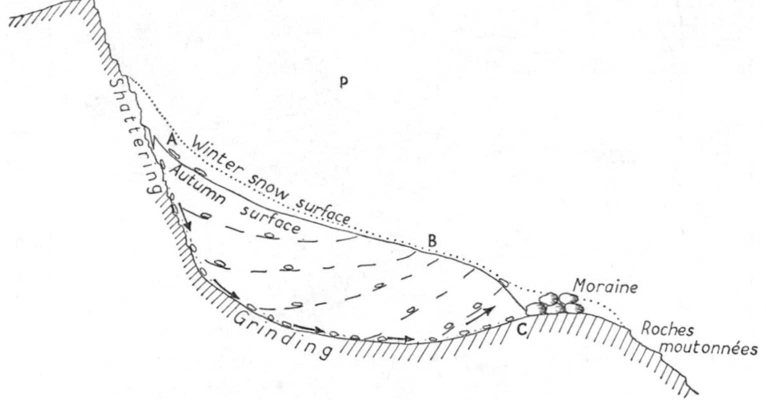

Fig. 194. The movement and erosion of a cirque glacier.

the release of pressure may allow the newly exposed rock to expand and form new joints parallel to surface of the ground. Joints of this kind can be seen in the granite-masses of Dartmoor and the Cairngorms.

The investigation of a small Norwegian cirque-glacier, Vesl-Skautbreen, in the Jotunheim, showed both on the surface and within that it moved primarily by pivoting, as it were, about an axis *P*. The maximum velocity, which was near the bed in the middle part of its course, rose towards the surface at *B*, near the tongue. This form of movement may help to account for the basin, which is such a characteristic feature of cirques. The motive force is the weight of the fresh accumulation of snow near *A* each year, together with the annual loss by ablation which is a maximum near *B*.

Most of the débris derived from the head-wall grinds along the bed, but any that falls on to the glacier, together with the dust that blows on to it in late summer when the surrounding heights are free from snow, travels down through the glacier. The broken lines indicate successive positions occupied by this dust and debris at intervals of, perhaps, ten to twenty years. These annual layers can usually be seen on the lower part of a cirque-glacier where they outcrop.

A similar rotational movement may form an important part of the general ice-movement within a cirque when the glacier is larger and flows out of the cirque into the valley below; it may help to account for the preservation of the step in such circumstances.

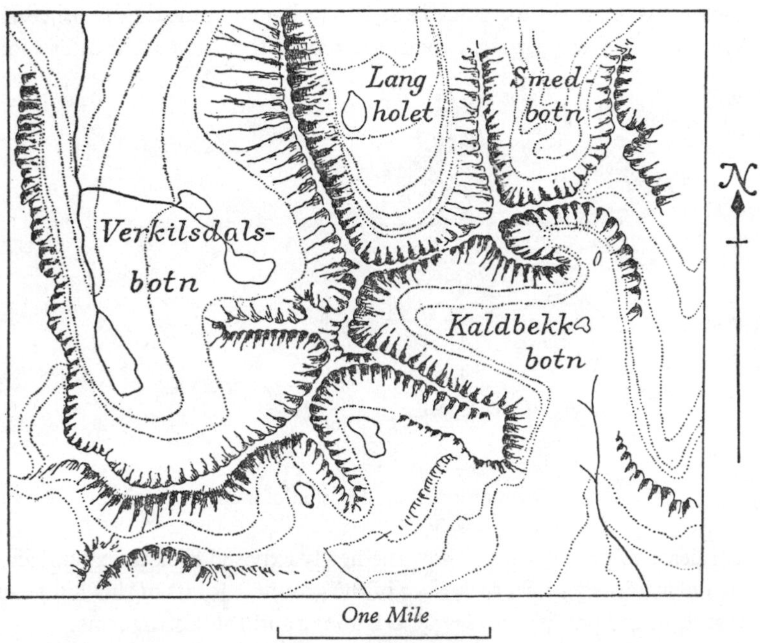

Fig. 195. Pyramidal peaks and razor-edges in the Rondane, Norway.

If a number of cirques eat headwards into a mountain mass the head-walls meet, forming arêtes—razor-edged ridges—which lead upwards to pyramidal peaks (fig. 195). In this way one of the most characteristic features of glaciated mountains arises.

Therefore cirques which may originate as slight hollows high up on the mountain side, or at the heads of river-formed valleys, develop eventually into features which are largely responsible for producing the surface relief of the greatest mountain ranges on the earth (pl. 14).

The floor and sides of glacial valleys are smoothed, and prominent crags are rounded, but the smoothed and rounded surfaces are marked by grooves and striations in the direction in which the glacier flowed (pl. 17*a*). Projecting spurs are sometimes sharply truncated and the valley is straightened (fig. 196).

When a little hill of rock rises up in the path of the glacier it is not usually worn away completely. The side which faces up the valley is smoothed and striated, while the opposite side remains rough and rugged. The side against which the glacier flows is ground down by the stones embedded in the ice, but on the downstream side the glacier pulls away any blocks which may be sufficiently loosened by the development of joints. If the ice is not too thick, thaw-freeze processes might powerfully assist this action.

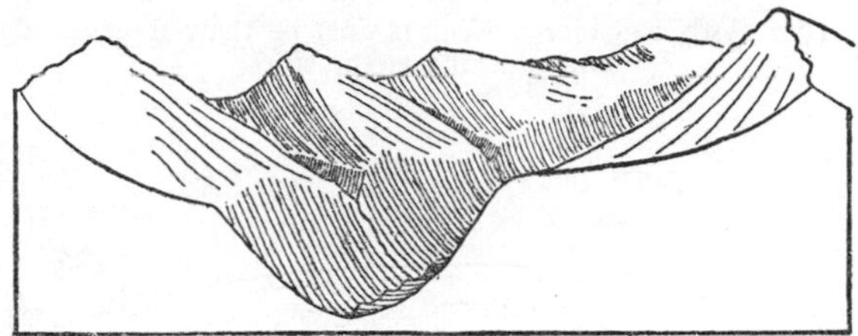

Fig. 196. Truncated spurs and hanging valleys.

Such hillocks of rock, rounded on the upstream side and rough on the other, are called *roches moutonnées* and are to be seen in almost any glaciated valley (pl. 18*a*, *b*). Owing to their form the appearance of the valley sometimes differs greatly according to the point of view. Looking down the valley we see the smoothed surfaces, and all the little inequalities are rounded and convex. Looking up the valley it is the rough sides that we see and the general effect is one of ruggedness.

The origin of some of the characteristic features of glaciated valleys is debatable. It must be remembered that there was usually a normal river-valley along which the ice advanced in the Ice Age. It is therefore difficult to estimate the amount of erosion done by the river and the amount done by the glacier. The typical U-section, however, is probably formed by two actions. The glacier, owing to its great bulk and pressure, wears away a considerable volume from the sides as well as possibly the bottom of the valley, a process aided by water running down the valley sides and melting its way down between the glacier and the rock, and later freezing. This would shatter the valley sides just below the surface of the ice. The thickness of a glacier is also important. A thin one (fig. 197) may do relatively little down-cutting but a fair amount of valley widening by freeze-thaw and removal, whereas a thick glacier, especially in constricted parts of its valley, seems able to do a great deal of erosion of the bed as well (fig. 198).

The frequency of roches moutonnées on the floor of the upper parts of a glaciated valley (fig. 199), suggests that plucking is a potent form of glacial erosion. When the glacier is thin and crevassed this plucking may result from the freezing of water in the cracks in the rock. When the ice

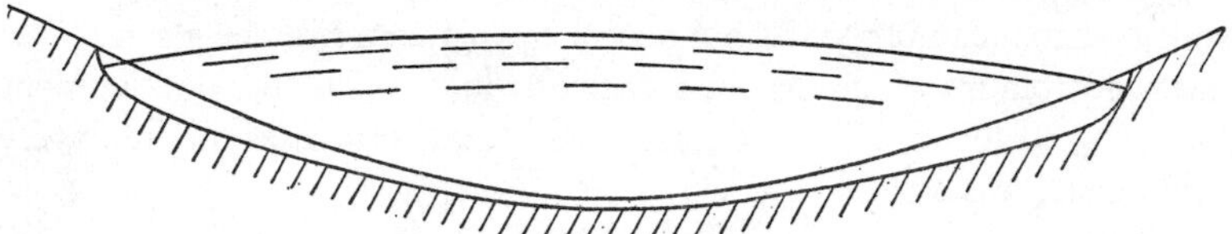

Fig. 197. A thin glacier eroding mainly by thaw-freeze wedging and plucking at the sides.

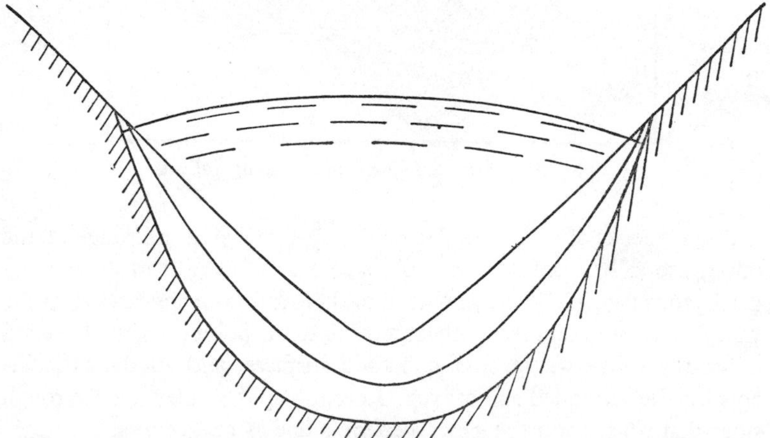

Fig. 198. A thick glacier eroding by thaw-freeze wedging and plucking at the sides, and by grinding, and perhaps plucking, at great depths.

is thick and the rock is jointed, blocks can be dragged away from the vertical faces. Plucking is, perhaps, not an ideal term for this process because the ice ordinarily presses against the vertical faces. The great vertical pressure, and the drag of the ice, on the projecting top of a roche moutonnée, may give rise to stresses which enlarge vertical joints. These stresses may even serve as a trigger-action and help to crack sparsely-jointed massive rocks. However this plucking occurs, it seems to remove more material than does grinding, since the parts of the valley floor subjected to plucking have been lowered most.

In, for example, Glen Nevis (pl. 18) plucked surfaces resembling roches moutonnées occur both on the valley sides and floor, suggesting that plucking helped in widening as well as in deepening the valley. That there was water present when the ice still occupied the glen is indicated by the half pot-holes high up on the plucked faces (pl. 18*b*).

An ordinary glacier need not fill the valley in which it flows, and above the surface of the ice the sides of the valley are worn by other agents. Frost usually plays an important part in the erosion; rain, streams, and above all melting snows, assist. Consequently, when the glacier disappears, the characteristic smoothing and striation reach only to a certain height. Above the former level of the ice the sides of the valley are often very rough, with rugged crags and deep gullies carved by mountain torrents.

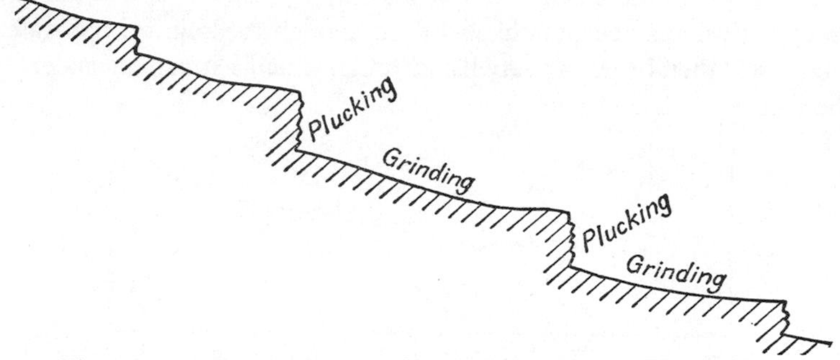

Fig. 199. Roches moutonnées forming a stepped profile near the head of a glaciated valley.

Loose blocks (erratics), often of enormous size, are scattered at intervals along the floor and sides of the valley, sometimes in very insecure positions. Some of these may have fallen from the crags above; but others are made of a different kind of rock, and have been brought down by the glacier. Occasionally they form a definite line upon the hill-side, corresponding with a former lateral moraine. But since the glacier has usually dwindled away very gradually, the position of its lateral moraines varies, and the blocks are therefore more often irregularly scattered (pl. 17*b*).

The terminal moraine is often visible, forming a crescent-shaped mound across the valley. Sometimes there are several terminal moraines, each of them marking a pause or temporary re-advance in the gradual retreat of the glacier.

In places the bottom of the valley may be filled with boulder-clay, a stiff clay with boulders of various sizes, some striated, scattered through it. This appears to have been the material at the bottom of the glacier, deposited in places where the movement of the ice was arrested in somewhat the same way as the sand or mud brought down by a river may be deposited in a sheltered hollow.

Lakes are a common and characteristic feature of glaciated valleys. Sometimes they have been formed by the blocking of the valley by a mass of boulder-clay. Occasionally a terminal moraine serves as a dam to hold the water up; but such a dam, being made up largely of loose blocks, is not always watertight, and is, moreover, liable to be breached by the overflow from the lake. In some cases at least, the glacier has scooped out a hollow in the solid floor of the valley, and the lake lies in a true rock-basin, not simply a part of the valley dammed up by glacial deposits.

In course of time the lake may be filled up by peat and silt, or the outflowing river may cut its channel deep enough to drain off the water. There will then be left a peaty flat, through which a stream meanders to the former outlet.

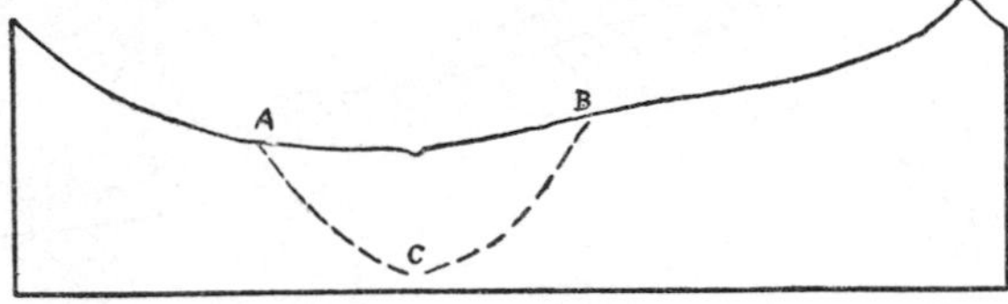

Fig. 200. Formation of hanging valleys by glacial erosion.

In mountain districts the valley of a tributary stream often opens high up the side of the main valley, and below the opening the tributary forms a series of rapids and waterfalls down the slope. Such tributary valleys as these are known as hanging valleys (fig. 200).

Hanging valleys are especially abundant in glaciated regions and apparently therefore glaciers have assisted in their formation. The obvious explanation is that the main valley has been eroded so rapidly that the tributary was unable to keep pace with it. Most authorities attribute the extra erosion to the glacier that formerly occupied the valley. Originally the bed of the main river was at the level shown in fig. 200. The glacier has eroded the part *ABC*, and the tributaries now enter the main valley at the level of *A* and *B*. Some lowering of the tributary valleys, especially if they carried small glaciers, must, of course, be allowed for (see description of pl. 15*b*).

Hanging valleys, however, are not confined to glaciated districts and do not necessarily require glaciers for their formation. If for any reason the main valley is eroded more rapidly than the tributary valleys, the latter will hang to a greater or less extent. If for example the main stream runs along a line of fault its erosion may be very rapid. Moreover, when a waterfall cuts its way backwards and leaves a gorge, the tributaries below the waterfall will enter the gorge at a high level, and for a time at least their valleys will be hanging valleys.

Some observers believe that glaciers are very ineffective as agents of erosion, and if this be true the formation of hanging valleys may be explained in a different way. When a valley is filled by a glacier up to the level *AB* (fig. 201) the sides of the valley beneath the glacier are protected from water erosion, but above the ice they are exposed. Streams will be

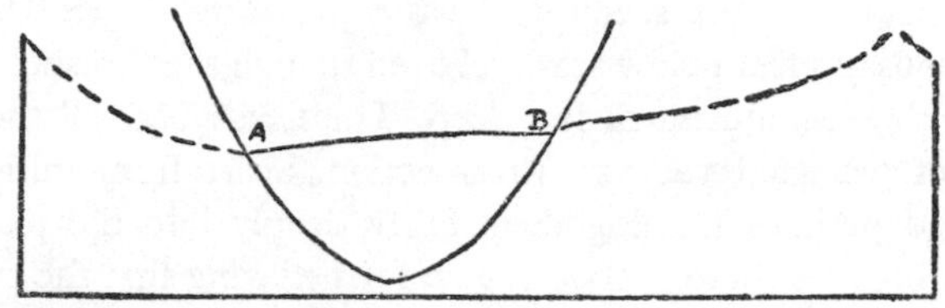

Fig. 201. Formation of hanging valleys by glacial protection.

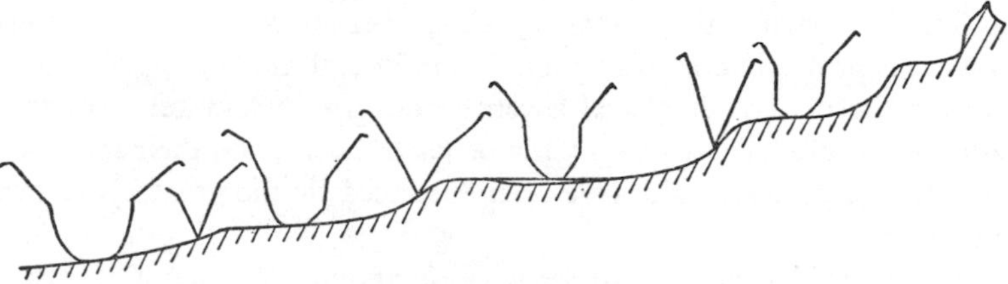

Fig. 202. Typical long profile and cross-sections of a glaciated Alpine valley.

formed on the sides of the valley and will cut backwards producing valleys (as indicated by the broken lines) in the ordinary way. But these tributary valleys cannot be cut below the level of the ice in the main valley, and therefore they open out at that level. When the glacier disappears they will be hanging valleys.

But this is an extreme view and is rarely held today. There is more support for the suggestion that glaciers can erode but are less effective agents of erosion than rivers. Perhaps the strongest evidence that these authorities produce is the existence of V-shaped cross-sections in valleys of the Alps and elsewhere, which once carried great glaciers. A typical glaciated Alpine valley is shown in long profile in fig. 202, to which the cross-sections have been added at significant points on the profile. When the gradient is gentle the section is U-shaped, but when the gradient is steep the section is often V-shaped, sometimes with a tendency to the U-form above the V.

The advocates of glacial erosion do not seem to have paid sufficient attention to these V-sections, an excellent example of which occurs in the Rhône Valley just downstream from Gletsch.

Against this view that rivers are more effective than glaciers as agents of erosion is the undoubted evidence of the little erosion that has been accomplished since the Ice Age by quite large streams in the glaciated parts of Britain, Norway, and elsewhere. One proof of the power of thick glaciers to erode seems to be the presence of great fiords cut several thousand feet below sea-level even though the thresholds, where they join the sea, are much less deep. The fiords bear all the characteristics of glaciated valleys. River action, apart from initiating the valleys and perhaps incising them fairly deeply into the plateaux, is ruled out because there is good reason for believing that the thresholds are of solid rock. Faulting may apply locally as an explanation of fiords, but it leaves unexplained the fact that true fiords are confined to areas which have suffered heavy glaciation.

The V-section noticeable along the steeper stretches of some glacial valleys is probably due to river erosion in interglacial times. Moreover, during the periods of glacial advance powerful melt-water streams in summer would have flowed swiftly beneath the ice, and their speed and destructive power would have been enhanced by the great hydrostatic pressure.

The coincidence between steep gradients and V-sections in glacial valleys certainly suggests a relationship between the two, but does not explain the steep gradients or steps. These probably originate in a variety of ways, but they are so widespread in glaciated mountains that they seem to be a necessary concomitant of glacial valley erosion. They vary greatly in size from large roches moutonnées to steps a thousand or more feet high. The majority can be attributed to hard outcrops, others to valley junctions where the main glacier has cut deeper than the tributaries. Still others—particularly in the Alps—seem due to river rejuvenation heads or nick points which the glaciers have subsequently enlarged and steepened. Others, again, are closely related to narrow parts of the valleys. After passing these narrows, the glacier can scour out its bed, rather like the scouring action in a stream below a mill-dam.

Glaciated lowlands. In the Scottish Highlands, in the Lake District, and in Wales all these characteristic features of a glaciated region are visible, and there can be no doubt that most of the valleys were formerly occupied by glaciers. But even in the lowlands there is evidence of the action of ice. Wide tracts of country are covered with boulder-clay. Here and there large blocks of rock lie on the ground, and these blocks are often entirely different from any of the rocks in the neighbourhood and have evidently come from a distance. In Yorkshire, for example, there are many boulders of granite, precisely similar to the granite of Shap in Westmorland. Such far-travelled masses of rock are called erratic blocks (cf. p. 349).

According to the view which is most widely held, the whole of northern Europe, down to the latitude of the Bristol Channel, was at one time covered by an almost continuous ice-sheet like that of Greenland, and it was this ice-sheet that spread the boulder-clay over the plains and scattered the erratic blocks. Often the boulder-clay has blocked up pre-existing valleys and diverted the courses of the rivers. The Vale of Pickering in Yorkshire is a wide valley running from west to east and opening out upon the coast. It seems to offer a direct and natural route for a river flowing eastwards into the North Sea. But the Derwent rises at its mouth, within a short distance of the sea, flows westwards in the Vale and breaks through the hills that form its southern bank, and finally flows into the Ouse. The mouth of the Vale is blocked by boulder-clay. It was probably dammed up still more by ice, and a lake was formed. The lake overflowed on its southern side, and the outflowing stream cut the channel by which the Derwent now reaches the Ouse.

Similarly the upper Severn, which used to flow into the Dee, was diverted southwards through the Ironbridge gorge. By the time the ice retreated the gorge had been cut down sufficiently for the river to keep to its new course.

The surface of the boulder-clay is very uneven, with low rounded hills and shallow irregular depressions. The depressions are often occupied by lakes. In England the lakes have usually been silted up or else drained by the outflowing streams; but in eastern Prussia the original character has not yet been lost, and the boulder-clay forms a low plateau bearing scores of shallow and irregular lakes upon its surface.

The unevenness of the boulder-clay forces the streams upon it to take tortuous and unexpected courses. Sometimes, too, a river bifurcates and the two branches flow in very different directions. In time these irregularities tend to be removed by the erosion of the rivers themselves, and in England this has happened to a very considerable extent. In Sweden it is not so long since the ice retreated, and bifurcations and other irregularities are more frequent.

CHAPTER XII

WIND

In the British Isles the wind is often violent, and, upon the coast, by producing waves and currents in the sea, it is indirectly the cause of considerable changes in the shoreline; but inland its effect upon the form of the surface is small compared with that of rain and rivers. Nevertheless, even here it transports dust and the finer particles of soil from place to place. The remains of Roman and other ancient buildings are often buried beneath the soil, and the burial is due in part to the action of the wind.

In England, however, the surface is usually covered with grass or other vegetation and it is seldom perfectly dry. The moisture causes the loose particles to adhere to one another, the roots of plants bind the soil together and their stems and leaves protect it from the wind. Only on some of the barer heaths and on sandy shores above high-water mark are the effects of the wind at all conspicuous.

In drier regions it is different. There is no dampness in the surface soil and but little vegetation to interfere with the action of wind; and in an actual desert the wind becomes one of the most important of the agents of land sculpture.

Wind, like running water, transports, corrades, and deposits; but it is different from running water both in its mode of action and in its effects. It has not the power of a rapid river and cannot move such heavy fragments as a river often does; but its strength is independent of the slope over which it blows, and it can carry material upwards as well as downwards. Here and there a turbulent stream may throw sand and mud upon its banks, above the general level of the water, but the upward movement is never more than a few feet. Wind on the other hand whirls the finer particles to great heights, and in desert regions it often blows clouds of dust across a mountain range.

The material carried. The wind can carry with it any loose material which lies upon the surface and which is sufficiently light and fine. In a temperate climate such material may be produced by rivers, by the waves of the sea, or by the ordinary processes of weathering. In a dry climate rivers are generally absent, and the weathering is due mainly to changes of temperature and to dew. The surface of the rock is broken up by the changes of temperature and the wind itself may then assist by causing the smaller pieces to knock against one another. Dew causes decomposition in many kinds of rock and the products of the decomposition are usually soft and powdery.[1]

The fineness of the loose material produced by the weathering will depend partly upon the nature of the rock; but also to some extent upon the wind itself, for as the particles are blown along they hit against one another and against the ground and are therefore broken up still further.

Transport. The power of the wind as an agent of transport is shown quite clearly even upon our own shores. During a gale the wind will often blow the smaller pebbles along the beach, and in gusts it may even move fragments of considerable size. The sand is blown along in a series of hops and the larger particles are rolled along the surface. Each time a grain lands it either bounces again into the air or splashes up other grains. As soon as a grain leaves the surface it is impelled forward by the wind. The sand, therefore, moves forward in a series of asymmetrical

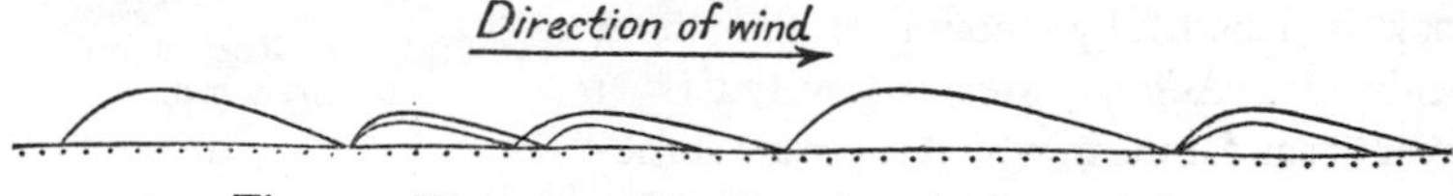

Fig. 203. The movement of sand grains in a wind.

hops (fig. 203). The tracks have been photographed in a wind tunnel by Bagnold whose experimental work has greatly advanced our knowledge of the movement of sand and the growth of dunes. This saltation of the sand grains exerts a great drag on the air, the velocity of which falls off very rapidly as the ground is approached.

The distance to which wind can carry the smaller particles is very great. Dust from the Sahara is often blown into southern Europe and occasionally it even reaches our own islands. The 'red rain' which fell in February 1903 at several places in Great Britain seems to have owed its colour to particles of dust brought from Africa by the wind.

The dust from volcanic eruptions is carried still greater distances, partly because it is very fine, partly because it is thrown high up into the air—well into the stratosphere—where the winds are stronger than on the ground. Volcanic ash from Iceland has fallen in the north of Scotland, and the finest of the dust from the Krakatoa eruption was carried several times round the globe before it settled (see p. 371).

Erosion. The material transported by the wind, like the sand and pebbles carried by a river, becomes an instrument of corrasion wearing

[1] Blackwelder and other workers emphasise the importance of chemical weathering rather than shattering resulting from temperature changes.

away the surface with which it comes in contact. In desert regions the exposed rocks are fretted, the harder bands standing out and the softer bands being more deeply worn. The effect is very well shown in the statue of the Sphinx in Egypt.

Much of this differential erosion can be attributed to sandblast. Since the heavier material is swept along the ground and only the smaller fragments are carried up into the air, the corrasion is greatest near the ground and decreases rapidly upwards. A projecting crag will therefore be gradually cut away at the base. If the direction of the wind is constant, only the windward side will be worn away; but if the direction is variable, the crag will be undercut all round (fig. 204).

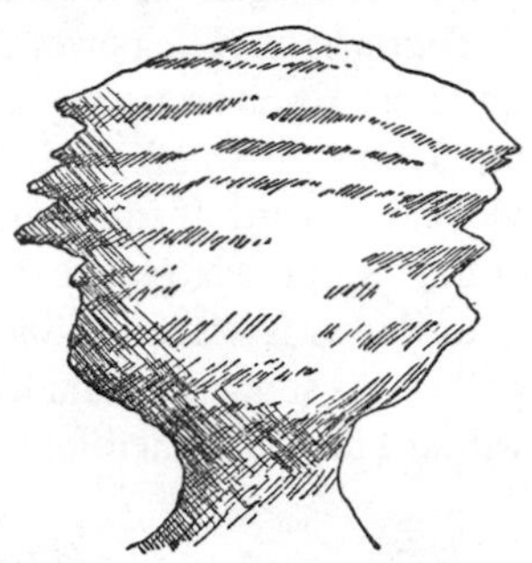

Fig. 204. Rock worn by the wind.

The erosion of a horizontal surface of rock is beautifully shown in the Sinai peninsula. A large area is covered by a layer of sandstone in which there are sometimes many manganese concretions. The sandstone is gradually worn away by the wind, but the concretions are harder and more resistant. They accordingly stand out above the surface, and on the leeward side of each is a little mass of the sandstone protected by the concretion from the wind (fig. 205).

Fig. 205. Wind erosion in the Sinai peninsula.

Wherever the erosive action of the wind is great and deposition small, the solid rock will be laid bare and a rock desert will be formed. If the beds are horizontal, the softer strata will be worn away until a hard layer is exposed.

In the hard rock erosion is assisted by dew, and takes place chiefly along the joints, where the dew is sheltered from the sun. The hard rock is cut through at the joints, down to the next soft bed of rock beneath. By the combined action of dew and wind the hard layer is gradually undermined and falls, until only a few caps are left resting upon pedestals of the softer rock. Finally, even these are completely removed, and the next hard bed is exposed and is eroded in its turn (fig. 206).

Sometimes the erosion proceeds in a different way. The surface of the rock is broken up by changes of temperature and the ground is covered by a layer of fragments, which serves as a protection to the rock beneath. Erosion is not concentrated at the joints, but the fragments continue to break up and the smaller particles are carried away by the wind. Deserts of stones formed in this way occupy large areas in the Sahara and Arabia.[1]

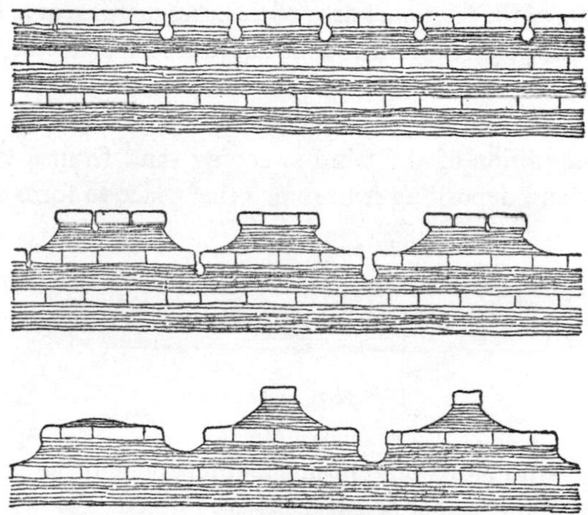

Fig. 206. Stages in the erosion of horizontal strata by the wind. (Cf. also pls. 20, 21.)

Deposition. Sooner or later the material carried by the wind must be deposited. It may be dropped when the wind dies down, and fall either on the land or into the sea; or it may be drifted into a sheltered hollow or banked against an obstacle.

To a certain extent the material is sifted according to its coarseness. The fine dust can be carried by lighter winds than the sand and travels farther. A mountain range is a barrier to the sand, but the dust may be blown completely over it.

Partly on account of this sifting and partly on account of the nature of the rocks which supply the material, there are deserts of sand and deserts of loam. Both are due to deposition and thus are different in their mode of origin from the rock deserts and stony deserts already described, in which erosion predominates. There are, for example, many valleys in South Africa which have been partly filled up by wind-blown sand.

[1] In the Sahara, however, vast areas known as *Reg* or *Serir* are covered by rounded pebbles, probably the remains of sheets of alluvial material laid down by floods which occurred in past periods of greater rainfall.

Sand-dunes often occur isolated in an area otherwise bare of sand, but where sand is abundant they form close together and frequently merge into an undulating surface consisting of a succession of dunes with depressions between. For a dune to form, there may be an initial patch of sand or some other obstacle, or some variation in the underlying bed-rock. The wind causes sand grains to hop along over a rocky or stony part of the desert, but on reaching the patch or obstacle the wind speed drops because of the frictional drag of the sand drifting over it. Thus the wind leaves the patch of sand at a much reduced speed, carrying little or no sand away, so that sand is added to the patch. This addition is continued by winds from varying directions and so we have the apparently anomalous condition of the wind sweeping sand from a large area of stony desert and depositing it in some other place to form a dune.

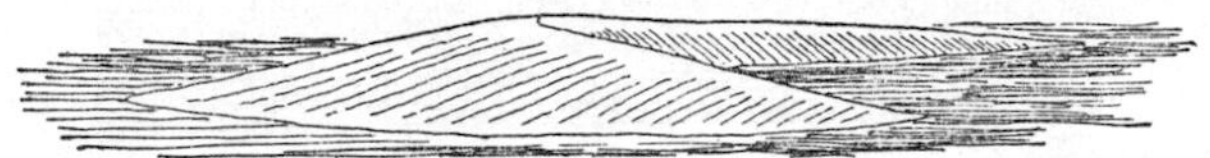

Fig. 207. A barkhan.

When the wind blows only from one direction and the sand supply is adequate crescentic dunes or barkhans are formed. The wind blows the sand not only over the dune but also round it. Therefore the sides of an isolated dune are prolonged as horns in the direction towards which the wind is blowing, so in plan the dune becomes crescent shaped. The sand is blown up the relatively gentle windward slope and falls down the steep, sheltered leeward side forming a slipping cliff. In this way the sand-dune travels slowly forward (fig. 207).

If the winds are variable the dune becomes a shapeless heap and its movements are irregular.

When dunes are crowded, two or more may unite and may lose their crescent shape. In the Indian desert two distinct types of sand-hills are conspicuous. In one type (fig. 208*a*) there is a ridge of sand at right angles to the prevalent wind, with a steep slope on the leeward and a gentle slope on the windward side. But the windward slope is not uniform; it is divided by little valleys into a series of spurs at right angles to the main ridge. Possibly these hills are formed by the coalescence of several barkhans, and possibly each spur may originally have been the windward slope of a separate dune.[1]

[1] It is worthy of notice that many of the smaller hills are horseshoe-shaped and ook like barkhans formed by the north-east monsoon, though it is the south-west monsoon which is the stronger here.

In the other type (fig. 208*b*) the shape is entirely different. Each hill is a long and narrow ridge running in the direction of the prevalent wind. Both sides are steep and the leeward end is also steep. The crest of the ridge rises gently from the windward to the leeward end. It is in fact like an ordinary dune enormously elongated in the direction of the wind. Here and there two neighbouring ridges are connected by a short transverse ridge.

The formation of these elongated sand-hills appears to be connected in some way with the strength of the wind; for they are confined to the western and seaward margin of the desert, where the force of the south-west monsoon is presumably at its maximum.

In the Libyan Desert longitudinal or seif-dunes are sometimes continuous for a hundred kilometres or more. They may occur to the lee-

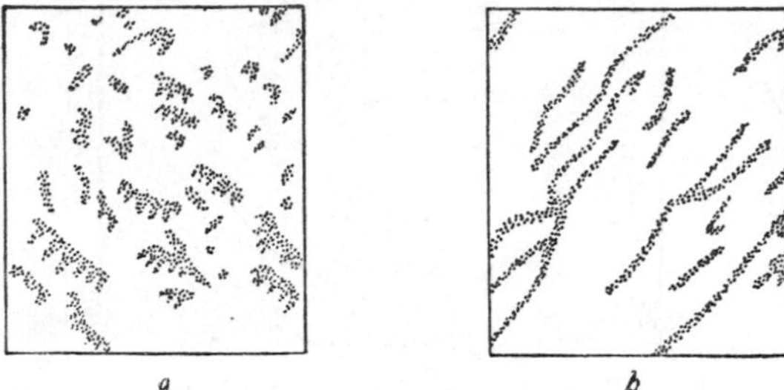

Fig. 208. Sand-hills in the Indian desert.

ward of a gap in the hills through which the wind blows. Parallel series often have bare desert between them. At the crest sometimes one side is steep and sometimes the other, according to the direction of the last cross wind to blow. These dunes form where there is abundant sand and when powerful cross-winds blow from a direction other than that of the more persistent prevailing winds which cause the general drift of the sand, i.e. the wind is not uni-directional as in the case with barkhans. Prevailing winds strong enough to drift the sand have a higher velocity along the bare strips than along the dunes. There is, therefore, a constant tendency for eddies to form and to carry the sand from the bare patches towards the sandy strips. Extensive areas of longitudinal dunes occur in Australia.

On the edge of a sandy desert the forward movement of the dunes has often devastated areas which once were fertile, and in Egypt and Syria ancient buildings and cities have been buried beneath the sand. Even in our own islands the dunes of a sandy shore sometimes encroach upon the cultivated fields; and on the southern shores of the Moray Firth the sand-hills have penetrated a forest, and overwhelmed the once fertile Culbin estate (pl. 19*a*).

In the Landes of Gascony the destruction caused by the advancing dunes became so serious that measures were taken to prevent their movement. Certain herbaceous plants with spreading roots were sown upon the dunes to bind the sand temporarily and to prepare the way for permanent plantations of coniferous trees. The method proved completely successful and the dunes are now fixed.

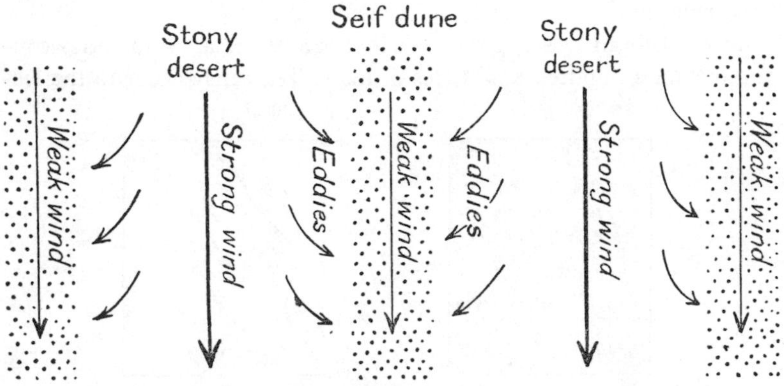

Fig. 209. Eddies from the prevailing wind adding sand to seif-dunes.

Even in actual deserts, however, the movement of the sand is often entirely superficial and the great dunes do not alter their positions. In some cases it may be because the winds are variable; in others it is because the dunes serve as reservoirs of water. Rain is rare, but when it falls it soaks at once into the sand. Evaporation is confined to the surface layers and lower down the sand is more or less moist. Damp sand is not easily disturbed by the wind, and accordingly it is only the superficial sand that moves. The larger the dune the more completely is the water in its depth protected; and thus in some regions the smaller sand-dunes move while the larger ones are practically stable, and dunes which have become fixed by vegetation may subsequently be consolidated by the infiltration of calcareous material, and survive a change of climate. Such dunes, as well as sand-blast pitting, sometimes afford evidence of past desert conditions in areas now humid.

Loess. Desert sand consists mainly of particles varying between 0·02 and 0·8 mm. in diameter. Material of this grade possesses no cohesion when dry, but if the grade falls below 0·02 mm. the grains cling together even when dry. This change of grain size corresponds with that from sand to loess grains, and so this property of cohesion probably accounts, in a large measure, for the very different landforms produced by loess and sand. Although loess grains are easily carried by the wind once they are in the air, they are not readily picked up from a bed consisting entirely of such material.

Loess deposits spread far beyond the limits of the desert regions and eventually come to rest in areas of greater rainfall and more abundant vegetation. Extensive deposits occur in Central Europe, China, and America, where the rainfall is fairly abundant. But the remains of animals found in the loess suggest that it was formed when the climate was drier than it is at present.

In China, where the deposit is of enormous extent and thickness, the loess is a fine calcareous loam, yellowish or buff in colour. It is penetrated by innumerable vertical and very narrow tubes, probably produced by the rootlets of the grass which grew upon the surface while the deposit was forming. The loess is still soft, and deep valleys have been cut in it by streams. Since it is very porous the rain sinks quickly into it, and the surface is dry. Partly for this reason and partly because the loess breaks most readily along the vertical tubes, the sides of the valleys are often almost vertical or rise in a series of precipitous steps.

Somewhat similar deposits occupy many of the depressions between the mountain ranges of central Asia. In general where there are no rivers the surface is nearly level, but towards the mountains it rises gently, frequently extending high up the flanks of the ranges.

The deposits in Europe extend from west to east over the north European Plain between the great end moraines of the Baltic Heights and the mountains of central Europe. It is a fertile deposit and greatly aids agriculture, but it is not thick enough, nor is the climate suitable, to give rise to the characteristic landforms of the loess of China. It consists of the finest material ground down by Quaternary glaciers and washed out by glacial streams. Later, when steppe conditions prevailed, it was re-sorted by the wind before being finally deposited. A separate deposit of loess was laid down in each of the inter-glacial periods of the Quaternary Ice Age.

CHAPTER XIII

INFLUENCE OF CLIMATE UPON TOPOGRAPHICAL FEATURES

Climatic zones. The shapes of hills and valleys are determined to a very large extent by the agents of denudation which are at work upon them, and the nature of these agents depends mainly on the climate. Where, for instance, rain is frequent, denudation is due chiefly to water; where rain is rare, wind and changes of temperature are of far greater importance. Consequently, the topographical features of a country are greatly influenced by its climate.

It will be useful therefore to consider briefly the general processes of earth sculpture from the geographical point of view; and for this purpose the globe may be divided into regions according to temperature and rainfall, as follows:

Equatorial zone and the monsoon regions. Temperature high; rainfall heavy.

Tropical dry regions. Temperature high: rainfall small.

Temperate zones. Temperature moderate; rainfall moderate.

Polar regions. Temperature low; precipitation mainly in the form of snow.

But no sharp boundary can be drawn between these regions. Moreover, the temperate zones, in particular, are far from uniform in character. They include areas of very low rainfall, while in the mountainous districts the rainfall may be excessive; the average temperature is always moderate, but the range of temperature may be very small or very great.

Earth sculpture in temperate zones. In temperate regions whereever there is at least a moderate rainfall the greater part of the work of erosion is carried on by rivers. Weathering is due partly to the chemical action of water, with carbon dioxide, and other substances in solution, partly to the mechanical action of frost. Where the former predominates the rocks decay and rounded surfaces are produced; where the latter is more important, angular fragments are broken off and rugged crags are common. In either case the loose material is carried downwards by running water and finds no permanent resting-place until it reaches the sea. The valleys are river-valleys and, even on a hill-slope where there is no actual stream, it is chiefly running water, during showers of rain, that washes down the soil and weathered rock. Thus not only the valleys but also the sides of the hills usually show the curve of water erosion; and this is the most characteristic feature of a temperate climate. The hills rise gently from the plains and the slope increases gradually towards their summits. In the lowlands, where chemical weathering prevails, the hill features are smoothed and rounded off; but in the mountains, where frost plays a more important part, jagged summits and rugged slopes are frequent (pls. 14, 15*a*).

Earth sculpture in tropical dry regions. In a tropical desert water is generally absent. There is no vegetation to hold the soil together and wind accordingly becomes the principal agent of transport and erosion. The breaking up of the rocks is due mainly to changes of temperature and there is but little decay. The broken fragments are therefore angular, and the hills, unless they are made of some soft rock like shale, are rugged. They often rise abruptly from the plain whether it is one of deposition or of solid rock. The abrupt angle between plain and hill is characteristic, but not fully explained. The loose material is carried downwards by gravity, by the wind and by occasional storms of rain; but there are no rivers to bear it to the sea, and it collects in the depressions and gradually fills them up. The lower hills may be completely buried, and only the tops of the higher ranges may be left uncovered. The loose material is still further broken up by changes of temperature and distributed by the winds, and forms extensive plains, diversified by sand-dunes. The curve of water-erosion is seldom seen, and the characteristic features are wide plains of broken rock or sand or loam, with hill ranges rising abruptly like rocky islands in a sea. (See pls. 20 and 21 which illustrate four successive stages.)

Earth sculpture in the equatorial zone. In equatorial regions the rainfall is excessive and the vegetation luxuriant. The temperature is high and uniform. On account of the warmth and moisture, together with the acids produced by the decomposition of dead leaves and plants, decay of the rocks is rapid, and the depth of the soil, or covering of weathered rock, is usually great. The most prominent parts, because they are the most exposed, decay most quickly and all angularities are rounded off. Owing to the dense growth of vegetation the loose material is not easily removed; and in spite of the presence of running water, the hills very commonly show the convex shape characteristic of chemical weathering.

Earth sculpture in polar zones. In polar regions there is no running water except in the height of summer. There is no decay of the rocks, but the rocks may be broken up by changes of temperature or at certain seasons by frost. Owing to the absence of vegetation the wind may become an important agent of denudation. Therefore, in many respects the topographical features are often not unlike those of a tropical desert. The hills are equally abrupt, without any well-marked curve of water-erosion, and on the lower-lying ground there may be the same accumulation of loose material.

Much, however, depends upon the amount of snow. Where the snowfall is heavy, as in Greenland and Spitzbergen, the whole region may be covered by an ice-sheet, or glaciers may descend from the mountains to the coast. Much of the loose material is carried away to sea, and the topographical features, concealed beneath the ice, must be those of a glaciated region. Any peaks, however, which may pierce the covering of snow and ice, show the jagged summits and angular outlines characteristic of the action of frost (see pls. 16*a*, *b*).

General observations of earth sculpture. Thus each of the four chief types of climate has its own characteristic topographical features; but the typical forms are liable to modification. A resistant rock will always tend to project, and may form steep slopes and rugged crags in the wettest of regions. A rock that allows the rain to sink rapidly into it may show little indication of the curve of water-erosion even in a temperate climate, and may present some of the features of a desert region. The flat-topped hills of Egypt are very different from the rugged ranges of Baluchistan though both show the abrupt slopes of a region destitute of water. In the former the strata are horizontal, in the latter they are strongly folded. Glaciers and glaciated valleys occur in the higher mountain ranges of low latitudes, and in the north of Europe and America even the lowlands still retain the features impressed upon them by their former Arctic climate.

It should perhaps be added that much of the temperate zone, as the term is usually understood, has a far from temperate climate. It includes, in central Asia, some of the largest deserts in the world and in north-eastern Siberia the most extreme climate known. In the former the topographical features are naturally those of a desert; in the latter they are to a large extent those of a polar climate with a small snowfall, but modified by the presence of rivers.

CHAPTER XIV

VOLCANOES

Condition of the earth's interior. In mine-shafts and well-borings the temperature usually increases with the depth. The rate of increase is far from uniform but a large series of observations gave an average rise of about 1° F. for each 64 feet of descent. How far downwards the increase continues is still uncertain, but if it is maintained unchanged the temperature of the interior of the earth must be above the melting-point of any of the rocks of the earth's surface.

These and other considerations led the earlier geologists to conclude that the interior must be liquid and that the solid crust is a comparatively thin layer floating upon the molten mass. But in the interior of the earth the pressure must be great, owing to the weight of rock above, whether this rock is solid or liquid; and increase of pressure raises the melting-point of most kinds of material. The behaviour of the earthquake waves suggests that the deep interior has certain important properties of a liquid. But, in the main, the earth behaves as if it were solid.

The strongest argument in favour of the solidity of the earth is derived from the tides. If the interior of the earth were liquid it would be affected by the moon in much the same way as the waters of the ocean, and the outer crust would yield to the movements of the molten material beneath. If it yielded as much as the water does the tides would probably be imperceptible; and if to a lesser extent, the apparent height of the tides would be reduced by the amount of the movement of the crust. From the heights of the tides as actually observed, it has been calculated that the amount of yielding is very small, and that the earth as a whole is as rigid as a solid ball of steel of the same size. The natural inference seems to be that by far the greater part of the interior is solid.

It is, however, certain that molten rock or lava rises at times from below and is poured out over the ground; and beneath the surface there must be reservoirs of molten rock or else of rock which melts when the pressure upon it is removed.

Formation of volcanoes. Volcanoes are formed by the escape or attempted escape of this material. It is possible that water percolating through the crust comes into contact with the molten or potentially molten rock, and the sudden conversion of the water into steam forces the lava upwards and causes the eruption. In support of this view it has been pointed out that most volcanoes are situated near the sea, and that volcanic eruptions are generally accompanied by the emission of enormous clouds of steam.

Another and more likely suggestion is that release of pressure due to earth movements is the primary cause of the eruption of the molten material, and certainly volcanoes are most abundant in regions where earth movements are proceeding. The heat and continued activity of a volcano are due to the chemical reactions produced by the more volatile gases which rise to the top of the magma or molten material. Further heat may result from reactions between the magma and the rocks forming the crater. The whole question is one of great complexity and cannot be discussed more fully here.

A typical volcano is a conical hill, from the top or sides of which eruptions take place at intervals. The hill is the product of the eruptions. It is formed of the material thrown out, which is naturally deposited most thickly near the outlet and less thickly at a distance (pl. 24*b*).

In most volcanoes there is a funnel-shaped hollow at the top of the cone, and this hollow is called the crater. The bottom of the funnel opens into the channel or pipe through which the erupted material finds its way to the surface. When the volcano is not in action, the pipe is usually plugged by solidified lava or by fragments which have been thrown up into the air and have fallen back into the crater (pl. 24*a*).

Sometimes an eruption takes place in the sides of the volcano and forms a secondary or parasitic cone with a crater of its own.

Products of eruption. The material thrown out during an eruption may be solid, liquid, or gaseous.

It is generally believed that the great masses of cloud which rise from an erupting volcano consist mainly of condensing steam; but this is not always so, and according to M. Brun the clouds emitted during eruptions in Java and elsewhere contain no more water-vapour than the surrounding air. He believes that they consist chiefly of ammonium chloride.

There can be little doubt, however, that water-vapour is sometimes present in enormous quantities. Volcanic eruptions have frequently been followed by deluges of rain, and the rain appears to be formed by the condensation of the vapour emitted from the volcano, together with atmospheric moisture precipitated in the powerful convection currents produced by the heat of the volcano. A thorough examination of the clouds sent out during an eruption is impossible.

Amongst other gases which have been detected in considerable quantities hydrochloric acid, sulphuretted hydrogen, sulphur dioxide, hydrogen, and carbon dioxide are perhaps the most important. Inflammable gases such as hydrogen and some of its compounds are occasionally in sufficient quantity to produce actual flames; but in most eruptions the appearance of flaming at the top of the cone is caused chiefly by the red-hot fragments thrown up into the air and the reflection of the glowing lava upon the rising column of cloud.

The gases issuing from a volcano are for the most part dissipated into the air and have little effect upon the volcano itself. They may, however, act chemically upon the rocks in the neighbourhood of the channel through which they escape, or they may produce by their reactions with each other deposits of sulphur and other minerals in and near the crater.

The liquid products of the eruption are of much greater importance. They consist of molten rock and form the streams of lava (pl. 22*b*) which flow out of the crater or out of fissures in the side of the volcano. Some lavas contain a high proportion of silica and are said to be acid; in others the percentage of silica is comparatively low and these are known as basic. Acid lavas have a high melting-point and are usually very viscous, and therefore they flow slowly and do not travel far. Basic lavas melt at a lower temperature and are generally very liquid; and a basic lava stream moves rapidly and may flow for many miles before it solidifies.

Sometimes the surface of a solidified lava is smooth; but more often it is very rough. If the lava is viscous, the surface becomes ropy like that of a stream of flowing pitch. Frequently, too, both in acid and basic lavas, escaping gases make the upper layers of the stream vesicular or full of little holes, like a piece of bread. Moreover, the outer surface cools and solidifies first, forming a crust, which is continually being broken up and carried forward by the moving stream beneath. The fragments of the crust, if they are vesicular, are known as scoriae.

Consequently, a lava-flow of recent date has usually a very rough and irregular surface, and its upper layers are full of holes and crevices into which the rain can penetrate. Partly for this reason weathering is rapid, and often produces a covering of rich and fertile soil.

In some volcanoes the liquid lava wells up quickly, filling the crater and overflowing without any great disturbance. But most eruptions are accompanied by explosions, which are often violent. In such cases vast quantities of broken rock are thrown into the air and fall back into the vent or cover the country around. At the birth of a volcano the fragments are pieces of the rock through which the pipe of the volcano passes; but at a later stage they are for the most part fragments of lava. The solidified lava that commonly plugs the channel of a quiescent volcano must be blown out before the molten rock beneath can rise into the crater. Sometimes the whole top of the hill is blown off by the explosion and sometimes an entirely new channel is opened on the sides. No doubt, too, in many cases there has been partial solidification in the molten reservoirs beneath, and the solidified rock is thrown out during the explosion.

In most eruptions, therefore, a large amount of fragmental solid material is ejected, and showers of dust and stones fall over the surrounding area. The larger pieces form breccia, a name applied to deposits of large and angular fragments; the smaller pieces are known as cinders or volcanic ash, or, if the material is very fine, volcanic dust.

The liquid lava may also be blown into the air and may solidify in drops before it reaches the ground. Volcanic bombs are masses of lava which have been thrown out in this way in a more or less liquid condition, and have assumed a rounded or pear-shaped form as they fall.

Owing to the torrential rains which sometimes accompany an eruption the volcanic dust may be washed down as a stream of mud, causing as much destruction as a flow of lava. In the great eruption of Vesuvius in A.D. 79, Herculaneum was overwhelmed by a stream of volcanic mud which has since become compacted into solid rock.

Forms of volcanoes. The form of a volcano depends largely upon the material of which it is composed.

In some cases there is nothing but a cavity produced by the explosion and around it a ring-shaped mound consisting of the fragments of rock thrown out. *Crater rings* of this type, with a small lake within the hollow, may be seen in the Eifel district.

More often the fragments of rock and lava are piled up till they form a hill of considerable size. Naturally the accumulation is greatest immediately round the vent and gradually decreases outwards, and a volcano formed in this way is conical in shape. Successive eruptions deposit layer after layer of ash on the sides of the cone, and thus on the flanks of the volcano the beds dip outwards. But in the crater itself the ash falls inwards, forming beds which dip towards the centre.

Volcanoes of this type, consisting entirely, or almost entirely, of fragmental material, are known as *ash* or *cinder cones* (fig. 210). In shape they are often almost perfect cones, but the cone spreads out towards the base so that in profile the sides are curved instead of straight (pl. 23*a*). The curve is concave upwards and is remarkably like the form produced by water-erosion. Near the vent the coarse fragments are piled so thickly that the cone slopes at 30–40°, i.e. at the steepest angle at which such loose material can come to rest; and fragments falling at the top or on

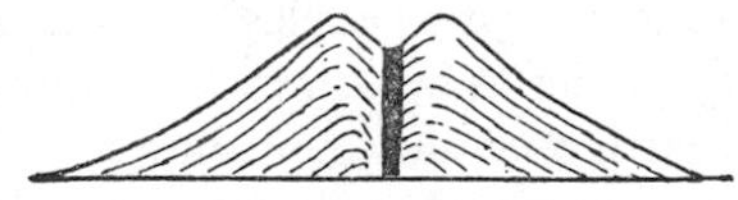

Fig. 210. Ash cone.

the sides roll down the slope. Farther away from the vent the accumulation decreases and the hill is formed, not of fragments which have rolled down the sides, but of the material which has been thrown outwards from the volcano and has fallen from the air.

If a strong wind blows during an eruption, the cinders or ashes will fall more thickly on the leeward side of the vent and the cone will be unevenly developed. Unsymmetrical volcanoes may be formed in this way in regions where the winds are constant; or even where the winds are variable, if the cone is due to a single eruption.

Volcanic eruptions, however, are not always explosive. In some volcanoes, called *lava volcanoes* (figs. 211, 212), the lava rises slowly and is poured out quietly. Puffs of gas and vapour may escape from the molten rock, but they cause very little disturbance.

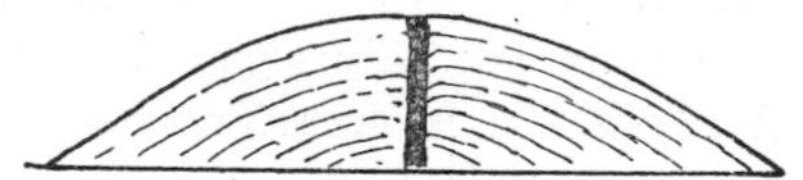

Fig. 211. Acid lava volcano.

Fig. 212. Basic lava volcano.

When this is the habitual type of eruption there are no fragmental deposits and the volcano is formed entirely of streams of lava. Such volcanoes are usually dome-shaped rather than conical, but the form of the dome varies according to the nature of the lava.

If the lava is acid and viscous it behaves like a mass of paste squeezed through an opening, and the dome is very convex, with steep sides and often without a crater (fig. 211).

If the lava is basic and fluid, it flows readily and for great distances. The diameter of the volcano is therefore great but the slope of its sides is gentle, and the form is that of a very flat dome. The crater is simply the hollow left when the lava in the pipe subsides (fig. 212).

Mauna Loa and Kilauea in the Hawaiian Islands are excellent examples of lava volcanoes. Mauna Loa is 13,675 feet high, but the angle of slope is only about 6°. Kilauea is about 4040 feet and lies upon the flanks of Mauna Loa. It is not, however, a subsidiary cone receiving its lava from the same source, for eruptions in Mauna Loa cause no disturbance of the liquid lava which is always visible in the crater of Kilauea, nearly 10,000 feet below. Kilauea must be an independent volcano which has been partly overwhelmed by the flows from Mauna Loa.

In both volcanoes the crater is a broad and relatively shallow pit with vertical sides and a terraced floor. On the lowest platform in the crater of Kilauea there are lakes of very fluid lava, constantly boiling. Now and then a crust forms on the surface for a time, but soon breaks up and is engulfed. The floor of the crater is itself a thicker crust resting upon the lava in the pipe, and the lakes are really holes in this crust through which the lava appears. The level of the floor is not always the same, but rises and falls with the lava in the pipe.

Outflows of lava may take place either from the crater itself or from the sides of the volcano. But even in the latter case there is as a rule no violent explosion. The lava appears to melt its way quietly through the rock, until it reaches the open air. In this respect lava volcanoes of this type are very different from such volcanoes as Vesuvius and Etna.

The great volcanoes are generally *composite volcanoes*, consisting partly of ash and partly of lava, in irregularly alternating beds. In the early stages of their growth, the form is conical, as in a simple ash volcano; but the shape is usually not so perfect, because the streams of lava flow out unevenly. As the height of the volcano increases, the column of lava in the central channel is compelled to rise higher and higher to reach the crater. The pressure that it exerts upon the walls of the channel increases until at length it is easier for the lava to force its way through the sides of the hill than to rise up to the crater. In large volcanoes, therefore, the streams of lava usually issue from fissures in the flanks, and subsidiary cones are often formed (pl. 25*a*).

Volcanic eruptions. If a volcano has remained quiescent for a long period, the channels through which the lava escaped become choked either by solid lava or by fallen fragments. When the next eruption occurs, the old channels must be cleared or new ones must be opened. Usually the pressure inside increases until at length there is a violent explosion. The top of the hill may be blown off, or the explosion may occur upon the flanks. In either case a gigantic cavity is formed, and in the middle of this a new cone may be piled up. The large cavity is sometimes known as a caldera.

The history of Vesuvius illustrates these changes. In the time of the Romans the mountain had the form of a truncated cone with the top hollowed out into a great amphitheatre (fig. 213*a*). There were then no records of any eruptions; but presumably the top of the cone had been blown off in some prehistoric explosion. In A.D. 79 the volcano again became active and a great explosion destroyed half the wall of the amphitheatre (fig. 213*b*), and buried Pompeii and Herculaneum in volcanic ash and mud. The other half of the wall still stands as a semicircular ridge, while in the midst of the broken hollow a new cone has since been built up with a crater at its summit (fig. 213*c*). The semicircular ridge round one side of the new cone is called Monte Somma.

In Etna a similar explosion must have occurred at some very early date, probably before the appearance of man upon the globe. It was not the top of the hill, however, that was blown off, but a portion of the side, and an immense hollow, now known as the Val del Bove, was formed on the flanks of the volcano.

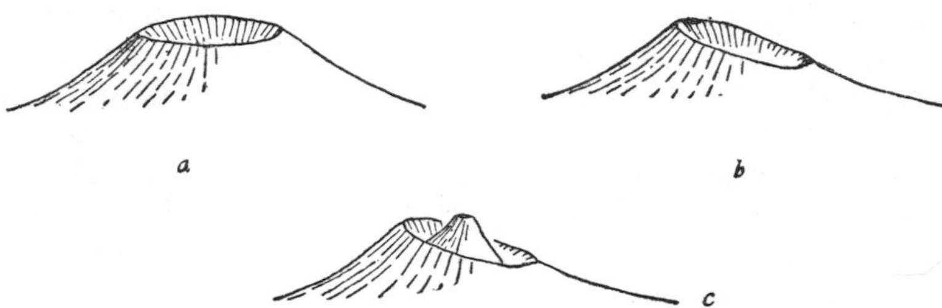

Fig. 213. Stages in the history of Vesuvius. *a*, probable shape before A.D. 79; *b*, shape after the eruption of A.D. 79; *c*, beginning of the new cone.

One of the greatest eruptions of modern times was that of Krakatoa in 1883. Krakatoa is the principal island of a little group in the straits of Sunda, between Java and Sumatra. The whole group is the remains of a great caldera formed by some ancient explosion and partially submerged. Upon the rim and in the midst of the caldera subsidiary cones had arisen, but the whole group had been quiescent for about 200 years. Premonitory earthquakes occurred in 1878 and succeeding years, and in May 1883, eruptions began and gradually increased in intensity. On 26 August a succession of most violent explosions took place and continued till the morning of the 27th. The ashes and cinders thrown up darkened the sky for miles around and, falling in the sea, obstructed the navigation of the straits for days. The noise of the explosions was heard almost all round for a distance of about 2000 miles and it was even audible at Rodriguez, nearly 3000 miles away. About two-thirds of the island disappeared.

The group of islands was not permanently inhabited and the actual eruption caused little loss of life. But the disturbance produced great waves in the sea which swept along the coasts of Java and Sumatra and drowned many thousands of the inhabitants.

The fine ash was shot many miles upwards and reaching the region of the upper winds was carried several times round the globe. It extended even as far as our own islands and was the cause of the extraordinarily brilliant sunsets observed in the autumn of 1883.

Another disastrous eruption of modern times was that of Mont Pelée, in the island of Martinique, in the year 1902. About the same time a similar eruption took place in the neighbouring island of St Vincent. The prominent feature in both eruptions was the sudden outburst of a dark and heavy cloud, consisting of hot gases and incandescent dust, which rolled down the mountain side with great rapidity. Everything that lay in its path was burned and destroyed and the town of St Pierre at the foot of Mont Pelée was overwhelmed in a few minutes. Less violent eruptions broke out at intervals for several months and when they had begun to subside a remarkable spine-like projection rose slowly from the crater of Mont Pelée to a height of 700 feet or more above the cone. It was formed by the partially solidified and pasty lava in the neck which was gradually forced outwards by the pressure within. The spine, however, was unable to resist the action of the weather and rapidly crumbled away.

Fissure eruptions. Volcanic eruptions sometimes take place not from a single vent but along a line of considerable length. In such cases the channel communicating with the interior is evidently not a pipe but a fissure, and the eruption may occur simultaneously throughout the whole length of the fissure or at numerous points along it. The eruption of Laki in Iceland in the year 1783 was of this type, the fissure being about 20 miles in length. The eruption of Tarawera, in New Zealand, in 1886, appears to have taken place from a fissure about 9 miles long.

The Tarawera eruption was violently explosive and large quantities of ash were ejected, but fissure eruptions generally seem to be characterised by the absence of explosive action. The principal feature is the quiet welling out of molten lava which may spread over many miles of country (pl. 25*b*).

Fissure eruptions are rare at the present day, but in the past they have taken place on a gigantic scale. The basaltic lavas of the Deccan in India, covering an area of about 200,000 square miles, and the lava-flows of the Snake River plains in the United States, about 200,000–250,000 square miles in extent, appear to have been poured out from fissures. In our own islands, the basalt flows of the north-east of Ireland and the Hebrides are of a similar type, and are merely the remains of an enormous lava-field which probably extended as far as Greenland.

Solfataras. Long after a volcano has ceased to eject lava and ashes and has become practically extinct it may continue to emit steam and gases of various kinds. It is then said to have reached the solfatara stage, the term being derived from the volcano called Solfatara, near Naples, the last recorded eruption of which occurred in A.D. 1198.

Volcanoes in the solfatara stage are common in all the great volcanic districts of the globe.

Geysers. In some parts of the world where volcanic action is still going on or has taken place in recent geological times, hot water and steam are thrown out at intervals in the form of a fountain, sometimes rising to a height of 100 or 200 feet. These intermittent fountains are called geysers and have long been known in Iceland. There are excellent examples also in the Yellowstone Park in the United States, and in New Zealand.

In the case of the Great Geyser in Iceland the water rises through a cylindrical pipe-like channel which opens in the middle of a saucer-shaped hollow. When the geyser is not erupting, the basin is filled with water at a temperature of 170–190° F., while at a depth of a hundred feet in the pipe the temperature is about 260°. At intervals the water in the basin and the upper part of the pipe is thrown upwards into the air along with clouds of steam.

The cause of the eruptions is that the column of water in the pipe is heated down below, and the channel is so long and narrow that convection does not take place freely. Consequently, the temperature below continues to rise while the water at the surface is still comparatively cool. Since pressure raises the boiling-point, the water towards the bottom of the column must be heated far above 212° before it begins to be converted into vapour. But when the necessary temperature is reached, the change takes place and the water above is forced upwards and begins to flow away. The escape, even of a little water only, at once reduces the pressure at the bottom of the column and accordingly the water there is rapidly converted into steam, forcing the whole column above it into the air.

The phenomenon is sometimes illustrated accidentally in the chemical laboratory when a narrow test-tube full of water is heated at or near the bottom. If the tube is clean and the water has already been boiled so as to free it from dissolved gases, it not uncommonly happens that the water is ejected violently, owing to the sudden formation of steam at the bottom of the tube in the manner described.

Hot springs. In other cases the heated water flows out continuously, without any explosive action whatever. Hot springs of this type are common in volcanic districts, but they are found also in many places where there are no signs of volcanic activity. The springs of Bath, for example, have a temperature of 120° F. (pl. 23*b*).

Mud volcanoes. If the erupted waters are muddy instead of clear, a conical mound of mud may be formed, with a crater at the top. Mud volcanoes are found in Sicily, New Zealand, and other volcanic regions, and here they probably represent the last phase of volcanic activity. But they occur also in the Crimea, at Baku on the Caspian, in southern Baluchistan and other districts, where no true volcanoes exist. In these cases the water is forced outwards, not by any kind of volcanic action, but by the production of gases beneath the surface in other ways. At Baku the volatile hydrocarbons given off from the petroleum-bearing beds beneath are probably the primary cause of the mud-eruptions. In other places gases are produced by the decomposition of organic matter or by other chemical changes (pl. 22*a*).

Distribution of volcanoes. Volcanoes are not scattered irregularly over the globe. Most of those that are now active lie within certain well-defined belts and by far the greater part of the earth has been free from volcanic action since man appeared upon its surface (see fig. 127).

These belts coincide to a large extent with the belts of crumpling which have formed the great mountain ranges of the present day, but the coincidence is not complete. There are, for instance, no volcanoes in the Himalayas, and on the other hand there is no sign of recent folding in Iceland.

At the present day it is upon the borders of the Pacific that volcanic activity reaches its maximum development. A line of great volcanoes may be traced up the Andes and through Central America and Mexico. In the United States and Canada there are a few active vents, but in the ranges of the west there are many which have not been long extinct. Living volcanoes reappear in Alaska and the line is continued through the Aleutian Islands, Kamchatka, the Kurile Islands, Japan, Formosa, and the Philippines to the Moluccas group.

Another belt of volcanic activity, meeting the line already described about the Moluccas, runs through Sumatra, Java, and the Sunda Islands generally. Barren Island, in the Andamans, which is still occasionally active, and some extinct volcanoes in Burma, mark the north-westerly termination of the belt, while towards the east it is continued, with several interruptions, through New Guinea, the Solomon Islands, the New Hebrides, and New Zealand to Mount Erebus on the Antarctic continent. It should, however, be observed that owing to the large gaps, it is by no means clear that there is any real connection between the different volcanic regions in the portion of this belt east of the Moluccas.

The islands in the midst of the Pacific are all either volcanic or made of coral, and in many of the groups eruptions still take place. There are active volcanoes, for instance in the Sandwich Islands, the Tonga Islands, and the Samoa group. The Fiji Islands are an example of a group which is of volcanic origin, but in which volcanic action has now ceased.

The great belt of folding which runs from west to east across Europe and Asia, like that surrounding the Pacific, is also associated with volcanic activity, but not to the same extent. In Italy and the neighbouring islands, Vesuvius, Etna, Stromboli, and Vulcano are still active, and several other vents have erupted in recent times. Santorin in the Grecian Archipelago has been the scene of many outbursts. Farther east there are numerous volcanoes of gigantic size, but they are either extinct or in the solfatara stage. Ararat, for example, and many other mountains in Armenia and Asia Minor, are volcanic. One of them, Nimrud, near Lake Van, is said to have erupted in 1441. Elbruz and Kazbek in the Caucasus and Demavend south of the Caspian are also old volcanoes, and the last still sends out sulphurous gases. In the region where the boundaries of Persia, Afghanistan, and Baluchistan meet, there are several volcanic cones of considerable size and one or two of them emit steam and other vapours. But these appear to mark the present easternmost limit of volcanic action in this belt of folding. In the time of Humboldt active volcanoes were said to exist in the great mountain chains of central Asia, but all recent exploration tends to show that the reports were erroneous. There seem, however, to be a few extinct vents.

A shorter line of volcanoes, also associated with recent folding of the earth's crust, occurs in the West Indies, where the Lesser Antilles are largely volcanic. Most of the vents are extinct, but several of them still show signs of activity. Their nearness to the Andes and to Central America suggests that they may form a branch of the Pacific belt, but it is not clear that there is any real connection.

The remaining volcanoes of the globe appear to have no relation to the belts of folding, and in general show no definite linear arrangement. Iceland is the last surviving remnant of a great volcanic area which in earlier times extended from Greenland to the north of Ireland. The Azores, Madeira, Cape Verde Islands, and Canary Islands are all volcanic, but the volcanoes for the most part are now extinct. In the Azores, however, there have been several eruptions in historic times, and Teneriffe in the Canary Islands has erupted even during the last few years. Ascension Island, St Helena, and Tristan da Cunha are all volcanic but have long been extinct.

In Africa there are a few volcanic centres. In the Cameroons there was an eruption in 1909. A considerable number of volcanoes lie in or near the great rift-valley which extends from the Jordan down the Red Sea and through the east of Africa. Kenya and Kilimanjaro are volcanoes, though probably they are now extinct. A small cone south of Lake Rudolf has recently been in eruption and also one or two south of Albert Edward Nyanza. There are also records of an eruption in Arabia near Medina in the year A.D. 1256.

There are many volcanic cones in Madagascar, but no record or definite tradition of eruption. In the Comoro Islands, however, the Grand Comoro has been active several times since the islands were discovered. In Réunion, the Ptone de la Foumaise is still frequently in eruption. Mauritius and many other islands in the Indian Ocean are volcanic but now extinct. Far to the south in Kerguelen Island there are still signs of activity.

Extinct volcanoes. It would take up too much space to enumerate the volcanic districts of the past; but leaving out of consideration the more remote geological periods, some of the European areas may be noticed here.

In the north-east of Ireland, in Skye, Mull and other islands of the Hebrides, there are enormous flows of basaltic lava of Tertiary age. They belong to the volcanic area which, as already mentioned, once stretched as far as Greenland. The flows, apparently, came from fissures and not from distinct volcanoes.

In the Eifel district, west of the Rhine, and in the Auvergne, a part of the Central Plateau of France, there are many volcanic cones which are almost as perfect as when they were in eruption. Others have suffered from subsequent denudation.

Several extinct volcanoes, which are geologically of modern date, lie on the eastern side of the Rhine; and there are others also in Bohemia and on the inner border of the Carpathians.

CHAPTER XV

LAKES

General conditions necessary. During a heavy shower the little hollows in the surface of the ground are usually filled with water and form temporary pools. When the rain ceases, the pools disappear; some of the water evaporates, some of it sinks into the earth. But as long as more water enters the hollow than can escape in this way, the hollow will remain full.

In a climate such as ours the annual rainfall exceeds the annual evaporation. Therefore, in general, every hollow, unless it is in porous rock, or unless there is some underground escape, is filled with water till it overflows. If the hollow is shallow, it cannot hold much water in proportion to its area, and it may dry up completely in the summer. If it is deep, the water will not all evaporate even in the driest seasons, and a permanent lake will be formed.

It is not necessary, however, for the formation of a permanent lake, that the rainfall over the lake should be greater than the evaporation from it; for the water is not all derived from the rain that falls directly into the lake. Much of the rain from the surrounding area drains into the hollow, and provided that the total amount received is equal to the loss, the water will never disappear. Consequently, permanent lakes may and do exist even where the evaporation is greater than the rainfall.

In the tropical dry belt the rainfall is small and evaporation rapid. Even the larger depressions in the ground are therefore usually dry. If, however, they receive the drainage of a wide area, and especially if there are mountains round about, they may be covered with water at certain seasons. But even in these cases the annual supply does not usually exceed the loss, by evaporation and otherwise. Most commonly a temporary lake is formed when the snow upon the mountains melts, but in the dry season the lake becomes a swamp or disappears entirely. Even when a permanent lake is formed, the hollows are seldom completely filled and rarely overflow, and the lake accordingly is without an outlet.

Before a lake can be formed there must evidently be an actual hollow, completely surrounded by higher ground. If the supply of water is sufficient the hollow will be filled to the level of the lowest part of its rim and there the surplus water will overflow.

A hollow may be formed, whether the original surface was even or uneven, by deposition, by erosion (using the term in its widest sense), or by earth movements; and lakes accordingly may be produced in any of these three ways.

LAKES DUE TO DEPOSITION

Deposition does not always take place uniformly, and the surface of a newly formed deposit may therefore be uneven. If it is exposed to the air the hollows may be filled with water, and lakes will be formed which are completely surrounded by the deposited material. In cases such as these the lakes are due entirely to deposition.

More often, however, the origin of the hollow is more complex.

Artificial reservoirs are usually constructed by building a dam across a river-valley; and a great many natural lakes have been formed in the same way. Glaciers or other agents have deposited material in a valley, in such a fashion as to make a natural dam. The hollow is then due partly to the erosion of the valley by the river, partly to the formation of a dam by deposition. Since it is the dam that completes the hollow, such lakes may be classed as due to deposition.

In a few cases the material deposited is solid rock. It may, for instance, be a stream of lava now solidified, or a deposit of sinter or travertine from a spring. But usually the material is derived from the denudation of pre-existing rocks, and the deposit is an accumulation of fragments of various sizes. It may consist of angular blocks, boulders, pebbles, sand, or clay. If it is made up entirely of large fragments the water can escape between them and no lake will be formed. But even a small proportion of clay may be sufficient to block the interstices and to make the whole accumulation impermeable. Moreover, percolating water may deposit silt between the fragments and may occasionally convert a leaky barrier into one that is watertight. When the fragments are small, capillary attraction tends to hold the water between the grains, and thus even a bank of sand offers considerable resistance to the flow of water through it.

Marine deposits. The sea often throws up a bank of shingle about high-water mark, and sometimes there is a small lagoon or salt-water lake between the bank and the sea-cliff. Owing to the permeability of the shingle the lagoon is usually dry at low tide, but occasionally silt or decaying seaweed makes its bed sufficiently impermeable to hold water permanently.

Lagoons on a larger scale are produced in the manner described in ch. IV, pt. III by the formation of spits of sand or shingle across bays or across mouths of the rivers. Breydon Water at the mouth of the Yare, represents an example of this process.

Sand-hills also may cut off arms of the sea and convert them into lagoons, or may block the mouths of rivers. In the Landes of Gascony, in Holland, and in other low-lying districts many lakes and marshes behind the line of sand-dunes on the coast have been formed in this way.

Alluvial deposits. The lagoons of deltas and the ox-bow lakes of meandering rivers have already been described; but occasionally a stream may form a lake in another way.

In a hilly district, the torrents running down the valley sides often carry with them, especially in flood time, enormous quantities of soil and broken rock. As the torrent flows out upon the floor of the valley, its velocity is checked and it deposits its burden as a delta. Very often the delta turns the main river in the valley out of its natural course. Sometimes the amount of material is so great that the river is unable to carry it away, and in time the delta is built completely across the valley. It then becomes a dam. The water above is ponded back and a natural reservoir or lake is formed. Sty Head Tarn, for example, owes its existence to a delta from the Gables. (See note, p. 384.)

Screes. In precisely the same way a valley may be more or less completely blocked by the screes descending from the crags above. Hard Tarn, on the flanks of Helvellyn, and Ffynnon Frech, on Snowdon, are dammed by screes.

Landslips. Much larger lakes than these have often been formed by landslips blocking up a river-valley, but not in our own country. Such lakes are usually only temporary, for the dam consists of loose fragments piled haphazard, and has no great strength. As the water rises behind it the pressure upon it increases. When the water overflows, the dam is rapidly weakened by erosion and suddenly bursts, letting out a flood of water into the valley below. The unexpected floods which not uncommonly occur in the upper part of the Indus are believed to be due to this cause.

Glacial accumulations. More lakes probably are due to the action of glaciers than to any other cause. In our own islands it is where the signs of former glaciation are most conspicuous that lakes are most abundant; but not even Cumberland or the Highlands can compare with Finland for the number and size of its lakes. In southern Finland they cover nearly half the country. In the one-time Government of Novgorod, it is estimated that there are 3200 lakes, and it is in this part of Russia that moraines and other indications of a former ice-sheet are still most evident.

The lakes in a glaciated region are due in some cases to deposition and in others to erosion. It is with the former that we are now concerned.

The original surface of a moraine or of a spread of boulder-clay is usually very uneven and, when it is first exposed, water collects in the hollows and forms lakes. As a rule such lakes are very irregular in shape and of no great depth. In our own islands most of them have long ago been silted up; but on the plateau of boulder-clay in north-eastern Germany many hundreds still remain.

These lakes are completely surrounded by glacial deposits, but more often the glacial material forms a lake by blocking up a river-valley. The terminal moraine of a glacier is a natural dam and, when the glacier retreats may hold the water above it as in an artificial reservoir. For several reasons, however, a terminal moraine is seldom very effective as a dam. The stream which issues from the end of the glacier tends to keep a passage open while the moraine is forming, and the dam accordingly is often incomplete. Moreover, the terminal moraine consists chiefly of angular blocks loosely heaped together. It is not often watertight and it is not solidly enough constructed to resist much pressure or erosion. Consequently, few lakes of any great size or depth are dammed by terminal moraines; but a considerable number of small lakes have been formed in this way. Bleawater Tarn in the Lake District, for example, is dammed by a semicircular moraine at the mouth of the cwm in which it lies.

A far more effective barrier is often formed by the boulder-clay deposited beneath a glacier or ice-sheet. It is not laid down evenly throughout the whole length of the valley but the deposit is thicker in some places than in others. When the ice disappears the valley is partially blocked and water collects above the places where the accumulation is thickest. Windermere and Ullswater, the lake of Llanberis and many others are probably due, in part at least, to barriers of boulder-clay blocking up the valleys in which they lie.

As a rule the stream that leaves the lake still runs down the original valley; but sometimes the valley is so completely blocked that the water overflows at the sides or even at the head of the valley, and finds some other course to the sea. In this case the actual outlet may be over solid rock, and at first sight it may appear that the lake lies in a hollow eroded in the rock.

The glacier itself may form a barrier which holds the water up. Where two glaciers meet there is sometimes a small triangular lake in the angle between them. In Greenland the inequalities on the surface of the ice due to projecting nunataks often lead to the formation of pools of water which may be of considerable size. Much larger lakes are sometimes found, both in Greenland and elsewhere, where a glacier crosses the opening of a valley that is free from ice. Unless the temperature is above the freezing-point for a considerable part of the year no lake will be formed, but many glaciers extend far below the snow-line. The valley of the glacier itself may be filled with ice while the side valleys are occupied by running streams. As a rule these streams flow out upon the glacier and fall down crevasses, but sometimes the drainage of the lateral valley is completely blocked and a lake is formed. The Marjelen See in the Alps is the best-known example.[1] It lies in a lateral valley opening into the valley of the Aletsch glacier. Sometimes the water can escape

[1] An overflow tunnel has now been constructed which limits the height to which the lake can rise, and so minimises the floods when the waters periodically escape under the glacier.

through crevasses in the glacier; but often the dam of ice has been so high and perfect that the lake has overflowed a col into the neighbouring valley of the Viesch glacier. Since there is always a free outlet over the col, the water can never rise to any greater height, and a beach or terrace is formed at the level of the col.

The Parallel Roads of Glen Roy, north-east of Ben Nevis, were formed in this way. They are terraces or beaches evidently due to the action of waves and marking the height to which the water reached. Each terrace is on the level of a col over which the water could escape. The mouth of the valley was dammed by ice and a lake was formed. When the ice was at its greatest extension all the cols except the highest were also blocked, and the water stood at the level of the uppermost terrace. As the ice retreated the second col was opened and the water fell to its level and produced the second terrace. Next the third and lowest col was freed from ice and the lowest terrace was formed. Finally, the dam at the mouth disappeared and the lake ceased to exist. Streams entering the lakes built small deltas which correspond in level with the beaches. The streams subsequently cut through the deltas and left them exposed on the hillside (pl. 10*b*).

Volcanic deposits. In a volcanic district a stream of lava may flow across a valley and dam up a river. Lac d'Aydat near Clermont-Ferrand was formed in this way.

Crater-lakes are much more common. The crater of a volcano is a natural hollow in which water might be expected to accumulate. But in most cases the walls consist to so large an extent of loose volcanic ash that they are not watertight. Moreover, since the crater is usually at the top of the hill, the only water that reaches it, after the volcano becomes extinct, is the rain that falls directly into it. Consequently, the majority of craters are dry. There are, nevertheless, a considerable number of crater-lakes in the Eifel, the Auvergne, and elsewhere; but most of them are in craters formed by explosion rather than by accumulations of volcanic ash.

Organic deposits. Even animal or vegetable deposits may occasionally give rise to lakes. The lagoon of an atoll is a kind of lake and owes its origin to the reefs built by coral polyps. In forest-covered districts rivers are sometimes blocked by floating trees washed down during floods. If one of these becomes jammed so that it cannot move, it may cause an accumulation of logs which for a time will form a dam. Above the dam there will be a temporary lake; but sooner or later the dam will give way and the water will escape. More permanent lakes of the same kind are produced by the dams constructed by beavers across some of the rivers of north-western Canada.

LAKES DUE TO EROSION

Lakes sometimes lie in hollows which are completely surrounded by solid rock. They are not dammed by accumulations of loose material, but are in actual rock-basins. Such lakes may exist in the course of a river; but it is evident that the hollow was not worn by the corrasive action of the river itself. For unless the hollow is very shallow and the river very turbulent the water at the bottom must be practically still, and deposition instead of corrasion must take place. It is only at the foot of a waterfall or where the water swirls round in an eddy that a river can corrade a hollow below the general slope of its bed. Such hollows are always small and it is not too much to say that no rock-basin of any considerable size or depth can be due to the corrasive action of running water.

If, however, the river flows across an outcrop of rock that is soluble in water, it may by solution form a basin. Even if it makes no actual hollow in its bed, the solvent action of the rain and of the river itself upon its banks may widen the channel to so great an extent as to produce a sheet of water which may be called a lake. It is probable, for example, that the expansions of the Shannon known as Loughs Ree and Derg are due to solution of the limestone over which the river flows.

Erosion by wind. Though water ceases to corrade when in a hollow, there are other agents which are not limited to the same extent. Both wind and glaciers can carry fragments upwards and consequently they can corrade when moving up a slope. Either of these agents, therefore, can erode a rock-basin of greater or less extent.

Where there is no vegetation small depressions are often produced by the irregular erosive action of the wind, and during a storm of rain they may be filled with water. This, however, is in desert regions and permanent lakes will not be formed. In moister climates the influence of the wind is less; but the weathering of rock-surfaces is often very uneven, and since the weathered material is usually soft it may be removed by the wind, leaving hollows, which are capable of holding water. These hollows, however, are small and shallow, and it is not possible to point to any rock-basin even of moderate size that has been formed in this way.

Erosion by glaciers. Some writers assert that glaciers are almost ineffective as erosion agents. They allow that a glacier may remove any loose and weathered material over which it flows, but they deny that it is capable of eroding a rock-basin except, perhaps, a very small one. It has, however, been pointed out already that lakes are most numerous in glaciated regions. Many of these lakes owe their origin to the damming of river-valleys by glacial deposits, but many others lie in basins hollowed out in solid rock. Loch Coruisk in Skye may serve as an example. It is entirely rock-bound, and soundings show that it consists of two distinct basins separated by a rocky barrier. No valley worn by water can have this form, for the floor of such a valley must slope continuously to the sea. Glacial striations, roches moutonnées and other signs prove that the valley was once occupied by a glacier; and it is natural to attribute the erosion of the basins to the action of the glacier.

It must not be supposed, in cases such as these, that the valley itself was excavated by ice. There was a river-valley first. In the Glacial Period it was occupied by a glacier. The glacier did not make the valley but modified its form. In particular it hollowed out the two rock-basins, which cannot be due to the action of the original river.

Solution. When a river flows over rock that is soluble in water, a lake, as already explained, may be formed by solution of the rock. But solution does not take place only at the surface. Underground streams dissolve limestone, salt, and other soluble material, and often excavate long and spacious caverns (see ch. VII, pp. 292, 293). If the roof of a cavern falls in there will be a depression in the ground above and in this depression water may accumulate as a lake.

Many of the meres of Cheshire are probably due to this cause. Beneath the surface there are beds of salt, and the presence of brine-springs shows that the salt is being removed by underground water. Where the process is hastened by pumping up the brine, subsidences frequently occur, and from time to time new lakes are formed or the old ones increase in size.

Deposits of salt are comparatively rare and it is in limestone districts that the effects of underground water are most frequently observed. But although the limestone is dissolved and depressions are produced in the ground above, it is not often that lakes are formed; for owing to the fissured nature of most limestones the water can usually escape by some underground channel. Occasionally, however, the opening of the channel may be plugged by glacial or other material, and the water will collect in the hollow. Or if there are beds of shale as well as limestone, impervious hollows capable of holding water may be formed.

Volcanic explosions. In the Eifel district there are many circular cavities in the ground produced by volcanic explosions. Sometimes they are surrounded by volcanic ash, sometimes only by the fragments of rock thrown out by the explosion. They are craters, but craters which have been hollowed out rather than built up; and since their walls are of solid rock they can hold water.

The majority of crater-lakes lie in craters of this type. The Laacher See in the Eifel district and Lake Avernus near Naples are well-known examples.

LAKES DUE TO EARTH MOVEMENTS

It is easy to see that a hollow capable of holding water can be produced by bending or fracturing of the earth's crust, and there is no doubt that some lakes owe their origin to this cause.

The Dead Sea is one of the best examples. It is not dammed by loose material but lies in a true rock-basin. The surface of the water is 1292 feet and the bottom 2592 feet below the level of the Mediterranean. No such depression as this can be due solely to subaerial erosion, for no erosive agent could remove material from so deep a hollow. The valley of the Jordan is a narrow strip of country which has sunk down between two parallel faults or fractures. From the Waters of Merom southwards for a distance of more than 150 miles this strip is now below the level of the sea; but it did not sink down evenly. The deepest part of the depression is at the Dead Sea, and it is there that the water collects.

Lakes Nyasa and Tanganyika and many other smaller lakes in eastern Africa lie in similar faulted strips and have been formed in a similar way.

Probably the Great Lakes of North America are also partly due to earth movements, but the earth movements were of a different type. Around the shores there are terraces formed when the water stood at a higher level. Originally these terraces must have been horizontal, but they are not horizontal now. The crust of the earth has been bent since they were formed. Such bending must certainly modify the shape of the lakes and may have been the original cause of their formation.

There is some evidence, too, that the larger lakes of the Alps are due, in part, to bending of the surface. With few exceptions they lie in river-valleys just where the valley opens out upon the plains. It has been suggested that the valleys, like normal river-valleys, once sloped continuously to the sea, but the weight of the mountain mass caused the earth's crust to sag beneath it. Owing to this sagging the slope of the valleys at the foot of the hills was reversed and consequently the lakes were formed. In support of this view it is said that near the lakes the old river-terraces, which must have once sloped towards the sea, now slope towards the mountains.

Note (see page 379). Breydon Water is part of the old estuary of the Yare dammed by the spit on which Yarmouth stands. Many of the broads in the Ant and Bure valleys are now regarded as artificial—the result of peat digging in mediaeval times. (See J. N. Jennings, *R.G.S. Res. Ser.* **2**, 1952, and J. M. Lambert, *Trans. Norfolk and Norwich Nat. Soc.* **17**, 1953, 223.)

CHAPTER XVI

FLOODS AND STORMS: THEIR PHYSIOGRAPHICAL EFFECTS

The processes of erosion and deposition discussed in this book usually act slowly, and it is not easy to appreciate that they are capable of doing all the work ascribed to them. A volcanic eruption, or a dust storm in a desert are convincing evidence to an observer that natural agencies can produce great changes in a short time. But in a country such as our own, the physiographer is perhaps more impressed by the slowness with which change takes place. Lyell's doctrine of Uniformitarianism—the processes of the present are the key to the past—is hard to appreciate and it is difficult to believe that wide valleys have been carved by the sluggish rivers now flowing in them, or that steep cliffs of hard rock have been eroded by waves.

In the few years since the second World War we have experienced several violent storms, which have, locally, left their imprint on the landscape. They include the great sea-floods on the east coast in 1953, the severe damage done, particularly to railways and roads, in south-eastern Scotland in 1948, the destruction of much of Lynmouth in 1952, and the tremendous rainfall near Weymouth in 1955. They are not to be regarded as particularly unusual; there have been many such events in the past. The great storms at Louth in 1920 and Norwich in 1912 are other instances, and many others could be cited.

In this chapter, emphasis is laid on the physiographical effects of storms. The amount of work done by them may be most impressive and shows clearly how enormously processes are speeded up on such occasions.

Dorset storm, 1955. On the night of 18–19 July 1955, there was violent rain between 4.30 p.m. and 2.0 a.m. in parts of Dorset, the heaviest being near the Hardy Monument on Black Down. It produced high floods in all the small streams, some of which left their beds, and the Wey rushed through the streets of Upwey. At Weymouth 7·2 inches of rain fell in 24 hours, and probably as much as 12 inches fell at Black Down—most of it between the hours mentioned above. At Martin's Down 11 inches were recorded, and this was accepted as the largest amount ever recorded for a rainfall day in these islands.

The small streams on this part of the Dorset coast run down to the beach and then trickle through the shingle. The storm caused them to cut right through the shingle to its rocky foundation, and to form small deltas. The depth of the cuts in the shingle varied between 3 and 6 feet. On the steep hill-side near Falcon Farm, Ringstead, the soil, covered with bracken and shrub, was so saturated that it slipped bodily, exposing a scar about 25 yards square—a fine example of solifluction. The little stream cascading to the sea at Osmington Mills drains about three square miles of country, on which about seven inches of rain fell in the same number of hours. All this water had to find its way out through a narrow and rather steep gorge. Débris showed that the water flowed at 12 feet above its normal level, and bridges and gardens of houses were washed away. The cascade deepened its bed by 4 or 5 feet, and new sections of the Jurassic rocks were exposed.

At Coryates, there is a gap through the Portlandian ridge which was formed by capture of a stream running parallel to the ridge on its northern side by a small stream on the south side of the ridge. The old north side valley is now dry, but during the storm its upper part, Hell Bottom, became a raging torrent which emptied through the western arm of Coryates' Gap, and then rushed on to Coryates hamlet. In so doing it scoured out the gap

which now looks like a desert wadi, and exposed a long clean section of Portland Sand cementstones and loams, destitute of vegetation or soil. In the main gap the water undermined the west side, causing solifluction and slipping, so that Portland Sand loams are exposed from road level almost to the top of the hill.

All this district had been studied in detail by W. J. Arkell who also wrote:

I have known the little gorge of the Osmington stream intimately for some 20 years and all that time there has been no sign of its lowering its bed or eroding the hillsides; on the contrary, it has become progressively more choked with decaying vegetation. But on the 18 July, in a single night, all the forces of denudation started up for a few hours; the terminal cascade was lowered several feet; the bed of the stream was deeply scoured and many tons of boulders and other debris were shot over the cascade into the sea; meanders were altered and the banks undercut and trimmed back at many points; and the whole catchment was lowered by the removal of soil in sheet floods, as hillwash and by solifluction. (*Proc. Dorset Nat. Hist. and Arch. Soc.* 77, 1955, 90.)

Exmoor storm, 1952. The storm on Exmoor and the flooding of Lynmouth on 15 August 1952, were notable, unfortunately, for the loss of life they caused: twenty-three people were killed and 1250 rendered homeless. The first half of August was wet, and the ground was saturated when the storm occurred. There was considerable rain all that day, but most fell between 8 p.m. and 1 a.m. on the 16 August during a heavy thunderstorm. In an automatic gauge at Longstone Barrow, 9·1 inches were recorded in 24 hours, and 7·58 in. fell at Challacombe. The heaviest rain was over a small part of the northern and north-eastern slopes of Exmoor. All the rivers flooded rapidly, but damage resulting from floods was limited to about 250 square miles—an area enclosed by Dunster, Tiverton, South Molton, and Lynmouth. Since the ground was already saturated, the floods rose rapidly, and their rate of fall was also rapid. At 9 p.m. water was flowing down Lynmouth High Street, and was rising six inches every quarter of an hour; the level had begun to fall by 11 p.m.

The East and West Lyn join at Lynmouth, and together drain an area of some 38 square miles. Kidson calculates that some 3100 million gallons fell on this area, and that since the ground was already saturated the loss through percolation was small or even negligible, and that caused by evaporation was almost certainly far below the normal for an August day.

> If the rate of flow in the Lyns is calculated on the basis of two-thirds of the day's rainfall falling in the five-hour period...(and this is a conservative estimate) the following short period rates result: West Lyn 5,375 cusecs.; East Lyn 13,088 cusecs....This gives the two streams combined over a period of a few hours a rate of flow almost as great as the record figure...for the Thames. (*Geography*, **38**, 1953, 1.)

Both streams drain steep country, and it has been estimated that about 40,000 tons of boulders were moved into the Lynmouth area. It is virtually certain that fallen trees and boulders created dams, and that when the torrents overcame them, surges were produced which travelled at high speeds and did great damage. It was the impression of all observers that the sudden bursting of these temporary dams was the worst feature of the floods. The West Lyn changed its course in Lynmouth itself as a result of one of these bursts, and the plan of the town, causing the virtual canalisation of the river, was one of the factors favourable to the destruction wrought by the flood.

> ...the floods in the Exmoor region serve to re-emphasise the nature of the processes by which a river carves out its valley. The West Lyn in a single day moved more than 50,000 tons of boulders, some of which weigh more than 10 tons, and it is estimated that the deltaic deposit on the right bank of the East Lyn river in Lynmouth contains some 200,000 cu. yards of boulders, débris and soil, most of it brought down at some time by the West Lyn river.

On Exmoor landslides of two types were produced. Most of the slides were caused by soil and vegetation, completely saturated, being stripped off a surface of rock or drift which had been lubricated not only by the storm-rain, but by the rains of the previous two weeks. The other type, limited to one notable example, resulted from the downhill flow of saturated material.

Slaty débris from a deep hole poured down a slope of fifteen degrees, clearing its path of bracken and mantling the grass with debris. On reaching the small tributary valley at the foot of this slope most of the débris was diverted down the valley to pour into the main valley, but some was carried across and up the opposite slope to mantle completely the lower end of the interfluve. Such a remarkable uphill flow indicates that the movement was sudden and rapid, and in the nature of a mudflow rather than a slide. (J. Gifford, *Geography*, **38**, 1953, 9.)

Louth storm, 1920. The severe thunderstorm at Louth on 29 May 1920 began soon after 1 p.m., and the little River Lud rose rapidly to 15 feet above its normal level in some places, and a torrent 200 yards wide swept through the town. Buildings were destroyed and twenty-two persons were drowned. The heavy rain fell between one and five o'clock, and just west of Louth 120 mm. fell on a small area in the twenty-four hours ending at 9 a.m. on 30 May. Over the area enclosed by the 100 mm. isohyet mud was washed from fields and collected on the downslope sides or corners and deep furrows were cut. Here, as at Lynmouth, much of the damage was almost certainly caused by the bursting of temporary dams formed by timber jamming bridges.

Chiltern storm, 1936. Exceptional rains in chalk districts are not uncommon. One occurred in the Chilterns on 17 May 1936. Records of rainfall are scanty; 1·64 inches were measured at Radnage, but greater amounts are thought to have fallen at the two centres of the storm—near Fingest and at Piddington, both situated in coombes about 3 miles apart. The country is fairly steep at both localities. At Fingest a delta-fan was formed consisting of 'a flat-topped lobe of clean washed sand, 36 feet long, 12 feet wide and 3 feet high, fringed by an extensive lower-lying spread of mud. The whole delta covered an area of about 100 square yards. At its narrower end, or origin, there was a gully 6–9 feet wide and 1 foot deep eroded in the plough land.' The rain, having flooded various fields, concentrated in a small gully, and became a devastating torrent, which for a short time was largely absorbed by a swallow-hole, which soon became choked, and then circumvented. The torrent did not cross any outcrop of sand, so that the sand forming the delta was derived wholly from the fields.

Near Piddington the main London–Oxford road was blocked by a delta fan measuring 120 × 60 × 6 feet. The gravel was mixed, and included flints reaching 9 × 6 inches. The sand-matrix was mainly composed of microscopic flint chips. The delta was the work of a torrent which had been canalised by a sunken lane leading down to the Piddington valley where the lane and the Oxford road join.

The torrent had developed considerable erosive and transporting power; it had stripped off the gravelly surface of a lane to a depth of six inches or so, exposing Clay-with-flints. When I saw the torrent it looked like the dry bed of a mountain torrent. Gullies a foot deep had been excavated at the sides of the lane; in places the hedge-row banks had been undermined. At the back of the delta-fan the torrent had gouged a hollow 3–4 feet deep.

Many dry valley floors in the Chilterns are covered with gravels of precisely the same character as that forming the Piddington delta, and may well have been formed when there was little if any vegetation, and heavy floods washed down the loose and deep flint soils produced under peri-glacial conditions. (K. P. Oakley, with notes by C. D. Ovey, *Records of Bucks*, **14**, 1945, 265.)

Floods of south-eastern Scotland, 1948. The floods in south-eastern Scotland on 12 August 1948 attracted much interest because of the damage done to railways and roads. The previous week was wet, and there was heavy rain on 7–8 August, thus the ground was saturated. On the 12 August, 6 inches fell in the Tweed basin, and over 5 inches in parts of the Merse. Five inches also fell on the hills between the Tyne and the Whiteadder. The storm was associated with a depression, the centre of which was off the Norfolk coast, but the complete combination of factors which produced the storm has not been adequately explained. (See C. K. M. Douglas, *Met. Mag.* 78, 1949, 10.)

The terrain over which the rain fell is varied and includes the Lammermuir Hills. No comprehensive measurements of erosion and deposition appear to have been recorded immediately after the storm and a general survey was not made until a year later by A. T. A. Learmouth (*Scot. Geog. Mag.* **66**, 1910, 147), who noted the effects of erosion, transport, and deposition of material, particularly the thick deposits of gravel which were left on the meadows (haughs) along the rivers. Numerous landslides occurred, especially on slopes of about 1 in 3. Few of them took place in woodland, but when they did so, they left a deeper and more extensive scar. In the Lammermuirs the old cones of dejection in the gullies received large additions. On the other hand the local farmers did not regard the loss of soil by erosion as particularly serious, but it was noted that for some days after the storm the sea was discoloured by the Old Red Sandstone soils for at least 2 miles from the shore. A. Scott (*Scottish Agriculture*, **29**, 1950, 125) wrote:

> Rivers broke their banks and swept over the haughs with such strength that they lifted from the beds surprising quantities and kinds of material. At Allanton on the Whiteadder, 20,000 tons of material, a figure arrived at by direct measurement, was lifted from the bed and bank of the river and spread over an area of about 5 acres. Blocks of stone of between 4 and 5 tons were deposited on the haugh. At Edrington, on the same river, 25,000 tons of material, with a lesser weight of stones, were similarly spread over the haugh.

The power of the floods can perhaps best be appreciated in the valley of the Eye. This stream drains a basin of about 13½ square miles and is usually insignificant. Yet it destroyed seven main-line railway bridges and several road-bridges. Once again, the effect of trees uprooted along the banks of the river was a major cause of the damage. They formed dams, which led to surges when they burst and so to the underscour of the foundations of the bridges.

***Llyn Eigiau dam-burst, 1925*.** The effect of a dam-burst in North Wales was studied by W. Fearnsides and W. H. Wilkinson (*Geogr. Journ.* **72**, 1928, 401). In November 1925, following heavy rains, the water from the Llyn Eigiau reservoir escaped by forcing a passage under the retaining wall. The water followed the course of the Afon Porth-llwyd and piled up above the Coed Ti dam. The burst in the wall of the reservoir lowered the level of the water 11 feet, which meant that at least 110 million cubic feet of water emerged through the breach, immediately outside which it spread out and for the first 100 yards uprooted neither heather nor grass. A little lower down the waters concentrated in streams and lifted the peat in cakes which floated away. The water also dug deep runnels in the boulder-clay, and the main stream cut 10 to 20-feet ravines. Lower down where the valley becomes more gorge-like, erosion was much more active, and in parts the channel was lowered 10 feet, and trees and thousands of tons of stones were dumped above the Coed Ti dam, which was built (see fig. 214) to collect the water from various leats, and to hold the spills from the higher ones. It was already overflowing on 26 October as a result of heavy rains.

Because of the burst in Llyn Eigiau pressures were brought to bear on the Coed Ti dam which it was never designed to stand, and, soon after 8 p.m. on 2 November, it gave way, and some 12 million cubic feet of water were released.

For about half a mile below Coed Ti, the slope is less than 1 in 10, and the flood spread out so that its cross-section was rather more than 5000 square feet. In this stretch it removed trees and a bridge as well as soil and loose rock. Then the slope became 1 in 8 and 1 in 6 above the Rhaiadr, and the cross-section was reduced to about 3000 square feet. Only blocks of more than 10 cubic feet remain, and, on the top of the Rhaiadr, one block weighing 200 tons was inverted. Oddly enough, there is no record of any effective corrasion.

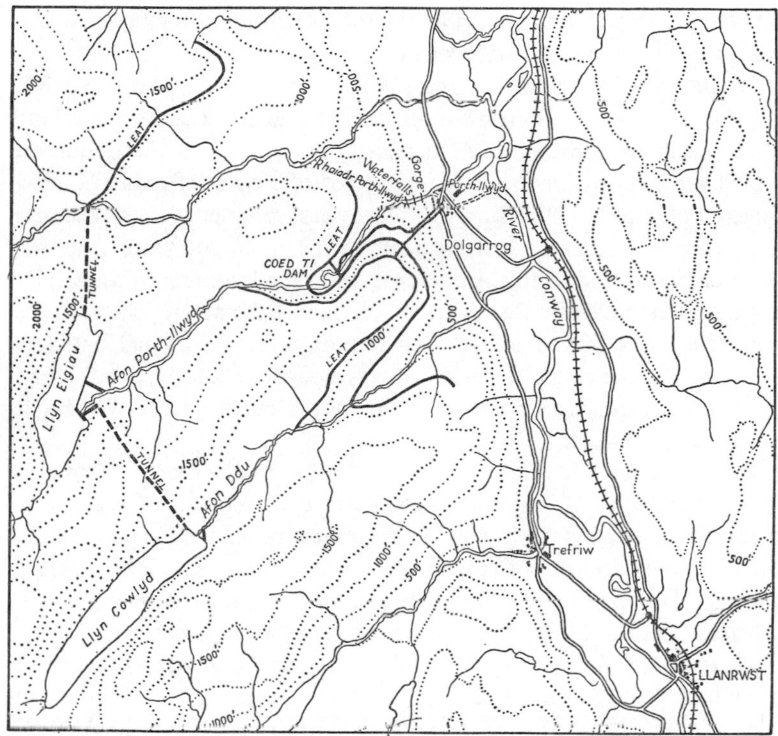

Fig. 214. Map of Porth-llwyd valley and Dolgarrog.

Below the Rhaiadr there were striking changes. The stream falls about 200 feet over a slope of 1 in 2, then flows over an inclined ledge before reaching the ravine with the falls, and so completes a total fall of about 500 feet with an average gradient of 1 in 4.

From this steep slope, within the tract of the... waters every projecting block, not firmly embedded or attached as rock *in situ*, was rooted out and swept away. What before the flood was a wooded ravine, well occupied with trees and fallen boulders, now presents a complete if almost inaccessible clean-scoured exposure of solid rock. Where the waters at the foot of the first precipitous descent fell against the bank of boulder-drift which marks the crossing of a slightly divergent pre-glacial channel, they undercut and removed some tens of thousands of tons of moraine....The stream course for a distance of about one hundred yards was shifted laterally...about thirty feet.

Below the Rhaiadr the pounding and erosion of the solid rock increased, but, in the steep narrows in the waterfall gorge, there seems to have been no change. It was estimated that the total quantity of rock eroded was only a few hundreds of cubic yards.

In the ravine, the slope is about 1 in 4, and it decreases to 1 in 6 below the gorge. This rapidly checked the rush of the torrent and a huge cone of dejection was formed which, as a result of the action of distributaries, was remarkably symmetrical for about 60° of a circle of radius about a quarter of a mile. Porth-llwyd village was completely buried under 20–40 feet of boulders. The gradient lessens about 200 yards from the apex of the cone, and this, in its turn, caused a lessening in the size of the boulders carried to that part. Nevertheless, for about 300 yards the main road was buried under 6–10 feet of stones and small boulders derived from the glacial deposits. It was estimated that the flood-débris left within a quarter of a mile of the works of Dolgarrog was about 4 million cubic feet.

Storms at sea often do considerable damage on the coast, but even so it is difficult to find any measurement or even estimate of damage to coasts faced by cliffs cut in hard and resistant rocks. On the other hand, the effect of storms on soft, incoherent rocks is often great. The ordinary annual loss along boulder-clay cliffs like those of Holderness and North Norfolk is of the order of one or two yards in most places.

East coast floods, 1953. One of the most severe storms on our east coast took place on the night of 31 January–1 February 1953. The storm was primarily caused by a depression which advanced from the Atlantic into the North Sea around the north of Scotland. It attained its minimum pressure (968 mb.) when it was in the northern part of the North Sea. It was followed by an anticyclone, and when the depression entered the North Sea violent northerly winds accompanied it and swept down the east coast of England. Fortunately, they blew from just a little west of north so that, except on the north-facing shores of the Moray Firth, Norfolk, and Kent, they were slightly offshore. South of the Border, the wind speeds were not excessive, but off north-eastern Scotland they reached hurricane force, and thus the water was extremely rough all over the North Sea basin. (*Geogr. Journ.* **119**, 1953, 280.)

The storm was accompanied by a tidal surge which reached record heights on our coast. A surge is defined as 'a water movement which is quickly generated and whose effects are soon over... The rapidity of generation, the notable rise (or fall) of the sea-level and the manner in which the surge travels, are characteristics which distinguish it from other meteorological disturbances of sea-level.' The way in which a surge is generated, and its method of propagation, are rather like those of a bore. In the North Sea, the time of high (or low) water is progressively later as it travels southwards along our east coast. The surge followed the same direction, and superimposed itself on the tide. Fortunately, it did not coincide with the top of the tide—it was about 3 hours later—nor was the tide, although a spring tide, a particularly high one. Nevertheless, the recorded tide at Aberdeen was approximately 3 feet, at Immingham 7 feet, at Southend nearly 8 feet, and at Dover 6 feet, higher than that predicted. These abnormally high waters were associated with unusual wave-action, and the locus of wave-attack was in consequence anything up to 10 or 12 feet higher than usual. In some places this meant that for a short time the waves covered defence works and attacked the cliffs above the level of defending walls.

The worst effects of the storm were on low-lying coasts, especially in Lincolnshire, Norfolk, and Essex. Sea-walls were overtopped and severe flooding took place on low-lying ground. The houses at places like Mablethorpe and Sutton in Lincolnshire, at Jaywick near Clacton, and at Canvey Island suffered severely, and 307 people lost their lives. The effects on the Lincolnshire beaches were spectacular. For long stretches, the sand was completely swept away from the beaches and the underlying deposits exposed. Much of the sand was swept either seawards, or southwards; much was thrown over the walls and promenades and piled up around houses to a depth of 3 or 4 feet or even more in places. In Lincolnshire where the beach and natural dunes were widest the damage was less. A little north of Mablethorpe and also south of Skegness the damage was relatively slight. Along the narrower beach between these two places it was severe. The sand took a long time to return to these beaches. Repeated surveys of seventeen sections between Mablethorpe and Gibraltar Point between February 1953 and April 1957 showed that by the latter date in all but three sections the beach had regained normal conditions.

At Hunstanton and on the north coast of Kent, the storm was onshore, and damage to promenades, sea-walls, and buildings was locally severe. On the north coast of Norfolk, flooding of embanked marshland was perhaps the most conspicuous overall effect. The main dunes at Scolt Head Island were cut back 8–10 yards; the great shingle bank of Salthouse was breached, a factor which helped in the serious damage that took place there; the narrow line of dunes between Eccles and Winterton was reduced in width to about one-half, and a breach was made at Palling. Sea-walls were overtopped and breached all round the coast, and flooding of low-lying ground on the open coast and its estuaries caused a great deal of damage to property, industry, agricultural land, and stock.

But despite the violence of the storm, it can be argued that far less damage occurred than might have been expected. Along the Suffolk coast the cliffs are all made of soft materials. All the way from Benacre to Southwold the cliffs were pared back; at Covehithe where they are between 10 and 30 feet high the loss was phenomenal. At the low north end of the cliffs they were cut back more than 80 feet, and a little farther south, cliffs 30 feet high were cut back 30 feet horizontally. On the other hand, at Dunwich, a place that has suffered serious erosion throughout historical times, no damage whatever occurred apart from flooding of the marshes at the north end of the cliffs, and, even at Minsmere, about a mile and a half farther south, only a foot or so was taken off the cliffs. This variation in the amount of damage is noteworthy and characteristic; erosion varies much from one place to another even along what appears to be a simple stretch of coast.

The River Alde (see p. 267), in spite of the flattening of the shingle and breaches in the sea-walls, did not flow out to sea at Slaughden, nor did the southern end of Orford shingle spit suffer unduly. In 1897, in another great storm, about one mile of the southern end of the spit was cut off.

If the winds had been from the north-east damage would have been far more severe, and to obtain some idea of what might have happened we must turn to Holland where the wind was directly onshore. There the worst effects of the storm occurred in the delta-lands of the Rhine. The low-lying islands of Walcheren, Schouwen, Over-Flakkee and others were severely damaged. In Schouwen much of the embanked land lies at a low level, and once the banks had been breached the sea rushed through the breaches and flooded wide areas. The flood itself did all too much damage to sea-walls and agricultural land, and the ebb and flow of succeeding tides widened and deepened the breaches so that their repair was a major operation. For months after it was possible to sail through the larger breaches at high water in a ship as big as an ordinary Thames tug. The storm drove the water up the mouths of the Rhine and Scheldt, and Rotterdam itself was seriously threatened. The death roll in Holland was very high; 1487 people lost their lives. The Dutch authorities are now to build dams across the mouths of the rivers between

Walcheren and North Beveland, North Beveland and Schouwen, Schouwen and Goree, and Goree and Voorne. This is a more difficult problem than the enclosing of the Zuider Zee, but it will make the defence of the delta from wave-attack far more secure.

Effects of wind action in England. The effects of wind action in these islands are usually best seen on our coasts where wide beaches are exposed at low water. But wind is sometimes destructive inland, especially on light soils. The Fens and Breckland suffer much in this respect. Blowing is aided by the absence of clay and humus to act as binding material, by lack of rain, and by the absence of wind-breaks. The peat fens, for example, have to all intents and purposes no clay. April and May are usually the worst months; the crops have scarcely had time to cover the ground, which is often very dry at this time of year. The worst effects are on agricultural land once the surface has been prepared as a seed bed for sugar beet and other crops. A severe wind may remove perhaps four inches of soil and dump it in ditches and dykes. Unfortunately, the crop-plants, too, may be removed from the ground.

The events described in this chapter are all recent. Few reliable records of physiographical effects of storms exist for those which occurred even fifty years ago, and scarcely any for earlier times. Yet storms have taken place, and at times have been severe, as in the fourteenth century. After the final melting of the Quaternary ice-sheets, there was much storminess and before the spread of a more or less complete plant and tree cover it produced great changes in the landscape. In viewing our scenery today we must try to evaluate the effects of changing climates and meteorological conditions since the Ice Age as well as the less spectacular ones of the present day.

CHAPTER XVII

SOILS

Physical geography and ecology. Most of the creatures on earth live in the ocean and in smaller bodies of water. Outside the hydrosphere, life is concentrated in a relatively thin layer, rarely more than a few tens of feet thick, where the atmosphere and lithosphere adjoin. This layer consists of the plants covering the land, the soil inhabited by their roots, and the various animals and organisms, some of them of microscopic size, living on the vegetation and in the soil. All of them are directly or indirectly affected by the physical environment, and the entire make-up of the layer, the biosphere as it is sometimes called, depends on the nature of the underlying rocks of the lithosphere, the relief, and the climate. All these vary from place to place over the land surface of the globe, and the constitution of the biosphere varies accordingly over short and long distances.

For each species of plants there is a certain set of conditions in which it best thrives, and each species can tolerate a certain range of soils and weather. Some plants are killed by frost and are therefore confined to frost-free parts of the world, others are unable to resist drought and are found only where they can obtain water from the soil throughout the year. Many plants have adapted themselves to severe seasons by having an annual resting period, when they shed their leaves or when life is preserved in the seed ready to germinate with the coming of spring or the rainy season. Others are more highly specialised and can tolerate very difficult physical conditions, but are unable to meet the competition from plants that are less hardy where soil and climate are favourable to both. As a result of these variations in adaptation and tolerance, any particular combination of soil and climate tends to be associated with a certain assemblage of plants, that is, a characteristic vegetation.

By tracing the stages in the colonisation by plants of a piece of fresh ground, such as might be exposed by a landslip, it is possible to illustrate how the vegetation adapts itself to the soil and climate it finds. Algae and other lower plants first colonise the bare ground, and seeds are carried there from plants in the neighbourhood by the wind, birds, and other means. They germinate and, if the habitat is suitable, begin to grow. Gradually the number of plants and the number of species represented increases, until the plants begin to come into contact with one another and form a more or less complete cover. At this stage one species competes with another for the light and water on which they so much depend, and those best adapted to the particular conditions grow most strongly. They survive while the others are ousted, until an association of species evolves that is more or less characteristic of that habitat.

From this illustration it might appear that the vegetation developing in any place is almost entirely dependent on the soil and climate conditions that it happens to find there. This is far from being the case. The vegetation is capable of modifying both. The character of the soil is in time largely determined by the plant cover, and the climate in the soil and in the vegetation is very different from that of the free air.

A sequence of vegetational changes taking place on a salt marsh has been described in an earlier chapter. In the initial stages, wet muddy flats frequently covered by the tide are colonised by *Zostera*. Silt is deposited around these plants and other obstacles to the free movement of the water, and on the higher and somewhat firmer ground thus formed other plants begin to establish themselves. The plant cover thickens, more silt accumulates largely as a result of the presence of the plants, and as the marsh builds up to levels at which it is covered only by the highest tides, species less tolerant of submergence begin to flourish and the marsh may eventually be used for grazing. In this case the vegetation has itself been largely responsible for modifying its own habitat in the course of time.

A similar sequence of steps in the plant succession is followed in fresh-water swamps of the kind that once existed in the Fenland between Cambridge and the Wash, and the stages can be deduced both from the plant remains occurring at different levels in the peat there, and from the vegetation pattern in a portion of undrained fen that has been artificially preserved at Wicken near Ely. Some of the plants growing in fresh water a few feet deep are completely submerged, others have floating leaves or aerial shoots. At the edges of pools reeds such as *Phragmites* and *Scirpus* grow and gradually spread outwards, and as the water near-by shallows with the accumulation of mud and dead plants, sedges such as *Cladium*, and the fen rush, *Juncus obtusiflorus*, begin to dominate the vegetation. The process continues and various flowering plants and grasses take root. Because the ground is so moist, the remains of the dead plants do not decay completely, and the level of the marsh builds up until shrubs and trees appear, first willow and later birch and alder. Ultimately, fen woodland or carr is formed. This succession differs from the salt-marsh succession in that the constructional process is largely brought about by the accumulation of the plant débris itself, while in the salt-marsh it is caused mainly by debris from an outside source. Both result in the evolution of *organic soils*, but the salt marsh soils usually contain much more mineral silt and sand.

Having noted these two examples of how vegetation modifies the environment in the course of time, and builds up the soil material in which it is rooted, we can turn back again to the landslip as an illustration of the evolution of a plant cover adapted to its environment, and consider the changes that are likely to follow those already described, in a warm or temperate humid climate.

The plants grow by absorbing energy from the sun and using it to convert water, mineral salts and nitrogen from the soil, and carbon and oxygen from the air, into the organic matter of which their roots, stems and leaves are composed. When the plants die they fall to the ground and decay. This organic matter together with that from the die-back of roots is attacked by small animals and by bacteria and other organisms of microscopic size, and the complicated organic compounds are broken down into a wide range of simpler substances, some gases and some mineral salts. Many of these are soluble in water. Some of the partially decayed plant and microbial remains give rise to a relatively stable colloidal complex known as humus. This is insoluble in water but may disperse under certain circumstances. The first plants growing on the landslip had to depend on the limited amounts of plant food in the weathered rock, but as one generation of plants succeeds another the nutrient resources increase. The products of breakdown of the plants are dissolved by percolating rain water and the acid water attacks mineral particles in the weathering rock, releasing more calcium, phosphates and other necessary salts for the use of succeeding generations of plants. The weathering of primary minerals also produces clay which assists in the retention of nutrients. In time, various small animals come to live amongst the plants and in the soil; spiders, rodents and earthworms. They burrow in the soil, mix up the organic matter with the mineral particles of the weathered rock, and with their excreta and eventually their dead bodies, add to the humic material in the soil. The breaking down of the organic material is performed mainly by bacteria, of which there are numerous species, and commonly several hundreds of millions of individuals to each cubic inch of soil. They are most active under certain conditions, and thrive best in soils neither too acid nor too alkaline, with temperatures between 60° and 120° F., and an adequate moisture content. With the development of a soil layer, new species of plants less tolerant of the severe conditions that originally existed begin to survive. After taking advantage of the shelter afforded by the more hardy pioneers in their early stages of growth they eventually replace them. Shrubs and trees appear and some plants wither in their shade. But the soil benefits from the minerals, brought up from a great depth by the roots and released from the leaf-fall. It deepens, acquires certain structural features of a kind to be described later, and the woodland is inhabited by a new faunal population. Eventually, soil and vegetation together reach a state of balance or dynamic equilibrium. The vegetation is said to have reached its climax, with large and complicated plants dominant. The soils are called mature soils and show well-developed profiles.

Throughout such a development, the plant cover, the soils and the creatures living in them are constantly acting and reacting one on the other, and it is difficult if not meaningless to consider the evolution of any one of the three apart from the others. The complex has for most purposes to be considered as a whole. To the study of the interrelationships involved, the name ecology is often applied.

It is impossible to eliminate man and his works from a subject of this kind. Throughout the last million years, human societies have exerted an increasingly greater influence on the biosphere. At first they burned the forests and woodlands in the course of hunting forays, and the vegetation in some critical areas, for example, at forest margins, was probably converted into a fire-climax instead of a natural climax a very long time ago, certainly hundreds and possibly thousands of years. Later, flocks and herds of domesticated animals grazed wide areas of grassland and, where woodland had been burned, prevented trees from recolonising the land by eating young shoots and damaging saplings. Cultivation of the soil, first by shifting cultivators and later by settled farmers, has transformed the landscape of large parts of the world.

Man has created in his farmlands special environments suited to the requirements of the hundred or more species of plants he finds most useful, and where they do not have to meet competition from other plants. Until quite recently crop production involved impoverishment of the soil. When land had been cultivated for a few years it was abandoned and regained fertility as the natural vegetation took over once more and humus was restored. This use of the land is wasteful of time and labour and soil, but it persists in many parts of the world and especially in the less densely populated parts of the tropics. Similar systems were once the rule almost everywhere, but in Britain as in most other advanced countries the aim of the modern farmer is to build up the soil to a level of productivity higher than that attainable under a natural plant cover, by careful cultivations, crop rotations, drainage, and manuring with mineral and organic fertilisers. The soils and vegetation of these countries are man-made and differ greatly from what they would be under natural conditions. This is true not only of the cropland but also of the pastures and forests and even the moorland.

It is now within the power of the engineer, forester, and agriculturalist to modify the soils and vegetation profoundly and no doubt they will employ the means at their disposal more and more as time goes on. Nevertheless, the economic advantages to be gained from clearing, draining, irrigating, and fertilising depend very largely on the inherent physical and initial biological conditions. The activities of man modify the soil-vegetation complex but they are themselves influenced by the nature of this complex. In fact, man can be regarded as one of the active principals in ecology, and a great deal of human geography is concerned with viewing him in this light.

It follows that physical, human, and biogeography are not independent subjects but they overlap over wide fields of knowledge. We are mainly concerned here with the borderland of physical geography where biological influences are of the highest importance. Here the soil is regarded as the focus of the ecological system and amongst the matters discussed, it attracts the most attention.

The soil and its evolution. Soil is made up not merely of finely divided particles of rock. It is a complicated mixture of mineral particles derived from weathering rock, organic material derived from dead plants and animals, and living things that include the roots of large and small plants and various animals. It is permeated by gases and by water containing many substances in solution. Within the soil these various components react on each other, so that the soil material is in a constant state of both synthesis and decomposition. Solutions move through the pore spaces in the soil, plant roots penetrate downwards and later die and decay, and earthworms take in soil and pass it through their systems. Within the soil mass everything is in motion, but the nature of the soil as a whole may remain fairly constant. However, should the vegetation be modified, perhaps as a result of a change of climate or perhaps as a result of human interference (which is a more likely eventuality), the amount and composition of the organic matter returned to the soil alters, the animal population is transformed and the soil, adjusting itself to the new conditions, alters in nearly every respect.

Because of the constant circulation of substances within the soil and its response to changes in the environment, some writers have been induced to regard the soil as a living body. Certainly it is much more than weathered rock. Weathering involves simplification. In the cases of igneous and metamorphic rocks the rather complicated minerals formed at high temperatures and pressures are broken down into simpler substances. For example, a fresh granite may be formed of crystals of quartz, felspar, biotite and muscovite (black and white mica). After chemical weathering (p. 284) the quartz remains little altered as grains of siliceous sand, the muscovite breaks up into exceedingly small flakes, and the biotite decomposes. The felspars break down to give various ionic solutions and colloidal suspensions. These are carried away in percolating waters, or clay minerals are precipitated from them. The granite breaks down into a mass of gritty clay, stained red or brown in colour by the oxidation of iron from the biotite.

The formation of a soil on the other hand is more of a constructive than a destructive process. For example, individual particles of mineral and organic matter are bound together into lumps or aggregates and the soil is said to acquire a structure. Each layer in the soil acquires special properties and is exploited for particular purposes by the plant roots living in it. The processes involved in the building of the soil are of a complicated nature. Humic acids play a very important part in binding particles together into aggregates, but the chemical and biological reactions involved in soil formation are not well understood in spite of the immense amount of data that has been collected with reference to them, and if they were understood a full explanation would not be possible in a brief account of this kind, because it would have to presuppose a good acquaintance with many branches of science on the part of the reader.

An ideal vertical section at the surface of the lithosphere shows a passage from fresh rock, it may be at a depth of a few inches, or it may be at hundreds of feet in the humid tropics, through a layer of weathering rock where simplification is the rule, to the soil where constructive biological processes are at work. There is often no clear distinction between the weathering layer and the soil; one merges into the other. Sometimes the situation is complicated because the solid rock has been covered with drift, that is by sedimentary deposits such as boulder clay or river alluvium, and the soil is derived from this parent material which is in a comminuted state before it is further weathered *in situ*. Occasionally the situation is still more complicated—the existing soil-forming processes taking place on the remains of ancient soils which may well have evolved under conditions quite different from those of the present and which have been, as it were, fossilised.

The character of the soil depends a good deal on the nature of the parent material. Soils derived from sandstones are normally coarse-textured and free-draining, while those formed from shales are heavier and often poorly drained. Soils developing on youthful volcanic rocks are often richer in various mineral salts required by plants than are those derived from quartz-rich acid gneisses. Soils formed over limestones are usually alkaline—but some are black and rich in humus while others are red and rich in iron. In spite of the fact that the role of the parent material is occasionally dominant, the soil qualities attributable to it are usually regarded as being subordinate to those acquired over a long period of years, and accounted for mainly in terms of the various climatic conditions prevailing during the soil's evolution.

When soil formation has been in progress for no more than a few years the parent material is hardly altered at a depth of an inch or two. As the vegetation develops and organic material is incorporated in the surface layers, plant roots and soil water perform their work and important changes begin to take place. A pit dug a few feet deep shows a section called a soil profile and, in a soil past its first youth, this normally shows more or less distinct horizontal layerings called horizons. These horizons may differ from each other in colour or texture or in other features visible in the field, or the distinctions may only become apparent when chemical or other laboratory analyses have been made. The horizons are commonly designated by the letters *A*, *B* and *C*. In a podsol soil, of the kind found under coniferous forests, a dark coloured surface layer containing abundant plant remains and humus overlies a pallid layer. From both of these percolating water carries material away in solution and suspension and they are known together as the eluvial or *A* horizon. Immediately below is the illuvial or *B* horizon where substances are precipitated and it is often rather highly coloured. The *B* horizon merges into a zone of weathering, the *C* horizon. In this country it is often difficult to pick out the horizons, either because the soils are immature or because they have been disturbed by past farming. Indeed, this system of naming soil horizons is not easily applicable to most soils and the whole question of its continued use is at present under review.

A soil develops more quickly in warm, humid, conditions under which chemical reactions and plant growth are rapid, than in a cool or dry climate; and a mature profile will evolve more readily in parent material that is already finely divided than it will over solid rock. Even under optimum conditions the time required for a soil to reach maturity is usually considerable. Under certain favourable circumstances, however, it is possible to estimate the date when soil-forming processes must have begun, and by comparing soils of several different ages, all formed over the same parent material and supposedly in the same climate, to deduce the sequence and rate of changes, at any rate in the earlier stages.

In the chapter on shorelines, some mention was made of the accumulation of sand-dunes on low-coasts where sand is blown landwards from inter-tidal flats (see pl. 19*b*). Where dunes are extending towards the sea it is occasionally possible to calculate the age of different parts of the dunes from a study of historical records and old maps. Salisbury traced the development of the dunes near Southport in this way, and was then in a position to describe the development of the vegetation and soils on dune sand over the last few hundred years. The mounds of sand or embryo dunes on the beach are colonised first by sea couch-grass (*Agropyrum junceum*), and as they grow to form a frontal dune, marram (*Ammophila*) and lyme grass (*Elymus dunarius*) become established.

They push up through the sand as it continues to accumulate, and they assist sand accumulation by reducing the speed of the wind as it blows over the dune, causing it to deposit its load. This continues until eventually a new foredune builds up on the seaward side, cutting off the supply of sand and giving shelter from the wind. The older dune is now more stable and various mosses, lichens, and rooted grasses are able to grow on it. At first the soil is rather alkaline on account of the sea-salt and the particles of shells in the fresh sand blown up from the flats. But when the supply of fresh sand is cut off, percolating rainwater dissolves the salt and calcium carbonate, and after perhaps two centuries they have been leached away almost entirely. Over the same period the organic material in the soil increases and it becomes more acid. A pit reveals several inches of dark topsoil resting on what appears to be raw yellow-brown sand. In this country the dunes are eventually occupied by some form of scrub or heath or else they are planted with conifers. In the latter case the acidity becomes more marked and the soil begins to assume some of the characteristics of a podsol, a type of soil that is described below.

The ages of soils at the heads of some of the glacial valleys in the Tyrol have been ascertained by making use of historical records of the advances of glaciers responsible for the moraines between which the soils are located. The boulders are colonised in time by various lichens and algae but otherwise remain little altered. On the finer material in the hollows a variety of plants becomes established in the course of a century, soil acidity develops, the proportion of clayey material increases and the nitrogen content builds up; but the whole process is a slow one.

The eruption of Krakatoa, to which reference is made on p. 371, allowed scientists to make some interesting observations on the speed of colonisation by plants and the evolution of soils on fresh volcanic rocks near the equator. The eruption covered the nearby island, Lang Eiland, in volcanic dust more than 100 feet thick in some places. Less than fifty years later it was found that the youthful ash was covered by a luxuriant plant cover including more than a hundred different species, and analyses showed that it had already progressed a long way towards being converted into a true soil. Similarly, after an eruption on the island of St Vincent, in the West Indies, it was found that fertile soils had developed on what had been sterile ash thirty years before.

These three examples give some indication of the differing rates at which soil profiles and vegetation develop under unlike climatic conditions and in different parent material. But they cover only a relatively short interval of time. In fact, it has proved difficult to trace datable soils representing the various stages in the evolution of the most widely recognised mature soil profiles, and their history is not well understood, especially in so far as the chemical and biochemical reactions involved in the development of the soil horizons are concerned. The whole situation is complicated by the fact that climatic and vegetational changes took place while these soils were forming. Nevertheless, it is possible to distinguish several broad groups of soils which are more or less well-defined and to show that each group is associated with a particular set of climatic conditions and a certain kind of plant cover.

Climatic and vegetation regions. The climate of a place is the sum total of the weather experienced there, and it includes not only normal conditions and seasonal fluctuations, but also abnormal happenings such as very heavy storms and prolonged droughts. Places with similar climates can be grouped together into climatic regions. The delineation of such regions is an arbitrary matter, since there are no clear climatic boundaries in nature—one type of climate grades into another. In defining their regions, climatologists have often used natural vegetation as a guide, and have then applied climatic statistics in an attempt to express the vegetation boundaries. Generally, they have used temperature to distinguish regions in high latitudes, because it is the critical factor there as far as plant growth is concerned. At temperatures below 42° F. plant growth practically ceases, and below 32° F. plants sensitive to frost are damaged or killed. In low latitudes, temperatures fall to freezing-point only at high altitudes, and availability of water is the main factor that limits the growing season. Annual losses of water by evaporation from tropical lakes and moist soils are three or four times greater than in this country, so that the chances of droughts occurring are high. Soils in hot countries dry out, at least in the surface layers, if the rainfall in any month is less than about four inches, and only plants with long roots penetrating deep underground are able to thrive in the protracted dry seasons. In low latitudes, therefore, rainfall is the most important factor used for defining climatic regions.

Soils are affected by the same kind of climatic factors. Temperature differences are important because they influence biological activity and the rate of chemical weathering, especially the rate of breakdown of organic matter. The amount and direction of water moving through the soil is one of the primary controls in the development of a soil profile. Moreover, the soil is to a large extent a function of the vegetation. It is not surprising, therefore, to find that maps showing the main types of soil and their distribution over the world bear a strong resemblance to those showing climatic regions (see fig. 215). But within each climatic

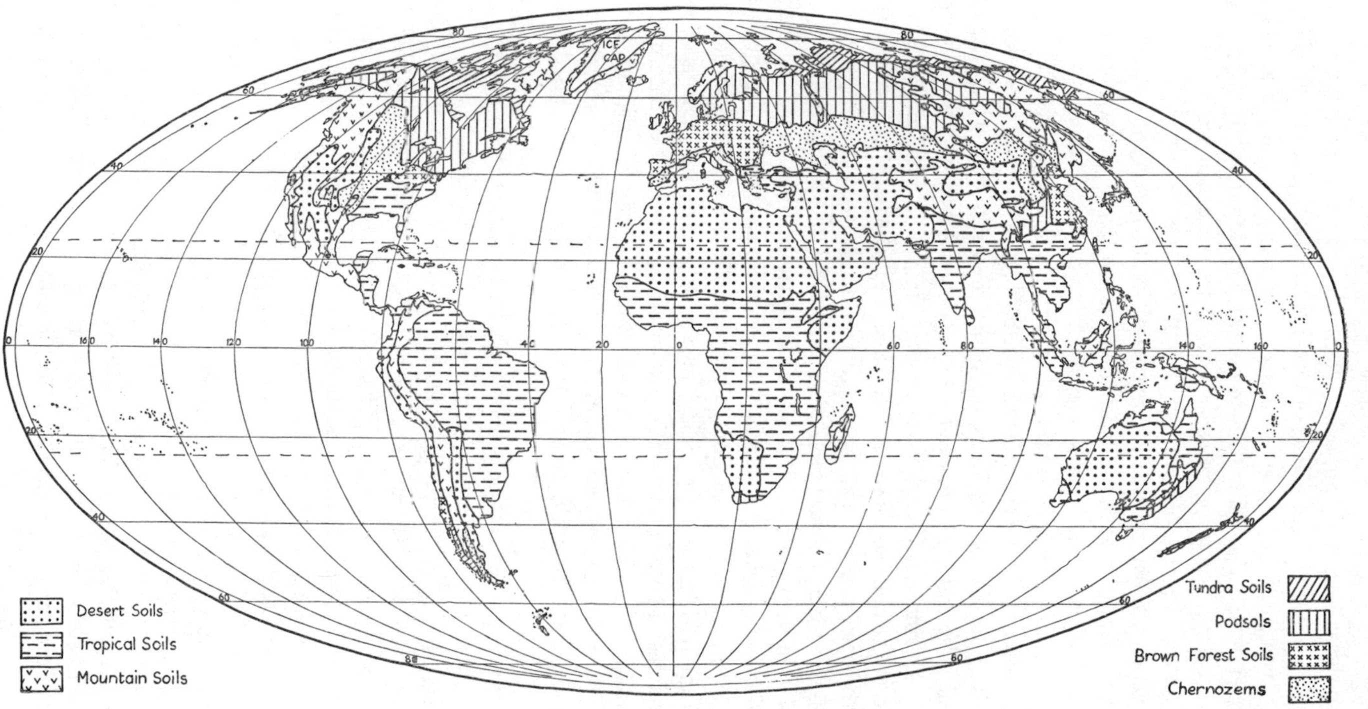

Fig. 215. Soil map of the world.

region the soils are far from being all the same, because of differences in parent material and the effects of topography. Such discrepancies only become apparent on large-scale maps of small areas (see fig. 216). It is, however, worth discussing their origin in a little more detail at this stage before continuing to make some generalisations about soil-vegetation relationships in each of the main climatic regions.

A geological drift map is an approximation to a map showing parent material. On a world scale this would have some faint resemblances to a map showing climatic regions. Large parts of the humid temperate lands have been covered by ice-sheets and retain a mantle of glacial deposits; these vary greatly in texture from stiff boulder clays to outwash sands, according to the mode of deposition and the rocks over which the ice passed. The drier steppe country was widely covered with wind-blown loess. During the glacial advances and retreats in high latitudes, the deserts were at times more extensive and at times smaller than at present and the parent material at the margins of the deserts commonly consists of old wind-borne desert sand, now established under grasses and trees. Finally, in the high rainfall areas of the equatorial rain forest, the monsoon lands and savannas, soil-forming processes have been going on for a very long period, and many of the existing soils include material derived from the horizons of very ancient soils preserved on the remains of old peneplains. There is then some parallelism between the distribution of parent material of different kinds and the existing climatic regions, but it is by no means exact, and within the broad classes of drifts mentioned there are important variations that are all reflected in the soils derived from them.

The relief of the surface is another factor that plays an important part in producing variations in the soil over short distances (see fig. 217). Very often the land-forms and the parent material in an area are closely related. The outwash fans and eskers and other deposits laid down by running water in glaciated regions are sandy, while the till plains are commonly clayey. Again, the parent material in lands where planation surfaces have been preserved at different levels is commonly older and more completely weathered on the older, higher surfaces than on the lower, younger ones.

Soils also vary from place to place, although both the parent material and the climate remain uniform, according to their positions on the slopes. The slope of the ground influences the movement of water in the soil, and also the rates and results of soil erosion and deposition. (Soil erosion here refers to geological erosion under the natural plant cover; it does not mean the accelerated erosion of the soil, caused by man's

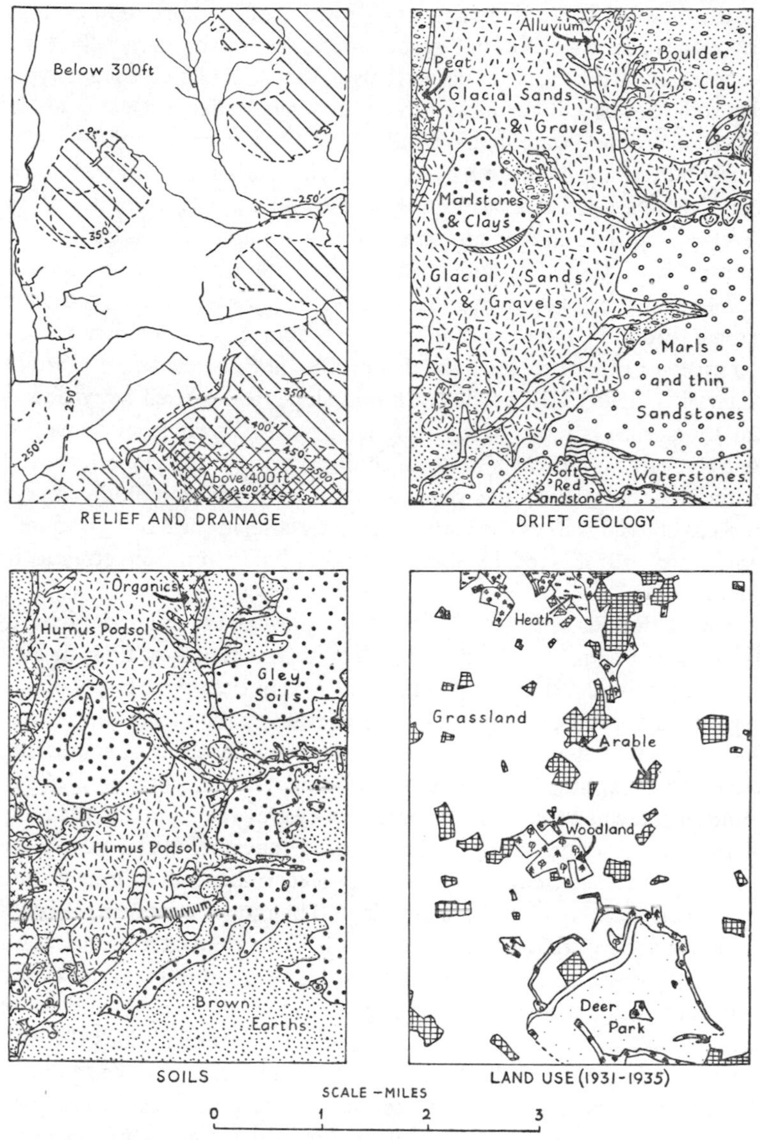

Fig. 216. Maps of a part of Shropshire covered by surveys of drift-geology, soils, and land use. The patterns of the physical elements are evidently inter-related, but the pattern of land use shows no clear relation to that of soils.

interference. This is discussed later.) Mature soils usually develop most readily on gently rolling terrain, where erosion of the soil is slow and yet drainage is adequate. On flat ground, drainage is poor, especially if the parent material is somewhat impervious so that soils of a distinctive type, gley soils, develop. They include a mottled layer called a 'G' horizon in a zone of alternate waterlogging and drying, above a grey or blue permanently waterlogged subsoil. On steep hillsides, soil and weathered material are eroded away as rapidly as they form; mature profiles never develop, and the soils remain shallow but well-drained. In undulating country with slopes of intermediate declivity there is sometimes a regular sequence of soils from hillcrest to valley bottom, forming a soil catena. From the hill crests soil material is constantly being removed by soil creep or other processes, so that profiles are shallow and the parent material is close to the surface. In mid-slope, soil carried away downhill by erosion is replaced by material brought down from above, so that the soil may be in a state of equilibrium. At the slope foot, soil material accumulates; the deep soils thus formed commonly merge into old alluvial soils of the valley floor and these, in their turn, into soils which are still affected by the deposition of alluvium from streams in flood.

In well-drained sites water moves down through the soil under gravity and either escapes laterally to the surface in stream beds or finds its way to the water-table. During a period of drought the upper layers of soil dry out as a result of evaporation and of transpiration from the vegetation and water moves up towards the surface as a result of capillarity. Such water commonly contains salts of iron, alumina, silica, or alkalis in solution and when the water evaporates they are precipitated in the body of the soil or at the surface. The upward movements can take place through a vertical thickness of about 3 feet, rather less in gravels and sands, considerably more in loamy clays. The rate of movement is faster in coarse than in fine textured material. When the water available for capillary lifting drops below a critical level, upward movement ceases and then salts that have accumulated may be washed down again and out of the soil with the next heavy rain. But under desert conditions the soils are not washed out by rain, and if the soil water is fed by some means so that upward capillary movements continue, perhaps as a result of seepage from higher ground, or artificial irrigation without adequate drainage, the salts accumulate. Saline soils are normally found in depressions, especially in basins of inland drainage, and they support special kinds of salt-tolerant vegetation. Depressions in more humid regions receive much more surface water and if lakes do not form, the soils are likely to be of a peaty nature on account of the incomplete breakdown of the plant débris under the wet, anaerobic (airless), conditions.

Having outlined some of the factors that can complicate the soil pattern and result in local variation of soil profiles, we can consider the relationship between climate, soil, and vegetation on a regional basis.

The tundra. Beyond the Arctic Circle, and farther south in the east of Canada and Siberia, the low temperatures throughout the year and the short growing season are tolerated by only a limited number of small plants or dwarf varieties of larger ones. Mean annual temperatures are below freezing and the subsoil below a depth of a few feet is frozen permanently, and has been given the name *permafrost*. The top layer of soil and rock débris thaws out in the early summer when erosion on slopes is strong on account of mudflows and slips. An abundant load is made available to strong floods of water fed by melting snow and there is active deposition over the wide plains flooded by the rivers in their lower reaches. When the cold returns in early autumn, the ground freezes again, the upper layers first and then those below, and throughout this period frost action and the accompanying physical weathering are very strong.

In the drier upland sites violent wind erosion in the summer, and melt-water in the spring, sift out the fine material, and leave behind a mantle of stones. Any plants that manage to survive form dense cushions and their roots, bunched closely together underneath, are like the raw humus of a podsol profile which is described below.

Where the rainfall is somewhat higher, perhaps ten inches, some trees survive, but the dominant cover is made up of lichens and mosses. The mosses conduct heat slowly and during the summer thaw ice may remain under clumps of moss when it has melted under patchy bare ground. The surface of the ground is commonly hummocky as a result of this process. The seasonal freeze and thaw gives rise to other ground patterns. The finer material forms rounded hummocks of earth a few feet or several yards in diameter, within a network of stones. Exactly how this comes about is not known although there are several theories purporting to explain it. Mosses, sedges, grasses and low bushes colonise the edges of the stone rings.

In flat or basin-shaped areas mosses may form a more or less closed cover, and dark coloured peaty soils may accumulate. Poor drainage and the accumulation of peaty soils are assisted by the frozen subsoil impeding the downward movement of water.

Representatives of tundra types of soil and vegetation can be found at high altitudes in this country. They are most widespread in Scotland, notably above 3000 feet on the Cairngorms. Frost polygons and stone stripes, both of which are types of patterned ground that form over a frozen subsoil, have been found at low levels in this country, notably in the Breckland area of East Anglia, where they are survivals from a colder period.

Podsol soils of high-latitude coniferous forests and heaths. Coniferous forests extend in a broad belt across Northern Europe and the U.S.S.R. and cover large tracts of North America, south of the Arctic Circle. The growing season is short, mean annual temperatures are below 32° F. in places and the subsoil is then permanently frozen. But mean annual temperatures may be as high as 45° F. and coniferous forest still the dominant vegetation if the summer temperatures are too low for deciduous woodland.

Beneath the trees the ground is covered with herbs and mosses and occasionally cranberries and bilberries. The surface-layer of soil is raw humus or 'Mor'. This consists of only partly decayed plant remains. They accumulate because temperatures throughout most of the year are too low for the active life of organisms, such as bacteria, capable of breaking down organic material which is naturally resistant to decomposition. The leaf-fall of the trees contains few bases and such quantities that are released are leached away by water percolating down through the soil for much of the year. Consequently, the top-soil is acid, its fauna rather specialised, and earthworms are absent. Only a few species of bacteria are present; various kinds of fungi are abundant, but they are less effective in mineralising organic matter.

The upper peaty part of the *A* horizon overlies a bleached layer often about 6 inches thick that forms the most characteristic feature of the podsol profile. The name podsol is derived from the Russian word for ash; Russian peasants believed the bleached layer to be ash left behind by forest fires in the past. In fact it is the insoluble residue left behind after strong leaching by acid waters percolating down from the layer above. It is a dead horizon, and the tree roots are mainly confined to the peaty soil above, and to the upper parts of the horizon below.

The *B* horizon is very variable but is commonly about a foot thick and is made up of a thin dark layer where particles of humus have been precipitated from descending water, and a thicker brown layer of iron accumulation that passes down into weathering rock. Under moorland or heath vegetation, and especially where a pebbly layer happens to occur in the *B* horizon, iron and humus together form a tough metallic layer a fraction of an inch thick at the top of the usual iron-stained horizon.

Podsols in Britain are mainly confined to the mountainous north-west, where the raw humus tends to be of a peaty character, but in a slightly different form they occur over sandy parent material in the south-east, where active leaching and a lack of lime make up for the lower rainfall (see fig. 217). They can be seen on the heathlands of the Breckland and also on Hindhead Common in Surrey.

Although podsols do not give fertile cropland, they can become quite productive after adequate dressings of lime and fertiliser and, sometimes, draining. Draining occasionally involves deep ploughing to break up the impervious ironstone layer and may also be necessary to improve pastures or to allow heathland to be planted up with trees. Under cultivation, podsols acquire some characteristics of the more amenable brown forest soils.

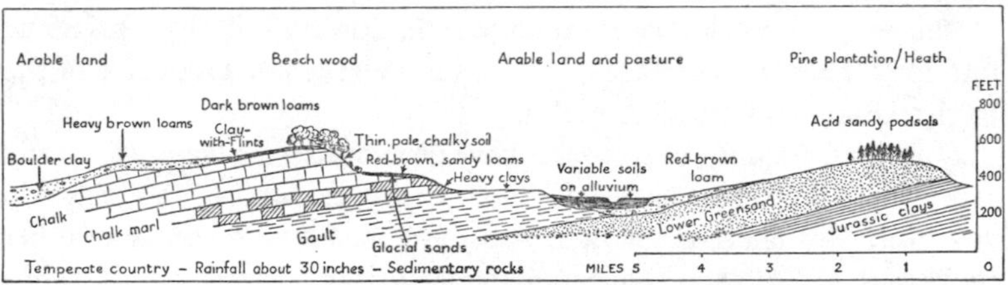

Fig. 217. Soils of temperate regions.

Brown and grey soils of the deciduous forests of high and middle latitudes. Under climatic conditions somewhat less severe than those of the coniferous forest belt, deciduous woodland with such trees as oak and beech as dominants becomes the climax vegetation. The higher temperatures of summer, and the warmer springs, result in the soil drying out for short periods, and in slight upward movements of soil water. The leaf-fall from deciduous trees is richer in calcium and phosphates than are pine needles, and is much more readily decomposed. In place of the sour soggy 'Mor' of the coniferous forest, there is a brown or grey-brown layer containing well-decomposed mild humus or mull. It is only slightly acid, and on account of the great activity of earthworms and other creatures is intimately mixed with the mineral part of the soil. Owing to the rapidity of decomposition under these conditions, the whole cycle involving plant growth, decay, and the uptake of material in the tree roots, continues at a greater rate than in the podsols of the coniferous forests.

Within the *A* horizon there is no bleached layer, but the mull grades down into a brownish (*B*) horizon which merges into the weathering rock. The colours are somewhat greyer in climates more continental than those of this country.

Just as there are outliers of podsols and coniferous woodland in Britain south of the main podsol zone, so are there outliers of brown forest soils in the north-west. They are usually associated with lime-rich parent material.

Brown forest soils are much more attractive to the agriculturalist than are podsols. Locally they possess a well-developed crumb structure that is ideal for plant growth, and with careful attention they can be raised to a high level of productivity. But to produce crops successfully year after year they have to be farmed carefully.

Chernozem soils of the steppes of mid-latitudes. The soils which are by nature the richest and most productive of all, and retain their fertility for many years in spite of extractive agriculture, have developed on the grassy steppes of sub-humid to semi-arid lands in the continental interiors. They are the Black Earths, the great wheat producers of the Soviet Union and North America.

Over wide areas the chernozems have developed from loess, and nearly everywhere the parent material is fairly heavy, calcareous, and relatively youthful. But chernozems have also developed over a variety of other rocks, and climate and vegetation appear to have played at least as important a part in their formation as parent material.

The steppes have an annual precipitation of between 10 and 20 inches. Winter snowfall is important there because the melt-water percolates deeply and provides much of the soil water used by the plants in the following summer. In winter, the cold is severe and biological activity practically ceases for several months. With the coming of spring the soils tend to puddle as the frost leaves them, and then the grasses begin to grow swiftly. Summers are very hot, and the rain falls in heavy showers at intervals of several days. The grasses grow long and elaborate root systems in an attempt to combat the drought, but eventually they die. Their systems of fine rootlets remain only partially decomposed on account of the dryness of the soil, and this probably has important effects on the soil characteristics.

The most striking feature of the chernozems is the very dark *A* horizon, sometimes as much as 5 feet thick. It is black when wet, and it contains a large amount of organic matter derived from the grasses and their roots, which has become incorporated in the soil to a great depth by the work of a rich fauna of earthworms and burrowing animals.

The passage downwards to the light grey or brownish-grey *B* horizon is a gradual one. This horizon has a rather coarse, blocky structure; it sometimes contains lime concretions and occasionally a layer of gypsum beneath them.

The prairie soils of North America lie east of the main chernozem belt where the climate is more humid. Forest grows in areas still farther east which seem to be no more humid than the prairie soils. But on the latter, for some reason that is not clear, the vegetation is grass and the soils are similar to the chernozems.

Agriculturally soils of this type are attractive. The chernozems have been made by and for grasses and they are admirably suited for the production of cereals. The soil particles are bound together into aggregates varying in size between a pea and a nut. The origin of this crumb structure is not known for certain. The crumbs may have been formed by local drying out near the grass rootlets. They may owe their strength to the adhesive effects of organic colloids flocculated by calcium. Whatever its cause, the crumb structure is a valuable property because it allows good circulation of water and air, and is very favourable to plant growth. The chernozems retain their structure well, as compared with other soils, but after some decades of cultivation, if little has been returned to the soil and much extracted, the structure breaks down and severe erosion by wind and water follows. The black dust of the storms that sometimes sweep across the Great Plains when cold air advances in the spring is largely derived from the chernozems. Fortunately, the great depth of the organic horizon means that recuperation of the soils is rapid under careful treatment, unless erosion has been unusually destructive.

Tropical soils. The three groups of soils that have been described above, podsols, brown forest soils and chernozems, occupy fairly distinct belts stretching across the great glaciated and peri-glacial plains of Europe and North America. Parent material and age are fairly uniform and the main factors that distinguish the soils appear to be climate and vegetation. Much of the early scientific work on soils was carried out in Russia and the United States where there was a good deal of interest in assessing the potential agricultural value of the new lands that were being opened up for cultivation about a century ago. The ideas that the early scientists derived from their studies of the three soils mentioned have influenced the science of pedology since then and there has been a tendency to extend the types of classification evolved to other parts of the world where they may not be so applicable. In low latitudes parent material is more variable than on the northern plainlands, the period of soil formation varies enormously over short distances, and any classification based on climate or vegetation is of only limited value. Moreover, the volume of information on tropical soils that was available until a few years ago was not great, and although much has been collected since the end of the Second World War it remains to be systematised. Experts are still unable to agree on any classification of tropical soils that can be widely applied.

Considered as a whole tropical soils have certain properties in common that distinguish them broadly from soils of high latitudes. In general they have a low content of organic matter. In the deserts this is largely on account of the sparse vegetation. Under forest, the annual addition of dry matter probably varies from a few tons to each acre in savanna woodland to some tens of tons in the rain forest. But at the high temperatures experienced organic matter is rapidly oxidised. With mean annual temperatures in excess of 80° F. organic material does not accumulate except in a few waterlogged sites.

In hot countries termites take the place held by earthworms in temperate lands as far as soil-forming processes are concerned. There are several species of these creatures; some are edible, several are very destructive of wooden buildings, clothes, and books. They play their part in soil formation by chewing up the woody parts of plants, thus preparing them for attack and further breakdown by micro-organisms. But they also have a great effect on the structure of the soil. In most woodland and open areas there are a few or several termite heaps to each acre. Some form red or yellowish spires 20 feet high; these are usually found on deep, well-drained, sandy loams. Different types of soil can be picked out by the shapes of the heaps made by the differing species of termite living in them. Over shallow ironstone soils, the termite heaps are often shaped like large brown toadstools; open stretches of coarse gravelly soil are commonly interrupted by low volcano-shaped mounds a few feet in diameter. Since from time to time the heaps collapse and new ones are built on different sites, entire areas must be affected by them in the course of a few centuries. The complicated systems of passages often penetrate several feet below the surface, since in any one nest there is a greater proportion of it below than there is above ground. Analysis of the material in the heaps shows that it is often richer in nitrogen, less acid and more clayey than the soil from the surroundings.

A little earlier it was mentioned that tropical soils may have evolved over a long period, possibly tens of thousands of years. During such a long time the climate and vegetation have alternated in some places between arid desert and humid forest, and soils dominated by one or the other are intermingled. Only occasionally is there a wide extent of soil with a fairly uniform appearance. In the following paragraphs soil descriptions are highly generalised.

The soils and vegetation of Mediterranean regions. The topography of lands with cool wet winters and hot dry summers of the Mediterranean regions is complicated. Arid valley bottoms alternate with mountain ridges. The soil patterns are consequently intricate. Furthermore, these lands, at least in the old world, have always been attractive to man. Both the vegetation and the soils have been much altered by clearing of the original woodland, by the grazing of goats and sheep, and by farming, terracing, and erosion. The woodland has been replaced by shrubby vegetation with a few tall trees and a ground cover made up of a variety of herbaceous species. In recent decades some Australian trees, notably the eucalyptus, have been successfully introduced to the Mediterranean regions of the other continents.

In many paintings of the south of France, the bright red colour of the soil is a striking feature of the scenery, and indeed Terra Rossa soils are very typical of these regions. They are commonly underlain by limestones but not invariably so; consequently the red colouring may owe its origin to ancient soil-forming processes rather than the underlying rock, and it has been suggested that the parent material is the remains of old tropical soils.

The *A* horizons of the Terra Rossa are usually poorly developed, normally less than 4 inches thick, and their organic matter content is low. Such a thin layer is easily eroded away and in most cases it is a lower (*B*) horizon thus revealed that gives the characteristic bright red colour to the slopes.

Desert and semi-desert soils. About 30 per cent of the land surface of the earth can be said to have desert soils, soils that must be irrigated if they are to produce crops. Under natural conditions they support only a sparse cover of cactus, sagebrush, or thorny bushes, with a denser cover of tall grasses, acacias and palms in the valley floors. The production of humus is limited in amount, because the plant remains are scarce and are often dried out before humification can take place. Chemical weathering is restricted by the lack of water; physical breakdown of mineral material is active on account of the big daily ranges of temperature, and by the crystallisation of salts rising in solution, but its effects are mainly confined to the surface layers.

Erosion is active in the desert under natural conditions because there is no protection from the vegetation, and consequently soil development is slight and the soils differ little in appearance from the parent material.

The largest part of the landscape consists of rocky slopes from which the fine particles have been washed out or blown away, and the soils, if this term can be used here, consist mainly of gravel and gravelly sand. The stony material consists of tough fragments from the underlying rock, commonly coated with varnishes of silica or iron and manganese. Sometimes these hard coatings form crusts up to a quarter of an inch thick, and the rock inside sometimes weathers to a powder and the desert surface is littered with the rough fragments of the crusts.

A pebbly or gravelly surface hinders wind erosion and the soils are relatively stable. But on open sandy plains or dunes the 'soil' is shifted by every strong wind. Plants are often entirely lacking except at the margins of dunes, where water derived from rain falling on the absorbent sand seeps out and supports a narrow band of vegetation.

Soils in shallow depressions have a higher content of clayey material than those at higher levels, but they are often highly saline. Their profiles are not usually well developed. Sometimes there is a surface crust a few millimetres thick, formed by lichen and fungi, which is rather impervious and hinders the percolation of rain water. At the centres of depressions, salt accumulates on the surface and is glaringly white in the strong sunlight.

In many areas a tough layer of material, consisting largely of silica over sandstones or of calcium carbonate over calcareous rocks outcrops at the surface. These layers seem to be the result of some soil-forming processes of the present or in some cases of the past.

From what has already been said about desert soils it will be evident that they are not naturally as fertile as is sometimes supposed, and they need more than water if they are to produce good crops. Usually they are saline, lack both organic matter and nitrogen, and are often difficult to cultivate because of tough layers at or near the surface.

The intertropical savannas and forests. In low latitudes, high forest is the vegetation climax where the mean annual rainfall exceeds about 50 inches and the dry season lasts less than about three months. In areas with less rain and more strongly marked dry seasons the climax seems to be woodland with grasses. In the high forest the trees form canopies with their branches and leaves at two main levels, and some very tall trees, called emergents, rise above the upper canopy. In the wetter areas the forest is largely made up of evergreen species, but towards the drier margins deciduous species are numerous. The savanna woodland has a single canopy of a height at about 50 feet. As the rainfall diminishes the trees form a less complete cover and towards the desert margins consist mainly of thorny species, and grasses become dominant in some places.

Although it is rash to generalise about the fertility of tropical soils, it can be said that those formed under deciduous high forest are amongst the most attractive to cultivators. They are less thoroughly leached than those under the evergreen rain forest and they receive a greater supply of organic matter in the form of leaf-fall than those of the savanna. In many parts of the tropics deciduous high forest has been largely cleared by cultivators and replaced by economic tree crops such as oil-palms, or by savanna woodland that differs little in appearance from the natural savanna. Once the high trees are cleared, grasses come in and they burn in the dry season. The fires destroy the young shoots of high forest trees and allow only fire-resistant trees to survive. Savanna woodland of this kind, derived from high forest, is sometimes called a fire climax.

The soils under high forest, with the exception of those derived from recent volcanic rocks, are usually strongly leached and are consequently deficient in bases and are more acid than the soils of the savanna lands. In all the tropics, the soils deteriorate after a few years when the vegetation is cleared so that the supply of organic matter is not maintained, and the ground is exposed to the sun. In spite of the prolific plant cover the soils are not inherently very fertile. Permanent cultivation is mainly confined to those areas that are flooded annually and thereby receive plant nutrients from outside.

The appearance of the soils varies greatly from place to place. In hilly country underlain by well-drained rocks, very deep red or orange soils develop. They have a thin, dark humic topsoil but show no other clear horizons.

Basaltic lavas, shaley limestones and other lime-rich, clayey parent material occupying areas of low relief commonly give rise to deep, dark-coloured soils sometimes called Black Cotton soils. They are similar in appearance to chernozems but are very different in fact. In spite of their colour they seem to have but a low content of organic matter and are too heavy for most native farmers to cultivate.

Much of tropical South America, India, Africa, and Australia consists of dissected upland plains. The plains are ancient peneplains, the outcome of long-continued erosion, and are underlain by material that has been thoroughly weathered.[1] The soil on the valley slopes is formed from fresher rock, and that of the valley bottoms from alluvium. The

[1] The name laterite is often given to soils that have suffered prolonged leaching and as a result lack bases and even silicates. The name was first applied by Buchanan in India a century ago to certain mottled clays from which bricks are made by cutting the material into blocks and drying them; hence the word laterite, from *later*—a brick. But laterite has since been applied to all kinds of red soils and weathered rock, and at the present time, it is used most widely for the tough iron rich layers, often derived from old soil profiles, which are more accurately known as ferricrete.

succession of soils from slope crests to valley bottoms has already been described above as a catena, and various catenal arrangements of soils are found over these dissected plains, their patterns depending on the present and past climates and the nature of the parent materials (see fig. 218).

In southern Africa and Brazil the old plainlands are at high levels where both the soils and vegetation are affected by temperatures ten, twenty or more degrees lower than those at sea level in the same latitudes. Grasslands occupy the high plateaus of Kenya, Abyssinia, the Cameroons and parts of southern Africa. The soils appear to be quite productive but are liable to be affected by erosion under cultivation, unless effective soil conserving measures are taken.

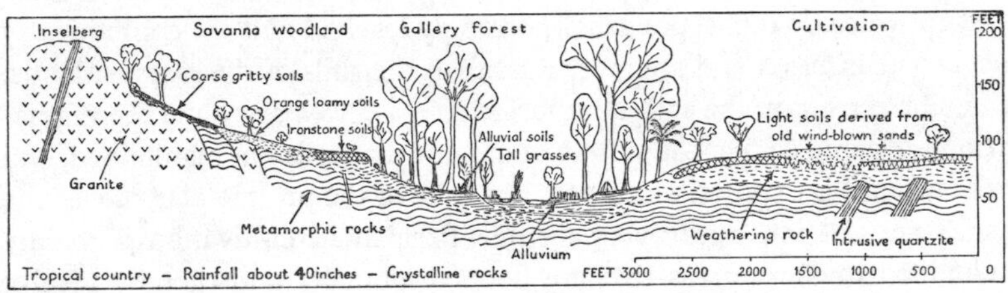

Fig. 218. Soils of tropical regions.

Soil erosion accelerated by man. So far it has been assumed that the soils and vegetation in the various regions of the world are adjusted to the existing climates, and in general this is the case. But the climate of the world has fluctuated considerably in geologically recent times; ten thousand years ago much of Scandinavia was still covered by an ice-sheet, and since then there have been periods when northern Europe has been milder than at present and when in Africa the deserts have been at times larger and at times smaller than now. As a result natural vegetation in critical areas is commonly in an unstable condition, and it is often difficult to decide how far changes in the plant cover are the work of man and how far they have been caused by a change in climate. Critical areas exist near the poleward limits of trees, near the tree-line on mountain sides, and at the desert margins.

Both the soil and the plant zone above it have their own climates which differ greatly from that of the air above. Within a forest the humidity is usually greater than outside because of transpiration from the leaves, temperatures are more equable, and wind speeds seldom exceed a few miles an hour. When the forest is cleared all this changes.

Amongst the changes that result from destruction of the natural vegetation, the most important as far as the soil and man are concerned is probably the speeding up of the processes of erosion and deposition by wind and running water. Erosion of the soil is a natural process, and the shaping of the land surface can be regarded as largely a matter of soil formation and soil erosion. But under a natural plant cover of grass or trees the movements are gradual because the vegetation slows down the winds to a speed at which they are unable to pick up soil particles, and the soil is capable of absorbing the rain falling in all but the heaviest storms. When vegetation is cleared the soil loses the canopy of plants and the layer of decaying plant remains that normally takes the impact of raindrops. The drops break up the soil aggregates, fine particles block the passages in the soil down which water normally percolates, water collects in pools on the surface and begins to run downhill, picking up soil particles as it gathers speed. In time the soil exposed to the sun and receiving no leaf-fall, loses its structure; the soil crumbs break down and the volume of material carried away by the water flowing over it increases. Eventually, soil losses from cultivated land may be a hundred or a thousand times those under the natural cover, and the soil-forming processes cannot keep pace with them. The *A* horizons may disappear entirely, and then the run-off on the more clayey *B* horizons is greater still, and deep gullies sometimes cut down into the weathering rock. If the soil is lost in this way, it can only reform over a long period of time during which pioneer plants colonise the area once more and the long sequence of soil formation is repeated.

In the dry lands, where the soils are derived in many cases from material that was originally deposited from the wind, erosion by the wind is the main danger resulting from depletion of the plant cover. In order to shift particles of sand size, wind speeds near the ground must be of the order of 15 m.p.h. Even a sparse grass cover will keep speeds below this level, and it is this braking effect, rather than the binding effect of the roots, that is important in, for example, the stabilisation of sand dunes by grasses. Once the retarding effects of trees and grasses are removed and the soil aggregates break down into individual particles then wind erosion can begin, and duststorms and sandstorms follow.

Rapid erosion, including erosion that has been accelerated by man's clearing the vegetation, usually takes place in short periods, at long intervals of time, and as a result of extraordinary weather conditions. It is often difficult to tell how far erosion in the examples described in ch. XVI, pt. III should be attributed to the weather and how far to man's own fault. The blame must be shared.

Again the results of accelerated erosion are often most serious in places with severe climates, or where the climate is known to have fluctuated from time to time. The apparent deterioration of the conditions in the lands bordering the Sahara is still a matter for dispute; it has been attributed to desiccation of the climate on the one hand and to the work of goats on the other. Similarly, the erosion of certain large systems of gullies in New Mexico has been blamed on desiccation, on over-grazing by cattle, and on certain unusually heavy storms. These controversies underline the close relationships existing between the climate, vegetation and soil, between erosion and man's work.

CHAPTER XVIII

MARINE LIFE IN RELATION TO THE PHYSICAL-CHEMICAL ENVIRONMENT

The physical and chemical natures of the oceans and of the atmosphere above them have a profound effect on the food resources of the sea. In order to understand fully the distributions of these resources it is necessary to have a complete knowledge of the ecology of the sea, but as yet our knowledge is very incomplete and many of our conclusions are tentative. Taking the definition of ecology as the science of all the relations of all the organisms to all the environment and realising that these relationships are reciprocal, it can be seen that the subject is one of vast proportions, especially as the animals and plants living in the sea are so abundant and diverse and the environmental conditions so variable. Moreover, modern oceanography is barely a century old and the scientific study of sea fisheries in particular is only just over sixty years old.

The marine ecological cycle. The ecological cycle in the sea is shown in fig. 219. The essential producers are the microscopic planktonic plants (phytoplankton) and as these need light they are found near the surface of the sea where they use the available nutrient salts in the water. The herbivores which graze down the phytoplankton consist mainly of planktonic animals (zooplankton) and a few fish, such as the menhaden, which occupy a place in the sea analogous to, say, sheep on the land. Some of the bottom-living animals (benthos) are also herbivores as they filter phytoplankton from the water. The strong swimming animals (nekton) form the third link in the chain. The primary carnivores feed on the zooplankton and consist of pelagic fish, such as herring and mackerel, as well as such large animals as the basking shark and the whalebone whales. Most of the other carnivores have longer and more complicated food chains. The cod, for example, is a bathypelagic fish and feeds on zooplankton, pelagic fish and benthic animals; whilst the halibut feeds on bathypelagic fish and large crustacea. Moreover, some of the benthic animals are carnivores and act as scavengers living on food provided by the death and decay of both herbivores and carnivores. Predatory animals such as sharks, whales, seals and, of course, man him-

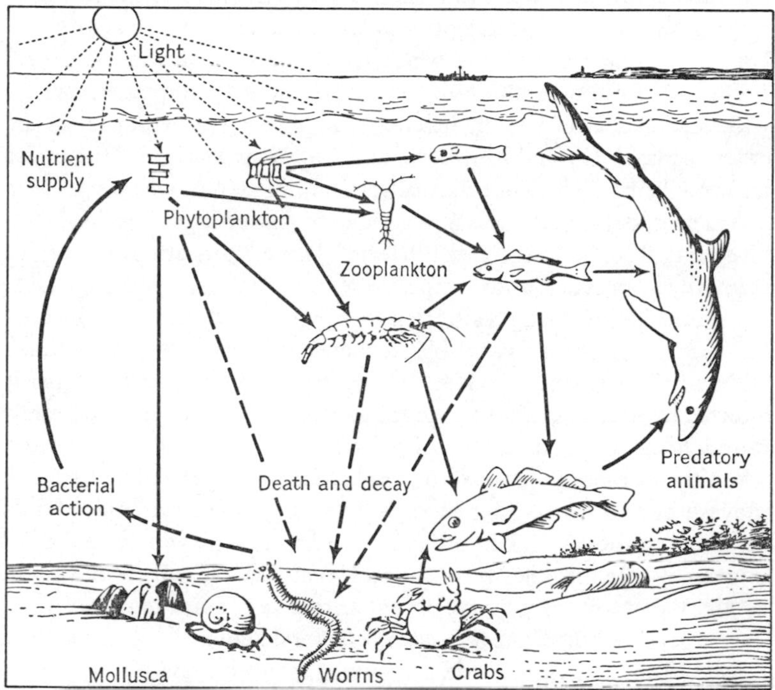

Fig. 219. The marine ecological cycle.

self feed on the fish. The ecological cycle in the sea is completed by the decomposers and transformers: marine bacteria break down the bodies of dead plants and animals, as well as the excreta of living animals, and transform this material into forms suitable for use by the phytoplankton once more.

The physical and chemical environment affects all points in this chain and some of the relationships are general. These we will discuss first before turning our attention to the more specialised relationships influencing the world's fisheries. It is often difficult to separate the effects of the different physical and chemical factors acting upon a population of organisms, as these factors do not operate separately in nature but directly or indirectly in groups. However, an attempt will be made here to discuss them under separate headings, while at the same time the effects of associated factors are pointed out.

Pressure. The pressure in the sea increases by about 1 atmosphere every 10 metres depth so that at the bottom of the ocean basins the pressure is enormous, but it does not crush organisms and prevent them from living there since it is the same inside their bodies as outside. That organisms can live at great depth was proved conclusively in 1951 by the Danish *Galathea* Expedition which trawled up sea anemones and sea cucumbers from a depth of 10,500 metres off the Philippine Islands.

Several species of benthic invertebrates have a wide depth range and extend from the littoral zone down to the abyss and some species of fish and zooplankton carry out diurnal vertical migrations over distances of 400 metres, but nevertheless most species of marine organisms have definite vertical limits to their distribution. These limits are probably due primarily to such factors as temperature, light and food. Although there is some evidence that pressure has a physiological action on invertebrates and fish without swim-bladders little is known about it. Animals with air-filled cavities, such as fish with swim-bladders, are seriously affected by pressure, however, and as a result this type of animal is rarely found living at great depths. The swim-bladder supplies buoyancy: when the fish moves downward the bladder is compressed and when it moves upwards the bladder expands, so that gas must be removed from or added to the bladder in order for the fish to maintain control of its buoyancy equilibrium. It is thought that these changes in volume brought about by vertical movement stimulate the fish to return to its former level and therefore the pressure factor definitely limits the vertical range of fish with swim-bladders. Diving mammals and birds have the added problem of breathing, but whales and seals are adapted to deal with this. Whales regularly dive to 400 metres and have been known to become entangled with submarine telegraph cables at a depth of 1000 metres.

The marine environment can be divided into various zones on the basis of depth. These zones are shown in fig. 220. The pelagic division includes the whole mass of water and consists of a neritic province and an oceanic province: the boundary between the two provinces occurs at the edge of the continental shelf, at about 200 metres depth. The oceanic province can be subdivided into epipelagic, bathypelagic and abyssopelagic zones. The benthic division includes all the ocean floor and consists of two systems, the neritic and the deep-sea, the dividing line again being at 200 metres depth. In the neritic system are the littoral and sub-littoral zones. The littoral zone usually has strong wave and current action and enough light for plant growth. Below it is the sub-littoral zone starting usually at 40–60 metres depth. The tidal zone forms the upper part of the littoral zone. In the deep-sea system are the archibenthic and abyssobenthic zones, the dividing line being between 800 and 1100 metres.

Light. In the sea light becomes altered both qualitatively and quantitatively: 10 per cent or more of the light reaching the surface is lost by

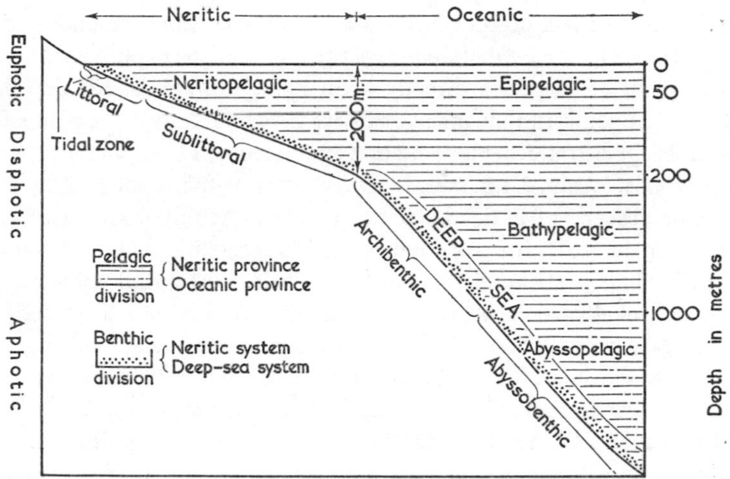

Fig. 220. The chief divisions of the marine environment.

reflection, and in passing downward through the water its intensity and spectral composition are modified. Even pure water absorbs light rapidly compared with air, and the yellow, orange and red components are absorbed more quickly than the blue, green and violet. Suspended material in the water, including living organisms, increases the extinction, and in temperate and coastal seas the green component is usually the most penetrating. The depth at which the light intensity is reduced to 1 per cent of its surface value represents the approximate lower limit of growth for planktonic plants, and it varies greatly. In the Caribbean Sea it is 110 metres, on continental shelves in temperate seas it is about 40 metres, and in coastal areas it is 15 metres or less. In general, benthic plants will not grow at depths at which the light intensity is less than 0·3 per cent of the surface value, and the maximum depth for such growth varies from 160 metres in the Mediterranean Sea to 10 metres in shallow, marginal, temperate seas. At about 250 metres depth the light intensity is reduced to 0·001 per cent of the surface value; at 500 metres the limit for vision of fish is reached; and below 1000 metres there is no perceptible light from the surface. The water column can thus be divided into three zones based on the light factor. The euphotic zone is uppermost and has sufficient light for photosynthesis. It rarely extends beyond 100 metres, and below it is the disphotic zone with insufficient light for photosynthesis but sufficient light for animal responses. This extends to 800 metres depth where the aphotic zone begins. The aphotic zone receives no light of biological significance from the surface.

The major effect of light in the sea is on the chemical reactions concerned largely with the metabolism of the organisms as in photosynthesis. Thus plant life depends directly upon light, and animal life depends indirectly upon it in that the animals are dependent upon the plants for food. Light also affects pigmentation and in animals brings about colour adaptations. Animal life can, however, exist, without solar light, and light or absence of it has been one of the most important factors in moulding the structural development and the adaptations of most marine animals. This is strikingly shown in the weird anatomical adaptations, especially of abyssal fishes, that enable animals to survive in faintest light or utter darkness. These adaptations are tactile structures, food-procuring contrivances or light-producing organs. Bioluminescence is very common among marine animals and is found in thousands of species.

Light is also an important factor in the movement of marine animals. Many forms of zooplankton make a diurnal migration, moving from the deeper water towards the surface as darkness approaches and descending again towards dawn. This migration can have a range of several hundred metres, but it varies with different species and the presence of a sharp temperature gradient in the water column can also limit its extent. Light is the chief motivating factor and its main influence seems to be that of changing intensity upon the organisms' optimum light requirements. This effect is modified by such factors as gravity, temperature and the animals' need for the plant food that is located in the upper layers. Plankton-eating fish take part in this diurnal migration and it thus may affect the distribution of such important species as the herring. The migrating population is of such a size that it has been detected by ships' echo-sounding equipment over wide areas of the ocean and it appears on these instruments as a false bottom that moves up and down daily.

The planktonic animals also undergo a seasonal migration but the pattern of this varies greatly. Some forms descend during the summer and are nearer the surface in spring and autumn, and it has been sug gested that light is the causative factor. However, other forms seek deeper water during the winter; but this may be due to temperature, as will be explained below. Again, some species ascend to the surface in summer and there occurs a local swarming which is associated with spawning close to localised areas of phytoplankton production. Some fish also show a seasonal change of depth, but it is not clear whether this is related to light or temperature or food supply.

Salinity. Marine plants and animals can be divided into two groups according to their tolerance to changes in salinity. *Stenohaline* organisms are sensitive to relatively small changes. The animals of the open ocean normally fall into this category, and if they are carried by currents into coastal or estuarine waters of low salinity they may perish. *Euryhaline* organisms, on the other hand, have a tolerance to a wide range of salinity and are therefore characteristic of coastal areas and estuaries. The degree of euryhalinity varies greatly in different species and no sharp line distinguishes stenohaline and euryhaline forms. Some species can withstand big changes in salinity if they can become adapted slowly, but few species can undergo a rapid yet big change.

The limits of distribution of a species are sometimes sharply defined by salinity toleration. For example, in San Francisco Bay the wharves in the upper part of the bay were built without protection against the native wood-boring mollusc, *Bankia setacea*, as this species is unable to grow in salinities below 10‰ such as frequently occur in the region. In 1913 the European shipworm, *Teredo navalis*, was introduced into the area and it was found to be actively destructive at salinities as low as 6‰. So much so that in a few years it had caused destruction amounting to 25 million dollars.

Temperature. Temperature is probably the most important physical factor in the marine environment. It acts directly upon the physiological processes of organisms, especially upon the rate of metabolism and the reproductive cycle. Indirectly it affects other factors, such as the concentration of dissolved oxygen in the water, viscosity and density, all of which also influence life in the sea.

The range of temperature in the sea is small compared with that in the air and there are no temperatures too high or too low for active life of some kind. Again temperature changes in the sea are smaller and slower than on land, and animals can avoid unsuitable temperatures by making a short journey to a different depth provided that other factors do not prevent them. Most of the animals living in the sea are cold-blooded, however, and any change in temperature of the water is immediately accompanied by a change in the internal temperature of the organisms living in it. Regulatory mechanisms such as occur in terrestrial forms are lacking and as a result the vital physiological processes are affected. Despite the small range of temperature occurring in the sea there are temperature barriers that segregate faunas and floras into fairly well-defined geographical regions whose limits are controlled by latitude, depth of water, and the general circulation of the oceans. As salinity also assists in segregation, water masses with distinctive temperatures and salinities contain distinctive faunas and floras so that it is possible to distinguish both major and minor biogeographical regions in the sea. A striking example of the effectiveness of temperature in segregating faunas occurs in the region of the Wyville Thomson Ridge, over which water from the Gulf Stream flows into the Norwegian Sea. The bottom waters of this sea have a sub-zero temperature, so that on the southern slope of the ridge the 4° C. isotherm is at 1500 metres depth and on the northern slope it is at 600 metres. An analysis of the benthic fauna of each slope has shown that only 11 per cent of the 433 species enumerated are common to each side. Further, the species which are common are not taken at the same depth on each side, but at depths bathed by waters of approximately the same temperature.

When the temperature gradients are not so well-defined the faunal zones are not so clearly delimited and wide transition zones occur. In the North Atlantic Ocean the isotherms diverge towards the east and converge towards the west, as shown in fig. 224. The temperature gradients are more clearly defined on the western side of the ocean and as a result faunal boundaries tend to be obliterated on the eastern side but not on the western. Thus 36 per cent of the fishes found north of the Arctic Circle in the Norwegian Sea are also found in the Mediterranean. Consequently the European Atlantic fishery has much more regional scope than the American one.

Organisms can be divided into two groups depending on their degree of tolerance to temperature changes. *Stenothermic* forms are tolerant only to small temperature changes whilst *eurythermic* forms can tolerate large changes, but there are many gradations between the two. Each species has an upper and lower limit of temperature tolerance and also an optimum temperature, but these are not always the same for all stages and functions of life. We have to distinguish between *reproductive eurythermy* (or *stenothermy*) during the spawning periods and the egg and larval developmental stages, and *vegetative eurythermy* (or *stenothermy*) during all other periods of life. The distribution of many marine animals is largely dependent on the influence exerted by temperature upon breeding. Each species has a fairly well-defined spawning time that appears to depend mainly on temperature, and the temperature limits are much more narrow for the reproductive processes and for the survival of eggs and young than they are for other stages of life. This means that the spawning time must be adjusted to the season. Winter-spawning animals of warm waters can only live in colder waters by adjusting their spawning to the summer, and conversely summer-spawning animals of cold waters can only live in warmer waters by adjusting their spawning to the winter. The very mixed fauna of the European continental-shelf seas is believed to be mainly due to such adjustments since these seas have big seasonal variations in water temperature; as great as 15° C. in the North Sea.

It is also possible for both high-latitude and subtropical phytoplankton to grow in temperate latitudes, depending on the season and other factors, provided that, during the resting stages they are carried in by currents at the proper season or that they can survive the 'off' season in order that they may germinate in the growing season.

The faunas of the colder waters of the northern and southern hemispheres contain many elements in common. Some cold water stenothermic animals can, however, find suitable temperatures in the tropics by seeking greater depths, if they are sufficiently euryhaline and eurybathic. Thus a continuous distribution can result, the cold water forms being found near the surface in high latitudes and at progressively greater depths as the equator is approached.

This tropical submergence of some species shows that temperature can control the vertical as well as the horizontal distribution of marine animals. Just as in the horizontal plane sharp temperature gradients can segregate faunas, so in the vertical plane a thermocline can cause segregation. In arctic waters the range of temperature between deep and shallow water is small and some species of benthic fauna range from the littoral zone to the abyss. In lower latitudes the vertical temperature range is greater and the boundaries between littoral and deep-water fauna are more clearly defined.

Temperature affects the rate of metabolism of marine animals and plants. It increases greatly as the temperature rises within favourable limits. Moreover, as the optimum temperature is nearer the upper limit of temperature tolerance than the lower, a small rise in temperature from the optimum is more likely to be lethal to cold-blooded animals than is a greater fall. The latter can in fact lead to an extension of life by slowing up vital processes at times when the food supply is small. For example, the copepod, *Calanus*, descends to seek colder water at depths of 200–300 metres in the Norwegian Sea in winter when the food supply is at a minimum, and so conserves its energy at the lower temperatures to be found at that depth. In spring it migrates to the surface to spawn at a time when food is abundant.

Temperature also affects the rate at which calcium carbonate can be precipitated by marine animals to form shells and skeletons. This process is carried on more rapidly in warmer water than cold and hence organisms that use calcium compounds are more abundant in tropical waters, as is shown for example by the distribution of coral reefs. Again, among the foraminifera the calcareous-shelled species of warm waters are replaced in cold northern waters by arenaceous types. Among the pteropods some cold-water forms have either no shells or very thin shells in contrast to the warm-water forms.

Finally, temperature appears to affect the size of marine animals and the numbers of species living in an area. Cold-water animals frequently grow to a larger size than their warm-water counterparts. The increased density and viscosity of cold water enables larger planktonic forms to keep afloat. But, temperatures also lengthen the time required for cold-blooded forms to reach sexual maturity and cold water thus permits a longer growing period with resultant larger size. In lower latitudes the more rapid turnover of generations, the more nearly optimum conditions, and the relative absence of big seasonal temperature changes bring about the production of a greater number of species of most animal groups than is the case in higher latitudes with their more severe and selective conditions. Since it is the abundance of individual edible species and not the variety of species that matters, it follows, in general, that the tropics are less likely to develop large-scale fisheries than higher latitudes.

Oxygen. Oxygen is necessary for the maintenance of the life processes of all organisms, and for all forms, except anaerobic bacteria, it is available for metabolic processes only when it is in solution in the free state. The concentration of dissolved oxygen in the sea is much less per unit volume than in the air and it is irregularly distributed. Nevertheless, the ocean is well supplied with oxygen for marine breathing organisms, even in the abyss. Oxygen-rich water is carried downwards by wind-stirring and, below the limit of wave-action, by eddy transfer across current boundaries in the vertical plane, and by the massed sinking of water at convergences and in regions of winter-cooling. Deep permanent currents carry this water, which has sunk to intermediate levels or even to the bottom, great distances towards and even across the equator (fig. 91). The saturation value for dissolved oxygen in sea water increases as the temperature of the water falls; surface water in the tropics contains about

4 ml. of oxygen per litre, but in high latitudes it can contain about 8 ml. As this latter water sinks there is depletion of its oxygen owing to the respiration and decomposition of organisms, but in no part of the Atlantic Ocean does its value fall below 3 ml. per litre, although in certain parts of the Pacific, for example off lower California at 300–1000 metres depth, it falls to zero. Thus animals living in the depths of the sea receive oxygen through a direct flow of water from the oxygen-rich seas of high latitudes.

In special circumstances seas may have very low oxygen concentrations if the circulation is largely or entirely cut off and decomposing matter accumulates. The Black Sea is a classic example. Wind-stirring to any depth is prevented by a surface layer of fresh water coming from the Danube and the other large rivers that drain into the sea. Subsurface exchange with outside water is prevented by the shallow sill of the Bosporus. Organic particles use up the oxygen as they sink, and below about 150 metres depth no measurable oxygen is found. Anaerobic decomposition produces hydrogen sulphide and animals are not found in the depths where oxygen is absent. Similar conditions are found in some Norwegian fiords but on a smaller scale.

PRIMARY PRODUCTION

Conditions for plant growth in the sea. The production of organic matter in the sea and on the land depends upon the ability of the plants to use the energy of sunlight, and the processes whereby organic compounds are synthesised are the same in both cases. Carbon dioxide and water are required for the synthesis of carbohydrates and for building up fats and proteins, but, whereas land plants obtain carbon dioxide directly from the air, marine plants obtain it from the water. The roots of land plants take up nutrient salts in solution from the soil. Marine plants float in the surface layers of the sea, and sea-water is in general a weak solution of nutrient salts such as phosphates, nitrates and silicates. It also contains trace elements, which are indispensable to marine plants. The concentrations of the nutrients are low, as shown in Table 14, but nevertheless, marine plants can use these weak solutions.

Conditions for photosynthesis in the sea depend upon the depth to which the light reaches and upon the concentration of nutrient salts. The depth to which the light reaches varies with the altitude of the sun and hence with latitude, and also with the transparency of the water: in coastal waters the transparency is much less than in the open ocean. Thus near the land seaweeds do not generally grow at depths much greater than 30 metres in temperate latitudes, but at depths down to 100 metres in the tropics. Some of the kelps reach great dimensions and in places they are harvested for the manufacture of such substances as alganin and iodine and for use as fertilisers, but the seaweeds represent only a small part of the primary production of the sea.

Table 14

Element	Parts per million by weight
Phosphorus	0·001–0·10
Nitrogen (dissolved gas not included)	0·01 –0·7
Silicon	0·02 –4·0
Copper	0·001–0·01
Iron	0·002–0·02

The bulk of the primary production in the sea is carried out by the phytoplankton, which drift passively in the surface layers and may occur in such quantities as to make the water feel slimy to the touch and green or even red in colour. These plants can use the light in a surface-layer the thickness of which varies from 10 to 100 metres and they must be able to maintain themselves in this zone. As living protoplasm is heavier than pure water and the shells are even heavier, adaptations are required to prevent or retard sinking. The rate of sinking of such a body depends upon the ratio of surplus weight to friction. As the latter is determined chiefly by the size of the surface area of the body and as the easiest way of obtaining a relatively large surface area is to reduce the absolute size, most phytoplankton are minute.

The marine plants must, of course, have a suitable environment to live in. It must satisfy their limits of temperature and salinity tolerance and, although different species may have different temperature and salinity preferences, both the warmest and coldest seas are able, when other factors are favourable, to produce a characteristic flora. Indeed, the resting stages of some neritic species of high latitudes are so resistant to low temperatures that they are viable even after having spent unfavourable periods frozen solidly in ice. Thus temperature and salinity conditions do not directly inhibit production or render parts of the sea sterile.

Of more importance as limiting factors are the motion of the water in the vertical plane and the availability of nutrient salts. The currents and turbulence in the upper layers of the sea must not be too strong or they will carry the plants out of the euphotic zone. Again, the nutrients that are absorbed by the phytoplankton in the surface layer are not returned to the water until these organisms are eaten or die: then they are returned by decomposition or by excretion from animals. The dead organisms and excreta sink, however, and the return takes place in the deeper layers. In shallow waters it occurs on the sea-bed. The surface layer would therefore soon become sterile if there was no transfer of the nutrients from the deeper layers to the upper ones, but natural processes operate in order to achieve this. In fact, the ocean must be 'ploughed' to maintain productivity and as, in general, the nutrient content increases with depth, the deeper it is ploughed the greater is the yield. But the forces that can bring about ploughing do not operate with equal efficiency all over the oceans: there are regions of high production on the one hand and oceanic deserts on the other.

Wind stirring. There are three agents that bring about vertical mixing in the sea; the wind, winter cooling, and tidal streams. The direct stirring action of the wind varies with its strength and the latitude: it rarely exceeds 120 metres depth in equatorial regions and 50 metres in high latitudes. It is important if the euphotic zone is shallow. Marginal seas, such as the North Sea, are among the world's richest fishing grounds, and nearly 2 million tons of fish are taken in the North Sea each year. These seas receive a large run-off from the land and the rivers bring down fertilising materials which make them nutrient-rich, but what is equally important is that their fertility is maintained by annual ploughing. The stirring of the water column by the wind during the winter replenishes the nutrients in the euphotic zone by bringing them up from the layer near the sea-bed and from the sea-bed itself. At the same time the reduction in the intensity of solar radiation in these areas in winter results in a narrowing of the euphotic zone, and the stirring inhibits the production of phytoplankton by carrying it below this zone. With the coming of spring the euphotic zone deepens, the stirring is reduced, and the water column becomes progressively stratified. Thus conditions become suitable for phytoplankton production and the so-called 'spring-flowering' occurs, the growth of the population being extremely rapid. Eventually one of the nutrients in the surface layers becomes exhausted and the spring outburst ends. The warming of the surface waters as summer approaches leads to the thermal stratification of the water column with warm, nutrient-poor water above the thermocline and cool, nutrient-rich water below it. This relatively stable structure prevents the transfer of nutrients from the deeper water to the surface and at the same time the herbivores graze down the phytoplankton, whilst remnants of plants and animals sink to the bottom, to decompose or provide food for benthos and ultimately for bottom fish. In autumn when stronger winds occur, stirring starts again, nutrients are returned to the surface layers and an 'autumn-flowering' takes place. This is not of the same magnitude as 'spring-flowering', however, and the increased stirring and reduced illumination of winter eventually stop diatom growth and the nutrients are brought to the surface once more.

This cycle, which is shown diagrammatically in fig. 221, is modified according to local conditions. In some temperate seas winter cooling assists the wind in stirring the water column and may increase the depth

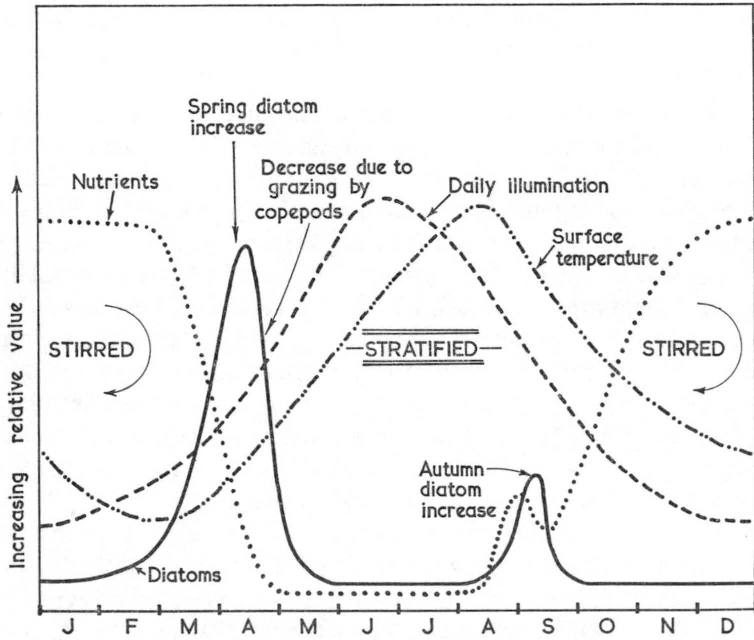

Fig. 221. The cycles of nutrient salts and phytoplankton in temperate seas.

to which the sea is ploughed. In very shallow seas where the tidal streams are strong the turbulence is such that stratification of the water never occurs and ploughing goes on all the year round. In such seas the transparency is usually low owing to run-off from the land and wave-action stirring up the bottom sediments. The euphotic zone is therefore very shallow, but it deepens as summer approaches: the water clears as wave-action decreases and at the same time the intensity of solar radiation increases. Eventually the zone extends to the sea-bed and phytoplankton growth then increases rapidly. The southernmost part of the North Sea falls into this category, but it is to some extent unique in that it receives fertilising matter in fairly large quantities owing to the discharge of

London's sewage into the Thames. The large amount of mixing that goes on in the southern North Sea ensures that good use is made of this supply of nutrient, so that this small area is able to support big fisheries, about 100,000 tons being caught annually.

In the tropics there is plenty of light all the year round and the euphotic zone often extends below the bottom of the wind-stirred layer. There is a pronounced stratification of the water column and only little nutrient travels upwards by eddy transfer from the deeper waters into the zone of light influence. This is particularly true of the Sargasso Sea, which consequently has such a small amount of production that it is regarded by some authorities as an oceanic desert. A similar area is found in the North Pacific to the west of Lower California. Recently a radioactive carbon technique has become available to determine the speed of carbon fixation by the phytoplankton. Some of the rates are given in table 15, which shows that the Sargasso Sea has the lowest. These figures must be used with caution, however, as they are the results of isolated experiments. Production in temperate and high latitudes takes place in a short spell of intense growth in the spring and in a less intense one in the autumn: in tropical latitudes it goes on at a slower rate but throughout the year. Thus, until measurements have been made of the productivity at all seasons in all seas, it is difficult to make a sound numerical comparison of the total amounts of production in high and low latitudes, but it seems that the tropics contain some of the world's least fertile seas.

Upwelling. There are, however, certain tropical regions that have an exceptionally high fertility. These are brought about by a secondary effect of the wind that causes deeper ploughing than the direct effect. When the wind blows over the ocean a wind current is set up and owing to the rotation of the earth the total transport of water by this current is directed at right angles to the wind; to the right of it in the northern hemisphere and to the left of it in the southern hemisphere. Only a shallow surface layer is transported by the wind action: the depth of this layer increases as the wind speed increases and decreases as the latitude increases. Off a coast where the transport by the wind current is directed away from the coast, the surface layer will be carried offshore and must be replaced by water which upwells from some depth and which is therefore rich in plant nutrients.

The process of upwelling has been studied in most detail off the coast of California in connection with the important sardine fishery that has arisen there since the late 1920's. From February until July the prevailing wind is from the north and hence parallel to the coast. Thus surface water is transported away from the coast and is replaced by nutrient-rich water which upwells from a depth of 200–300 metres. This water has a greater density than that which it replaces and this leads to a lowering of sea-level in the region of upwelling. It is a very slight lowering but enough to make the currents offshore flow southwards. These induced currents sweep the nutrient salts and the phytoplankton southwards into the region where the temperature is right for the sardine to spawn. Thus the sardine larvae are provided with an ample supply of food. The sardine catches vary from 500,000 tons a season to about 100,000 tons. The intensity of upwelling varies from year to year, depending upon the wind conditions. It is thought that this is a factor helping to determine the size of the sardine brood in a particular year, and that the fluctuations in brood strength from year to year are at least part of the cause of the variations in catch.

The main regions of upwelling in the world are shown in fig. 222. They are largely confined to seas equatorwards of the 40° parallels and to the west coasts of continents. As they occur where the wind has an offshore component they are nearly all found near hot semi-desert and desert land areas. The most extensive region of upwelling is off the coast of Chile and Peru. It stretches up to 200 miles offshore and these waters are probably the most fertile in the world. Although they produce food for great quantities of fish there has not been any commercial fishing of any magnitude until recently. Nevertheless, the fish indirectly influence the economy of Peru, because of the guano deposits on the offshore islands that are the homes of an enormous population of fish-eating birds. Upwelling also takes place off the west coast of South Africa and the highest rate of carbon fixation given in table 15 comes from here. Guano is exploited and there is also a possibility that a big pilchard fishery can be developed. Upwelling also occurs off Morocco which is a productive area with great quantities of fish such as pilchards. Little is known about the regions of upwelling off north-west Australia and Brazil, which are regarded as areas where tuna fisheries could be developed, or about conditions along the coasts of Somaliland and Arabia where the south-west monsoon causes periodic upwelling.

Upwelling takes place in the Pacific along the equator. To the north of the equator the prevailing easterly wind causes a transport to the right, that is, to the north: to the south of the equator it causes a transport to the left, that is, to the south. A divergence near the equator results, but the position is complicated by the North Equatorial Current and the Equatorial Counter Current which cause a further divergence in lat. 10° N. Because of these divergences water upwells and brings up nutrients that make these areas very productive, as is shown by the high

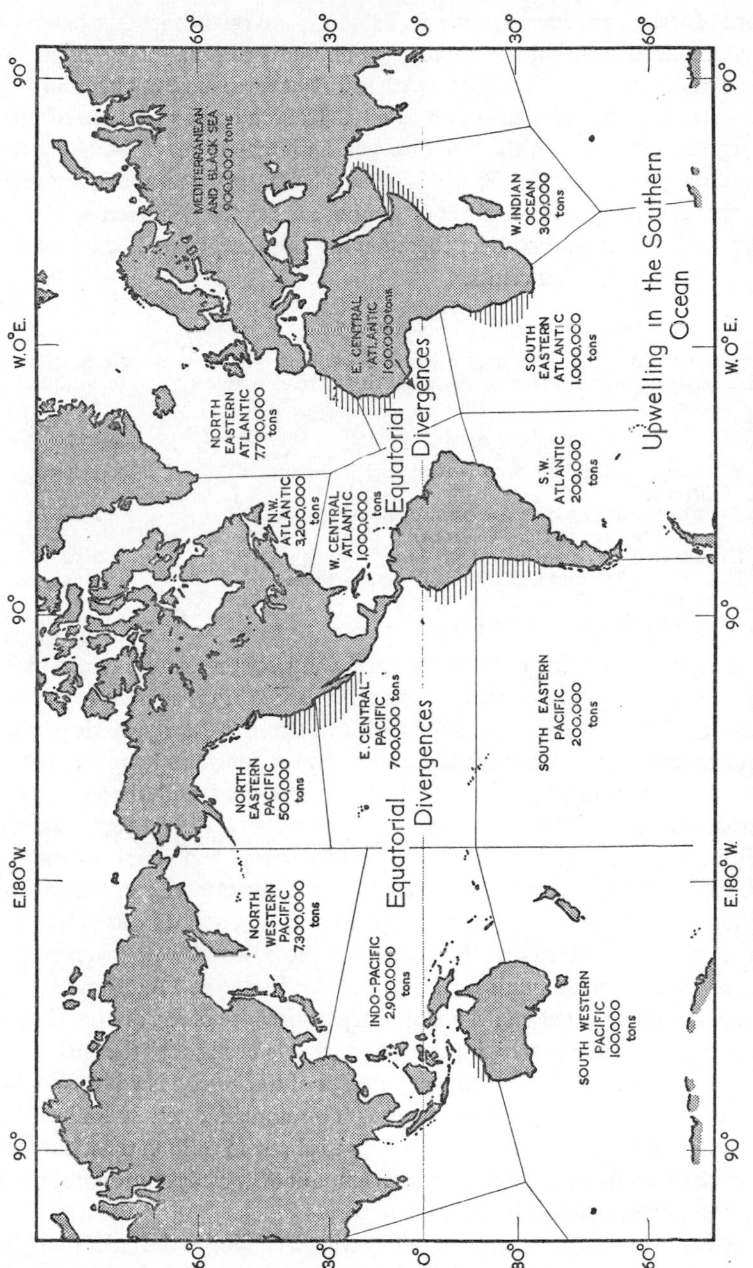

Fig. 222. The main regions of upwelling and the distribution of the world catch of fish.

rate of carbon production given in Table 15, and by the fact that Japanese and Californian fishermen catch large amounts of tuna there. A similar pair of divergences occurs in the Atlantic, but these have not been so well investigated or exploited commercially. In both oceans a region of convergence lies between the two divergences in about lat. 5° N. along the boundary between the South Equatorial Current and the Equatorial Counter Current. These areas of sinking are relatively barren of plants, the surface waters that meet there having been impoverished by earlier exhaustion of the nutrients.

Table 15.

The organic gross production below 1 sq. metre in various regions. (Based on results obtained with a recently developed radioactive carbon technique.)

Area	Grams of carbon per day
Area of upwelling off South-West Africa (Benguela Current)	0·46–2·50
Area of upwelling off west coast of South America (Northern part of Peru Current)	1·02
Pacific Ocean: equatorial divergence	0·50
Pacific and Atlantic Oceans: sub-tropical areas	0·15
Sargasso Sea	0·05
Mouth of English Channel	0·47

Near the Antarctic continent easterly and south-easterly winds blow out from the land-mass and cause a westward surface current to prevail near the land. Between lat. 40° and 60° S. strong westerly winds prevail and cause an eastward surface current. In the southern hemisphere the wind currents transport water to the left of the wind, and, therefore, this eastward current has a northerly component and a divergence results. There is consequently a climb of deep water from 3000 metres depth to about 200 metres depth. This deep water consists partly of water that sinks around Greenland and partly of water that flows out along the bottom of the Straits of Gibraltar. It flows southwards across the equator to be mixed with Antarctic Bottom Water and Antarctic Intermediate Water. It contains much nutrient because of the decay of sinking organisms and this high nutrient content is brought to the surface in the Antarctic. The large whale population of this region is witness to the resultant productivity of the region. The annual catch is limited by international agreement and it amounts to about 1¼ million tons, but this is probably only a fraction of the total amount of organic matter produced by the phytoplankton in the region.

Winter cooling. In high latitudes winter cooling is the chief ploughing agent and in many places it leads to deep stirring. The depth to which the surface water can sink depends upon the vertical distribution of temperature and salinity at the point where cooling occurs. In the area between Labrador, Greenland, and Iceland, the salinity of the water column in late winter is practically constant from surface to bottom, and the temperature of the deep water is about 3° C. Cooling of the surface water to 3° C. can therefore lead to its sinking to depths of 3000–4000 metres and to its being replaced by nutrient-rich water from those depths. Farther north the basins of the Norwegian and Greenland Seas are filled with water of constant salinity and of a temperature near −1° C. When the surface water in the western and central parts of these seas is cooled to this temperature in winter, it sinks and is replaced by deep water. These seas formerly had large whale fisheries, but the stocks have been depleted as a result of over-exploitation, and a large fishery for herring is now the main form of commercial enterprise, the Norwegians alone taking 1,000,000 tons of this fish in 1953.

In the northern part of the Atlantic Ocean at the extremities of the Gulf Stream system, water of high salinity is carried into regions with low winter air temperatures. It already has a high density on account of its high salinity, and when cooled in winter it attains such a density that it sinks to great depths. This process occurs around Greenland and Iceland and along the coasts of Norway and Spitsbergen. In the North Pacific, on the other hand, the Aleutian Islands prevent the saline water of the Kuroshio from reaching such high latitudes. Moreover, excessive precipitation reduces the salinity of its upper layers and when cooled in winter the surface water sinks only to 300 metres. However, the nutrient content in the North Pacific increases more rapidly with depth than in the North Atlantic, so that this shallow ploughing is sufficient to maintain fertility. Intensive mixing also takes place in these oceans where currents meet, for example, off the northern islands of Japan where the warm Kuroshio meets the cold Oyashio and to the south of the Grand Banks of Newfoundland where the warm Gulf Stream meets the cold Labrador Current. Both these regions support important fisheries.

The effect of ice. In high latitudes the ice régime influences primary production considerably. The Barents Sea has a large stock of cod and other fish exploited by many nations, the total annual catch being about 1,200,000 tons. The depth of the sea varies between 100 and 400 metres and winter cooling allows ploughing to take place right down to the sea-bed. In late winter and early spring the northern and eastern parts of the sea are covered with ice which hinders light from penetrating to the water below, especially if the ice has a thin snow cover. Thus plant production cannot occur in these areas until the ice thins in late spring and summer. The melting of the ice then results in stratification;

a cold, shallow, surface layer of water of low salinity overlies warm water of high salinity. This layer is shallower than the euphotic zone, and phytoplankton can develop rapidly. A wave of phytoplankton production therefore follows the ice as it melts with the onset of summer. The zooplankton spawns near the ice-edge and successive spawnings follow the melting ice. The capelin, a pelagic fish feeding on animal plankton, follows the zooplankton northwards and this fish in its turn is pursued by the cod. Seals breed on the edge of the pack ice when it is at its furthest southward extent in March and April, and follow it northwards in summer, feeding on zooplankton and fish, and whales also come to feed. Thus the ice-edge becomes the scene of great activity in spring and summer.

The melting of the ice is not steadily in one direction since the ice-limit is blown to and fro by winds from different directions. Moreover, air temperatures change rapidly in these regions in spring. Thus, after the initial outburst of phytoplankton and the consequent depletion of the nutrients in the thin, low salinity, surface layer, the water column may be stirred by wind action and cooling and the surface layer replenished with nutrients. When warmer and calmer conditions prevail the thin surface layer forms again and another phytoplankton outburst occurs. This process makes the best use of the nutrients in the sea and helps to account for its great productivity.

Tidal mixing. A ploughing effect is noticeable in some inlets. In the St Lawrence estuary the channel is nearly 200 fathoms deep, but the narrowing of the estuary leads to the tide attaining an amplitude of as much as 17 feet. When the tide is flooding the mass of water in the estuary attains such momentum that when it reaches the end of the deep channel, near the mouth of the Saguenay river, the deep water which is cold, salt, and nutrient-rich is forced to the surface and raises the level of it. There results a surface flow seawards for many miles along the southern shores of the estuary even during flood tide. A local outcome is a considerable fishery for herring and other salt water fish, but there is a more distant effect. As the cold salty water from the depths with its store of nutrient is discharged seawards by the Gaspé Current, it mixes with the river water, which is denuded of nutrients but which, owing to its low density, provides a hydrostatic force for removing the mixed water rapidly from the mixing point. The potent mixed water has a comparatively low density and spreads out at the surface on reaching the open Gulf of St Lawrence. Here the rotation of the earth diverts it into the broad, shallow, southern portion where steady plant production occurs giving rise to extensive fisheries.

Total primary production in the sea. At first sight one might expect the primary production in the sea to be much greater than that on land; because the ocean surface has more than twice the area of the land surface; because marine plants can live in a relatively thick surface layer whilst land plants use the light in a very thin one; and because, apart from the area perpetually covered by pack-ice, there are no sterile surface areas in the sea comparable with the mountains, deserts and glaciated regions on land. The total amount of production varies from

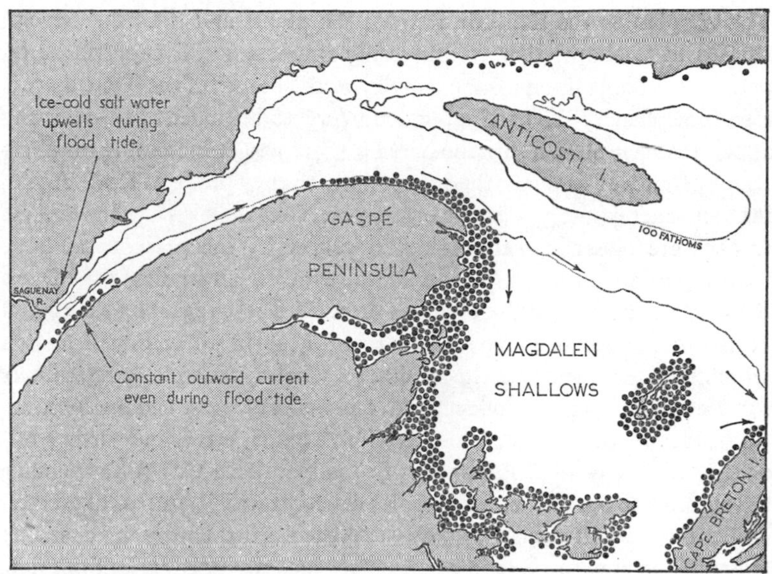

Fig. 223. The annual catch of fish in 1929 in the St Lawrence estuary in relation to upwelling and currents. Dots represent 300,000 lb. of fish.

region to region and in most areas from season to season, and these variations depend upon the amount of light available for photosynthesis, the availability of nutrient salts, and the presence or absence of various ploughing agents. The latest estimates of the total primary production of the sea based on the results obtained with the recently developed radioactive carbon technique only put marine primary production about equal to that of land at $1{\cdot}5 \times 10^{10}$ tons of carbon per year. However, the value of the primary productivity of the sea as human food is smaller, since man cannot make direct use of the plants and has to make indirect use of them by catching fish. Between the fish caught and the marine plants there are several links in the ecological cycle, and at each link only one-tenth to one-twentieth of the food consumed is stored, so that the food value of the fish represents only between $\frac{1}{1000}$ and $\frac{1}{10000}$ of the food value of the plants. For this reason the possibility of harvesting the marine plants has been seriously considered by some authorities. The total world catch of fish at present amounts to about 26,000,000 tons and the chief regions of capture are shown in fig. 222.

THE ZOOPLANKTON

The zooplankton is the link between the plants and the fish. Several studies have shown that commercially important fish concentrate on patches of zooplankton. For example, off the mouth of the Tyne there is a summer fishery for herring, and surveys with modern fish-detecting apparatus have shown that the herring aggregate in increasing numbers about patches of *Calanus*, the copepod which they prefer as food. Again, in the mackerel fishery which is centred on Newlyn in spring, the highest catches are taken in water coloured yellow by the presence of large numbers of *Calanus* and *Pseudocalanus*. Norwegian studies in the Davis Strait have shown that the blue and fin whales congregate on the coastal banks in regions of great swarms of krill, shrimp-like organisms, on which they feed; and that the smaller sei whales, which have finer filters for capturing copepods, collect in the regions of greatest *Calanus* production. The sperm whales, which feed on squids, are found farther offshore. Similarly English workers in the Southern Ocean have shown that there also the blue and fin whales concentrate in the areas of greatest krill production. The zooplankton varies greatly in quantity and character from area to area and that in a particular place similarly varies from time to time. These changes affect commercial fisheries and are to some extent the result of physical and chemical factors. Moreover, the eggs and larvae of fish have a planktonic existence and the factors that affect them at this stage have a vital effect on the size of fish stocks.

Adaptation. The animal plankton like the phytoplankton is adapted for drifting passively in the water, and is microscopic or semi-microscopic in size, although there are some notable exceptions such as jelly-fish. Special structural adaptations are provided. Some forms contain air cavities or light materials such as oils. For example, the Portuguese man-of-war, a siphonophore, has a pneumatic float, and many fish eggs contain droplets of oil. Again the water content of many planktonic animals is high, particularly in jelly-fish, and skeletons when present are thin. Some forms have developed spines and other appendages that hinder sinking, whilst other organisms have such a slow rate of sinking that a small amount of swimming helps them to maintain their position in the water column.

The density of the planktonic animals is close to that of the water in which they live and it is possible that the small changes of density which occur in the sea might make all the difference between sinking and floating. A change of 2 per cent is enough to make haddock eggs sink. The viscosity of the water is only slightly affected by the salinity, but it decreases with increasing temperature, so that sea-water at 25° C. offers only half the resistance it would at 0° C. Thus at higher temperatures the effect of decreased viscosity is added to that of lowered density and, it is as an adaptation to this that many planktonic animals in warmer water bear more bristles and feathery structures which retard sinking. The effect of viscosity is also shown by the tendency of planktonic organisms to accumulate at levels where appreciable changes of viscosity occur, but here again the direct effect of temperature in limiting the distribution of zooplankton is also a governing factor. Viscosity is also of importance to the phytoplankton. Marked temperature gradients in the euphotic zone retard the rate of sinking, and accumulations of plants can occur there. Moreover, warm-water forms have thinner shells and a more slender build than cold-water forms.

Indicator species and water-masses. A water mass can have a characteristic zooplanktonic fauna depending on its temperature and salinity, and certain species of zooplankton can even be used as indicators of the distribution of a particular water mass. A striking example of this relationship between water-mass and zooplankton is found to the west of the British Isles. Some Mediterranean water that flows into the Atlantic along the bottom of the Straits of Gibraltar is carried northward along the European continental slope at a depth of 600–1200 metres and eventually upwells into the upper layers to the west of Scotland. It carries with it a typical but exotic fauna that can be caught with nets as far north as the Shetlands, but this fauna is reduced by the mixing of the water-mass with others as its progresses northward and the degree of survival of the original fauna is a measure of the purity of the inflow.

At the mouth of the English Channel it has been possible to distinguish three types of water on the basis of their plankton communities. Most of the Channel is occupied by coastal water of a lower salinity than the oceanic water to the westward. Three species of the arrow worm, *Sagitta*, allow three water types to be distinguished: *S. setosa* is found in the coastal water, *S. serratodentata* in the open ocean water, and *S. elegans* in oceanic water mixed with coastal water. The boundary between the *setosa* water and the *elegans* water used to be in the neighbourhood of

Plymouth, so that the mouth of the Channel was occupied by *elegans* water which was richer in nutrient salts and plankton. Since 1929, however, the boundary has lain much farther to the west, and the water off Plymouth has been much poorer in plankton. At the same time there has been a reduction in the number of young fish of many kinds present in the plankton and a decline in the once prosperous Plymouth herring fishery that used to occur at about Christmas. A similar phenomenon has recently been observed off the coast of Scotland where there has been a progressive southerly movement of the main centres of the herring fishing during the years 1946–53. At the same time increasing quantities and earlier appearances of a number of planktonic animals have indicated progressively larger and earlier oceanic inflows from the north.

Currents. The zooplankton drifts passively in the surface water and is at the mercy of the currents which can transport a particular species into an unfavourable environment so that extinction follows. Thus all the Arctic organisms carried southwards by the Labrador Current are killed when the water in which they are living is mixed with warm water in the Grand Banks area: conversely all tropical zooplankton carried northwards by the Gulf Stream are killed if they are swept by eddies into the cold water. On the other hand, the currents can bring about the widespread dispersal of exotic planktonic forms from their centres of production, successful propagation taking place en route if the course of the current is sufficiently long. Further, the currents can maintain an endemic population. For example, in some land-locked bays and fiords the oscillating tidal streams maintain a characteristic population. Large eddies which are more or less permanent also maintain a stock of zooplankton in some seas. In the Gulf of Maine in summer an anticlockwise eddy provides a tolerably uniform environment which allows the endemic *Calanus* population to complete their whole life-cycle from egg to spawning adult while being swept around the Gulf. This process is also important in the vertical plane. In the Southern Ocean in summer the larvae of *Euphausia superba*, a shrimp-like food of the whale, are carried northwards at the surface in a layer rich in plant food, but later on the animals migrate downwards and in winter are carried southwards again in the warmer sub-surface flow before they rise to mature and spawn.

The difference in rate and sometimes in direction between surface and sub-surface currents can help to spread a species. The larvae of the jellyfish, *Velella*, sink into the depths to develop before rising to the surface again. Thus, it moves differently from its parent and the species is spread as widely as possible. When the differences in rate and direction are superimposed upon a vertical diurnal migration pattern interesting planktonic distributions result. For example, species that make diurnal vertical migrations can become segregated horizontally from species that do not when their migrations take them upwards into water with a different rate or direction of flow. On the other hand some species use the vertical diurnal migration to maintain their geographical position. The daily migrations of *Euphausia frigida* and *E. triacantha* in the Southern Ocean extend over a range of 200 metres. At night these organisms travel northwards in the surface flow: during the day they are returned southwards in the sub-surface current.

Many of the benthic animals in the littoral zone produce planktonic eggs and larvae and thus take advantage of water movements to obtain as wide a distribution as possible. During this dispersal many larvae are eaten by predators or are carried into unfavourable environments and perish, but to overcome these hazards of the pelagic phase each individual produces vast numbers of young and many of these find favourable settlement areas. Even then the new stage of life is still dependent upon currents to maintain tolerable living conditions with respect to aeration, disposal of toxic wastes, and supply of planktonic food.

Benthic animals, such as oysters, remain established in tidal rivers and estuaries although the planktonic larvae might be expected to be carried away as the net water transport in such regions is always seaward. In certain estuaries a denser, saltier water near the bottom moves landwards whilst the greater surface flow is seaward. Some barnacles take advantage of this by having larvae that in the early stages drift seawards in the surface layer; as the larvae approach the settling stage they concentrate near the bottom and are carried landwards again. In other estuaries the older oyster larvae drop to the bottom on the ebb tide and rise into the water on the flood.

The eggs and larvae of fish are temporary members of the zooplankton and it is during the pelagic phase that the success or failure of a particular brood is largely decided. As we have already seen, temperature conditions must be favourable at spawning and during the egg and larval stages, owing to the direct effect of temperature upon the reproductive processes and to the indirect effect of temperature upon the flotation of the eggs through its influence on the viscosity and density of the water. Currents then transport the larvae from the spawning areas to the nursery grounds. The classical example of this transport is provided by the European eel. Young elvers ascend the rivers of Europe in spring and after several years' life in fresh-water streams and lakes the full-grown eels, with the approach of complete sexual maturity in autumn, disappear into the sea to spawn. For many centuries the destination of these eels was a mystery, but in 1904 Johannes Schmidt began investigations that lasted over several years. He was able to show by plotting the distribution of smaller and smaller larvae that the eels spawn deep in the water south-east of Bermuda, and that the larvae are drifted eastwards in the Gulf Stream system to reach the European shores after 2½–3 years. How the mature eels find their way across 2000–3000 miles of sea to the spawning area is still unknown. The American eel breeds in an area that overlaps the spawning area of the European eel and the larvae of the two species drift in the same current. The metamorphosis of the American eel takes place after one year when the larvae are opposite the American shore and these larvae are then orientated towards the mouths of the American rivers. The European eel larvae drift on towards Europe because they require a longer larval life.

Variations in the speed and direction of the currents which carry the planktonic larvae of cod, haddock, plaice, and other commercially important fish can cause destruction of the larvae of considerable economic import. For example, the cod in the Barents Sea spawn at the Lofoten Islands in March and April. The larvae are drifted towards the nursery grounds on the Spitsbergen Shelf by the West Spitsbergen Current and towards the nurseries in the south-eastern part of the Barents Sea by the North Cape Current. Observations during recent years have shown that the strength of the West Spitsbergen Current at the critical time when the larvae are being transported varies from year to year, and that the success of the brood of cod spawned in a particular year depends largely upon the strength of the current at that time. Plaice spawn in the southernmost part of the North Sea in the early part of the year and the eggs and larvae are transported north-eastwards to the sandy shallows off the Dutch, German, and Danish coasts. This kind of ground appears to be essential to the young plaice as soon as it reaches that stage of life in which it seeks the bottom. In some years the current does not run so strongly to the north-eastwards and under a northerly wind régime it is even reversed. It is reasonable in this instance to suppose that the success of a particular brood depends to some extent on the rate and direction of the flow through the southern North Sea and that the degree to which different nursery grounds are colonised in a particular year is similarly affected.

Other larval hazards. There are other hazards than those imposed upon the larvae by the currents. The larvae require planktonic food. In the early stages this consists mainly of phytoplankton, and investigations of the plaice in the southern North Sea have shown that larvae which develop in areas without such food grow weakly and perish, whilst others which develop in areas with such food grow strong and straight with well-developed brains and guts. The quantities of available planktonic food probably do not vary greatly from year to year, but the time of its main production may sometimes be earlier and sometimes later than usual. The success of a brood of fish depends to some extent on whether spawning coincides closely with food production. The time of the latter

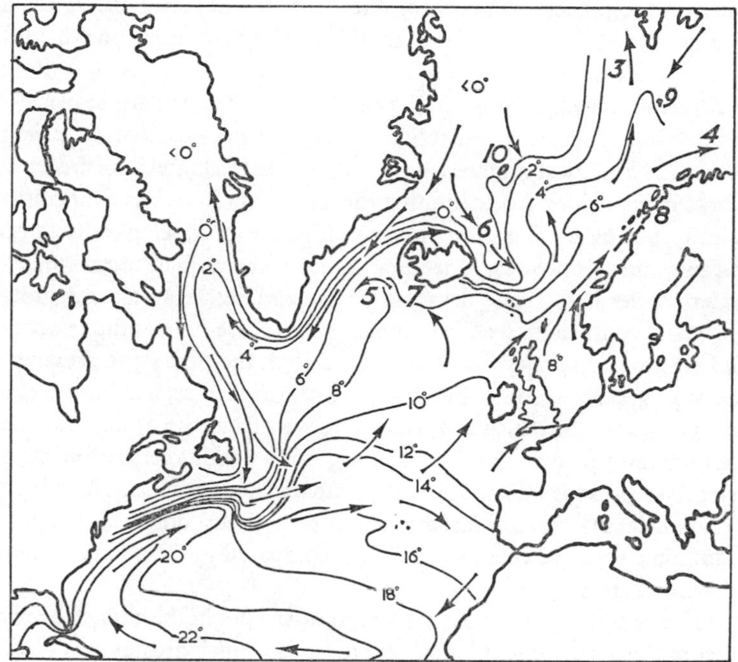

Fig. 224. The temperature distribution at 100 metres in the North Atlantic (drawn by Helland-Hansen) and the system of currents.

1. Labrador Current
2. Norwegian Coastal Current
3. West Spitsbergen Current
4. North Cape Current
5. Irminger Current
6. East Icelandic Current
7. Vestman Is.
8. Lofoten Is.
9. Bear Is.
10. Jan Mayen

depends in its turn upon those physical conditions that control phytoplankton outbursts.

The success of the spawning of some planktonic animals also seems to depend upon its timing relative to phytoplankton production, and evidence is accumulating to show that increasing numbers of phytoplankton provide a stimulus essential for the spawning of animals. The swarming of copepods to spawn near the ice-edge in the Barents Sea already described is an example of this phenomenon. The degree of failure of the spawning and larval development of a species which is a member of the permanent plankton is reflected a few weeks later in the size of the adult stock. This is important economically if the species is a key item in the diet of fishes. As an example of this process it has been possible to establish a direct correlation between the abundance of mackerel caught in the western English Channel in May and the amount of sunshine in the preceding February and March. The latter affects phytoplankton production and so affects the stock of copepods on which the mackerel feed.

Species development. Many euryhaline and eurythermic species of animals have become cosmopolitan owing to their persistent dispersal by currents. For most animals, however, the scattering effect of currents works in opposition to the limiting effects of such factors as temperature, salinity, and light. It is thought that the species-producing centres occur in the warm-temperate and tropical areas, as the ratio of warm- to cold-water species is high and as many genera and higher systematic groups are nearly confined to tropical waters. From these centres the temperate and cold-water species have evolved through the persistent pressing of the warm-water animals by currents into border regions where conditions become further and further removed from the optima for these stenothermic forms. In the more rigorous conditions in the border regions the less tolerant species are eliminated and certain strains adapted to the selective conditions are developed. Thus only relatively few planktonic species become established compared to the abundant fauna of warm waters.

There is a greater number of planktonic species in the antarctic region than in the arctic, possibly because there is a much greater area of confluence between warm and cold waters in the southern hemisphere. There is a further factor to consider, however. Cold-water species evolving outwards from warm-water species may do so either by dispersal to the north or south or by submergence into the deep, cold water of the tropics. The deep current system of the Atlantic is such that it carries these deep-water forms southwards to the antarctic surface region but not northwards.

THE BENTHOS

The littoral zone. In the littoral zone there is an ample supply of food for animals since conditions are suitable for the production of plants, both floating and attached, and for making these plants available to the benthic animals both by direct and indirect routes. A considerable amount of organic matter is also brought into the zone from the land, and most littoral areas have a good water circulation, owing to the effects of tide, wind, seasonal or diurnal convection, and irregularities in the bottom topography. Thus the zone has an abundance of benthic animals.

The zone is outstanding for the great variety of the physical-chemical conditions that affect the habitats of the benthic animals. There are marked gradients of temperature and salinity and these properties can undergo great seasonal and diurnal fluctuations. Moreover, the actions of waves, tides, and currents are important, and many different materials form the substratum. It is possible therefore to distinguish communities of animals whose distributions are limited by the physical factors: depth, temperature, salinity, and substratum. In shallow water it is easy to see the fauna associated with a particular substratum. A rocky bottom has a rich growth of algae attached by holdfasts and a variety of snails, mussels, sea anemones, starfish, and other invertebrates which are attached to the bottom by sucking or cementing devices. If the coast is exposed the shells of molluscs are sturdy; sea urchins bore into the rock for protection; and crabs, worms and brittle stars use narrow crevices and undersides of rocks as retreats. On the other hand, animals with thinner shells live on a muddy bottom; e.g., burrowing bivalves with a large foot for digging and an elongated siphon for extension above the mud in order to take in water containing food and oxygen; and burrowing worms that make temporary or permanent tubes lined with a secretion. Many mud-inhabiting animals are detritus feeders and eat the mud for the organic matter it contains or suck up detritus that has settled on top of the mud. Similar variations of the fauna are found offshore depending on the nature of the substratum, but the offshore fauna on any particular substratum can be distinguished from the shallow water associations on the same substratum.

Not only does the substratum influence the organisms, but the organisms can also influence the substratum. Some break down rock by boring into it and others secrete acid that disintegrates empty shells. In some cases the substratum is built up. The deposition of calcium carbonate by calcareous algae and coral polyps, the building up of successive layers of mussels to form a mat, and the binding together of loose sediments by eel grass, *Zostera*, are examples of this process. Change of the level of the substratum by these processes leads to changes in the fauna and flora inhabiting it.

The tidal zone. The tidal zone forms the upper part of the littoral zone and the animals and plants living in it are subject daily to alternating spells of exposure and submergence. The timing and height of the tide change daily and so affect the depth and duration of submergence. Thus an animal living near the spring tide high-water mark will be covered only for a short time every two weeks, but an animal living near the spring tide low-water mark will be exposed only for a correspondingly brief time. Despite these severe conditions the tidal zone has a dense population and a varied fauna and flora including seaweeds, barnacles, and mussels. At low water land animals and birds feed in the area and at high water fish and crabs move into it. To overcome the effects of exposure the permanent inhabitants have various adaptations. Sea anemones can endure a considerable drying of their tissues without harm, forms with shells close up, other forms burrow into mud or move into crevices, and among crabs the species living higher up the shore have a smaller number of gills and a higher ratio of body to gill volume in order to retard the loss of water from the respiratory surfaces.

A zonation of plants and animals occurs from low-water mark to high-water mark, the vertical limits of each zone being determined by such factors as resistance to exposure, wave action, type of substratum, and competition. On rocky shores there are three main zones. The *Littorina* zone is found near the spring tide high-water mark and is characterised by snails and some salt-resistant terrestrial plants and animals; the Laminarian zone stretches from the spring tide low-water mark downwards and is characterised by Laminarian seaweeds; between the two is the Balanoid zone characterised by barnacles. Similarly, a zonation occurs on muddy and sandy shores.

Variations in physical factors depending largely on meteorological conditions can have devastating effects on some species in the zone. Unusually cold winters in normally mild areas can cause a high mortality among such important shellfish as mussels and cockles. Very hot summers can also cause mortality amongst the latter. Heavy seasonal rains may lower the salinity and this may affect commercially important species. In the Fal Estuary, for example, damage occurs to the oyster beds during excessively rainy seasons and large fluctuations in salinity can stop 20 per cent of the ripe females from spawning properly. Reduced salinity combined with low temperature is especially deadly to the oyster, and heavy losses in the Essex estuaries have been observed to occur following a thaw when there has been a heavy run-off of cold melt-water. There is also some evidence to show that silt stirred up in the run-off can cause uffocation.

As the tidal zone is strictly limited in area, competition for food and for settlement space is intense. Many pelagic larvae fail to find a suitable substratum and perish. For this reason oystermen make sure that there is a suitable substratum on which the oyster larvae can settle by dumping large quantities of broken shell. The severe competition for food and space also results in such valuable shellfish as the oyster having many predators such as the American slipper limpet, the common starfish, and various tingles, barnacles and worms.

Horizontal distribution of the littoral fauna. The seas can be divided into faunal regions on the basis of the species, genera, and families of animals found within their littoral zone. The animals considered include not only the littoral benthos but the pelagic animals that are confined by their life histories to the coastal zone. The regions are shown in fig. 225. They are not sharply defined and transitional areas occur. Water temperature and salinity are two of the chief factors determining the limits of the regions, and comparison of fig. 225 with fig. 70 shows how closely the water-masses and the faunal regions are related. The continents and broad expanses of deep water act as barriers. The eastern part of the Pacific Ocean, for example, owing to its great depth prevents the spreading of the littoral fauna through the abyssal zone and because of its width stops the successful transport of the pelagic larvae of littoral animals across it. The littoral fauna can be divided broadly into three divisions: arctic, tropical, and antarctic: between these are gradations such as boreal and temperate. Each division can be subdivided longitudinally: the tropical fauna although homogeneous in many respects (e.g. coral-reef formation), can be divided into Indo-West Pacific, Pacific Tropical American, Atlantic Tropical American, and Tropical West African.

Deep-sea benthos. The boundary between the littoral and the deep-sea faunas depends on such factors as temperature, light, depth, and food supply. It thus lies at different depths in different latitudes. Moreover, many species are eurybathic and this prevents the boundary from being precise. Most of the deep-sea benthic animals are mud-dwellers and only animals with long appendages, broad bases, and other adaptations can live without becoming smothered by the mud. The deep-sea benthic species are widely distributed and their horizontal distribution increases directly with increasing depth owing to the more uniform temperature conditions existing at great depths. Benthic deep-sea genera are usually cosmopolitan, but submarine ridges such as the Wyville-Thomson Ridge can exert a great influence in limiting distributions.

Abundance of benthos. Since most of the benthos feeds on particles of organic matter, such as living phytoplankton and zooplankton or detritus from dead organisms and faeces which fall from the upper

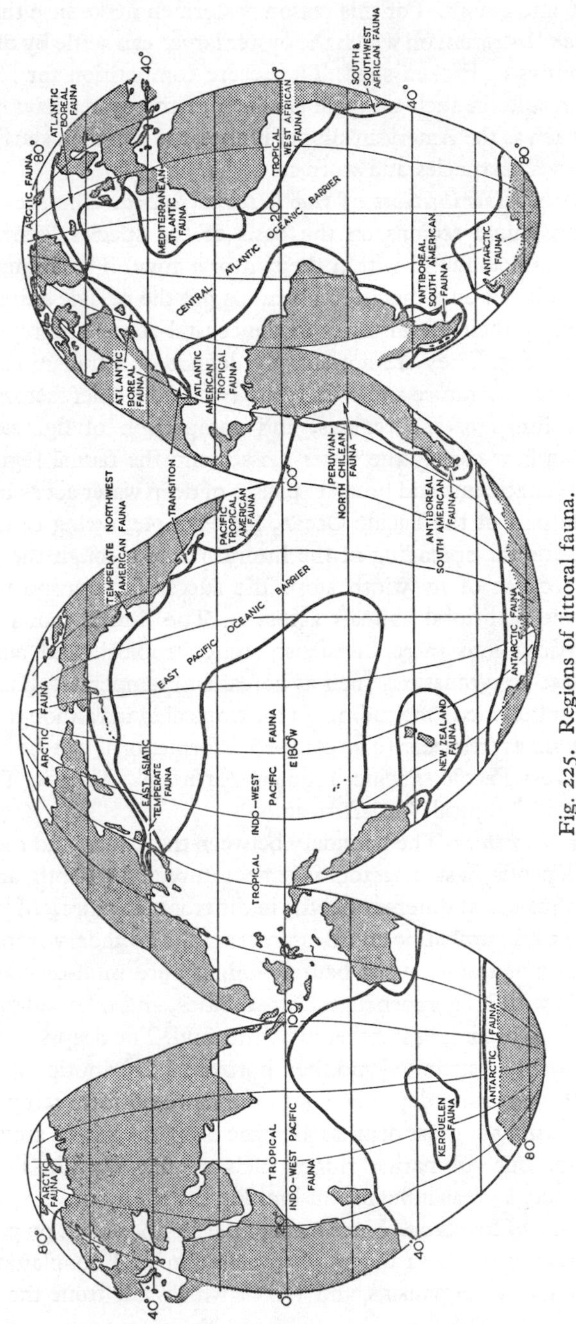

Fig. 225. Regions of littoral fauna.

layers, the abundance of benthos is related to production in these layers. In the deep ocean abyss much of the falling material is broken down or eaten before it reaches the bottom, and abyssal forms get their food from the decay of bathypelagic and abyssopelagic animals that have in turn been fed by organisms living in the epipelagic zone. For these reasons deep-sea benthic animals are scarce over most of the ocean. In oceanic regions where production in the upper layers is great, however, there is an abundance of deep-sea life. Such a region occurs near Kerguelen and the rich accumulations found there lie under the Antarctic Convergence. This is an area of sinking towards which the productive surface waters of the Southern Ocean are directed.

Benthos is found in the greatest quantity on the continental shelf. The shelf seas of temperate and high latitudes have been shown above to be productive of plankton. Their depth is such that the falling material does not decay before it reaches the bottom, although the abundance of benthos varies from place to place. In the Barents Sea, for example, the greatest quantity of benthos is found under the area of maximum plankton production—close to the position of the ice edge in late spring. The amount of benthos that can be produced in these seas is shown by a Danish quantitative estimate of the abundance in the Kattegat of the benthic animals considered to be plaice food: in an area of nearly 3500 square miles 230,000 tons of first-class food and 380,000 tons of second-class food are produced annually. As such bottom-living fish as the plaice, as well as demersal fish like the haddock, use the benthos as food, the relative abundance of suitable benthic animals is a factor affecting the size of the fish stocks in a region. In the area investigated in the Kattegat the quantity of plaice food is considered to be sufficient to produce nearly 13,000 tons of plaice annually. Fish may have a favourite form of benthic food that is limited to a certain type of substratum, and can therefore be influenced in their distribution by the nature of the bottom.

THE NEKTON

The continental shelf. Demersal fish spend most of their lives on or near the sea-bed and are rarely found in depths greater than 300 fathoms. The depth zones occupied by different species vary: plaice and soles usually less than 40 fathoms; cod, haddock, and whiting mainly in less than 100 fathoms; halibut, skate and hake at some seasons between 200–300 fathoms. These fish can only be caught on the continental shelf and most of them in depths of less than 100 fathoms. Fig. 61 shows that the area between the 100-fathom line and the coast occupies only about

5 per cent of the earth's surface and the importance of the shelf seas in the world's fisheries is at once apparent. The width of the shelf varies greatly; off mountainous coasts it may be nearly absent but off areas with broad lowlands it may be very wide. The main shelf seas of the world are to be found off western Europe, in the East China and Yellow Seas, around the Arctic basin, between Siam and Northern Australia, in the Bering Sea, off Patagonia, and along the east coast of North America. Those around the Arctic basin are largely covered by ice for most of the year and, with the exception of the Barents Sea, are of no commercial importance. It is in those of the temperate and sub-arctic regions that the world's most important demersal fisheries occur.

Availability for capture. Fishermen have a considerable lore on the parts that various physical factors play in determining the success or failure of their voyages. For example, it is thought that the pattern of the East Anglian autumn herring fishery is affected by the state of the moon, and consequently the tides, and by the type of wind régime that prevails in a particular year. The mechanisms that bring this about are not clearly understood. We have already seen how the abundance of food, both benthic and planktonic, causes aggregations of fish, and have examined the physical factors governing the distribution of food. Shoaling also occurs at spawning time and we have seen that spawning often only occurs in a narrow range of temperature that is largely responsible for controlling the distribution of a species. Any variations in temperature from year to year not only assist in bringing about fluctuations in annual brood strengths but they can also affect the availability of fish for capture. The cod which spawn in the Vestfiord in the Lofoten Islands in spring do so in midwater in a layer where the temperature is between 3° and 6·5° C. The depth and thickness of this layer varies from place to place and the temperature distribution in the area in spring varies from year to year, depending on certain physical factors such as air temperature and the degree of winter cooling that it brings about, and the strength of the Norwegian Coastal Current.

The migratory routes along which fish travel to spawn are held by some authorities to be influenced by the pattern of currents in the sea. The contranatant theory of migration holds that in their longer migrations the fish swim in a direction opposed to that of the current. The cod which spawn at the Lofoten Islands come from the Spitsbergen Shelf and the eastern part of the Barents Sea, migrating respectively against the West Spitsbergen Current and North Cape Current to do so: those which spawn at the Vestmann Isles off south-west Iceland come from the northern coasts of Iceland and from Greenland, and migrate respectively against the clockwise circulation around Iceland and the Irminger Current. Such an arrangement ensures that the fry and spent fish are drifted back to the areas from which the spawners originally came.

A spawning migration of a different type is undertaken by the herring which spawn off south-western Norway in the early months of the year and so form the basis of an important fishery. These herring spend the summer feeding in the plankton-rich and fairly warm surface layers of the Norwegian Sea between Iceland and Jan Mayen. With the approach of winter they descend into the colder, deeper waters in order to conserve their resources. This cold water moves south-eastwards as the East Icelandic Current and the herring move with it, passing north of the Faroes to be checked when the current meets the warm water coming from the Atlantic between the Faroes and the Shetlands. This check is probably due to the change of temperature because after a few days the fish eventually strike eastwards for the Norwegian coast. The larvae are drifted northwards by the Norwegian Current and westwards into the Norwegian Sea by the eddies that occur along the western side of this current, so that this life cycle takes advantage of a circular current system (see fig. 224).

Temperature can play a part in making fish available for capture outside the spawning season, especially in areas where there are steep temperature gradients dividing water in which the fish are comfortable from water where conditions are lethal. Cod on the Spitsbergen Shelf live for three-quarters of the year in water warmer than 2° C. and concentrate in shoals of commercial importance in pockets of warm water more or less surrounded by cold water. In some cases the cod are on the bottom and are roofed in with cold water. In summer, however, the fish can move into temperatures of about 0° C. Much attention has been paid in recent years to the way in which the distributions of warm and cold water determine the distribution of cod on this shelf as it is an area of great economic importance. The position of the vital temperature barrier at any time depends upon the state of balance between the Atlantic and Arctic water-masses and this in its turn depends upon those meteorological conditions that control winter cooling, and upon the strength of the West Spitsbergen Current. It undergoes an annual cycle but its position at any season varies from year to year, and so the pattern of commercial fishing is affected. The temperature barrier also plays an important role on all the great cod fishing grounds, as these are located along a front, which is the meeting place of cold and warm currents and stretches from the Grand Banks of Newfoundland past Greenland and Iceland to the Barents Sea and Novaya Zemlya.

Lethal effects of temperature and salinity. The reason for the lethal effect of low temperature on teleost fishes, such as cod, is understood fairly well and it is known that salinity plays a part. Sea water has in general a salinity of about 35 parts per thousand: fish blood has a salinity of 15 parts per thousand. Thus the osmotic pressure is not the same inside the fish as outside and a pressure difference of about 13 atmospheres tends to extract water from the fish's tissues and thus to salt it down alive. A regulatory mechanism in the gills prevents this. The marine plants and invertebrates do not face this problem because their internal fluids have the same osmotic pressure as the water in which they are living, and in some cases even a higher one. The elasmobranch fishes, such as sharks and rays, also have a higher pressure. If the salinity of the water changes rapidly and by a large amount, the regulatory mechanism of the teleost fish may break down and cause death. Some fish, however, move from salt to fresh water and back without harm. The change is more gradual, but studies of the stickleback, which lives in estuaries and spawns in fresh water, indicate that the activity of the thyroid gland is also involved. It appears that this fish cannot stand the saltier conditions of the estuary when this gland is active. Recent studies of the Spitsbergen cod have similarly shown that when the thyroid gland is inactive in summer the fish can maintain control of its salt content even if it goes into cold water. At other times of the year when the gland is active it is unable to maintain control if it enters water below 2° C.; its blood develops a high salt content which can be lethal.

Large and sudden changes of temperature can be lethal to fish. The severe winters of 1929 and 1947 in the southern part of the North Sea led to abnormally low water temperatures and were catastrophic in that large quantities of fish, such as sole, cod, and plaice, were killed. Off the coasts of Peru and Ecuador the warm water of the Equatorial Counter Current is in February and March normally carried a few degrees south of the equator as a south-flowing current known as El Niño. Occasionally it extends beyond Callao (12° S.) where cooler waters usually prevail. This extreme development can lead to the wholesale destruction both of fish and plankton, and of the guano birds that feed on them. The decay of all these dead organisms liberates hydrogen sulphide which blackens the paint of ships and gives the phenomenon its name, the 'Callao painter'.

Oceanic weather and oceanic climate. Just as the atmosphere has a weather and a climate so has the ocean. The oceanic climate is defined by the average conditions. The oceanic weather, on the other hand, consists of the day-to-day conditions. The climate of the sea like that of the atmosphere fluctuates. The warming of the air in arctic and sub-arctic regions during the past forty years results from the greater transport northwards of warm air masses brought about by an intensified atmospheric circulation. This more vigorous atmospheric circulation has also intensified the oceanic circulation and brought about a greater transport northwards of warm water masses. Thus an oceanic climatic fluctuation has taken place and has caused changes in the distribution of marine animals. Atlantic benthic forms have extended their distribution on the Spitsbergen Shelf far to the north and have replaced arctic forms. At the same time the cod stocks of the Barents Sea, the Spitsbergen Shelf, Iceland and Greenland have all increased.

It is well known that the Hansards from Lübeck used to catch herring in the Baltic for salting and so obtained much of their wealth, and that in the fifteenth century these fish suddenly disappeared. As a result the North Sea herring fishery became more important—to the advantage of the Dutch and the detriment of the Hanseatic League. These changes have been explained by one authority as being caused by a long-period tidal cycle. The recent atmospheric climatic fluctuation is known to have resulted in the bottom waters of the Baltic becoming increasingly more saline. This has allowed the cod and sprat to increase in numbers in the southern and central part of the sea and to enter the Gulf of Bothnia for the first time; so much so that the Baltic cod fishery has become the second biggest in Europe, surpassed only by the Lofoten fishery.

NOTE (see p. 301)

The continued existence of the re-entrant angle at *E* (fig. 157) results from the ability of the stream to remove the waste supplied from above down a gentler slope than soil creep is able to do, and still have energy available for down-cutting. Thus much of the energy of the headwaters is used in headward recession. This retards vertical down-cutting and encourages the development of the concave curve of erosion.

Each curve is drawn below the preceding one because when the river in, say, the stage *EKB*, is at a distance *HB* from the mouth, the calibre of the load is finer, and perhaps the discharge is greater, than when at *H* in the stage *GHB*. This finer load can be carried to the sea down a gentler slope. The calibre of the load at *K* in stage *EKB* would be similar to that at *H* in stage *GHB* if *EK* approximately equals *GH*. When eventually the amount of high ground is greatly diminished the graded reach will recede farther inland, but probably never to the source, since there will always be a stretch along which the load is being picked up. This stretch must remain steeper than the next downstream where transport predominates. A steeper gradient is necessary for a stream to pick up loose articles from its bed than to maintain them in motion. A high gradient is necessary if the load is derived from solid rock or from the reduction of large boulders in the stream's course.

As erosion continues the smaller mass and calibre of the load enables it to be carried down gentler gradients, leading to the stage *LB*. The later stages shown in Fig. 157 require far more time for their development than the earlier profiles.

If slope, discharge, and resistance of strata render the stream unable to erode at its source, erosion must await increased power, following increased discharge, and will begin farther downstream. If discharge increases by means of tributaries, then one of the first results may be the formation of a nick at each junction. These nicks will recede upstream.

BIBLIOGRAPHY

PART I. THE ATMOSPHERE

BOTLEY, C. M., *The Air and its Mysteries*. Bell, 1938.

BRUNT, D., *Weather Study*. Nelson, 1941.

FRANKLIN, T. B., *Climates in Miniature*. Faber and Faber, 1955.

GARBELL, M. A., *Tropical and Equatorial Meteorology*. Titman, 1947.

KENDREW, W. G., *Climatology*. Oxford University Press, 1957.

KENDREW, W. G., *Climates of the Continents*. Oxford University Press, 1953.

MANLEY, G., *Climate and the British Scene*. New Naturalist Series, Collins, 1952.

MILLER, A. A., *Climatology*. Methuen, 1943.

PETTERSSEN, S., *Introduction to Meteorology*. New York: McGraw-Hill, 1941.

SCORER, R. S. and LUDHAM, F. H., *Further Outlook*. Allan Wingate, 1954.

SUTCLIFFE, R. C., *Meteorology for Aviators*. H.M. Stationery Office.

Admiralty Weather Manual. H.M. Stationery Office.

The Meteorological Glossary. H.M. Stationery Office.

The Observers' Handbook. H.M. Stationery Office.

The Weather Map. H.M. Stationery Office.

PART II. THE OCEAN

BOURCART, J., *Géographie du Fond des Mers*. Paris: Payot, 1949.

CARSON, R., *The Sea Around Us*. Staples, 1951.

DAVIS, W. M., *The Coral Reef Problem*. American Geographical Society, Special Publication, No. 9. 1928.

HARDY, A., *The Open Sea—The World of Plankton*. New Naturalist Series, Collins, 1956.

MARMER, H. A., *The Tide*. New York: D. Appleton. 1926.

RUSSELL, R. C. H. and MACMILLAN, D. H., *Waves and Tides*. Hutchinsons, 1954.

SCHOTT, G., *Geographie des Atlantischen Ozeans*. Hamburg: C. Boysen. 1926.

SCHOTT, G., *Geographie des Indischen und Stillen Ozeans*. Hamburg: C. Boysen.

STREET P., *Beyond the Tides*. University of London Press, 1955.

SVERDRUP, H. V., *Oceanography for Meteorologists*. Allen and Unwin, 1945.

SVERDRUP, H. V., JOHNSON, M. W. and FLEMING, R. H., *The Oceans, Their Physics, Chemistry, and General Biology*. New York: Prentice Hall, 1942.

UMBGROVE, J. H. F. *The Pulse of the Earth*. The Hague: M. Nijhoff. 2nd ed. 1947.

Admiralty Manual of Tides. H.M. Stationery Office, 1941.

Oceanography. National Research Council, Bulletin No. 85, Washington D.C., 1932.

Geology of Coral Reefs. Snellius Expedition, Vol. v. pt. 2. P. H. Kuenen, 1933.

The Great Barrier Reefs of Australia. See papers in the *Geographical Journal*, 74, 1929, pp. 232–57 and 341–70; 76, 1930, pp. 193–214 and 273–97; 89, 1937, pp. 1–28 and 119–46.

PART III. THE LAND

BAGNOLD, R. H., *The Physics of Blown Sand and Desert Dunes*. Methuen, 1941.

BRADE-BIRKS, S. G., *Good Soil*. English Universities Press, 1944.

CLARKE, G. L., *Elements of Ecology*. New York: Wiley, 1954.

COLLET, L. W., *Les Lacs*. Paris: Doin, 1925.

COTTON, C. A., *Climatic Accidents*. New Zealand: Whitcombe and Tombs, 1942.

COTTON, C. A., *Volcanoes as Landscape Forms*. New Zealand: Whitcombe and Tombs, 1944.

EARLE, K. W., *The Geological Map*. Methuen, 1936.

ENGELN, A. D. VON, *Geomorphology: Systematic and Regional*. New York: Macmillan, 1942.

FLINT, R. F., *Glacial Geology and the Pleistocene Epoch*. New York: J. Wiley, 1947.

GRAHAM, M. (Editor), *Sea Fisheries: Their Investigation in the United Kingdom*. Arnold, 1956.

GULCHER, A., *Coastal and Submarine Morphology*. Methuen, 1958.

HOLMES, A., *Principles of Physical Geology*. Nelson, 1944.

JACKS, G. V., *Soil*. Nelson, 1954.

JEFFREYS, H., *Earthquakes and Mountains*. Methuen, 1935.

JENNY, H., *Factors of Soil Formation*. New York: McGraw-Hill, 1941.

JOHNSON, D. W., *Shore Processes and Shoreline Development*. New York: J. Wiley, 1919.

KING, L. C., *South African Scenery*. Oliver and Boyd, 1942.

LAKE, P. and RASTALL, R. H., *Textbook of Geology*. Arnold, 1941.

MARTONNE, E. DE, *Traité de Géographie Physique*, vol. II. Paris: Armand Colin, 1935.

ODUM, E. P., *Fundamentals of Ecology*. Philadelphia and London: W. B. Saunders.

RAMSBOTTOM, J., *Popular Book of Botany*. London and Melbourne, 1953.

RUSSELL, SIR E. J., *The World of the Soil*. New Naturalist Series, Collins, 1957.

STEERS, J. A., *The Coastline of England and Wales*. Cambridge University Press, 1948.

TAIT, J. B., *Hydrography in relation to Fisheries*. Arnold, 1952.

TANSLEY, SIR A. G., *Introduction to Plant Ecology*. Allen and Unwin, 1946.

UMBGROVE, J. H. F., *The Pulse of the Earth*. The Hague: M. Nijhoff, 2nd ed., 1947.

INDEX

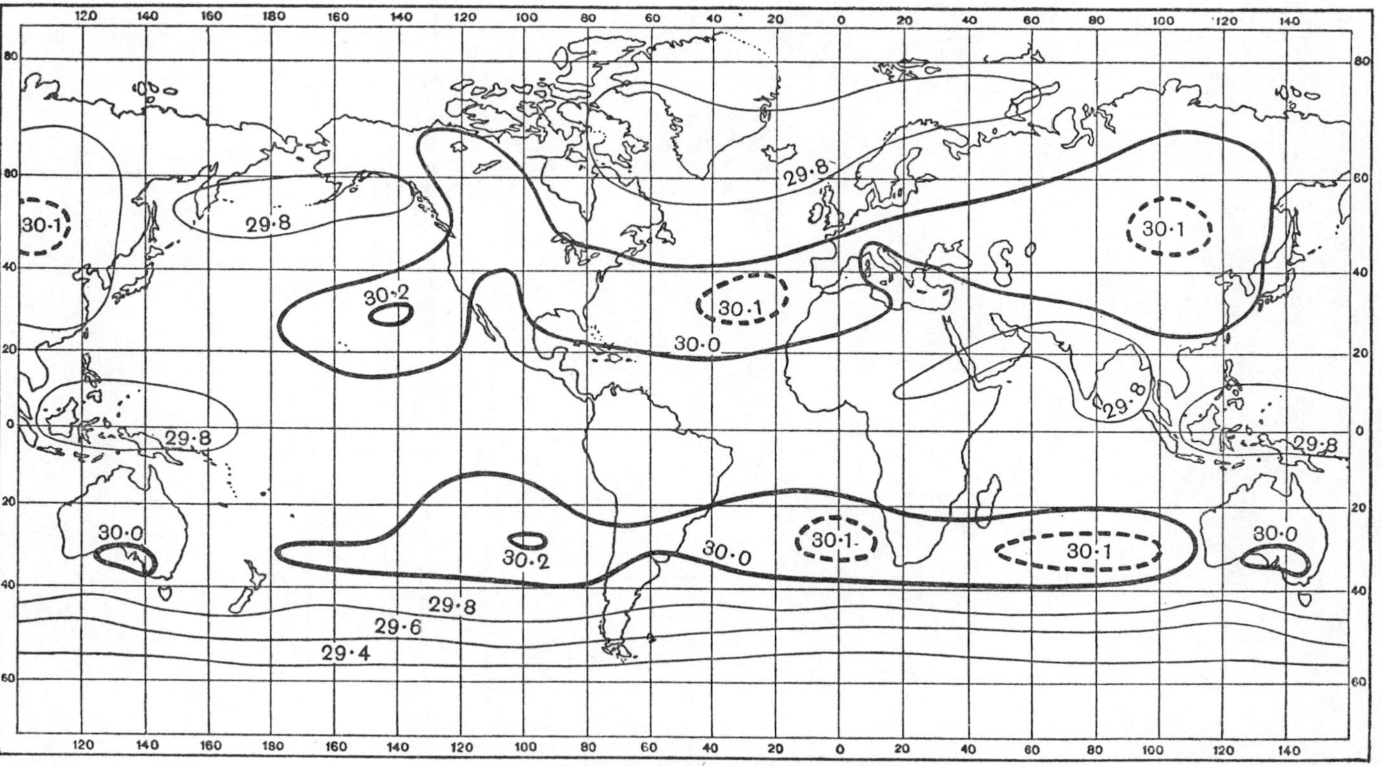

Mean annual isobars

Isobars shown are approximately 995, 1002, 1009, 1016, 1019, 1023 millibars

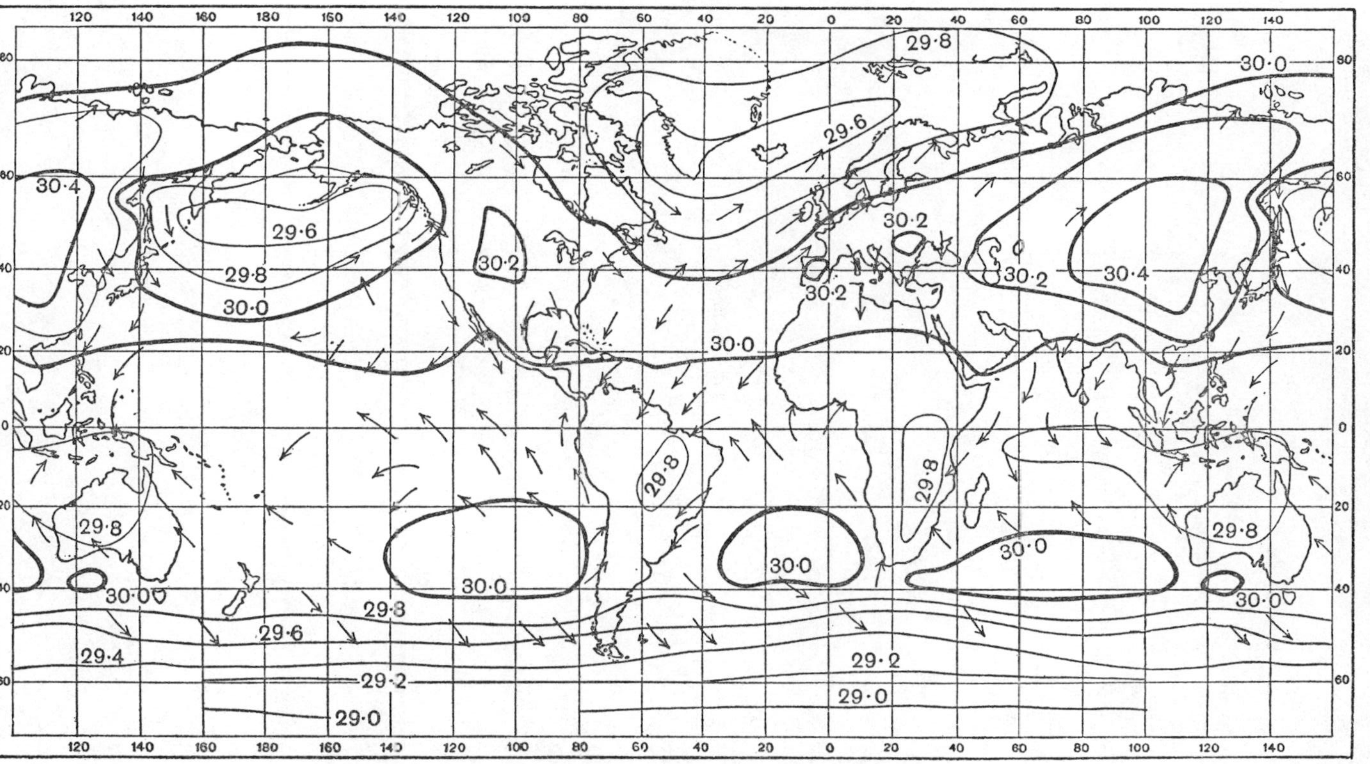

January isobars and winds

Isobars shown are approximately 982, 989, 995, 1002, 1009, 1016, 1023, 1030 millibars

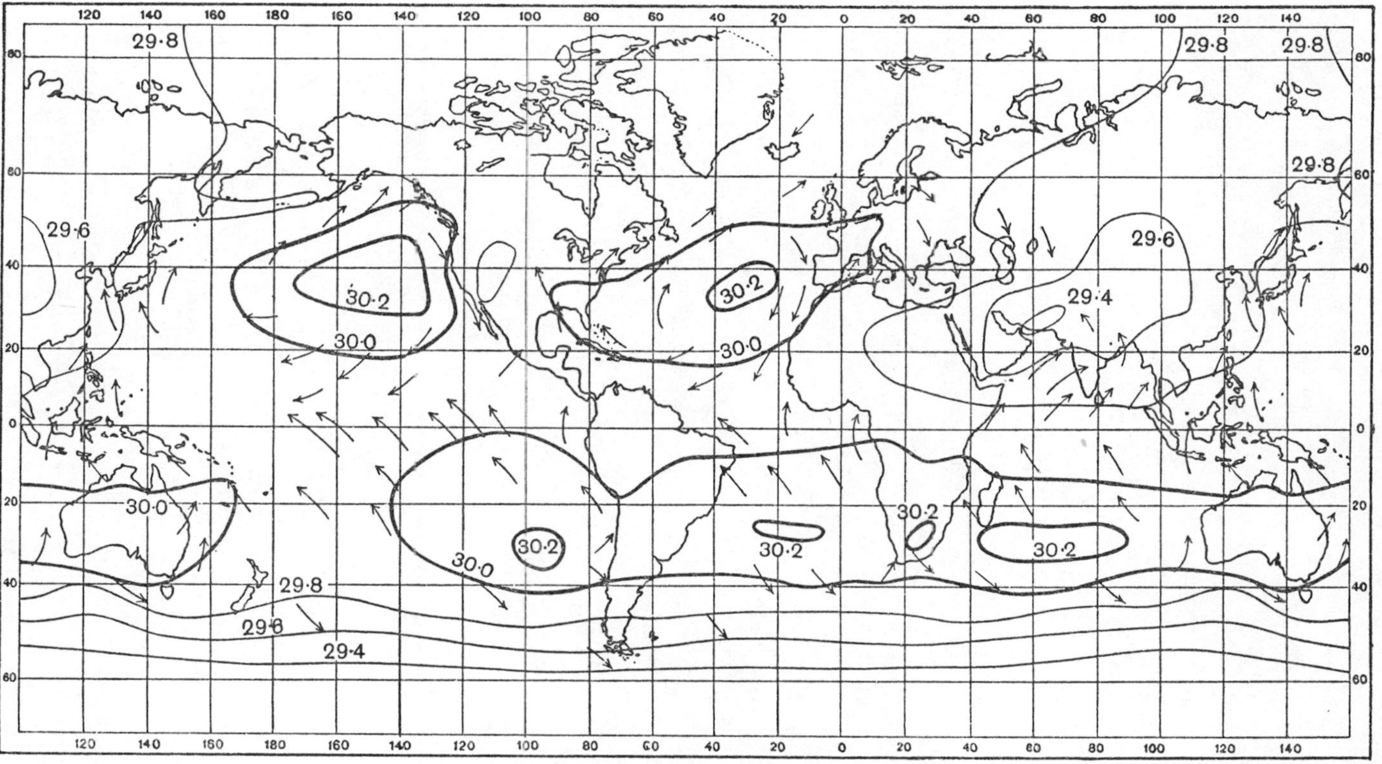

July isobars and winds

Isobars shown are approximately 995, 1002, 1009, 1016, 1023 millibars

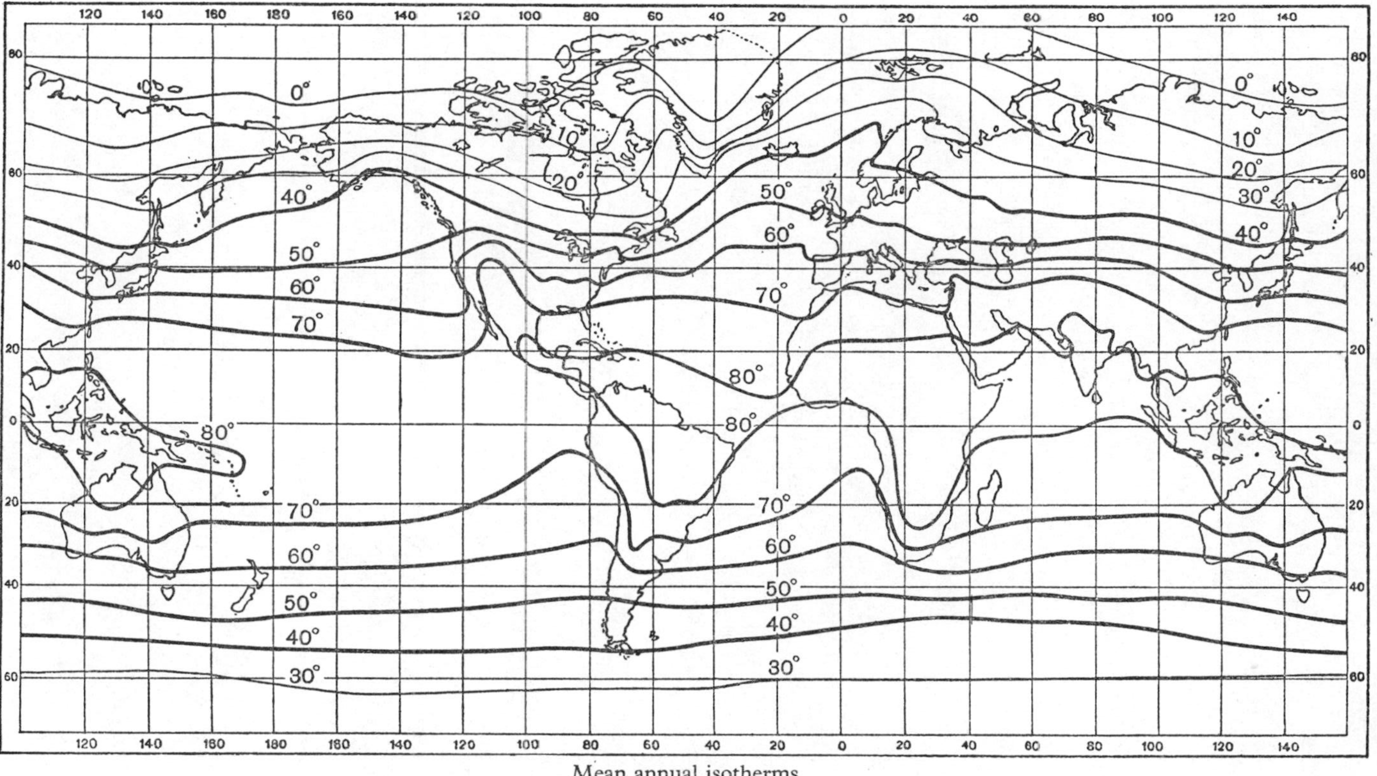

Mean annual isotherms

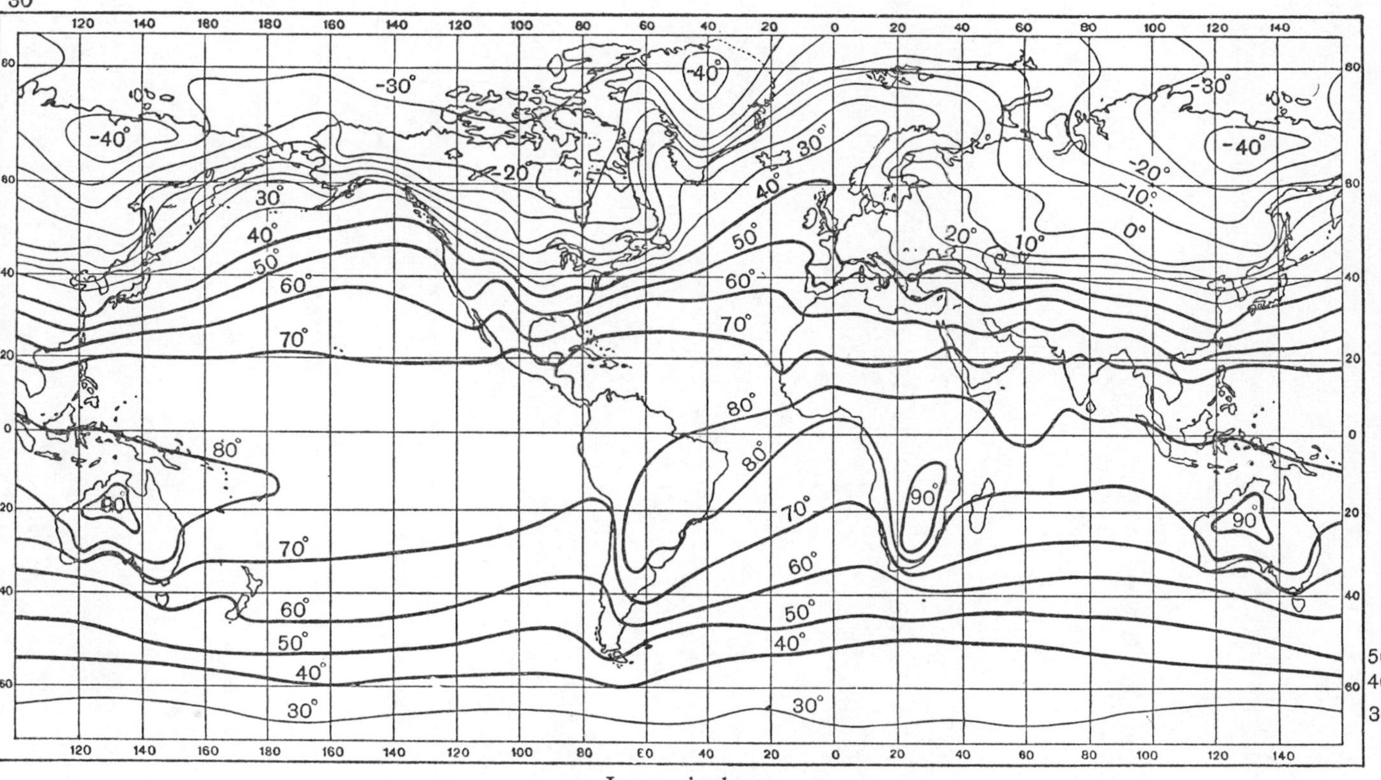

January isotherms

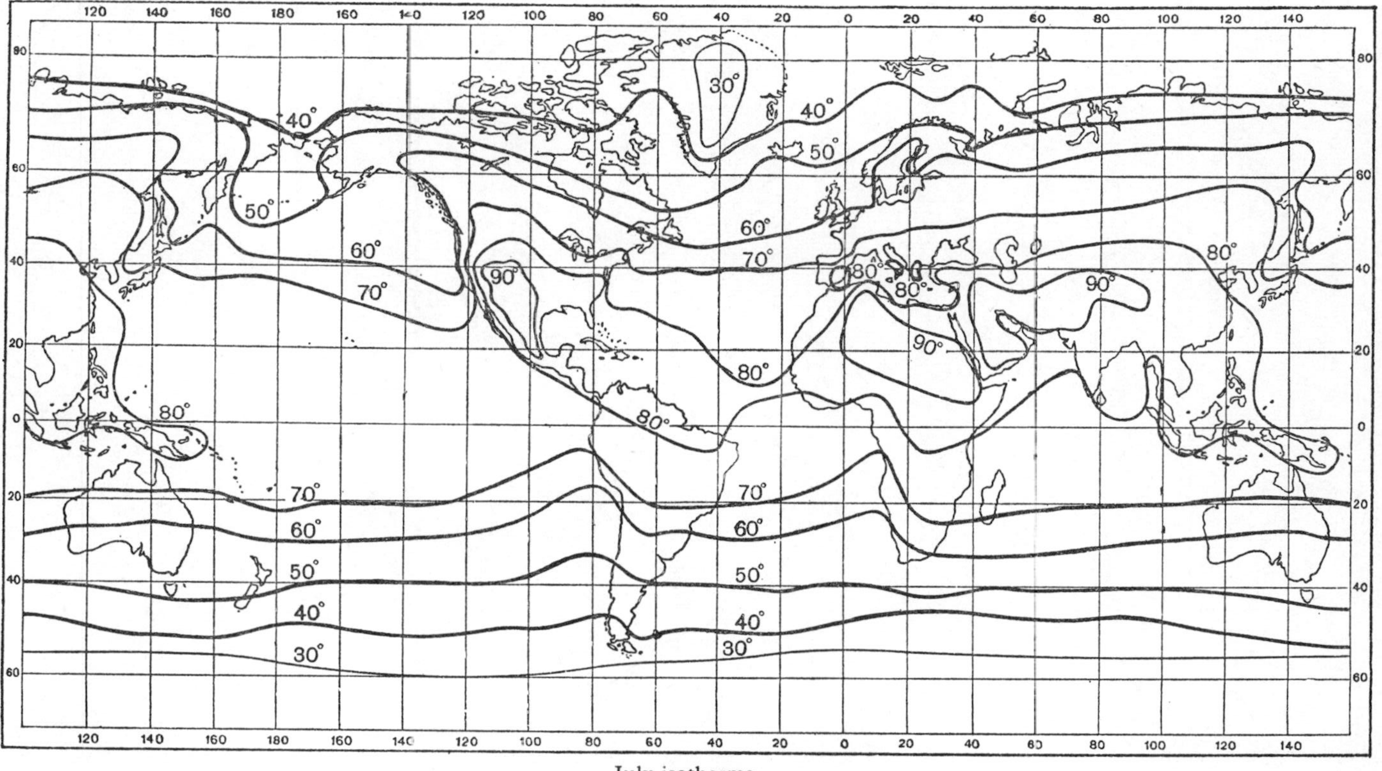

July isotherms